Penguin Education

Penguin Modern Psychology Texts
General Editor: B. M. Foss

Introducing Psychology
An Experimental Approach

D. S. Wright, Ann Taylor
D. R. Davies, W. Sluckin, S. G. M. Lee and J. T. Reason

Introducing Psychology
An Experimental Approach

D. S. Wright, Ann Taylor, D. R. Davies,
W. Sluckin, S. G. M. Lee and
J. T. Reason

Penguin Books

Penguin Books Ltd, Harmondsworth,
Middlesex, England
Penguin Books Inc., 7110 Ambassador Road
Baltimore, Md 21207, U.S.A.
Penguin Books Australia Ltd,
Ringwood, Victoria, Australia

First published 1970
Reprinted 1971
Copyright © D. S. Wright, Ann Taylor, D. R. Davies, W. Sluckin,
S. G. M. Lee and J. T. Reason, 1970

Made and printed in Great Britain by
Richard Clay (The Chaucer Press) Ltd,
Bungay, Suffolk
Set in Monotype Times New Roman

Contents

6 Contents

8 Contents

Editorial Foreword

This is a textbook of Experimental Psychology. The term 'experimental psychology' has been used for several decades to refer to scientific psychology, which uses mainly experimental methods, as opposed to kinds of psychology based mainly on philosophic or therapeutic considerations. The contents of the book are therefore concentrated upon that core of scientific psychology which is central to academic courses in most parts of the world.

A book of this kind has a large amount of material to draw from. In 1968, *Psychological Abstracts* referred to nearly twenty thousand psychological articles and books published in one year. There are few individuals who can cope with the spread of the subject, even at introductory level, and Penguin Books have been most fortunate in obtaining the services of a group of authors who are all members of the same department of psychology. The editing of Ann Taylor and Derek Wright has resulted in an integrated scholarly document.

The book makes at points a particularly British contribution. It inclines to empiricism and has a rather strong emphasis on human cognitive psychology. Also there are certain kinds of psychology which have been developed strongly in Britain over the last few years. The study of animal behaviour has been enriched by the work of the European ethologists. This work has been amalgamated with that of the animal psychologists, so providing a whole new repertoire of techniques and explanatory concepts which are being used also in the study of human behaviour. In Britain, probably more than anywhere else, psychologists have been studying complex human behaviour, as manifested in skilled performance, for thirty years, and the results of this work have influenced many other branches of psychology, for instance the current interest in vigilance, attention and short-term memory. All these topics are dealt with at some length.

For undergraduates, the value of many introductory text books is exhausted before the end of the first year. At the same time, there are many more advanced texts which deal exclusively with particular specializations within psychology, such as physiological, developmental and social psychology. What appears to be lacking is a textbook which would be of service to undergraduates through most of the course, and yet have fairly general coverage. The authors have met this need by sampling representatively some of the main areas of interest within psychology, and dealing with each in greater depth than is customary. Each chapter provides the reader with a sound starting point for the detailed exploration of one of these areas of interest, and is supplemented by an extensive bibliography. Although the authors have had student readership primarily in mind, the general reader will find this book useful if he wants to find out what contemporary psychologists are doing.

B.M.F.

Preface

The writing of this book has been an education for the authors. It has provided a unique opportunity for each of us to share a common focus of interest with colleagues whose specialist concerns differed widely from our own. But it has also posed a number of problems, foremost among them being the difficulty of reaching an agreed structure and policy for the book. The original intention was to take a fresh look at psychological textbooks and present a new integration of the subject. It became plain that multiple authorship does not readily lend itself to the achievement of such a goal. In trying to reach agreement we found ourselves moving steadily closer to the conventional approaches. At the same time, however, we came increasingly to realize that novelty of approach is not always a virtue; indeed it can easily be misleading for someone coming to the subject for the first time. Once we had given up the idea of novelty for its own sake, agreement followed quickly.

The reader will notice a comparative absence of theoretical discussion. This is deliberate. The creation of large-scale general theories has gone out of fashion in psychology now in favour of limited and precise theories dealing with specific problems. To deal adequately with these would be impossible. We have therefore tended to place the emphasis upon the analysis of concepts and the reporting of empirical findings. In doing this we have kept in mind that any text on a growing science must be in the nature of a report of work in progress, and we have tried to achieve a balance between established topics and areas where there is considerable uncertainty and controversy.

Psychology bridges the gap between the biological and the social sciences. Accordingly the general movement of the book is from the structural and biologically given determinants of behaviour, through the analysis of human functioning and the importance of the non-social environment, to the social determinants of behaviour. If we had tried to be entirely consistent in this, however, we would have imposed an artificial structure on the subject. The more detailed the study of any problem in psychology, the more it links up with other problems. Faced with the choice between attempting to say something about all aspects of psychology and dealing with selected areas in some depth, we have opted for the latter course. Individual chapters represent largely independent forays into the subject, and their organization and content to some extent cut across the pattern of the book as a whole.

Nevertheless we have rejected the idea of presenting a collection of isolated chapters, and have tried to retain the notion of an integrated textbook. The following procedure was adopted: each chapter, or part of a chapter, was initially written by one author. This first draft was then edited and revised by two members of the group, Ann Taylor and D. S. Wright, in collaboration with the original author. The task before the editors was to integrate the chapters into a coherent whole, and to soften as far as possible any obtrusive stylistic differences between authors.

Although there is a sense in which the responsibility for the whole book is collective, at the same time the final responsibility for the content of each chapter rests with its original author. The distribution of responsibility among chapters is as follows: D. Roy Davies, Chapters 5, 6, 7, 17 and parts of 15; S. G. M. Lee, Chapters 1, 2 and 20; J. T. Reason, Chapters 13 and 19; W. Sluckin, Chapters 8, 11 and 12; Ann Taylor, Chapters 9, 10, 14, 16 and parts of 15; D. S. Wright, Chapters 3, 4, 18, 21, 22 and 23.

D.W.

A.T.

Part One
Introduction

Chapter 1
Psychology

For centuries, man has been trying to make sense of his experience of himself and of others. To this end he has elaborated a complex language of psychological terms. One distinction – deep-rooted in this language – is that between 'mind' and such allied terms as 'soul' and 'spirit' on the one hand, and 'body' on the other. This distinction corresponds to the familiar fact that many of our activities – the ones we call mental – such as thinking, planning and wishing, are not visible to others and remain private unless we choose to communicate them. Our bodily activities, including speaking, are public; our thoughts, intentions and feelings are hidden from others.

This fact of experience appears to have given rise both to metaphysical doctrines about the nature of man and to the notion of a simple demarcation between the subject matters of psychology and physiology. Psychology is the study of the mind, whereas physiology deals with the bodily machine through which the mind acts. We need not here concern ourselves with purely philosophical problems. It is, however, pertinent to ask whether psychology can be adequately defined as the study of mind. And of course our answer must depend upon how we interpret the notion of mind.

One consequence of the conceptual dichotomy of mind and body has been the tendency to define each without reference to the other. The extreme of this is the 'dualism of substance' conception of the nature of man, in which mind is said to be the functioning of a non-material substance or entity which temporarily inhabits the body. The philosophical difficulties encountered by this extreme position are considerable. From the point of view of psychology it generated the assumption that, although the observational and experimental methods of natural science are appropriate for studying the body, the obvious method for the psychologist is introspection. What is now called 'armchair psychology' consisted in 'looking inside', describing what was found, and generalizing to other people.

The decisive development in the history of psychology was the application of the general methods of the natural sciences to the study of mind. With this went an abandonment of any sharp distinction between what is mental and what is bodily, and the recognition that introspection, by itself, is not a satisfactory route to knowledge. Introspection, as the central method in psychology, was discarded for several reasons. It does not provide public evidence, and the psychologist is not properly entitled to infer from his own introspection to the experience of other people. Any attempt to make use of other people's introspections also runs into difficulties. Where attempts are made to get others to agree on a code to describe sensations or experience, obvious artifacts of 'indoctrination' appear. Everyone might agree to describe a feeling in a certain way, but there is no proof that the subjective realities of the participants really coincide. This is not to say that introspective report has no place in contemporary psychology; on the contrary, its use is very common. But it does mean that the verbal report of subjects is interpreted in a context of other, non-verbal behaviour. For example, the verbal report by a subject 'I feel sick' may or may not be reliably associated with a feeling of sickness, and there is no way for anyone else to check this. But such statements can constitute useful evidence for the psychologist if he has grounds for thinking that such utterances are regularly associated with certain physiological conditions or with certain kinds of behaviour.

In their reaction against introspection, some students of the subject have gone to the extreme of denying that the psychologist can take any account at all of mental events. They argue that since it is only people's behaviour which is public, observable and recordable, a scientific psychology should confine itself to such phenomena. J. B. Watson, an early and influential behaviourist, adopted, between 1913 and 1919, the position that consciousness was useless as an object of scientific study. For him, thinking was a by-product of such 'real' behaviour as the 'subvocal tremor of the larynx' and as such could be safely ignored. Today, however, such an extreme position has few advocates. It is true that psychologists are behaviouristic in the sense that they accept that the only data they can profitably work with are observations and measurements of behaviour; but the definition of behaviour they adopt includes semantic aspects of language, communication and the subject's self-report of his feelings and motives. The existence of mental processes is not denied. The crucial difference between contemporary psychologists and the early introspectionists is that the former try to limit their reference to mental processes to those occasions when they can be inferred from, or are necessary to explain, behavioural data.

We have used the word science several times already and it would seem useful to look at the term more closely. Science is what scientists *do*. The stress is on method rather than upon any particular collection of facts; and methods are guided by aims. These aims have been listed by G. W. Allport (1947) as 'understanding, prediction, and control above the levels achieved by unaided common sense'. Let us look at these purposes of scientific method more closely: the first two are almost inextricably linked, logically. Any successful prediction of an outcome implies some understanding of the processes antecedent to that outcome, though there may be great differences in the amount of understanding shown. Compare the primitive man who very successfully predicts that the sun will rise on the morrow with the astronomer who just as successfully predicts an eclipse of the sun twenty years in advance. The first is a purely actuarial prediction, based on a simple invariant repetition; the second is based on sophisticated physical theory, sophisticated because many more predictions of different kinds can be derived from that theory. The primitive man's fiery god who gets up in the morning in the east is not a very powerful theoretical tool. It is obvious that one of the scientist's tasks is the setting up of adequate causes to account for the events he observes. The psychologist, often sensitive about the status of his relatively new science, tends to stress prediction; understanding (the establishment of adequate theory) tends to lag behind, and this is the point of J. A. Deutsch's (1960) comment: 'Of facts there is already too much in psychology, of evidence too little' (p. 16).

'Control' is the third purpose of scientific method that Allport listed. To the physicist or chemist this element is of vital importance, in that here is shown the mastery over his environment for which the scientist is striving. In psychology, control over human behaviour tends to have unpleasantly authoritarian connotations, and, even with experimentation, grave ethical issues are raised by the use of human subjects. However, the applied psychologist, in such fields as industrial or clinical psychology, is usually concerned to demonstrate 'control' by the improvement of his subjects' work or health.

Other elements enter into the scientific investigation of nature. The scientist must be concerned with repetitive events in his environment. The single instance does not lend itself to scientific manipulation. Experiments must be replicable and, on second or further occasions, give very much the same results in order to be valid. Scientific knowledge is public knowledge and everyone with sufficient training should, theoretically, be able to demonstrate the inter-relationships of its variables for himself. Whether a person has thought a particular thought at a particular time is at present scientifically unverifiable, for it is private knowledge; the reaction times of a subject to various stimuli are measurable and public, and are therefore appropriate scientific data. It is here that the value of Francis Galton's dictum 'count whenever possible' becomes apparent and hence we have the widespread use of statistical methods in modern psychology. We have to be reasonably sure that any reactions elicited in an experiment are not merely due to 'chance' (events outside our experimental control) and, in order to be sure, we have not only to count them but also to compare them with chance expectations. The nature of experimentation will be dealt with more fully in Chapter 2. For the moment, we have other aspects of the general problem of the nature of psychology to consider.

Two points of view dominate science: the empiricist and the hypothetico-deductive. No perfect differentiation can be made between these in practice, but, briefly, the empiricist approach is to look first for regularities among observable phenomena and then to infer conclusions from them. For example, it is a reasonable empirical observation that people living in Africa tend, on average, to be darker than those living in Europe. A hypothesis, on the other hand, derives from an explanatory theory which may be true or false, but which is made up by the investigator and which he will then test by some kind of experimental procedure. Thus the statement 'People living in Africa are darker because the sun is hotter there and they are sunburnt' might be tested by exposing Europeans to more sunlight and seeing whether they grow permanently darker in colour. With the method of hypothesis and deduction, greater power of generalization is obtained, and progress is apt to be faster, though it must be remembered that the hypothesis is usually based, in the first place, on some empirical observation.

So we have in science a continuous process of observation, the setting up of hypotheses, proof or disproof, further observation or experimentation and so on. There is no final certainty or absolute truth in the natural sciences. We acquire a theory which works well until further facts are discovered. We then modify or abandon the theory for another and attempt to find the instances where it, in turn, is not applicable. One of the hallmarks of a scientific theory is that it is testable. As Popper (1963) has said: 'A theory which is not refutable by any conceivable event is non-scientific. Irrefutability is not a virtue of a theory (as people often think) but a vice. . . . Every genuine *test* of a theory is an attempt to falsify it, or to refute it' (p. 36).

What? How? When? Why? These are the kinds of questions that initiate scientific inquiry. It is with the last of them that we are apt to experience the most difficulty. 'Why?' is usually, though not always, a question about causation, and we can have many different kinds of causal explanation. Ask a child of four why the trees have leaves and you might get the answer 'So as to be pretty' or 'To look nice'; ask an untutored, primitive man and you may be told: 'Because there is a spirit in the tree who wishes to keep cool.' The first explanation is finalistic in that the phenomenon is 'explained' in terms of its end result; the second is animistic, in that human motivation is ascribed to the tree. Neither account would tend to lead to further research. By contrast the scientist's explanation is in terms of specifiable, independent and antecedent conditions. He has no single 'cause' to offer. His explanation of the leaves will involve long and complex sequences of events, physical and chemical, concerning not only the tree but also its environment. Ultimately, he will have to choose the 'cause' which he thinks most appropriate for his particular interest and the furtherance of his work, fully aware of the arbitrary nature of this choice and realizing its limitations.

In summary, then, we are saying that psychology is the application to human behaviour, including speech, of the observational and experimental methods of science; and its aim is to locate the antecedent conditions associated with particular forms of behaviour, and to explain these relationships through theories which may or may not take account of what are ordinarily understood as mental processes.

But the psychologist's interests are not limited to human behaviour. Many of the experiments cited in this text were carried out on animals. It is therefore worth asking why psychologists study animal behaviour as well. Of course, such study is worth-while in its own right. But it is clear that a great deal of animal experimentation is undertaken in order to help us understand human behaviour better. How can it do this?

That man differs from the other animals in important ways is obvious. Both in structure and functioning he is much more complex. His behaviour is more malleable and plastic, and less determined in its particular detail by genetic factors. As a consequence of his prolonged infancy, he exhibits a greater intraspecific variability in behaviour. With his greater mental time span, his possession of symbolic language, transmitted culture and technology, he is less dependent upon his immediate stimulus environment.

But at the same time there is an underlying evolutionary continuity between man and other animals. In his scientific role, the psychologist assumes that these differences are due to the greater complexity and elaboration of man's structure and functioning. It is characteristic of the scientific approach that it is piecemeal; one limited and localized problem is taken at a time. There is a preference for investigating aspects of behaviour in their simplest form first and thereby accumulating a body of knowledge from the standpoint of which more complex aspects can be tackled. Not only can animals provide such simpler forms of behaviour but they are also more convenient experimental subjects. It is possible to assert more rigorous experimental control of animal subjects; genetic factors can be controlled through breeding, and experiments can be performed on their developmental and physiological processes which would be impracticable with human subjects.

This does not mean that we can easily extrapolate to human behaviour the results of animal experimentation; the species differences are such that extrapolation must always be extremely cautious and tentative. But animal experimentation can provide useful hypotheses for subsequent testing on human subjects. And we can go further. For obvious reasons it is impossible to study many problems of human behaviour in a rigorously experimental way; instead, we have to rely upon data which leave the direction of causation inconclusive. For example, surveys have shown that the children of mothers who were highly anxious during pregnancy tend themselves to be rather anxious later on. Surveys of this kind do not allow us to conclude that it was the maternal anxiety which 'caused' the later anxiety in the children. If, however, carefully controlled experiments on animals clearly imply such a causal connexion, we may feel strengthened in our belief that such a causal interpretation is valid for human beings as well. Though, of course, we still have not demonstrated it.

The present book, then, while certainly not abandoning the term mind and what it stands for, endeavours to deal with the concept in the manner espoused by Hebb (1966):

Thus the method of psychology is to work behavioristically, constructing a theory of mind that is based on the objective facts of behavior. This means that we know mind, and study it, as the chemist knows and studies the properties of the atom. Atoms are not observed directly; still less the electrons, protons, neutrons and so forth that – theoretically – compose the atom. The chemist has ideas about the atom which he can test by experiment, and modify in accordance with the results. . . .

For psychology, our problem is to construct in imagination the complex machinery of mind that will account for what we can observe people doing, for the difference between higher and lower animals, and so forth. Our present theories are far from adequate, and a most important goal for the student is to learn to use theory without believing it himself, or being dogmatic when talking to others. A theory can be 'good' without being 'true'; that is, it may be on the right track and close enough to the truth to have useful applications, and still be a very rough approximation that will have to be corrected and extended before it agrees fully with the facts. We may or may not reach that latter stage in the next millennium; in the meantime, psychology like other sciences is developing steadily by the use of theory combined with observation and experiment (p. 10).

Other disciplines study men and animals and some even concentrate on their behaviour. Can these be demarcated from psychology? This is largely a matter of convenience, for natural phenomena do not divide themselves into neat, mutually exclusive categories; in biology, for example, there is an obvious unity of life – some processes are very similar to each other throughout living matter – and psychology is, in our view, very much part of biology. However, no man today can possess a complete knowledge of all disciplines, so it is probably useful here to attempt to distinguish, crudely, some of the other disciplines which border upon and overlap with psychology:

1. Philosophy studies the mental processes of man and their embodiment in language, but its concern is with the logical relationships between ideas and the reasons which can be offered to justify holding them, rather than with factors which exert a causal influence upon thinking.
   2. History studies the past behaviour of man with a view to determining the sequence of events and the factors which have helped to shape them. In so far as inferences are made about causal determinants of behaviour, it might be regarded as in part a field of applied psychology.
   3. Sociology and social anthropology study the social institutions of mankind, often comparatively, and it is difficult to draw any very clear line between these disciplines and some aspects of social psychology. Unlike the latter, however, they do not use experimental methods.
   4. Zoology studies animals in their entirety, excluding man. It is based on taxonomy and experiment, and behaviour *per se* does not constitute a very large proportion of its content, unlike
   5. Ethology which is a development of the last fifty years. This constitutes the attempt by zoologists to study animal behaviour under conditions more natural than those of the laboratory (but often using experimental techniques) with particular emphasis on

the place of such behaviour against the background of evolution. It does not differ, essentially, from comparative psychology.

6. Psychiatry is the discipline concerned with the diagnosis and treatment of mental disorder which has grown out of the practice of medicine. The psychiatrist is a medically qualified person who has had additional training in abnormal psychology. His work may overlap with that of the clinical psychologist, who is qualified in psychology but not normally in medicine.

7. Finally we have anatomy, physiology, genetics and cytology. All these disciplines have great relevance for the study of man and animals. They are not, at present, greatly concerned with 'molar' patterns of *behaviour*, but more with 'molecular' events of cell structure and interactions, growth and the functioning of internal mechanisms of the body. Their explanations of living function tend to be at 'lower', more 'basic', levels than those of psychology or sociology.

The distinction between molecular and molar levels of analysis raised by the last group of disciplines presents for psychologists the problem of differentiating levels of explanation. It is possible to offer either '*same level*' or *reductionist* types of explanation of behaviour. When we explain a subject's behaviour in terms of the behaviour of others and the general features of the stimulus situation, we are engaging in a 'same level' explanation. But it is also possible to explain behaviour, in principle anyway, by describing in detail the sequence of neural and chemical events which are correlated with it. This would be an example of a reductionist explanation.

The further down the phyletic scale that one moves, the more satisfying is the explanation of behaviour in reductionist terms. The behaviour of an *Amoeba* or *Paramecium* is probably fairly completely accounted for in terms of its biochemistry. This reductionist explanation is theoretically possible for human behaviour as well, but such is the complexity and dependence upon myriad interactions of human behaviour that it will be a very long time before cellular explanation can account for its more complicated patterns, and, even then, the answers may not be very useful. To illustrate this let us suppose that a steam train regularly leaves Euston Station for

Scotland at 6 p.m. every Sunday. This can be quite satisfactorily explained in terms of the units of energy involved, the 'behaviour' of the particles of steam, the pressure of the driver's hand on the throttle, etc. Useful, but not necessarily what we want to know. We may legitimately be much more concerned with the reasons behind its timing (dependent upon decisions made by British Rail, which, in turn, may be dependent upon past passenger demand) or even with the conformist attitudes of the drivers in obeying their orders. These 'higher' and 'less basic' levels of explanation may be considerably more use to us than a physicist's account of the phenomenon of the train's journey.[1]

One additional consideration which is against the full acceptance of reductionism in psychology is that of human *experience*. It would be meaningless to the human subject to have to describe the experience of falling in love in terms of the changes in his body cells. We have an agreed language for talking about changes in cells, and also a vocabulary which makes it possible for us to collect from human subjects their reports of the gross physical sensations and thoughts that accompany falling in love; what we lack is a way of translating one language into the other. Fortunately, we do not need to choose finally between these two levels of explanation. Psychologists will select that level which is most fruitful for their purposes.

We have stressed above some of the differences between psychology and other disciplines; it is nevertheless essential for the modern psychologist to have some knowledge of disciplines other than his own. He must understand the relevance of the critical tools of philosophy to his methodology and construction of hypotheses and theories. Men and animals are, almost without exception, social rather than solitary and many of their actions are dictated by the presence of others and the structure of their social group; hence sociology and social anthropology are also relevant. Without some acquaintance with anatomy, genetics, cell biology and, especially, mammalian physiology, the psychologist will be handicapped in certain aspects of his subject. The close relationship between 'mind' and the brain necessitates some study of the central nervous system

1. We are indebted for this example to Professor C. A. Mace, a notable anti-reductionist.

and here it is almost impossible to draw hard and fast lines between neurophysiology and some aspects of psychology.

We have considered briefly how the psychologist goes about his job and where his interests coincide with, and differ from, those of other scientists. It would be appropriate at this point to give a summary and comprehensive account of what his interests are. Unfortunately, this is no easy task as readers of this book will discover. We could with some justification characterize present-day psychology as a collection of specialisms, united only in the logic of their methods, within which individuals worry over limited sets of problems, construct theories whose field of application is restricted to these problems, and maintain little more than a general interest in what is going on elsewhere in their discipline. The practice of carving up university courses into chunks labelled Learning, Perception, Physiological Psychology, Behaviour Genetics, Personality, Social Psychology, Developmental Psychology and so on, both reflects and tends to perpetuate this image of a discipline broken down into specialisms.

Although this image of the subject has a basis in fact, it is to some extent misleading. There is a continuous tendency for the study of one circumscribed aspect of behaviour to end up by involving many others. For example, the student of visual perception is very likely to find himself also concerned with processes of maturation, learning, thinking and social influence and, of course, physiology. In addition, the concepts and principles evolved in studying limited problems have often provided in their turn a fruitful basis for approaching a much wider range of issues. For instance, the study of motor skills has provided a conceptual framework within which to analyse thinking and social interaction. In short, though psychology is a group of specialisms, the boundaries between them are far from distinct, and one of the most common sources of impetus to research has been the application to one specialism of ideas developed in another.

But if the constant interaction between specialisms is a source of vitality within the subject, it is a problem for writers of textbooks. The present text does not depart significantly from the conventional classification of specialisms, but nevertheless the task of reducing overlap between chapters was not easy, and the reader is warned that the arrangement of material is to some extent arbitrary.

The underlying structure of the book is based upon the assumption that psychology has its roots in biology and that it spans the gap between the other biological sciences and the social sciences. In Part Two we consider the influence upon behaviour of what is biologically given. This part includes chapters which relate heredity, maturation, and physiological structure and functioning to behaviour. It closes with a chapter on 'biological motives' which prepares the way for Part Three in which we focus upon environmental determinants of behaviour. This section opens with a discussion of perceptual processes, for environmental influences are mediated by the way an organism perceptually structures its environment. This is followed by chapters on the effects of early experience, learning processes, the development of skills and remembering. This last chapter leads on to the discussion of symbolic processes, which is the concern of the chapters on language and thinking in Part Four. In Part Five we turn to an examination of the more general ways in which people differ. After exploring the methods of measuring individual differences, we continue with a discussion of the notions of intelligence, personality and normality. In the last part of the book, we consider some of the ways in which people affect the behaviour of each other, beginning with a chapter on some mechanisms of social influence, which is a description of recent work in which basic principles of learning have been extended to the two-person situation. This is followed by a review of certain aspects of socialization and the book ends with a chapter on persuasive communications and the determining influence of group membership upon an individual's behaviour. The reader will discover that, although specific chapters are given over more or less exclusively to an examination of heredity, development, physiological structure and learning, the general issues raised by them tend to recur throughout the book.

Excluded from the book is any account of the main fields of applied psychology. These are: clinical (the diagnosis and treatment of mental disorder), occupational ('fitting the man to the job' or, in the case of ergonomics, 'fitting the job to the man'), educational (research into educational processes and the treatment of educational difficulties) and such occupations as advertising and market research. It is true that research in these applied fields has given rise to important theoretical considerations; but in general their concern is with effecting changes in people's behaviour rather than discovering the principles which make behaviour understandable.

Finally, it has been said that the major factor unifying the various specialisms within psychology is the logic of its methodology. It is this which is the strongest unifying bond of the present book. It is therefore appropriate, before turning to the main body of the book, to examine the nature of empirical observation and experiment. This is the substance of the following chapter.

Chapter 2
Scientific Method in Psychology

Observation

The need for selection

The psychologist, like all other scientists, is surrounded by millions upon millions of events in nature, and his task is to study some of them and to try to build a theoretical framework on the basis of his study, which will serve the three purposes of understanding, prediction and control. We have already considered, in Chapter 1, the distinctions between psychology and other disciplines which determine which types of events will engage the psychologist's attention; his interest will be in certain kinds of behaviour and perhaps – though not necessarily – in humans rather than in animals. But even within these limits, the number and diversity of 'behavioural events' force the psychologist to delimit further the objects of his observation; and he must also proceed somehow from the simple observation of events to the formulation of some manageable set of *generalizations* which can serve as the material for theorizing.

The process that takes us from a collection of facts to a set of generalizations is called *induction*. It has been well described by Medawar (1963), who writes:

What induction implies in its cruder form is roughly speaking this: scientific discovery, or the formulation of scientific theory, starts with the unvarnished and unembroidered evidence of the senses. It starts with simple observation – simple, unbiased, unprejudiced, naïve, or innocent observation – and out of this sensory evidence, embodied in the form of simple propositions or declarations of fact, generalizations will grow up and take shape, almost as if some process of crystallization or condensation were taking place. Out of the disorderly array of facts, an orderly theory, an orderly general statement, will somehow emerge (p. 377).

However, there are problems associated with this inductive approach to knowledge. Medawar points to three main weaknesses:

1. There is no such thing as unprejudiced observation. In this he would be supported by a great deal of evidence from psychology (see Chapters 9 and 10). People see and, above all, *interpret* what they see, differently. We are all biased by our earlier experiences.

2. Induction does not enable us to *prove* general propositions, though it may enable us to discern relations among sense data.

3. The sum of inductive statements is totally unable, logically, to lead to generalizations which are more than the sum of those statements.

While we would regard this third criticism as arguable, the first has very definite pertinent truth for the psychologist and brings us up against the many faceted problem of control of observation.

Initially, then, we have to delimit *what* is to be observed; we have deliberately to sample the sense data surrounding us. We have neither the time nor the capacity to pay attention to everything and the entities that we observe will depend upon an initial 'hunch' or guess that new relationships are likely to emerge from the scrutiny of particular groups of people, samples of behaviour and so on. It is here that 'serendipity' or 'inspiration' enters psychology as it does every other science. To cite Medawar (1963) again: 'Hypotheses arise by guesswork. That is to put it in its crudest form. I should say rather that they arise by inspiration; but in any event they arise by processes that form part of the subject matter of psychology and certainly not of logic, for there is no logically rigorous method for devising hypotheses' (p. 378).

The fact that our subjects are usually human makes our problem of delimitation even more complicated. Humans differ from one another in many more respects than do, say, domesticated rats or molecules of the same metal; it is by no means clear *a priori* which differences are likely to repay study. One way of describing the possible choice of variables for study is by their classification into *stimulus, response* and *organismic* characteristics. Effectively, the psychologist may choose one (or more) of four courses. He may examine the relation between certain stimulus variables and certain response variables – for example, the relation between noisy or quiet working conditions and efficiency of work. He may examine the relation between certain organismic states and certain response variables – for example, to see whether the age, sex, state of hunger, attitude or 'personality' of an individual is related to some aspect of his behaviour. He may examine the relation between certain response variables and others – to see, for example, whether people who are good at academic work are also good at physical games. Finally, the psychologist may examine the relation between certain stimulus characteristics and certain organismic states – for example, the relation between an unhappy family life in childhood and susceptibility to neurosis in adult life.

Two further points should be made about this analysis. First, the measurement of organismic characteristics is very often inferred from response characteristics, rather than directly obtained (see, for example, Chapter 17), so that the distinction between response and organismic variables is not always distinct. Second, studies of any of the kinds quoted above imply *comparison of different individuals* by correlational or experimental methods; we shall return presently to this point.

Observer bias and the definition of variables

We have already mentioned that, in observation, allowance must be made for the possible biases of the observer. As individuals we see and interpret events uniquely – the so-called 'personal equation' of the physical scientist. How can we combat these built-in imperfections? (a) We may use more than one observer, and here we are often helped by the use of photographic, acoustic or other permanent records of behaviour. (b) Our knowledge, to fall within the canon of science, must, as we have seen, be *public* knowledge, and our observations should be replicable upon another occasion by any other qualified worker. This means that we must be able to *describe* adequately what we observe, which is much more difficult than it sounds. In psychology our data are so complex that they can seldom be adequately described in the universal scientific language of mathematics and we are bedevilled by the possible differences in meaning of the same word to two different psychologists.

'Intelligence' is a case in point. It would be difficult to get any two psychologists to agree on an exact definition of the term (see Chapter 18), though a particular act might well be similarly classified by both as 'intelligent' or 'unintelligent'. But the idea of intelligence has proved to be a concept of great practical value to psychology and we would not wish to abandon it. Following the example of other scientific disciplines, we tend to take refuge in an *operational* definition of intelligence – 'intelligence is what is measured by intelligence tests'. We can agree on this, and mean the same thing by 'intelligence tests', but there are snags. As Popper (1957) writes:

A host of interesting problems is raised by *operationalism*, the doctrine that theoretical concepts have to be defined in terms of measuring operations. Against this view, it can be shown that *measurements presuppose theories*. There is no measurement without a theory and no operation which can satisfactorily be described in non-theoretical terms. The attempts to do so are always circular; for example, the description of the measurement of length needs a (rudimentary) theory of heat and temperature measurement; but these, in turn, involve measurements of length (p. 189).

We have, too, the danger that forced agreement may be reached between observers because they have both been indoctrinated in a particular fashion, and that this indoctrination may be based on fallacy, so that the data are forced into a particular descriptive framework regardless of its appropriateness or theoretical truth. One example of this is the charge levelled by academic psychologists against the followers of Freud. In the closed system of psychoanalysis, goes their argument, evidence for 'the unconscious', the 'superego', 'the dream world', 'repression', etc., is bound to emerge from the data, for it is through these spectacles that the Freudian analyst, indoctrinated in his training, is bound to look. Be this as it may, the psychologist is always poised between the Scylla of artificial agreement (convenient but spurious) and the Charybdis of unique descriptions ('true' but not comparable one to another).

As scientists, we are interested in *repetitions* in the behaviour of our subjects; but, if we look narrowly and intensely enough, these can be shown not to exist. A subject blows his nose several times. We are usually content with this kind of description of a person's actions, but if we look at the series of actions more closely we find that each act was, in detail, different from the others. If we had more than one subject we would find differences between the nose-blowing of each. Despite these detailed differences we rely on the fact that there are sufficient common elements in each situation for us to treat 'blowing the nose' as a useful category of action and useful correlational facts may emerge; for example, the hypothesis that 'people who have colds blow their noses more often than those who have not' (in Western society, at any rate) is easily tested and likely to be confirmed. In other situations the problem of assessing which responses are, and which are not, *functionally equivalent* may be much more difficult; consider the difficulty encountered by the layman as well as by the psychologist in identifying the consistencies, and inconsistencies, in an individual's behaviour which may be taken to indicate his 'personality' (see Chapter 19).

Idiographic and nomothetic approaches

There are two ways in which we may build up samples of events for study. First, we may record a great many different examples of the behaviour of one subject, and examine the pattern or profile that emerges. This is the *idiographic* approach (see Chapter 19), and an outstanding example of its use is given in a study by Baldwin, of which G. W. Allport (1947) writes:

Although the study has not yet been published in full, attention should be called to an unusual attempt to quantify the structure of personality of *one individual* life on the basis of a collection of personal documents. . . . The materials consisted of a revealing collection of letters from a widow written during the last eleven years of her life, setting forth her abnormal attachment to her son, the story of his death and her loneliness and reflecting her gradual deterioration of strength and hope. The method, employing an adaptation of the chi-square technique, [1] determined the frequency with which any two ideas were related in the writer's mind. A portrait resulted

1. A statistical technique applicable to *nominal* data: see Chapter 17.

of a dramatic personality, aesthetically sensitive, scrupulous in financial matters, possessive of her son's affection, suspicious and full of hatred towards women.

The method is of considerable importance representing, as it does, a contribution to the exact analysis of the structure of the unique single personality on the basis of personal documents. It sets forth a new conception of a 'population' for statistics: a population of events and traits within the boundaries of one person. If the initial promise of this method is fulfilled it will supply an important bridge between the statistical and clinical points of view (pp. 35–6).

The idiographic approach has an immediate emotional appeal to most people today, as for three hundred years the emphasis of Western thought has been upon the uniqueness of the individual, and there is in all of us the tendency so pleasantly described by William James in 1902:

The first thing the intellect does with an object is to class it along with something else. But any object that is infinitely important to us and awakens our devotion feels to us also as if it must be *sui generis* and unique. Probably a crab would be filled with a sense of personal outrage if it could hear us class it without ado or apology as a crustacean, and thus dispose of it. 'I am no such thing,' it would say; '*I am myself, myself alone*' (p. 9).

Despite the appeal of this 'study within the unique', it has one major drawback. It does not enable us to generalize beyond the single case, though it may suggest hypotheses that can be tested in other subjects.

As a result of this last difficulty the psychologist usually adopts the second, *nomothetic* approach (see Chapter 19), using numbers of subjects and comparing the responses of many individuals with those of their fellow subjects. This method enables us, within the limitations of the representativeness of our sample, to generalize about people and to predict with some accuracy future *group* results, but it does not help us much with prediction of the behaviour of the *individual* subject. With neither method is the psychologist able to have his cake, in predictive terms, and eat it. As Allport (1947) writes, possibly rather overstating his case:

The problem of the prediction of 'personal adjustment' is one to which various social scientists . . . have given attention. Studies . . . have had to do with predictions of marital adjustment, of parole success, of juvenile delinquency. In these studies the method employed is to find variables *frequently* present in marital success, in parole violation, or in juvenile delinquency. If enough of these variables are found to be present in a *new* case, then this is designated in advance as a likely success or likely failure. So long as large numbers of cases are concerned, there is no flaw in this reasoning. The prediction is like that of life insurance companies, and in the long run is dependable in the sense that actuarial predictions are always dependable.

Where this reasoning seriously trips is in prediction applied to the single case instead of to a population of cases. A fatal *non sequitur* occurs in the reasoning that if 80 per cent of the delinquents who come from broken homes are recidivists, then this delinquent from a broken home has an 80 per cent chance of becoming a recidivist. The truth of the matter seems to be that this delinquent has either 100 per cent certainty of becoming a repeater or 100 per cent certainty of going straight. If all the causes in his case were known, we could predict for him perfectly (barring environmental accident). His chances are determined by the pattern of his life and *not* by the frequencies found in the population at large. Indeed, *psychological causation is always personal and never actuarial* (p. 156).

As we have suggested, there may be overstatement here, but an interesting critique and expansion of the ideas can be found in Meehl (1956). Most psychological experiments or correlational procedures are nomothetic in type, and the uniqueness of each response is to some extent neglected in favour of similarities or responses between people.

The design of studies

The correlational method

We have used the terms experiment and correlation and these form the most powerful weapons in our psychological armoury. To quote Woodworth (1938):

To be distinguished from the experimental method, and standing on a par with it in value, rather than above or below, is the comparative and correlational method. It takes its start from individual differences. By use of suitable tests it measures the individuals in a sample of some population, distributes these measures and finds their average, scatter, etc. Measuring two or more characteristics of the same individuals it computes the correlation of these characteristics. . . . This method does not introduce an 'experimental factor'; it has no 'independent variable' but treats all the measured variables alike. It does not directly study cause and effect. The experimentalist's independent variable is antecedent to his dependent variable; one is cause (or part of the cause) and the other effect. The correlationist studies the interrelation of different effects (p. 3).

We will be discussing the meaning of some of the terms in the preceding paragraph later in this chapter – meanwhile let us take a more simple-minded look at what happens when we correlate data. Let us imagine that ten different subjects are given on three different occasions three different tests, with the following results:

Test X		Test Y		Test Z	
Subject	Score	Subject	Score	Subject	Score
A	90	A	99	A	17
B	85	B	94	B	23
C	80	C	89	C	24
D	75	D	84	D	30
E	70	E	79	E	32
F	65	F	74	F	35
G	60	G	69	G	36
H	55	H	64	H	40
I	50	I	59	I	41
J	45	J	54	J	44

(These are artificial figures and would be highly improbable in real life. They will serve to demonstrate, simply, some of the facts of correlation.)

With tests X and Y it is immediately apparent that our subjects have shown a very close similarity of result; indeed, were we to allocate ranks to the results of the candidates on tests X and Y it would appear that the relative rankings on the two tests were identical, in that A would be first in each instance, B second, etc. In statistical terms we would have a *rank-order correlation* of +1 (the highest possible coincidence). If we were to take into account the actual scores, rather than ranks, the correspondence would not be as exact, but in either case the hypothesis that tests X and Y had much in common would be highly tenable.

Now with test Z we have a very different result. In terms of rank order the subjects are exactly reversed, if we compare test Z results with those from either of the other tests. A, instead of being first, is last; B second to last rather than second, etc. Here we have a perfect negative rank-order correlation of -1 (the highest correlation possible in the opposite direction). Scores on Z are obviously related systematically to scores on X or Y – but the relation is negative.

Had our figures simply been random with no relation (either positive or negative) between the orders of subjects on the tests, our correlations would have been approximately zero; in other words, no correlation would have emerged.

Now rank-order correlations are only one kind of correlation, but on the basis of these what can we conclude from our results so far? We can say with confidence that tests X and Y have something in common, and that test Z measures an opposite tendency. But we cannot say that the success of A on test Y was in any sense *caused* by his success on test X. This is the basic limitation of correlation as a method, a limitation of which every psychologist, and indeed every scientist, must be aware: *correlation does not imply causality*.

An amusing example underlining this point is given by Kurtz (1965):

From the fact that there is a significant relationship between two variables it does not necessarily follow that variation in one causes variation in the other . . . an observed relationship between two variables in this type of study may be the result of their relationship to some third factor. An impressive illustration of this point, cited by Snedecor (1956), is the nearly perfect negative correlation, $r = -0.98$, observed between the birth rate in Great Britain and the production of pig iron in the United States during the period from 1875 to 1920. Surely neither of these two variables affected the other directly; the relationship apparently came about because these two quantities both varied as a function of time during the period in question, one increasing, the other decreasing (p. 209).

This is an obvious example, but it is surprising how often both psychologists and laymen deliver themselves of statements like:

'Babies who are weaned early can be shown to be more acquisitive in later life than those who are late weaned. Therefore early weaning is the cause of adult greed.' In such an instance there might well be a third variable (for example, rejection by mother) which was causal in both phenomena.

There are other factors which can affect the truth or falsity of our conclusions. It is obvious that if we use a very small number of subjects chance correlations are much more likely to occur. We could show empirically that a particular rank order of only two subjects was very likely to appear on a second occasion merely by spinning a coin to decide the ranks. How are we to tell whether our correlations are meaningful, or whether they might well have oc-cured by chance? Here we have to resort to validatory statistics to help us.

If two sets of scores are unrelated, but both vary as a result of 'irrelevant' factors, it is likely that the correlations obtained from them on different occasions will not be exactly zero but will *vary around* zero, having, typically, low positive or negative values. When, therefore, a given value (positive or negative) is obtained in a psy-chological investigation, the problem is to decide whether this value is one which might well represent a chance variation from zero, or whether its size is such that this 'chance hypothesis' is unlikely. In other words, we must calculate the *statistical significance* of the value obtained.

The obvious way of calculating the chance-occurrence probability of a given value would be to carry out, many hundreds of times, correlation of two sets of scores (equal in number to the sample involved in our 'experimental' correlation) which are unrelated – for example, sets of figures selected at random. We could then calculate the number of times that our 'experimental' value occurs in this series of 'chance' values, expressing it as a percentage, or alterna-tively as a proportion of 1·00. Thus an 'experimental' value which was also obtained, say, ten times in 250 correlations of random figures could be said to have a chance-occurrence probability of 4 per cent, or 0·04.

In practice, the probabilities of values have been definitely stated, for most individual statistical tests, in *statistical tables*, calculated both from empirical data and from consideration of the statistical concept of the *normal distribution* (discussed in Chapter 17). By consulting the appropriate statistical table (taking into account the size of the sample from which his value was obtained) the scientist can see whether his obtained value is one with a high or a low probability of occurrence by chance. If the value is likely to occur by chance, he cannot conclude that the sets of scores in his sample are meaningfully related. If the chance probability is very low, it is reasonably safe to dismiss the 'chance hypothesis' – in statistical terms, the *null hypothesis* – and to conclude that the relation observed in his scores is a meaningful one. This does not necessarily mean that his *interpretation* of the relation is supported (see the discussions of correlation and causality, above, and of experimental design, below). The estimate of probability simply indicates whether it is wise to accept the finding as a 'real' one.

Clearly, whether a given probability level is regarded as 'high' or 'low' is to some extent a matter of taste. It is an accepted convention that if the probability of chance occurrence is *above* 5 in 100, then the correlation is not regarded as significant. If the probability of chance occurrence lies between 5 per cent and 1 per cent (or 0·05 and 0·01) the correlation is regarded as significant, but only to the extent that we should proceed further with our line of inquiry – we do not regard such a finding as confirming the relation, but as an indication that further research along the lines of the hypothesis might well be profitable. If the chance probability is less than 1 per cent (or 0·01) the correlation is accepted as highly significant.

In the correlations between the results of tests X, Y and Z above, the expectations of gaining a perfect correlation with ten subjects would be well below 1 in 100, and so we would accept both the positive and negative rank order correlations as statistically significant.

Again, it should be stressed that the significance levels quoted here are *arbitrary*. In the experimental literature, a probability level of 0·05 is in practice very often quoted as inviting total confidence in the finding obtained, while the 10 per cent, or 0·10, probability level, while not accepted as demonstrating significance, is often remarked upon as an indication that the line of research concerned should be pursued further.

In this chapter we have been talking about the problems of the description and control of variables – the disciplining of ourselves and the sorting of our data. We have considered, very briefly and superficially, some of the problems associated with personal bias, the adequate definition of variables, prediction, adequate sampling, the error of attributing causality on the basis of correlation, significance and statistical checking against chance. We have stressed the need for caution and the control of data. In the next section of this chapter we will be considering and illustrating the use of experimental method proper, where the control of variables is maximized.

The experiment

It is the difficulty of ascribing a causal role to any variable that leads us to the use of *experiment*, for by the establishment of adequate experimental control we put ourselves in a position to say: 'If x had not occurred y would not have happened; therefore x is causally related to y.' A typical method of conducting a study of this kind is to draw up two groups of subjects who differ with respect to x – which may be called the *independent variable*. To return to an earlier example, if the investigator is interested in the effect of noise upon efficiency at work he may assign half of his subjects to work in noisy conditions and half to work in quiet conditions. The independent variable then is the background noise – the characteristic in which the experimental situation of individual subjects is made to differ. The measure which the experimenter takes of 'efficiency at work' is then termed the *dependent variable*, since it is hypothesized to be dependent upon the independent variable – that is, the variable independently manipulated by the experimenter. Incidentally, manipulation may take the form either of employing two or more different values of the independent variable, or of varying simply whether it is present or absent (the presence or absence of distraction while at work, for example). When one group of subjects receives a zero value of the independent variable it is commonly referred to as a *control group*, while subjects receiving a positive value of the independent variable constitute the *experimental group*. See, for example, this usage in Chapter 14 (Table 6, p. 359).

An alternative method, and one often adopted, would be to test each of the subjects involved under *both* conditions of the independent variable: this procedure avoids some disadvantages of the first, but also incurs some problems of its own.

There are some variables whose effect upon performance may interest us, but which cannot be directly manipulated by the experimenter: sex and age are obvious examples. In the case of such variables the experimenter does not assign subjects to one condition or another; subjects already possess certain characteristics which automatically place them into one category or another. Strictly speaking, the term 'experiment' applies to a study in which the experimenter himself manipulates the independent variable; when the variable to be investigated is one with respect to which subjects 'assign themselves' to groups, the study is not an experiment but a *systematic observation*. Most (though not all) studies concerned with correlation are of this latter type. Here, we shall use the term 'experiment' to cover any study of the effect of one variable (however manipulated) upon another.

It should incidentally be noted that many experiments involve the manipulation of several variables, rather than one only. We shall not deal with them here; the principles of experimental design are basically similar, although the designs needed become much more complex.

In any experiment there are various sources of error which have to be taken into account. These are of two kinds – non-systematic or random, and systematic. Random errors enter into every experiment, particularly in psychology where the subjects of experiment are complex organisms. Unexpected interruptions, switches of attention, changes of mood, individual differences in skill or susceptibility to fatigue, motivation to perform the task – all these and many other factors may give us differences of performance on the dependent variable. However, we have methods of controlling some of these random sources, if not all: for example, the use of sound-attenuated rooms, temperature control, the matching of groups in terms of their abilities before the application of the independent variable, and so on. In practice, it is impossible to match groups perfectly. We usually content ourselves with the assumption that random sources of error will cancel themselves out in the scores on the dependent variable, if the subjects have been assigned to their groups by some 'lottery' procedure. No one has ever performed a perfectly controlled experiment in psychology and nobody ever will; it is largely a matter of taking all reasonable precautions to control or balance out random sources of error, and then to be aware of any effects that any remaining ones may have had on our results.

Much graver faults occur if systematic errors are uncontrolled. Examples of these would be the failure to test the groups under the same conditions – a control group tested after a heavy lunch will behave very differently from an experimental group that is hungry. This would, of course, be quite acceptable if the independent variable was amount of feeding, but not otherwise. Again, if we placed all female subjects in one group and all males in another, any differences in the dependent variable might well be the result of this sex difference rather than of the experimental treatment. In effect, we would be compounding 'independent variables' and would find it difficult to discriminate between their possible effects.

The techniques of control are very numerous, but can be grouped under four main headings: elimination, constancy, balancing and randomization. The meanings of these terms are fairly self-evident. Unexpected interruptions, for example, can be *eliminated* as a source of error by testing the subject in a sound-proofed room, locking the door, pulling the blinds and posting notices outside which urge quiet on passers-by. Some variables cannot be eliminated but can be *held constant* – for example, the age of subjects, or ambient illumination during a perceptual task. Some variables, again, cannot be eliminated or held constant: suppose, for example, we wish to test the preferences of newborn infants for pattern (see Chapter 10). One method adopted to this end has been to present the infant with two patterns at a time and to observe the time spent by the infant in fixating each pattern (Fantz, 1961). It could be that the child has a preference for the left-hand object of a pair, quite irrespective of any pattern; thus the positioning of the patterns must be controlled. It cannot be eliminated or held constant, since the objects must both be presented, and cannot be presented simultaneously in the same place. The variable must be *balanced*: that is, the experimenter must ensure that each pattern used is presented for half its presentations on the left-hand side, and for half its presentations on the right-hand side, of the pair. In more general terms, balancing ensures that although the extraneous variable may vary in value from trial to trial, its variation is nevertheless the same for each condition of the independent variable. We cannot elaborate further on methods of balancing, or on methods of *randomizing*, which can be regarded as an approximation to balancing; accounts are given by, for example, A. L. Edwards (1960), Hyman (1964), Kurtz (1965) and McGuigan (1960).

Finally, the usefulness of a finding – in particular the generality with which it can be accepted – is crucially dependent upon the nature of the *sample* upon which it is based. Suppose, for example, that we wish to test a hypothesis concerned with the behaviour of children. Ideally, to test this hypothesis we should have as subjects children of both sexes, of all ages and intelligence levels, from all types of home background and from all national groups. Since this is impracticable, we should strictly speaking alter our hypothesis to fit our sample, so that it now has reference to, say, children of specified age and intelligence, from specific neighbourhoods of a specific town. In fact this is probably being too strict, and we can generally work within the common-sense notion that if, on *a priori* grounds, we have no reason to think that the variables of central importance will be substantially affected by our limited sampling, we can proceed with some confidence that the sample is reasonably representative – in this case, of 'children'. Further discussion of the methods and difficulties of sampling will be found in the references quoted above.

The controls adopted in the scientific study of behaviour are rigorous, and we are generally agreed that they must be so; but the requirement of rigorous control has often been felt effectively to prohibit the study of some areas of interest, while the investigation of other areas is open to the charge of artificiality. While this difficulty applies in some measure to all sciences, the problems for psychology are most acute, particularly in respect to the study of personality, psychopathology and, to a lesser degree, social behaviour. Nevertheless, most experimental psychologists share a belief – or at any rate a pious hope – that in the controlled observation of behaviour some reconciliation is possible of the demands of richness and precision. This book, too, testifies to that belief; it is for the reader, ultimately, to decide whether the belief is justifiable.

Part Two
Structure and Behaviour

We said in Chapter 1 that psychology has its roots in biology and that it spans the gap between the biological and social sciences. Accordingly we shall begin by examining behaviour from the biological point of view. In this part of the book it will be our business to look at the general question of how behaviour is shaped by those innate, constitutional or biologically given qualities of organisms which have evolved through natural selection.

The biologically determined characteristics of an organism are given with its genetic structure, or genotype. The simplest and most direct question we can ask, therefore, is whether genetic structure and behaviour are related. Chapter 3 takes up this question. As the reader will discover, answering it is far from easy. It is first necessary to be clear what is meant by the inheritance of behaviour and what kinds of evidence would demonstrate its existence. We shall endeavour, therefore, to state precisely the questions the behaviour geneticist asks and how he sets about answering them. This will be followed by a brief survey of some of the results of animal and human studies.

One of the fundamental defining characteristics of living organisms is that they develop. In Chapter 4 we examine the notion of development as it applies to behaviour. Since our interest here is in the developmental process in so far as it is constitutionally determined, we must also consider the ideas of maturation and growth. These terms are often used loosely, and our first task will be to attempt a definition of them. We shall look more closely at the kinds of evidence that justify the concept of maturation and end by considering certain general principles of development that have been suggested by research findings.

The third way in which we can study the influence of constitutional factors is by examining the relations between physiological structure and process and behaviour. Before we look at these relations, however, the structure itself must be described. In Chapter 5 we offer a summary account of those physiological structures that have been found most significant for the understanding of behaviour, namely the structures that make up the nervous system.

With this behind us we turn, in Chapter 6, to a review of the experimental evidence of the relationships between brain structure and behavioural functioning. The main areas of the brain are taken in turn. Then in Chapter 7 we examine those physiological processes which underlie the emotional and motivational aspects of behaviour.

Finally, in Chapter 8 we again take up the topic of motivation, but this time from the point of view of its behavioural definition and its instigation by both environmental and internal stimulation. This shift of emphasis to the interaction between environmental and constitutional factors prepares the way for Part Three which deals more directly with the influence of the environment.

Chapter 3
Behaviour Genetics

Introduction

The general problem

It is well known that the physical structure of an organism is to a large extent determined by its genes. To put it more technically, morphological phenotype is a function of genotype where by *morphological* we refer to shape or patterning, by *phenotype* we mean all the observable features of an organism at a given point in time, and by *genotype* we mean that total set of genes which is present in every cell. Individual differences in morphological phenotype, both between species and within species, can therefore be attributed primarily to differences in genotype. This is not to deny that environmental variation may also be associated with structural differences; a grossly uncongenial environment, prolonged inadequate nutrition, or disease can have permanent structural consequences. But it does mean that, when the environment is 'normal' in the sense of providing the conditions necessary for healthy growth, structural differences between and within species are more closely connected with genotypic differences than with such variation in environment as can occur within the 'normal' range for the organism.

The concern of the behavioural geneticist is to examine the relationship between genotypic variation and differences in *behavioural phenotype*, that is, in the functional properties exhibited by organisms. An organism functions in a context and as a result of stimulation from this context, and therefore to some extent this functioning is shaped by the context; behaviour represents the more or less adaptive transaction between an organism and its environment. We may therefore expect that behavioural difference will be somewhat less closely associated with genotypic difference than is structural variation. But the fact that behaviour is always the functioning of a structure which remains relatively constant from one situation to another, and which is under genetic determination, makes it probable that the influence of genotype upon behaviour will be discernible.

It might be thought that comparisons between species would give us the strongest evidence of genetic influence upon behaviour. Though in general this may be true, there are two complications. First, behavioural differences between species cannot be dissociated from environmental differences; two species may co-exist in the same physical environment, but the behavioural significance of that environment will be quite different for them. Second, one of the respects in which species differ, as a result of their differing genotypes, is in the plasticity or flexibility of their behaviour. Because of his genetic endowment, man is the most malleable of animals; his behaviour is most modifiable through learning. It is because of this genetically determined modifiability that some psychologists have held that genotypic differences between people are not important determinants of behavioural differences between them. The argument that because structure is under genetic determination therefore behaviour will in some measure also be, has less force in the case of human beings, for whom the distinguishing feature of their structure is the capacity for highly variable functioning under the stimulus of environmental change.

Two consequences have followed from these complications. In the first place, behaviour geneticists have concentrated upon the effects of genotypic difference within a species rather than between species. If the focus is upon one species, it is easier to exercise experimental control over environmental factors and thus isolate, in some degree, the effects of genotype. In the second place, students of genetic influence upon human behaviour, and that of other species to a lesser extent, have had to deal with *general* characteristics of behaviour, or broad *behavioural traits*, rather than with specific responses. The concept of behavioural trait is discussed in detail in Chapter 19. Briefly, it is based upon the fact that individual differences in certain forms of behaviour remain stable from one situation to another. We call a person intelligent, not because on one occasion and in one situation he exhibits behaviour which meets our criterion, but because he does this habitually and in varying circumstances. It is the influence of genotype upon behavioural trait that the behaviour geneticist investigates.

The specific questions asked by the behaviour geneticist

More precisely he asks the following questions:

1. Is there an association between individual differences in a behavioural trait and the genotypic differences of the same individuals? Do genotype and phenotypic behavioural trait *co-vary*? This is the initial question and the answer establishes whether, in explaining the variability of a particular form of behaviour in a population, we need to take account of hereditary differences.

2. *To what extent* are genotypic differences related to behavioural differences? What are the relative contributions of heredity and environment to the observed behavioural differences? Plainly, the answers to these questions must always be relative to the range of environmental and genotypic differences sampled in a particular investigation. But it may be possible to show that some behavioural traits are less susceptible to the influence of environmental variation than others.

3. What is the genetic mechanism involved in the production of a given behavioural difference? Is the difference due to forms of a single gene, or is it due to a number of genes acting in a cumulative fashion? Is there evidence of a dominant–recessive relationship between different forms of the same genes?

4. What is the nature of the physiological structure and process which intervene between the primary, local action of the gene and the behavioural trait manifested by the whole organism?

5. In what ways do genotype and environment interact in the production of behavioural differences? For example, the effect of a given environment might be to increase the intellectual functioning of all people. But it might also have a differential effect, making the innately more intelligent better still, and at the same time, perhaps

because it is overstimulating, actually depressing the level of performance of the innately less intelligent. Conversely, an environment which stimulates the innately dull may be insufficiently interesting to promote effectively the intellectual development of the innately bright.

This last question raises an issue which needs further elaboration. Phenotype, whether structural or behavioural, is always a function of the interaction of both genotype and environment. The effects of genotype and environment are not additive but multiplicative, in the sense that, without an appropriate environment, there can be no phenotype. To emphasize the point, it is worth listing some of the complex interactions which occur in the 'gap' between genotype and behaviour. Though genetic material does not all have the same function, the primary effect of those genes which control structural development is the production of enzymes. Thereafter, the following interactions occur: (a) between the effects of similar or different forms of the same genes at corresponding loci on a pair of chromosomes, (b) between the effects of different genes, (c) between the cell and its environment and (d) between the total multicellular organism and its environment. Just as it is the environment which determines whether potential genetic effects are actualized, so it is the genotype which determines which aspects of the physical environment are behaviourally significant.

These considerations make plain the absurdity of saying of a particular person's intelligence, for instance, that more of it is due to heredity than to environment. How is it, then, that we can even raise question 2 above, and what is the significance of the estimates made by many investigators of the relative importance of heredity and environment? To understand the justification for the question and the context which makes answers to it meaningful, it is necessary to be clear on two points. First of all, as we have said, the behaviour geneticist is not studying the single organism, but is trying to find out whether, and how much, in a specified population of organisms, *differences* in genotype *co-vary* with, or are associated with, *differences* in behavioural trait. Second, in analysing the results of an experiment he has to make use of various statistical procedures. He uses, as models to facilitate his analysis, those parts of statistical theory which suit his purposes. Central among these is the statistic called the *variance* or σ^2.

The variance is a single value which represents the degree of variability, scatter or dispersion of a set of scores; it is the average of the squared deviations of each score from the average score. For an adequate account of this statistic, the reader must consult one of the standard textbooks (e.g. A. L. Edwards, 1967c). For the present, the importance of this statistic resides in the following fact: if individual differences in a variable A can be attributed to two other independent variables X and Y, then the variance of the scores measuring A can be analysed into three components, one which represents the amount of the variance of A which is due to X, and the other the amount due to Y, together with a third, interaction component, which represents that amount of the variance of A which is due to the interaction of X and Y. These three components are additive and together make up the total variance of A. Now the behavioural geneticist knows that the behavioural variability in the population which he has measured is a function of both the variability of genotype and the variability of environment. It is therefore possible for him, using the variance statistic as his model, to write the following theoretical equation:

$$\sigma_B^2 = \sigma_H^2 + \sigma_E^2 + \sigma_{EXH}^2$$

where:

σ_B^2 is the total variance of a given behavioural trait

σ_H^2 is the amount of σ_B^2 which co-varies with genotypic differences

σ_E^2 is the amount of σ_B^2 which co-varies with environmental differences

σ_{EXH}^2 is the amount of σ_B^2 which can be attributed to the interaction of heredity and environment.

It must be reiterated that this is a purely theoretical equation. In practice, the problem of giving numerical values to the components of the equation is considerable. It would be necessary to have adequate measures of both genotypic and environmental differences, and we should need to modify the equation to take account of error in measurement. But the point remains that, so long as we are talking about the variability of a trait in a population, it is in principle quite possible to say that more of it is due to genotypic than to environmental differences.

It has been argued (Loevinger, 1943) that since we know that the effects of genotype and environment are not additive, it is inappropriate to apply a mathematical model which assumes that they are. The short answer is that, since the model is the best available, we have no choice. But it is possible to go further. In so far as this criticism has force, it is relevant only to the misapplication of the statistical model. The function of statistical analysis is to summarize in a convenient way the relations between sets of scores; to make inferences about the mode of operation of the factors involved is to go beyond the mathematical analysis, and cannot be justified by it. The assertion that differences in a trait are more closely associated with genotypic differences than with environmental does not conflict with a recognition of the fact that the two determinants interact continuously; for the former is a statement about the variance of a trait in a population, the latter a statement about the processes operating in each individual case.

For the remainder of this chapter, we shall consider some of the work which has been done in this field. No attempt will be made to give an exhaustive account. Instead the emphasis will be upon the problems that arise and the methods adopted to meet them, with particular reference to the questions listed above. Furthermore, we shall be primarily concerned with the direct experimental approach to the genetic determination of individual differences within a species. Other sources of evidence which bear upon the general question of hereditary influence, such as interspecies comparisons, studies of maturation and the correlating of physiological structure and function with behaviour, will be dealt with in other chapters.

Broadly speaking, the experimentalist is faced with three problems: (a) he must select a behavioural trait which can be reliably measured and which is not trivial; (b) he must be able to manipulate systematically the variable of genotypic difference; and (c) he must be able to control environment. Genes, of course, cannot be manipulated directly. In animal studies, control of genotypic difference is inferred from the nature of the breeding programmes adopted; in human beings it is inferred from the nature of familial relationships, or, as in the case of identical twins, from crucial phenotypic similarities. Since the study of animals and of human beings must necessarily involve somewhat different approaches, they will be considered separately.

Animal studies

The work of Broadhurst

The simplest way to introduce the reader to experimentation in this field is to take as illustration a particular group of experiments. The series chosen was performed at the Maudsley Hospital under the direction of Broadhurst. It has been selected because it is certainly one of the most sophisticated and extensive studies yet done, and it deals, in one way or another, with each of the questions listed at the beginning of the chapter. Though a full account of this work is to be found in a number of publications, the best starting point for the student is Broadhurst (1960).

Broadhurst began by replicating the earlier work of C. S. Hall (1951) under more rigorously controlled conditions. The behavioural trait investigated was that of emotionality in rats, as measured by the 'open-field test' (see Figure 1). This test consists essentially of a fear-inducing situation which yields two measures of intensity of response: rate of defecation, and latency and extent of ambulation, or readiness to explore. Because it might be questioned whether these measures are valid indices of what is usually meant by the term 'emotional', Broadhurst substituted the labels 'reactive' for 'emotional' and 'non-reactive' for 'unemotional'.

The experimental manipulation of genotypic difference in animals can be achieved in two related ways: by the *method of selective breeding*, in which the experimenter breeds out of a population of animals two strains that differ consistently on the behavioural trait; and by the *comparative method*, in which strains which have already been selectively bred for some other characteristic such as coat colour are tested for significant differences on the behavioural trait. The second is complementary to the first, and bears witness to the fact that breeding for one trait often results in breeding for others as well. Both methods were used by Broadhurst.

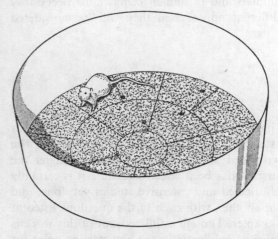

Figure 1   The open-field test of emotionality. The animal (here, a rat) is taken from its home cage, placed in the open area shown and subjected to mildly frightening noise and light stimulation. Measures of the animal's response include the number of faecal pellets eliminated and the amount of exploration or movement about the area; the floor is marked off in sections to allow a measure of movement. (Adapted from Broadhurst, 1963, Plate Ia)

In the experiment on selective breeding, extreme reactive animals were mated with each other, as were extreme non-reactives drawn from the same population. This was then repeated for subsequent generations. Mating schedules can be such as to maximize or to minimize inbreeding. Schedules that maximize inbreeding increase the over-all genotypic similarity within each strain and over-all difference between strains, and therefore increase the likelihood of breeding for other traits; schedules that minimize inbreeding make it more likely that the two strains will only differ on those genes relevant to the trait being investigated, and that in other respects they will be genotypically similar. The former procedure was adopted in Broadhurst's study, though his opinion is that, on balance, the latter is probably preferable. In practice, it is not easy to keep consistently to either.

Reactive and non-reactive animals had to be reared under as nearly identical environmental conditions as possible to ensure that differences between them could only be attributed to the breeding procedure. In Broadhurst's experiment, feeding, handling and physical environment were rigorously controlled. Important among environmental influences is the influence of the mother. To control for this, the offspring were cross-fostered, which means that half the offspring of reactive mothers were exchanged at birth with half the offspring of non-reactive, thus keeping the influence of the reactivity of the mother the same for both strains. The only way to control for the intra-uterine environment is to transplant some of the foetuses and this is not practicable. However, Broadhurst was able to test for the influence of this factor retrospectively. As soon as two relatively pure strains had been bred, it was possible to mate reactive fathers with non-reactive mothers and non-reactive fathers with reactive mothers. The offspring could then be assumed to be genetically similar and to differ only in their intra-uterine environments. When it was found that the two sets of offspring did not differ significantly on the behavioural trait, it could be concluded that intra-uterine environment was not a significant factor in this experiment.

The results of the main experiment are given in Figure 2. It is clear that, within a few generations, Broadhurst had bred two strains of rat which differed significantly and consistently on the behavioural trait. This fact is powerful evidence of the genetic influence upon the trait.

Breeding experiments of this kind do not permit any general assessment of the relative importance of heredity and environment for the obvious reason that environmental variation has been to a very large extent excluded. It is, however, possible to compare two traits for degree of genetic influence, when experimental conditions are comparable, by calculating the heritability quotient or h^2. This value is the ratio between the variance due to breeding procedures and the total variance. If this ratio is high for a given trait, it means that it is relatively easy to breed strains which differ systematically on it and that therefore the genetic influence is strong. In

Broadhurst's selective breeding experiment, heritability was found to be high for one measure, defecation rate, and somewhat lower for the other, ambulation scores. It should be noted that in his experiment using the comparative method, the heritability quotients were somewhat different.

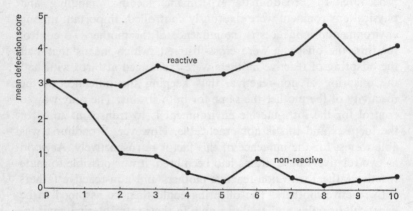

Figure 2   Results of selective breeding for high and low defecation scores. The graph shows the mean scores of the reactive and non-reactive groups from the parent generation through successive generations. (From Boadhurst, 1960, p. 51)

An examination of the logic and experimental method involved in analysing genetic mechanisms is beyond the scope of this chapter and the reader is referred to Fuller and Thompson (1960) for a clear account. Essentially, however, it consists of deriving predictions from a genetic hypothesis and testing them by mating schedules involving more than one strain of animal. From his own experiments, Broadhurst was able to conclude that an additive, polygenic system – that is, a large number of genes acting cumulatively – underlies emotionality in rats, and that the trait is not sex linked in any significant way.

A preliminary move in the investigation of the physiological structures and functions intervening between gene action and behaviour is to compare strains which are breeding consistently for a particular behavioural difference on other measures, both behavioural and physiological. However, if a physiological difference is found between two strains, it does not necessarily follow that this physiological difference is closely connected with the behavioural trait being investigated; this conclusion would only be justified if it could also be shown that the *only* genotypic difference between the strains was that specific to the behavioural difference, and this is difficult to ascertain. However, it does establish an initial likelihood that the physiological and behavioural variables are functionally related. The reactive and non-reactive strains have been subjected to a large number of further tests, both behavioural and physiological, and a number of differences have been discovered (Eysenck, 1964b). Reactive rats have been found to be heavier, to have a lower basal metabolism and a higher level of cholesterol in the bloodstream, and so on.

The final question concerns the interaction between genotype and environment. Experimentally, this means rearing different strains of animal under varied conditions to see if the conditions differentially affect the strains. In Broadhurst's main experiment, such an interaction was ruled out by maintaining a uniform environment for both strains. But in a later study (Levine and Broadhurst, 1963), reactive and non-reactive rats were compared for the effects of handling in infancy. Though for various reasons the outcome was not too clear, the evidence suggested that handling had a greater effect in reducing emotionality in reactive rats than in non-reactive ones.

Other studies

So far we have considered only one behavioural trait, that of emotionality. It is time to look briefly at the rest of the work that has been done.

The other behavioural trait which has received most attention, at least in selective breeding experiments, is 'intelligence' in rats, as measured by capacity to learn mazes (maze brightness). Two major studies (Heron, 1935, 1941; Tryon, 1940) have both found strong evidence of the influence of genotype upon this trait. Subsequent experiments have compared maze-bright and maze-dull rats on other measures and though it seems clear that maze brightness is not an isolated trait but part of a syndrome of traits, the precise nature of the syndrome is as yet unclear. Thus Searle (1949) found that the strains differed not only on cognitive tests but also on motivational ones; maze-bright rats showed stronger food motivation and lower spontaneous activity, so that they were less distracted by alternatives in the maze. Thompson and Bindra (1952) found no difference in emotionality between their maze-bright and maze-dull strains. On the physiological side, Tryon's maze-bright and maze-dull rats were used in experiments by Krech, Rosenzweig and Bennett (1956) which provide evidence of a relationship between cholinesterase activity in certain parts of the brain and performance in a learning situation. Subsequent experiments have demonstrated the following: that it is possible to breed strains of rat which differ systematically in cholinesterase activity (Roderick, 1960); that an enriched environment leads to an increased level of cholinesterase activity; and that there is an interaction effect between genotypic difference and environment in the determination of cholinesterase activity (Bennett et al., 1964). For a criticism of these experiments, see Hirsch (1964). The interaction between genotypic and environmental differences in the production of learning ability in rats has been examined in several studies. Hughes and Zubek (1956, 1957) supplemented the diet of bright and dull strains of rat in certain ways from weaning for forty days. The result was a significant improvement in learning by the dull rats, an improvement which lasted at least three months after the cessation of the dietary supplement; there was no improvement in the performance of the bright rats. Cooper and Zubek (1958) raised bright and dull rats in enriched and restricted environments, and compared their performance on learning tasks with a control group reared in 'normal' laboratory conditions. The results showed that bright animals were not improved by the enriched environment, and were retarded by the restricted environment; dull animals, on the other hand, were not affected by the restricted environment, but were considerably improved by the enriched environment.

Most of the other studies in this field have used the comparative method, and have served primarily to establish the influence of genotypic difference upon a behavioural trait. Many different species have been used and many different behavioural traits investigated. The following is a brief, illustrative sample: duration of crowing in cocks (Siegel, Phillips and Folsom, 1965); exploratory activity in mice (Thompson, 1953); various aspects of sexual behaviour in mice (McGill, 1962); emotionality in mice (Lindzey, 1951); and various aspects of social behaviour in dogs (Scott and Fuller, 1965).

Human studies

General remarks

Investigation into the influence of heredity upon human behaviour faces difficulties not encountered in animal studies. The direct manipulation of genotypic difference through breeding and the direct control of environment are not possible. Genotypic difference cannot be measured directly, nor are there any precise measures of environmental difference; indeed, it would be necessary first to know what aspects of environment are relevant before such measures could be constructed. However, the experimenter is not helpless. On the one hand, the principles of genetics enable him to infer degrees of genotypic similarity between people on the basis of their familial relationships. For example, the genotypic similarity between pairs of siblings is on average greater than the genotypic similarity between first cousins, or unrelated people. On the other hand, though environment cannot be precisely measured, it is possible to infer that some environments are more similar than others. For example, there is some plausibility in saying that siblings reared together experience more similar environments than siblings reared apart. The task before the psychologist, then, is to seek ways of showing that similarities on a behavioural trait are associated with similarities in genotype under conditions in which it is reasonable to claim that they are not also associated with similarities in environment. Since to do this he has to make a number of more or less plausible, but unproven, assumptions, it is hardly surprising that conclusions drawn from human studies are less firm and more vulnerable to criticism than the conclusions drawn from animal studies.

One of the earliest approaches to the problem was to report evidence on the way certain characteristics, such as high ability or mental defect, tend to run in families. Thus, Galton (1869) examined the frequency with which the relatives of eminent men themselves achieved eminence, and he showed that the remoter the relationship, the lower the frequency. As evidence for a genetic effect, such studies are inconclusive, since close relatives are likely to experience a similar environment. If we are to make justifiable inferences from a comparison of close and distant relatives, it must be under conditions in which we can be fairly sure that environmental variability is not affecting the results.

This has been attempted in a variety of ways. Since the most popular method has been to make use of twins, this method will be examined in detail here.

The twin method

Identical twins, since they derive from the same fertilized ovum, have identical genotypes. Fraternal twins derive from two separate fertilized ova, and therefore are no more alike genotypically than ordinary siblings. Yet both types share the experience of being twins. The argument then goes as follows: similarities on a trait between both identical and fraternal twins are due to both similarities of genotype and environment; but if identical twins are *more* similar to each other than are fraternal twins, this must be because of their greater genotypic similarity, and this difference in degree of similarity on the trait can be taken as evidence of the influence of genotype upon it. The argument can be summarized as follows, when I_a and I_b refer to members of a pair of identical twins, and F_a and F_b members of a pair of fraternal twins:

$I_a - I_b$ is due to environment
$F_a - F_b$ is due to environment and heredity.

Therefore, if $|F_a - F_b| > |I_a - I_b|$, then the difference must be due to the greater genotypic similarity of the identical twins.

A variant of this method is to compare identical twins who have been reared apart with both identical and fraternal twins reared together. Since it is implausible to claim that twins reared apart experience more similar environments than twins reared together, we can argue that, if identical twins reared apart are more similar than fraternal twins reared together, and if they are not much less similar than identical twins reared together, we have strong evidence of the influence of genotype upon behaviour. In practice, of course, it is difficult to find identical twins who have been separated early, and have grown up apart.

In making their comparisons, most investigators have used the correlation coefficient as their index of similarity between twins. A test measuring the relevant behavioural trait is given to both members of every pair of twins in the sample. The scores of one member of each pair are then correlated with the scores obtained by the other member of each pair. A high positive correlation means that the differences between members of pairs of twins tend to be small in relation to the variability between pairs. If the correlation coefficient for identical twins is higher than the coefficient for fraternal twins, it means that the differences within pairs of identical twins tend to be smaller than the differences within pairs of fraternal twins, provided of course that the variability between pairs is the same for both sets.

Intelligence and personality

Using the method of twin comparison, numerous studies have sought to demonstrate a genotypic influence upon intelligence. It is impossible to list them all here. Fortunately, Erlenmeyer-Kimling and Jarvik (1963) have reviewed some fifty-two studies involving subjects from many different countries, and of different generations, ages, ethnic grouping and socio-economic level. They found that the median correlation coefficients were as follows:

for identical twins reared together   0·87
for identical twins reared apart   0·75
for fraternal twins reared together   0·53.

In general, the average difference between fraternal twins reared together was one and a half to two times as great as the average difference between identical twins reared together.

So far, few studies have used twin comparisons to examine the relationship between genotypic difference and personality difference. Two papers (Eysenck, 1956; Eysenck and Prell, 1951) report results for the personality dimensions of neuroticism and extraversion–introversion (for a discussion of these dimensions, see Chapter 19). Identical twins reared together correlated 0·85 on neuroticism and 0·50 on extraversion; the corresponding coefficients for fraternal twins were 0·22 and −0·33. In a later study of the same personality dimensions, Shields (1962) obtained the following results:

	Identical apart	Identical together	Fraternal together
Extraversion–introversion	0·61	0·42	−0·17
Neuroticism	0·53	0·38	0·11

The coefficients are lower than for intelligence but fraternal twins are consistently less similar than identical twins. Gottesman (1963) found that identical twins reared together were more similar than fraternal twins on fifteen out of the seventeen scales of the Minnesota Multiphasic Personality Inventory (see Chapter 17 for an account of this test). The twin method has also been extensively used in the study of psychopathology (see Shields and Slater, 1961).

Results of this kind are often accepted as powerful evidence of the influence of genotype upon intelligence and personality. However, in assessing just how strong this evidence is, there are important qualifications to be made. Consider first the comparison between identical and fraternal twins reared together. The conclusion that the greater behavioural similarity between identical twins is due to their greater genotypic similarity is based upon the assumption that this greater similarity is *not* due to the fact that they experience an environment that makes them more similar. It is doubtful whether this assumption is justified. Earlier investigators found evidence of environmental pressures towards both greater similarity and greater difference among identical twins. For example, identical twins were more often mistaken for each other, were in each other's company more, and more often shared the same friends than was the case with fraternal twins; but on the other hand they were also more often observed to adopt different roles (one twin becoming the 'ambassador' for the pair), and the frequency of differential handedness was greater among them. It has sometimes been hopefully concluded that these factors cancel each other out. But when we do not know what aspects of environment are decisive for the trait in question, and when the evidence is so scanty, this conclusion is hardly warranted. Moreover, in a study (Husen, 1959) in which a very large sample of the population was involved, it was found that identical twins were much more anxious to stress their similarity and much less likely to be competitive. Furthermore, Husen found no difference in handedness between the types of twin, and in answer to the question, 'Who usually decides what you are going to do when you are together?', identical twins were much more likely than fraternal twins to reply, 'Both of us.' The problem is complex and difficult; but on balance the safest assumption seems to be that identical twins do experience more similar environments than fraternal twins and that a consequence of this could be greater similarity on intelligence and personality tests. The question we must then ask is whether this greater similarity in environment is a sufficient explanation of the consistent and markedly greater behavioural similarity. In the absence of definitive evidence, our judgement is bound to be influenced by the expectations we form on the basis of other findings involving different assumptions.

The most striking of these other findings is that identical twins reared apart are more similar on measures of intelligence and personality than fraternal twins reared together. In Shields's study (1962) they were even found to be slightly more similar on personality measures than identical twins reared together. It does seem very unlikely that identical twins reared apart share more similar environments than fraternal twins reared together. But even this assumption is not entirely beyond question. Identical twins reared apart are not in competition with each other as fraternal twins reared together often appear to be, and they may not experience environments which differ much on trait-relevant variables. It is plain that environment can affect performance on intelligence tests, for identical twins reared apart are less similar than identical twins reared together; and when identical twins reared apart are considered alone, there is a high correlation between degree of difference in educational advantage and degree of difference in intelligence (Anastasi, 1958). Finally, because identical twins who have been separated early in life are so rare, the use of them in research is especially vulnerable to criticism of a different kind. In order to draw general conclusions from comparing different types of twin, not only must the twins be representative of the population, but the different sorts of twin must be *equally representative*. It should be added that, in recent studies, steps have been taken to meet this criticism. Again we have to judge whether considerations such as these are sufficient and plausible enough to provide an alternative account of the results.

It should now be clear that, in the absence of precise measures of relevant environmental factors, comparisons between twins, and indeed between other groups such as siblings reared together and apart, cannot provide conclusive evidence of genotypic influence. With sufficient ingenuity, it is usually possible to produce some hypothetical explanation in terms of environment. But, at least as far as intelligence is concerned, the cumulative effect of studies involving different comparisons, so that no single environmental explanation can suffice for all of them, makes it at least highly probable that individual differences on the trait are partly a function of genotypic difference. Though there have been fewer studies of personality, it may be justly said that for some personality measures, the evidence points in the same direction.

Recent developments

In so far as intelligence is concerned, 'few psychologists nowadays would be inclined to contest the mere fact of mental inheritance' (Burt, 1958). It is when we ask about the mode of transmission of the genetic factor and the proportion of the population variance which can be attributed to it that we find controversy. Comparisons between types of twin do not help us to answer these questions. It is true that formulae have been devised for estimating the heritability of a trait (see Fuller and Thompson, 1960, pp. 112–14) on the basis of twin comparison, but the reliability of estimates derived in this way depends upon the assumption that identical twins do not experience an environment which makes them more similar than fraternal twins, and this assumption we have been obliged to query.

If these other questions are to be answered, a more general approach to the problem is needed and already some preliminary attempts have been made to supply it. Burt and Howard (1956) have developed a 'multifactorial theory' of inheritance and applied it to intelligence. This is too complex to be outlined in detail here, but essentially it consists in adopting a particular genetic theory, or model, and then predicting the correlations between all kinds of familial relationship which would follow from it. If the predictions fit the observed correlations closely, this may be taken as support for the accuracy of the theory. Burt and Howard found such a 'fit' in their preliminary study and conclude that the evidence favours a polygenic system, adjusted for partial dominance and assortative mating, which will account for nearly 80 per cent of the variance. Of course, such a result would only apply within the genetic and environmental limits of the population sampled in the study.

In the field of personality difference, Cattell and his associates have developed a 'multiple variance analysis' approach (Cattell, Blewett and Beloff, 1955). This is a technique for handling a variety of particular familial comparisons at the same time and calculating the ratios of the variance due to genetic and to environmental differences. The approach is flexible and permits, for example, distinguishing between the ratios for variability *within* families and the ratios for variability *between* families. In the examples of its application provided, Cattell used the junior version of his own 16 Personality Factor Test, and found that some of the personality dimensions were mainly a function of environment and others of heredity, and that the pattern varied depending on whether the focus was upon differences between families or upon differences within families. A fuller account of Cattell's work will be found in Chapter 19.

It is likely that Burt and Cattell have given a new impetus to research in this area, but since their methods require large numbers of subjects and complex statistical treatment of results, it may be a little time before we shall know. But perhaps the greatest need at present is for accurate measures of environmental influences. Only these will make possible close analysis of the interactions between genotype and environment. In this respect, one of the most promising approaches, which will be discussed in the next chapter, is the use of twins in developmental studies. Individuals of a known degree of genetic similarity can be closely observed in their interactions with controlled environmental factors and the consequences of such interactions specified in detail. Though large-scale statistical studies serve an essential function, the price paid for them is a certain remoteness from the actual behaviour of people.

Further reading
P. L. Broadhurst, *The Science of Animal Behaviour*, Penguin Books, 1963.
C. O. Carter, *Human Heredity*, Penguin Books, 1962.
J. L. Fuller and W. R. Thompson, *Behavior Genetics*, Wiley, 1960.
G. E. McClearn, 'The inheritance of behavior', in L. Postman (ed.), *Psychology in the Making*, Knopf, 1962.

Chapter 4
Maturation and Development

Introduction

In the previous chapter we examined some of the evidence which points to the existence of a functional relationship between genotypic difference and behavioural difference, *when behaviour is measured at a particular stage of development*. In the present chapter we shall be focusing upon the influence of genotype upon behavioural development. More precisely: are differences in genotype related to differences in the way behaviour changes over time in the same individuals?

The behavioural transactions between an organism and its environment are constantly being modified under the control of changing environmental stimulation on the one hand and biological processes of growth and ageing on the other. It is usual to label the changes due to environment as *learning* and the changes due to growth and ageing as *maturation*. It is of the greatest importance to be clear, however, that this conceptual distinction does not imply that there are two independent processes, one of maturing and one of learning, that somehow occur in parallel. The development of behaviour must be regarded as a single, continuous process. The notions of maturation and learning are convenient abstractions from this developmental process and serve to draw attention to the two main classes of influence that bear upon it.

In what follows, we shall inquire into how psychologists use the term *maturation* and into the kind of empirical evidence that justifies this usage; learning will be discussed in Part Three. The first part of this chapter will be concerned with conceptual analysis because the confusion surrounding the notion of maturation has been responsible for many fruitless controversies in the history of psychology.

The concept of maturation

In defining the concept of maturation, it is useful to contrast it with two other, overlapping terms – namely *development* and *growth*. There is a good deal of confusion and ambiguity in their usage. Some writers use them virtually interchangeably, and those who do differentiate their meanings are by no means in agreement. For the psychologist, the justification for maintaining distinctions between them must lie in the fact that each can be given a distinctive empirical reference. Since the terms can be given such distinctive references, there seems to be good reason for trying to separate them. (For other general discussions, see Ausubel, 1958; Bayley, 1951; D. B. Harris, 1957; Hebb, 1966; Kessen, 1960.)

Development

Of the three this is the most inclusive term. The concept of development refers to the fact that changes in the nature and organization of an organism's structure and behaviour are systematically related to age; 'a characteristic is said to be developmental if it can be related to age in an orderly and lawful way' (Kessen, 1960, p. 36).

Such a definition naturally raises the question whether there can be non-developmental changes in behaviour. To say that behavioural change is age-related is to say that in some sense it is cumulative and irreversible. Having once attained puberty, or learned to walk or to read, there is no going back to the condition which existed before these events. And each of these events is the necessary condition of further developments in behaviour. What kind of behavioural change would then be classified as non-developmental? Clearly it would be any learning which is reversible in the sense that it could be 'unlearned', and which could occur equally well over the whole age range. It could be argued that no learning meets these criteria: later learning always builds upon and is affected by early learning; and it could be said that there is never complete 'unlearning' since a learned response which appears to have been forgotten has presumably left some permanent and irreversible trace in the organism. But this is to be too academically precise. Much learning, especially in human beings, can occur equally well over a wide age range and does not appear to be an important condition for later learning. For practical purposes we can designate learned responses of this kind as non-developmental.

We call behavioural change developmental, then, when it follows an invariant sequence over age. To take an obvious example – in the development of motor skills in children, sitting precedes crawling which in turn precedes walking, and so on. Each stage prepares the way for the next and the order of the stages is always the same. Such development is the fruit of the intimate and subtle interaction between spontaneous structural changes on the one hand, and the different experiences and learning made possible by systematic environmental change on the other.

Growth

Growth refers, of course, to *incremental increases in amount* of a characteristic. But some psychologists have included in the term other features of the developmental process, such as changes in organization and the emergence of 'new' forms of behaviour. This, however, is to make the term effectively synonymous with development. Growth is best exemplified in such physical characteristics as height, heart size and gland weight. Growth curves have been plotted for a great many physical characteristics and, although there is considerable variation among individuals, the curves do, on average, follow predictable patterns (see Shock, 1951). The concept of growth has also been applied to behavioural traits in the hope that similar stable patterns would be found. However, the application of the term to behaviour is less safe. It is only justifiable to talk of the incremental growth of intelligence when what we mean by this is that, with increased age, individuals solve more difficult versions *of the same kind of problem* that they were solving earlier. But to talk of the growth of intelligence in a more global sense may be misleading, for there is reason to think that the nature of intelligence, in this wider sense, changes with age. To extend the term to age changes in personality traits is even more problematic, for it is highly questionable whether, for example, aggression is the same kind of trait in childhood as it is in adulthood. The essential requirement for evidence of growth is that the same measure be applied at different ages and yield an increase with increased age. It follows that growth in a characteristic ceases when the maximum level is reached.

Maturation

Maturation is the least easy to define. Gesell (1929) defined it in terms of those phases and products of development which are wholly or chiefly due to innate and endogenous factors. But, of course, no developmental change is wholly due to genetic influence. Both genotype and environment are necessary conditions of all development, but neither is sufficient; and, as was said at the beginning, development is a single process, not two parallel ones. Some writers (e.g. Hebb, 1966) have loosened the term to include, besides innate factors, the influence of those environmental conditions which are the essential prerequisites of the realization of genetic potentiality. Others adopt an operational approach and, like Ausubel (1958), define maturation as 'development that takes place in the demonstrable absence of specific practice experience' (p. 80). But rarely, if ever, can we 'demonstrate' the absence of specific practice. It seems wisest to recognize that precise circumscription of the term is impossible. Its central function is to refer to genetic control of the patterning and sequential ordering of development; maturation is genotype in action. Despite arguments to the contrary, there is still some value in contrasting maturation and learning so long as we remember that this is simply a convenient way of classifying different antecedent conditions of the single process of development.

Some writers (e.g. Bayley, 1951) would limit the term to progress towards maturity or adulthood. The implication is that maturation ceases when the optimal development level of a trait is reached. This is inconsistent with the term as understood here. There is evidence that genetic influences affect development throughout the life cycle. Kallman and Sander (1949) conclude from their study of twins over the age of sixty years that genotype plays a basic role in determining the ability to maintain physical and mental health into senescence.

Finally, we can usefully distinguish behavioural from physiological maturation. Since behaviour occurs 'between' an organism and its environment, and since the genetic influence upon behaviour is mediated by physiological structure and functioning, behavioural maturation can be defined as behavioural development in so far as it is determined by physiological maturation. The development of physiological structure is, of course, dependent upon an adequate physical environment. Moreover, variations in environment can affect the timing of the process and the ultimate level reached in growth (Tanner, 1962). But the *sequence* in which physiological structures develop seem to be very much under the control of genotype. The order in which the structures develop is highly constant within a species and resistant to wide variations in environment. Studies have shown that the timing of the onset of menstruation is much more similar for identical than for fraternal twins (Tanner, 1962). Patterns of growth in at least some features, such as height, show a 'target-seeking' quality. Tanner (1963) observed that when growth in height is slowed down by illness, there tends to follow a period of accelerated growth until the individual 'catches up' with his growth curve. There is good reason, therefore, for assuming that, given an adequately supportive environment, the differences between individuals in their physiological development are very much a function of their genotypic differences. It follows that one of the ways of investigating behavioural maturation is to study the way in which behaviour change is correlated with physiological development.

A striking feature of physical growth is that in general it follows a negatively accelerated curve. With the exception of the adolescent spurt, growth is fastest in the very beginning and gradually slows up. It is not surprising, therefore, that students of behavioural maturation have tended to concentrate upon the earliest stages of development, for it is then that the effects of physiological maturation are most visible.

So far we have only been concerned with the definition of certain terms. The psychologist is interested in the concept of maturation only in so far as the results of empirical studies require it for their adequate evaluation. Comparatively few studies have been explicitly designed to demonstrate the existence of behavioural maturation, and these stem mostly from the period, now part of history, when investigators tended to adopt somewhat extreme points of view – either that maturation is unimportant, or that development is more or less wholly due to it. In recent years, developmental psychologists have assumed the operation of both maturation and learning and have sought to understand the nature of their interaction rather than to demonstrate the presence of either.

In the following section, we shall give some examples of the different kinds of study which seem to demand the concept of maturation for their adequate description and explanation.

The empirical basis for the concept of maturation

Irrefutable evidence of behavioural maturation is hard to obtain. This is because it cannot be separated from the effects of environmental change. Environment does change systematically with age. This is especially true for children. The caretaking procedures of adults are deliberately varied as the child grows older and this could not only provoke changes in the child but also be the effect of those changes in the child which are due to maturation. Nevertheless, there are grounds which support the use of the concept. Six kinds of evidence have been selected for discussion here. They do not all offer equally strong justification for assuming the presence of behavioural maturation, and one or two provide only tenuous support. A brief description of them will be given first and then each will be discussed more fully with illustrations.

The first source of evidence is studies which correlate changes in physiological structure with the appearance of new forms of behaviour. The importance of maturation is manifest if the emergence of certain forms of behaviour is contingent upon specifiable structural developments. Second, the fact that the sequential ordering of behavioural development is constant within a species points to the influence of maturation provided we have no reason to think that the phases of this development are environmentally initiated. Third, there are studies in which subjects with known genetic similarities and differences are tested at regular intervals over a period of development. If similarities and differences in the timing and patterning of behavioural change parallel genetic similarities and differences, we have the most direct evidence of 'genotype in action'. Fourth, attempts have been made to exclude the possibility of learning and to show that behavioural development nevertheless occurs. Fifth, there are the studies which show that the same learning procedures have different effects at different ages. Last, there is the evidence that individual differences in a behavioural trait remain relatively constant through development.

1. All organisms have a life cycle, the pattern and timing of which is genetically controlled through the mediation of physiological maturation. There are two ways in which this process influences behaviour. Certain levels of physiological development are a necessary condition of the appearance of certain classes of behaviour; when these behaviours appear for the first time, they may already be structured and patterned in a species-specific manner. This is most evident in the early stages. The first appearance of reflex responses is contingent upon neural maturation, as is the pattern of these reflexes (see Carmichael, 1954, and Coghill, 1929, for a detailed account). The maturation of the sexual function is a necessary condition of sexual reproduction. In lower species, whose behaviour is relatively stereotyped, maturation also determines the *form* this sexual behaviour will take when it emerges; the higher the species, the less the form of the behaviour is maturationally determined. In monkeys, for example, gross social deprivation in early life can radically affect the form of behaviour to the extent of making reproduction highly unlikely; though even in this species, it may be assumed that, within the 'normal' limits of environmental variation, physiological maturation plays an important role in determining the structure of sexual behaviour when it occurs. Among human beings, however, though puberty is a necessary condition of sexual reproduction, the patterning of sexual behaviour is, within the limits set by anatomical structure, much more determined by social factors than by maturation. Even the common assumption that at puberty

a maturationally determined increase in heterosexual interest occurs has not been demonstrated. It is true that a change of interest does occur. In an early study, Stone and Barker (1939) compared pre-menarcheal and post-menarcheal girls of the same age, educational and social status, and found that post-menarcheal girls had significantly stronger heterosexual interests. But, as the authors point out, this could be a function of the social expectation that they should have greater heterosexual interests with the onset of menstruation. There is evidence that interests, values and social behaviour vary systematically throughout the life cycle (see Pressey and Kuhlen, 1957); but though common sense suggests that maturation plays a part in this, it cannot be offered as clear evidence of maturation until cross-cultural studies have shown this to be stable across societies which differ in the relevant social expectations.

2. The influence of maturation is also discernible in the way in which the sequential ordering of behavioural development remains constant, at least within the normal range of environmental difference. In human beings, the best evidence of this has come from the work of Gesell and his associates, who studied the motor development of children over the first years of post-natal life. Babies were examined at frequent intervals and under standard conditions, and their behaviour very precisely recorded. The sequential patterning of motor development was found to be remarkably constant; indeed, it was sufficiently constant for Gesell to formulate a number of 'principles of developmental morphology' to describe the sequence (Gesell, 1954). An example is the principle of cephalocaudal progression, previously observed by Coghill and others, which refers to the tendency for the more developed forms of motor behaviour to occur first in the region of the head and only later in lower regions of the body. It is true that Gesell did not examine the effects of gross environmental abnormality upon this sequence; but his observations were so refined and detailed that it is hard to believe that environment played an important part in determining the sequence. Moreover, there is evidence that gross restriction of movement in the early stages may not affect the outcome, though it may interfere with the patterning and timing of the intermediate stages. Dennis

and Dennis (1940) compared babies who, in accordance with cultural practice, had been strapped tightly to a cradle board for the first three to six months of life with babies allowed freedom, and found no difference in the age of onset of walking.

Another example is speech development. In recent years, research into the development of language strongly suggests that maturation plays a crucial part. Lenneberg (1967) has summarized this research and his argument is briefly as follows: though exposure to language is an essential condition of speech attainment, children are not normally taught to speak; yet by the age of about three years they have usually acquired a considerable skill in it and the sequence of steps in the achievement of this skill remains invariant even though children may differ widely in the amount of speech stimulation they receive; moreover, if for some reason speech development is delayed, children still go through the same stages in its acquisition. The content and structure of the speech to which the child is exposed will, of course, influence the content and structure of his own speech; but provided he is exposed to speech of some kind, the timing of his speech development follows its own course. In short, what occurs over the first three years is not so much a change in the environment as a change in the child's capacity to learn from the environment.

3. The most direct experimental approach to the study of behavioural maturation involves the control of genotypic difference. Scott and Fuller (1965) reared five breeds of dog under controlled conditions and found that the timing of certain critical phases of early development was related to genotypic difference. With human beings, the obvious method is the use of twins. Gesell and Thompson (1941) have reported the results of an intensive developmental study of one pair of identical twins from early infancy through to puberty. The twins were frequently given tests of motor, mental, linguistic and social behaviour, during which the authors made extensive use of film. Though it is impossible to draw general conclusions from one pair of twins, particularly without fraternal twin controls, the developmental profiles were strikingly similar. This was especially true of motor development, where the similarities were so close that

the differences that did occur were small enough in the authors' judgement to pass for similarities in a comparison of unrelated children, or even siblings. A recent, better-controlled study has been done by Freedman and Keller (1963). Making use of observations and film, they found that, over the first ten months of post-natal life, identical twins were significantly more similar in the timing and patterning of behavioural development than fraternal twins. The method adopted by these investigators deserves to be used much more than at present.

4. Some experiments have sought to exclude all significant environmental influence for a period of time to see whether changes in an organism's behavioural repertoire have occurred without the effects of environment. The classical experiments of this kind were done by Carmichael (1926). He anaesthetized *Amblystoma* (a kind of newt) shortly before the swimming responses would normally appear. Control *Amblystoma* were allowed to develop in the usual way. When the control *Amblystoma* had been swimming freely for five days, the experimental group was released from the anaesthetic. Within thirty minutes, they were swimming as well as the controls. Later experiments (Carmichael, 1927) suggested that the thirty minutes could largely be accounted for by the time taken for the effects of the anaesthetic to wear off. These experiments have sometimes been taken as evidence that structural maturation can occur without practice of the relevant function. However, Fromme (1941), in a similar series of experiments, showed that practice is necessary for the optimal functioning of a structure. That this is so does not alter the fact that the experiments demonstrate the importance of maturation.

5. A further type of study which at least points to the effect of maturation is that in which the same learning procedure can be shown to have different outcomes at different stages of development. The demonstration that such a difference exists does not necessarily entail an explanation in terms of maturation; but the relevant studies do carry the implication, in various degrees, that maturation may be involved. One method is that of 'co-twin control'. In the

well-known study by Gesell and Thompson (1929), one of a pair of identical twins was given practice in climbing stairs while the other was kept away from stairs. Shortly after the trained twin had reached a high level of proficiency, the other was allowed to climb the stairs. She was found to reach an equal level of skill in a much shorter period of time. The improved learning capacity in the delayed twin cannot be attributed wholly to maturation, since, though unable to climb stairs, she had plenty of opportunity, as had the trained twin, to practise the component elements of the stair-climbing pattern at other times. However, the fact that she was able to recombine these elements into a new pattern more quickly suggests that maturation was at work. In a similar study, using two pairs of twins, McGraw (1940) showed that twins who were given training in bladder control from an early age were no better than their co-twins whose training was delayed until well after the age of twelve months.

There is a very great deal of evidence to show that certain experiences and forms of learning have their optimal effect when the developing organism has reached a stage of readiness for them. We know, for instance, that the formation of the first social attachments in children, and learning to walk, to speak and to read are all contingent upon the attainment of certain levels of development. There is also evidence that in some instances, if the learning is delayed much beyond this optimal period, it may be less easily acquired, or not acquired at all. Investigators commonly assume that this readiness to learn, or special susceptibility to experience, is at least partly a function of maturation. However plausible this assumption is at a common-sense level, its demonstration is extremely difficult. To illustrate, we can consider the development of learning in monkeys. Zimmerman and Torrey (1965) have reviewed the experimental evidence which shows that for some tasks adolescent and adult monkeys learn more rapidly and effectively than young animals under conditions in which experience of the task is held constant. This superiority of the older animals could be due to the fact that efficient performance of the task is dependent upon specific forms of prior learning which the young animal has not had the opportunity to acquire; or it could be due to the facilitating effect of greater physiological maturation; or both factors could be equally important. To be sure that maturation is an important factor, it would be necessary to demonstrate either that specific antecedent learning is not necessary, or, if it is, that it has already adequately occurred in the young animals, or that in the intervening period of development, certain relevant physiological changes have taken place which are not themselves dependent upon particular forms of learning.

6. There is one final type of study which is relevant to the concept of maturation and that is the study which seeks to show that behavioural differences at a later period of development are predictable from differences at an earlier stage. In this type of study, a group of subjects is tested at regular intervals from early childhood through to adulthood. Performance at the earlier stages is correlated with performance later. (An excellent review of these studies will be found in Bloom, 1964.) A number of such longitudinal studies of intelligence have been made, all of which are in agreement that differences in intelligence, as measured by tests, have a quite high degree of stability over a long period of childhood and adolescence.

The results for one study are plotted graphically in Figure 3. A detailed discussion of these results and the findings of other studies will be found in Bloom (1964). The fact that correlations for the first year are zero or very low is due to the difficulty of creating measures which can be realistically applied to both early infancy and later childhood. This in turn stems from the fact that the nature and organization of intellectual functioning are probably not the same at the two stages.

Though studies of this kind offer firm evidence that differences in intelligence between children remain fairly stable over a long period of development, they provide no clue why such stability should occur. There are two possible explanations. On the one hand it might be a maturational effect in that genotypic differences between children presumably remain absolutely stable throughout life. On the other hand it might be due to the fact that differences in environmental stimulation remain constant throughout development. In order to demonstrate that the stability in intelligence is a function of maturation it would be necessary to show that such stability still obtains under conditions in which it is known that differences in the relevant environmental factors are not stable. At present we are a long way from such a demonstration, for valid and reliable measures of the relevant environmental variables do not exist.

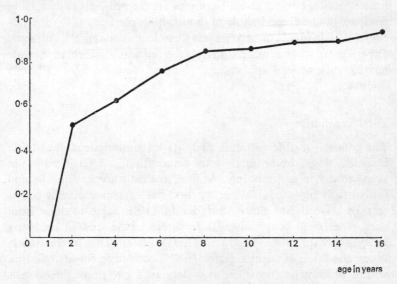

age in years

Figure 3   Correlations between I.Q.s measured at different ages with I.Q.s at age eighteen years. (Data from Bayley, 1949)

Some characteristics of the developmental process

Besides investigating the innate and environmental conditions which shape development, psychologists have also attempted to character- ize the process itself by formulating various descriptive principles of behavioural development. These principles are useful because they draw attention to some of the observable features of the process and point the way to a general theory of development. As yet there is no accepted general theory and it would be a mistake to suppose that the principles put forward constitute one. But they are a useful way of representing those developmental consistencies within and between species which await explanation in terms of a general theory.

Not all the principles put forward are equally useful. Some have very limited applicability, such as the principle of cephalocaudal progression quoted earlier, which is relevant only to the earliest stages of behavioural development. Others are so general as to have little empirical content at all. Examples are the principle of increasing complexity and the principle of diminishing plasticity (i.e. the tendency for individuals to become less flexible and adaptable with age). Others more or less succeed in being empirically informative while having some general application. Three of these will now be briefly discussed.

1. Differentiation

The concept of differentiation finds its least ambiguous illustration in embryology. Immediately after conception, the fertilized ovum starts to divide and multiply. At first, the cells are structurally and functionally indistinguishable. As the total aggregate of cells begins to take a significant shape, so individual cells begin to differ from each other. Cells progressively differentiate in the sense of becoming increasingly specialized in structure and function. This differentiation is one condition of the aggregate of cells becoming a single organism, within which cells may differ as widely as, for example, blood cells and nerve cells.

At the level of cellular development, differentiation can be defined with some precision. In extending the term to behavioural development, some of this precision is lost, but there is much evidence that the extension is justified. Coghill (1929) was one of the first to document this principle in the field of behaviour. He observed that in the behavioural development of *Amblystoma*, the first responses tended to be total and diffuse, involving the whole organism, and that only later was the organism capable of more precise, local responses. As Coghill puts it: 'The limb arises in complete subjugation to the trunk. It can do nothing except as the trunk acts. From this subjugation, it struggles as it were for freedom.' And again: 'Behaviour develops from the beginning through the progressive expansion of a perfectly integrated total pattern and the individuation within it of particular patterns which acquire various degrees of discreteness.'

Gesell (1954) reports evidence of a similar differentiation of local responses from original total responses in the behaviour of babies during the first year of life. When a young baby reaches for an object, he is likely to do so with arms, legs and even head; later he will reach for it with one arm only. Bridges (1932), also in a study of babies, has reported evidence that the emotional responses of joy, fear and anger are progressively differentiated out of an initial response of general excitement.

The concept of differentiation has also been applied to more long-term aspects of development. Werner (1948) has attempted to conceive all mental development in this way. Witkin and his associates (1962) have traced the way children's experience of themselves and their environment becomes progressively articulated with age. The child's conception of the human body appears initially to take the form of a general, schematic impression which subsequently becomes differentiated as the component elements are increasingly articulated. There is also evidence that the development of intelligence can be conceived in terms of the differentiation of special abilities out of a more unitary general ability. The relevant studies have mostly used factor analysis, and have been designed to show that more factors are needed to account for individual differences in adolescence than in childhood. However, the studies are not all in agreement and the issue is still unresolved. (For useful discussions of this problem, see Bayley, 1955, and Burt, 1954.)

2. Integration

As cells differentiate in structure and function, so the survival of each cell, and of the whole structure, depends upon the co-operative integration of these different functions. The activity of different organs must be co-ordinated in the service of the organism as a whole and the need for such co-ordination is directly related to the degree of autonomy achieved by the particular organs. That is, the complexity of integration is a function of the complexity of differentiation. In higher organisms, one type of cell, the nerve cell, has been differentiated largely to serve this co-ordinating, integrating function.

Psychologists have applied the concept of integration to behavioural development in order to bring out the observable fact that local reflex units become combined, through learning, into more complex patterns and sequences. In the past, some psychologists adopted a somewhat doctrinaire attitude and claimed that this was indeed *the* way in which behaviour developed. They were in turn opposed by advocates of the principle of differentiation. Though the controversy generated much research, its unreality soon became apparent. Both principles are needed, for each presupposes the other. Moreover, there is an inherent imprecision in both, for it would be difficult to establish that a particular response was really a total response, or that it was entirely local (Kuo, 1939).

It is not difficult to find evidence to support the use of the concept of integration. All learning can be conceived in these terms. Developmentally, it can be evident in the way component skills are organized into more complex patterns, as in learning to walk or play a game; it can be seen in the combination of speech sounds into words and sentences, and in the way abstract concepts are formed through the process of classification. At a more general level, personality theorists make much use of the term to describe the way attitudes, values, motives and opinions tend, with more or less success, to be consistent and coherent (G. W. Allport, 1961). The whole process of psychological development in children and adolescents could be said to be in the direction of greater autonomy and self-regulation, and greater independence of social support and influence.

3. Successive stages

A number of psychologists have described development as proceeding in stages; others have criticized the use of the concept as arbitrary and misleading. This dispute is in some respects a new form of an older controversy, namely, whether behavioural development is continuous or saltatory (i.e. occurring in sudden jumps). This earlier controversy has largely died down through the recognition that development can validly be described as both continuous and discrete, depending upon the perspective of the observer. For example, at the appropriate stages of readiness, the young child will learn to walk with apparent suddenness. From only being able to crawl, he will, in a matter of weeks, be walking quite well. However, when the process is examined in detail, a long period of preparation will be evident. The development of walking can be described as both gradual and sudden. We could put the point another way by saying that growth in a particular characteristic is always continuous and gradual, but that changes in the patterning and organization of growing elements may be relatively sudden.

A necessary condition of the use of the concept of stage is that the limits of a stage can be more or less precisely delineated in a non-arbitrary way. It follows that the term cannot be applied to the process of quantitative, incremental growth, for its use would be arbitrary. But it can be usefully applied to the more qualitative aspects of development, such as changes in behavioural organization, the emergence of new forms of behaviour and the disappearance of old.

A further condition which must obtain if the concept of stage is to be *developmentally* relevant is that the sequential ordering of those qualitative changes which empirically index particular stages must be constant. The age at which individuals enter a given stage may vary; what matters is that all individuals normally go through the same stages in the same order.

The developmental theorists who have made most extensive use of the concept are probably Freud, Gesell and Piaget. Freud (1905, trans. 1949) conceived of the development of the 'sexual instincts' in children in terms of an invariant sequence of stages. Each stage is defined by that area of the body which, at the time, is the salient focus of erotic sensation. The first centre of pleasure is the mouth. By the end of the second year, though the mouth is still an important source of pleasure, the anus is now a more salient centre of erotic concern. Then, by the age of about four or five years, the focus has shifted to the genitals. The primacy of the genitals is at this time precarious and temporary, for, according to the theory, from about this time until puberty, the child is presumed to enter a stage of latency, during which sexual interests recede in importance as a consequence of socially induced repression. Finally, at puberty or shortly afterwards, with increased sexual drive, the primacy of the genitals is firmly established and lasts until old age. These stages of sexual development are presumed to underlie the pattern and quality of the growing child's social relationships. Future adult character is held to be partly explicable in terms of the relative importance which the stages have for the child, and failure to develop properly through these stages is thought to be the basis of later sexual perversions and neurotic disorders (see also Chapter 19).

Though Freud's developmental theory has proved fertile in such fields as the study of family relations and psychopathology and has led to much research which might not otherwise have been done, considered from the point of view of the concept of stage, it has a major weakness. Freud's use of the term meets the second of the criteria mentioned above, in that the stages are presumed to be invariant and universal; but it fails to meet adequately the first. It is extremely difficult to deduce from the theory what sorts of behaviour would be unequivocal evidence that the child had moved from one stage to another. The theory is too loosely related to observable behaviour for an adequate testing of it to be easy or even possible. This probably follows from the fact that its original formulation was not based on systematic observation of children but upon the memories of adults.

Gesell's approach was quite different. With a minimum of theoretical presupposition, he closely observed the behaviour of children and, so to speak, allowed this behaviour to reveal its own stages. For the resulting account of development see, for example, Gesell and Ilg (1949). Gesell's use of the concept does meet the two criteria we have described. But because his stages are so numerous and remain essentially a convenient way of organizing observations, they are not integrated into a general theory in the way that Freud's psychosexual stages are. On the other hand, Gesell's work, because of its great precision, has facilitated the construction of measures of 'intelligence', or mental maturity, in infancy.

The psychologist who has made the most elaborate and systematic use of the concept of stage is undoubtedly Piaget. Piaget investigated in great detail the qualitative aspects of the development of thinking. He has been concerned with defining and classifying the structures which thought takes at different periods of development. Aspects of

Piaget's work will be described later (see Chapter 18; for a full account, see Flavell, 1963). For the present, all that need be said is that the stages Piaget discovered were empirically determined and, at least under normal circumstances, seem clearly to be invariant in sequence; indeed, one of the criteria Piaget used for defining a stage is its constant position in a sequence of stages. Furthermore, Piaget integrates the structures characteristic of each stage into a general over-all theory which is modelled on logic and epistemology.

There are other descriptive principles to be found in the literature. But enough has been said to show that, as the characteristics of the developmental process become defined with some precision, so it is possible to compare individuals in terms of the developmental level they have reached – their developmental age. Individuals of the same chronological age may differ widely in developmental age. There is good ground for saying that the total pattern of development is unique to the individual. As research continues, it becomes increasingly possible to specify an individual's developmental age, in relation to others, and this is much more informative than his chronological age. The implications for a society where such things as education and law are based upon the notion of chronological age are considerable.

Further reading
N. Bayley, 'Development and maturation', in H. Helson (ed.), *Theoretical Foundations of Psychology*, Van Nostrand, 1951.
L. Carmichael, 'The onset and early development of behavior', in L. Carmichael (ed.), *Manual of Child Psychology*, Wiley, 2nd edn 1954.
D. B. Harris (ed.), *The Concept of Development*, University of Minnesota Press, 1957.

Chapter 5
The Structure of the
Nervous System

We turn now to a direct examination of the relation between physiological structure and neural processes on the one hand and behaviour on the other. Psychologists are concerned with the physiological processes which occur within an organism, and especially within the brain, because such study considerably extends their understanding of behaviour. The range and quality of an organism's behaviour is largely determined by the way in which the organism is built; increasing our knowledge of structure leads to more complete understanding of function.

The body structure of mammals can be divided into various subsystems – for example, the endocrine and nervous systems. Of the two, the nervous system has interested psychologists most and we shall deal with it first. Although the nervous system is a functional unity, it is convenient to subdivide it. There are three classificatory systems commonly used, each relying upon a different kind of criterion.

The first is based upon spatial location and is the division between the *central nervous system* (CNS) and the *peripheral nervous system* (PNS). The CNS consists of the brain, the brainstem and the spinal cord; the peripheral system consists of all those nerve fibres which enter or leave the brainstem and the spinal cord and connect them to the rest of the body. The two systems are shown schematically in Figure 4.

The second is a functional classification, and distinguishes the *somatic nervous system* from the visceral or *autonomic nervous system* (ANS). The former consists of the CNS and those peripheral nerve

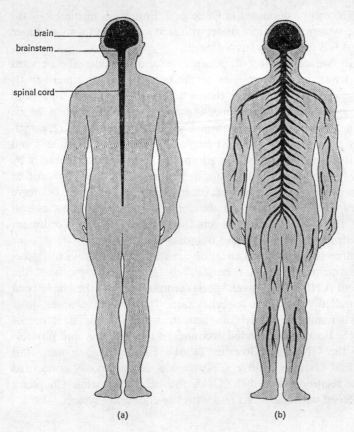

brain

brainstem

spinal cord

(a)   (b)

Figure 4   (a) represents the central nervous system — brain, brainstem and spinal cord (the brainstem in fact extends into the brain); (b) is an impressionistic representation of the peripheral nervous system and also shows the central nervous system.

fibres that convey messages from the sense organs to the CNS, and from the CNS to the striate or striped muscles of the body. The ANS consists of those parts of the CNS and PNS which have connexions with various glands and with the smooth muscles of the heart, the lungs and other internal organs of the body (the distinction between striate and smooth muscles need not concern us here). Some glands form part of the endocrine system, which, together with the ANS, will be discussed in Chapter 7. Functions mediated by the somatic system are mainly under voluntary control; those mediated by the ANS are mainly involuntary.

Finally we can shift our perspective and consider the nervous system from the point of view of the organism's adjustment to its environment. We then have the threefold division into input and output systems, and the connecting and controlling system which intervenes between them. The input system, or system of *receptors*, receives information from the external or internal environment and transmits it in the form of nerve impulses to the brain, generally by way of the spinal cord. The output system, or system of motor or *efferent* nerves, conveys information, again in the form of nerve impulses, from the brain, via the spinal cord, to the muscles and glands. The CNS, which connects the two, integrates, co-ordinates and controls the incoming and outgoing information.

All three systems of classification are important, but, in the selective treatment that must necessarily be given the topic here, the CNS and ANS will be given special emphasis, since they have been most studied in relation to behaviour. The present chapter deals with two main topics: nervous transmission, and the structure of the CNS. For more extended accounts of the anatomy and physiology of the CNS, see Bowsher (1961), Field, Magoun and Hall (1959) and Gardner (1963). Chapter 6 is more directly concerned with the relation between the CNS and behaviour, while Chapter 7 is concerned with the ANS and with the endocrine system.

Nervous transmission

All organisms are made up of cells and different types of cell have become specialized to perform different functions. Thus sense organs, such as the eyes and ears, contain receptor cells, cells which are sensitive to environmental stimulation in the form of energy change; effector cells in the muscles are specialized for contraction, while effector cells in the glands are specialized for secretion. As a consequence of having become specialized to perform different functions, cells also differ in structure. For example, receptor cells in the eye, which are responsive to changes in photic stimulation (that is, changes in the intensity or wave-length of light), differ both structurally and in the functions they perform from the receptor cells for audition in the ear.

Cells within the nervous system, known as nerve cells or neurones, are specialized for the conduction of nerve impulses from one cell to another, the point of transfer being known as a *synapse*. Neurones may link two segments of a sensory system, two segments of a response system, or two segments of a larger system of neurones connecting a sensory system and a response system. However, some neurones have become specialized to receive stimulation directly from the external environment – for example, olfactory receptors, where neurones act to all intents and purposes as receptor cells.

Neurones are not the only kinds of cell in the nervous system. In addition there are glial cells, or *neuroglia*, which provide mechanical support for the neurones and tend to be wrapped around them. Glial cells, of which there are several varieties, considerably outnumber the neurones they support and probably assist in neuronal metabolism, although they may also function in learning and memory.

Neurones are found both in the PNS and in the CNS, the majority of them within the latter. It has been estimated that there are fifteen to twenty thousand million neurones in the entire nervous system and ten thousand million in the brain. Neurones are of variable size and shape and average one-tenth of a millimetre in diameter. The fibre processes of neurones (see Figure 5) also vary in diameter and in length. Most neurones connect with several hundred other neurones, so that the influences brought to bear on any one neurone are extremely numerous and the chances of tracing all, or even a few, of the connexions of a single neurone are very remote. However, although nerve cells are very small and their connexions extremely complex, much has been learned about their structure and functioning through a variety of anatomical, histological and physiological techniques.

The use of the light and electron microscopes and of staining methods makes it possible to estimate the number and type of nerve cells coming from different parts of the brain, the size of a particular cell and the extent of its fibre processes. Individual nerve cells can be removed from the nervous system and electrically stimulated. In this way, it has been possible to measure the velocity of a nerve

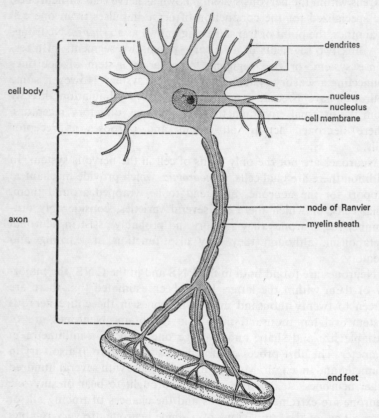

Figure 5   Diagram of a nerve cell or neurone with its fibre processes (dendrites and axon)

impulse travelling along a nerve fibre. Recordings can also be taken from inside the cell membrane by means of micro-electrodes. The micro-electrode is inserted into the cell through the cell membrane which seals itself around it. Micro-electrodes are also used for recording activity from positions inside or near nerve cells in the brain of a living organism, particularly from cells in the outer layer of the brain. In such cases the micro-electrodes are usually suspended, making them effectively weightless, and they are able to move with the brain. Nerve cells in the brain of living organisms can also be stimulated electrically or chemically. Finally, the fluid within the cell membrane can be extracted and chemically analysed.

Neurones resemble other cells in their basic structure: they have a nucleus and a cell membrane, and contain a watery solution known as intracellular fluid or cytoplasm.

The enlarged head of the neurone in Figure 5 is the cell body or soma and its extensions are of two types, *dendrites*, of which there are several, and a single *axon* which can have offshoots known as *collaterals*. At the end of the axon are small enlargements known as *end feet*, terminal boutons or synaptic knobs, which make connexions with other cells. These connexions constitute the synapse referred to earlier.

Axons, also termed nerve fibres, may have two types of covering – a thin membrane on the outside, known as *neurilemma* and between this and the fibre a white fatty substance called the *myelin sheath*. Neurilemma is found almost exclusively around fibres in the peripheral nervous system and it takes part in the regeneration of fibres which have been cut or damaged in some way. Thus, in general, fibres outside the CNS can regenerate, whereas those within it cannot. Myelinated fibres are found in the CNS and outside it; they are generally larger nerve fibres. At regular intervals, of about 1 mm, the myelin sheath is interrupted and the cell membrane laid bare. These points are known as *nodes of Ranvier*, after their discoverer, and it appears that the nerve impulse does not proceed continuously along the myelinated nerve fibre but effectively jumps from node to node, thus travelling at a faster rate than continuous progression would permit. The larger the diameter of a nerve fibre the faster the nerve impulse travels, the fastest speeds being around 300 feet per second and the slowest around three feet per second.

The most important function of the axon is to conduct impulses away from the cell body and dendrites. Usually axons connect with the dendrites of a receiving neurone, although in some cases they may connect directly with the cell body. The dendrites receive nerve impulses, the axon transmits them, while the cell body is involved in both functions.

The nerve impulse involves two sets of inter-related events, electrical and chemical. When the neurone is in the resting state, that is, when it is not carrying a nerve impulse, a potential difference of about seventy millivolts exists across the cell membrane. This means that the inside of the cell membrane is negative, by about seventy millivolts, with reference to the outside. When a stimulus is applied to the neurone, provided that the stimulus is *above threshold* – that is, at or above a certain minimum intensity – this potential difference is reversed, with the result that the inside of the cell membrane becomes momentarily positive with respect to the outside by about thirty millivolts.

In addition to the fluid inside the cell membrane, the intracellular fluid, there is a fluid which surrounds and bathes the neurone; this is the extracellular fluid. Both these fluids contain electrically charged particles known as ions, which are formed as a result of the dissociation or breaking apart of chemical substances dissolved within them. The reversal of potential which represents the nerve impulse appears to be a consequence of the effects of stimulation on the permeability of the cell membrane. During the period of stimulation the membrane becomes permeable to the positive sodium ions outside the cell. When a sufficient concentration of positive sodium ions have passed through to the inside of the cell, the reversal of the resting potential takes place and the membrane is said to be depolarized. Almost as soon as this depolarization of the membrane has occurred, polarization, that is the resting state, is re-established and the nerve impulse passes to the next segment of the axon. The impulse is thus an electrochemical disturbance which spreads along the cell membrane, segment by segment, lasting for about a millisecond (1/1000 s) at any one point.

A synapse has already been referred to as the point of transmission between the end feet of an axon of one cell and the cell body or dendrites of the cell with which it connects (see Figure 6). Chemical transmitters convey the nerve impulse from the transmitting to the receiving cell, the energy required for the transmission process being supplied by enzyme-producing structures, termed *mitochondria*, in the end feet of the transmitting cell.[1]

Axons and dendrites differ somewhat in their response to stimulation. The effect of excitation in the dendrites is graded, resulting in a varying electrical potential being produced as a consequence of varying stimulation. This means that a weak stimulus produces a

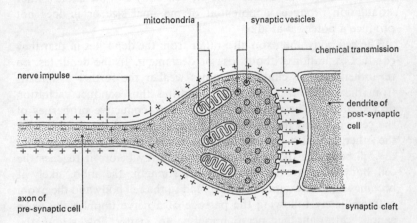

Figure 6   Diagram of a synapse. The 'synaptic cleft' is bridged by chemical transmitter molecules released by the synaptic vesicles. The mitochondria provide the energy for the whole process of transmission. The nerve impulse in the presynaptic axon is thus thought to cross the synapse on 'chemical carriers'. (After A. Besterman in *The Science of Man*, vol. 2, BBC, 1963, p. 16)

weak effect and a strong stimulus a strong effect. Since several hundred axons may converge on the dendrites of a neurone, the strength of stimulation depends largely on how many axons are transmitting nerve impulses to the dendrites at a particular time. The electrical potential which can be recorded from the dendrites is graded because it is proportional to the strength of stimulation. Graded potentials appear to play an important role in some parts of the CNS and we shall refer to them again later.

1. Most commonly, synaptic transmission occurs between the axon of one neurone and the dendrites of another, although it can also take place between an axon and a cell body.

The axon and the cell body, on the other hand, operate on the *all-or-none principle*. This means that, provided the stimulation reaching the cell body and the axon from the dendrites is above threshold, an ungraded potential is produced in the cell body and the axon. The amount by which stimulation from the dendrites exceeds the threshold of a particular neurone thus makes no difference to the size of the potential produced in the cell body and the axon. Either stimulation produces a potential of maximal size or it does not produce a potential at all.

The cell body and axon also differ from the dendrites in that they conduct excitation without loss or decrement. In the dendrites, on the other hand, excitation becomes weaker the further it spreads from the point of stimulation. Dendrites thus conduct excitation decrementally. The result of the different conductive properties of the cell body and the axon on the one hand, and the dendrites on the other, is that a dendrite may be excited at some distance from the cell body and the excitation may die away before it reaches the cell body. The greater the stimulus strength, the more likely it becomes that the excitation will spread to the cell body and the axon.

Immediately following the passage of a nerve impulse the axon cannot carry another nerve impulse, no matter how strong the stimulus may be. This very brief period is called the *absolute refractory period* and it sets an upper limit to the rate at which the neurone can conduct nerve impulses (the fastest rate of firing in a single axon is around 1000 per second). Immediately after this period a nerve impulse can be produced in the axon if the applied stimulus is strong enough, and this period, which again is a very brief one, is called the *relative refractory period*. In the relative refractory period a stimulus needs to be stronger than normal to produce a nerve impulse in the axon. The threshold of the neurone is thus raised during this period, although it should be mentioned that, for large diameter nerve fibres, the refractory period is shorter and the resting threshold lower. After the relative refractory period the neurone returns to the resting state (see Figure 7).

The term threshold refers to the strength or intensity of stimulation required to produce a nerve impulse in a neurone. The threshold of any one neurone fluctuates from moment to moment so that a stimulus which produces a nerve impulse on one occasion may not do so on another. A convention is followed in defining thresholds such that if a stimulus of constant intensity produces a nerve impulse in a particular neurone on 50 per cent of the occasions when it is applied, then it is said to be at threshold for that neurone. If the threshold is raised then it means that a stimulus which normally

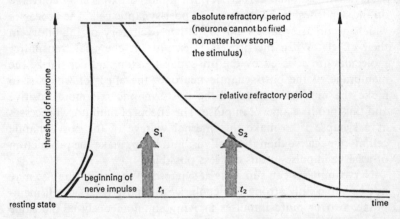

Figure 7 The absolute and relative refractory periods. S_1 and S_2 are two stimuli of equal strength. At t_1 the neurone is not fired; at t_2 it is fired

produces an impulse 50 per cent of the time may now, for example, produce an impulse only 25 per cent of the time: that is, the stimulus is less likely to fire the neurone. Conversely, if the threshold is lowered, then that same stimulus may, for example, produce an impulse 75 per cent of the time. Some drugs, such as novocain, raise the thresholds of neurones whereas others, such as strychnine, lower them.

Because of the all-or-none principle, the strength or intensity of a particular stimulus bears no relation to the size of the potential produced in an axon. This suggests that information about stimulus intensity is conveyed not by the size of the nerve impulse but in some other way. Such information appears to be conveyed by a frequency code, that is, the number of impulses produced per unit of time. A stimulus nearly always produces a train of nerve impulses, unless it lasts for a very short time, and a strong stimulus can fire the axon at an earlier point in the relative refractory period and can, therefore, produce a greater number of impulses (see Figure 7). In addition, there is evidence that some fibres in the various receptor systems fire spontaneously in the absence of stimulation, and this topic will be discussed briefly in the next chapter.

As was mentioned earlier, several hundred axons may converge on the dendrites of the receiving or post-synaptic cell. The processes which occur at synapses can be either excitatory or inhibitory in their effects. When the process is excitatory, chemical transmitter molecules are released by the pre-synaptic axon and depolarize the membrane of the post-synaptic neurone, the effect of which is to make the internal voltage of the post-synaptic cell more positive and thus produce a nerve impulse. The effects of inhibitory processes at a synapse is to make the internal voltage of the post-synaptic cell more negative than it usually is, and hence make the production of a nerve impulse in this cell less possible.

Nerve impulses can summate at synapses. Where one impulse may not be sufficiently strong to depolarize the post-synaptic cell membrane, two or more impulses arriving simultaneously at the same area of cell membrane along different axons raise the probability of firing of the post-synaptic cell. Summation becomes crucial when the threshold of the post-synaptic cell is raised, for example, during the relative refractory period, and the time of arrival of nerve impulses at the post-synaptic cell membrane is thus important in determining whether or not summation occurs.

Nerve fibres frequently travel together in groups of as many as several million from one point in the nervous system to another. These groups or collections of nerve fibres are known as pathways, tracts or bundles within the CNS and as nerves outside it. Cell bodies also collect together in distinguishable groups having a similar appearance and similar connexions. Such groups of cells in the CNS are known as nuclei and in the peripheral nervous system as *ganglia*, and two or more *nuclei* or ganglia are connected if tracts of nerve fibres run between them. The connexions between nuclei can be either direct or interrupted by synapses. Where fibres conduct excitation in the same direction and are laid down in parallel, there is a high probability of the excitation being transmitted from one synaptic level to the next. This means of conduction is very reliable and highly efficient. The conduction of nerve impulses may also be diffuse; fibres may start out together but travel in different directions so that impulses in different fibres cannot sum their effects at the next synapse. Large areas of the brain are given over to diffuse conduction systems and Hebb (1958) discusses their importance in 'voluntary' activity, together with the importance of parallel conduction systems in 'sense-dominated' behaviour. We shall return to these different conduction systems later on.

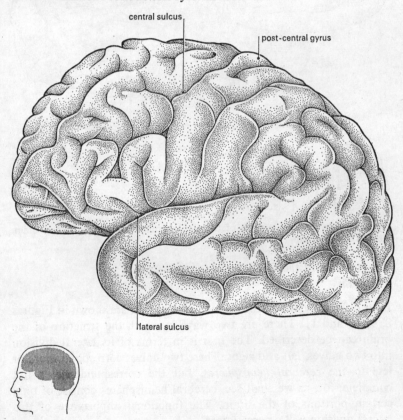

Figure 8 The external surface of the left hemisphere of the human brain

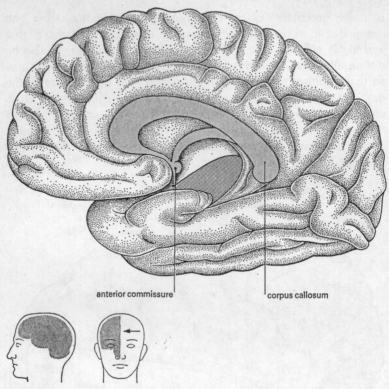

anterior commissure   corpus callosum

Figure 9 The internal surface of the right hemisphere of the human brain, viewed from the side

The structure of the CNS
The brain

Four different views of the surface of the brain are shown in Figures 8, 9, 10 and 11. There are two ways in which the structure of the brain can be described. The first is in terms of its lateral division into two halves, left and right. These two halves correspond more or less to the *cerebral hemispheres*, but the correspondence is not complete, for, as we shall see, cerebral hemispheres consist of only certain portions of the brain. The functional importance of this lateral division will emerge later.

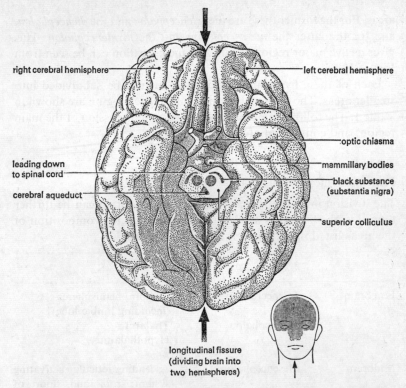

right cerebral hemisphere

left cerebral hemisphere

optic chiasma

leading down
to spinal cord

mammillary bodies

black substance
(substantia nigra)

cerebral aqueduct

superior colliculus

longitudinal fissure
(dividing brain into
two hemispheres)

Figure 10   The undersurface of the human brain. The cerebellum is not shown.
Immediately below the optic chiasma is the pituitary stalk or infundibulum.
The two circles below the black substance represent the red nuclei

The second approach is longitudinal, and specifies the structures
which make up each half of the brain. However, the structures which
make up one half are also represented in the other half, so that each
half is, as it were, a mirror image of the other. For this reason, the
outline which follows will be based on the longitudinal classification,
and the lateral classification will be, for the moment, ignored.

Longitudinally, the brain can be divided into three parts, the
forebrain, the midbrain or *mesencephalon* and the *hindbrain*. The
forebrain and hindbrain can each be subdivided into two major

areas. For the former these are the *telencephalon* and the *diencephalon*, and for the latter the *metencephalon* and the *myelencephalon*. This gives us five major regions in all, and their location can be seen from Figure 12.

Each of these five major regions can in turn be subdivided into smaller areas. The principal constituents of each region are shown in Table 1. The following pages are devoted to a discussion of the main regions and constituent areas.

Table 1

Principal regions of the brain

The division into forebrain, midbrain and hindbrain can be further refined to the five areas shown in column 2, and the composition of the areas listed in column 2 is shown in column 3.

1	2	3
Forebrain	Telencephalon	Cerebral hemispheres (including limbic lobe)
	Diencephalon	Thalamus Hypothalamus
Midbrain	Mesencephalon	Ascending reticular activating system; roof and floor of midbrain
Hindbrain	Metencephalon	Pons, cerebellum
	Myelencephalon	Medulla

1. The telencephalon. The telencephalon is the major, frontal portion of the brain and consists of the two cerebral hemispheres. The cerebral hemispheres possess an outer covering of nerve cells, which varies in thickness from about 1·5 to 4·5 millimetres, known as the *cerebral cortex*, cortex meaning rind or bark. Considerable changes have taken place in this outer layer of cells in the evolution from the lower organisms to man. Fish, for example, have no cerebral cortex and it is not until the early reptilian stage is reached that cells

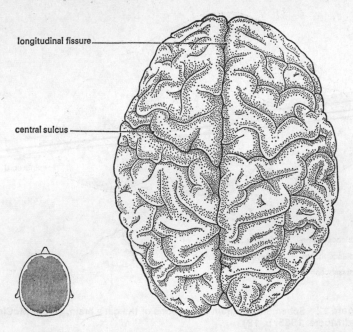

Figure 11 The human brain viewed from above, showing the longitudinal fissure

appear on the surface of the cerebral hemispheres forming a cortex. This first layer of cells is termed 'old cortex' or *paleocortex* to distinguish it from 'new cortex' or *neocortex* which develops later in the evolutionary scale. The paleocortex is more primitive in structure than the neocortex and is primarily concerned with the mediation of olfactory functions (that is, the sense of smell), although its functions change considerably with further evolution. The first cortex having non-olfactory functions appears in birds, but only assumes great importance in the regulation of behaviour in mammals. In man the neocortex reaches its greatest size in relation to the rest of the brain. These evolutionary changes in the brain are shown diagrammatically in Figure 13.

The evolution of the neocortex until it covers the outer surface of the cerebral hemispheres has meant that the paleocortical structures

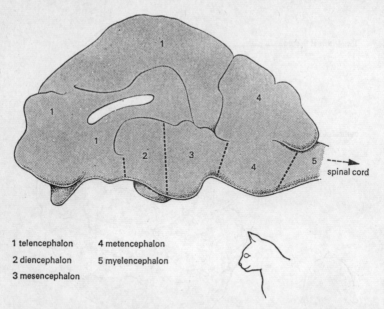

Figure 12 Schematic diagram of divisions of the cat's brain. (From McCleary and Moore, 1965, p. 19)

1 telencephalon
2 diencephalon
3 mesencephalon
4 metencephalon
5 myelencephalon

spinal cord

have been displaced to positions within the cerebral hemispheres. Because of their earlier association with smell, these structures are sometimes known collectively as the *rhinencephalon* or *olfactory brain*, although in higher mammals their functions have little to do with olfaction. We shall be returning to these functions later on.

The surface area of the neocortex greatly exceeds the inner surface area of the skull cavity into which it is fitted, and the neocortex folds backwards and forwards over the subcortical structures of the cerebral hemispheres and brain stem. The result is that various wrinkles or convolutions are produced in the neo-cortical layer. These convolutions take the form of ridges known as *gyri* (singular *gyrus*) or fissures known as *sulci* (singular *sulcus*) and they provide useful landmarks for subdividing the brain into areas known as *lobes*. Figure 14 shows the left cerebral hemisphere, viewed sideways on, subdivided into lobes. The two sulci which are marked,

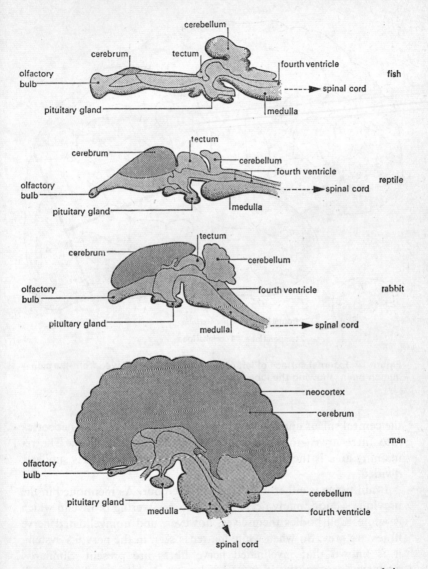

Figure 13 Evolutionary changes in the relative size of different parts of the brain

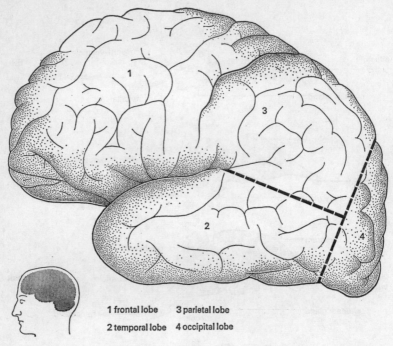

1 frontal lobe   3 parietal lobe
2 temporal lobe   4 occipital lobe

Figure 14 External surface of left cerebral hemisphere viewed from the side —
human brain, showing the lobes

the central sulcus and the lateral sulcus, serve to divide the neocortex
into three areas, the frontal, temporal and parietal lobes. The remaining area is the occipital lobe. The right hemisphere is similarly
divided.

Brain tissue is either grey or white in colour. As mentioned in the
previous section, many nerve fibres have a covering of myelin which
is white. Cell bodies themselves, however, and unmyelinated nerve
fibres are grey. So when white matter is seen in the nervous system,
it is known that myelinated nerve fibres are present. Similarly,
whenever grey matter is seen, it is known that it is made up of cell
bodies or unmyelinated nerve fibres.

The neocortex chiefly comprises grey matter, arranged in six layers of which the outermost or most superficial layer is made up primarily of dendrites. These dendrites belong to motor cells (sometimes termed *pyramidal*) which alternate with sensory or *granular* cells in the middle four of the six neocortical layers. The innermost neocortical layer contains interconnecting neurones, whose axons end in the more superficial layers of their own, or the opposite, hemisphere. Neurones in the neocortex are, in general, much smaller than those found in other regions of the nervous system. Their axons tend to be much shorter than those found elsewhere and their dendrites are typically more numerous and more complexly intertwined.

The brain consumes about one-fifth of the oxygen used by the whole body and nerve cells die within a few seconds without oxygen. In addition, the brain receives a very rich blood supply, about one-sixth of the total cardiac output, and the grey matter of the cortex contains the usual network of small blood vessels that permeate all organs of the body, bringing in nutrients and carrying out waste products. The grey matter of the cortex receives a richer blood supply than the white matter.

The brain and spinal cord also possess a further fluid supply, the cerebrospinal fluid, which surrounds the brain and fills various cavities within it, known as ventricles, and also the hollow core of the spinal cord, the spinal canal. The function of cerebrospinal fluid, in so far as it is known, appears to be mainly nutritive, and it also acts as a protective cushion for the central nervous system. Figure 15 shows a diagram of the ventricular system.

Viewed from above, the two cerebral hemispheres are separated by a valley or cleft known as the median longitudinal fissure or sulcus, which runs from the front to the back of the brain. At the bottom of this fissure a large group of myelinated fibres, about 100 million in number, runs across from one hemisphere to the other, connecting mirror-image points in the two hemispheres. The *corpus callosum*, or great cerebral commissure, as it is also known, is the principal interconnexion system between the two hemispheres.

The rhinencephalon, or olfactory brain, has already been referred

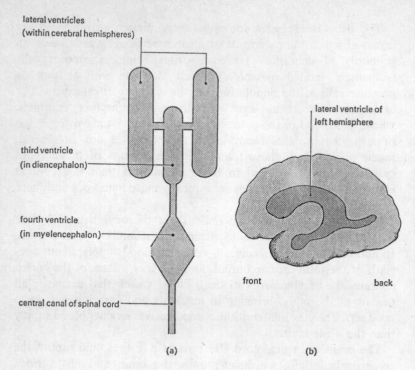

lateral ventricles
(within cerebral hemispheres)

lateral ventricle of
left hemisphere

third ventricle
(in diencephalon)

fourth ventricle
(in myelencephalon)

front

back

central canal of spinal cord

(a)

(b)

Figure 15   Diagram of the ventricular system. The gaps on either side of the
fourth ventricle in (a) represent the means of communication between the
fourth ventricle and the sub-arachnoid space which lies between the skull and
the brain and which also contains cerebrospinal fluid. (b) shows an outline of
the lateral ventricle projected onto a lateral view of the left cerebral hemisphere.
(After Bowsher, 1961, pp. 12 and 40)

to as lying within the cerebral hemispheres. The rhinencephalon is
one of the most primitive parts of the cerebral hemispheres, and the
structures comprising it can be divided into two groups. The first
group contains the olfactory bulbs (the receptors for the sense of
smell from which the olfactory nerves arise) and the olfactory nuclei,
to which these nerves project. The second group of structures in
the rhinencephalon make up the *limbic lobe*, a term coined by
Broca in 1878, which has developed evolutionarily in close association with the olfactory areas, although the structures in the limbic

lobe of higher mammals have lost their direct connexion with the receptors for the sense of smell.

The structures in the limbic lobe are the *septal area*, the *cingulate gyrus*, the *hippocampus* and the *amygdala*. The term limbic lobe is applied to these structures because, taken together, they form a ring on the inner surface of each cerebral hemisphere (see Figure 16)

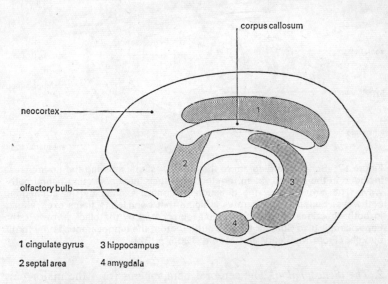

1 cingulate gyrus   3 hippocampus

2 septal area   4 amygdala

Figure 16 Schematic diagram of the inner surface of the right hemisphere of the cat's brain showing the limbic lobe (shaded areas). Structures within the limbic lobe, together with the olfactory bulb, make up the rhinencephalon. (From Morgan, 1965, p. 53)

around its junction with the diencephalon (limbus means 'edge' or 'perimeter'). The structures in the limbic lobe have many input and output connexions with the neocortex and with subcortical structures in the diencephalon and the brainstem.

The limbic system is a functional rather than a structural unit, since it includes some brain regions which lie outside the rhinencephalon. Figure 17 is a schematic diagram of structures within the limbic system.

The limbic system is thought to be primarily involved in motivational and emotional behaviour or in remembering, although other interpretations are available. We shall discuss these alternatives in the next chapter.

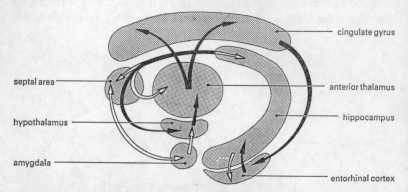

Figure 17   Schematic diagram of the limbic system, showing the neural areas included in the limbic system together with their interconnecting neural pathways. The arrows show the direction of control exerted by the connecting pathways; double-ended arrows indicate that connecting fibres exert effects in both directions. The closed circuit represented by the black arrows is the Papez circuit (see Chapter 6). The outflow from the hippocampus is the fornix bundle. (From McCleary and Moore, 1965, p. 32)

2. The diencephalon. The cerebral hemispheres form the major part of the forebrain. The remaining region is the diencephalon, or 'between brain', which consists primarily of two structures, the *thalamus* which forms the upper half of the diencephalon and the *hypothalamus* which forms the lower half (see Figure 18). The cavity of the third ventricle separates the two thalami (that of the left hemisphere and that of the right) from the two hypothalami, and is thus also included in the diencephalon (see Figure 22). The diencephalon surrounds the top of the brainstem (that part of the brain below the cortex and above the spinal cord), and the connexions between the cerebral hemispheres and the brainstem are channelled through this region.

The *thalamus* consists of many nuclei or groups of nerve cells connected with one another, with the hypothalamus, with structures

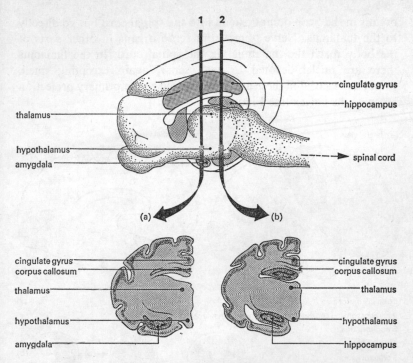

Figure 18 Diagram of cat's brain – right hemisphere, medial view. (a) and (b) represent sections at points 1 and 2 as they would be seen looking head on. The relative positions of the thalamus and the hypothalamus are shown by dots. (From McCleary and Moore, 1965, p. 25)

in the brainstem and spinal cord, and with the rhinencephalon and neocortex. It has been suggested that the organization of the thalamus is the key to the organization of the cortex and also that 'the true definition of a functional cortical area depends not upon the fortuitous folding of its surface into sulci and gyri, nor upon its cytoarchitecture (though this is related) but upon its specific projection from a particular thalamic nucleus' (Bowsher, 1961, p. 66).

Nerve fibres from the various sense organs, with the exception of those from the olfactory bulb, all pass through the thalamus on their way to the cortex. Nerve fibres coming to the thalamus from sense organs in the head do not extend into the spinal cord but go directly to the thalamus. Nerve fibres from sense organs in other parts of the body reach the thalamus via the spinal cord. In the thalamus there are nuclei devoted to each sense, again excepting smell. Impulses received in these areas are relayed to the primary projection areas of the cortex (see Figure 19).

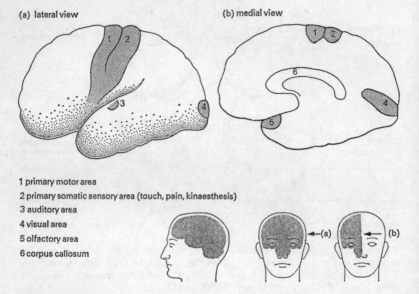

(a) lateral view   (b) medial view

1 primary motor area
2 primary somatic sensory area (touch, pain, kinaesthesis)
3 auditory area
4 visual area
5 olfactory area
6 corpus callosum

Figure 19   Primary sensory and motor areas of the human cerebral cortex. (After Bowsher, 1961, p. 55)

Each of the different senses has its own primary projection area in the cortex. Olfactory input is relayed extrathalamically to its projection area on the underside of the temporal lobes. It can be seen from Figure 19 that the primary projection area for vision is located in the cortex of the occipital lobe, for audition in the temporal lobe and for smell, as already mentioned, on the underside of the temporal lobe. The area for taste, thought to be in the parietal lobe, is not shown. In addition, Figure 19 shows the projection area, in the post-central gyrus, for the somaesthetic or bodily senses, which comprise the senses of touch, temperature, pain and kinaesthesis, all of which appear to have separate receptors, including different ones for the sensations of heat and cold. The receptors for the kinaesthetic sense are found in the muscles, tendons and joints of the body and they provide feedback about, for example, the position of the limbs in space.

The motor cortex, in the pre-central gyrus, is the cortical division of the skeletal or voluntary motor system and is of special importance in producing muscle movements. We shall return to it in the next chapter. For the present we will note that, together with the sensory projection areas, it can be classified as *extrinsic cortex*. This classification is based upon the fact that these areas receive projections from *extrinsic thalamic* nuclei. Extrinsic thalamic nuclei are those nuclei within the thalamus which receive input from outside the thalamus; *intrinsic thalamic* nuclei receive input from within the thalamus.

Referring back to Figure 19 it can be seen that there are large areas of the cortex which lie outside the sensory projection areas and the motor cortex. In man these comprise the largest areas of the cortex. These areas are usually called the *association areas*, and they are generally divided into two, the frontal association area, located in the frontal lobe, and the parietal-temporal-occipital, or PTO, association area, overlapping the three lobes that make up its name. The term 'association area' was coined by early students of the brain who thought of the association areas as a series of transcortical paths from one of the specialized areas (sensory or motor) to the other. Current opinion holds that this is too simple a picture (see, for example, Hebb, 1958; Pribram, 1960a and b), and some of the reasons for this will be discussed in the next chapter.

The primary motor and sensory areas of the cortex, as well as the hypothalamic–rhinencephalic areas of the cortex (the frontal association area) receive their specific point-to-point projections from thalamic nuclei whose own input is extrathalamic. The PTO association area, on the other hand, receives its specific projections from the thalamic nuclei whose input is intrathalamic. Figure 19 represents two views of the brain, lateral and medial, divided into sensory and motor areas. Figure 20 shows the same two views of the brain in terms of their thalamocortical projections. It can be seen that a large area of the temporal lobe receives no major projection from the thalamus. However, this region of the temporal lobe is connected to the PTO association area by transcortical fibres known as association bundles.

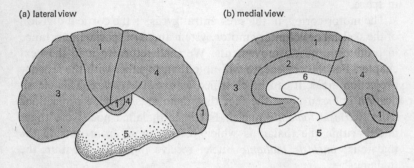

(a) lateral view   (b) medial view

1 primary motor and sensory cortex (projections from ventral group of thalamic nuclei)

2 projections from mammillary bodies and hippocampus via anterior thalamic nuclei

3 projections from hypothalamus via dorsomedial nuclei of thalamus

4 projections from ventral thalamic nuclei via lateral-pulvinar group of nuclei (cognitive association cortex)

5 non-thalamically dependent cortex with some projections from pulvinar (interpretive association cortex)

6 corpus callosum

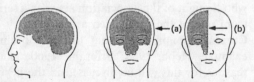

Figure 20   Projection zones of thalamic nuclei on the cerebral cortex. (After Bowsher, 1961, p. 65)

The PTO association area, which is thalamically dependent, can be described as 'sensory' or 'cognitive' association cortex, whereas the area of temporal lobe which is not thalamically dependent can be described as 'interpretive' association cortex. Interpretive association cortex appears to be involved in memory processes which are dependent, to some extent, upon the connexions of non-auditory temporal cortex with the rhinencephalic structures that lie beneath it.

Like the thalamus, the *hypothalamus* ('hypo' meaning below) consists of a group of nuclei, each nucleus being represented in each hemisphere (see Figure 21). As mentioned earlier, the third ventricle separates the hypothalamic nuclei of the left hemisphere from those of the right. The hypothalamus is situated below and a little in front

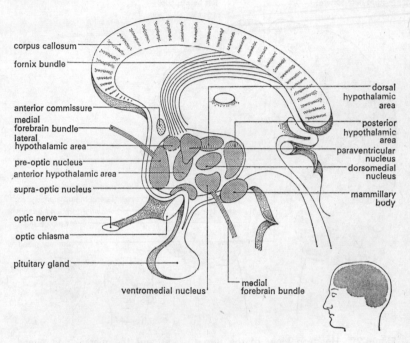

Figure 21 Schematic diagram (lateral view) of the hypothalamus

of the thalamus (see Figure 22). The forward (anterior) end of the hypothalamus is bounded by the *optic chiasma*, a junction point in the visual system at which some of the fibres from each eye are sent, via the thalamus, to the visual projection area of the contralateral hemisphere. The posterior limit of the hypothalamus is marked by the mammillary bodies, usually included with the hypothalamus. Throughout the length of the hypothalamus there are two fairly distinct zones. The nuclei of the medial hypothalamic zone, including the mammillary bodies, surround the cavity of the third ventricle while on both sides of the medial area are the fairly scattered nuclei of the lateral hypothalamic area. Many short connecting fibres pass between these two zones.

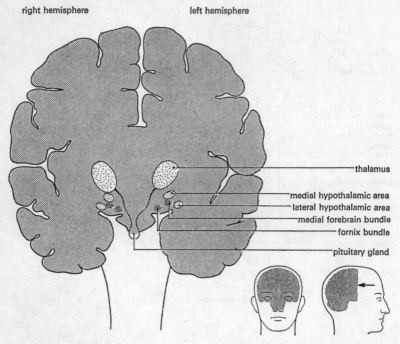

Figure 22   Head-on view of the two thalami and the medial and lateral hypothalamic areas. Note that the hypothalamus is divided into medial and lateral areas by the medial forebrain bundle. The third ventricle runs from the thalamus to the pituitary gland

Through the lateral hypothalamic area runs the medial forebrain bundle, which connects the brainstem, the lateral hypothalamic area and structures in the rhinencephalon. The medial hypothalamic area receives input from the hippocampus in the rhinencephalon and also sends fibres to the pituitary gland, which is attached to the under-surface of the hypothalamus (see Figure 22). The hypothalamus controls the endocrine glands via the pituitary gland. In addition there are two-way connexions between the hypothalamus and thalamus, and between the hypothalamus and the cortex of the frontal lobe in the pre-motor area. The hypothalamus is also richly innervated by collateral fibres from the various sensory pathways and it receives the richest blood supply of any part of the brain.

In view of its many connexions with other regions of the brain, its connexions with sensory pathways, its proximity to the third ventricle and its very rich blood supply, it is not surprising to find that the hypothalamus, although only about half an inch across, appears to function as an integrating system for many different kinds of behaviour. For example, it controls the water balance and regulates the temperature of the body. It regulates, to a large extent, the activity of an involuntary motor system, the autonomic nervous system, and thus in part regulates glandular activity. As the most important neural centre regulating endocrine secretions, it plays a large part in regulating metabolism, particularly of fats and carbo-hydrates. In addition, the control of blood pressure, via the auto-nomic nervous system, involves the hypothalamus. It also appears to play an important role in the mediation of eating, drinking and mating behaviour and is involved in emotional behaviour.

3. The mesencephalon. The mesencephalon or midbrain is a relatively small area which forms a bridge between the forebrain and the hindbrain. The fourth ventricle, which, in the midbrain, narrows to a passage known as the *cerebral aqueduct*, divides the midbrain into a roof (tectum) and a floor.

The roof contains four groups of nuclei, known as the *colliculi*. The two superior colliculi are situated in the anterior end of the midbrain, nearer the forebrain, and the two inferior colliculi are situated in the posterior end of the midbrain, nearer the hindbrain. Both the superior colliculi, for vision, and the inferior colliculi, for hearing, are junction points along the pathway from the sense organ concerned to the thalamus. In addition, both pairs of colliculi receive fibres from, and transmit fibres to, the spinal cord.

The floor of the midbrain is an interconnecting system between the forebrain and the hindbrain, and it contains bundles of ascending sensory fibres and of descending motor fibres. It also contains nuclei which send fibres to those muscles of the eyeball concerned with eye movements, as well as other nuclei, the red nucleus and the substantia nigra (black substance), which are concerned with other motor functions.

4. The metencephalon. The metencephalon contains two main areas, the *cerebellum* and the *pons*. The *cerebellum*, or 'little brain', is a structure that resembles the cerebral hemispheres in that its outer surface, the *cerebellar cortex*, consists of grey matter which is highly convoluted, and its interior is made up of white matter together with clumps of grey matter consisting of various nuclei.

Fibres enter the cerebellum from three sources, the cerebral hemispheres and the brainstem, the vestibular nuclei (concerned with the sense of balance and equilibrium) and the spinal cord. Fibres from the cerebellum go via the midbrain to the thalamus and thence to the motor cortex, to various motor nuclei in the midbrain, to the reticular formation (see below) and to the spinal cord.

The functions of the cerebellum appear to be those of a feedback mechanism which controls and guides movement. It is thus a part of the motor system. Damage to the cerebellum is apparent mainly during movement and produces 'intention tremor' (Snider, 1958).

The pons ('bridge') is characterized by very thick bundles of fibres which run across it from one side or hemisphere of the cerebellum to the other. Within the pons are various nuclei which are involved in sensory and motor functions, and various ascending and descending fibre tracts.

5. The myelencephalon. There are two areas of the myelencephalon which are of importance here – the *medulla* and the *reticular formation*. The medulla joins the spinal cord to the higher centres of the brain. In the medulla the majority of the dozen sets of cranial nerves (which perform various sensory and motor functions for organs in the head) enter and leave the brainstem, and the medulla contains several nuclei associated with these nerves. The medulla also contains nuclei associated with the autonomic nervous system which are involved in the processes of breathing and heart action.

The reticular formation is a core of nervous tissue, about five centimetres in length, which is located in the centre of the brainstem, and clustered around the central canal. It runs through the medulla, the pons and the midbrain, and at its upper end it connects with the hypothalamus and the thalamus in the diencephalon. It is surrounded by ascending and descending fibre tracts. The term 'reticulum' means network, and the reticular formation consists of a collection of predominantly short nerve fibres of small diameter, criss-crossing in all directions. Synapses and dendrites are abundant.

The reticular formation appears to possess two distinct subsystems. Some groups of reticular cells have axons which project down into the spinal cord, and these are known as reticular-spinal neurones. Others have axons which project to higher levels of the brainstem, and some reticular cells appear to have axons with two-way connexions, one branch passing downwards and the other upwards. The reticular cells which send projections into the spinal cord make up the *descending reticular system*, which has primarily motor functions, while those which have upward projections form the *ascending reticular activating system*, or ARAS, whose functions are primarily sensory.

The ARAS, with which we shall be mainly concerned, is a polysynaptic pathway which connects to a group of nuclei in the thalamus, and thence, by diverse routes, to the whole cortex, particularly the frontal lobe. This projection is diffuse and is not point-to-point as is the case with the projections of those thalamic nuclei concerned with the specific sensory systems. This thalamic extension of the ARAS is known as the *diffuse thalamic projection system* or DTPS. In addition, the ARAS connects with structures in the rhinencephalon and the lateral hypothalamus via the medial forebrain bundle.

The reticular formation receives branches or collateral fibres, as well as direct projections, from all the sensory pathways, and in addition, it receives fibres from the cortex and from structures in the rhinencephalon. Figure 23 is a schematic diagram of the principal input and output connexions of the ARAS.

When sensory impulses feed into the ARAS they increase its level of electrical activity, commonly called the level of *activation* or

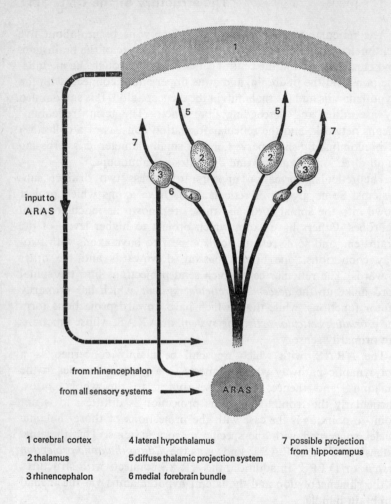

Figure 23 Schematic diagram of the major connexions to and from the ascending reticular activating system (ARAS)

1 cerebral cortex
2 thalamus
3 rhinencephalon
4 lateral hypothalamus
5 diffuse thalamic projection system
6 medial forebrain bundle
7 possible projection from hippocampus

input to ARAS

from rhinencephalon
from all sensory systems

ARAS

arousal. The ARAS in turn transmits this level of activation to the hypothalamus and rhinencephalon via the medial forebrain bundle and to the cortex by way of the DTPS. Through these two pathways the ARAS is able to influence considerably the level of activation or arousal of these structures. Thus the electrical activity of the ARAS can be modified by sensory input and by its connexions with other parts of the brain, and it can itself modify the level of electrical activity in the cortex, the rhinencephalon and the hypothalamus.

The behavioural consequences of these modifications of electrical activity will be mentioned in the following chapter. Briefly, the ARAS appears to be concerned with the maintenance of wakefulness (Magoun, 1958), and damage to it produces coma and eventually death.

The spinal cord

Just as the brain is divided into two hemispheres, each dealing with the opposite side of the body, so is the spinal cord similarly divided, each half sending and receiving fibres to and from one side of the body.

The spinal cord has two main functions – conduction and control. First, it acts as a conduction path between the brain and the periphery. Nerve impulses travelling from sensory receptors enter the spinal cord at various levels, depending on what part of the body they come from, and then proceed up to the brain. Motor fibres coming down from the brain to the effectors (the muscles and glands of the body) leave the spinal cord for the periphery, again at the level appropriate for their final destination.

Spinal cord pathways are of different lengths. Long tracts connect the spinal cord with centres of the brain and are situated primarily in the periphery of the cord. Shorter tracts, known as intersegmental tracts or ground bundles, connect different levels or segments of the spinal cord. The name of each tract, with some exceptions, is made up first of the place where the tract arises and second of the place where the tract ends. The reticulospinal tract, for example, arises in the reticular system and terminates in the spinal cord.

The spinal cord, as well as acting as a conduction path between the brain and the periphery, also mediates simple reflexes. There are many different kinds of reflex, some handled by the spinal cord alone, known as *spinal reflexes*, and others involving the brain, known as *suprasegmental reflexes*. In some spinal reflexes, only one segment of the spinal cord is involved, while in others several segments take part. Since spinal reflexes do not involve the brain, they can still be elicited when the connexions between the brain and spinal cord are severed.

In this chapter we have been concerned with the structure of neurones and of the CNS; in consequence very little has been said about behaviour. In the following chapter, therefore, we shall be concerned with brain function and its behavioural consequences.

Further reading
S. P. Grossman, *Physiological Psychology*, Wiley, 1967.
K. H. Pribram (ed.), *Brain and Behaviour*, 4 vols., Penguin Books, 1969.

Chapter 6
The Brain and Behaviour

Methods used in the study of brain–behaviour relationships

There are four principal methods used in the study of brain–behaviour relationships:

1. *Extirpation* or the ablation or removal of parts of the brain.
2. The *recording of electrical changes* taking place in the brain during behaviour.
3. The *electrical or chemical stimulation* of parts of the brain.
4. The *clinical observation* of patients who have suffered brain damage.

Extirpation

By this is meant the removal of some or all of an animal's cortex, the cutting of connexions between areas of the brain, or the putting out of action of some subcortical structure. Either the animal's performance on some standard task is measured before and after the operation, or the performances of operated and unoperated animals are compared, the two groups being matched as carefully as possible on all other variables. Experimental extirpation is not carried out on human beings, but occasionally situations arise, either as a result of accidental brain injury or as a result of brain operations to relieve behavioural disorders, which permit essentially the same type of observation to be made on human beings.

The term for an injury to the nervous system produced accidentally or by the extirpation methods is a *lesion*. Since one half of the brain is a mirror image of the other, structures of the brain are bilaterally represented. Lesions can thus be bilateral, when, for example, the hypothalamus on both sides of the midline is destroyed, or unilateral, when only the hypothalamus of one hemisphere is affected.

There are two main methods of producing lesions in the nervous system. One method, as has been mentioned, is simply to remove the requisite part. This method is only possible when the region to be extirpated is directly accessible. For deeper structures within the brain, again for example the hypothalamus, it is more difficult simply to remove the desired area. To make a lesion in a deep structure a wire, insulated except for the tip, is passed through the brain into the structure. Once the wire has been guided into position by means of a method known as stereotaxis, a D.C. current is passed through it of sufficient strength to produce a lesion in the tissue at the uninsulated tip of the wire.

In studying the effects of brain lesions on behaviour it is important that bilaterally symmetrical lesions should be made, and in the case of deeper structures of the brain this is a difficult procedure. The difficulty can be overcome by using split-brain animals (see Sperry, 1961, 1964) in which the connexions between the two halves of the brain, including the corpus callosum and other cerebral commissures, are cut. The two hemispheres of such split-brain animals have been shown to be independently capable of perceiving, learning and controlling responses. In such animals lesions need only be made in one hemisphere, since the two hemispheres are independent, and the intact hemisphere can be used as a matched control for the operated hemisphere. Temporary lesions can be produced chemically as well as electrically in that the application of chemical substances to the cortex can put it temporarily out of commission.

The recording of electrical changes

There is always some measurable electrical activity in the living brain, even when stimulation is apparently absent. The second group of methods of investigating brain function is to record this activity and attempt :o relate it to behavioural variables. Three methods are commonly used, the *electroencephalogram* (or EEG), the method of *evoked potentials* and *micro-electrode techniques*.

The EEG provides a measure of changes in the electrical activity of the brain in the form of an EEG record. In order to obtain such a record, metal discs or electrodes slightly smaller than a sixpence are secured with paste to the scalp of a human or animal subject. The electrical activity of the brain, recorded indirectly from the scalp, is picked up by these electrodes and transmitted to an amplifier, and from here to a pen write-out which traces the record on a moving sheet of paper. The EEG provides a continuous record of the voltage fluctuations taking place on the surface of the brain, even though these changes are recorded from the scalp. They can also be recorded directly from the surface of the brain by means of the electrocorticogram or ECG. EEG tracings represent a recording of the summed electrical activity of millions of neurones in the cortex and provide information about the state of activity of the brain as a whole.

Two measurements are commonly used to analyse an EEG record: first, the amplitude or size of the waves and, second, the number of waves per second. Broadly speaking, the more relaxed a person is the greater the amplitude and the lower the frequency of the waves; this is known as high-voltage slow activity. The lower the amplitude and the higher the frequency (low-voltage fast activity) the more likely the subject is to be in an excited state, as Table 2 shows. (For further details of the EEG, see, for example, Hill and Parr, 1950.)

The second method of recording the electrical activity of the brain is to insert thin wire electrodes, similar to those used for making lesions in the deeper structures of the brain; but in this case no current is passed through the wire. By this method it is possible to take recordings from smaller groups of neurones than is possible with the EEG. For example, if a wire electrode or a group of such electrodes inserted into an animal's cortex indicated increased electrical activity when a light was flashed into the animal's eyes, it could be concluded that the small area of cortex around the tip of the electrode or electrodes was responsive to light stimulation; further, the latency between stimulation and response can serve as an index of the length of the nervous pathway involved. By first placing the electrode in one small area of the cortex and then in another while, for example, a tone is sounded, cortical areas responsive to the auditory stimulus can be mapped. If a specific stimulus,

Table 2

Psychological states and their E E G, conscious and behavioural correlates. (From Lindsley, 1951)

Behavioural continuum	Electroencephalogram	State of awareness	Behavioural efficiency
Strong, excited emotion; fear, rage, anxiety	Desynchronized: low to moderate amplitude; fast mixed frequencies	Restricted awareness; divided attention; diffuse, hazy; 'confusion'	Poor: lack of control, freezing up, disorganized
Alert attentiveness	Partially synchronized: mainly fast low-amplitude waves	Selective attention, but may vary or shift; 'concentration' anticipation; 'set'	Good: efficient, selective, quick reactions; organized for serial responses
Relaxed wakefulness	Synchronized: optimal alpha rhythm	Attention wanders – not forced; favours free association	Good: routine reactions and creative thought
Drowsiness	Reduced alpha and occasional low-amplitude slow waves	Borderline partial awareness; imagery and reverie; 'dream-like' states	Poor: unco-ordinated, sporadic, lacking sequential timing
Light sleep	Spindle bursts and slow waves (larger); loss of alpha	Markedly reduced consciousness (loss of consciousness); dream state	Absent
Deep sleep	Large and very slow waves (synchrony but on slow time bases); random irregular pattern	Complete loss of awareness (no memory for stimulation or for dreams)	Absent
Coma	Iso-electric to irregular large slow waves	Complete loss of consciousness; little or no response to stimulation; amnesia	Absent
Death	Iso-electric: gradual and permanent disappearance of all electrical activity	Complete loss of awareness as death ensues	Absent

such as a light or a tone, evokes an electrical response in the brain, this response is known as an evoked potential (see Chang, 1959).

The third method of electrical recording is to record with the aid of micro-electrodes the activity of single neurones in the nervous system, as was mentioned earlier in this chapter. For further information see Frank (1959).

Stimulation methods

The third method of studying brain–behaviour relationships is again similar to that used for making lesions: thin wire probes are inserted into the brain. Neurones are stimulated into action by electrical current and they can be fired by putting an electrical current near them. Thus particular regions, usually groups of nuclei, can be activated by means of electrical stimulation, and it is possible, for example, to evoke fear-like responses or movements of the body by stimulating certain areas of the brain. It is a fairly common view that the firing pattern of neurones stimulated electrically does not exactly replicate the 'natural' firing pattern, but approximates very closely to it. The effects of electrical stimulation are often blurred or mixed and some investigators have preferred to use chemical stimulation in which a chemical substance is injected into a chosen brain site.

Clinical observation

The final method we shall mention is that of systematically observing patients who have suffered brain damage. This method faces two main problems. First, the clinician is not always sure of the exact location and extent of the brain damage; second, it is not always possible to compare performance on various behavioural tests of brain-damaged patients after the injury with performance before the injury occurred. A good deal of evidence on the effects of damage to various parts of the brain has nevertheless been accumulated by this method.

Some problems of interpretation

Although the methods described above have provided a great deal of information about the relationship between areas of the brain and different kinds of behaviour, investigators have not always been in agreement concerning the interpretation of experimental results. There are several reasons for the ambiguity of such evidence. In the first place, there are considerable differences in the structure of the brain, both across species and between individuals of the same species, and these differences in structure are not easily observable, except by post-mortem examination. Second, in two members of the same species, lesions which may appear to involve the same part of the brain may in fact involve rather different functional areas.

In addition to these technical difficulties, the interpretation of ablation experiments presents other methodological problems. Behavioural changes observed after an operation do not necessarily imply that the behaviour is located in the part of the brain that has been removed or otherwise put out of action. The brain area in question may have been part of a larger circuit of nuclei and fibre tracts whose functioning has been disturbed or completely disrupted; it may have controlled the functioning of other brain areas which, following ablation, are now released from control; finally, the observed behavioural changes might result from malfunctioning of the brain area in question due to the formation of scar tissue rather than to a complete absence of its influence.

Furthermore, several non-anatomical variables have been shown to be important in determining the behavioural effects of brain lesions. In electrical-stimulation studies, the frequency and waveform of the stimulus have been shown to be important, as has the degree to which the effects of such stimulation extend beyond the target area (Olds and Olds, 1965). Then, in general, the effects of lesions made in infancy are much less severe than the effects of those made in adulthood (Harlow, Akert and Schiltz, 1964). In studies of the effects of brain lesions on learning and performance, the amount of training given on the task prior to the operation and the method of stimulus presentation have been shown to influence the post-operative behaviour (Orbach and Fantz, 1958). The conditions of rearing also play a part in determining the behavioural effects of brain damage (Smith, 1959), as does the way in which the animal is treated following the operation (Weiskrantz, 1956). The effects of lesions in particular parts of the brain also differ with the animal's position in the evolutionary scale. In general, the higher the animal's position on this scale, the more severe are the effects of damage to, for example, the cerebral cortex. This point is further discussed in later sections of this chapter.

Functional differences between the two hemispheres must also be considered when assessing brain–behaviour relationships. In Chapter 5 the two hemispheres were considered as essentially identical; but the organization of the human brain is both more complex and less symmetrical than that found in animals. It is more likely, therefore, that in human beings the behavioural effects of a lesion in one hemisphere will be different from those of a similarly placed lesion in the other. However, such differences between the effects of a similar lesion in different hemispheres depend to a great extent in man, and to a lesser extent in animals, upon the particular function studied. The way in which the two hemispheres interact to regulate different kinds of behaviour appears to differ for different functions.

For some kinds of behaviour, such as speech, one hemisphere appears to be dominant, with the result that damage to an area in one hemisphere (usually the left) produces a marked language deficit whatever the handedness of the individual, while damage to a corresponding area in the other hemisphere produces only a slight deficit, if any at all. For other kinds of behaviour, such as motor movements, it appears that each hemisphere controls the function cross-laterally. That is, muscle movements on the left side of the body are initiated by nerve impulses carried by nerve fibres originating for the most part in the motor cortex of the right hemisphere. Similarly, the motor cortex of the left hemisphere regulates movements on the right side of the body. This means that if damage to the motor cortex of the left hemisphere produces motor impairment, then this impairment will reveal itself on the right side of the body, and vice versa. The motor area of the cortex is organized within each hemisphere in such a way that different regions of the motor cortex control movements of different parts of the body. Thus damage to the corresponding areas of the motor cortices of the two hemispheres produces deficits differing in laterality but not in kind.

A further possibility is that some bilaterally corresponding regions of each hemisphere subserve qualitatively different functions. In such a case, patients with a lesion in the left hemisphere would show little or no deficit on task A but a marked impairment on task B, while patients with a corresponding right hemisphere lesion would show little or no impairment on task B but a marked impairment on task A; this *double dissociation of function* can also be demonstrated within the same hemisphere. For example, a number of experiments have shown that monkeys with lesions of the frontal cortex have difficulty with tasks requiring a delayed response but perform normally on visual discrimination problems. (Examples of visual discrimination and delayed-response tests are given on pp. 152–3 and 162.) Monkeys with equally large temporal lobe lesions, on the other hand, exhibit no deficit on delayed response tasks but perform badly on tests of visual discrimination (Harlow *et al.*, 1952; Pribram, 1954).

Teuber (1955) has argued that demonstrations of double dissociation provide the only really incontrovertible evidence that one part of the brain is more important than others in the regulation of a particular kind of behaviour. From this kind of evidence it is impossible to argue either that all lesions of similar size produce comparable behavioural deficits, irrespective of location, or that one type of test is more sensitive to the effects of brain damage than the other. However, the mere association of a behavioural deficit with a lesion in one brain area but not in another is not enough to demonstrate a qualitative functional difference, since such a result could equally well be interpreted in terms of the dominance of one hemisphere or of part of one hemisphere over other areas for the particular function concerned.

A full understanding of the mode of interaction between the two hemispheres must also take account of the apparent conflict between the view that functions are localized in single specific areas of the brain and the principles of *equipotentiality* and *mass action*. The principle of equipotentiality holds that different parts of the cortex may be functionally interchangeable, in the sense that, if one cortical area is removed, the function it subserves can be mediated by another cortical area. This principle originated with the work of the French physiologist Flourens in the nineteenth century, and was elaborated in a famous series of experiments carried out by the American physiological psychologist Karl Lashley (1926, 1929, 1931, 1935, 1943).

Lashley considered that the operation of the equipotentiality principle was to some extent constrained by the principle of mass action. This latter principle derives from a series of findings showing that the *degree* of impairment of certain functions is positively and significantly correlated with the *amount* of cortical tissue ablated in areas equipotential in the mediation of these functions. Areas of the brain which are equipotential for the mediation of a particular function can vary in size; they can be small regions of the brain or they can comprise the whole cortex, as Lashley considered to be the case for both learning and intelligence. Learning can still occur following fairly extensive cortical damage and the location of such damage is, within certain limits, unimportant. In his experiments on maze learning in rats, Lashley was able to show that the severity of the learning deficit was highly related to the percentage of cortical tissue ablated, irrespective of the locus of the lesion. He was less successful, however, in applying the principle of mass action to functions such as pattern vision and brightness discrimination. For a recent account of the history and current status of the principle of mass action the reader is referred to Zangwill (1960). As Zangwill points out, the equipotentiality principle need not be regarded as being inconsistent with a localization of function view of brain organization; the two hypotheses do not contradict one another.

It is also possible that one hemisphere duplicates certain functions of the other such that the ablation of a brain area subserving a particular function in one hemisphere would not lead to impairment of the function since the corresponding area in the other hemisphere would continue to regulate the behaviour in question. One hemisphere would thus be acting in effect as a 'spare battery' for the other. Such a relationship between the hemispheres would be an instance of the principle of equipotentiality and is suggested by many animal experiments where unilateral damage produces little or no impairment of function while bilateral damage produces severe deficits. In general, the relationship holds less well for man, where unilateral damage has a higher probability of producing some behavioural impairment.

Finally, it is possible that unilateral damage may produce a given functional deficit, and that bilateral damage in the corresponding regions of the brain may increase the *severity* of the deficit without altering it qualitatively. The effect of the two lesions would thus be additive and such an effect would provide a special instance of the principle of mass action.

With these difficulties of interpretation in mind, some of the main findings from studies of brain–behaviour relationships will now be briefly surveyed. Four areas, the *ascending reticular activating system*, the *hypothalamus*, the *limbic system* and the *neocortex* will be dealt with, in that order, because they are the most important areas concerned in the regulation of behaviour and because, in the past few years, knowledge gained about each of them has provided support for certain relatively new ideas of brain organization and of the way in which the brain as a whole can be considered to function. In brief, recent views of brain function have emphasized the importance of subcortical structures in the regulation of behaviour at the expense of the neocortex, and notions of neocortical functions have been considerably revised. This is not to deny the great importance of the neocortex in the regulation of behaviour but to affirm the importance of subcortical structures. Whereas previously the neocortex was usually considered to be all-important, and subcortical structures to be of relatively little significance, it now appears that subcortical structures are to be accorded more or less equal weight in the regulation of behaviour.

The ascending reticular activating system (ARAS)

During the discussion of electrical recording techniques, it was mentioned that there is always some measurable activity in the living brain, even when stimulation is, apparently, absent. Furthermore, when brain tissue is completely isolated neurally from other nervous tissue, it remains quiescent until it is stimulated, but once stimulation has taken place, the resulting neural activity persists for some time after the stimulation has ceased. Burns (1958), for example, found that a few strong electrical stimuli applied to the surface of an isolated slab of cortical tissue produced a series of bursts of neural activity which generally continued for many minutes after the stimulation had stopped. Cortical neurones thus appear to be inactive in the absence of continuous stimulation or input, although there are reports that spontaneous neural activity may be present in the cortex for occasional brief periods. In any case, such neurones seem able to be readily activated for prolonged periods by any input they may receive.

In the normal intact organism, the spontaneous activity of receptor mechanisms seems to provide the input that the cortex requires for its continual self-excitation. An example of such activity would be the spontaneous discharge of cells in the retina, the visual receptor at the back of the eyeball, or the discharge of cells at other points in the visual pathways to their projection areas in the cortex. Granit (1955) reviews evidence which implies that the spontaneous neural activity of sense organs makes them one of the brain's most important energizers or activators, and suggests that the neural structure through which such activation has its effects on the cortex is the brainstem reticular activating system.

EEG records taken from a sleeping subject differ from those taken from the same subject in the waking state. The record from a sleeping subject is characterized by high amplitude low frequency (high voltage slow) activity, although the details of the EEG record vary with the depth of sleep (the intensity of auditory stimulation required to awaken the sleeper being used as an index of sleep depth). Dement and Kleitman (1957) and Williams, Agnew and Webb (1964) have devised classification systems for scoring EEG sleep records in terms of sleep stages. Thus, to some extent, the EEG has been thought to provide a measure of the degree of wakefulness, since sleeping and waking, when considered in terms of the EEG, are thought to be quantitatively different rather than qualitatively different states.

However, there is some evidence, stemming from research on

dreaming on the one hand and from research on drug effects on the other, which seems to run counter to the above assumptions about the EEG. Aserinsky and Kleitman (1955) observed that during a night's sleep there were periods during which subjects exhibited rapid eye movements (REMs), and Dement and Kleitman (1957) demonstrated that these REM periods were periods of sleep in which subjects were probably dreaming, although there is evidence that dream reports can also be obtained when REMs are not present (Foulkes, 1964, 1966). During REM periods subjects were found to be very hard to awaken, although the EEG record resembled a wakefulness pattern much more closely than that of deep sleep. Because of this apparent discrepancy between the EEG and the behavioural data, REM sleep has become known as 'paradoxical' sleep and also, because of the brain mechanisms apparently involved, 'hindbrain' sleep (Jouvet, 1967). These data presented some difficulties for a view of the EEG as an indicator of degrees of wakefulness and sleep, since, if subjects were awake, as the EEG record indicated, it was difficult to understand how they could be dreaming and why they should be so difficult to arouse. Similarly, if they were asleep, as their behaviour indicated, it was difficult to understand why the EEG record indicated a state resembling wakefulness rather than deep sleep. For a review of recent experimental studies of sleep and dreaming see Foulkes (1966) and Jouvet (1967).

In addition, psychopharmacological studies (for example, Bradley and Key, 1958) have demonstrated that cats injected with the drug atropine show an EEG record which strongly resembles that of sleep – that is, high voltage slow activity – whereas behaviourally the animals are extremely alert and responsive. In summary, it appears that low voltage fast activity and high voltage slow activity can each be associated with either sleep or wakefulness. Thus EEG records alone would seem to be inadequate in inferring the presence of sleep or wakefulness; behavioural and perhaps also other physiological measures need to be taken as well.

The importance of taking other measures becomes even greater when considering the problem of consciousness, for which wakefulness is often used as a synonym. In general, activities such as perceiving or learning, thinking or remembering require the organism to be conscious, and a state of consciousness is, presumably, essential for most adaptive behaviour to occur. The ARAS plays an important part in the maintenance of consciousness, although the evidence for this statement comes largely from experiments implicating the ARAS in the maintenance of wakefulness.

In an early experiment, performed before the significance of the ARAS was fully realized, Bremer (1935, 1954), working with cats, found that if the brainstem was completely transected at its base, where it joins the spinal cord (a preparation known as an *encéphale isolé*) the EEG record continued to show signs of both sleep and wakefulness. If, however, the transection was made at the top of the brainstem (a preparation known as a *cerveau isolé*) the EEG record showed persistent signs of sleep and the animal could not be wakened for longer than a few seconds. These experiments of Bremer demonstrate the importance of sensory input to the brainstem for maintaining wakefulness, but they do not show by what neural mechanism this is accomplished.

The studies of Magoun and his collaborators during the late 1940s and 1950s (see Magoun, 1958) demonstrated the importance of the ARAS as the neural mechanism linking sensory input and cortical activation. Moruzzi and Magoun (1949), working with cats, found that the electrical stimulation of the mesencephalic reticular formation produced or accentuated both behavioural and EEG signs of wakefulness. Similar changes in the EEG record were produced by a sudden loud noise. Further, Lindsley *et al.* (1950) showed that the restriction of input to the brain achieved by cutting the specific sensory pathways in the brainstem while sparing the ARAS did not alter the sleep–wakefulness pattern of the EEG, whereas the transection of the ARAS at the same level, sparing the specific sensory pathways, produced only EEG sleep patterns (see Figure 24).

The ARAS is thus considered to be an important centre in the maintenance of the normal sleep–wakefulness cycle. However, the neocortex is also involved (Kleitman, 1939, 1963). In 1939 in the first edition of his important book, *Sleep and Wakefulness*, written before the significance of the reticular formation had been fully realized, Kleitman proposed what he called an evolutionary theory of sleep. It was so called because it regarded patterns of sleeping

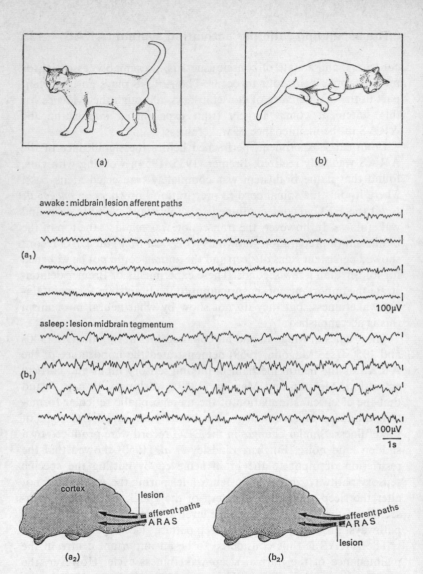

Figure 24 Effects of bilateral section of (a) the classical afferent pathways and (b) the ARAS in the midbrain. Cat (a) with bilateral section of the classical afferent pathways in the midbrain sparing the ARAS (a₂) stands awake with characteristic waking EEG (a₁). Cat (b) with midbrain ARAS interrupted, sparing the classical afferent pathways (b₂), lies somnolent with sleeping EEG (b₁). (After Lindsley *et al.*, 1950, p. 496)

and waking as dependent upon the evolutionary development of the cerebral cortex, especially in mammals. Kleitman distinguished between two kinds of wakefulness, a wakefulness of necessity and a wakefulness of choice. The first kind of wakefulness was said to be regulated by a subcortical centre and the second by the neocortex. Wakefulness of necessity is wakefulness which is maintained solely by sensory stimulation. It is found both in mammalian infants and in decorticate organisms (Kleitman, 1952) and characterized by a polyphasic alternation of sleep and wakefulness. Whenever a decorticate animal is freed from sensory stimulation arising in the external or internal environment, it lapses into sleep. This also seems to be true of the newborn human infant, who spends most of the twenty-four hours asleep with occasional short periods of wakefulness in which his bodily needs are satisfied. However, in adult mammals possessing an intact cortex, the alternation of sleep and wakefulness becomes a joint function of the subcortical waking centre and the cortex, and wakefulness of choice becomes superimposed on wakefulness of necessity. Wakefulness of choice is maintained by the direct or indirect effects of cortical activity on the subcortical waking centre. Such cortical activity, Kleitman suggested, is largely determined by an organism's adjustment to the light–dark cycle of the world in which it happens to live. The human organism, for instance, *learns* to postpone sleep to the night-time and to remain awake during the day, thus developing a monophasic cycle of sleep and wakefulness, as opposed to the polyphasic cycle of infancy (or of decortication).

The subcortical centre, mentioned above, thus has activating properties and, as has been indicated, is generally considered to be the ARAS, although the hypothalamus may also be implicated. Feldman and Waller (1962) found that certain brainstem lesions brought about sleep or drowsiness in cats while at the same time producing low voltage fast activity in the EEG record; other brainstem lesions produced high voltage slow activity although the animal was quite alert and responsive. For the implications of such studies for the understanding of neural mechanisms of sleep, see Routtenberg (1966).

One of the routes taken by the ascending pathway from the ARAS terminates in the thalamus and from the thalamus there arises a diffuse projection system to the neocortex, although there is some evidence which suggests that this diffuse thalamic projection system (DTPS) activates the cortex not by a direct ascending route but by an indirect descending route via the reticular system (Schlag and Chaillet, 1962). The DTPS has somewhat different characteristics from the other ascending route of the ARAS. While the ARAS appears to be a general arousal system concerned with prolonged periods of wakefulness, the DTPS appears to be an accessory mechanism that participates in more transient increases in arousal. For example, increases in arousal (as indicated by EEG records) produced by stimulation of the DTPS subside much more rapidly than those produced by stimulation of the ARAS (Lindsley, 1960). The arousing effects of the ARAS appear to be stronger than, and to take precedence over, those of the DTPS. When the DTPS is destroyed or its connexions with the neocortex severed, stimulation of the ARAS still brings about a neocortical arousal reaction.

The reticular formation also influences attention and discrimination. Paying attention to some environmental event involves the selection of that event or class of events and the rejection of others, since it is not possible for the organism to 'attend' to all the sensory stimuli which impinge upon it on any one occasion. A conceptual model of attention has been advanced by Broadbent (1957b, 1958). He suggests that *selective filtering* is performed on sensory events so that some events are allowed to travel up to higher levels of the central nervous system while others are not. Selection is carried out on the basis of certain characteristics of the sensory events, for example, the intensity or novelty of a stimulus, and of certain states of the organism, such as 'drive states'. The many psychological studies which give credence to such a model are reviewed by Broadbent (1958) and Treisman (1964). There are also neurophysiological studies which suggest that this selective filtering process is carried out by the reticular system (Hernández-Peón, 1961). For a critical review of some aspects of this work, see Horn (1965).

These experiments (and others, for example, Fuster, 1958) suggest that changes in the environment may be more readily detected by an animal that is aroused and attentive as a consequence of increased reticular formation activity produced by electrical stimulation. There are several aspects of the functioning of the reticular system that have not been discussed in this brief survey; in particular the effects of reticular activity on motor behaviour and on learning. For a fuller account of the relation of the reticular system to behaviour, see Samuels (1959), and for an account of the descending influences of the reticular system on motor behaviour, see French (1957).

The hypothalamus

Studies of the hypothalamus have yielded a reasonably consistent picture of its functioning. The hypothalamus contributes to the *initiation*, the *maintenance* and the *cessation* of behaviour prompted by various bodily needs, such as those for food and drink. Experimental manipulation of the hypothalamus, using stimulation and ablation techniques, influences the consummatory responses of eating and drinking associated with these needs or drives.

The satisfaction of many of the body's needs is such that a very fine balance is kept between output and intake, and this helps to ensure stability of the internal environment. This stability of the internal environment within rather narrow limits is essential to normal cell function, and hence to life, and is known as homeostasis. Because the hypothalamus is principally concerned in regulating the balance between output and intake, its mode of action is sometimes described as homeostatic. An example of a homeostatic mechanism is the domestic thermostat which can be set to maintain a certain room temperature. If the room temperature rises above this level, the thermostat shuts off and the room temperature falls to the level required; if the temperature falls below this level, then the thermostat remains on until that temperature is reached. The principle underlying the operation of a thermostat is that of negative feedback, and the hypothalamus appears to operate on a negative feedback principle, although its mode of action is considerably more complex than that of the thermostat.

An account of the body's control of water balance may make clearer the nature of homeostasis. Water is lost from the body in three main ways: through exhaled air, through perspiration and through the urine. The first two between them account for about 40 per cent of the daily water loss, although the loss through exhaled air is not very great. Thus the principal way in which water is retained in the body is by altering the urinary volume; this function is performed by the kidney where urine is manufactured and its constitution determined. A hormone secreted by the pituitary gland, known as vasopressin, acts on the kidney, checking the outflow of water. Without it the kidney allows water to be passed in large amounts.

Vasopressin is stored in the posterior lobe of the pituitary and can be released into the bloodstream in small or large amounts by hypothalamic action. Thus the amount of hormone released affects the urinary volume. The amount of water in the body appears to be signalled to the hypothalamus by the composition of the blood, in particular, by its osmotic pressure. As noted in Chapter 5, the hypothalamus is copiously supplied with blood. An increase in the intake of solids by the body raises the osmotic pressure of the blood which will draw water out of the intracellular fluid into the bloodstream unless the blood is diluted to regain its original osmotic pressure. Conversely, if the blood becomes diluted through an increase in liquid intake the osmotic pressure falls. In the former case the kidney is stimulated by vasopressin to retain water and in the latter case to lose it by the hypothalamus shutting off the release of vasopressin.

In addition to exerting its effect through the endocrine system, the hypothalamus also preserves homeostasis through the autonomic nervous system (ANS). The ANS and its functions will be discussed in the next chapter.

The sensitivity of the hypothalamus to changes in both the internal and the external environment is clearly important for the regulation of behaviour associated with the biological drives, although it should be noted that Hess (1954) emphasized that the functional areas in the hypothalamus overlap considerably and are poorly localized. However, as we shall see in the study of *eating behaviour*, fairly precise 'centres' within the hypothalamus have been located.

Control by the hypothalamus over eating behaviour has been demonstrated in a number of experiments. For example, electrical stimulation of part of the medial hypothalamic zone, in the vicinity of the ventromedial nucleus, produces a decrease in food consumption (Olds, 1958); while the effect of bilateral lesion in this area is to double or treble an animal's food intake – a condition known as *hyperphagia* (Hetherington and Ranson, 1942). Further, stimulation of an area in the lateral hypothalamic zone produces an increase in food consumption (Delgado and Anand, 1953), while lesions in this area produce a condition known as *aphagia*, in which the animal refuses to eat (Anand and Brobeck, 1951) and/or drink (Teitelbaum and Stellar, 1954). When both the ventromedial and lateral areas are ablated, the animal behaves as if only the lateral area had been removed – that is, it refuses to eat. The lateral area, as implied above, also appears to be involved in the regulation of drinking. The eating and drinking systems, though difficult to separate anatomically, seem to be neurochemically different; Grossman (1960), using various chemical agents which were injected into the lateral hypothalamic area at the same point, was able to elicit eating or drinking depending on the chemical used.

Satiated animals which are stimulated electrically or chemically in the lateral hypothalamic area will not only eat food if it is readily available, but will also perform a variety of responses in order to obtain food as a reward (N. E. Miller, 1961). Thirsty but food-satiated animals will even take food in preference to water when stimulated. In view of their willingness to work for a reward, the behaviour of such animals appears to be 'motivated' rather than merely reflexive and the general results of electrical stimulation in the lateral hypothalamic area parallel those of normally elicited hunger in a number of ways.

However, hypothalamic hyperphagic animals, although they eat a great deal more than normal animals, do less work to obtain food (N. E. Miller, Bailey and Stevenson, 1950) and the difference between the amount of work done by the two groups increases with the amount of work required. Thus, hyperphagic animals appear less motivated to obtain food. They are also more sensitive to the taste of food. If their food is adulterated with non-nutritive cellulose, their food intake decreases, whereas normal animals eat more to maintain their caloric intake (Teitelbaum, 1955). In addition, hyperphagic animals will detect the presence of quinine in their food at lower concentrations than will normal animals. Hyperphagia thus also involves an increased sensitivity to the palatability of food.

Following the removal of the ventromedial area there are two distinct post-operative phases. During the dynamic phase, hyperphagic animals double or treble their normal food intake and, in consequence, become extremely obese. In the static phase, food intake approximates to normal, and as a result, body weight is maintained at a constant level. Thus, hyperphagic animals ultimately regulate their food intake according to their weight as do normal animals, but the weight level is higher.

The opposite effects of stimulation and ablation of the lateral and ventromedial hypothalamic areas are shown in Table 3.

Table 3

Effects of stimulation and ablation of the ventromedial and lateral hypothalamic areas

	Ventromedial area	*Lateral area*
Stimulation	Decrease in food consumption	Increase in food consumption
Ablation	Increase in food consumption (hyperphagia)	Decrease in food consumption (aphagia)

Probably the most generally accepted explanation for the majority of these findings is the dual-centre theory put forward by Anand and Brobeck (1951). This theory provides a neat summary of evidence relating to neural mechanisms of eating behaviour, although it is open to some objections and some findings are not covered by the theory (see Ehrlich, 1964). It proposes that the lateral hypothalamic area is an 'eating centre' whose effects are excitatory and which initiates the eating response under appropriate conditions, while the ventromedial area is a 'satiation centre' which shuts off or inhibits eating when the animal has satisfied its need for food.

The dual-centre theory has been integrated into a more general view of hypothalamic function related to the biological drives by

Stellar (1954, 1960). The cornerstone of Stellar's conception of hypothalamic functioning is that both inhibitory and excitatory centres exist in the hypothalamus for each of the biological drives. Neural activity in an excitatory centre leads to the arousal of the relevant drive, while activity in the inhibitory or satiation centre occurs when the consummatory response associated with the drive has taken place. The level of the drive in question is thought to be reduced by the activity of the inhibitory centre depressing that of the excitatory centre, or, alternatively, by the inhibitory centre blocking the output of the excitatory centre. The effect of such activity of the inhibitory centre is held to terminate the arousal of the drive and also to terminate the associated consummatory behaviour.

This dual-control system of excitatory and inhibitory centres is clearly under the influence of many different factors, and Figure 25 illustrates some of these. Such influences could be blood-borne (for example, hormones or drugs circulating in the blood) or sensory (for example, the sight or smell of food or the role of stomach contraction in hunger). The hypothalamus is also open to the effects of activity in other parts of the brain and hence to the influence of learning. Learning presumably underlies the development of food preferences. In addition, the effects of the consummatory response of eating or drinking can also feed back to the hypothalamus and affect its activity: examples would be the distention of the filled stomach, food that has been digested and absorbed into the bloodstream, or the acts of chewing and swallowing. According to Stellar, it is likely that these various influences are equally able to initiate activity in the excitatory or inhibitory mechanism, that they interact in their effects and that they could have two types of effect, either starting or stopping neural activity in either inhibitory or excitatory centres.

Presumably these influences produce physiological changes in the hypothalamus, but it is not clear what specific physiological changes are responsible for changing the activity of neurones in the excitatory and inhibitory centres. In the case of eating behaviour, it seems probable that neurones in the excitatory centre are activated by a decrease in the body's food supply, while those in the inhibitory centre, the ventromedial area, are activated by an increase in this

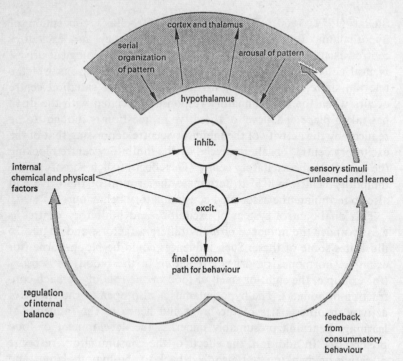

Figure 25 Schematic diagram of Stellar's model of the physiological factors contributing to the control of motivated behaviour. (From Stellar, 1954, p. 6)

supply. But how this activation is initiated is not clear. Further it is not known how neural activity in the excitatory area sets in motion the series of actions which culminate in the ingestion of food – for example, running through a maze with food as a reward.

Other parts of the brain, for example the *amygdala*, also appear to be involved in the neural control of eating. Bilateral ablation of this limbic system structure generally produces hyperphagia, although the effect is not as marked as in the case of hypothalamic damage (Morgane and Kosman, 1957, 1959). In view of these and similar findings, it has been suggested that the importance of the hypothalamus in eating behaviour, and presumably in the regulation of other drives as well, derives from the fact that it is a point of convergence for a great many fibre systems, all of which act on lower systems controlling eating (Morgane, 1961). It would therefore be expected that the effects of hypothalamic lesions are more severe because there would be fewer alternative pathways available following hypothalamic than following other types of brain injury.

An excitatory centre for drinking has been located in the anterior hypothalamus, and water-satiated animals will ingest considerable amounts when stimulated electrically or chemically in this area (see Andersson, 1953). However, no inhibitory area has been located, although lesions in the lateral hypothalamus, as already mentioned, can produce adipsia, a refusal to drink, and the regulation of food intake and that of water intake appear to be interdependent.

The neural control of mating behaviour appears to involve sensory or hormonal influences, as Stellar's model would suggest, and the anatomical, physiological and behavioural support of mating is dependent upon the presence of the proper sex hormones. The hypothalamus also appears to contain excitatory centres for mating behaviour, one hormonal and the other behavioural, but there is no firm agreement as to the existence of a hypothalamic inhibitory centre. However, lesions both in the hypothalamus and in other parts of the brain, in particular the amygdala, produce hypersexuality, suggesting that an inhibitory mechanism has been impaired; evidence has also been produced (Lisk, 1966) which suggests that an inhibitory mechanism concerned with sexual behaviour exists in the mammillary bodies of the hypothalamus of male rats. The way in which mating behaviour is regulated is clearly very complex, although Stellar has provided a possible conceptual framework for understanding it. For further discussion of the whole topic the reader is referred to Beach (1948, 1965), and Young, Goy and Phoenix (1964).

The limbic system

Early theories of limbic system functioning emphasized its role in olfaction; it was not until the 1930s that much interest was shown in the possible involvement of limbic structures in non-olfactory functions. In 1933 Herrick suggested that the limbic system might serve as a non-specific activator of all cortical activities and in the following year Kleist suggested that limbic system structures might be important in emotional behaviour. Three years later, on the basis of clinical experience with brain-damaged patients and of data from animal studies, Papez (1937) suggested that neural activity within the limbic system and, in particular, in the circuit that bears his name (see Figure 26) might underlie the experience of emotion; and in the late 1930s, Klüver and Bucy published the results of a series of experiments in which the behavioural consequences of temporal-lobe damage in monkeys, first investigated by Brown and Schaefer in 1888, were re-examined (Klüver and Bucy, 1937, 1938, 1939).

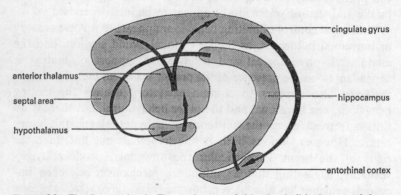

Figure 26   The Papez circuit. The pathways of this circuit (black arrows) form a closed loop running from the hippocampus to the hypothalamus, from the hypothalamus to the anterior thalamus and from the thalamus back to the hippocampus by way of the cingulate gyrus and the entorhinal cortex. (Adapted from McCleary and Moore, 1965, p. 32)

Klüver and Bucy removed both temporal lobes, including the amygdala, the entorhinal cortex (a rhinencephalic structure; see Figure 26, and Figure 17 in Chapter 5) and most of the hippocampus; the subsequent behavioural changes they observed have become known as the Klüver–Bucy syndrome. First, the monkeys were no longer particular about what they ate, eating food which was normally rejected and showing a tendency to put anything movable into their mouths.

Second, they seemed unable to recognize familiar objects in their cages – a condition described as visual agnosia. Third, they displayed increased sexual activity, much of it towards inappropriate objects, such as pieces of cloth. Fourth, they became tamer and safer to handle and, finally, they showed no fear, in that they would repeatedly put their fingers into the flame of a burning match. In this last example, changes with respect to fear rather than changes in the awareness of or sensitivity to pain have been inferred from the observed behaviour, largely because the electrical stimulation of certain of the brain areas removed in the Klüver–Bucy experiments can produce behavioural signs of intense fear, as will be mentioned later. These structures, then, appear to be involved in the mediation of fear, while pain appears to be mediated by different, although related, parts of the brain.

Later investigators have confirmed these results and have, to some extent, been able to locate more exactly the areas of the limbic system and temporal neocortex responsible for the changes in behaviour. It should also be mentioned that the Klüver–Bucy syndrome has been demonstrated, in modified form, following bilateral temporal lobe removal in man (Terzian and Ore, 1955). The main difference between human beings and monkeys in the effects of temporal-lobe removal appears to be that in man there are no oral tendencies, perhaps because monkeys normally make much more extensive use of their mouths in exploring new objects. However, Terzian and Ore found that food intake increased markedly and food preferences virtually disappeared. Second, there appears to be no failure to appreciate the meaning of objects and the uses to which they can be put, as there is in monkeys, although the patient studied by Terzian and Ore often failed to recognize people familiar to him. In addition, this patient showed some impairment of both spoken and written language and, finally, there was some evidence of hypersexuality, mainly in the form of exhibitionism and masturbation.

To oversimplify, the changes in eating behaviour, the placidity, the failures of recognition, the inappropriate sexual behaviour and the lack of fear characteristic of the Klüver–Bucy syndrome can be subsumed under three main headings: first, perceptual changes, probably due to the removal of temporal neocortex; second, changes in recent memory resulting from ablation of the hippo-campus; and third, to impaired avoidance behaviour (that is, behaviour motivated by the fear of unpleasant consequences) due to removal of the amygdala.

In the remainder of this section we shall consider more specifically the functions of the *hippocampus*, the *amygdala* and the *septal area* and *cingulate gyrus*. Further, we shall consider the importance of the loss of *temporal-lobe neocortex* which is often associated with damage to the limbic system, before moving to the final section of this chapter, in which the role of the neocortex is of central interest.

The hippocampus

Bilateral ablation of the hippocampus produces behavioural changes suggestive of some kind of *memory defect* both in animals and in man, although there has been considerable disagreement as to whether hippocampal removal results in post-operative deficits in the performance of pre-operatively learned tasks. Since in some studies the amygdala has been removed as well, it is also not clear to what extent the absence of this structure contributes to the post-operative changes. Furthermore, the wide variety of tasks used in studies of hippocampal function has made it difficult to disentangle the nature of the memory defect.

Patients with hippocampal lesions retain material which has been learned pre-operatively. Their occupational knowledge and skills remain unimpaired, language skills are undiminished and memories of early experiences are unaffected. However, there may be amnesia for events subsequent to the operation. Milner (1962) quotes an example of a patient in his late twenties whose family had moved house ten months after his operation. Ten months later he had not learned the new address although the old address was perfectly retained. Furthermore, he did not know where objects in daily house-hold use were kept and apparently would read the same magazine article over and over again without finding its contents familiar. In a formal testing situation, forgetting occurred the instant that his attention was diverted, although when not distracted his ability to sustain attention was extremely good. Apparently the item to be recalled had to remain the focus of attention, and once attention was shifted, recall was impossible. Hippocampal removal in man seems to result in short-term or recent memory defects, which also impair some kinds of learning. Thus the patient discussed by Milner (1962) showed no improvement in maze learning over a three-day period, although in a motor skill (mirror drawing) considerable day-to-day progress was made, suggesting either that the two tasks make differential demands on short-term memory or that hippocampal influences on memory may not be as general as previously supposed.

The nature of the memory deficit and its consequences for learning have also been investigated in animals. Hippocampal removal in animals produces deficits in what is known as *compound learning* but not in *delayed learning*. In compound learning, whether an animal is rewarded or punished depends on the response made to a stimulus sequence. For example, if the two stimuli separated by a brief time interval are the same, then the animal makes one response and is rewarded. If they are different, it makes a different response and thereby avoids punishment. In order to make the appropriate response in such a situation, the first stimulus must be retained and compared with the second. In delayed learning, on the other hand, the animal is trained to associate a particular response to one stimulus in order to obtain reward or to avoid punishment. However, the appropriate response must be delayed until a second stimulus is presented. No comparison of the stimuli is necessary for the formulation of the appropriate response. This response merely has to be withheld until the one for response, the second stimulus, is provided.

Hippocampal animals tend to be impaired in compound learning situations but not in delayed learning ones and the impairment is apparent irrespective of the sensory modality in which the stimuli are presented (Stepien, Cordeau and Rasmussen, 1960). It appears, therefore, that the type of memory deficit resulting from hippocampal damage reflects an inability to retain the characteristics of the first stimulus for later comparison with the second. In compound learning attention has to be diverted from the first stimulus in order to register the second. In delayed learning it is not necessary to register the characteristics of the second; attention can still be directed towards the first. However, the 'memory' hypothesis is only one of a number of hypotheses about hippocampal functioning. For a summary see Douglas (1967).

Other changes shown by hippocampal animals include impairment of reversal learning and an increase in general activity. This latter change also results from removal of the amygdala, to which we now turn.

The amygdala

The immediate consequence of bilateral amygdalectomy is a marked reduction in an animal's general activity, presumably attributable to the non-specific after-effects of the operation. However, this reduction in activity is not usually permanent and subsequently the animal may become hyperactive. Hyperactivity, when it occurs, appears to be the result of an increased awareness of and responsiveness to external stimulation, particularly in the visual mode. Objects in the environment are subjected to a great deal of investigation, both olfactory and gustatory (Schreiner and Kling, 1954).

The same general pattern, a decrease followed by an increase, occurs in drive-regulated behaviour such as eating or sexual activity. Immediately following the operation food intake is reduced, but thereafter many animals exhibit long-lasting hyperphagia. This increase in food intake apparently arises from the fact that amygdalectomized animals persistently take small objects into their mouths ejecting only those that are inedible. As far as sexual behaviour is concerned, hypersexuality usually develops as a result of amygdalectomy – especially in males. The major role in determining this change in sexual behaviour has been allotted to the pyriform cortex (Green, Clemente and De Groot, 1957), the removal of which often accompanies that of the amygdala. However, this explanation does not seem able to account for the entire effect (Wood, 1958).

The phenomena most frequently studied in relation to amygdaloid function are changes in *emotional behaviour* and in responsiveness to noxious or potentially dangerous stimuli. Such studies have been mainly concerned with a behavioural continuum varying from placidity to aggressiveness. Lesions in the amygdala can tame an otherwise wild animal and such effects have been observed in monkeys, non-domesticated cats and even in the lynx (Schreiner and Kling, 1953, 1954). However, some experimenters have found that damage to the amygdala produces an increase in aggressiveness and it is not entirely clear why such lesions produce these two opposing effects.

Different emotional responses also result from electrical stimulation of the amygdala. Over widespread areas of the limbic system electrical stimulation produces an 'attention' response and an increase in arousal, inferred from EEG desynchronization, for which, presumably, the connexions between the ARAS and the limbic system provide an anatomical basis. A more elaborate and apparently emotional response can be elicited from more restricted locations – for example, fear- and rage-like reactions both from the anterior or forward end of the cingulate gyrus and from the amygdala. These reactions may be produced in an abbreviated form or, by increasing the strength and duration of the electrical stimulation, the total response pattern can be elicited. In the case of fear-like reactions, the stimulated animal first shows the attention response, then crouches and begins to withdraw as if faced with danger. Finally, if the stimulating current is further increased, the animal turns and starts in flight; it will even attempt to hide if a suitable place is available. In the rage-like reaction the sequence of behaviour develops from the attention response to crouching and hissing and culminates in striking movements of the claws. Both the fear- and rage-like reactions are accompanied by an increase in autonomic activity. Since both types of response can be provoked by stimulation and ablation of the amygdala, it seems probable that this group of nuclei contains separate but overlapping zones which mediate, at least in part, these two types of emotional behaviour, although there are some results which do not appear to be covered by such an interpretation (see Goddard, 1964).

Amygdalectomized animals also show certain deficits in *learning*. They cannot learn to withhold a response when rewarded for withholding it; they cannot learn to avoid punishment by withholding a response (*passive avoidance learning*) or by learning a new response (*active avoidance learning*); and they do not show the suppression of response shown by normal animals when a fear-producing stimulus is presented during performance of a learned response (*conditioned suppression*). For a fuller account of the training procedures involved and of the deficits produced, see McCleary (1961).

Various interpretations of amygdaloid function have been made in the light of these results, although in spite of the great amount of data concerned with the amygdala it would appear that there is at present insufficient evidence to warrant the acceptance of any one interpretation. Goddard (1964) suggests that the amygdala is 'primarily involved in the active suppression of motivated approach behaviour' since animals in whom the amygdala has been removed 'do not know when to stop' (p. 102). Goddard also considers the amygdala to be important in the consolidation of the association between a neutral stimulus and a noxious event, and it is certainly true that the amygdala has many connexions with other areas of the brain, electrical stimulation of which appears to be 'unpleasant' (see Chapter 12). Weiskrantz (1956) takes the view that the effects of amygdalectomy on learning are primary and that these, within the context of the post-operative treatment of the amygdalectomized animal, determine the effects on emotional behaviour. Other investigators maintain that the differences in emotional behaviour, whether placidity or aggression, derive from underlying anatomical differences in the form of 'placidity' or 'aggression' centres within the amygdala. Damage to the 'aggression' centre produces increased placidity and vice versa. Another possibility is that the changes in emotional behaviour produce differential changes in the strength of different drives and that these differences in drive strength determine the ease of acquisition of conditioned responses.

The septal area and the cingulate gyrus

Lesions in the limbic system, as already mentioned, produce various abnormalities of fear-motivated behaviour. Damage to the cingulate gyrus, for example, results in many more trials being required before an animal can make an active avoidance response to a warning signal, and in more rapid extinction once the avoidance response has been acquired. However, damage to the cingulate gyrus does not markedly affect passive avoidance behaviour or conditioned suppression.

Septal lesions produce the opposite effect. Animals with such lesions seem unable to acquire a passive avoidance response and also fail to develop conditioned suppression in a normal manner. Instead of crouching tensely in response to a warning signal as unoperated animals do, animals who have sustained damage to the septal area continue to perform the task on which they are engaged. However, septal lesions do not disrupt active avoidance behaviour; if anything, such responses are acquired somewhat faster by these animals than by unoperated animals (King, 1958). Damage to the septal area also produces what is known as the septal rage syndrome, and this has been most commonly studied in rats, since they show very marked behavioural changes, becoming very wild and aggressive (Brady and Nauta, 1953; King, 1958). Rats also become hyper-irritable as a consequence of septal lesions; that is, an unexpected sound or tactile stimulus leads to an exaggerated startle response.

The rage pattern produced by damage to the septal area can be duplicated by a lesion in the anterior hypothalamus and counter-acted by a lesion in the amygdala. Conversely, an animal made placid by damage to the amygdala can be made vicious by damage to the anterior hypothalamus. Although these three areas – the septal area, the amygdala and the anterior hypothalamus – are all implicated in the control of aggressive behaviour, it is by no means clear how this control is exercised.

It has already been mentioned that electrical stimulation of the cingulate gyrus produces fear- and rage-like reactions. Stimulation of the septal area on the other hand appears to be positively re-inforcing: animals with electrodes implanted in the septal area and connected to a lever in a Skinner box will stimulate themselves electrically for long periods. Since a considerable literature exists on the effects of electrical self-stimulation in different parts of the brain and since there appear to be distinct positive and negative reinforcement systems in the brain which have been mapped using electrical self-stimulation techniques, a discussion of the main findings of this research is included in Chapter 12.

The contribution of temporal neocortex to the Klüver–Bucy syndrome

In monkeys bilateral removal of all temporal neocortex (except for the auditory projection areas), but sparing the limbic system structures beneath, has been found to produce many of the features of the syndrome (Akert *et al.*, 1961), a result which emphasizes the close anatomical and functional links between the temporal neocortex and underlying limbic structures (Meyer and Meyer, 1963). It might have been expected that temporal neocortical removal alone would have produced only perceptual disturbances, but Akert *et al.* found increased oral tendencies, increased placidity and an apparent loss of fear in addition to the expected sensory impairments. However, it must be noted that the perceptual and emotional changes in the Klüver–Bucy syndrome are not as independent as they might seem (Downer, 1961).

The nature of the perceptual deficit, which appears exclusively in the visual domain, has received considerable experimental attention. Although the temporal lobe as a whole appears to be involved in visual functions, the area of temporal neocortex which appears to be most intimately concerned is the inferotemporal cortex which lies on the underside of the temporal lobe. However, it is not necessary for this cortical area to be removed to produce disturbances of vision: severing its connexions with the rest of the cortex (by cross-hatching) is sufficient. Presumably the connexions between temporal neocortex and the primary visual projection area in the occipital lobe are the crucial ones. Severing the thalamic connexions of temporal neocortex on the other hand produces very little, if any, impairment of vision.

The visual functions which are impaired following bilateral removal of inferotemporal neocortex are, in the main, those concerned with visual discrimination learning and, in particular, with the retention of visual habits as measured, for example, by the animal's ability to remember which of two shapes or colours or patterns have been associated with a food reward in a previous learning situation. In some cases there is also impairment of the animal's ability to learn such a discrimination. Thus, impairment does not seem to be due to any purely sensory deficit, since such animals can perform tasks requiring a high degree of visual acuity, such as locating very thin threads, and there do not appear to be any 'blind spots' in their visual fields. The difficulty of the discrimination required determines, in part, whether or not impairment occurs. Monkeys normally find it easier to discriminate between two three-dimensional objects than between two painted patterns. Chow (1954) found that monkeys who had been trained on these two kinds of discrimination and in whom the inferotemporal cortex had subsequently been removed successfully retained a habit based on the first kind of discrimination but not one based on the second. His monkeys were also unable to re-acquire the second kind of discrimination. The amount of prior training has also been shown to be a factor (Orbach and Fantz, 1958). If monkeys are given extremely large amounts of training on a particular discrimination, then the habit based on this discrimination tends to be successfully retained post-operatively.

Thus inferotemporal neocortex appears to be involved in the retention and also, to some extent, in the acquisition of visual discriminations; deficits in these kinds of behaviour presumably underlie the visual agnosia which in turn is responsible for the failure to recognize appropriate fear objects, suitable food substances and compatible sexual partners.

The neocortex

In this section the role of the cerebral cortex in the regulation of behaviour will be briefly considered. As mentioned in the previous chapter, the cortex of each hemisphere divides into sensory projection areas, a motor area and two association areas, the frontal area and the parietal–temporal–occipital (PTO) area.

The amount of neocortex present in the brain increases with progression up the phylogenetic scale, as does the relative size of the association areas in the neocortex. The neocortex reaches its greatest size relative to the rest of the central nervous system (a process known as corticalization) in man and the higher mammals. Since higher mammals also tend to exhibit more complex behaviour it seems natural to assume that these two developments are related. This suggestion, that the emergence of more advanced forms of behaviour is due on the one hand to anatomical corticalization and on the other to a broad functional corticalization, an upward shift of control within the brain, is known as the *corticocentric* hypothesis. Functions which are regulated subcortically in lower animals are assumed, in higher animals, to be taken over and elaborated by the neocortex. Such a view can be expressed in at least two ways. The more extreme form of the hypothesis would be that, from the point at which the neocortex makes its first phylogenetic appearance, functions formerly regulated by subcortical centres are immediately transferred to the control of the neocortex. Alternatively it might be that functional control is shared between the subcortical centres and the neocortex, but that with evolutionary development the neocortex contributes a progressively greater share. On the first view one ought to be able to find functions which neocortical damage would impair equally in all species possessing neocortical tissue. The second view would imply that neocortical damage would affect the same functions to different degrees in different species. In general the evidence favours the latter alternative. But even where removal of the area of neocortex involved in the regulation of a particular function results in the abolition of that function, this is not to say that the function in question is 'localized' in that particular neocortical area and nowhere else. Most functions are subserved by a system of areas within the brain and of neural circuits connecting these areas. For some functions in some species destruction of one component of the system is sufficient to produce complete loss of function; for others more than one component needs to be destroyed.

The advantage of possessing large areas of neocortex is not simply that these areas aid subcortical centres in the regulation of behaviour. In addition, the anatomy of the neocortex, in particular the fact that much of it consists of divergent conduction paths with short, interconnecting nerve fibres, enables it to add flexibility to the list of functions regulated by subcortical centres. The importance of the neocortex is not so much that it provides new functions, although to some extent it does this too, but that it enables old functions to be performed in a new way.

In the first place, the divergent conduction paths of the neocortex make it possible for a response to be delayed, rather than elicited automatically. If the entire CNS consisted of parallel conduction paths, there would be no physiological basis for 'higher' forms of behaviour at all, since each above-threshold stimulus would automatically and immediately produce a response. Second, the divergent conduction paths of the neocortex make possible a screening of sensory inputs. Again, if this screening were not possible, as would be the case if there were only conduction in parallel within the CNS, then any intense and varied stimulation would produce an overloading of the nervous system resulting in a breakdown of behaviour. Third, as a consequence of the screening of stimuli, selective responding is possible and the ability to respond selectively is an important feature of 'higher' forms of behaviour. Finally, the great increase in the number of cells in the CNS provided by the neocortex enables a more precise control of function to be exercised by the nervous system; the neocortex can thus be regarded in one sense as the most specialized area of the brain, although this does not preclude a cortical area from involvement in more than one function.

A considerable body of evidence has accumulated in favour of the corticocentric hypothesis, at least for certain functions. Some of this evidence will now be briefly considered in relation to sensory and motor functions.

Sensory functions

Under this heading, the role of the neocortex in vision and audition will be briefly considered.

One of the implications of the corticocentric hypothesis is that the consequences for vision of removal of the striate area will become more severe as the phylogenetic scale is ascended. Very broadly, and with certain qualifications, this expectation seems to conform with the available evidence. Fish, without any neocortex at all, are capable of making visual discriminations between objects differing in size, brightness, colour or shape (Bitterman, 1965; Bitterman, Wodinsky and Candland, 1958). Furthermore, removal of the entire forebrain in fish has, apparently, no effect on the ability to acquire a new visual discrimination or to retain an old one (Hester, quoted by Teuber, 1960, p. 1614). In fish, therefore, visual discrimination processes must be handled subcortically and by structures less advanced than the forebrain. In birds, the removal of the thin layer of neocortical cells in the occipital lobe has no effect on the ability to discriminate visually (Layman, 1936) but the consequences of forebrain removal are less clear (Teuber, 1960). In the rat, cat, dog, monkey and man the ability to discriminate visual patterns is permanently lost following total bilateral ablation of the striate area (Neff, 1960).

However, the ability to discriminate differences in brightness appears to be very little affected by bilateral removal of the visual cortex in these animals, although the greatest degree of impairment is found in man. Other visual deficits are also apparent and Neff (1960) summarizes the evidence on the effects of visual cortex ablation on vision in the following way:

one would infer that animals such as the rat, cat and monkey, after ablation of the visual cortex, perceive a two-dimensional world; a world without depth; without contours, differing only in brightness gradients or perhaps of uniform brightness at any given instant but changing when eye and head movements lead to increase or decrease in luminous flux[1] (p. 1462).

The evidence briefly surveyed above has come from studies of adult animals. However, Doty (1961a) has demonstrated that if the primary sensory projection area for vision is completely removed in newborn kittens, then such animals, when adult, show no impairment of pattern vision; the CNS possesses a greater degree of plasticity when the animal is young. Further examples of this phenomenon are cited in later sections.

In discussing audition, three topics are briefly considered: the effects of auditory cortex removal on pitch, on loudness discrimination, and on the ability to locate the source of sound.

The majority of studies in this field of inquiry have used cats as subjects. Cats whose auditory cortex has been removed are able to discriminate the onset of a sound, and between intensities of sound

1. A technical term denoting, roughly, the total amount (strictly speaking, rate of flow) of light impinging on the eye.

(Kryter and Ades, 1943; M. R. Rosenzweig, 1946). Thus both absolute and differential intensity threshholds appear to be unimpaired. Following auditory cortex removal cats are also able to discriminate between equally loud sounds which differ in pitch (Goldberg and Neff, 1961). On the other hand, such animals have difficulty in discriminating between different tonal patterns – for example, high–low–high and low–high–low – or between two sounds of equal loudness and pitch but of different durations (Diamond and Neff, 1957; Neff, 1960). Finally, such animals lose the capacity for sound localization completely and seem unable to re-acquire it.

As in vision, it is pattern discrimination that is most impaired following removal of the relevant cortical projection area while intensity discrimination is relatively unaffected. There is some suggestion that the same conclusion holds for dogs and monkeys. But in man widespread damage to the auditory cortex results in total deafness.

The above results come from experiments using mature animals and again, as in vision, the effects of cortical lesions in immature animals are much less marked. Scharlock, Tucker and Strominger (1963) found that kittens, from whom large areas of cortical tissue inclusive of auditory cortex were bilaterally removed, were able to discriminate between different tonal patterns when tested at the age of six months. No difference was found between the lesioned animals and their litter-mate controls in the number of trials required to learn the discrimination. However, adult cats in whom similar lesions were made were completely unable to learn to discriminate between the two tonal patterns.

Motor functions

Figure 27 shows the neocortex divided into various areas on the basis of their cellular structure, that is, the number of distinguishable cellular layers within the neocortex at various points and the different types of cell found within these layers. The classification system shown in Figure 27 is one developed by the German physiologist Brodmann in the early years of this century and it assigns a number to each of these structurally distinguishable areas. However, not all of the regions distinguished by the Brodmann system are functionally distinct areas as established by ablation experiments or by electrical stimulation and recording techniques. The system is referred to here to distinguish the different regions within the motor area of the neocortex.

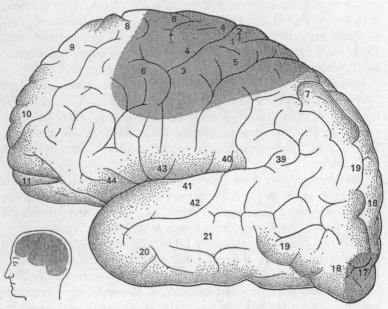

Figure 27   A schematic drawing of Brodmann's numbering of cortical areas. The shaded areas are discussed in the text and are as follows: pre-motor, motor and somaesthetic cortex nos. 1, 2, 3, 4, 5 and 6; visual cortex no. 17. (From Cobb, 1941, p. 72)

Area 4 forms the main body of the motor cortex although areas 1, 2 and 3 in the post-central gyrus are also part of the motor region of the cortex, at least functionally. So is area 6, in front of the central sulcus, which is known as the pre-motor area. Bilateral ablation of all the cortical areas primarily concerned with voluntary movement, that is, areas 4, 6, 1, 2 and 3, results in complete and permanent motor paralysis in monkeys, chimpanzees and man. Removal of these areas in rats, cats and dogs produces much less impairment of motor functions. As already mentioned earlier in this chapter, lesions of the motor cortex of one hemisphere reveal their effects on motor functions cross-laterally.

Even in man, however, some recovery of motor function is possible following damage to the motor cortex. It is not entirely clear whether this recovery is due to the functional reorganization of tissue remaining in the motor cortex or to the appropriation of some motor functions either by cortical areas outside the motor cortex or by subcortical centres. In monkeys, bilateral removal of area 4 alone results in less severe impairment from which there may be some recovery of function. Furthermore, if a unilateral ablation of area 4 is made and is followed some months later by the removal of the same area of the other hemisphere, the usual results of bilateral injury are not obtained. If, however, areas 1, 2, 3 and 6 are removed at the time of the first ablation of area 4 and, after a similar interval, the remaining area 4 is also removed, the results are the same as if a bilateral lesion had been made in the first place. In other words, the failure to obtain complete paralysis in the first instance must be due to the compensatory activity of the post-central gyrus, areas 1, 2 and 3, and the pre-central area, area 6.

Removal of areas 4 and 6 in infancy does not result in motor paralysis, at least in infant monkeys (Kennard, 1938, 1942). Thus, as in vision and audition, the age of the animal at the time of brain injury is an important factor in determining the degree of impairment. When monkeys in whom areas 4 and 6 have been removed in infancy reach maturity some motor paralysis does become apparent, but it is much less marked than if areas 4 and 6 are ablated at maturity. Some reorganization must therefore take place as the animal grows older. Stimulating drugs such as strychnine and thiamin have been shown to increase both the rate and extent of recovery of motor functions (Ward and Kennard, 1942), while sedatives such as phenobarbital produce a decrease (Watson and Kennard, 1945).

The association areas

The advantages of possessing neocortical tissue outlined above are particularly marked in the case of the association areas. As mentioned earlier, the relative amount of cortical tissue consisting of sensory and motor areas decreases as the phylogenetic scale is ascended. The proportion of cortical tissue devoted to the association areas is thus greater in man than in other animals. It is worth noting that many objections have been made to the use of the term 'association areas'. However, no satisfactory synonym has been forthcoming.

At one time the association areas were thought to consist of transcortical paths connecting the sensory and motor areas of the cortex. Although the association areas do consist in part of transcortical paths, these 'horizontal' connexions between sensory and motor areas are probably less important than the 'vertical' ascending and descending pathways which link different areas of the cortex via subcortical centres. In an experiment illustrating this point, Doty (1961b) attached electrodes to the skulls of cats so that the electrical contacts rested either in one of the outer layers of the cortex or on its surface. At least one electrode was placed in the primary visual projection area of the cortex (area 17) and a second in the motor cortex. Doty then employed a classical conditioning procedure (see Chapter 12): when the motor area of the cortex was electrically stimulated (the unconditioned stimulus) a discrete peripheral movement of one of the limbs occurred. This was the unconditioned response. By repeatedly pairing electrical stimulation of the visual area (the conditioned stimulus) with stimulation of the motor area, Doty was eventually able to produce a limb movement in response to stimulation of the visual area alone (the conditioned response). He then operated on the visual area in two ways, either severing its horizontal (transcortical) connexions with the motor area or its vertical (subcortical) connexions. In animals in whom the horizontal connexions were left intact but the vertical connexions cut, the conditioned response could not be obtained; but in those in whom the horizontal connexions were severed but the vertical connexions spared, it was possible to obtain the conditioned response. It thus appears that the vertical connexions are the more important ones.

The frontal association areas. The effects of damage to the association areas of the frontal lobe have been extensively studied both in man and in animals. In subhuman primates damage to the frontal lobes produces moderately severe consequences, while in man considerably more subtle behavioural changes result. Speculations as to the function of the frontal lobes in man range from the notion that this area is responsible for man's highest intellectual achievement (Halstead, 1947) to the more cautious statement of Hebb (1942) to the effect that there are very few adequately controlled studies in which a major behavioural deficit has been demonstrated to result from frontal lobe damage. Teuber (1959) suggests that deficits do occur but that they are more readily observable on simple sensorimotor tasks than on complex, cognitive ones.

There appears to be general agreement that performance on standard intelligence tests is relatively insensitive to frontal lobe damage. However, cognitive deficits do appear on pencil-and-paper, maze-learning tasks and on tasks requiring the recall of digits or of nonsense syllables (Scherer, Winne and Baker, 1955). Impairment associated with frontal-lobe damage also occurs on a card-sorting task (Wisconsin Card Sorting Test) in which cards can be sorted in terms of colour, form or number. The subject sorts in terms of colour for a while and then the sorting principle (inferred by the subject from the tester saying 'right' or 'wrong') is changed from colour to form to number and so on. Frontal-lobe patients make perseverative errors on this task; they persist in sorting cards in terms of a principle which is no longer correct (Milner, 1963, 1964).

As mentioned above, frontal-lobe patients also have difficulty with certain sensorimotor skills – for example, visual search (Teuber, Battersby and Bender, 1949) and the perception of sudden figural reversals (Cohen, 1959) – and in orientation to the body. In this last task, the patient, standing, faced a series of drawings of the human figure, also upright, one facing the patient, the other facing away from him. Parts of the human figures were numbered and the patient was required to touch the corresponding parts of his own body in the sequence indicated by the numbers. In summarizing the results of these experiments, Teuber (1964) has stated that following frontal-lobe damage in man, 'the essential alteration would be in some mechanism which enters into proper direction of voluntary gaze, on searching tasks, and into the proper maintenance of the perceived upright during changes of posture' (p. 438).

However, a disturbance of affect is often associated with frontal-lobe damage and this reveals itself as a motivational deficit when the subject is required to perform complex tasks. Thus, it is not entirely clear whether the rather subtle performance changes observed, on the Wisconsin Card Sorting Test for example, following frontal-lobe damage reflect a genuine loss in capacity or an unwillingness to perform the task as efficiently as possible.

The interaction of age with frontal damage is also unclear; that is, if frontal-lobe damage is sustained in the early years of life, are the effects less severe than if the damage is sustained at maturity? The evidence on this point is equivocal in that there are cases in which frontal damage sustained in youth has had little apparent effect and others in which the effects have been very marked. Wooldridge (1963) has suggested that the frontal lobes supply, in computer terminology, 'standby capacity' which is called upon by the rest of the brain when complex problems must be dealt with. He hypothesizes, following Hebb (1942), that one of the reasons why severe impairment of intellectual function does not normally appear after frontal damage may be that the performance of routine intellectual operations does not require standby capacity. The most difficult and demanding intellectual activities that individuals engage in are usually those involved in the learning of complex and abstract concepts; these activities would be expected to require standby capacity. Since most of this kind of learning goes on during childhood, it is possible that frontal-lobe damage would have more profound and easily observable effects in children than in adults, in contrast to the usual effects of brain damage and age.

In animals the most frequently studied deficit resulting from frontal-lobe damage is that revealed on delayed-reaction tasks. In such tasks the animals, generally monkeys, watch the experimenter place a peanut under one of two identical containers, but they are prevented from selecting the container with the peanut until after a few seconds' delay. In one of the first experiments in this field, Jacobsen (1935) showed that monkeys with frontal lesions were unable to perform this kind of task successfully and the inference was drawn that the frontal damage impaired 'recent memory'. However, later experiments, while not completely resolving the issue, have stressed that 'frontal animals' appear to be suffering more from attentional than from memory defects, since in other situations they are able to retain information as efficiently as control animals (Finan, 1939).

Monkeys with frontal-lobe damage are hyperactive and distractible. This distractibility can be reduced by the administration of sedatives and frontal monkeys are able to perform delayed-reaction tasks when under light sedation (Pribram, 1950; Wade, 1947). Darkness during the delay period, which presumably reduces distractibility, also facilitates performance on this task (Malmo, 1942). A different kind of investigation has examined the role of spatial factors in the delayed-reaction performance of frontal monkeys. In Jacobsen's original experiment, the animal was faced with two containers, one on his left and the other on his right. Later experiments have used only one container which the experimenter either baits or leaves empty in full view of the monkey. Following the delay, the animal's task is either to reach, if the container was baited, or not to reach, if the container was left empty. This is known as a go/no-go problem and comparisons of this situation with the traditional delayed-reaction situation have shown that frontal monkeys can solve the former problem but not the latter (Mishkin and Pribram, 1956). Frontal monkeys do make some mistakes on the no-go trial, however; these take the form of responding when a response is not called for, suggesting some inability to inhibit or suppress responding.

The capacity to perform delayed-reaction tasks is age-related in monkeys (Harlow, 1959a). The effects of frontal lesions on delayed-reaction performance are, in consequence, also related to age (Harlow, Akert and Schiltz, 1964). Rhesus monkeys in whom bilateral frontal lesions were made at age five days, when the ability to solve the delayed-reaction problem is totally absent, or at age 150 days, when this ability is still poorly developed, showed little or no deficit on subsequent learning of the task, as Figure 28 shows. In contrast, animals who sustained the same operation at the age of two years showed a marked deficit.

PTO association area. Some of the deficits arising from damage to the temporal lobe have already been mentioned in an earlier section.

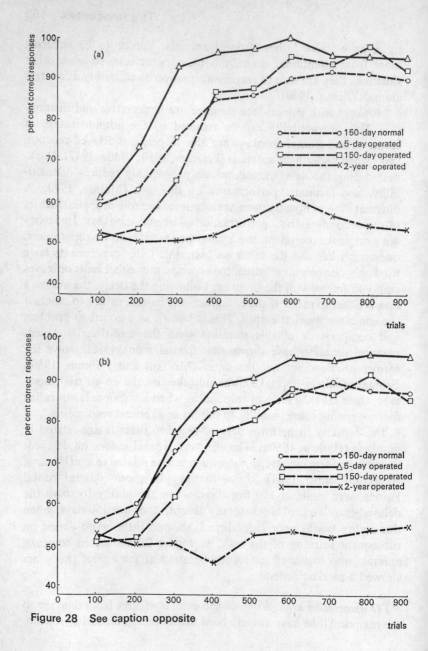

Figure 28 See caption opposite

In man this area, together with part of the parietal and occipital represented only in one hemisphere; generally the dominant hemisphere for speech is the left. Language deficits in right-handed patients are almost always consequent upon left hemisphere damage, although in left-handed people similar deficits appear to result from an injury to either hemisphere. It is possible that bilateral cortical representation of language skills occurs more frequently in left-handed patients than in right-handed ones (see Piercy, 1964, p. 312). A technique for detecting hemisphere dominance in speech has been developed by Landsell (1962). Sodium amytal is injected into the carotid artery of one side of the brain; this produces a greater degree of anaesthesia in the injected hemisphere. If disruption of speech also occurs, the injected hemisphere is the dominant one for speech. Severe left hemisphere brain damage sustained in the early years of life rarely retards language development, and removal of the damaged hemisphere in later life does not appear to produce language deficits. Thus the dominance of one hemisphere over the other in language functions probably occurs gradually, and the two hemispheres seem to be initially equipotential for the mediation of speech.

The most common language deficit is aphasia, of which there are several types, although the manifestations of aphasia are extremely diverse and the classification into types is something of an over-simplification. There are two general categories of aphasia, sensory and motor. On the sensory side there is auditory aphasia, an inability to comprehend speech, and visual aphasia, or alexia, in which the deficit takes the form of an inability to read and understand written language. Malfunctions on the motor side are of three main kinds: in verbal aphasia there is impairment of the ability to form and produce words; in nominal aphasia the patient experiences difficulty

Figure 28   The effects of pre-frontal lesions on delayed-response performance in monkeys at different ages. (a) Performance of the operated groups and the 150-day normal group on 900 zero-second delayed-response trials. (b) Performance of the operated groups and the 150-day normal group on 900 5-second delayed-response trials. (From Harlow, Akert and Schiltz, 1964, pp. 134 and 135)

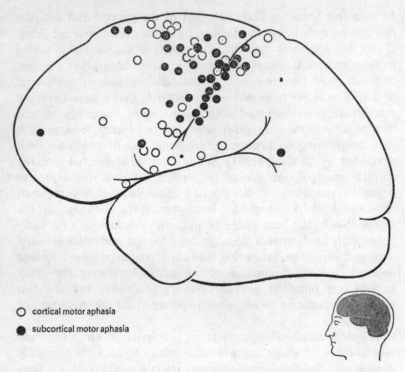

O   cortical motor aphasia

●   subcortical motor aphasia

Figure 29   Localization of lesion in cases of motor aphasia. (From Conrad, 1954, p. 495)

in naming objects or people; and in manual aphasia, or agraphia, there is an impairment of writing. Other kinds of defect which are sometimes considered with the aphasias are the agnosias, a collection of defects which have in common an inability to recognize familiar objects, and the apraxias, which have in common an apparent loss of memory for a familiar sequence of actions which make up a particular, usually fairly low-level, skill.

Figures 29 and 30 are reproduced from a study of localization of brain damage in cases of motor, sensory and nominal aphasia (Conrad, 1954). Damage to the frontal and temporal lobe appears to be associated with motor aphasia, damage to the parietal and

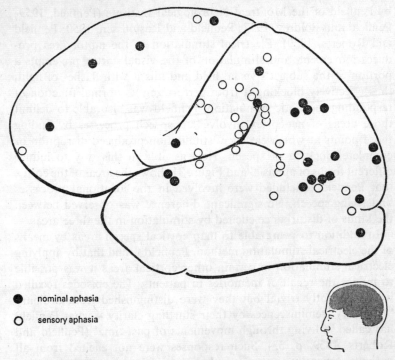

nominal aphasia

sensory aphasia

Figure 30   Localization of lesion in cases of sensory aphasia, together with cases of nominal aphasia. (From Conrad, 1954, p. 495)

temporal lobes with sensory aphasia, while damage to the parietal and occipital lobes is associated with nominal aphasia. It is worth mentioning that damage to the appropriate region of the motor cortex or to the descending motor pathways can produce articulation deficits or complete loss of speech, since the muscles of the larynx are no longer adequately innervated. This speech deficit is quite distinct from the aphasias, where it is the ideational processes underlying speech which appear to be primarily disrupted.

Much important work has been done in mapping the functional areas of the neocortex in man using the electrical stimulation method by Penfield of the Montreal Neurological Institute (Penfield, 1959; Penfield and Boldrey, 1937; Penfield and Rasmussen, 1950; Penfield and Roberts, 1959). Electrical stimulation of the motor area produces movement, and stimulation of the visual cortex pre-empts a portion of the subject's visual field and fills it with flashes of light, thus effectively blocking it from performing its normal function of responding to photic stimulation. Penfield was also able to delimit those areas of neocortex involved in speech processes by finding those points at which electrical stimulation produced disruption or complete blocking of speech. He was able in this way to induce different forms of aphasia, and Figure 31 shows the areas of the cortex that Penfield concluded were involved in the ideational processes underlying speech. No significant difference was observed between the kinds of disturbance elicited by stimulation in the three areas.

In addition to being able to map cortical speech areas by means of the electrical stimulation method, Penfield found that by applying electrical stimulation in certain other cortical areas it was possible to induce the recall of memories in patients. The episodes recalled were frequently trivial but they were distinguished from ordinary 'voluntary' reminiscences by their startling clarity – what Penfield has called 'a living through movements of past time' (Penfield and Roberts, 1959, p. 53). Such responses were not elicited from all patients, generally appearing only in patients with a past history of epilepsy involving damaged tissue in the vicinity of the area from which the recall was elicited. However, Piercy (1964) has stated:

Penfield's suggestion that these evoked experiences amount to a playback of the stream of consciousness cannot be accepted simply on the basis of the patient's conviction that memory was involved. Identifying paramnesia attaching to a visual hallucination is an equally plausible explanation (p. 337).

Finally, damage to the parietal lobe in man often appears to affect fairly specialized route-finding skills, while damage to the nonstriate occipital cortex primarily affects visual functions. In animals, damage to the PTO association area affects discrimination learning, although other functions are sometimes impaired as well (see Pribram, 1960a and b).

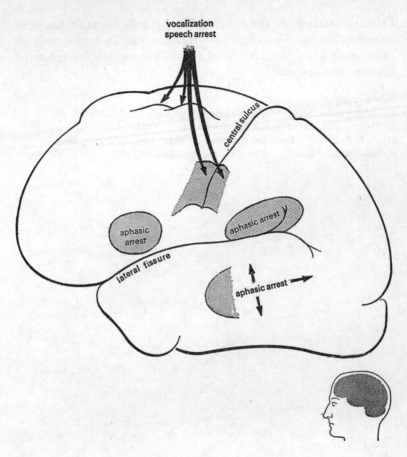

Figure 31 Summary of areas in which stimulation may interfere with speech or produce vocalization in the dominant hemisphere. (From Penfield and Rasmussen, 1950, p. 107)

Little has been said in this chapter about studies of interhemisphere integration in animals and the role of the corpus callosum in effecting communication between the hemispheres (see Myers, 1961; Sperry, 1961, 1964; Trevarthen, 1962). Similarly, little space has been given to the development of the human brain from birth to maturity (see

Magoun, Darling and Prost, 1959). Finally, little attention has been given to the role of psychophysiological techniques in the study of emotion in man; the next chapter briefly considers the topics of emotion and arousal.

Further reading
D. Bindra and J. Stewart (eds.), *Motivation*, Penguin Books, 1966.
S. P. Grossman, *Physiological Psychology*, Wiley, 1967.
K. H. Pribram (ed.), *Brain and Behaviour*, 4 vols., Penguin Books, 1969.
P. Teitelbaum, *Physiological Psychology*, Prentice-Hall, 1967.

Chapter 7
The Autonomic Nervous System and Behaviour

The physiology of the ANS and the endocrine system

The autonomic nervous system

Autonomic means self-governing and the activity of the ANS is largely independent of direct neocortical influences, although the neocortex affects the output of the ANS indirectly, mainly via the hypothalamus. The ANS consists of a network of motor fibres originating principally in the hypothalamus and conveyed to their destinations in the peripheral nervous system by way of the spinal cord. These motor fibres are connected to the smooth muscles of the visceral organs, such as the heart and the stomach, and to various glands (see Figure 32).

The ANS has two divisions, the *sympathetic* and the *parasympathetic*, fibres of the former division coming from the middle section of the spinal cord and of the latter from the two ends. The majority of the structures connected to the ANS are innervated by both sympathetic and parasympathetic fibres. This *reciprocal innervation*, as it is called, provides a mechanism for maintaining the activity of a given structure within fairly narrow limits, since the two divisions of the ANS exert somewhat opposing effects. In general, the sympathetic division exerts effects which increase energy expenditure whereas the parasympathetic division exerts effects which promote energy conservation. The effects of sympathetic dominance appear in situations requiring rapid action – for example, a situation perceived as involving danger; such situations have been described as demanding 'fight or flight' on the part of the organism. Indicators of sympathetic activity are, for example, increases in heart rate, respiration or sweat gland activity. Parasympathetic dominance

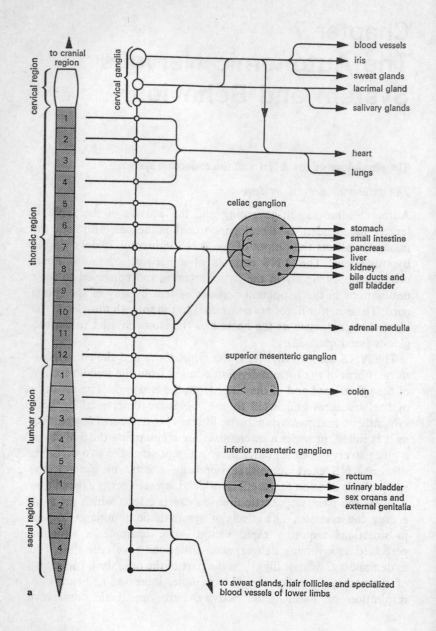

cervical region

to cranial region

cervical ganglia

→ blood vessels
→ iris
→ sweat glands
→ lacrimal gland
→ salivary glands

1
2
3
4
5

thoracic region

6
7
8
9
10
11
12

→ heart
→ lungs

celiac ganglion

→ stomach
→ small intestine
→ pancreas
→ liver
→ kidney
→ bile ducts and gall bladder

→ adrenal medulla

lumbar region

1
2
3
4
5

superior mesenteric ganglion

→ colon

sacral region

1
2
3
4
5

inferior mesenteric ganglion

→ rectum
→ urinary bladder
→ sex organs and external genitalia

a

→ to sweat glands, hair follicles and specialized blood vessels of lower limbs

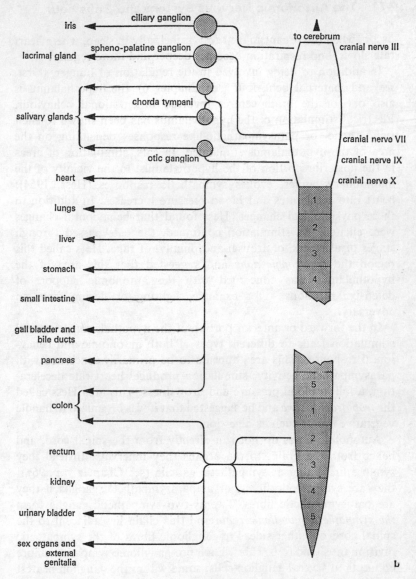

Figure 32 Highly simplified diagram of the autonomic nervous system and the parts of the body that it serves; **a** shows the sympathetic division and **b** the parasympathetic division

occurs when the organism is at rest, principally in sleep, where heart rate slows, and respiration becomes deeper and more regular.

In addition to being involved in the regulation of hunger, thirst, sex and maternal behaviour (see Chapter 6), the hypothalamus is also one of the brain centres involved in emotional behaviour. Electrical stimulation of the hypothalamus has been shown to elicit sympathetic- or parasympathetic-like responses depending on the area of the hypothalamus stimulated. In cats, stimulation of areas in the posterior portion of the hypothalamus, in the vicinity of the mammillary bodies, evokes sympathetic responses (Hess, 1954); heart rate accelerates and blood pressure increases. In addition to these physiological changes, Hess found that behavioural changes were elicited. As stimulation continued, the cats passed through stages of alertness, of arousal and, finally, of rage. Hess called this region the *ergotrophic zone* and suggested that this area of the hypothalamus was concerned with the autonomic support of defensive reactions – for example, fighting or fleeing from an adversary.

In the forward or anterior portion of the hypothalamus, electrical stimulation leads to different types of both autonomic and behavioural responses. This area appears to be primarily concerned with parasympathetic activity; stimulation produces heart rate deceleration, a fall in blood pressure and drowsiness. This area Hess called the *tropotrophic zone* and he suggested that it was organized to handle vegetative events such as digestion.

Autonomic fibres do not run directly from the spinal cord, and hence from the brain, to the organs they innervate. Instead they synapse first either at sympathetic ganglia (see Chapter 5, p. 96) if they are sympathetic fibres, or at parasympathetic ganglia if they are parasympathetic fibres. Twenty-two sympathetic ganglia form *the sympathetic ganglionic chain* and this chain lies adjacent to the spinal cord on either side. Pre-ganglionic fibres of the sympathetic division thus tend to be short. Each pre-ganglionic sympathetic fibre connects to several ganglion cells, some within the ganglion nearest to its level of exit from the spinal cord and some in ganglia above and below this level. From sympathetic ganglia, post-ganglionic fibres run to the organs innervated by the sympathetic division.

Parasympathetic fibres have their ganglia too, but these are near the organs they innervate; parasympathetic pre-ganglionic fibres thus tend to be long and post-ganglionic fibres to be short. Both sympathetic and parasympathetic pre-ganglionic fibres are myelinated, while post-ganglionic fibres are not.

At both sympathetic and parasympathetic ganglionic synapses, transmission is effected by the release of the substance *acetylcholine*. Post-ganglionic cells are thus said to be stimulated *cholinergically*. However, while post-ganglionic sympathetic and parasympathetic fibres are alike in the nature of the synaptic transmission which stimulates them, they differ with respect to the mode of chemical transmission which occurs thereafter: that is, the transmitter substance liberated by post-ganglionic parasympathetic fibres is different from that liberated by post-ganglionic sympathetic fibres. Parasympathetic fibres stimulate their structures cholinergically. Sympathetic fibres, on the other hand, stimulate the structures they innervate *adrenergically*, that is, through the release of *noradrenalin* (to be discussed later). However, there are some exceptions to adrenergic innervation by post-ganglionic sympathetic fibres. One such exception, to be discussed below, is the *adrenal medulla*; another is the sweat glands, which are innervated only by sympathetic post-ganglionic fibres, although the mode of stimulation is cholinergic rather than adrenergic.

Stimulation from sympathetic fibres accelerates the heart beat while stimulation from parasympathetic fibres tends to slow it down. Parasympathetic activity promotes digestive processes and increases gastric contractions; sympathetic activity inhibits them. However, the sweat glands and blood vessels both receive sympathetic stimulation only, the former cholinergic and the latter adrenergic. In the latter case it appears that sympathetic fibres account for both *vasoconstriction*, a reduction of blood vessel diameter, and its opposite, *vasodilation*, and it is possible that there are two kinds of adrenergic substances responsible for these two opposing effects.

As was noted above, the sympathetic division is most active in situations calling for the expenditure of bodily resources and the parasympathetic division is dominant in more peaceful states, such as sleep, in which bodily resources are conserved. However, when

one division of the ANS is dominant, the other is not inactive.
Sympathetic division activity, as well as parasympathetic activity,
occurs during sleep. Since both divisions are always active in varying
degrees, it is not always possible, by observing changes in one
measure of autonomic activity, to draw a firm conclusion as to
which division is primarily responsible for the effects. It is therefore
preferable to state that certain changes in autonomic activity reflect
the apparent dominance of the sympathetic division, while others
reflect apparent parasympathetic dominance.

Sympathetic division activity is more *global* in its effects than is
parasympathetic division activity. One reason for this is a structural
one; there is much more overlap between sympathetic division inter-
connexions. There is also a chemical reason. Increased sympathetic
division activity increases the secretion into the bloodstream of
adrenalin and noradrenalin from the adrenal medulla and these
exert effects on all other sympathetically innervated organs, adding
to the effects already produced by direct sympathetic connexions.

The endocrine system

The endocrine system modulates ongoing processes occurring in the
internal environment by the emission of chemical stimulators, known
as hormones, directly into the bloodstream. This distinguishes
endocrine or ductless glands from *exocrine* or duct glands – for
example, the salivary glands, which secrete the hormone ptyalin
through salivary ducts. Hormones circulating in the blood affect
cellular activity, modulating the rate at which cellular processes take
place, rather than initiating new processes. The number and amount
of hormones present in the bloodstream vary with environmental
demands. The endocrine system is shown in Figure 33.

The *pituitary gland*, which divides into two quite distinct parts, the
anterior and posterior lobes, lies beneath the hypothalamus and is
joined to it by the pituitary stalk or infundibulum. The anterior lobe
secretes six hormones and the posterior lobe at least two. The pituitary gland controls the activity of the endocrine system as a whole,
stimulating other endocrine glands into action by the release of
hormones, although the adrenal medulla, for instance, is stimulated

into action by nerve impulses travelling along fibres of the sympathetic division of the ANS, of which it is in fact a part. The *thyroid gland*, together with the *parathyroid glands*, is mainly concerned – through the agency of its hormone thyroxin – with growth processes.

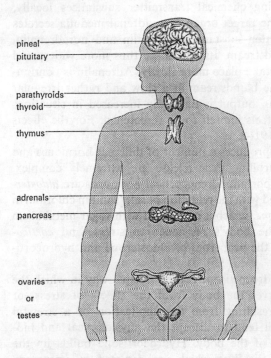

pineal
pituitary

parathyroids
thyroid

thymus

adrenals
pancreas

ovaries
or
testes

Figure 33   The endocrine system. (From Hoskins, 1933, p. 19)

The *pancreas* is concerned with the secretion of insulin, and the *gonads* (the ovaries and the testes) are the sex glands, whose hormones play an important role in shaping sexual behaviour and in the development of secondary sexual characteristics.

The endocrine glands which have been most intensively studied in relation to behaviour, in particular emotional behaviour and behaviour under stress, are the *adrenal glands*. There are two adrenal glands, one lying above the left kidney and the other above the right, and they both receive an extremely rich blood supply. Each adrenal gland consists of an outer layer, the adrenal cortex, and an inner core, the adrenal medulla, which is an outgrowth of the sympathetic division of the ANS.

The sympathetic division of the ANS, as we have seen, achieves its effects by liberating chemical transmitter substances locally, directly stimulating the target organ. The adrenal medulla secretes two of these transmitter substances, adrenalin and noradrenalin, directly into the bloodstream. Its effects are thus more widespread but they also tend to take place more slowly. Adrenalin is continuously released into the bloodstream at a slow and rather irregular rate, but the adrenalin output is markedly increased in situations where the individual feels himself to be threatened. For the effects of adrenalin, see pp. 191–2.

The adrenal cortex produces a number of different hormones and the mechanisms controlling their release are extremely complex. Three of the more important adrenocortical hormones are *aldosterone*, which is concerned with the retention of salt (sodium chloride) in the body, *hydrocortisone*, which is concerned with sugar metabolism and in mobilizing the body's resistance to stress, and *corticosterone*, which shares the properties of aldosterone and hydrocortisone.

The secretion of hydrocortisone is the principal way in which the adrenal cortex preserves the body from the effects of stress, or repairs the damage resulting from the application of a stressful stimulus. Such stimuli tend to disrupt the physiological and biochemical equilibrium of the body. Hydrocortisone builds up the reserves of sugar in the liver which are depleted in emergency situations by the action of the adrenal medulla. Hydrocortisone maintains these reserves by breaking down into sugar the proteins contained in muscle and by preventing further protein increases until the emergency situation is over.

The measurement of autonomic variables

Because the measurement of autonomic variables involves certain difficulties, in this section problems of measurement and interpretation of autonomic changes will be discussed in some detail.

Cardiovascular variables

The circulation of the blood through the arterial system of the body is effected by the intermittent pumping action of the heart. This pumping action can vary both in strength (stroke volume) and in rate (the heart rate). The expansion of the heart muscles during what

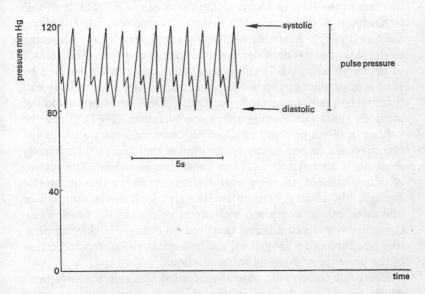

Figure 34   Typical blood pressure readings, showing systolic and diastolic blood pressure. The difference between the two is pulse pressure. (From Lywood, 1967, p. 135)

is known as the *diastolic phase* allows blood to enter the heart and the length of the diastolic phase determines the amount of blood that is available for distribution when the heart muscles next contract during the *systolic phase*. The arterial blood pressure is determined in part by the output of the heart and consists of a mean value upon which are superimposed pulsatile changes corresponding to the diastolic and systolic phases (Figure 34). The maximum value is known as the systolic and the minimum as the diastolic blood pressure. The difference between the two is known as the *pulse pressure*. Methods of measuring blood pressure are described by Lywood (1967).

Circulatory exchange is also determined by the diameter of the arteries and veins through which the blood flows. If the output of the heart remains constant, an increase in the diameter of the blood vessels supplying a particular organ (vasodilation) results in an increase in the flow of blood within the organ. An example of this is blushing. A decrease in the diameter (vasoconstriction) reduces the blood supply available to the organ and results in a whitening of the skin, usually considered a characteristic of fear. The volume of blood present in different parts of the body can be detected by plethysmographic methods which make use either of a pressure cuff (pneumatic plethysmography; see Lader, 1967) or of photo-electric methods (photoplethysmography; see Weinman, 1967). Since the volume of blood present in the body is constant, constriction of the blood vessels in one organ system means that the blood normally available to that system has been transferred elsewhere. The volume of blood present in peripheral systems, such as the limbs (for example, the fingers) or in internal organs such as the stomach or intestines, can be compared with blood volume in the head. Vaso-constriction and vasodilation also produce changes in skin temperature (see Plutchik, 1956) which can be used as an indirect indication of the presence of dilation or constriction.

Heart-rate changes are generally recorded on an *electrocardiograph* which provides a tracing of the electrical activity of the heart muscles. These changes can be counted manually but automatic recording devices are also available. Figure 35 is a representation of the heart-rate cycle as it appears on an electrocardiographic record. The cycle can be divided into five parts, each representing either a positive or a negative deflection from the baseline. The R-wave represents the heart beat. Other measures of cardiac activity are discussed by Brener (1967).

Although respiration rate is not a cardiovascular measure, it is usual when recording heart rate to take measures of respiratory variation as well. This is because in some cases heart-rate changes may be due to respiratory variations. When one breathes in, heart rate increases; when one breathes out, it decreases. This phenomenon is known as *sinus arrhythmia*, and tends to vary with age, being more marked in younger individuals. Body movements also tend to bring about changes in heart rate and these also need to be controlled, although such effects are usually clearly apparent in the heart-rate record. Finally, it should be mentioned that in addition to changes in heart-rate level, changes in the *variability* of the heart rate can also be recorded.

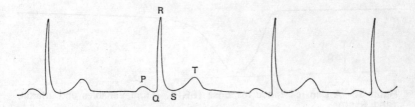

Figure 35   A heart-rate record showing the five phases of the heart-rate cycle, conventionally labelled P, Q, R, S, T. (From Brener, 1967, p. 105)

Electrodermal measures

Several measures of changes in the electrical properties of the skin have been used in psychophysiological studies. The two most common are *skin resistance* and its reciprocal, *skin conductance*; a more recent addition is *skin potential* (Venables and Sayer, 1963). The first two measures are obtained by passing an electrical current between two points on the skin surface and by measuring the resistance of the skin to the passage of the current. The resistance varies with the activity of the sweat glands: the greater the amount of sweating, the lower the resistance and vice versa. Thus, in general, an increase in resistance is expected when an individual is relaxed and a decrease when he is excited. The resistance value is measured in ohms (named after the originator of that unit of measurement) and is obtained, in accordance with Ohm's Law, by dividing the voltage (in volts) by the current (in amps).

Two measures of skin resistance can be taken. The first is the baseline resistance, or the skin-resistance level, which undergoes gradual shifts over a relatively long period of time. The second is the skin resistance response, also known as the galvanic skin response (GSR) or the psychogalvanic reflex (PGR). This can be defined as a change in the waveform of the skin response, in which a negative deflection is followed by a positive deflection (see Figure 36). Although skin-resistance responses occur as a result of stimulation,

Figure 36   A skin-resistance response (SRR). (From Venables and Martin, 1967, p. 55)

they may also occur in its absence. The measurement of skin potential does not depend upon an externally applied current. As with skin resistance, two measures can be derived, the number of skin potential responses and a measure of basal level. The many problems involved in the measurement of skin resistance are discussed by Montagu and Coles (1966) and Venables and Martin (1967).

Other measures used in psychophysiological studies include *muscle tension* (Lippold, 1967) and changes in *gastric motility* (Russell and Stern, 1967). Changes in *pupil size* have also been recorded.

A general problem in the evaluation of autonomic responses arises from the fact that autonomic responses to stimulation appear to be a function of the pre-stimulus or resting level. The resting level, therefore, needs to be taken into account when assessing the effects of stimulation. This relation was first discussed in any detail by Wilder (1957), and was called by him the *law of initial values*.

One method of dealing with this problem is to express the response to stimulation as a percentage of the resting level but it is questionable whether an increase of 10 per cent in the heart-rate response to stimulation has the same meaning for an individual whose resting value was seventy beats per minute as for one whose resting value was ninety beats per minute. Various other transformations have been proposed as solutions to this problem but none of them has been completely satisfactory (Benjamin, 1963; Lacey, 1956). The relationship between pre- and post-stimulus levels of response thus remains as a problem to be borne in mind in the evaluation of autonomic responses.

Autonomic response patterns

As will be seen in later sections, most investigations of the relation between autonomic responses and behaviour have recorded several autonomic measures rather than relying on just one or two. In the search for autonomic changes characteristic either of stimulus situations or of individuals, reliance has thus been placed on *patterns* of autonomic response. Some examples will now be briefly considered.

Responses to novel stimulation

If a relaxed individual is exposed to an unexpected and intense stimulus, for example a sudden loud sound, signs of increased sympathetic nervous system activity become apparent. At the same time changes in EEG activity take place and various motor reactions – for example, blinking and muscular flexion – occur. The changes in sympathetic nervous system activity include an increase in heart rate and blood pressure, a temporary change in the level of skin resistance or conductance, a reduction in the blood volume of the extremities (peripheral vasoconstriction) and an increase in the flow of blood to the head, and pupillary dilation.

Various names have been applied to the collection of changes just described. In what has become known as the *emergency theory* of emotion, Cannon (1932, 1936) argued that a massive sympathetic nervous system discharge occurs whenever bodily resources have to be mobilized and vigorous muscular activity is required for the purposes of fight or flight. Cannon considered that the secretion of adrenalin by the adrenal medulla, prompted by nerve impulses from the sympathetic division of the ANS, liberated reserves of glycogen from the liver (to be consumed by the muscles in the form of glucose) and in this way provided the energy required for coping with emergency situations. On this view emotion is a biologically advantageous mechanism because it enables more efficient, or at least more energetic, evasive action to be taken when the organism is threatened. As will be seen in a later section, Cannon also took the view that different emotions, or at least those involved in fight (anger) and flight (fear) could not be distinguished on the basis of their concomitant response patterns. Not only is this second view challenged by more recent evidence, to be reviewed below, but a careful inspection of the effects of adrenalin on the circulation, heart rate, blood sugar level and on the utilization of oxygen (Arnold, 1960) suggests that the increased level of adrenalin associated with fear may have debilitating effects rather than energizing ones. Although it is possible that the physiological changes associated with anger promote increased muscular power and efficiency, those associated with fear appear to produce the reverse effects. Arnold (1960) states,

this long look at the physiology of adrenalin shows that the subjective feeling of weakness during acute or chronic fear is supported and explained by objective evidence. Adrenalin and sympathetic stimulation do not improve muscular performance. Rather they reduce efficiency by increasing lactic acid formation and by interfering with glucose and oxygen utilization (p. 220).

The emergency reaction of Cannon is also seen in non-emotional situations such as the response to sudden stimulation already mentioned. The same reaction, or a very similar one, has also been called the *startle reaction* (Landis and Hunt, 1939), the *startle reflex* (Sternbach, 1960), *the defence and orienting reactions* (Sokolov, 1960) and *activation* (Duffy, 1962; Lindsley, 1951). The electroencephalographic response is known as *EEG activation*, *EEG desynchronization* or, if alpha activity is predominant, as *alpha blocking*.

The main difference between the startle reaction, the startle reflex and the emergency reaction lies in the amount of time required for the various physiological indices to return to the pre-stimulus level. The startle reflex, like the startle reaction, lasts only for a few seconds, although there are some interesting individual differences in recovery times (Sternbach, 1960). The emergency reaction generally takes somewhat longer to build up and to subside.

The startle reaction thus tends to precede the emergency reaction which follows when some appraisal of the stimulus situation has been made. However, the startle reaction itself can be divided into two different classes – the defence reaction and the orienting reaction.

The defence reaction and the orienting reaction can both be elicited by non-signal stimuli of brief duration. By 'non-signal' is meant that the stimuli in question are completely devoid of any reinforcing properties. An example of such a stimulus would be a tone. The orienting and defence reactions resemble one another in some respects but differ in others. They are similar in that they both consist of unlearned motor, autonomic and central nervous system responses. Further, both reactions are independent of stimulus quality; that is, they are not confined to any particular class of stimuli. They differ in that orienting responses tend to be evoked by stimuli of low or moderate intensity, while defence responses result from the administration of relatively intense stimulation. Second, unlike the defence reaction, the orienting reaction is elicited by any *change* in stimulation – for instance, both the onset and offset of a stimulus. Third, the defence reaction tends to be intensified by stimulus repetition, while the orienting reaction diminishes very rapidly (habituation or adaptation) whenever a particular stimulus is repeated (see Figure 37). Thus, broadly speaking, the orienting reaction is a response to stimulus change; the habituation or adaptation reaction, a response to stimulus repetition; and the defence reaction, a response to stimuli outside the 'normal range' of intensities.

Sokolov (1960, 1963) has suggested that whether the orienting reaction or habituation occurs in response to a stimulus is determined by the comparison of that stimulus with a neuronal model established in the cerebral cortex by previous stimuli. If the stimulus matches the cortical model, habituation occurs. If they are discordant, the orienting reaction is elicited. In one experiment, Sokolov habituated EEG and autonomic responses to a tone of fixed loudness, pitch and duration; using the same subjects and keeping other parameters of the stimulus tone constant, he then reduced its duration and obtained an orienting reaction to the period of silence. Sokolov hypothesized that the cortical model preserves information about all stimulus parameters for comparison purposes. If one of them is discordant, the orienting reaction is then set off by excitatory mechanisms. When the stimulus matches the model, inhibitory mechanisms prevent the orienting reaction from occurring.

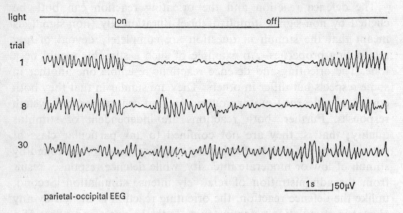

Figure 37   EEG desynchronization produced by a three-second visual stimulus presented at regular intervals for thirty trials. Note the habituation (diminished response) with repeated stimulation. (From Obrist, 1965, p. 265)

Response patterns associated with different activities

The late R. C. Davis and his colleagues at the University of Indiana, in the course of several studies of autonomic response patterns associated with simple stimuli and responses, have been able to identify several different configurations of autonomic response (Davis, 1957; Davis, Buchwald and Frankman, 1955). Some of these are shown in Table 4.

E — 1 is a pattern associated with mild exercise, in which subjects repeatedly pressed a key in response to a signal. N represents the pattern of responses to variations in the intensity of an auditory stimulus. This pattern was also found with simple visual stimulation but cutaneous stimuli (C), especially pressure and warmth, produced

Table 4
Configurations of autonomic response. (From Davis, 1957, p. 735)

Pattern	E – 1	N	P	C
Palmar sweating	+	+	+	+
EMG	+	+	+	+
Pulse rate	+	+ –	–	–
Volume pulse	–	–	–	–
Pressure pulse		– +	–	+
Finger volume *		–	–	+
Chin volume *		+	–	+
Respiration rate	+	–	–	+ –
Respiration amplitude	+	+	–	– +

Double signs indicate diphasic effects.
* That is, the volume of blood recorded in a finger or at the chin.

a different pattern in which the volume of blood in a finger (not the responding finger) increased rather than decreased. Finally, the P pattern represents the response to a more complex stimulus situation in which male subjects looked at pictures of nude women. Other pictures seemed to produce a different effect. For example, an unpleasant picture of a starving man produced not only less response than did those of nude women but also a different response pattern. Pressure pulse and the two respiration measures all increased instead of decreasing as in the P pattern.

These four patterns are examples of *stimulus–response specificity*: that is, different stimulus situations appear to produce different patterns of autonomic response. The work of Davis and his colleagues has been complemented and extended by Lacey and his co-workers who have demonstrated that different response patterns are associated with environmental intake and rejection. In situations apparently requiring the external environment to be rejected – such as mental arithmetic or the Cold Pressor Test, in which the subject's hand is repeatedly immersed in icy water – skin conductance, blood pressure and heart rate all increase. However, in situations in which attention must be paid to the external environment, such as watching a flashing light or listening to a tape-recorded play, skin conductance and blood pressure increase while heart rate decreases. Lacey suggests that the performance of tasks which emphasize cognitive functioning are accompanied by heart rate increases, while the performance of tasks emphasizing perceptual functioning are accompanied by decreases in heart rate (Lacey, 1959; Lacey *et al.*, 1963). There is some neurophysiological evidence suggesting that increases in heart rate serve to diminish transmission along sensory pathways and thus to decrease the effectiveness of external stimuli. Presumably the opposite effect occurs with a decrease in heart rate.

However, there are also consistent individual differences in the characteristic patterns of autonomic response exhibited in a wide variety of stimulus situations. This patterning represents the relative predominance of different physiological reactions in the response to stress. Thus it is possible to speak of 'blood pressure reactors' and 'gastro-intestinal reactors', for example, where the blood pressure reaction or the gastro-intestinal reaction is the most marked in response to stress. The order of magnitude of less dominant responses also tends to be stereotyped for the individual. This principle of *individual response stereotypy* derives initially from studies of patient groups which demonstrated that for psychiatric patients with bodily symptoms, for instance head and neck pains, the physiological measure underlying the symptoms, in this case muscle tension, was specifically responsive to activation by any stressful stimulus (Malmo, Stagner and Davis, 1950). More recently, Engel (1960) and Engel and Bickford (1961) have demonstrated that both stimulus–response specificity and individual response stereotypy can occur simultaneously in the same individuals.

Autonomic response patterns and emotion

Since the concept of emotion is such a central one in the study of behaviour, it is perhaps as well to treat it, initially, in historical terms. Two theories, appearing at approximately the same time in the late nineteenth century, have exerted important effects on subsequent thinking about emotion. The first of these theories, that of William James (1884, 1890), has been an important influence partly because

the criticism of James's position by Cannon (1927, 1931) has stimulated a great deal of empirical research. The second theory, that of
Lange (1885), has been important because of its influence on activation theories of emotion (Duffy, 1941; Lindsley, 1951; Wenger, 1950).
The two theories are often considered together as the James–Lange
theory of emotion although, in fact, they are somewhat different.

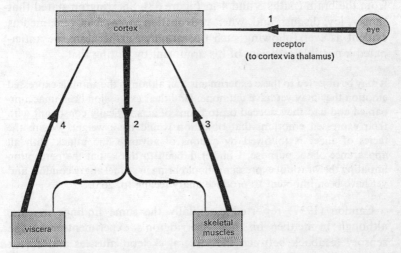

Figure 38   Schematic diagram of James's theory of emotional experience
(see text)

James attempted to explain the relationship between visceral
changes and emotional feelings and the main point made by his
theory is that emotional experience is consequent upon visceral
changes. To summarize James's theory very briefly, certain stimuli
evoke visceral responses via the autonomic nervous system, and
motor responses via the skeletal motor system, and these two classes
of response themselves act as stimuli which bring about emotional
feelings in the brain. This theory is depicted in Figure 38. The
essentials of this theory are expressed in James's well-known statement that 'we are afraid because we run, we do not run because we
are afraid'. Emotional experience is thus the appreciation of changes
occurring in the viscera or the motor system, and these changes are

initiated directly by the perception of an appropriate stimulus, 'the exciting fact' as James terms it.

Sherrington (1906) objected to James's theory on the grounds that he had observed emotional behaviour in dogs deprived of a large part of the sensory feedback from the viscera and skeletal musculature; all the viscera and most of the skeletal musculature were isolated from the brain (paths 3 and 4 in Figure 38). Sherrington stated that 'anger, joy, disgust, and, when provocation arose, fear, remained as evident as ever following such operation'. Furthermore, he anticipated a possible criticism of his argument by stating that,

it may be objected to these experiments that although the animals expressed emotion they may yet have felt none. Had their expression been unaccompanied and had they not led on to trains of acts logically consonant with their expressed emotion, that objection would have weight. Where the facies of anger is followed by actions of advance and attack with all appearance of set purpose, I find it difficult to think that the perception initiating the wrathful expression should bring in sequel angry conduct and yet have been impotent to produce angry feeling (p. 265).

Cannon (1927) reported essentially the same findings in cats, although in neither his nor Sherrington's experiments was the sensory feedback between the viscera, skeletal muscles and cortex completely eliminated. Nevertheless, no impairment of emotional expression was observed. It has been pointed out by Hebb (1946a, 1949) that James did not claim that emotional *expression* but that emotional *experience* would be lost if the sensory feedback between viscera, skeletal muscles and cortex was reduced or abolished. Sherrington's answer to this point has already been cited. In addition, clinical observations on human beings do not suggest that there is any diminution of emotional experience, as inferred from patients' behaviour and verbalizations, following fairly severe losses of visceral and motor feedback (Cannon, 1927; Dana, 1921).

A second objection to James's theory made by Cannon (1927) is that (a) different emotional states – for example, anger and fear – show the same patterns of autonomic discharge and are not therefore distinguishable on this basis, and (b) non-emotional states – for example, those resulting from physical exercise or exposure to high temperatures – are accompanied by similar patterns of autonomic activity to those found in emotional states. However, since James stated that emotional experience was not dependent upon the feedback from particular visceral organs and specific skeletal muscles but upon the total pattern of visceral and motor discharge, James's hypothesis could be refuted only if it could be shown that the patterns of physiological discharge prior to the experience of fear were exactly the same as those preceding the experience of anger, or that those preceding anger were in no way different from those consequent upon physical exercise. Although there is little evidence on such points, what there is suggests at least that the emotions of fear and anger can be differentiated physiologically.

The relevant studies are those by Ax (1953), Lewinsohn (1956) and J. Schachter (1957). In spite of the different measures taken, the different ways in which these measures were scored and the different situations from which the experiences of fear and anger were inferred, there is some agreement among the findings. Broadly speaking, and, with certain qualifications, diastolic blood pressure appears to increase from the resting level to a greater extent in anger than in fear, while heart rate, cardiac output, palmar conductance, respiration rate and frontalis muscle tension all appear to increase more in fear than in anger.

Funkenstein, King and Drolette (1957) have suggested that anger is accompanied by a greater secretion of noradrenalin as opposed to adrenalin, whereas fear and anxiety (little or no distinction is made between them) are characterized by a greater secretion of adrenalin as opposed to noradrenalin. Thus the physiological response patterns associated with anger should be similar to those following the injection of noradrenalin, while the injection of adrenalin should produce physiological response patterns resembling closely those observed in fear.

Martin (1961) concludes from a survey of the physiological reactions accompanying injections of adrenalin and noradrenalin that in general the former leads to increases in palmar conductance, systolic blood pressure and heart rate, and decreases in diastolic blood pressure, hand temperature and salivary output. Fewer measures have been taken in studies of the effects of injected noradrenalin, but such effects include increased diastolic and systolic blood pressure and no change or a slight decrease in heart rate. Wenger and his colleagues (1960) found that injections of adrenalin produced a marked increase in cardiac output (rate and stroke volume) while noradrenalin produced a decrease; both drugs were found to decrease the flow of blood to the skin, but it was inferred that adrenalin constricts the blood vessels of the skin to a lesser extent than noradrenalin, while constricting to a greater extent the blood vessels supplying the skeletal musculature. However, Wenger reported that no feelings of emotion accompanied injections of either drug. It thus appears that, in spite of some overlap, there are differences between the effects on physiological responses of adrenalin and noradrenalin, at least at the dosage levels used in the above experiments, and that there is some correspondence between the physiological changes seen in fear and anger and those which follow adrenalin and noradrenalin injections. However, an important factor in the analysis of emotional responses, namely the appraisal of stimuli, is missing from the experiments just mentioned. We shall return to the problems involved in the 'artificial' induction of emotional states and their concomitant physiological reactions (see p. 195).

However, there is some evidence which suggests that the relationship between fear and adrenalin-like reactions, and between anger and noradrenalin-like reactions, is rather a dubious one. Levi (1965) showed his subjects a series of feature films, some of which (such as *The Devil's Mask*) were considered anxiety- or fear-arousing, as assessed by subjects' ratings, while others (such as *Charley's Aunt*) were not; another film, *Paths of Glory*, seemed to contain both anxiety- and aggression-arousing features. The urinary excretion of adrenalin and noradrenalin was measured before and after each film and before and after a control film consisting of landscapes and scenery. *The Devil's Mask*, rated as the most anxiety-arousing film, increased both the adrenalin and the noradrenalin level and, although *Paths of Glory* produced ratings high in anxiety and in aggression, the associated adrenalin level was similar to that produced by *Charley's Aunt* – which was rated neither as anxiety- nor as aggression-arousing. Levi suggested that there is a positive correlation between the intensity of emotional arousal, whatever the expressed emotion may be, and the urinary excretion of adrenalin and possibly also that of noradrenalin.

Even supposing that an outside observer, using polygraphic recordings and computer analysis, can distinguish reasonably accurately between the physiological changes associated with fear and anger, can the individual experiencing the emotions do so? This is the basis of Cannon's third criticism of James's position. Cannon argued that the visceral organs are poorly supplied with nerve fibres and hence transmit little information. It would therefore be difficult to make fairly subtle discriminations between patterns of visceral activity, or indeed to be aware of them at all. While it appears to be the case that the viscera proper may contain few fibres that mediate pain sensations, there is plenty of evidence that visceral organs contain stretch, pressure and temperature receptors, and differential stimulation of these receptors is presumably reflected in such common expressions as 'a sinking stomach' and 'a lump in the throat' – both of which are often linked to different emotional states. In any case, James appears to have been concerned with changes in sympathetic, parasympathetic and somatic nervous system activity in addition to purely visceral changes, if these can be distinguished.

However, an experiment by Mandler and Kahn (1960) shows that individuals find it impossible to discriminate between small changes in their own heart rate. In this study subjects were asked to guess which of two lights would come on next, by pressing one of two keys. Unknown to the subject, one light went on when his heart rate increased by at least two beats per minute, the other when it decreased by the same amount. After 5000 presentations, there was no evidence that subjects had learned to make the discrimination. The visceral changes accompanying emotional states are usually of considerably greater magnitude than the small changes in heart rate investigated in the above experiment, although it is presumably a difficult task for individuals to discriminate differences in their own autonomic patterns.

There are considerable differences between individuals in the degree to which changes in their own physiological states are reported. Subjects given a questionnaire listing common physiological changes and asked how often they observed such changes taking place in themselves were found to differ markedly in their responses. When these self-reports were correlated with the magnitude of physiological changes occurring in response to a laboratory stress situation, the over-all correlation was found to be low but positive. However, when subjects were divided into extreme groups on the basis of their questionnaire responses and the intermediate group omitted from the analysis, highly significant differences in physiological reactivity emerged. Those subjects who reported observing physiological changes frequently were much more reactive in the stress situation, while those subjects who reported a low incidence of such changes were much less reactive (Mandler and Kremen, 1958; Mandler, Mandler and Uviller, 1958). These results suggest that some subjects at least are fairly accurate monitors of their own internal states, although it is also notable that *patterns* of physiological response seem to be more highly correlated with subjects' reports of visceral activity than any single autonomic measure (Mandler, 1960). Mandler suggests that 'if people react to anything referentially in their visceral upheaval, it is likely to be a rather global, general condition of arousal' (Mandler, 1960, p. 318).

Cannon also suggested that the effects of visceral changes are transmitted to the brain too slowly for them to be a direct source of emotional feeling, since there is evidence (Lehmann, 1914) that (a) reports of emotional feeling occur extremely quickly after the presentation of an emotion-provoking stimulus, and (b) that specific autonomic changes almost always follow the verbal report. It is of course always difficult to correlate verbal reports with other indicators, but the evidence reviewed by Lehmann does suggest that in adults at least the verbal report of emotional experience cannot be determined by visceral changes. However, later evidence (Newman, Perkins and Wheeler, 1930) suggests that there are two distinguishable experiences (one fast and one slow) separated by the visceral response consequent upon the presentation of an emotion-provoking stimulus. But studies of emotional behaviour in infants and children provide some grounds for thinking that the emotional expression of pain and fear, and perhaps other emotional states as well, follows the presentation of an appropriate stimulus much less rapidly than in adults; in other words, the Jamesian position appears to hold in very young organisms (see Kessen and Mandler, 1961; Schneirla, 1959). It is thus possible that in infants the experience of a particular emotion is determined to a great extent by visceral changes. Adults, on the other hand, have learned to apply the verbal report to the stimulus situation directly without waiting for the occurrence of visceral changes.

However, what remains to be explained is why the visceral changes themselves occur in some stimulus situations and not in others. In infants the autonomic nervous system, like other bodily systems, is much more labile than it is in later life, and mild stress situations produce much greater autonomic changes (see Steinschneider, 1967). Presumably some diminution of autonomic activity occurs as a function of maturation and as a result of the developing organism's learning to exercise some control over his own autonomic activity and to suppress it in many non-stressful situations.

The final objection made by Cannon to the Jamesian position was that the 'artificial' induction of those visceral changes known to occur in emotional states does not produce reports of emotional experience nor emotional behaviour. Specifically, he argued that the injection of adrenalin which, as already mentioned, is a sympathetic nervous system activator, should produce emotional feelings. However, adrenalin does not appear to affect either the activity of the parasympathetic or the somatic nervous system which James also considered to be important in producing emotional experience.

In the experiment of Wenger et al. (1960), cited above, the injection of adrenalin and noradrenalin did not produce any spontaneous reports of emotional feelings. In earlier studies, for example Marañon (1924), it had been found that some subjects injected with adrenalin and questioned about their emotional states reported 'as if' emotions, while others reported no emotional feelings at all. About a third of Marañon's subjects said that they felt as if they were afraid or as if they were awaiting good news. When Marañon talked to them about emotionally toned events, then the emotional feelings were reported without qualification. Thus the provision of situational or instructional cues, coupled with visceral changes, can shape emotional behaviour. This point emerges very clearly in an experiment performed by S. Schachter and Singer (1962).

Schachter and Singer, in commenting upon Marañon's procedure and results, make the point that his subjects were aware that they were receiving an injection of adrenalin and that they probably knew something of its effects. That is, they knew why they felt the way they did. However, if an individual was unaware that he had received an injection of adrenalin, although in fact he had, he would have no readily available explanation for his physiological state. The verbal label that he would use to describe his internal state in the absence of an appropriate explanation would, Schachter and Singer hypothesized, be determined by his interpretation of the situation in which he found himself. However, if an individual knows very well why he feels the way he does, then he is unlikely to label his feelings in terms of new interpretations of the situation. Finally, given the same situation without visceral arousal, the verbal label applied to the internal state is unlikely to be an emotional one. For Schachter and Singer, emotional feelings are a joint function of a state of physiological arousal and an appropriate cognition.

In Schachter and Singer's experiment, volunteer subjects came to the laboratory ostensibly to participate in an experiment concerned with the effects of a drug, 'suproxin', on vision. The drug was in fact adrenalin. Subjects were divided into four different groups. Those in the first group were correctly informed what the effects of the injected drug would be, namely to produce mild hand tremor, to increase heart rate and to bring about a flushed feeling in the face. Those in the second group were misinformed about the effects of the drug; they were told that it would produce numbness in the feet, itching sensations and a slight headache. Those in the third group were given no information about any side effects the drug might have, while those in the fourth group, who were also given no information, were given an injection of saline solution as a placebo.

The second and third parts of the experiment were identical for all groups. Each subject was shown to a waiting room where another subject was waiting to participate in the experiment. This subject was actually a confederate of the experimenter. The confederate behaved in exactly the same way on every occasion. In one experiment, concerned with the induction of euphoria, the confederate behaved in a manner designed to make the subject euphoric, while in a second experiment, concerned with the induction of anger, the confederate tried to make the subject angry. Finally, subjects were given a scale on which to rate their feelings of euphoria or anger and their pulse rate was taken.

In the euphoria experiment, the misinformed group was the most euphoric, as judged from their rated behaviour in the waiting room and from their self-ratings on the questionnaire, followed by the ignorant group, the placebo group and the correctly informed group, in that order. In all subjects who had received injections of adrenalin, pulse rate increased from the pre-injection level to the post-injection level at the end of the experiment, while the means for the placebo group showed a decrease over the same period. Apparently, therefore, the drug succeeded in increasing one index of physiological arousal. But the three groups who received the active drug, and whose arousal levels were increased to much the same degree, behaved in very different ways in the same stimulus situation. The only factor which seems able to account for this difference is the kind of information the groups were given beforehand. The observed results are compatible with Schachter and Singer's analysis of emotional feeling and it thus appears that cognitive factors are an important determinant, along with visceral arousal, of the way in which emotional experience is labelled and of the resulting behaviour.

The experiments considered so far under the heading of emotional behaviour have mainly been laboratory studies which have attempted to induce short-term emotional states in artificial settings, although they have provided a great deal of useful information about the determinants of emotional responses under such conditions. However, differences appear to exist between physiological reactions accompanying chronic and acute emotional states. Mahl (1952, 1953), for example, has shown that in dogs and monkeys who are chronically afraid, hydrochloric acid secretion increases, while during laboratory-induced fear situations it does not. Bindra (1955) has shown that in chimpanzees there appear to be distinct differences between the physiological reactions resulting from short- and long-term exposure to the same stimulus situation. Psychiatric studies of soldiers in the Second World War have demonstrated that the physiological and psychological symptoms of men who broke down early in combat were markedly different from those of men who broke down after a considerable time in the combat area. Finally, animals whose characteristic mode of response is fearful, such as rabbits, appear to have different noradrenalin–adrenalin ratios from animals whose mode of response is typically aggressive.

However, it also seems fairly clear that whatever the differences may be between the physiological concomitants of chronic and acute emotional states, many of the principles established in the laboratory with reference to acute states also obtain when chronic states are considered. For example, the principle of stimulus–response specificity in different emotional states also seems to operate in patients suffering from chronic emotional disorders.

Wolf and Wolff (1943), for instance, were able to study over a long period a patient with a chronic stomach fistula, in whom the blood flow to the stomach as well as gastric activity could be observed in different, naturally occurring, situations. Whenever this patient was afraid, the stomach lining became white, being virtually drained of blood, and gastric contractions were considerably reduced. When he became angry or resentful, blood flow to the stomach increased, producing a reddening of the stomach lining, and gastric activity was elevated.

We now turn to a second view of emotion, that of Lange (1885). His view differs from that of James in that little or no emphasis is placed on emotion as a mental event. Instead, the bodily changes (particularly those occurring in the viscera) which accompany emotional states are thought to define an emotion completely. Thus, for Lange, emotion is vasomotor disturbance. A more recent statement of Lange's view can be found in Wenger (1950) and Wenger, Jones and Jones (1956) who define emotion as 'activity and reactivity of the tissues and organs innervated by the autonomic nervous system. It may involve, but does not necessarily involve, skeletal muscular response or mental activity' (p. 343). Furthermore, 'change in emotional behavior is altered activity or reactivity in a part of one, or more, tissue or organ innervated by the autonomic nervous system' (p. 344).

Such a viewpoint has two implications: first, that emotions can be differentiated on the basis of their associated autonomic response patterns, and second, that the intensity of emotion can be inferred from the magnitude of response of one or a group of autonomic measures. As we have seen, some degree of success has been achieved in relating different emotions to different autonomic response patterns; in the following section we shall briefly examine some ways in which the magnitude of autonomic response has been related to the intensity of emotion.

In fact it would be more accurate to say that the studies which we shall be mentioning are concerned with relating the magnitude of physiological response to the intensity of behaviour. One of the theorists who has been principally concerned with such an approach has been Elizabeth Duffy who has argued that the concept of emotion should be abandoned and that 'the phenomena loosely referred to by this term should be studied in their own right as separate aspects of response occurring in continua rather than in discrete categories' (Duffy, 1941, p. 283).

Duffy suggests that the most characteristic feature of the condition called emotion is a change in energy level. This may be an increase or a decrease depending upon whether or not the individual is highly motivated to obtain some goal. If progress towards the goal is either blocked or facilitated, then the energy level increases. If, on the other hand, no attempt is being made to reach a goal, then the energy level will fall. A second feature of emotional behaviour is that it is often disorganized and poorly controlled. An angry individual may temporarily lose control of movement and his speech may be difficult to understand. This is also true of an individual who is depressed. Third, emotion is generally characterized as being, or being accompanied by, some unique quality of consciousness. Duffy argues that this unique quality represents an easily discriminable change in energy level, and emotion thus differs from other responses in degree but not in kind.

Arousal

Duffy's statements about emotion have drawn attention to the idea that behaviour can be regarded as varying along a continuum of intensity (Duffy, 1962; Lindsley, 1951) and attempts have been made to describe behaviour in these terms and to specify the physiological changes taking place at crucial points on this continuum. Underlying changes in the intensity of behaviour are thought to be changes in an internal state known as activation or arousal (Duffy, 1957; Malmo, 1959; Welford, 1962), and we now turn to a consideration of arousal. Many studies have been concerned with the relationship between arousal and performance at various tasks and it is these studies that we shall emphasize.

The dependent variables used as performance measures in studies of the relationship between arousal level and performance have been the speed, intensity and accuracy with which responses are made, as well as assessments of the quality of performance and the degree to which different responses are co-ordinated.

The various physiological indices of arousal level show, in general, positive intercorrelations, although these do not appear to be sufficiently high to warrant any one measure being used as an adequate index. Furthermore, there is some evidence which suggests that the correlations between the same physiological measures in the same individual in the same stimulus situation on different occasions may be low (Kaelbling et al., 1960), although other evidence (Lacey et al., 1963) suggests the reverse.

Gray (1964) has divided definitions of arousal into three groups. First, there are definitions in terms of the intensity with which behaviour occurs; second, those in terms of the intensity of the motivational factors to which the organism is subject; third, those in terms of the level of alertness of the organism. It is certainly true that definitions of arousal differ, at least in emphasis, and this disunity springs in part from the very wide range of independent variables used by different investigators in this field.

The independent variables which have been studied and which, it is hypothesized, influence the level of arousal, may be grouped under three headings. First, some variables appear to influence the *liveliness* of an individual; others influence his *effort*, while others again affect what might be called his *arousedness*.

The effects of liveliness are seen in the spontaneous fluctuations of an individual's efficiency throughout a twenty-four-hour cycle and it is generally assumed that these cyclic changes in performance are related to diurnal changes in other bodily rhythms, such as body temperature. There is some evidence which supports this assumption (Kleitman, 1952, 1963). The effects of liveliness are most readily observed when situational and motivational determinants of the level of arousal are held constant and the principal independent variable to be manipulated in studying these effects is the time of day at which the subject is tested.

The performance measure may be a simple one, such as strength of grip or simple reaction time, or more complex, such as discrimination reaction time or performance in a letter cancellation task. Blake (1965) showed that cancellation performance varied with body temperature at five different times of day, being lowest at 8 a.m. and highest at 9 p.m. In addition, he observed a positive correlation across subjects between performance and body temperature at each time of day. Kleitman (1952) found that the body temperature curves of different subjects reached their peak at different times of day and that these peaks coincided with periods of optimum performance on a sensorimotor task. Colquhoun and Corcoran (1964) and Blake (1965) found an interaction between the performance of two temperament groups and time of day.

Effort is a difficult term to define. Ryan (1953) suggests that the term refers to 'the experience of the individual as he works. He feels at one time that he is "working hard", at another that he is "working slowly and easily". Effort also includes the experience of difficulty in maintaining one's attention upon a boring task, and the strain or stress in performing an unpleasant or distasteful job' (p. 109). Ryan makes the point that defining effort in this subjective manner disturbs many psychologists but undoubtedly this subjective aspect is an important one (see also Murrell, 1967). A difficulty is that effort is presumably also subject to spontaneous fluctuations and can also be influenced by situational determinants; for example, if the experimental situation is an extremely unpleasant one, the subject is unlikely to expend much effort on the experimental task unless he has to. Effort thus appears to be an attitudinal or motivational variable which is influenced by the presence or absence of incentives and the type of instructions given. The amount of effort expended is also related to how challenging or demanding a task is and is considered to increase with the number and type of operations a subject has to perform and the rate at which he has to perform them.

The third term, arousedness, denotes the extent to which an individual is stimulated by the experimental situation and is the consequence of the amount or variety of stimulation to which he is exposed. It is in this sense that most investigations have used the term 'arousal'. In any task situation, stimulation may be provided by the task and by the extra-task environment, although it is not always clear precisely what factors determine whether or not a task is stimulating. Welford (1965) suggests that arousal level is raised by 'any task which is in some way challenging or demands an effort' (p. 3). Arousedness is determined by the amount and variety of sensory input and by the arousal level of the individual, and there are several experiments showing that the general level of efficiency is affected by the conditions of stimulation in which the individual is working; for example, his performance is affected by whether he works in noise or quiet, by whether he has been deprived of sleep or has slept normally, by the incentives under which he is working and so on.

McGrath (1963) studied the efficiency of sailors detecting small differences in the intensity of a light when they were working in a steady, low level of noise or while listening to a varied background of sounds consisting of office noise, footsteps, music and so on. Efficiency was significantly greater in the second condition.

It is important to note that in this experiment the task was an unstimulating one and that it was carried out under unstimulating conditions. Subjects were isolated in booths and the only extra-task stimulation was provided by the monotonous low-intensity noise in the background or by the varied auditory stimulation. The reason for this emphasis is that many theorists (for example, Hebb, 1955; Welford, 1962) have argued that efficiency does not continue to improve as the arousal level increases. Instead, efficiency improves up to a certain point and thereafter declines. The relationship between arousal level and performance is thus considered to take the form of an inverted U-shaped curve, as Figure 39 shows.

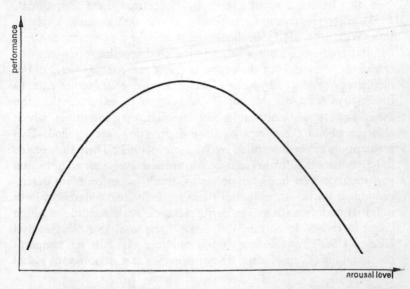

Figure 39 The hypothetical inverted-U relationship between performance and arousal level

If the inverted-U model is correct, then the beneficial effects of increasing stimulation will apply only at low levels of arousal, and the effects upon performance of different factors which raise and lower the arousal level (as measured physiologically) – for example, high-intensity noise and sleep deprivation – should produce an interaction (Broadbent, 1963). Such an interaction, between the effects on performance of noise and sleep deprivation, has been demonstrated by Wilkinson (1963) and Corcoran (1962). Wilkinson showed that on a serial reaction task, noise increased the efficiency of sleep-deprived subjects but not that of subjects who had slept normally, whose performance deteriorated slightly. Wilkinson (1961) also showed a similar interaction between the effects of sleep deprivation and incentives.

Wilkinson used white noise (that is, noise of mixed frequencies taken from a wide range of the frequency spectrum) at an intensity of 100 decibels (dB), an abnormally high level of stimulation. Among individuals who have had a normal night's sleep such a noise level is known to bring about inefficiency in certain tasks (Broadbent, 1953). Sleep deprivation has similar effects on the same kinds of task (Wilkinson, 1965). Both stresses thus impair performance when administered singly, but when administered together each tends to cancel out the effects of the other. It seems reasonable to regard the inefficiency produced by noise alone as being due, at least in part, to too high a level of arousal. It might thus be expected that the adverse effects of noise would be intensified when incentives, which also cancel out the effects of sleep deprivation, are applied. This assumption has been verified by Wilkinson (1963). There thus seems to be evidence that further increases in arousal level, after an optimum performance level has been achieved, result in performance deterioration. It is also possible that there are individual differences both in initial performance and in performance in noise conditions which could be related to chronic differences in arousal level. Davies and Hockey (1966), for example, found an interaction between temperament and the effects of noise on performance at a monotonous visual task.

The physiological evidence relevant to the inverted-U model is not very considerable. Stennett (1957) recorded skin conductance and muscle tension and was able to demonstrate an inverted-U relationship between arousal level measured in these ways, and induced by different levels of shock and reward, and performance on a tracking task. One of the most frequently used measures has been induced muscle tension (Courts, 1942). Shaw (1956), for example, reported evidence for the inverted-U model when the relationship represented was that between induced muscular tension, produced by squeezing a dynamometer, and the perception span for digits or the number of digits reproduced after tachistoscopic presentation.

Schnore (1959) reported that during visual tracking and mental arithmetic, in one instance under 'low arousal conditions' and in another under 'high arousal conditions', 56 per cent of his forty-three subjects showed a significant correlation between the various physiological measures which he employed. These were muscle tension, heart rate, respiration rate, systolic blood pressure, skin conductance, skin temperature and grip pressure. The measures which differentiated consistently between high- and low-arousal conditions were muscle tension, heart rate, respiration rate and systolic blood pressure.

Some authors, for example Corcoran (1964), have maintained that the level of effort and the level of arousal are quite distinct, although many of the physiological measures, in particular muscle tension, which have been used as indicators of effort (Ryan, 1953), have also been used as indicators of arousal or activation (Duffy, 1962). The problem of distinguishing between muscle tension as an indicator of effort on the one hand and of arousal on the other is especially acute when considering the question of whether sleep deprivation raises or lowers the level of arousal (Corcoran, 1964). Wilkinson (1960) found that subjects whose performance on a continuous adding task showed least effects of sleep deprivation also showed the greatest increase in working muscle tension over the pre-task resting values. This result was interpreted as showing that these subjects were able to maintain a high level of performance under conditions of sleep deprivation because of their greater expenditure of effort.

In this chapter we have considered only a small sample of the many studies concerned with the relation between the ANS and behaviour. Little consideration has been given to pyschophysiological studies of sleep (see Foulkes, 1966) or to possible individual differences in psychophysiological functioning (see Sternbach, 1966) or to autonomic responses to pain (see Sternbach, 1968). Psychophysiological methods are being increasingly used in a number of areas in psychology, but the role of the ANS in behaviour still remains to be made fully explicit.

Further reading
M. B. Arnold (ed.), *The Nature of Emotion*, Penguin Books, 1968.
K. H. Pribram (ed.), *Brain and Behaviour*, 4 vols., Penguin Books, 1969.
R. A. Sternbach, *Principles of Psychophysiology*, Academic Press, 1966.

Chapter 8
Needs and Drives

Throughout Part Two, our interest has been centred upon the influence of organismic variables – such as genotype, maturation and physiological structure – upon behaviour. In the preceding chapters, most of the studies quoted have been based upon an experimental design in which the organismic variable has been directly manipulated – for example, by breeding strains of rat or ablating areas of the cortex – and the effect of this upon behaviour recorded. In this concluding chapter of Part Two, there is a slight shift in perspective. We shall still be mainly concerned with the influence of constitutional factors, but the emphasis will be upon how these factors *interact with environment* in regulating behaviour.

In particular, we shall be looking at motivation. The idea of motivation is ambiguous. In one sense, motives are a particular class of *reasons* for doing something, as when we talk about the motives for a crime. In a broader and looser sense, the word 'motive' simply refers to that which *causes* an individual to behave in any way at all. Peters (1958) has provided a valuable analysis and clarification, from a philosopher's point of view, of this and other distinctions that can be drawn. However, the empirical psychologist is not primarily concerned with conceptual analysis. His starting point is the fact that organisms are active, that this activity is instigated by stimulation and that it frequently has both a discernible *direction*, in the sense that it appears to be goal-seeking, and a measure of *intensity*, in the sense that the goals can be pursued with more or less vigour and persistence. The instigation for directed behaviour derives both from the internal state of the organism and from external stimulation; such instigation is a function of the complex interaction of these two sets of conditions. The task before the student of motivation is to define these instigating conditions, to relate them to the various directions and intensities which behaviour can manifest, and to explain the relationships he finds.

The relative importance of internal and external conditions for the instigation of directed behaviour can vary, though it must be presumed that both are necessary. For some forms of directed behaviour the internal state of the organism can be readily identified as the primary instigating condition. When this is the case, psychologists have found it convenient to designate the internal condition as one of *need*. The concept of *drive* is used to refer to the purposive activity which is initiated by both the internal state and external stimulation. As will be shown later, many drives appear to be initiated more by external stimulation than by any clearly definable state of need.

Variations in the internal state of the organism are to a large extent regulated by the mechanism of homeostasis. The physiological nature of the homeostatic mechanism was discussed in some detail in Chapter 6, in connexion with the functioning of the hypothalamus. It is its relevance to the understanding of motivation which concerns us here. In the broadest outline, the steady functioning and adaptability of organisms, such as ourselves, are possible because of the physical and chemical stability of the immediate environment of all the living cells in the body. This environment, consisting of blood and lymph, is known as the *internal environment*. Early studies make it clear that (a) certain specifiable characteristics of the internal environment are the normal and optimal conditions of physiological functioning, and that (b) when these conditions are upset physiological and behavioural mechanisms are set into action whereby the equilibrium is restored. Typically, the level of sugar in the bloodstream necessary for efficient functioning is periodically restored by food intake, the requisite amount of fluid in the body is kept constant by the mechanism of thirst, the maintenance of the correct chemical composition of the blood is helped by the operation of the various, so-called specific hungers, and so forth. Cannon used the term 'homeostasis' to refer both to the state of physiological equilibrium of the body and to the tendency, characteristic of so much of the activity of living things, to keep on continually restoring this equilibrium.

Many of the restorative processes show themselves as recurring rhythms or cycles of activity. One such process, in diurnal organisms, is waking up in the morning and falling asleep at night, over and over again. Another consists of becoming hungry, feeding to satiation, gradually getting hungry again, and so on. Sex activity, too, tends to go in cycles. All such behavioural cycles are rooted in the physiological functioning of the body, the so-called *endogenous rhythms*.

Disturbances of equilibrium are normal occurrences, as some substances in the bloodstream are used up and others accumulate. Some disturbances also arise from changes in the external environment, to which the organism must continually attune. Thus, disequilibria of one kind or another develop; and these are often subjectively felt as needs – for example, a need for warmth, or hunger or the sexual urge. While the word 'need' refers in one sense to experiences of a particular class, it is also nowadays used in an impersonal way. Thus, it is quite customary to refer to the physiological disequilibria themselves as needs; these are often described as homeostatic or *biogenic needs*. And it has been suggested that such needs are the ultimate springs of all action.

One consequence of this suggestion is that features of behaviour, human and animal, which cannot be readily seen as arising from homeostatic needs, have been assumed by many theorists and investigators to derive indirectly from these needs, namely through learning. This has stimulated animal behaviour research concerned with establishing how various acquired behaviour tendencies are built upon initial biogenic needs. At the same time other observational and experimental studies have indicated that some tendencies – for example, investigative behaviour or affectional behaviour – do not always appear to spring from biogenic needs of the type described above, depending perhaps upon their own 'built-in' mechanisms. This situation has been a challenge to anyone interested in theories of motivation.

However, some needs never manifest themselves as drives, and some drives are certainly not based on physiological needs. Thus, oxygen deficiency, the lack of certain vitamins, or exposure to carbon monoxide, do not bring forth drives for corrective action. On the other hand, animals and people will sometimes actively seek saccharine, although the body has no need for it; see, for instance, experiments reported by Sheffield and Roby (1950). Furthermore, animals, and especially human beings, often acquire strong drives that are physiologically harmful: for alcohol, for drugs and for various forms of maladaptive action. It could be argued that such drives are a manifestation of homeostasis in a very broad sense of the word; for the word 'homeostasis' is not an unambiguous one. Some psychologists have extended the concept to cover all motives, including curiosity and aggression. Such extensions imply that the organism and its environment are being conceived of as forming a single system, which can be in a state of equilibrium or disequilibrium. Though this way of looking at all motives can be illuminating, it is apt to be untestable, and therefore ultimately unfruitful.

Many more-or-less convenient classifications of motives are possible. For example, we can distinguish between those which are cyclic and those which are not. In the latter category are those motives which have to do with the continued adaptation of the organism to changes in the external environment. Animals avoid excessive cold and heat, and withdraw from painful stimulation; human beings go further by putting on or removing clothes, and by taking a variety of steps to relieve pain. The needs that instigate action of this kind are not normally cyclic and are induced by environmental conditions. The typically cyclic activities are internally rather than externally aroused, for instance, by the recurrent needs for sleep, food and elimination. Sexual motivation, however, does not easily fit into either of these categories. It is to some extent cyclic, and depends ultimately on the presence of sex hormones, male and female, in the bloodstream. On the other hand, it is clear that this drive is moulded, and sometimes profoundly so, by a range of environmental factors. Like sex, the parental drive in some of its forms has roots in the physiology of the endocrine system, but can be considerably modified by environmental conditions.

A more frequently used classification is that between *basic* drives and those others which, however strong they may be, are acquired or learned by organisms in the course of their lives; sometimes the labels 'primary' and 'secondary' are used for these two kinds. This classification runs into the problem of providing criteria for distinguishing between the innate and the learned. However, though this is a controversial and difficult matter, there are a number of motives which are sufficiently universal and which appear without any discernible opportunity for them to be learned, for us to be fairly confident that they are 'inbuilt'. These motives include, of course, those called 'self-preservative' and 'species-preservative'. But there are other drives, such as the tendencies to be active and to explore (curiosity), and the tendency to form attachments to living things (proximity seeking), which do not spring from biogenic needs in the narrow sense, but which none the less appear in the light of the evidence to be primarily innate rather than acquired.

In this chapter, our interest is in the basic drives. Treatment must, of course, be selective. We shall begin with the drives dependent upon the familiar biogenic needs of thirst and hunger, and the sexual need. The discussion will be brief, for the homeostatic mechanisms underlying them, particularly thirst and hunger, have been described in some detail in Chapter 6.

We shall then turn to what might loosely be called *cognitive drives*: that is, drives which appear to be primarily instigated by environmental conditions. It is not easy to label some of these drives for they are not clearly differentiated from each other. There is first what can be called *general stimulus seeking*, or behaviour which is directed towards maintaining an optimal level of general stimulation. Treatment of this will be brief since the topic is also discussed in Chapters 9 and 13. Then there is *proximity seeking*, or approach tendencies instigated by certain stimuli experienced at an early stage of development. This also receives further attention in Chapter 11. Third, there is *curiosity*, or approach tendencies generated by novel stimuli. Last, the chapter will close with accounts of fear and aggression.

Thirst and hunger

The problems that have engaged research workers concerned with thirst and water intake have mainly been two: (a) the factors, additional to water deprivation, that affect thirst, and (b) the character of the internal stimuli within the body responsible for thirst. The background studies to the first problem are typified by the work of Siegel (1947); this investigator deprived rats of water for periods up to forty-eight hours, and he found that the water drunk five minutes afterwards (an operational measure of thirst) varied in what is termed a *sigmoid* fashion as a function of the duration of deprivation; that is, thirst increased relatively slowly during the first six hours of deprivation, then faster between six and twelve hours, and then again more slowly. Apart from the lack of water, thirst is considerably affected by the salt needs of the animal and by its hunger; and research in this field is continuing (see Deutsch and Deutsch, 1966; Grossman, 1967).

In order to determine the precise role of various internal stimuli in thirst, different organs of animals have been manipulated; for example, the throat would be made dry, the stomach would be filled with water without the animal drinking, etc. These physiological studies have so far made it possible to conclude that the general dehydration of body tissues, rather than any specific parts of the body, is the main factor instrumental in bringing about thirst; but exactly how this process works, and what is the precise role of the brain in it, we are not quite sure (Miller, 1957).

Contractions of the empty stomach were shown by Cannon to be a factor in hunger. Later studies, however, indicated that the chemical composition of the blood of a food-deprived organism influences the hypothalamus which controls the appetite for food; a destruction of an appropriate area of the hypothalamus abolishes hunger, and electrical stimulation of this area induces eating in food-satiated animals. But, as smell and taste stimulate the cerebrum, it, too, is involved in influencing hunger (see more about the brain and the appetites in Chapter 6). At the behavioural level, investigations have been conducted to relate food deprivation quantitatively to eating activity, and further to determine the influence on hunger of variables ranging from water deprivation to the social environment (see Deutsch and Deutsch, 1966; Grossman, 1967).

Much research has been devoted to the so-called *specific hungers*, i.e. hunger for special kinds of food rather than food in general. It is well known that animals develop specific hungers, for example, for substances containing salt or calcium, to accord with their physiological needs, although the matching between needs and appetites does not appear to be perfect. It is also known that in human beings the liking and desire for different types of food is very greatly influenced by cultural and social factors.

We may well ask whether the natural tendency to like what is good for one is lost in people. To investigate the facts in young children, C. M. Davis (1928) gave three infants for six to twelve months after weaning the opportunity of cafeteria feeding, that is, a free choice of a wide range of dishes. The children did very well, having on the whole chosen a balanced diet for themselves. But the ability of animals, let alone human beings, to select food that is good for them cannot always be relied upon, because (a) some vitamin and mineral deficiencies do not bring forth specific hungers, and (b) food habits, however acquired, have been found to be very persistent. To find out how and when such persistent behaviour tendencies develop has been the task of students of learning, and especially research workers in the field of early learning.

The sexual drive

The sexual drive is associated with the presence in the bloodstream of sex hormones: androgens in the male and oestrogens in the female (see Beach, 1948). Much as the drive depends on these hormones in higher mammals, and especially in human beings, it is not entirely controlled by them. The removal of testes and ovaries (which, in addition to producing sperm cells and ova, also secrete sex hormones) does not necessarily abolish sex behaviour and drive altogether. In any case, sexual arousal depends in part on tactile stimulation and reflex responses mediated in the vertebrates, including man, by the lower spinal cord (these responses are co-ordinated by a particular region of the hypothalamus). The higher up the evolutionary scale, the greater is the role in sexual behaviour of the cerebral cortex (Beach, 1947).

In so far as we may talk about sexual need, this depends on the internal state of the organism and blood chemistry in particular. The drive state is, however, dependent also on the presence of appropriate stimuli: visual, olfactory, auditory, etc. In subhuman species the role of these stimuli is readily seen in the inflexible patterns of sexual behaviour; the appearance of the male releases a particular behaviour pattern in the female which in turn evokes the courtship of the male, which elicits the next response of the female, and so on. Instinctive behaviour patterns of this kind in certain insects, in some fish (especially the three-spined stickleback), and in different bird species are described by Tinbergen (1953). In the higher mammals, sexual behaviour is less rigid, being modified by the individual's experience and learning. Social factors influence human sexual drive and behaviour a great deal: for example, standards of feminine attractiveness vary from culture to culture, and so do codes of acceptable and respectable behaviour.

Parental behaviour is related to the sexual drive in that in many species it is controlled by hormonal secretions. In some species only the female looks after the young, in certain species only the male, and in many others the task is shared by both parents. The maternal drive in mammals depends to a considerable extent on the presence of the hormone, prolactin, in the bloodstream; it has been found that injecting prolactin into adult virgin female rats tends to make them accept and care for infant rats. In human beings any physiologically rooted parental drive, such as there may be, is highly overlaid by psychological influences deriving from upbringing and cultural milieu.

The seeking of stimulation

Powerful homeostatic drives such as hunger or pain avoidance are absolutely necessary for survival and the sexual drive is a *sine qua non* for the preservation of the species. Clearly, there may be some other 'built-in' behaviour tendencies that help individual and species survival. Many patterns of behaviour clearly have this effect, but it may be asked which of them are innately instigated. Observational and experimental studies have shown that various features of behaviour, not directly associated with homeostasis in the narrow sense, appear to be rewarding in themselves or intrinsically motivating. To this category belong activities associated with the seeking of stimulation, including early filial responses of the young (proximity seeking), as well as investigative tendencies (curiosity) displayed by most animals, including man. This is not to say that such tendencies may not be developed and strengthened through experience.

The very possession of sense organs favours their use. Sensory deprivation studies indicate that animals and people require some optimal level of sensory stimulation if they are to function normally (see the survey of many such studies by Brownfield, 1965). The finding that living creatures both positively need and actively seek stimulation is somewhat at variance with the more traditional type of behaviour theory. For the implication of homeostasis and the associated theoretical outlook is that organisms, in seeking to satisfy their needs, seek to reduce stimulation. In fact, while some mechanisms ensure that the level of internal and external stimulation is kept down, other mechanisms, which we may call stimulus-seeking drives, maintain the tendency to avoid a deficit of stimulation.

Proximity seeking

Evidence of proximity seeking comes from studies of approach and following behaviour of newly hatched or newborn animals of various avian and mammalian species (see, for example, Sluckin, 1964). The so-called precocial young, that is those that are capable of locomotion very soon after hatching or birth, tend to approach any object, or a source of sound, that stands out against the background. If this salient object is one that moves away from a neonate animal, then the animal tends to follow it. The approach and following tendencies may be observed in animals so very young that it is unlikely that such behaviour could have been acquired through reward learning. Indeed, the responses themselves are a starting point of learning; for animals so responding to certain stimuli gradually become attached to them so that later the animals choose the familiar stimuli in preference to any strange ones.

Systematic studies of young primates have shown proximity seeking to be the normal pattern of behaviour. Harlow and co-workers, studying the growth of affectional behaviour in young rhesus monkeys, found that textures such as cloth are intrinsically attractive to the infant animals. The monkeys cling to such 'cloth mothers' whether rewarded or otherwise, as if the contact itself provided them with comfort (see, for instance, Harlow and Zimmermann, 1959, and Chapter 11). It is doubtful whether contact comfort is equally sought after by human babies. But even though babies do not always crave for contact, they behave as if they persistently sought stimulation – visual, auditory, tactile, etc. Certainly in the first few months of life proximity seeking is much in evidence, while proximity avoidance of unfamiliar objects and people shows itself only later (Schaffer and Emerson, 1964).

Curiosity

Motivational theories between about 1925 and 1955 were dominated by a rather simple view of human and animal nature. According to it, all behaviour could be regarded as evoked by homeostatic needs, or by sex, or by painful stimulation; and if not arising directly from such sources, then – it would be said – it is elicited by conditioned stimuli. Thus, a small number of innately based drives plus a great deal of learning would account for all motives. But in the light of the more recent studies it began to look as if organisms could be active even in the absence of any instigating conditions listed by the traditional drive-cum-learning theories. Such activity might be described as *spontaneous*, or as intrinsically motivated, or as deriving from certain 'extra' drives (see Hunt, 1963).

When animals and people wander about, look here and look there, explore and investigate, then they may be considered to be curious. But motives other than curiosity might be invoked to account for such activity. There may be behind it an urge for locomotion perhaps, or a seeking of stimulation. However, curiosity does suggest itself as a possible drive at the back of any activity that has the appearance of being exploratory (Berlyne, 1960). And we cannot be sure that activity which is not manifestly homeostatic or learned is other than exploratory.

If in the first place we are to deal with tangibles, then it is difficult to give the concept of curiosity any priority. For in observing behaviour we can only assume it. But we can observe behaviour, including activities which we would be inclined to call exploratory or investigative. We cannot know anything about the intentions inherent in such activities, unless the subjects of our observations tell us about them; therefore to call these activities exploratory may well be misleading. However, we may nevertheless use the label on the understanding that we are not committed, at least not initially, to any particular view about the nature of the behaviour.

Now behaviour which has been called exploratory, or investigative, began to be studied systematically by comparative psychologists in the early 1950s. Such behaviour differs from what is known as appetitive behaviour in that it does not culminate in any consummatory act such as, for example, eating or mating. But, somewhat like appetitive behaviour, exploratory activity is essentially variable. Its variability, if that is the right word, is characterized by approach responses, followed by withdrawal, then by further approach, and so on. In this way most features of the environment are first inspected and then avoided, and perhaps later approached and avoided again; and such activity tends to die down gradually, until such time as the organism is confronted with further novelty. So the pattern is often somewhat like this: the animal or person exploring the world around him first moves towards whatever is unfamiliar, then moves away from it towards the next unfamiliar thing, and continues in this manner, being attracted by novelty and tending in consequence to shun anything approached recently.

Some students of behaviour of this type consider that it can manifest itself in its simplest form as alternation activity in two-choice situations; that is, when repeatedly confronted with a T-maze or Y-maze, the exploring subject will alternate between the right-hand and left-hand turns, going first one way, then the other way, and so on. A subject that is not exploring will, by contrast, not exhibit any such consistent alternation sequences and may even choose all the time one or the other of the two pathways. The behaviour of rats in T-mazes was extensively studied by Kay Montgomery. In one series of experiments she set out to investigate whether the typical rat's alternation could or could not be ascribed to 'exploratory drive' (Montgomery, 1952). For there might be at least one other plausible explanation of this behaviour pattern, namely that it is due to what Hull called *reactive inhibition*. Reactive inhibition is an avoidance of body movements recently made, i.e. an inhibitory reaction to those movements. Montgomery asked whether maze alternation resulted from an avoidance of movements recently made or of places recently visited. She concluded that the latter was the case; and in a later paper she reported that on the assumption of novelty seeking one could predict the rat's activity better than by postulating that reactive inhibition governs the animal's conduct in new environments.

What is more, Montgomery (1954) showed that the exploratory tendency in rats is so strong that it can provide a basis for learning in the way that biogenic needs do. That is, the opportunity to explore unfamiliar regions can act as a powerful incentive to learn discriminations between stimuli that lead, or do not lead, to the goal of exploration. Studying rhesus monkeys, Butler (1953) found that these animals, too, could readily learn to cope with discrimination problems 'on the basis of a visual-exploration incentive'. In the experiment monkeys actually learned to choose between yellow and blue colours for the reward of viewing their surroundings for a short while. Butler (1954) also studied the influence of different incentive conditions on the extent of visual exploration. Monkeys were found to be more interested in viewing and hearing other monkeys than in viewing moving objects, food, etc.; but viewing anything new was preferred to seeing the same old monotonous environment.

Investigative behaviour, or curiosity, is not confined to some sensory modalities only. Tactile exploration is a common occurrence in human beings and in subhuman species. Harlow and co-workers studied the manipulatory activity in monkeys and postulated a 'manipulation drive', innate rather than acquired (e.g. Harlow, Harlow and Meyer, 1950). It was later found that object discriminations could be learned by monkeys 'on the basis of manipulation motives'. Similar visual-exploratory motives were also hypothesized by Montgomery and by Butler; and these motives, in view of their strength, persistence and spontaneous onset, were considered not to have been derived from any other primary drives. Curiosity did not appear to be a second-order drive, conditioned upon hunger or sex (Harlow, 1953).

Some later experimentalists and theoreticians expressed a similar view. Miles (1958) carefully controlled the history of some kittens to ensure that their exploratory and manipulatory activities were never associated with drive reduction, such as feeding or pain avoidance. Yet, at eight weeks of age, exploration and manipulation were sought by the animals for their own sake, and could be successfully used as incentives for Y-maze learning. White (1959) argued that exploration could not be put on a par with drives in the traditional sense of the term for a number of reasons; he pointed out that exploration is not discernibly related to body tissue needs, it does not normally culminate in a climax and it is not seemingly reinforced by any need reduction.

However, some workers do see a similarity between curiosity and biogenic drives. Shillito (1963), for instance, concluded from a study of voles that the exploratory drive is, like other drives, capable of some satisfaction – namely, by the reception of sensory stimuli. On the other hand, Halliday (1966) found that rats were equally exploratory in a new environment whether or not they had just previously been exploring something else. This finding could be taken as indicating that such motivation was less like hunger or thirst than like fear which can always be aroused by certain new stimuli. The problem to be empirically studied is which new stimuli evoke exploration and which evoke fear. But questions posed by fear-motivated behaviour are the subject of the next section.

Fear

The word 'fear' generally denotes an emotion which everyone knows from personal experience (the physiology of this emotion is discussed in Chapter 7). This feeling is often accompanied by characteristic modes of behaviour, in accordance with circumstances. When we observe acts such as running away or 'freezing' in other people or in animals, we are inclined to regard them as signs of fear. We may well ask whether the varieties of behaviour thought of as indicative of fear have all some common identifiable physiological features. This is a problem concerning both psychology and physiology. The problem at the behavioural level is to decide when to give the label of fear to acts of behaviour, that is, how to define fear operationally in terms of particular responses. Clearly we have some latitude in deciding what is and what is not to be called fearful behaviour. In practice, however, there is a consensus of opinion in regarding certain responses, and primarily withdrawal, as representing fear.

It is in the tradition of ethological theory that fear is an innate response to certain releasing stimuli (see Tinbergen, 1948). Thus, it was reported by Tinbergen that hawk-like shapes overhead evoke fear reactions in birds on the ground – for example, in turkeys and wild ducks. It was later questioned whether such stimuli are as highly specific as had originally been thought (see Green, Carr and Green, 1968; Hirsch, Lindley and Tolman, 1955; and Martin and Melvin, 1964). It has also been said that responses such as wing flapping, taking shelter, etc., depend to a degree on some earlier experience of being attacked. On the whole, it seems doubtful whether fear is initially attached only to highly specific stimuli; but more experimental research is needed to settle the question.

Still, it is impossible to doubt that certain fears have an innate basis. Walk and Gibson (1961) showed this clearly in the case of fear of falling. In their experiments they used as subjects inexperienced rats, chickens, kids, lambs, piglets, turtles, kittens, puppies, monkeys and human infants. They all showed clear signs of fear of falling off a 'visual cliff' (see Chapter 10). It may be wondered whether there are other similarly rooted fears.

A view for which there is a great deal of observational support is that fear is simply brought about by intense stimulation (Schneirla, 1965; Thorpe, 1963). This view, too, asserts that fear depends on a built-in mechanism; although the role of learning in fear is not played down. One problem is to define intense stimulation independently of the behaviour of the organism exposed to it. Otherwise the intensity of stimulation is inferred from the presence of fear responses, and fear responses are ascribed to intense stimulation – which would make the explanation of fear circular. Still, there is evidence that many inexperienced young animals respond to stimulation of any type, in any modality, either by approach, whenever stimuli are weak, or by withdrawal, when stimuli of the same kind are stronger.

Barring really intense stimulation, such as loud bangs and bright flashes of light, fear responses become attached to some stimuli, but not to others, as a result of learning. Here there is some confusion in the use of the terms 'fear' and 'anxiety'. Sometimes anxiety is distinguished from fear in that, while the latter has a definite object, anxiety is considered to be generalized or 'free-floating' (see, for example, Miller, 1951). Other authors make the distinction on other grounds; Mowrer (1939), for instance, regards anxiety as simply an acquired fear. Such acquisition of fearful or anxious behaviour is based on the organism's avoidance of pain stimulation. Of course, there is plenty of evidence from everyday life and from experimental studies that fears can be acquired that way (Miller, 1948a). What must be denied, however, is that all fear is thus learned.

What is sometimes referred to as the incongruity hypothesis is the theory of the origin of fear that supplements the evidence that fear is brought about both (a) by intense stimulation, and (b) by learning that some non-intense stimuli signal pain. Hebb (1946b), having studied the reactions of chimpanzees to many types of stimuli, concluded that fear is a function of the individual's earlier perceptual experience. Strange objects that evoke most fear are those that are sufficiently like familiar objects to arouse habitual processes of perception, but at the same time are sufficiently unlike anything familiar to 'disrupt the central neural patterns laid down by previous stimulation'. More recently Hunt (1963) contended that congruity with past experience results in boredom, while incongruity evokes fear.

In keeping with this view is the finding of Sluckin and Salzen (1961) that young nidifugous birds (that is, birds which are mobile and capable of leaving the nest very soon after hatching) become attached to familiar visual stimuli – become imprinted to them – but show fear of anything to which they are not imprinted. This is fear which is acquired as a result of prior experience, but which is not acquired directly through conditioning. Schaffer (1966) studied extensively the development of the fear of strangers in human infants and showed that an explanation in terms of the incongruity hypothesis is one that is the most appropriate. In general, it is clear that fear reactions arise in more ways than one. It is for empirical research to determine how all the factors responsible for fear interact in various types of situation.

Aggression

The term *agonistic* behaviour is sometimes used to refer to certain activities of animals and man that seemingly aim at aggressing against, or withdrawing from, other individuals. Agonistic behaviour is, of course, associated with emotions such as anger and fear. We have seen that fear is sometimes evoked by unfamiliar stimuli and sometimes by ones that are, as it were, only too familiar, having previously been associated with pain. Is aggressive behaviour towards other individuals also evoked by their strangeness or by the knowledge that they are a threat? Such a suggestion would be too facile and too summary.

Situations that bring about aggression may be considered under three main headings. First, aggression can be evoked (particularly in certain fish, reptiles and birds) by certain releasing, or unconditional, stimuli; this is the case when the sight, or smell, or any other sign of prey sets off predatory activity in carnivores; or when the presence of another male of the same species leads to territorial fighting. Second, aggression occurs in certain frustrating situations, as in self-defence; sometimes, when goals are unattainable, generalized aggression directed anywhere and everywhere is displayed by the frustrated individual, animal or human. Third, aggression in some situations is an acquired, conditioned or learned response; it is the mode of behaviour which has proved to be advantageous to the individual or one that has resulted from specific training. Let us, then, consider each of these types of situation.

Predatory behaviour is basic in some species. James Fisher (1964) has described such interspecies, or *interspecific*, aggression in a lively, if somewhat anecdotal, manner. Intraspecies, or *intraspecific*, aggression has been vividly described with all its ritual by Eibl-Eibesfeldt (1961). The fact is that such aggressive behaviour is well-nigh universal among vertebrates. Individuals compete, of course, for food, nesting sites, etc.; and fighting serves to space out individuals. There is also much aggression during breeding seasons when males compete for mates. Much of this fighting is differently ritualized in different species. The rituals ensure that a minimum of damage is done. Thus, the fittest are selected for breeding, compatible with the survival of the largest possible numbers.

Lorenz (1966), using his extensive knowledge of natural aggressiveness in animals, drew conclusions about aggressive behaviour in people. He considered that intraspecific, instinctive aggression is all the more apparent in man because his powers of attack, at one time only slight, are now enormous. What is more, man lacks adequate mechanisms for diverting his natural aggression: and there are not enough opportunities for sidetracking it. However, Hinde (1967) points out that the evidence for the 'spontaneity' of human aggression is quite inadequate. Far from being spontaneous, aggressive behaviour often appears to be evoked by situations of one kind or another. But the main weakness of Lorenz's theorizing lies in the inadequate attention which he gives to experience as a factor affecting the development of aggressive modes of behaviour. Even in the case of animals, rearing conditions have been shown in many experiments to influence quite profoundly the later aggressive activity.

When is aggressive behaviour simply a response to particular stimuli? Is such behaviour always the result of a non-attainment of goals? Freud tended to believe that one of the effects of frustration was aggressive action. But a theory that aggression was primarily due to frustration was put forward by Dollard et al. (1939) and by Miller (1941). In this view aggression is directly related to the strength of each drive from which it originates, to the degree of interference to which each drive has been subjected and to a number of separate but associated frustrations. However, none of these factors is readily assessable, and still less, measurable.

Aggressive responses to frustrating situations are, in the first place, directed towards agents which appear to be at the source of the frustration. But there is often a marked displacement of aggression from the threatening onto the innocuous persons or things. Instead of attacking the parent or boss, the individual might use violence against the innocent spouse or child, or resort to damaging objects such as clothes or crockery. In this way acts of aggression may be said to be consummatory or, in psychoanalytic terms, cathartic.

The frustration–aggression theory has not been stated in sufficiently quantitative terms to be properly testable. While fitting some observable facts, it does not fit others. For one thing, frustration can have certain other, well-known effects, such as regression to earlier modes of behaviour (see, for example, Barker, Dembo and Lewin, 1943), or fixation of habits (see Maier, 1949). Again, there is evidence that often aggression is whipped up in the individual as it occurs, rather than being discharged through catharsis (Berkowitz, 1962). In general, it is clear that aggression does not necessarily arise from frustration even though experimental evidence indicates that it often does (Yates, 1962).

Above all, aggression can be learned. N. E. Miller (1948b) trained rats to be aggressive. When given an electric shock, rats leap up; Miller had the shock turned off when the animals struck one another; in this way, quite quickly the rats learned to fight. Bindra (1959) pointed out how seemingly innate aggression could, in fact, be acquired by animals; for there is little doubt that in many cases aggression is continually reinforced. There is some evidence that antisocial aggression among delinquent boys is partly due to the fact that parents have in the past praised them for being aggressive (Bandura and Walters, 1959). Some aggressive acts feature within the early behavioural repertoire of young animals and human beings; it undoubtedly often pays the big and the strong to deploy aggression; thus aggressive behaviour may be greatly built up in, at least, some individuals. Learning, however, is considered in later chapters.

Further reading
D. Bindra and J. Stewart (eds.), *Motivation*, Penguin Books, 1966.
R. C. Birney and R. C. Teevan (eds.), *Instinct*, Van Nostrand, 1961.
G. A. Cicala (ed.), *Animal Drives*, Van Nostrand, 1965.
W. H. Thorpe, *Learning and Instinct in Animals*, Methuen, 2nd edn 1963.

Part Three
The Use of Experience

Part Two of this book dealt principally with constitutional
influences upon behaviour. In this section we shift our emphasis
to elaborate upon three related points raised in Part Two: that
behaviour is influenced by environmental as well as endogenous
factors; that an organism *learns* and retains what it has learned;
and that there is an interaction between maturational and
experiential factors in the determination of behavioural
changes.

The importance of the environment in determining behaviour
lies in its significance for us rather than, directly, in its real nature:
environmental stimuli which are *not perceived* cannot directly
influence behaviour, and when stimuli are misinterpreted by the
perceiver they will influence his behaviour in accordance with their
assumed rather than their veridical nature. Chapters 9 and 10
will therefore be concerned with the nature of perception, its
organizational characteristics and the determinants (learned or
unlearned) of such organization. In Chapter 11 we shall consider
evidence for the importance of environmental characteristics in
early, as distinct from adult, life and their consequences for later
behaviour; and in Chapter 12, the process of adaptation to the
environment, or learning, which such evidence implies. Finally,
Chapters 13 and 14 deal with certain further modifications of
learned behaviour; Chapter 13 is concerned with skilled performance
and Chapter 14 with remembering and forgetting.

Some aspects of these topics – such as the physiology of
sensation, learning and memory, and the possible significance of
early social experience in the development of intelligence and
personality – will barely be dealt with here. To some extent they

have been or will be the concern of other chapters: see, for example, the discussion in Chapter 6 of the role of the reticular system in discrimination and that of the hippocampus in learning and memory, and the discussions of intelligence and personality in Chapters 18 and 19.

Chapter 9
Perceptual Organization

Introduction

It is obvious that man does not live in isolation but in an environment; that is, he is surrounded by other people, things, events. It is also true that his behaviour is governed by environmental events or characteristics as well as by his own structure and innate propensities to action (if any). The very food which he must eat to live is an environmental object.

The influence of the environment can be thought of in two ways. In the first place, the mere fact of outside stimulation – of 'things happening around one' – seems to be important in determining efficiency of behaviour; the functioning of the organism is influenced by the intensity of environmental stimulation, irrespective of the exact nature or 'meaning' of the stimuli. Either too little or too much stimulation may disrupt behaviour. In the second place, it is clear from everyday observation that different environmental events have different results upon behaviour. The car driver reacts differently at traffic lights according to whether the lights on his side are at red or at green. If a knife looks blunt we pick it up casually; if it looks sharp we handle it with care.

This distinction between the general and the specific effects of outside events upon behaviour is reminiscent of an older distinction, at present rather unfashionable, between sensation and perception. It has been said that these terms describe different aspects of, or different phases in, the impact of stimuli upon the organism. The account of environmental influence implied in such a distinction is roughly as follows. In the first place, if external events are to influence behaviour they must in a sense become internal; an event must be 'taken in' before we can react to it. Events are 'taken in' via one or more of the special senses, as they are commonly termed: sight, hearing, taste, smell and the cutaneous senses of pressure, pain and temperature. Stimuli impinge upon the sense organs – for instance, the eye or the ear – and are thence relayed, in most cases, along specific neural pathways to the higher centres of the brain. Once they are 'inside' they are interpreted on the basis of experience, and the appropriate response or responses made. Thus stimuli are said to be first sensed and then interpreted, and the first process is described as sensation and the second as perception.

There are, however, difficulties in making this distinction. For example, what sort of process is the 'interpretation' which is said to be involved in perception? Is this a process of conscious inference from patterns of stimulation about the nature of external objects? If so, should not the process more properly be called judgement – a kind of thinking which follows, but is not logically part of, the process of receiving stimulation? If on the other hand we mean by interpretation a kind of automatic inference which is not necessarily conscious, how are we to decide when it is necessary to say that it has occurred? How are we to tell which perceptions involve sensation and which, if any, do not but are 'given', in the sense of being completely determined by the sensation which produces them? And if we decide that all sensation has to be interpreted, on what basis do we need to distinguish between the two terms, sensation and perception, and what do we gain by the attempt? Experimental studies of perceptual phenomena (some of them reviewed in the following chapter) suggest that in some respects more, and in some respects less, 'interpretation' is involved in perception than one might suppose; but the definition of 'interpretation' is both difficult and crucial to the argument.

The distinction between sensation and perception is, then, difficult to maintain consistently and has in consequence tended to disappear from theoretical analyses of perceptual processes. The term 'sensation' is generally retained in speaking of sensory physiology while 'perception' is applied fairly generally to the whole range of experience from detection of a flash of light to estimates of the nature of complex stimuli. Some psychologists would so far extend the term as to apply it, in the field of 'person perception', to the process whereby we form impressions of the personality characteristics of other people. Perhaps the majority would consider the latter activity as one involving judgement rather than perception, and would restrict the term's usage rather more, but the boundaries of definition are wide and fluid (for further discussion of this topic, cf. Boring, 1942; Hochberg, 1964).

The distinction proposed earlier in this chapter between the specific and the non-specific influence of the environment does not have such obvious logical difficulties as that between sensation and perception, and is useful as a starting point in considering the importance of the environment to the understanding of behaviour. In this and the following chapter we shall consider, first, the importance of stimulation *per se* and possible reasons for its influence; second, the different effects produced by different stimuli and ways of accounting for them.

The importance of non-specific stimulation

We have already suggested that the amount of stimulation which an organism receives from its environment is related to the efficiency of its behaviour; it appears that there is an optimal amount of stimulation needed to maintain efficient behaviour and that disruption may occur if stimulation either greatly exceeds or falls short of the desirable amount.

A number of experiments have been carried out in the United States and Canada to observe the effects of sensory deprivation – that is, severe reduction of sensory stimulation. The experiments carried out are not uniform in procedure but most of them have in common that subjects (normally college students who are paid for taking part) are required to stay in isolation in sound-proofed cubicles, wearing opaque goggles and with arms and hands bandaged to cut down tactile cues. One alternative method is that employed by Lilly (1956) who kept his subjects suspended in water at body temperature, blindfolded and wearing breathing apparatus, so that not only environmental but also kinaesthetic cues were drastically reduced. After a period of time spent under these conditions, which may be anything from one to four days, subjects typically exhibit certain disturbances in behaviour which vary in severity according to the exact procedure employed and the length of the isolation period. The most general report of subjects is that after a time in isolation it becomes harder to occupy oneself with organized trains of thought; concentration is difficult and instead 'the mind wanders'. Some subjects drift further into a confused state in which they cannot tell whether they are waking or sleeping and in which they become emotionally labile, experiencing considerable swings of mood. Occasionally – and more often in some experimental situations than in others – visual and auditory hallucinations occur, ranging from fluctuations in light intensity to complex and colourful everyday scenes. There is also some distortion of the alpha rhythm of the EEG, which becomes slower and irregular in form. In many cases such disturbances are still in evidence for as long as forty-eight hours after the termination of the experiment (see Solomon et al., 1961).

It must be admitted that there are not inconsiderable differences among the results obtained by different investigators and among the effects of sensory deprivation upon different subjects. One study has shown that subjects who are very highly motivated to stay in the experimental situation do not report the typical disturbances in experience (Ruff, Levy and Thaler, 1961); the same has been reported of subjects who are described prior to the experiment as 'mature and non-neurotic' (Goldberger and Holt, 1961), although little evidence has as yet been produced to relate personality factors to the ability to tolerate sensory deprivation (Zubek, 1964). Nevertheless it appears generally true to say that subjects under conditions of reduced sensory input function below their normal level of efficiency. The same can be said of subjects in less extreme situations than these; decrement in efficiency has been shown to occur during the performance of monotonous tasks such as radar observation, where the observer is required to detect very infrequent signals in an environment otherwise rather lacking in stimulation. Such tasks have been simulated in the laboratory, where they are commonly termed vigilance tasks. Performance in a vigilance task may be improved if an additional source of stimulation is introduced – for instance, the provision of pictures and projected slides at which the subject may look while listening for an auditory signal (McGrath, 1963). The idea of 'music while you work', if the task is monotonous, is basically a sound one.

Citing vigilance tasks in this context brings us to an important difficulty of interpretation. A distinction can be made (see, for example, Zubek, 1964) between *sensory deprivation*, which involves drastic reduction of sensory input, and *perceptual deprivation*, in which the patterning of sensory input is reduced although the absolute level of input is not necessarily low. Thus subjects undergoing sensory deprivation would be kept in darkness while those undergoing perceptual deprivation would be required to wear translucent goggles, which allow diffuse, but not patterned, light to reach the eye. Many studies in fact involve some elements of both types of deprivation; studies of behaviour during monotonous tasks, considered in this connexion, should clearly be classed under the heading of perceptual deprivation. Other studies of this type have been concerned with the perceptual delusions and hallucinations sometimes reported by aircraft pilots isolated in the cockpit (A. M. H. Bennett, 1961; Clark and Graybiel, 1957), and with the similar experiences suffered to a lesser degree by some motorway drivers and to a more severe degree by hospital patients who, for instance, are confined for long periods in an iron lung. There are clearly analogies between these experiences and those undergone by subjects in the laboratory who submit to perceptual deprivation; and on the whole the evidence suggests that there is, if anything, more severe disturbance of organized behaviour in situations of perceptual deprivation than in situations of sensory deprivation – an odd finding, since sensory deprivation of course necessarily involves perceptual deprivation also.

These considerations, then, would suggest that disruption of behaviour is brought about by the monotony or homogeneity of the stimulus situation rather than by an absolute reduction in stimulus input; or, conversely, that the environment is important not because it supplies a certain level of stimulation but because it supplies changing stimulation. However, the maintenance of any percept is dependent upon the stimulation, by the same perceptual element, of many different receptors; a single receptor under constant stimulation becomes periodically fatigued and incapable of conveying information to the cortex. If one observes a completely homogeneous visual field, or *Ganzfeld* (Cohen, 1957), the field disappears from vision after a few seconds and fluctuates in and out of vision thereafter; and similar phenomena occur when a visual stimulus is experimentally stabilized so that it falls constantly upon the same area of the retina (Pritchard, 1961). Thus a monotonous environment may in fact be one in which the absolute level of sensory input is lower than normal; perceptual deprivation may necessarily involve sensory deprivation, as well as the reverse.

However, while too little stimulation can disrupt behaviour, too much may also be harmful. Experiments dealing with the effects of excessive stimulation – sensory overload – are few in comparison with the number dealing with the opposite condition. Sensory overload can involve either the stimulation of several sensory modalities at the same time, or intense stimulation of one modality, though some writers (e.g. Lindsley, 1961) would restrict the term to one or other of these situations. Roughly speaking, the first situation described leads to disruption of behaviour because of the extreme 'distraction' involved, while the second does so because it produces extreme discomfort.

When subjects are required to perform two different tasks at the same time their performance of both tasks is often, though not always, impaired; the more difficult the tasks are, the greater the degree of impairment. Similarly, if subjects perform moderately difficult tasks while listening to loud noise their efficiency declines, but the effect is not as marked with easy tasks, which in some cases actually show improvement (Broadbent, 1957a, 1963). It is not easy to disentangle the distraction effect suggested here from the 'arousing' effect of extraneous stimulation mentioned earlier. One might explain the differential effect of noise upon tasks of differing difficulty in terms of distraction, in terms of arousal, or in terms of an interaction of the two. Some experiments are in this respect fairly unambiguous: in these experiments intense stimulation is administered in one (or more) sense modalities and the effects upon human or animal subjects are noted. Intense stimulation is painful and can produce marked effects upon behaviour. Subjects exposed to short periods of intense noise have reported muscular weakness and excessive fatigue, feelings of dizziness and sometimes burning of the skin (Allen, Frings and Rudnick, 1948). Intense auditory stimulation can be shown to kill some insects (Allen, Frings and Rudnick, 1948) and to produce fatal seizures in rats (Bevan, 1955).

Thus behaviour, and in particular the integration of behaviour, is affected by the intensity of environmental stimulation to some extent independently of its nature. Moreover, when sensory deprivation or overstimulation occurs in early life its effects are likely to be long lasting if not permanent; this will be discussed later in Chapter 11.

Specific effects of stimuli

Discrimination: sensitivity and experience

A scientist interested in the perceptual ability of animals is faced with the obvious problem that animals have no speech. Therefore he cannot present, say, a visual stimulus and ask the animal to describe what it sees; he must find another way of determining the limits of its visual ability. A method commonly adopted in this situation is to teach the animal to respond in a specific way to a certain stimulus; the animal is then presented with a stimulus which differs in certain respects from the one used in training, and observed to see whether it responds as to the original stimulus, or differently, or not at all. This (with qualifications) tells the experimenter whether the animal is able to 'tell the difference' between the two stimuli.

This method highlights perhaps the most basic characteristic of human or animal perception – that the organism can discriminate among stimuli and respond differentially to them. Detection is itself a form of discrimination. When we 'notice' an external object we are rarely perceiving something where there was nothing before; there is virtually always environmental stimulation of some sort and there is constant neural activity in the receptor system, so that when we notice something we observe not the onset of stimulation but a change in stimulation. Thus the detection of an object involves the ability to discriminate between a stimulus complex which contains that object and one which does not (for a fuller account of this 'signal detection' theory of perceptual threshold, see Green and Swets, 1966). There are nevertheless limits to the discrimination of which an organism is capable. We can distinguish between two notes when they are far apart on the musical scale, but when they are closer together than a half- or quarter-tone the task of distinguishing them is much more difficult. If a tone is very faint we may not hear it: that is, we may not be able to distinguish between two possible situations, one in which background noise alone is present and one constituting both background noise and the note for which we are listening.

What determines the limits of our ability to discriminate among stimuli? The above example suggests two answers. In the first place, ability is clearly limited by the sensitivity of the perceptual apparatus involved (both at a central and at a peripheral level). Only certain stimuli can be received and transmitted; stimuli must be of or above a certain intensity and of a certain kind – for instance, visual stimuli of a wave-length which falls within the visible spectrum, or auditory stimuli of an audible frequency to the listener (the visible and audible spectra of the human observer are in fact extremely limited – see Geldard, 1953). The fineness of the discrimination which can be made between stimuli is similarly limited by the accuracy and sensitivity of the receptor system. On the other hand, ability to discriminate is to some extent a function of practice and interest. The trained musician is more likely to observe that a note is flat, not natural, than is a musical illiterate, and a keen ornithologist 'learns' to make fine distinctions among species of birds which appear identical to the untrained. The implication is not that enthusiasm and practice improve perceptual acuity but that, with experience, the distinguishing characteristics of stimulus classes are well learned and more readily observed.

Thus when we fail to discriminate between two different stimuli it may be because the stimuli are too similar for us to be even potentially capable of telling them apart or because we are not sufficiently familiar with either to be able to make the discrimination. If stimuli are very different one can discriminate between them independently of their familiarity, but the more alike stimuli are, the more practice and attention is needed to tell them apart. In the case of detection, the fainter or more ambiguous a stimulus is, the more influential is experience in determining its ease of recognition. Experiments attempting to show the influence of experience upon perception have therefore employed techniques which render the stimulus ambiguous: subjects may be asked to identify stimuli presented visually at very dim illumination or via a tachistoscope – a device which enables stimuli to be shown for very brief time intervals, usually small fractions of a second; or auditory stimuli may be presented at very low intensity or accompanied by masking noise. Using techniques such as these it has been found, for instance, that common words are more readily identified than words (of the same length) which occur less frequently in the language and therefore have occurred, presumably, less frequently in the subject's experience (Howes and Solomon, 1951; Postman and Rosenzweig, 1956); that subjects recognize words which are related to their own interests (and are therefore more familiar to them) more readily than other words (Postman, Bruner and McGinnies, 1948); and that subjects attending to words played into one ear notice when their own name is spoken into the other ear, although they are normally unable to report ordinary words presented to the ear to which they are not attending (Moray, 1969; Treisman, 1964).

The effect of experience, it is usually argued, is to establish in the perceiver a *set* or readiness for some stimuli rather than others. As a result of differential experience he is set to attend to some stimulus characteristics rather than others and also to attempt certain identifications rather than others when stimuli are ambiguous. If a word, tachistoscopically presented, is only partly perceived, the perceiver will think first of 'probable' words (that is, words which have been frequently encountered in the past and which therefore appear likely to be encountered again) in trying to fit a word to the partial information derived from the stimulus. Only if 'probable' words are found unsatisfactory is he likely to consider 'improbable' words as possible identifications. Such *response bias*, or differential readiness of hypotheses, will be discussed further in the context of motivated perception (Chapter 10).

As Maltzman (1962) has pointed out, a perceptual set can be established rapidly, by instructions or by immediate context, as well as by prolonged experience. If subjects are told that they will be shown tachistoscopically words of a particular kind (for example, names of animals) and are then shown a nonsense word, they will 'identify' it as an animal name; other subjects will interpret the same nonsense word as belonging to a different category if that category has been specified in instructions (Siipola, 1935). Similarly, if subjects are instructed to attend to a specific stimulus characteristic (for example, the number or spatial arrangement of items) and are asked after presentation of the stimulus to report on all its characteristics, they are generally unable or less able to report accurately characteristics other than that to which they have been set to attend. In an intermediate situation, Postman and Leytham (1951) have shown that subjects who, without explicit instructions, are required to identify words which are all of the same kind (that is, are all trait adjectives), they develop a set for such words which results in delayed recognition of words which are not of this kind (although the set is apparently very quickly abolished by presentation of one or two words which are not congruent with it). Leeper (1935) has also shown, in a classic study, that a subject's perception of an ambiguous figure may be affected by prior experimental experience of a figure which stresses one aspect of the test figure rather than another. Whether established gradually by pre-experimental experience or, implicitly or explicitly, in the laboratory, a set can thus be shown to determine to a considerable extent the ease and the nature of stimulus recognition, although it is not always clear whether the effect demonstrated is strictly speaking 'perceptual' or whether it rather represents variation in response readiness or immediate memory (see, for example, J. Brown, 1960; Maltzman, 1962).

In the case of word identification, experience must clearly be a crucial factor in ease of recognition since the significance of verbal stimuli is basically arbitrary and must be learned; but in other cases it may be extremely difficult to decide which limiting factor, if not both, is responsible for a failure to discriminate. For instance, how does one explain the failure of a 'tone-deaf' person to distinguish one musical note from another? Is he genuinely lacking in auditory perception, or does his inability reflect lack of interest in and lack of experience of music? Without exhaustive laboratory tests and a fairly detailed life history it is difficult to arrive at any conclusion. This difficulty in choosing between an explanation in terms of the 'given' sensory apparatus and one in terms of experience, attention and interest recurs constantly in the psychological study of perception and with reference to virtually every perceptual phenomenon; it will be the concern of much of the following chapter.

Perception beyond sensation

Apart from the basic fact of discrimination, the most striking characteristic of perception is surely that there are certain aspects of it which cannot readily be explained in terms of sensory physiology. Our ability to discriminate pays tribute to the efficiency of the perceptual apparatus; but when one considers closely the phenomena of everyday perception it becomes obvious that the appearance of things does not correspond exactly to the patterns of stimulation which they produce at the receptors and at the sensory cortex. One familiar example of this apparent lack of correspondence is that of perceptual constancy; another, that of the perceptual illusions.

The term 'perceptual constancy' refers to a variety of phenomena which have in common the fact that we usually see an object more or less 'as it really is', even when it is presented under unusual or distorting conditions. A man usually looks more or less man-sized, whether he is near or far away, and a house looks real and not a toy, even when seen on the horizon. Yet the stimulus patterns produced at the retina and at the visual cortex by the same object at different distances are vastly different in size; the fact that our immediate impression of their size corresponds more closely to real than to retinal size is referred to as size constancy. Similar phenomena are apparent in regard to other object characteristics. A plate on the dinner table looks round to the person sitting behind it, although its retinal shape, for that person, is almost certainly elliptical (shape constancy), a sheet of white paper looks white both in sunlight and in shade, although the light reflected from its surface will vary enormously under the two conditions (brightness constancy).

In size constancy and shape constancy the perception of depth or distance is clearly crucial. Many experiments, as well as everyday observation, have shown that accuracy in estimating the size or shape of an unfamiliar object is reduced sharply if cues to its distance from the observer are eliminated – for instance, when the object is viewed through a small aperture or narrow tunnel which blocks its surroundings from sight. The retinal pattern of stimulation, however, is two-dimensional and cannot literally represent three-dimensional space.

The perceptual illusions also provide examples of 'perception beyond sensation', but with the difference that they represent inaccurate rather than accurate perception of real objects. Certain illusions have become standardized and are regularly used in the psychological study of such phenomena; some of these are shown in Figure 40. An illusion occurring in everyday life is the so-called 'moon illusion'; the moon commonly looks smaller when it is at its zenith than when it is at the horizon. This illusion was known in Ptolemy's time and has been of enduring interest to students of perception, not least because it appears at first sight to contravene the 'law' of size constancy. It appears also to be a genuinely 'psychological' phenomenon, since there are no good physical reasons for the difference in appearance (although one or two have been suggested: for example, the relative distances of zenith and horizon moon from the observer, or differences in the degree of refraction of the moon's image through the atmosphere at zenith and horizon). Moreover, the illusion can still be experienced when photographs of the moon in different parts of the sky, rather than the moon itself, are viewed. For one discussion of these points, see Kaufman and Rock (1962).

There is no universally accepted explanation of these phenomena. One conceptually interesting line of attack is the attempt to explain the illusions as special cases of perceptual constancy. Gregory (1966) has argued, for instance, that when the naïve subject is shown the Müller–Lyer illusion (see Figure 40a) he receives an impression of depth.[1] It is (at any rate largely) a learned impression, by way of

1. Gregory (1966) should be consulted for an exact account; his theory is more complex than the statement given here.

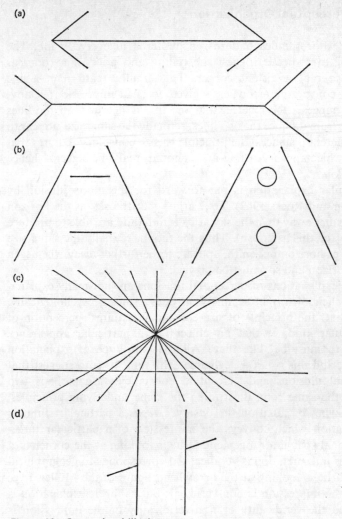

Figure 40   Some visual illusions
(a) The Müller–Lyer or 'arrowhead' illusion: the horizontal lines, in fact equal, appear different in length.
(b) Two forms of the Ponzo or 'railway lines' illusion: of the two equal lines, or circles, the upper appears larger than the lower.
(c) The Hering illusion: the horizontal lines, although straight and parallel, appear curved.
(d) The Poggendorf illusion: the diagonal line is in fact on a single plane, but appears too high on the right-hand side of the figure for continuity

analogy with stimulus patterns encountered in everyday life. The diverging arrowheads suggest the ceiling and floor of a room as they appear at a distant corner. The stimulus pattern of a line between converging arrowheads gives no such impression; if anything it suggests the reverse, that the line is nearer than the lines receding from it. Since the two lines, retinally the same size, appear to be at different distances, the principle of size constancy requires that the line which appears further away should 'really be bigger' – hence the illusion.

A similar explanation is put forward for the moon illusion by Kaufman and Rock (1962). They argue that the sky at the horizon looks further away than the sky at its zenith (and are able to produce evidence for this assertion). Thus the moon, retinally the same size whether at horizon or zenith, appears to be further away when seen at the horizon and so 'must be bigger'.

These explanations of perceptual illusions are not really explanations in their own right at all. What does it mean, psychologically, to say that 'the principle of size constancy requires' perception of a particular kind, or that an object has a particular appearance because it 'must be' like that? All that this type of explanation achieves, and this is not a negligible achievement, is to suggest that perceptual illusions and perceptual constancies are perhaps two sides of the same coin, illustrating the same underlying principles. In both types of situation the observer views a particular stimulus configuration which conveys the impression of a particular three-dimensional spatial arrangement. If he is looking at the corner of a room this interpretation is veridical – it corresponds to geographical reality. If he is looking at the arrowhead figure of the Müller–Lyer illusion the impression is non-veridical; but as far as explanation is concerned the veridicality or non-veridicality of the impression is irrelevant. The task of the psychologist is to discover the reason – perhaps common to both cases – that a particular impression is produced. For a further illustration of this point, see Figure 41.

Whatever explanations are offered for the phenomena of illusion and constancy it can be said that they are descriptively alike as examples of a general truth: that perception, in the sense of our awareness of outside events, is *organized*. Further, this organization can seldom be regarded as 'given' purely by the sensory impression of outside events. Complex patterns are immediately apprehended in terms of the environmental objects which produce them. The organization involved in perceiving even simple environmental objects has been pointed out most notably by the Gestalt school of psychology, which assumed prominence in the field of perception

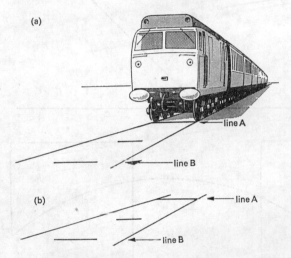

Figure 41 Constancy and illusion compared. In both pictures (a) and (b) line A appears longer than line B, although they are in fact equal in length. This phenomenon in picture (a) is termed constancy; in picture (b) it is termed illusion. The difference is that line A can be interpreted as 'really' longer than line B (because the lines are incorporated in a representational context which implies depth) in picture (a), not in picture (b)

in the early decades of the twentieth century and has never altogether lost it; it is worth considering this account in a little detail. The German term 'Gestalt' means in English 'form' or 'pattern'; Gestalt psychology, which may be said to have been founded in the University of Frankfurt by three men, Max Wertheimer, Kurt Koffka and Wolfgang Köhler, started from the basically philosophical assumption that 'the whole is more than the sum of its parts' and that the proper approach to the understanding of behaviour should be the study of experience in all its complexity, rather than the molecular

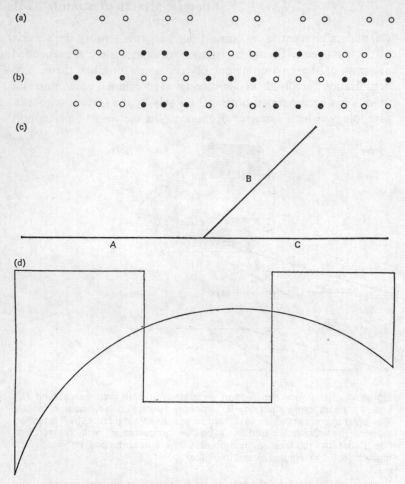

Figure 42 Some principles of perceptual organization
(a) Proximity: the dots in this arrangement are readily seen in groups of two, according to their spatial proximity.
(b) Similarity: these equally spaced dots are seen as falling into horizontal groups of three, similar units being grouped together.
(c) Direction: although lines B and C are closer to one another than are A and C, the immediate impression is of one horizontal line, A + C, with an oblique line, B, meeting it – not of a line A and an angle B + C.
(d) Good curve: a 'special case' of the law of direction. The curve segments are seen as a single continuous curve, not as parts of three independent figures, in spite of the law of closure (see below)

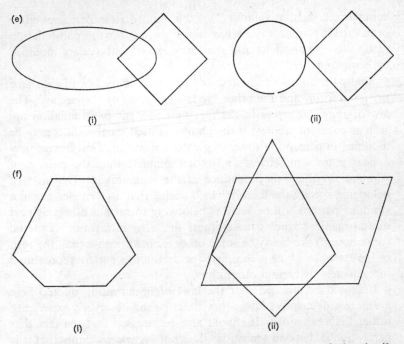

(e) Closure: where possible, figures are organized into symmetrical and self-enclosed units. Figure (i) is viewed as two overlapping units rather than three. Figure (ii) is usually seen immediately as a circle and a diamond; in fact both forms are incomplete.

(f) The 'good Gestalt': the form shown in (i) is present also in (ii), but is recognized only with some difficulty; the difficulty can be explained by recourse to several of the principles above. (From Wertheimer, 1923)

study of sensations and actions then common in the psychological laboratory. To demonstrate the complexity of even commonplace perceptual behaviour, so readily lost in the analysis of 'pure' sensation, the Gestalt psychologists, notably Wertheimer (1923, trans. 1938) and Koffka (1935), collected a number of examples of perceptual organization which were said to illustrate the general laws of perception. Some of these are illustrated in Figure 42. The most important general principles are probably proximity, similarity, direction, good curve and closure, and F. H. Allport (1955) has summarized them as follows: '. . . that immediate experiences come organized in wholes; that certain items "belong" to one constellation rather than to another; and that experienced features are modified by being together.'

Really these laws can be reduced to two: one the law of *Prägnanz* or 'good form' and the other the law (or laws) of 'belonging'. The law of *Prägnanz* refers to the fact that patterns of stimulation are seen as coherent wholes; if the pattern is itself incoherent it may be modified in perception towards greater coherence. Thus figures may appear more symmetrical and more complete than the pattern of stimulation which they produce at the sense organ. The laws of belonging specify the factors which decide that a given element in a stimulus pattern will be seen as belonging to certain others as part of an organized whole: these are its similarity in form or its spatial (or temporal) proximity to some other elements rather than the rest, or the extent to which it completes or continues a pattern represented incompletely by certain other units.

It should be stressed that the laws of organization quoted here are purely descriptive laws; they describe the observer's experience rather than explain it. It should also be stressed that the fact that perception is 'beyond sensation' does not *necessarily* imply that it is ultimately determined by experience rather than by the nature of immediate sensory input; as we shall see, the Gestalt psychologists themselves stressed the importance of 'built-in', unlearned factors in perceptual organization. Others also have attempted to explain organization in terms of sensory input, notably Gibson (1950), who pointed out that the perception of depth can be described largely in terms of certain features of the stimulus pattern itself. In the following chapter we shall consider, in some detail, the relative emphasis placed upon learning and experience by different theories of perception and the sorts of evidence upon which these contrasting theories rely for support. We shall also consider a no less controversial question: the extent to which *selective perception* (for example, variations in ease of recognition and in response characteristics of the kind reviewed above) may be determined by motivational as well as experiential factors, and the other possible interpretations of the evidence underlying this hypothesis.

Two morals can be drawn, although prematurely, from the work to be reviewed. First, most of the evidence upon which theory has been based is concerned with visual perception only, a fact which obviously places fairly severe limits upon the generality of any theory of perception. Second, we shall see that it is safer, and perhaps ultimately more profitable, to attempt to describe perceptual phenomena than to attempt to explain them.

Further reading

J. E. Hochberg, *Perception*, Prentice-Hall, 1964.
M. D. Vernon (ed.), *Experiments in Visual Perception*, Penguin Books, 2nd edn 1970.
D. J. Weintraub and E. L. Walker, *Perception*, Brooks-Cole, 1966.

Chapter 10
Determinants of Perception

Theories of 'the appearance of things'

Man's environment can be defined in three ways. In the first place, there is the 'geographical environment', as Koffka (1935) termed it: that is, external objects 'as they really are'. Second, there is the sensory pattern produced by objects at the receptors and at the sensory cortex: this Koffka termed 'proximal stimulation' to distinguish it from the 'distal stimulation' of the geographical environment. Third, there is 'what we see' – the appearance of objects to us, the way we describe them. Koffka termed perception in this sense the 'behavioural environment' – objects as they are to us. The geographical and behavioural environments may be identical, as in the case of perfect constancy; or they may be different, as in the case of illusions. Obviously all three factors are interdependent, but they are also logically separate. The understanding of objects as they really are is the concern of the natural scientist; sensory physiology is primarily the concern of the physicist and the physiologist. The psychologist's basic interest is in the behavioural environment, and in the other two aspects of perception only in so far as they throw light on the third.

It is impossible to explain why things appear as they do simply in terms of their real nature, because perception is often illusory and because some 'real' characteristics of objects – such as three-dimensionality – cannot be directly represented at receptor areas such as the two-dimensional retinal field. On the other hand, it is also impossible to explain why things appear as they do simply in terms of the proximal pattern to which they give rise, in view of such phenomena as perceptual constancy.

It has often been suggested that our perception of objects represents a compromise between their real nature and their impression upon the sense organs; for example, the perceived size of a distant object is generally less than its real size but greater than the size of the image it projects upon the retina. This tendency for size (and other) estimations to represent some point between retinal and real values has been termed 'phenomenal regression to the real object' (Thouless, 1932), and many reviewers of the evidence have claimed that compromise is a fundamental characteristic of constancy phenomena. It appears, however, that whether or not compromise occurs is to some extent dependent upon the particular experimental techniques adopted. Under some circumstances observers may show overconstancy – for instance, they may report a particular stimulus object to be not only bigger than its retinal size but also bigger than it really is. Thus a general principle of compromise does not seem tenable even with regard to constancy; it is, moreover, difficult to see how such a principle could apply to other examples of perceptual organization. The appearance of things seems to be solely determined neither by the physical nature of distant objects, nor by the sensory stimulation they evoke, nor by a compromise between the two; yet it is both coherent and, usually, accurate, and requires lawful explanation.

Theories to account for 'the appearance of things' are of two kinds and have in common overwhelming emphasis upon visual perception; hence the corresponding bias of this chapter. The first approach both ante-dates and post-dates the second. It was favoured by the British empiricist philosophers of the eighteenth century, for example Hume and Berkeley, and has also been adopted by recent and contemporary psychologists, notably Hebb (1949, 1966). It may for simplicity be termed a 'learning' theory.

The learning theory of perception as propounded by Hebb is briefly that, apart from a primitive awareness of figure–ground relations, perceptual organization is gradually acquired by the young organism through an elaborate process of learning. At first the newborn animal perceives only blotches against a background – in William James's (1890) famous term, 'one blooming, buzzing confusion' – and is incapable of all but the grossest distinctions between stimuli. Identification of different objects is gradually acquired as the result of experience. A possible physiological mechanism is suggested by Hebb (1949). He proposes that when two or more cortical neural cells are fired in conjunction, repeated association in firing brings about structural changes in the neurones which facilitate their interconnexion: perhaps growths upon the dendrites or at the synapses, which provide a greater surface area. Thus there are established in the sensory cortex assemblies of cells which are likely to fire in conjunction; as perceptual experience accumulates, complex and stable patterns of firing are set up which Hebb terms 'phase sequences'. Different sensory patterns evoke different phase sequences which arise partly because of the specific contemporary stimulus pattern and partly because of the neural associations built up through experience. It is this communality of phase sequences which enables us to identify a newly encountered object as being, say, triangular and not square.

More complex perceptual organization is the result of more learning, often involving more than one sense modality. It is maintained, for instance, that size constancy is the result of extensive learning of the relation between retinal size and distance. When the naïve organism views a box at different distances from it, the box appears to be bigger or smaller according to its distance and thus its retinal size; but if the box is touched it is sensed to be the same size whether very close to the observer or at arm's length. In other words, we learn that objects do not shrink when they are further away from us, and we also learn, through experience, to judge accurately the size of an object from its retinal size taken in conjunction with its apparent distance. Distance is in turn judged from various visual cues which we have learned to appraise through their relation to tactile and kinaesthetic sensation.

Other theorists beside Hebb who share essentially this approach to the explanation of perceptual organization include Ames (1951) and Brunswik (1956). Ames's theory is named 'transactionalism', in that he understands perceptual organization to result from interaction – transactions – between man and his environment. Brunswik's theory has been termed 'probabilistic functionalism', since he conceives of perception as essentially an interpretative function based upon the perceiver's assessment of the probability (in the light of experience) that a given proximal stimulus will correspond to a particular distal object. These views, and other theories of perception, have been summarized and discussed by F. H. Allport (1955).

The other approach to perception is that of the Gestalt psychologists; and at first sight it seems an impossible approach to maintain. It is that perceptual organization is innate, in the sense that it is not dependent upon learning and that it is ultimately explicable in terms of sensory reception. How can this view be reconciled with the evidence already presented that the characteristics of perception cannot be directly inferred from proximal stimulation – evidence which has been stressed by the Gestalt psychologists themselves? There are two answers to this question (which are really the same answer, differently put). In the first place, it is argued, the apparent contradiction between stressing the importance of proximal stimulation and stressing the importance of organization and context can be easily overcome if one considers that the perceptual context itself is a matter of proximal stimulation, as much as is the object within the context (for an elaboration of this principle with regard to the perception of depth, see Gibson, 1950). Thus perceptual organization is to be explained in terms of the whole pattern of stimulation at retina and cortex at a given time, not merely the stimulus pattern produced by the object alone; and if the whole pattern is considered, it is claimed, the characteristics of proximal stimulation will be found adequate to account for the appearance of things.

The second answer which the Gestalt psychologists propose goes further in attempting a more thorough analysis of what is meant by 'organization' at the level of the sensory cortex. There is not room here for a detailed exposition of the Gestalt theory of cortical action, which has been well summarized elsewhere (e.g. F. H. Allport, 1955; Woodworth, 1948). Briefly, the theory rejects the assumption that the sensory cortex comprises discrete receptor neurones which are interconnected as the result of specific experiences (the switchboard model of neural action proposed by early 'learning' theories of perception). It considers rather that the cortex functions as a coherent *field*: a field of electrochemical activity in which a specific percept is represented not by neural activity in a specific locus but by neural activity which follows a specific pattern. We have already seen (Chapter 5) that there is a point-to-point correspondence between the locus of peripheral stimulation and the locus of cortical reception, at least in the case of vision and to some extent in the case of other senses; but electrochemical activity in the cortex, it is claimed, is not confined to the specific cortical receptors but spreads to adjacent areas, just as ripples spread across the surface of a still pool when a stone is dropped into its centre. The field is normally in a state of equilibrium; incoming stimulation upsets this equilibrium and a new stability of tension has to be achieved. The process of achieving cortical stability corresponds to the phenomena of organization and has been termed 'perceptual work' by Koffka (1935).

There are thus two sets of forces at work in the cortical field: cohesive forces which work to restore equilibrium and therefore may tend to distort perception, and restraining forces which result from the specific pattern set up by external stimulation and tend to preserve that pattern (for a fuller account, see Brown and Voth, 1937). What the observer actually 'sees' represents a compromise between these opposing forces. Sometimes the compromise represents accurately the external object: when, for instance, the object is symmetrical and is therefore, in physical terms, a stable form whose boundaries represent equalities of tension. When the object is not a 'good' shape in this sense, it may undergo modification in the field until stability of form is reached; thus its appearance will vary from its physical shape in accordance with the principle of good form. The patterns set up by a number of discrete objects in the perceptual field will also undergo modification according to the same principle; hence the phenomena of continuation, 'belongingness' and so on.

There are thus essentially two theories of perceptual organization. One stresses the influence of experience and the gradual building up of networks of connexions, in both the psychological and physiological senses. The other stresses the determining influence of innate processes of sensory reception. Naturally, not every theorist who stresses the importance of innate factors necessarily adheres to the Gestalt account of brain action; it is perfectly logical, for instance, to argue at a psychological level that perceptual organization is innately determined without specifying at all the physiological states and processes which might accompany it. It is also true that many psychologists would explain perceptual structure in terms of both innate and acquired characteristics. The accounts described above represent extreme positions whose psychological and physiological implications have been relatively fully elaborated and accepted by their advocates; thus they illustrate the extent to which such explanations may differ and at the same time, by their specificity, render these differences amenable to test.

There are some perceptual tasks (for example, those involving word recognition) which must be dependent upon learning because the identification of the stimuli is basically arbitrary (although constant within the culture). We have already seen (Chapter 9) that there are differences in the ease with which stimuli of various kinds are perceived, and that these differences can sometimes be explained in terms of prior experience or instructions; the final section of this chapter will be concerned with other examples of selective perception and with the factors which may be held to underlie this (necessarily acquired) selectivity. In the next section, however, we shall consider further our two explanations of the 'behavioural environment' – that is, of normal perceptual organization – and in particular the evidence which has been advanced for one explanation or the other.

Determinants of perception: learned or innate?

An enormous body of work testifies to the effort to decide between a 'learning' explanation of perceptual phenomena and an explanation in terms of unlearned organization. In this section we summarize the various methods adopted and point to the general conclusions which emerge.

Immediacy of impression

An obvious test between these hypotheses is introspection: consideration of 'what it feels like' to perceive simple or complex stimulus configurations. This was the kind of evidence first adduced by the Gestalt psychologists in support of their own position; and certainly if we are asked to report upon our own perceptual processes what generally emerges about perception of a particular stimulus complex is that 'it just appears to be like that', immediately and without conscious inference. However, this is hardly a crucial test. If an observer is unaware of any process of inference this does not necessarily mean that no such process occurs; it may rather be that the observer is simply unaware of its occurrence – he is not attending to it. The fact that most of us would find it difficult to give an accurate description of the motor processes involved in walking upstairs, and that we are not ordinarily aware of our sequence of actions when performing this rather complex skill, does not compel belief that the skill is innately organized.

The 'distorted room' designed by Ames (see Ittelson, 1952) illustrates this point. When we view a room like that shown in Figure 43,

Figure 43   Normally sized people viewed in a distorted room (see text). (Adapted from Gregory, 1966, p. 178)

We assume that it is a 'normal' room in which the two distant corners are rectangular and all four walls of equal height; but exactly the same appearance can be given by a room in which one of the far corners is further away than the other and in which the ceiling slopes upward (at a calculated angle) to the distant corner. There are, in fact, many different combinations of angularity and ceiling slope which would give the same impression to the observer, but the impression is 'immediately' one of rectangularity, and this impression persists even if, in a distorted room, two people are viewed at the far corners so that their different distances from the observer produce differences in retinal size. This immediate and persistent appearance of rectangularity must be a function of learning, derived from experience of 'everyday' carpentered environments. Immediacy of experience, therefore, would be decisive evidence of unlearned organization only in the case of an organism with no opportunity for learning.

Study of brain processes

Another obvious test of the two opposing theories, since they diverge so considerably with reference to accounts of brain action, is to study directly the brain processes concerned in perception. The methods which have been used to this end may be classified under three main headings. Some investigators have employed electrical recording techniques, recording either the electrical activity of the brain as a whole, using the EEG, or the activity of groups of cells, or even single cells, in the cortex and elsewhere, using implanted electrodes. These studies have investigated the potentials evoked in different areas of the brain by different patterns of sensory stimulation. Other investigators have made lesions in various areas of the brain, in particular the sensory cortex, and have examined the changes in behaviour, particularly in perception, following such lesions to determine whether the changes in behaviour are consonant with those predicted by either of the theories presented here. Other studies have investigated perception in brain-damaged patients, although one of the disadvantages of this method, and to a lesser extent of the lesion method, is that the exact locus and extent of brain damage cannot always be readily estimated.

Some experiments along these lines have provided limited support for the Gestalt position; others have produced contrary evidence. For a discussion of such findings, see F. H. Allport (1955), Hebb (1949) and Sperry and Miner (1955). More recently, Hubel and Wiesel (1962) have studied visual perception in cats, employing the technique of direct recording, with micro-electrodes, from cells in the striate cortex when the retina is stimulated by a point or pattern of light; and Young (1964) has conducted anatomical studies of the visual system of the octopus. The results of such studies (reviewed by Muntz, 1967) suggest that some characteristics of shape perception may well be 'built into' the visual cortex, in that there exist cortical cells which respond maximally only to patterns of light having a particular orientation – for instance, to a horizontal or vertical line of light – and which are inhibited by stimulus patterns differently oriented. Sutherland (1964) has discussed these findings in relation to shape discrimination in animals; they are also of interest in con-nexion with Hebb's (1949) suggestion that the perception of lines is, if not innate, at least of primary importance and very readily learned. There is therefore some evidence that orienting discriminations may be innate to the nervous system, but there is little direct support for the specific Gestalt hypotheses of cortical action, and some findings directly oppose them.

It should be noted that Lettvin et al. (1959) have reported the presence of specific receptors for various characteristics of visually perceived objects at the retina of the frog (a species which of course has virtually no neocortex but whose retinal structure is essentially similar to that of humans). The implications for human perception must be extremely slight, or at any rate obscure, since the two species are so widely different in respect to cortical development; but the finding is of considerable intrinsic interest, particularly in view of the fact that the retina is generally considered, from anatomical details, to be best regarded as a central rather than a peripheral structure (Polyak, 1941). It also, of course, underlines the caution needed in applying findings obtained with one species to an inter-pretation of visual processes in another.

There remain at least three bodies of work which can in a sense be regarded as investigating the brain processes involved in perception and which therefore deserve brief consideration here. All three are concerned chiefly with visual perception, and all three seek information by interfering in some sense with normal perception and observing the consequences; and the findings of all three have been used at some time in the innate–learned controversy.

1. The first type of study effectively aims at setting up illusions (distorting perception) by creating perceptual conditions in which they would be predicted on the basis of the Gestalt theory of cortical action. The *phi phenomenon* constitutes an example: the successive illumination of two lights in a horizontal or vertical plane may produce the impression of a single light moving to and fro between the light sources. This effect is said to be predictable in terms of the overlap of contours of flow produced by the two stimuli, which fuse in accordance with the principle of *Prägnanz* to produce the contours of a single, moving object. Other investigators have made predictions as to the cortical conditions which would be set up by presentation of a specifically patterned figure in the visual field, and have then predicted in turn the effect of such existent cortical configurations upon the appearance of a figure superimposed upon this background (Orbison, 1939) or subsequently presented (Köhler and Wallach, 1944). Studies of this kind (reviewed by Hochberg, 1964) offer some support to the Gestalt view, although there have been attempts (moderately but not entirely successful) to explain the results in other terms.

2. The second type of study is concerned with the characteristics of perception when the subject views the world through distorting spectacles. The lenses may be inverting or reversing prisms, so that the retinal image is turned upside down or laterally reversed; they may distort the curvature of objects, or render straight lines curved or bent at the retina; they may displace the visual field sideways so that the subject sees objects to one side of him when he 'looks straight ahead'. Accounts of work in this field, which has some seventy years' history, have been given by C. S. Harris (1965) and Kohler (1962).

The results of these studies have often been cited in support of an empiricist position, since it is found that subjects are normally able to adapt perfectly to the wearing of lenses after a few days' experience of them and apparently 'perceive the world the right way around'. Since adaptation occurs, it is argued, visual perception must be acquired through interaction with tactual and kinaesthetic cues to position. However, the argument is not logically compelling, since the fact that perception may be reoriented as a result of experience does not necessarily imply that the previous orientation was established through experience. Moreover as C. S. Harris (1965) has shown, the interpretation of subjects' reports is by no means unambiguous; it appears possible to argue not that visual perception is modified to fit the frame of reference provided by the subject's felt bodily position, but rather that perception of bodily position is modified to fit the visually changed world as it appears through lenses. Until this conflict of interpretation can be resolved it is difficult to assess the importance of the data for one or the other theoretical position.

3. Finally, it is interesting to consider studies of the characteristic perceptions resulting from stabilization of the retinal image. The maintenance of an image on the retina involves constant scanning and stimulation of many different receptors. When retinal stimulation is stabilized in location by, for instance, requiring the subject to wear a contact lens with an attached mirror and projection system (Pritchard, 1961), the image disappears after two or three seconds and may fluctuate in and out of vision thereafter. Pritchard has observed that these fluctuations have certain characteristics of interest to the Gestalt thesis. When a projected image is very simple – for instance, a line – it disappears rapidly, and reappears, as a single unit. When the image is more complex it may again fluctuate in vision as a unit, or parts of it may disappear and reappear independently of other parts. These partial units are usually 'meaningful' rather than completely fragmentary. Lines and corners function as units, as do potentially meaningful parts of complex wholes, and figure and ground – in the case of stimuli which can be described as having figure and ground elements – vary independently (see examples in Figure 44). It is also noteworthy that some irregular figures undergo successive modifications in appearance which are predictable from Gestalt laws of closure and good form, these modifications sometimes

involving not only selective appearance but actual distortion and 'hallucination' of parts of the modified figure. Initially meaningless patterns may come to acquire meaning.

These data may be taken in limited support of the Gestalt position. Hebb's theory would equally well predict the relative resistance and functional unity of meaningful stimulus patterns ('meaningful' here implying that they are relatively well learned), but has more difficulty in explaining the unified fluctuation of figures which are 'good' but not highly familiar (such as the amoeba-like shape in Figure 44).

Figure 44 Fluctuations in a stabilized retinal image. The left-hand diagram on each line represents the stimulus shown; others on the line indicate fluctuations in perception. Note the 'hallucination' of part of the figure on line 3. (From Pritchard, 1961, pp. 75–6)

For a discussion of the implications of this work for the two major theories, see Pritchard (1961). However, Pritchard's results are based on the reports of the subjects; and it is much easier to report the appearance of a meaningful unit than to describe accurately a randomly constituted recurring image. Thus, although Pritchard's subjects are said to be 'trained in introspection', we cannot altogether discount the possibility that the requirement of verbal report itself imposes meaning and organization upon the recorded data.

The direct or indirect studies of brain processes reported here have not, as yet, provided an unequivocal answer to the question of whether perceptual organization is innate or acquired. Other studies must also be considered which tackle the problem in a more obviously 'psychological' context.

Behavioural studies

A simple rationale underlies the diverse studies to be considered here. All follow from two basic premises:

1. If perceptual organization is innately determined, it should appear in the human or animal which has not had experience, that is, in the neonate. Conversely, if organization is acquired through experience it should not be evident in those observers – again, human or animal – who have had no opportunity to acquire it.

2. If perceptual organization is innately determined it should take essentially the same form for all perceivers, at least to the extent that they share the same sensory apparatus. Conversely, if organization is a function of experience one would expect differences among perceivers, to the extent that different perceivers have had different perceptual experiences. These differences may be appreciable among individuals of the same culture; they are even more likely when, for example, people of different cultures are compared.

From the first premise come studies which compare the perception of neonates with that which is expected of an adult of the same species; also, some studies examine the perceptual performance of subjects who, although not newborn, are without experience in the particular sensory modality of interest to the experimenter (for instance, the congenitally blind man who regains his sight and animals which have been reared in darkness). Representing the second approach, there are some studies comparing the perception of peoples of different cultures, and individual differences within a culture.

Studies of the neonate. Any investigation of perceptual ability in the neonate encounters the obvious difficulty that subjects cannot be expected to describe in words the appearance of objects presented as stimuli. A behavioural indicator of perceptual ability is required; the experimenter employs tests of discrimination. If the subject behaves differently with each of two or more stimuli, the stimuli must be distinct from each other in perception, and this must imply a certain degree of organizational ability in perception, the degree varying with the exact characteristics of the stimuli among which the subject is able to choose. If the animal is able to discriminate between objects of two different colours, the discrimination is evidence of a kind of 'organization', but there is good reason to suppose that this organization can be accounted for entirely in terms of retinal structure, since for the different wavelengths between which discrimination is made there exist anatomically separate and differentially sensitive retinal receptors. However, if an animal shows a preference for a shallow drop rather than a steep one, the discrimination involves a distinction between two complex stimulus patterns differing only in the specific organization of their constituent parts – that organization which gives an impression of relative depth. It is this type of discrimination which is of importance in the performance of the neonate.

The perception of depth has been studied in a series of experiments (for example, by Walk and Gibson, 1961) using young animals of several species – lambs, kids, kittens, chicks, rats, turtles – as well as young humans as subjects. Their apparatus naturally varied in detail according to the species tested, but essentially consisted of the 'visual cliff' (shown in Figure 45), which presents to a subject the choice between a 'shallow side' (that is, one giving the appearance of a shallow drop) and a 'deep side' (that is, one giving the impression of a steep drop), although in fact the surface of the apparatus is at the same level on both sides of the central platform.

Walk and Gibson (1961) tested young animals as soon as they were able to move about with minimal skill. With most species tested a clear preference emerged for the shallow side of the cliff; the animal would readily step on to the shallow surface and move about freely upon it, but would not move on to the deep side. The preference was not only definite but also seemingly resistant to learning, since if an animal were placed directly upon the deep side, so that it was supported by the glass surface but to the eye was suspended in space, it typically did not move about but would instead 'freeze', exhibiting apparent fear, and was no more likely to choose the deep side of the cliff when again placed on the central bar. Young rats, who showed no preference for either side when they were able to feel the glass surface with their vibrissae, nevertheless chose the shallow side when this tactual cue was removed by a modification of the apparatus. This finding incidentally underlines the indirect nature of the evidence with which we have to deal; the reason for a lack of discrimination

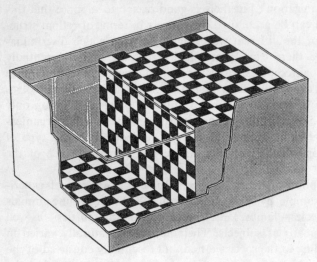

Figure 45   The 'visual cliff' used by Walk and Gibson (1961) in the study of depth perception

may be either that the animal lacks the ability to discriminate or that he is not exercising it. For this reason the only entirely crucial experiment is one in which no other cues to discrimination exist apart from those in the specific sense modality which the experiment is designed to study.

Human babies of ages ranging from six to fourteen months were also tested on the visual cliff. The technique employed was to place the baby upon the central bar and to observe whether it would approach its mother when she called, either from the deep or from the shallow end of the apparatus. Most of the babies tested would crawl to their mothers across the shallow side, but none moved on to the deep side (except for an occasional fall backwards on to it). Thus

It would seem that most human infants, as well as the young of many animal species, can discriminate depth as soon as they are capable of independent locomotion. However, the fact that testing must wait until locomotion is achieved, even if only for a few hours in the case of a domestic chick, is a serious drawback to this method. It is possible that perceptual learning could occur during the period between birth and the time of testing.

Some studies of perception in the human infant have considerably reduced this period from the six-month minimum of Walk and Gibson. For instance, Fantz (1961) has tested the preferences of babies aged from one to fifteen weeks for visual patterns shown to them, by the simple method of presenting the child with two patterns at a time and observing the length of time for which each was fixated. Even the youngest infants showed consistent preferences for some patterns over others, thus revealing themselves capable of discriminating one from another in a situation in which they were unlikely to have had appreciable experience with such patterns. Fantz also compared the attractiveness (in terms of length of fixation) of two diagrams, one a schematic drawing of a face, the other a 'scrambled face' containing the same elements as those of the first figure but differently arranged. The children tested showed a slight but consistent preference for the 'real' over the 'scrambled' face, while both were preferred to a third diagram comprising the same proportion of black to white as in the other two figures but with the black in a solid block (see Figure 46). Fantz concludes from this finding that

(a)   (b)   (c)

Figure 46 'Face' stimuli used in the study of fixation preference of babies. (a) A diagrammatic face; (b) a 'scrambled face'; (c) a black and white oval. (From Fantz, 1961, p. 69)

there is 'an unlearnt, primitive meaning in the form-perception of infants' (1961, p. 71). It is of course true that even young infants have almost certainly had the visual experience of a human face bending over the cot; but it is expecting much of the neonate's capacity for learning and categorization to argue that it has learned to discriminate between a face and a scrambled face in perhaps as little as a week. There would seem therefore to be some grounds for assuming some innate capacity for visual organization at any rate in predominantly 'visual' animals such as man.

Studies of the visually deprived. We have seen that it is difficult to reconcile the conflicting demands of an experimental situation appropriate to a test of the 'innate organization' hypothesis for a subject on the one hand perceptually naïve and on the other hand capable of unequivocal responses during testing. In the attempt to meet both requirements some investigators have reared animals in darkness from birth: that is, with no opportunity for visual experience but in otherwise favourable conditions for development of normal responses. Animals of various species have been reared in this way – rats, rabbits, pigeons and other birds, and primates such as the chimpanzee. A summary of studies is presented by Beach and Jaynes (1955).

It seems clear from these experiments that the visual ability of animals reared in darkness, when they are first exposed to the light, is considerably inferior to that of the normally reared animal. Riesen (1947), for example, has reported that a chimpanzee reared in total darkness for the first few months of life showed deficiencies of normal vision and took many times longer to learn simple visual discrimination tasks than animals normally reared. However, there is a complication in that animals reared without exposure to light are frequently found, on post-mortem examination, to have some degree of retinal degeneration and sometimes, after a prolonged deprivation, degeneration of the optic nerve. In other words, physical abnormalities of the optic system may result from visual deprivation and obscure the comparison between naïve and experienced animals. This difficulty can be surmounted by rearing animals in diffuse, unpatterned light; under such conditions of deprivation animals do not show anatomical degeneration, but do exhibit difficulty in avoiding obstacles and in the performance of visual discrimination tasks. Their performance, in fact, appears to be intermediate between that of the totally deprived and that of the normally reared animal.

However, Riesen (1947) also showed that a chimpanzee reared for seven months in darkness but admitted to a normally lighted environment for one and a half hours per day did not show impairment of visual ability, but performed in all observed respects like a normally reared animal. Thus while some visual experience may be necessary for efficient performance the experience needed is not extensive. Several studies have demonstrated that rats reared in darkness show no appreciable impairment in depth perception, and are capable of size, brightness and pattern discrimination after very little training. Walk and Gibson (1961) analysed separately the role of two factors in depth perception – *motion parallax* and *pattern density* – and found, in the case of both young and dark-reared rats, that motion parallax (the discrepancy between near and far objects in the speed at which they appear to move when the observer moves his head) appears to be an innate cue to depth. On the other hand, pattern density (the differential size and spacing of the elements of a patterned surface at different distances from the retina) appears to require learning before it can be utilized as a cue to distance in the absence of other cues.

It should be noted also that the effectiveness of visual stimulation in developing ability may depend upon the circumstances attending its experience. Held and Hein (1963), in one of a series of experiments, demonstrated the importance of *active*, rather than *passive*, visual experience by means of the 'kitten carousel' shown in Figure 47. Two- to three-month-old kittens were paired in the carousel, one in the restricting carriage and the other in harness, so that it could move about and so that the carriage moved with it. The kittens were put in the carousel for three hours a day and were otherwise reared in darkness. Thus both kittens received the same amount of visual experience; but for only one (the 'active' kitten) was visual experience correlated with movement. When the animals were tested after about ten days' training, the 'passive' kittens showed impairment on the visual cliff and in other tests of depth perception, while 'active' kittens showed no impairment. It is of course difficult to draw generalized conclusions since cats are blind at birth and (although the eyes open about nine days after birth) are not visually mature under normal conditions until about one month old. There are in such a case peculiar difficulties in distinguishing between maturation and learning and so in assessing the implications of the finding. Nevertheless, the finding strongly suggests that it is movement-produced rather than passively received stimulation which is important for the development of visual organization.

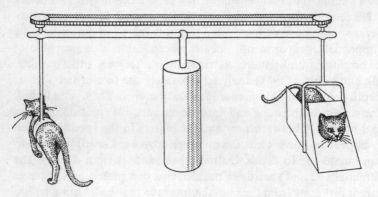

Figure 47   The 'kitten carousel' used by Held and Hein (1963)

No investigator has as yet reared a human subject in darkness from birth, but it sometimes happens that congenitally blind persons gain their sight, for instance, after an operation for removal of catar-act. Such persons might be considered to be in an analogous situation to the animal, reared in darkness, which is exposed to light for the first time. A number of case histories (sixty-five in all) dating chiefly from 1700 to 1928 were collected and published by von Senden (1932, trans. 1960), and Hebb (1949) relied heavily upon this evidence in arguing his theory of the learning of visual organization. The vision of these patients is reported to have been severely defective; they were for the most part initially capable only of very gross distinctions between figure and ground and took perhaps months to learn to distinguish between even simple shapes, while some were unable ever to proceed beyond this level of ability. This evidence would seem to support the idea that perceptual organization depends upon extensive learning; but as evidence it leaves much to be desired. The case histories are variable in the accuracy and detail of reporting, some providing only anecdotal evidence. The patients concerned also varied widely in age at operation, in the degree of visual experience (if any) prior to operation and in the amount and quality of vision granted after operation. Two factors in particular may have impaired performance. In the first place, when patients had learned, and had practised for many years, to perform various skills with the aid of senses other than vision, they found it extremely difficult to forsake their earlier methods and concentrate on learning to rely on visual cues; thus their old skills may have interfered with the learning of new ones. Second, largely because of inadequate psychological preparation for 'the new world of vision' in which they found themselves after operation, the patients appear often to have been confused, unsettled and intimidated by the new experience; unwillingness and inability to adapt to the new situation may therefore also have impaired performance. A more recent study (Gregory and Wallace, 1963) illustrates rather clearly the severe motivational disturbance which may follow operation and which may well affect visual performance for the worse. Thus in the case of human and animal alike it cannot be said with assurance that the visually deprived subject can be compared directly with the neonate, or that the perceptual development of a visually naïve adult is strictly analogous to that of the normal infant.

Studies of individual differences. A final method of testing the importance of learning in perception is to examine whether the differential experiences of perceivers are reflected in differential perceptions.

Some workers have compared certain perceptual characteristics of individuals of different cultures; most of the work in this field has been concerned with visual illusions and constancies. There would appear to be a few reasonably stable differences across cultures. For instance, Europeans have been found to show less shape and whiteness constancy than West Africans (Beveridge, 1935, 1939) and less size constancy than Indians (Thouless, 1932). On the other hand, they are more susceptible to perspective illusions than some other groups, for instance, the Zulu (Allport and Pettigrew, 1957) and Australian Aborigines (Gregor and McPherson, 1965). These findings are not easy to interpret. The commonest interpretation has been that non-European subjects tested are generally from 'non-carpentered' environments and are thus less susceptible to the interpretations of rectangularity which give rise to certain illusions (for example, the Müller–Lyer and Ames illusions) by association with room perspectives and other characteristics of urban living. However, Gregor and McPherson (1965) recently compared the performance of two groups of Australian Aborigines, one group living in a 'carpentered' environment – a relatively urbanized settlement – and the other in the open air with only very primitive housing structures; they hypothesized that the former group should be more susceptible to the Müller–Lyer illusion and the latter to 'extended vista' illusions such as the Horizontal–Vertical, but found no reliable differences between them, in a study which they claim to be the first to hold racial variables constant.

It might alternatively be argued that the differences obtained between racial groups may reflect differences in cultural attitude rather than in perceptual experience (although the two are of course likely to be closely related). Thouless (1932) has explained the difference between Europeans and Indians in size constancy in terms of culturally established artistic conventions. This argument gains support from comparison of individual differences in constancy within a culture. Thouless has shown, for example, that size constancy is less in artists than in other subjects, presumably as a result of differential training. Joynson (1958) has pointed out that constancy depends upon the adoption of a particular attitude, that of viewing the stimulus object realistically rather than analytically; it seems likely that individual differences in constancy, which have been related to personality differences (for example, by Ardis and Fraser, 1957), are a function of the attitude adopted by the observer rather than of perceptual organization in a narrow sense. The same may well be true of differences in susceptibility to perceptual illusions and may account for some of the observed differences in perceptual behaviour between children and adults (M. D. Vernon, 1962).

Some studies have compared the performances of subjects within the same culture who have undergone different experimental or extra-experimental experiences. It has been claimed, for example, that pictures of food appear brighter than other pictures of equal objective brightness when subjects are hungry, but not when they are sated; that poker chips are overestimated in size by children who have been able to exchange them for sweets, but not by children for whom the chips have had no value; that coins are overestimated in size as compared with plain discs of the same objective size, and that the overestimation is greater when subjects (again children) are poor than when they are rich (although this particular finding is controversial); that when one aspect of a reversible-perspective figure has been associated with monetary reward it becomes more readily noticeable than the other aspect, which has not been associated with reward. Such studies are reviewed by Dember (1961) and M. D. Vernon (1962). Incidentally, the last finding does not seem to work in reverse; punishing one of two possible percepts (for example, by administration of electric shock) does not make that percept less likely to occur and may have the opposite effect. This finding is of interest in connexion with 'perceptual defence', which is discussed later in this chapter.

Finally, there have been attempts to demonstrate individual differences in general 'modes of perceiving' which might be related to personality; for example, subjects have been classified as 'synthetic' or 'analytic' perceivers, as 'levellers' or 'sharpeners', as 'field dependent' or 'field independent'. All three dichotomies are based upon some notion of *perceptual integration*, although in rather different senses. The distinction between *synthetic* and *analytic* modes of perceiving refers to the extent to which perception of a stimulus is independent of its context, and would reveal itself, for example, in size constancy, in which the observer's estimate of size depends upon the extent to which contextual factors are taken into account. The distinction between *levelling* and *sharpening* is defined largely by the extent to which present stimuli are assimilated in perception to previous percepts – that is, one might say, the importance of the temporal context rather than the spatial. *Field dependence* or *independence* refers to the extent to which judgements of orientation can be based upon kinaesthetic cues in the absence of 'external' visual cues to verticality or in the presence of visual cues which are misleading. These schemes, and others, are summarized by M. D. Vernon (1962).

There is not space here to discuss these varied bodies of work; only one or two general points may be made. In the first place, some of these studies use as their measures not judgements of presented stimuli but judgements from memory, even if only from immediate memory. Second, many of them involve judgements of stimuli which have an arbitrary significance built in, and therefore necessarily learned, during the experimental session. Many, again, appear to be measuring differences in experimental or general attitudes, rather than directly perceptual differences; this is perhaps particularly true of studies of 'perceptual types'. Finally, even if perceptual behaviour may differ as a result of differential experience this may mean no more than that an existing perceptual organization has been modified through experience; it cannot demonstrate that no previous organization existed.

The results of these studies, then, cannot be conclusive, but they suggest two conclusions. One is that more of perception is learned than the Gestalt view allows; the other, that more of perception may be innately organized than is catered for by an extreme 'learning' theory. Depth perception and perhaps movement perception appear to be innate or at any rate very rapidly learned; and there is some evidence for an innate discriminability of certain spatial arrangements. Finer shape discriminations and appreciation of pattern density would seem to be dependent upon prior visual experience. Both of the positions from which this review started appear to be no longer tenable; but we have come a long way towards sorting out the role of experience in the perceptual organization of animals and men. As long as our evidence remains indirect, dependent upon inference from responses of the organism under study, it is unwise to rely too heavily for our understanding upon any one theoretical position.

Selective recognition and motivated perception

We have already seen in Chapter 9 that some learned percepts may be more readily identified than others as a function of experience: common words rather than uncommon ones, or one's own name in preference to other stimuli. The explanation which has so far been advanced is simply that we see most readily what is usual and, therefore, what we expect to see; in William James's (1890) phrase, 'perception is of definite and probable things'. Some psychologists, however, claim further that we see not only what we expect to see but also what we want to see. This claim has been usefully discussed by F. H. Allport (1955) under the heading of 'directive-state theory', since the assertion is that perception is to some extent directed by the internal states of the organism. We shall consider here the kind of rationale which may be advanced for the 'motivated perception' hypothesis, the type of evidence which has been advanced in its support, and some of the difficulties which occur in the attempt to appraise such evidence.

The motivated perception hypothesis

The notion of motivated perception is often, though not inevitably, related to the Freudian hypothesis of wish fulfilment, which has been applied to the field of perception by, for example, Murphy (1947). The child's impression of outside events is said to be *autistic*, governed by his present desires; the objects he 'sees' are those necessary to the satisfaction of his wants. When hungry, he 'sees' food, and his perceptual functioning has more to do with hallucination than with veridical apprehension of external objects. Very slowly the child learns to perceive only those objects which are really present, reconciling his fantasies with reality, since only real objects can ultimately satisfy his wants; however, the original element of hallucination (termed by Freudians 'the primary process') is not entirely lost. Although usually subordinate to realistic perception (the 'secondary process') it nevertheless comes into play in certain situations: in the absence of environmental stimulation, as in dreams, and perhaps in hallucinations under conditions of sensory deprivation; under conditions of ambiguous stimulation, when the nature of external objects is difficult to ascertain, either because stimuli are very near or below recognition threshold or because, as in the case of 'nonsense figures', their organization and meaning are by nature obscure; and, perhaps, when internal needs are very strong.

Under the last condition Murphy suggests that 'affective factors distort the cognitive picture of reality, so that the observer is markedly misled by the distortion' (1947, p. 366).

This is essentially a Freudian view, but it is not necessary to be an avowed Freudian to admit the possibility that such perceptual organization as is not laid down by the nature of sensory processes or by the communality of human (or animal) experience of the world may be affected by the more or less transient 'state' of the person at the time of perceiving. It can, for example, be argued by analogy with phenomena of learning and remembering that the association of certain percepts with reward or punishment may well influence the readiness with which these percepts are 'evoked' in the perceiver.

A wealth of evidence has been produced in support of the hypothesis that perception may be 'motivated'. Some of this evidence has already been quoted in the context of individual differences; it was noted that the appearance (for example, size or brightness) of stimuli presented above threshold may be affected by their motivational relevance to the perceiver. Another widely used procedure has been to compare the *ease of recognition* of neutral stimuli (usually words) with that of stimuli which have some relevance to the subject, when each stimulus is presented tachistoscopically or by some analogous procedure until it can be verbally identified. It has been reported many times (as we saw in Chapter 9) that recognition of stimuli is more rapid when they are related to some interest, value or need of the perceiver. For example, *hungry* or *thirsty* subjects recognize words related to their need more readily than other words; subjects with a high *need for achievement* (as assessed by personality measures; see Chapter 17) recognize success-related words more rapidly than other words, while the same is not true of subjects who appear to have relatively little need for achievement. Moreover, when stimuli are ambiguous, attempts at identification appear also to be influenced by motivational factors: when subjects guess wrongly at the identity of a word they tend to use as guesses words which are related to their own needs and interests. For instance, hungry subjects asked to 'identify' ambiguous or nonsense pictures tend to use more responses related to food than do non-deprived subjects.

Finally, McGinnies (1949), in a classic but ill-controlled study, and many other investigators using improved experimental designs and techniques (see Eriksen, 1954) have shown that subjects may take longer than 'normal' to recognize words which are of unpleasant connotation or are anxiety-arousing. The critical words used by McGinnies were socially taboo words, mainly sexual in connotation; other investigators have used words which are presumed to be unpleasant but not socially taboo, or words which are selected, on the basis of personality tests, as being associated with areas of anxiety for a particular subject or group of subjects.

Thus, it has been claimed, perception – in particular the ease of perception, but also the interpretation of ambiguous percepts – may be influenced by the needs and values of the perceiver in such a way that perception of related stimuli is enhanced; also, when threatening stimuli are presented, their perception may be 'warded off' – a phenomenon commonly termed *perceptual defence*, and often compared to the hypothesized Freudian mechanism of *repression*, the barring from consciousness of unpleasant material (for a fuller account, see also W. P. Brown, 1961, and Dember, 1961).

It has often been pointed out that there are *methodological flaws* in much of the evidence presented, and several studies appear, at least to the naïve eye, to be mutually contradictory. This is particularly true of studies of perceptual defence, some of which have actually demonstrated not decreased but increased ease of recognition for threatening stimuli; thus directive-state theorists must attempt to explain not only a difference in identification thresholds for neutral and critical stimuli but also opposing evidence as to the direction of differences, in what appear often to be essentially similar situations. For a close consideration of these difficulties and of possible resolutions see W. P. Brown (1961). It appears reasonable to conclude – though the statement here must be dogmatic – that enough evidence remains for motivated perception to command serious consideration as to its nature.

Difficulties of interpretation

A good deal of controversy has arisen over the interpretation of the evidence for motivated perception, and in particular over the interpretation of the perceptual defence phenomenon; the difficulties of interpretation merit consideration not only in this context but also more generally in relation to the nature of 'perceptual responses'. We shall consider some of the more important of these points.

The word frequency explanation. Some writers (for example, Howes and Solomon, 1950) have argued that the effect of motivation upon perception can be reduced to a simpler one, that of word frequency. Words which are related to interests and values of the subject are more familiar to him, because of selected reading and conversation, and may for this reason alone be recognized more readily. On the other hand, words which are associated with anxiety and threat are less likely to be encountered, partly because of social taboos on unpleasant material, partly because subjects will when possible avoid unpleasant situations and their concomitant verbalizations; these words are thus less readily identified because of their relative unfamiliarity, not because of their emotional connotation as such. However, perceptual defence is still obtained in some experiments in which the word frequency of neutral and anxiety-arousing stimuli is at least fairly well matched; moreover, the frequency effect appears itself to be greatest when very infrequent words are compared with relatively frequent ones, and is almost negligible when the less frequent words are still relatively well known, as is the case with many 'emotional' words used in perceptual defence experiments.

The logic of perception without awareness. It has also been claimed that the idea of motivated perception is logically absurd, since it implies that the perceiver somehow 'looks' to see if a given object is 'fit to be seen'. Some characteristics of the object must be perceived before it can be recognized as anxiety-arousing and consequently 'not identified'. Bruner and Postman (1949), among others, suggested a way round this paradox. They suggest that reception of a stimulus triggers off not one but a number of responses: one of these is the process of verbal identification, another is an autonomic, affective (positively or negatively emotional) reaction which can be measured via the psychogalvanic reflex (PGR). These responses may have different thresholds – that is, they may require different stimulus intensities, or different amounts of stimulus information, for the correct response to be elicited. 'Autonomic identification' of a stimulus may precede verbal identification, and an autonomic response to threatening stimuli may conceivably inhibit completion of the perceptual process and thus delay verbal identification, the indicator generally used to determine whether recognition has occurred. Thus it is argued that the notion of perceptual defence is not logical nonsense, and moreover, that there is some supporting evidence, from studies of *subliminal perception*, that autonomic discriminations can precede verbal discriminations in a perceptual recognition task. In a study by Lazarus and McCleary (1951), for example, subjects were required to identify nonsense words presented tachistoscopically; the words had previously been shown to subjects above threshold, half of them accompanied by administration of electric shock so that, it was hypothesized, they had become associated with discomfort and anxiety. When subjects tried to identify these syllables, simultaneous recording of PGR showed a greater autonomic response to previously shocked syllables than to non-shocked syllables, even at exposures below the level at which stimuli could be (verbally) identified. There seemed then to be evidence that autonomic discrimination can occur before verbal discrimination is achieved.

However, the evidence for subliminal perception is controversial; the strongest support for the effect comes from studies in which the subliminal stimuli are presented *above* the normal identification threshold but are, because of some experimental procedure, unnoticed by the subject. Moreover, Eriksen (1960) has argued that the lower threshold of autonomic, as compared with verbal, discrimination may simply reflect the relative difficulty of the two indicators of perception. The subject is usually required, in verbal report, to give complete and accurate identification of the stimulus, and often no account is taken of any *partial* recognition which may precede the final identification. Partial recognition may nevertheless be sufficient for identification of the affective nature of the stimulus, and thus for the evocation of an autonomic response of appropriate magnitude. Further, the correct verbal response may be one of a large number of responses; in the Lazarus and McCleary study, for example, the correct response is one of ten, but the 'correct' autonomic response is one of two – a comparatively great or a comparatively small reaction. Thus, if selection were made simply on a 'guessing' basis, the verbal response would be correct on about 10 per cent of the trials, but the autonomic response on about 50 per cent of the trials.

Perception and verbal response. Partly because of the difficulty of equating verbal and non-verbal measures of perception, it has been argued by various writers, in various terms, that motivated perception may be a verbal, not a truly perceptual, phenomenon. Howes and Solomon (1950) argued that subjects may see anxiety-arousing words as quickly as others but may hesitate to report them; this seems to be a likely criticism of some studies but not of others. Goldiamond (1958) claimed that differential recognition thresholds simply reflect a bias in the subject's readiness to produce various words as guesses when he cannot see what is being shown. A subject may be more likely to produce neutral or pleasantly toned words than to produce anxiety-arousing words; thus his guesses are more likely to be correct when neutral or pleasant words are in fact used as stimuli than when unpleasant words are presented. The effect upon ease of recognition is purely verbal, not perceptual in any real sense, since it is independent of the particular stimulus being shown and dependent simply upon the relatively chronic response bias of the perceiver. There is some evidence to support the response-bias interpretation of perceptual defence (M. Goldstein, 1962), and also support for a similar interpretation of the word-frequency effect (Goldiamond and Hawkins, 1958) and of the effects of set (Lawrence and Coles, 1954). On the other hand, some studies suggest that stimulus information and the expectation of the subject may play a more important role than such interpretations allow (Broadbent and Gregory, 1967; Minard, 1965; Smock and Kanfer, 1961).

Motivated perception, then, involves essentially a discrepancy between verbal identification and other indicators of perception – for example, the equivalent stimulus intensity of neutral and critical stimuli or other behavioural indicators such as the PGR. The problem of the accuracy of verbal indicators is not confined to motivated perception or, indeed, to the field of perception. The psychologist is always dependent upon recording and inferring from the overt responses of his subjects. When animals are used as subjects the experimenter concludes that discrimination has occurred when the animal reacts differently to different stimuli; in theory at least he cannot conclude when no discriminative response occurs that the animal cannot discriminate perceptually between the stimuli shown. Similarly, when an animal learns to discriminate between stimuli and, in general, 'learns to perceive', it is at least theoretically possible that what is learned is not the perceived difference among stimuli but the differential responses which should be made to them.

When the perceiver is human, the most common indicator of perception is verbal report: the subject is required to say 'yes' when he detects a stimulus or to name it when it is recognized. When an individual's recognition threshold varies because of set, motivation or more simply experience, variation may be the result not of differential visibility of stimuli but of the differential availability of the verbal labels which must be used in identification. Cultural and individual differences in perception may largely reflect cultural and individual differences in characteristics of verbal expression; the apparent lawfulness of perceptual experience is inevitably bound up with the lawfulness of the perceiver's language. The psychologist concerned with the study of perception must often, if not always, infer the characteristics of perception at secondhand, and has to be aware of this limitation upon the interpretation and the generality of his findings.

A final caution remains. We have spoken at length of the effects of learning and have reviewed some evidence that changes in perceptual organization are brought about apparently as the result of experience. We have said nothing about the process whereby experience and perceptual behaviour become correlated, that is, about the nature of learning. This will be our concern in the following chapters.

Further reading
W. Dember, *The Psychology of Perception*, Holt, Rinehart & Winston, 1961.
U. Neisser, *Cognitive Psychology*, Appleton-Century-Crofts, 1967.
D. R. Price-Williams (ed.), *Cross-Cultural Studies*, Penguin Books, 1969.
M. D. Vernon (ed.), *Experiments in Visual Perception*, Penguin Books, 2nd edn 1970.

Chapter 11
Early Experience

Kipling (1937) began his autobiography with the maxim, 'Give me the first six years of a child's life and you can have the rest.' The implication of this is clear: early years are formative years and thereafter personality is set. Such a view of human nature is held by many, ranging from Jesuits to Freudians. A variety of opinions has been expressed concerning the span of the formative period in life and the significance of the different types of early experience. To insist that early experience is all-important is an expression of faith; it is for empirical research to establish how important it is, and what precisely is important early in life in moulding the mature individual. Answers to such questions can only be pieced together as a result of many systematic observational and experimental studies. In this chapter we shall consider what is known about the effects of early experience; and we shall look at animal and human studies side by side. It will be seen that while some findings are clear-cut, others are only tentative; while a great deal of research has been done, far more will be needed before confident statements about the lasting effects of early experience can be made with justification.

Very generally, two aspects of early experience have been studied. Some workers have varied the amount of sensory stimulation received by young subjects and have observed the later effects of such variation upon behaviour. Others have been concerned with variation in rearing which is qualitative rather than quantitative – involving, for example, experience of certain stimuli rather than others, of various types of mothering and so on. Although the two kinds of study are only partly distinct (some variations in the type of early experience also involve variations in the amount of stimulation received) they will be dealt with separately here: the first under the title of *sensory stimulation* and the second under the heading of *social experience*. The latter is a useful title in view of the sorts of experiential manipulation and resultant behavioural change which have been of concern; however, we shall see that it may also be, to some extent, a misleading one.

Sensory stimulation

Additional stimulation

One way of studying in the laboratory the influence of early experience upon later behaviour of animals is to expose the young experimental subjects to a given type of stimulation, and compare them later with control subjects not so stimulated but otherwise treated in the same manner. This is done with a view to finding out how various kinds of early stimulation affect different modes of the animals' behaviour later in life: their activity, reactivity, learning abilities and so on. It is clear that considerable and continued physical differences between the experimental and control environments, such as differences in food supply, temperature and the like, are likely to have physiological repercussions and could, therefore, produce as a consequence some marked behavioural differences. However, probably more interesting psychologically are changes in behaviour other than those mediated by major physiological events resulting from altered physical conditions – that is, changes in later behaviour due to sensory stimulation of one kind or another occurring intermittently and not lasting very long.

A method adopted by a number of experimentalists has been to apply to animals such as infant mice or rats some such treatment as handling them for a few minutes a day, or 'gentling' (handling and stroking) them, or giving them electric shocks. Handled young animals have been found in adulthood to be more active but less 'emotional' (as indicated by lower defecation scores in the open-field test – see Chapter 3) than animals without this kind of experience (see, for instance, summary of findings in Denenberg, 1963). Furthermore, Levine (1956) and others in the late 1950s established that handling rats in infancy improves their later ability to learn, at any rate in certain types of task; and this has since been reported in other animals also. Somewhat more surprisingly, it has been found that occasional administration of electric shock to infant mice improves the ease with which they can later be conditioned (Denenberg, 1959; and for a discussion of *conditioning*, see Chapter 12). It is now clear that gentle handling, as well as painful shocks, helps animals to develop the capacity to cope with a wide range of stressful situations (see Levine, 1960).

At first sight, this might suggest that the more stimulation in infancy, the better for the behavioural development of the animal; and further, that stimulation as such, no matter what its nature may be, could be beneficial. It might even be wondered whether human infants would benefit from being talked to more than is customary, from frequent handling and from extra stimulation generally. The value of this, however, may be doubted. It would appear that extra stimulation in infancy results later in life in an improvement in the individual's ability to cope with stress and in his greater learning capacity only in certain circumstances – namely, when otherwise the infant, animal or human, would suffer from inadequacy of stimulation or some degree of sensory deprivation (see below).

Early sensory deprivation

Much has been learned about the effects of early experience from studies in which the experimental animal subjects have suffered from some form of deprivation. We shall briefly survey in this section the effects of rearing in a dull, monotonous environment, that is under conditions of perceptual deprivation; affectional deprivation will be considered in a later section. The problem facing researchers in this field is, in principle, relatively simple; it is to ascertain how important are certain perceptual experiences early in life for the development of various abilities. The experimental methods are essentially straightforward: deprived experimental subjects are compared later in life with control subjects on such traits as activity, curiosity, conditionability and adaptability. Studies of very severe and prolonged sensory deprivation are excluded from consideration; this is because under extreme conditions, for example rearing in complete darkness, some degeneration of sense organs is known to occur.

Such studies are of greater interest to physiologists than to psychologists who are primarily concerned with functional relations between behavioural variables.

Many studies were carried out in the 1950s with a view to investigating the effects of different environments during infancy, and particularly the effects of some form of restriction of early experience, upon adult behaviour; the experimental subjects were at first mainly rats. The findings in the main have been that animals with limited initial experience are later less active and markedly poorer at problem solving than control animals. Furthermore, it has been established that the lack of varied sensory input, such as limited visual experience, rather than the lack of motor experience, is the cause of the relative lack of ability in the mature animals; see, for instance, Hymovitch (1952).

A little later, dogs began to be studied. It was found that puppies raised in a restricted and unstimulating environment showed great 'curiosity' in their behaviour, but were apparently unable to profit from the experience afforded by exploration; they would be slow, for example, in withdrawing from painful stimulation, and (as in the case of rats) proved later to be poor learners. The effects of early sensory experience are quite persistent (see the summary of findings in Thompson and Melzack, 1956). In view of the findings concerning subprimate mammals, it may be a little surprising to note that monkeys reared in isolation have been found to be as good at many problem-solving tasks as feral monkeys. On the other hand, monkeys reared in isolation are less active than those reared in freedom; they also prefer later in life stimuli of relatively low complexity, they shun manipulative tasks and they show little curiosity. And such deprived animals are characterized later by grossly abnormal sexual and parental behaviour (Sackett, 1965).

Our knowledge of the lasting effects of an unstimulating environment in childhood upon the abilities of the human adult is somewhat uncertain. This is because no children are ever brought up in conditions of isolation and restriction equivalent to those used in animal studies. Furthermore, in assessing the influence of rearing conditions which are relatively unstimulating perceptually and intellectually, one must compare children brought up under such conditions with control-group children that are otherwise comparable. Thus, the experimental and control groups must be matched for genetic endowment – a well-nigh impossible task. Nevertheless, there is some evidence to indicate what the effects of cognitive deprivation in infancy may be.

Lack of varied experience in early childhood, insufficiency of cuddling, of verbal communication and so on, all result in a general retardation of physical and mental development (Dennis, 1960). This type of deficit of stimulation occurs inevitably in some otherwise good institutions in which sick or orphaned children have to stay for a long time. It is, however, very probable that lack of stimulation at one stage can be partially rectified by more stimulation and training in later stages. It is uncertain to what degree poverty of initial linguistic experience and of intellectual stimulation in childhood could have lasting adverse effects. Though such deprivation can do damage, human beings appear to be perhaps more resilient and adaptable, in so far as such comparisons are at all meaningful, than infra-human species.

'Social' experience

We turn now to consider those observational and experimental studies which compare the effects of *qualitatively* different early experiences. Studies of *imprinting* and of *socialization in mammals* may be regarded as an extension of 'additional stimulation' studies: that is, they are concerned with the effect of 'extra' exposure to specific stimuli. Similarly, studies of the importance of *parental care* represent an extension of deprivation studies, in that they consider the effects of deprivation of a specific (affectional) kind.

Imprinting

Certain effects of some infantile experiences are known as imprinting (see Sluckin, 1964). More specifically, imprinting, in the original and narrow sense of the term, refers to attachments which newly hatched birds of various species (but mostly ground-nesting) form quite speedily in relation to living things and inanimate objects simply as a result of being with them. The study of imprinting is bound up with the name of the pioneer ethologist, Konrad Lorenz, who, although not the first to observe such rapid learning, aroused great interest in it and attempted to describe its character relative to other aspects of animal behaviour (see the early paper in English – Lorenz, 1937).

Newly hatched chicks, ducklings, goslings and the like, tend to follow anything moving which they may encounter. The tendency to behave in this way is innate and probably because of this some writers have in the past referred to imprinting as instinctive. In fact, attachments which *develop out of* following responses, as distinct from the original following responses, are acquired. A fledgling can become imprinted to its own mother, or to any mother substitute such as an animal of another species, a person, a moving box, and even a stationary object. Thus, imprinting is a learning process. Some writers have been quite explicit about this, listing imprinting among simple learning mechanisms or animal training procedures.

Precocial species are those in which the newly hatched or newborn young have well-developed sense organs and are capable of loco-motion. The initial response of such young animals to stimuli of medium-range intensity tends to be approach. Lambs, kids, calves and other such young mammals, as well as chicks, ducklings, etc., approach sources of intermittent visual and other stimulation. Following responses are approach responses to receding objects. Some investigators have believed that following, in particular the effort expended in following, is essential to imprinting (see E. H. Hess, 1959). There is evidence, however, that sensory exposure to an object is the only condition that is necessary for imprinting to take place to that object, even though effort on the part of the animal is often needed to maintain visual contact with the object the characteristics of which the animal is learning (Bateson, 1966; Collins, 1965). This learning of the characteristics of a figure is, of course, necessary if a specific attachment to the figure is to occur.

But what, precisely, enables us to say that imprinting has taken place? One test of imprinting is the 'recognition' test. Young animals are exposed individually to some figure and later the responses of these animals to the figure are compared with the responses of control animals – that is, those without any prior experience of the figure. If the experimental animals are found to approach the figure more readily than the controls, then the initial exposure to the figure must have brought about a degree of imprinting to it. Another test of imprinting is the 'discrimination' test. In this case some experimental animals are individually confronted with one figure while others are confronted with another figure. Later each subject is tested with both figures together. If it is found that the animals' preferences are influenced by their prior experience in such a way that the familiar figures tend to be approached and the strange ones avoided, then imprinting is considered to have taken place during the initial confrontation.

Apart from showing itself as attachment to familiar objects, imprinting can lead to the courtship of familiar but biologically inappropriate figures. Some investigators consider that such *sexual imprinting* is one of the manifestations of the imprinting phenomenon, while others incline to the view that imprinted attachments and sexual imprinting develop separately. However this may be, many workers have reported cases of misdirected sexual approaches by males of various species of birds, approaches which appear to be directly due to early exposure to figures other than the usual mother figure. Unusual attachments do not by any means inevitably result in signs of sexual imprinting at maturity. However, rearing pairs of drakes together was found to lead to homosexual behaviour in these animals in later life; see, for example, Schutz (1965). Whether sexual imprinting of any kind can occur in mammals is quite uncertain.

Socialization in mammals

The development of social behaviour in birds has been studied both in relation to imprinting and in other contexts. In mammals the study of the formation of attachments has an entirely separate history from the study of imprinting, although the interests of these fields of research have in recent years tended to converge. Two main lines of investigation concerning mammals stand out: one has to do with the socialization and training of puppies, the other with the affectional development of infant monkeys. We shall deal with them in that order.

After many years of research an eminent student of animal behaviour, J. P. Scott, was able to conclude that certain kinds of early experience are crucial for the shaping of the later behaviour of dogs, and particularly for their sociability (see Scott, 1958a, 1962). Sociability in one sense may be assessed by the extent of the animal's fear reactions towards people. Experiments indicate that puppies become fully tame only if reared by people during the first three to four weeks of life. If allowed to run wild until about twelve weeks of age, then no matter how trained, such puppies will grow into somewhat timid dogs. Scott suggests that a distinction must be made between primary and secondary socialization. *Primary socialization* in dogs, and in other animals too, takes place in the first stages of active life. This is a process which normally attaches the individual to his species; but attachments may be formed to other species as, for instance, when dogs become tame in relation to human beings. *Secondary socialization* or later social learning is not considered by Scott to be of the same character; and it has repeatedly been reported to be less effective. We shall not here enlarge upon such evidence or upon Scott's definition of secondary socialization, which he views as a form of *instrumental learning* which is susceptible to *extinction*; these terms will be defined and discussed in Chapter 12.

One feature of primary socialization is of great interest, namely, its apparent independence of conventional rewards. While feeding during social training helps, it is not an essential factor in the development of sociability; the only necessary condition is social contact between the young animal and some person or persons. Thus, lasting social bonds which develop between the given individual and other animals or people depend less on reward learning than on familiarization with, or exposure to, others.

It may be added that it is thought that this is also the case with early human social learning. The dominant view in the 1940s and 1950s was that social learning in children depended on primary drive reduction – that is, that a tie to a mother and acceptance of her values were contingent upon the reduction of hunger and alleviation of pain which were attained through her. There is evidence that much social learning depends on such factors, but probably not all social learning, and especially not the earliest social learning.

Social ties in infancy would appear to develop primarily as a result of sensory experience of the social environment, and especially of the mother (see, for instance, Walters and Parke, 1965).

At any rate it has been shown that the love of an infant monkey for its mother – if one may use human terms in this context – is not 'cupboard love'. H. F. Harlow and co-workers established this conclusively in laboratory situations in which the food source was separated from the source of 'contact comfort'. The former was a wire structure provided with a milk supply obtainable through a protruding nipple – the wire mother, as it was called; the latter was a rather similar structure but covered with a towelling fabric – the so-called cloth mother. Infant monkeys were found to prefer the cloth mother, which provided the right 'feel', to the food-giving wire mother (see Harlow, 1959b; Harlow and Zimmermann, 1959). We have mentioned earlier the open-field test used to judge animals' fearfulness. Infant monkeys reared with wire and cloth mothers were so tested in a room larger than the familiar cage and containing some strange objects. Without the cloth mother an infant would huddle in a corner, showing the usual signs of fright. The presence of the wire mother had no effect on such behaviour, but an introduction of the cloth mother altered the infant's conduct radically. The baby monkey would first cling to the cloth mother and then begin to explore the strange environment, returning every now and then to the security of contact with her.

There is evidence that the very early experience of a monkey and in particular the attachments it forms to specific stimulus figures tend to have lasting effects. These lie partly in the specific preferences that the monkey has acquired and partly in the general behaviour of the animal later in life in such spheres as social and sexual. It has been argued that the ties, individual and species-specific, which primates develop are much like imprinting in precocial birds (Sackett, Porter and Holmes, 1965). The similarity of these learning processes is particularly clear in relation to the development of fear responses. As far as imprinting is concerned, it was reported in the earlier studies that the onset of fear coincided with the end of the so-called *critical period* for imprinting. It was believed that maturation brought about fear responses and that these inhibited following responses and, therefore, prevented further imprinting. It is now clear that fear is often entailed by imprinting in that the objects that are recognized as familiar are sought, but those that are recognized as strange are avoided or feared; likewise with the growth of affectional responses in infant monkeys: known objects, provided they have the 'right' texture, are sought and strange ones are initially avoided. Thus a teddy-bear and similar toys may be either loved or feared, depending on whether they are familiar or unfamiliar; and the same toy can, therefore, be a love-object to one monkey and a 'monster' to another (for further discussion, see Hebb, 1946b). However, the great importance of early experiences, as far as monkeys are concerned, lies in their long-term effects upon the animal's 'personality', as indicated in the next section.

Parental care

It is one thing to be deprived of a wide range of stimulation and another not to be given specific care and affection that parents, and especially the mother, normally provide. Studies of maternal deprivation in human beings have quite a long history. On the other hand, the effects of maternal deprivation in other primates have become the subject of research only relatively recently. It has been established that infant monkeys readily accept mother substitutes and cling to the so-called mothers as much as to real mothers or other adult animals. But it is clear that cloth mothers do not provide any true mothering; and unmothered infants, even if reared with inanimate mother surrogates, grow up into abnormally behaving adult monkeys. However, it is remarkable that the company of other infant monkeys makes up in many ways for any lack of mothering (Harlow and Harlow, 1962). The socially deprived monkeys have been found to be very disturbed in their later sexual behaviour; and unmothered females become themselves very inadequate mothers. One may wonder what the effects of the lack of maternal care and affection in human infancy may be. Obviously one must not jump to any conclusions from the study of monkeys to human beings. Fortunately one need not be tempted to do so because there is a great deal of information available from studies of deprived children. The findings are not always easy to interpret, and somewhat differing conclusions have on occasions been drawn from the same set of data.

The most extreme forms of parental deprivation occur either when a child is brought up in an institution, or when a child is separated from the parents, most commonly when it has to spend a long time away from home in hospital. An early systematic investigation of the effects of institutionalized upbringing was made in America by Goldfarb (1943). Fifteen boys and girls, ten to fourteen years old, who had been in an institution from the age of a few months until about three years of age, were compared with fifteen children (of comparable heredity so far as could be judged) brought up in foster homes. Detrimental effects of institutional upbringing were said to be apparent in almost every sphere of intellectual and social development. In England, Bowlby (1944) in his account of forty-four juvenile thieves, reported that, as compared with youngsters in a control group, the young delinquents had certain personality traits typical of those deprived in childhood of maternal care and affection; many of the delinquents had indeed suffered maternal separation of more than six months during the first five years of their lives. Spitz (1945, 1946) was much concerned with the effects upon the child of hospitalization and separation from the mother generally. He described the symptoms of what he called *anaclitic depression* in emotionally deprived children: apathy, slow development and so on. He found that recovery was rapid whenever the child was reunited with its mother after a short separation. However, after separations of over three months recovery tended to be slow and incomplete.

These early studies were conducted by psychoanalytically oriented workers and they tended to confirm the view that personality development is adversely affected by early deprivation of affectionate mothering occurring in broken homes, during separation from the mother and so on. Later studies brought out clearly the need for caution in interpreting data and in generalizing. Some earlier conclusions had to be qualified and modified. For instance, Bowlby *et al.* (1956), who studied children who had spent some time away from their mothers in a TB sanatorium, found them to be more often maladjusted than control-group children; however, the research showed that institutionalization did not commonly lead to the development of an affectionless or psychopathic character, as Bowlby (1944) had suggested. Indeed, many individuals who have suffered maternal deprivation are known – both from everyday observation and from systematic studies – to be well adjusted by every criterion which can be applied.

More recently attempts have been made at reassessing the effects of the deprivation of maternal care. We may ask in the first place what precisely is meant by maternal or parental deprivation. The term covers many distinct conditions, for example institutionalization, lack of adequate mothering, lack of ability to interact with mother figures, maternal rejection. And each kind of deprivation may be experienced at various levels of severity. Many questions concerning the effects of deprivation are controversial. For example, different views have been expressed about 'multiple mothering', that is, when the child is given care and affection by more than one person; such a controversy can only be resolved by further empirical studies. The question of the effects of *paternal deprivation* is now more actively investigated. Both maternal and paternal deprivation can have quite varied effects upon later behaviour. Many hereditary and environmental variables are relevant to the problems mentioned in this section; they are considered in some detail in the monograph by Ainsworth *et al.* (1962).

Critical periods

We have mentioned the critical period in imprinting; but critical periods are said to occur in other aspects of development of most higher animals, including man. Before psychologists became interested in critical periods, embryologists had found it necessary to think about development in these terms; they had noticed that certain physical abnormalities depended less on the character of the stimuli producing them than on the *time* at which the embryo was stimulated. Later the question arose whether the development of behaviour in the young also depended on the existence of certain sensitive or critical periods. Now the concept of behavioural critical periods is not identical with that of stages of development of behaviour: a developmental stage may be, but need not necessarily be, critical. And a number of claims have been made about the criticality of certain developmental stages.

It has already been noted (in Chapter 4) that Freud held that a child goes through a sequence of psychosexual stages, each of which is in effect a critical period for the development of various personality traits. The first twelve months or so of life are considered by the psychoanalytic school to be the oral stage, that is one when gratification is obtained mainly through the mouth. This is thought to be followed by the anal stage, the phallic stage and finally, the genital stage. Each stage is said to be characterized by certain modes of behaviour, which in due course give way to the interests and activities of the next stage. Furthermore, it is said that inadequate or excessive gratification and anxiety at any one stage result in a fixation of the characteristic feelings of the stage and of forms of behaviour deriving from those appropriate to that stage. Thus, greed in an adult would derive from oral fixation, conformity would be described as an anal fixation, and many other features of personality would be related in this manner to various early experiences of the child (see Chapter 19). Whether such an account of critical periods in personality development is true is quite uncertain. In order to be confirmed or refuted such suggestions must be tested by rigorous observations. And nothing like enough observational studies in this vein have yet been carried out.

The notion of critical periods in a more readily testable form has been put forward by Konrad Lorenz (1937) in relation to imprinting and by J. P. Scott (1958b) in relation to the early socialization of mammals. Concerning imprinting, all that need be added to what has been said earlier is that Lorenz and others found that it took place within a few hours, or at most during the first day or two, after hatching. Thereafter, it was generally accepted that imprinting could occur only during a strictly critical period some time early in the life of the individual, and that if it did not occur at that time then it never would. However, Guiton (1959) and others after him established that chicks kept in isolation remained capable of being imprinted to moving objects considerably longer than chicks reared in groups. The apparent shortness of the period of imprintability in communally reared chicks is due to the fact that such birds become imprinted to one another, and having become so imprinted, show fear of strange figures instead of approaching them. Thus it is misleading to think of imprinting as occurring solely during some short, genetically determined critical period; environmental factors influence the duration of the sensitive period and, generally, there are simply *more likely* and *less likely* times during which the formation of imprinted attachments is possible.

The acquisition of attachments by mammals has been said to occur mainly during certain sensitive periods in their development. Williams and Scott (1953) reported such critical periods in the development of social behaviour patterns in the mouse. Scott concentrated later on the study of socialization in the dog. He also surveyed findings concerning other animals (Scott, 1962) and concluded that the period of primary socialization, mentioned earlier in this chapter, is a critical one; during a short period early in life, experience determines who will be treated by the animal as its close relatives – members of its own species, or members of another species. Later, Scott (1963) equated the process of primary socialization in puppies, and in human infants, with imprinting. This is debatable. Even the view that primary socialization takes place during a critical period has been challenged (see Fuller and Clarke, 1966; Schneirla and Rosenblatt, 1963). Clearly, much more research is needed in this field of developmental psychology.

Early development of individuality

We may now draw together some of the findings surveyed above in order to consider the cognitive and affective development of the individual in relation to his earliest experiences. We have seen that it is fairly well established that the intellectual development of orphanage children is somewhat impaired. This may be because the institutional environment provides relatively little sensory stimulation and/or because the infant's intellect cannot function optimally unless motherly love is there to provide the necessary emotional stability. McCarthy (1954) has gathered evidence to show that institutionally reared infants are particularly retarded linguistically;

and language is, in turn, an important means towards further cognitive development.

The contrast between institutional and home environments may be regarded as a special case of possible 'cultural' differences in child-rearing practices. Both social, subcultural differences and national differences in methods of treating infants have been extensively studied. One particular in which cultures vary is the freedom of movement given to the young infant. While the Western way is to allow the baby to move its arms and legs freely, in parts of Eastern Europe swaddling is or used to be customary. Swaddling entailed a severe restriction of movement and it was sometimes combined with keeping the infant away from strong light and from contact with objects. Some American Indian tribes have also followed similar practices. It is fairly clear that motor development of swaddled children is not effectively retarded, although intellectual development might be.

However, it is the *personality* of the child which might be supposed most likely to be affected by early experiences typifying different cultures; and such evidence as is available favours the supposition. Strictures or permissiveness in upbringing in general, and in feeding habits and toilet training in particular, are thought to be markedly influential. Whiting and Child (1953) collated information about seventy-five primitive societies in order to test several specific hypotheses concerning personality development as a function of child-rearing practices. Cross-cultural investigations, and there have been several in recent years, have produced much factual and suggestive information; but such findings are too varied and often too controversial to be conclusively summarized.

Now many of the lines of investigation derive from psychoanalytic theory which attaches great importance to early experience, treating it as formative and crucial for personality development (see the useful summary in C. S. Hall, 1954). This chapter is not the place to discuss the speculative aspects of psychoanalytic thought; however, such thinking has given rise to experimentation aiming in part at testing specific aspects of Freudian theory. Perhaps somewhat surprisingly a great deal of work has been done with animals, no doubt partly because it is possible in laboratory studies to control closely the animals' early environment. Although such studies have not on the whole made it possible to confirm or refute conclusively many psychoanalytic tenets, they have added substantially to our knowledge of the lasting effects of early experience. Thus, mice have been studied in order to see whether single traumatic experiences, severe defeats for instance, would permanently influence the animals' behaviour. Experiments have also been carried out on mice to find out whether having to compete for food in infancy would influence the animals' behaviour at maturity. In fact, it turns out that severe defeat depresses the level of aggression later in life and that experience of competition raises it. However, perhaps the best-known studies are those which have set out to discover, using rats as subjects, whether frustration of the hunger drive in infancy would produce certain permanent 'personality' characteristics such as a tendency to hoard food. On the whole this proved to be so, even though research findings have tended to be somewhat equivocal (see Hunt *et al.*, 1947).

The mature individual, animal and human, has been moulded into what he is by the impact of his earlier experience upon his genetic make-up. Both specific early events and protracted early learning can be influential. The task of research is to discover all manner of lawful relationships between, on the one hand, happenings early in life and, on the other, later behaviour patterns in animals and in man. Work to this end may be said to have only just started. Our ignorance of the effects of early experience is still immense, but the prospects to all those engaged in this research are exciting.

Further reading
C. S. Hall, *A Primer of Freudian Psychology*, World Publishing Co., 1954.
G. Newton and S. Levine (eds.), *Early Experience and Behavior*, Charles C. Thomas, 1968.
J. P. Scott, *Early Experience and the Organization of Behavior*, Wadsworth, 1968.
W. Sluckin, *Imprinting and Early Learning*, Methuen, 1964.

Chapter 12
Learning

Generation by generation species adapt to changing conditions by natural selection. This adaptation includes the development of physiological bases for advantageous patterns of behaviour. An individual member of an animal species adapts to its environment mainly by learning how to cope with problems presented by changing conditions. Learning shows itself in modifications of behaviour, but many behavioural changes are the result of maturation or disease. Only adaptive and lasting changes, resulting from past experience and not due to maturation or disease, are ascribed to learning.

In common-sense terms, we learn when we get to know something we did not know before. To think of it this way focuses attention on the conscious aspect of experience. Learning may require following instructions, or it may need practice, or both. We learn when we acquire skills and habits – manipulative, intellectual, social. These are modifications of behaviour, generally, but not necessarily, accompanied by a consciousness of gaining knowledge or skill. We learn, in the broad sense of the word, most of the time when we are awake, whether or not we are actually aware of what is being learned.

Learning a subject at school, learning a motor skill such as riding a bicycle, learning how to behave well, learning to value money or to value friendship – how much in common have all these situations? Does the word 'learning' refer to some essential process or is it a label that points to a region of activities only vaguely delineated? It must be said that there is no real agreement among students of learning about such issues. Many of them, however, have attempted to describe and explain complex learning processes by reducing them to some prototype or prototypes of learning. These prototypes represent various learning situations that have seemed to be relatively simple and fundamental. Furthermore, these learning situations – Pavlovian conditioning, problem solving in animals, and some others, to be considered shortly – have been studied in minute detail. Again it must be said that such attempts at reducing complex learning to prototypical learning have not been crowned with unequivocal success. Nevertheless they have been highly illuminating and have been instrumental in advancing knowledge of learning processes.

To gain an understanding of learning we need not aim at well-rounded knowledge provided by a complete theory of learning. Theories there are in plenty and we shall briefly consider types of learning theory and some theoretical controversies later in this chapter. However, a view of learning may be adopted whereby varieties of learning situations are identified and the conditions that govern learning in these situations are specified (Gagné, 1967). Such an aim, if not very ambitious, is a practicable one. We cannot in this book set out to give a comprehensive survey of varieties and conditions of learning; we can and will, however, give a sample of learning situations that have been extensively studied. We shall begin with relatively simple learning, and then move on to more complex learning, the transfer of training and some theorizing about learning.

Simple learning situations

Classical conditioning

A training procedure, developed early in the century by Pavlov and extensively investigated since the 1920s has come to be known as classical conditioning. It may be noted that this type of learning was known in outline even before Pavlov's work; without the modern terminology, Jennings (1906) was able to describe such conditioning at some length. However, it was Pavlov who made a detailed study of it and constructed theories around it (see Pavlov, 1927). Classical conditioning is built upon *respondent behaviour*, as it is called by some writers, that is, reflexes which are directly elicited by certain stimuli. Pavlov used as a basis for conditioning the reflexive salivary response in the dog to the smell of food; other workers have used the pupillary reflex (contraction of the pupil in bright light), the knee jerk, sweating, nausea and so on. All such responses, occurring naturally, are called unconditioned (or unconditional) responses, known in technical literature as UCR or UR; stimuli which elicit such responses are described as unconditioned – in abbreviated form, UCS or US.

If some other stimulus, be it visual, auditory, olfactory, tactile, etc., is repeatedly presented at the same time as or shortly before some US, then this other stimulus will tend to acquire the power of evoking the response which initially could only be evoked by the US. In order to achieve this effect it may have to be co-presented with US anything from once to many hundreds of times. The stimulus thus co-presented with the US is called the conditioned stimulus, or CS. In this manner the sound of a bell, for instance, may be made to elicit salivation in a dog, or pupillary contraction in a human subject. The response to the CS is somewhat slower and weaker than that to US, and, so that we may distinguish it from UR, it is labelled CR, or conditioned response (sometimes called anticipatory or preparatory response).

The crucial feature of such training is that the conditioned and unconditioned stimuli are paired; the US reinforces the response to the CS. Without this *reinforcement*, the conditioned response would gradually become extinguished. *Experimental extinction* of CR may be deliberately achieved by providing it with no reinforcement. But such extinction is not necessarily permanent. After a time interval the conditioned response, that is, the response to CS, may make a reappearance, even though it is then weaker than directly after training. Such a reappearance of CR is described as *spontaneous recovery*.

Having been conditioned to respond to a given CS, the subject tends to generalize this response to other, similar stimuli; this is known as *stimulus generalization*. The more these other stimuli are like the CS, the stronger the CR; the relationship between the intensity of responses and the degree of similarity between new stimuli and the original CS is called the gradient of stimulus generalization. If the conditioned responses to the CS are reinforced, but the responses to a given stimulus similar to CS, which at first did evoke some responses, are not reinforced, then the subject will learn to discriminate between the two stimuli, responding to the former and not responding to the latter; this we call *stimulus discrimination*. The various features of conditioning just mentioned: reinforcement, extinction, recovery, generalization, discrimination, as well as several others, have been extensively investigated both in animals and man.

The original experiments in this field were based on the salivary reflex of the dog (see Pavlov, 1927). Later, other subjects as well as other types of response began to be used. Hovland (1937), for example, used human subjects; the US was a light electric shock to the subject's wrist, the UR to which is sweating; the magnitude of this response could be conveniently measured by electrical means because the more sweating the lower the skin resistance and, hence, the higher the galvanic skin response, or GSR (see Chapter 7). The CS in these experiments was a tone of a particular frequency which was paired a number of times with the electric shock to produce a CR to the sound of the tone, i.e. a GSR score. Using such procedures Hovland was able to demonstrate the necessity for reinforcement in conditioning, the extinction of the CR after the removal of reinforcement, spontaneous recovery of the CR, stimulus generalization to tones other than the one originally used (see Figure 48) and other features of conditioning.

Pavlov himself was interested in the physiological processes underlying conditioning. He postulated two complementary processes in the nervous system: *excitation*, as conditioned reflexes are formed, and *inhibition*, as responses to non-reinforced stimuli are prevented from occurring. According to this account, the spontaneous recovery of an unreinforced conditioned reflex would be due to a disinhibition of an inhibition. It is clear that this is no more than speculation; we are in a position to know with certainty some particular features of behaviour before, during and after conditioning but not the physiological functioning associated with these features.

To what extent does classical conditioning enter into everyday learning? There is some uncertainty about this, but it appears that many involuntary emotional responses are classically conditioned. Some students of behaviour believe that emotional responses of the autonomic nervous system become commonly associated with many initially neutral stimuli. Thus, fear, for instance, may easily come to be attached to any number of visual or auditory, or even tactile or olfactory, features of the environment (see, for example, Eysenck, 1964a). This could be the explanation of various common irrational phobias (see Eysenck and Rachman, 1965).

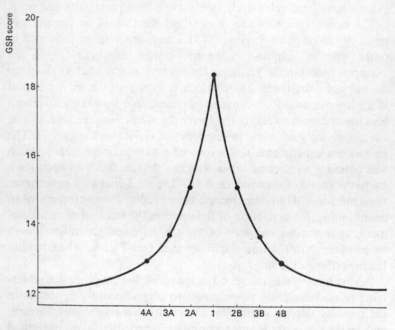

Figure 48   Stimulus generalization. Response was conditioned to stimulus 1 ; responses to other stimuli – tones of frequencies below and above CS – were progressively weaker as the stimuli diverged from CS. (After Hovland, 1937, p. 136)

At any rate, it has certainly been shown that some kinds of abnormal behaviour can be the result of conditioning experiences. Pavlov and his collaborators demonstrated experimental neuroses in dogs trained to make impossible discriminations. In one study, a dog was first conditioned to salivate when it saw a circle but not when it saw an ellipse. Then the difference between the two figures was gradually reduced until the dog's power of discrimination failed him. The behaviour of the animal then changed sharply: the dog squealed, barked and became violent. Animals under such conditions appear to be in a state of conflict over whether or not to respond. The ensuing breakdown of normal behaviour has been described as an experimental neurosis; but it is uncertain whether this type of breakdown can usefully be compared with any form of human neurotic behaviour.

Instrumental conditioning

Instrumental conditioning (known also as instrumental learning) is a training procedure which occurs frequently in everyday situations. It is normally built upon *operant behaviour*, to be distinguished from respondent behaviour mentioned earlier. Operant behaviour is 'emitted' by the organism, rather than elicited by any particular stimuli; it simply is the normal repertoire of the subject's activities. Instrumental conditioning consists of rewarding and/or punishing some acts and not other acts, thereby 'shaping up' behaviour in certain directions. This occurs as the rewarded acts tend to be stamped in and the punished ones stamped out. Roughly speaking, this tendency is what E. L. Thorndike (1911) called the 'law of effect'.

A particular instrumental training procedure developed by B. F. Skinner is known as operant conditioning; see Skinner (1938). Training of this kind involves the use of the Skinner box; this contains some simple mechanism which may be operated to deliver a limited amount of food or water. Such a box made for small mammals, commonly the rat, has a lever which the animal learns to press in order to obtain a pellet of food or a drop of milk; a box made for birds, usually the pigeon, has a disc which the bird learns to peck to obtain some grain. If the required response is not made, no reward is forthcoming. Thus the reward reinforces the response.

As reinforcement follows a particular feature of operant behaviour, this feature is produced more and more frequently; it is thus acquired or learned. Whereas in classical conditioning the unconditioned stimulus is the reinforcement, in instrumental conditioning the reinforcing stimulus is one that is associated with, and *follows*, some particular response, which initially is only one of the many responses within the organism's repertoire. If, after the operant response has been acquired, the reinforcement is no longer provided, then the response will gradually disappear. Behaviour extinguished in this way will, however, recover spontaneously to some extent after a time interval during which the subject has been away from the conditioning situation.

Whether the removal of reinforcement will result in a rapid or very slow extinction depends on the conditions of initial training. A number of experimental studies have shown that when some, but not all, occurrences of the requisite response are reinforced then, even though learning is slower, it is much more resistant to extinction. See, for instance, the findings of Jenkins and Rigby (1950) concerning the extinction of lever pressing in rats trained with *partial reinforcement* (see also Figure 49). Such intermittent rewarding occurs frequently in everyday situations; some of the most strongly established habits arise from learning under inconsistent reinforcement. Operant conditioning procedures have been developed using several different schedules of reinforcement, each having its particular effects; these schedules are discussed in great detail by Ferster and Skinner (1957).

The Skinner box is only one of many possible situations in which instrumental conditioning may be studied. Another one is the T-maze; in this simple maze the animal coming up to the T-junction faces a choice between turning to the right and turning to the left. The reward is to be found at the end of only one of the two arms. The animal learns by trial and error which way to turn and it may take it a few or a great many trials before it invariably makes the correct turn. In this situation the subject is instrumentally conditioned to make what is termed position discrimination. However, discrimination learning more often involves learning to choose one of two patterns, or one of two colours, entirely irrespective of their position.

Operant learning and discrimination learning described above are forms of reward training. Other instrumental conditioning procedures are avoidance training, omission training and punishment training (see Hilgard and Marquis, 1961). Avoidance training teaches the subject to respond to a signal in some particular way and thereby prevent a noxious stimulus from appearing. Omission training teaches the subject not to respond to certain stimuli by rewarding it for not so responding. Punishment training involves the punishment of the subject in some manner for certain acts; we shall consider further the role of punishment in learning later in this chapter.

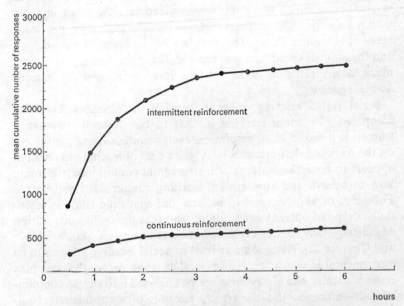

Figure 49 Rate of extinction in pigeons after intermittent and continuous reinforcement. Pigeons showed slower response extinction after intermittent than after continuous reinforcement. (After Jenkins, McFann and Clayton, 1950, p. 158)

Some procedures combine two or more of these types of training. For instance, the Yerkes box for learning position discrimination may provide a reward for the animal for taking one of the two paths and a punishment in the form of electric shock for taking the other. In the Lashley discrimination apparatus for training rats to choose between differently patterned cards, the animal is made to jump off a stand on to one of the two cards in front of it; jumping one way results in hitting an immovable card and falling into a net – a punishment of sorts – and jumping the other way shifts a card so that the animal lands on a platform and obtains its reward, usually a quantity of food.

An animal may readily be trained to make several correct choices in sequence, that is, to learn to run a maze. Mazes have been used in studies of animal learning since the beginning of the century. The original maze which white rats were trained to solve was contained within a six- by eight-foot rectangle and was modelled on the hedge maze in Hampton Court. The goal box of the maze contained food and the animals could be tested repeatedly for their ability to run the maze. Many different maze patterns have been used for various animal species.

Serial verbal learning, such as learning the alphabet, has been compared with maze learning in that in both situations what is learned is a sequence of responses, each response being contingent on the response that precedes it. A great deal of learning in children appears to have the features of instrumental conditioning: learning how to behave and how not to, learning simple skills and so on. Followers of Skinner tend to believe that academic study is essentially a type of operant conditioning and that the child's acquisition of language may also be explained in these terms (see Skinner, 1957; and Chapter 15). Also, some at least of social learning appears to be instrumental in character. However, that is not to say that complex human learning can always or often be analysed into simple component acts which exhibit the typical features of instrumental conditioning.

Indeed, relatively complex learning in animals, such as solving mazes, cannot readily be analysed into elementary instrumental acts, even though such learning may be put into the category of instrumental reward training, very broadly interpreted. It was suggested at one time that, in finding the way to the goal, an animal learns a chain of specific responses to specific stimuli at each junction within the maze. It later became clear, however, that animals do not just blindly learn series of muscular movements; an animal, like a human being, learns the topography of a maze and, having learned the layout, the animal can solve the maze whether it requires running or swimming or wading to the goal box (see Macfarlane, 1930; Restle, 1957).

Exposure learning

Although classical and instrumental conditioning differ in many ways, they are somewhat alike, especially in that they both unquestionably require reinforcement. There are, however, some experimental findings which indicate that learning, as distinct from the performance of what has been learned, does not necessarily depend on conventional reinforcement. Moreover, there is evidence to suggest that the exposure of the organism to sensory stimulation may in itself result in some learning. Whether we take the view that such exposure learning requires no reinforcement, or is self-reinforced, or is reinforced in some special way, depends in part on how we define the term 'reinforcement' which is not beyond controversy; we shall return later to this difficulty of definition.

Consider, to start with, a conditioning process whereby a subject learns to respond to, say, a particular sound – an initially neutral stimulus. Consider, further, a procedure prior to the classical conditioning whereby the sound is repeatedly presented to the subject together with another neutral stimulus, say, a light; such a procedure is known as *sensory pre-conditioning*. Now if after both some pre-conditioning and the conditioning sessions, the subject is tested with the light only, it may be found that it responds to the light, albeit weakly, even though no specific training to respond to it has been given (see review of such studies in Hilgard and Marquis, 1961). In our hypothetical experiment, the ability to respond to the sound alone is the result of conditioning; but the ability to respond to the light alone is the result of pre-conditioning or exposure of the organism to certain stimuli occurring together with those which are later conditioned. Thus, post-conditioning tests may be said to reveal the occurrence of some exposure contiguity learning prior to conditioning.

The effects of sensory exposure to relevant stimuli before actual training may be readily detected in many learning situations; such effects have been extensively investigated in animals learning to run mazes. In the usual experimental situations animals improve at running mazes if they are motivated to do so; thirsty rats will learn a maze if rewarded with water at the end of each trial run, hungry rats, if rewarded with food, and so on. Unmotivated, unreinforced animals do not show any overt learning. But, if just allowed to explore the maze, they nevertheless do learn it, although such learning is not immediately manifest. That the animals benefit from having been exposed to the environment becomes clear when they are properly trained to run the maze. Animals with prior experience of the maze learn it much more quickly than those without such experience. This was clearly demonstrated in such early experiments as those of Blodgett (1929) and Tolman and Honzik (1930). Such learning without reinforcement – learning which is inferred from subsequent behaviour – is known as *latent learning*, sometimes also called incidental learning (although the latter term is also used in a somewhat different sense to denote learning, in humans, which occurs without the intention to learn).

Learning resulting from sensory experience may show itself in yet other ways, especially in the young of precocial species of birds, and possibly mammals. Such learning, considered in Chapter 11, goes by the name of imprinting. It involves the learning of the characteristics of figures to which the young organism is exposed, i.e. the acquisition of the ability to discriminate between familiar and strange sensory stimulation. Imprinting, or the formation of attachments without conventional rewards, is of course procedurally different from classical conditioning or instrumental learning. We may take the view that behind this actual acquisition process there may be some form of exposure learning, that is, a modification of a disposition or potentiality for overt action.

Specific attachments are one possible result of exposure to fellow-beings. Another is imitation or *observational learning*. Here the subject does nothing to start with other than observe another, the *model*, doing something. Later, as a result of this experience, he may perform a sequence of responses made earlier by the model. For the subject, as distinct from the model, these are new responses which, not having occurred previously, could never have been reinforced. During the first two decades of this century the reality of observational learning in animals was much debated. Some workers claimed to have demonstrated it, but E. L. Thorndike and the early behaviourists denied that animals were capable of true imitation. Warden and Jackson (1935) showed conclusively that under certain conditions monkeys may perform better on selected tasks when given the opportunity to observe the successes and failures of models (demonstrators) on these tasks. More recent animal studies have confirmed the effectiveness of observational learning in animals, although the interpretation of such studies is sometimes in doubt (see K. R. L. Hall, 1963). Studies of children point in the same direction (see, for instance, Bandura, 1962). Observational or vicarious learning in children is discussed in some detail in connexion with social learning in Chapter 22.

Special problems of learning

How is the affection of a child for his mother acquired? It could be through classical conditioning – the sight of mother is a signal for food, and as such is valued. It could be through instrumental conditioning – the child's affection for his mother is well rewarded by the care and love she gives the child. It could be through imprinting – the child gets attached to his mother who is the most familiar figure in the child's environment. It could be all these things at once and more besides. Much that is learned in life cannot be ascribed without uncertainty to one or another of the known training methods. Does this mean that we cannot readily gain any understanding of everyday learning? Not at all; learning can be profitably studied in ways other than reductionist. Learning processes can be investigated to elucidate the various factors that help and hinder acquisition. Problems concerning learning may be stated, conceptually clarified and then tackled experimentally. In this section we shall consider some such problems.

Reinforcement

The term 'reinforcement' is not unambiguous. It is sometimes used to mean a *process* – the (hypothetical) strengthening of a response tendency, which can be measured by an increase in the frequency or probability of occurrence of that response. Thus, a response has been reinforced if it has become more likely to occur. In a somewhat different sense reinforcement may be used to denote a *technique* adopted by the experimenter: reinforcement of a response is the application of a *reinforcer* – some stimulus event which is expected to have the result of increasing the probability of the response which precedes it. For example, food administered to a hungry rat when it presses a lever in the Skinner box is a reinforcer because its administration increases the likelihood of the lever-pressing response. In this sense the US in classical conditioning can be regarded as a reinforcer, even though it precedes the response it reinforces; generally speaking, however, a reinforcer can be defined as 'a member of a class of events which, when they follow a response, strengthen the tendency for that response to occur' (Hill, 1963). Thus, whether reinforcement is defined in terms of a strengthening process or in terms of a training procedure, it is tautologous to say that reinforcement of a response increases its probability of occurrence, since this must be so by definition.

A few investigators have defined reinforcement, rather differently, simply as the presentation of a stimulus which provides the opportunity for learning. For example, in paired-associate learning, where the subject's task is to produce the second item of a pair when the first is presented alone as a stimulus, any presentation of both stimulus and response items together constitutes a 'reinforcement'; presentation of the stimulus item alone constitutes a 'test' (Estes, 1950).

Given that reinforcement is generally defined in terms of its consequences for behaviour, can we say anything more about the nature of reinforcers? Many investigators and theorists of learning have sought other respects in which reinforcers are alike, so that the characteristics of reinforcement can be more clearly understood. It has often been claimed that reinforcers serve to *reduce drive*, and that it is the reduction of drive associated with a response which increases its frequency. Some reinforcers, such as food and water, clearly can be thus described. Others, such as money for human subjects, might be described as having acquired reinforcing value through their association with primary drive reduction: these are sometimes called secondary reinforcers. In yet other cases, however, it is difficult to trace an association between drive reduction and an event which appears to be reinforcing – when, for example, exposure learning occurs or when people take up hobbies demanding the acquisition of knowledge and skills. Again, reinforcers can be described as *rewarding*: a definition which, apart from its appeal to common sense, is almost if not quite circular.

Alternatively, some theorists have claimed that the function of reinforcers is less to reward than to inform the responding subject, to manipulate his attention to various aspects of the learning situation, or to alter the learning situation to such an extent that the responses acquired in it are 'preserved' from the interference which might result from further responding in the same situation. Finally, it has been argued that different kinds of learning may involve different kinds of reinforcement and thus of reinforcers (see, for example, Hill, 1963; Mowrer, 1960a). It is, consequently, not easy to avoid circularity in the description of reinforcers; ultimately, what such events have in common is their effect upon behaviour.

Certain qualifications should be added here. In the first place, we have discussed reinforcement in terms of an increase in response probability; but some procedures may have the effect of decreasing, rather than increasing, the occurrence of associated responses. Further, certain procedures which on other grounds one might expect to decrease response probability may in fact increase it. These possibilities will be further discussed in the following section concerned with punishment.

Finally, while reinforcers are generally held to be externally applied stimuli whose effect is mediated by sensory reception, there is evidence that *direct electrical stimulation* in some parts of the brain may constitute positive reinforcement, in that animals will make responses which result in such stimulation. In other areas of the brain electrical stimulation may be negatively reinforcing, in that animals will make responses which avoid it.

Olds and Milner (1954) placed electrodes in various parts of the brain such that by pressing a lever, animals (in this case, rats) could deliver a brief burst of current to the part of the brain where the tip of the electrode was located. They compared the number of bar pressings when the current was turned off with the level when the current was turned on. With electrodes in some areas of the brain whether the current was on or off made little difference to the rate of bar pressing. However, with electrodes placed in other brain areas the rats learned to press the bar more and more rapidly.

In the same year, Delgado, Roberts and Miller (1954) found that brain stimulation could serve as punishment in a learning situation, that is, animals (in this case cats) would perform a variety of responses to avoid such stimulation. In the usual avoidance situation animals learn to avoid peripheral stimulation, for example, an electric shock to the feet, but, in general, there appears to be little difference between the rate of acquisition of avoidance responses to peripheral or central stimulation. Those areas which are positively reinforcing are principally areas of the midbrain, most of the hypothalamus, parts of the thalamus and the septal area. From the hypothalamus in particular an extremely high rate of bar pressing (as much as 8000 per hour) can be obtained and this can continue for periods of twenty-four hours or more, until the animal is exhausted. The placements which are negatively reinforcing appear to be in the reticular system and parts of the thalamus. In addition there are areas in which stimulation appears to be neither positively reinforcing nor negatively reinforcing and areas which are both. In this section we shall consider only positive reinforcement.

Although the majority of the work on the positively reinforcing effects of electrical self-stimulation has been performed with rats, similar effects have been produced in cats and monkeys, and human beings report feelings of pleasure when stimulated in these areas (Heath, 1955). Animals will also cross an electrically charged grid from which they receive a painful electric shock to obtain electrical stimulation of the brain and they will withstand a stronger shock to obtain electrical stimulation than they will to reach food when hungry (Olds, 1961). In general, stimulation of the brain seems to produce effects which are stronger than those produced by 'natural' reinforcing agents, such as food and water.

There are thus some similarities between the effects of electrical self-stimulation and those of 'natural' reinforcers, and the results of self-stimulation experiments have been taken as support for hedonistic theories of motivation and reward. However, there are also some important differences between the effects of the two kinds of reinforcement, natural and electrical. First, as already mentioned, little or no satiation of the drive for brain stimulation occurs: animals continue bar pressing to obtain brain stimulation until they are exhausted and the rate of bar pressing does not appreciably deteriorate. For habits based on food or water rewards, the rate of responding slows down when an animal has received enough food or water.

Second, very rapid extinction of the bar-pressing response takes place when brain stimulation is used as reinforcement. That is, if the current is turned off, bar pressing ceases almost immediately, whereas when food or water is used as reinforcement the rate of responding slows down gradually before ceasing altogether. Linked to extinction studies are studies of different reinforcement schedules in which, instead of receiving brain stimulation every time the response is made, the animal receives reinforcement intermittently. For example, an animal may be given reinforcement at regular intervals – say, every two minutes – regardless of its rate of response; this procedure is termed *fixed interval reinforcement*. Again, an animal may be reinforced after, say, every seventh occurrence of the response – *fixed ratio reinforcement*. Animals who are reinforced with food will respond at very high fixed ratios, for example, 100 unreinforced responses to one response reinforced; but for animals reinforced with electrical stimulation the ratios have to be much lower unless the animal is very carefully trained. Similarly, the time between successive reinforcements of food and water can be quite long and the animal will still keep responding, whereas in the case of electrical stimulation if the interval extends much over fifteen seconds the animal ceases to respond. It thus appears that the drive for electrical stimulation of the brain decays extremely rapidly when the animal is not receiving stimulation.

The third main difference concerns secondary reinforcement. Secondary reinforcement can be demonstrated in situations where a neutral stimulus, such as a tone, is paired with a primary reinforcer such as food or electric shock; in such cases the neutral stimulus alone comes to produce the same (positive or negative) effects upon behaviour as the primary reinforcer. But in general secondary reinforcement has been difficult to demonstrate using brain stimulation as a primary reinforcer. There is some evidence for it, but the evidence is not entirely free from other interpretations (see Gallistel, 1964).

It is not clear why the effects of electrical self-stimulation should in some respects resemble, and in others differ from, those of 'natural' reinforcers; for a theoretical account of the possible relation between self-stimulation effects and the neurological bases of drive and reinforcement, see Deutsch (1960) and Gallistel (1964).

Learning and punishment

We have said earlier that punished acts tend to be stamped out. This is perhaps a simple view, but one prompted by everyday observation of the way in which animals and children appear to learn. Are we, then, justified in thinking that punishment generally helps learning? The answer which emerges from empirical investigations is that it 'all depends'; that is, one general answer will not do. Whether punishment is conducive to learning or otherwise has much to do with the type of learning situation in question. Let us, therefore, turn to factual studies of different learning situations.

E. L. Thorndike (1932), well known for his researches into animal learning, subsequently investigated human verbal learning and reported that punishment in the form of criticism did not speed up the acquisition process. He used subjects who knew no Spanish, and presented them repeatedly with a Spanish word together with five English words. The subject's task was to guess which English word was equivalent to the Spanish one; and on giving a response, the subject would be told whether he was right or wrong. It was found, as might be expected, that the correct or rewarded responses tended to be repeated on later occasions whenever the subject was tested on the full list of 200 words; however, there was no tendency for the incorrect, punished response to disappear. Thus, the probability of reappearance of a given response increased when the response was awarded, but did not decrease when it was punished – a somewhat unexpected asymmetry of reward and punishment effects.

Thorndike's study proved influential. On the one hand, many educationalists began to take the view that punishment was unhelpful in school learning. On the other hand, experimentalists were stimulated to examine more closely the conditions under which punishment was ineffective. Tilton (1939) carried out under strict controls an experiment with nonsense syllables and found that rewarded items tended to be retained while punished ones were eliminated; thus, both reward and punishment were helpful in the learning of lists, and so common sense seemed to prevail again. Having later surveyed the research in this field, Postman (1962) concluded that 'sheer frequency of repetition produces only small amounts of learning', that 'reward reliably strengthens stimulus–response connexions and is the single most powerful determinant of learning', and that 'punishment does not weaken connexions directly: whatever beneficial effects punishment does have must be attributed to the variability of behavior produced by annoyers, which in turn leads to the substitution and reinforcement of correct responses' (p. 396).

While verbal reinforcement, such as saying 'right' or 'wrong', tends to have certain effects on the learning of lists of words or syllables, it could have somewhat different effects in the learning of concepts. This indeed was found to be the case by Buss and Buss (1956). In a series of experiments concerned with perceptual learning of concepts, these workers found that saying 'wrong' for the incorrect responses, and doing nothing in the case of correct ones, was an effective method of learning. It was more conducive to learning than saying 'right' for correct responses and saying nothing for the incorrect ones.

Nevertheless the ineffectiveness of punishment in some human learning situations has often been confirmed; and ineffectiveness has also been shown to prevail in some types of learning in animals. Estes (1944) reported an experiment in which rats were trained in a Skinner box to press a lever to obtain food. The experimental animals were then shocked whenever they pressed the lever; the control animals just received no reward. It was found that the punished group retained the response longer than the control group. Here punishment, far from suppressing responses, actually helped the retention of what had been learned.

Paradoxically, then, punishment can sometimes be rewarding. This can occur, for example, when electric shock has become firmly associated with food. In such circumstances the animal can learn discriminations for the secondary reward of shock. Human beings sometimes appear to seek punishment as if it were rewarding; and perhaps it can be in providing much sought after attention. But apart from such complications, punishment is the one instrument of learning in avoidance training, mentioned earlier. And a very effective instrument it is, for avoidance training has been found to be remarkably long-lasting after even a few punishing trials (Masserman, 1943; Solomon, Kamin and Wynne, 1953).

The belief that punishment is of doubtful value in learning is surprisingly widespread. Solomon (1964) has questioned 'persisting legends concerning the ineffectiveness of punishment as an agent for behavioral change', and also 'the inevitability of the neurotic outcome' of punishing procedures. Likewise, Church (1963), while surveying the varied effects of punishment, concludes that responses are very effectively suppressed in the presence of noxious (punishing) stimuli whenever these stimuli are directly associated with the responses; in simple words, we learn well from our own mistakes. And further, the closer the time of punishment is to the response, the more marked is the suppression; that is, punishment is best when it is immediate. However, the effects of punishment cannot be predicted without taking into account additional factors in the situation: the restrictiveness/permissiveness of the prior régime, the consistency/inconsistency of previous punishing acts, etc. It may fairly be said that punishment of specific acts is effective in learning, but general punitiveness is not (Marshall, 1965; Sears, Maccoby and Levin, 1957).

Mediating processes in learning

A great deal of human learning involves understanding what is being learned and thinking about it. Sometimes animals, too, behave as if they had some *insight* into the situation to which they are adapting. Köhler (1925) observed chimpanzees learning to pile up boxes on top of one another, or join sticks together, in a seemingly intelligent manner, in order to solve specific problems. Tolman (1939) reported *vicarious trial-and-error behaviour* in rats, 'crouching to jump at one door and then crouching before the other door, before finally jumping'; and rapid learning by rats tended to be preceded by such symbolic trial-and-error demeanour.

Human beings are aided in their learning by images, or ideas, or symbolic representations of sensory experiences. Much animal learning appears to be reflexive, or sense-dominated; but some of it decidedly looks as if it involved some symbolic processes – for example, problem-solving behaviour or observational learning. This type of evidence will be briefly discussed in Chapter 16. Although we have no means of knowing anything about such symbolic processes directly, we must presume them to intervene between stimulation and action. They are often described as *mediating processes*. In human beings, symbolic representations may likewise be regarded as mediating between sensory experiences and behaviour that is not under the sole control of sensory events.

The units, as it were, of mediation are specific mediating responses. We may distinguish between two sorts of such responses: the stimulus-producing and the observing (Hill, 1963).

By *stimulus-producing responses* are meant responses whose role in a behavioural sequence is to provide stimuli for further responses; Hull (1943) called such responses 'pure stimulus acts' and several theoreticians of learning have employed this or similar notions in explaining behaviour. There is, for example, a traditional distinction between *immediate* and *mediate* associations, particularly with reference to verbal associations (for a general discussion, see Jenkins, 1963). If we suppose, from various kinds of prior evidence, that a stimulus item A is associated with another item B; if we then require subjects to learn an association between another item, C, and item A, and then require them to learn an association between item C and item B, there will almost certainly be *facilitation* in the learning of the association C → B. The association C → A has been learned; the association A → B has been inferred already to exist; thus both prior associations *mediate* the acquisition of the new association C → B. We may suppose that item C, presented as a stimulus, evokes the response A, and that the response A *mediates* the production of response B, by serving as a stimulus for its evocation.

The notion of mediation has also been relevant in describing conditioning. For example, Hull (1943) hypothesized that when a stimulus complex is associated with a response complex, certain portions of the response complex tend to become *anticipatory* (basically via some form of stimulus generalization; we shall not be concerned with possible mechanisms here). If, for example, a rat is trained to run a maze for food, some of the feeding responses which occur in the goal box will become conditioned to maze stimuli which occur earlier in the maze-running sequence. Clearly, not all feeding responses can become anticipatory in this way, since some require the presence of food, while others would interfere with maze running, would therefore not be *reinforced* and would therefore be *extinguished*. Thus, only fractional parts of the 'goal reaction' become anticipatory: responses which do not interfere with the activity needed to reach the goal and which are light-weight in terms of energy expenditure. Nevertheless, such responses are *distinctive* to the goal reactions which they represent. They have *proprioceptive consequences*, and the proprioceptive perception of such responses can serve as a *cue* or stimulus for (and thus *mediate*) specific further responses. To stay with our example, maze stimuli at any point in the maze-running sequence may produce fractional anticipatory responses, specific to the final goal response, which provide a stimulus for the continuation (and appropriate variation) of the 'running' response sequence.

It must be stressed that 'mediating responses', and the 'mediated stimulation' to which they give rise, are hypothetical events. Sometimes an overt response can be seen as mediating further responses by its proprioceptive consequences – for example, in the *internal feedback* involved in much skilled performance (see Chapter 13). More often, what is meant by mediating response is some more or less implicit internal representational response which may be muscular, glandular, subvocal (in the case of humans possessing a language system) or even purely neural; it is impossible within so broad a specification to predict and test the occurrence of a mediating response in a specific situation. The notion of mediation has nevertheless been used quite widely to extend essentially stimulus–response (S–R) explanations of learning, and more generally of behaviour; for example, in explaining the phenomena of set and the acquisition and functioning of secondary drives, and in the analysis of meaning and purpose. For accounts, see Hill (1963) and Osgood (1953); we shall also refer again to the notions of mediation and internal representation in Chapter 16.

Mediating responses of the other sort are *observing responses* involved in paying attention. These responses are thought to underlie the *acquisition of distinctiveness of cues*, or learning to which cues in a given type of situation attention should be given. Such acquisition occurs frequently in everyday life, but can also be demonstrated in animal learning in the laboratory when a subject has to learn which aspects of a situation are crucial and which are incidental. Thus, observing responses are presumed to occur when an animal learns – to give examples – that moving a particular object regardless of its position is always rewarded, or that touching an object on the right regardless of its nature is punished and so on. Such learning depends in some way on a process known as transfer, and before we return to this subject of learning principles, we must consider the elementary facts and rules of transfer.

Transfer of training

Our interest in learning goes beyond the study of either acts of simple learning or the learning of complex tasks in isolation from one another. Indeed, a great deal of study has been devoted to the influence of one act of learning upon another, that is, to the transfer of learning from one task to another task. The general problem is one of assessing the benefit which is derived from past experience – what value has education, for instance, in preparing the child for adulthood. We may ask how useful is industrial or military training which, of necessity, is only up to a point concerned with tasks which will be tackled later. We may wonder whether one set of acquired emotional attitudes carries over to new processes of attitude acquisition. In order to attempt to answer such questions it is necessary to start at the root of the problem of transfer.

Our basic concern is the interaction between different learning tasks. Let us call the earlier task A, and the later task B. *Positive transfer* from A to B is said to occur when learning A facilitates learning B. *Negative transfer* from A to B is said to occur when learning A hinders learning B. To what extent do the two forms of transfer occur in everyday situations? There is evidence that there is some positive transfer of training in such activities as sport and in the acquisition of some manual skills; there is also positive transfer from some intellectual tasks to some other intellectual tasks. Negative transfer, too, occurs quite commonly – in general, when two tasks are superficially similar, though requiring, in fact, quite different responses.

Interaction between different learning tasks may also show itself in the way in which learning one thing affects the *retention* of another. Effects of this kind are known as retroaction and proaction, and are dealt with in Chapter 14. It should be noted that one of the tests of retention is delayed recall; one of the tests of learning attainment is immediate recall. Thus, since the dividing line between immediate and delayed recall is somewhat arbitrary, transfer phenomena cannot always be easily separated from phenomena of memory.

Certain rules of transfer may be given in terms of the stimulus and response elements of the learning tasks between which transfer is possible. Consider a task such as learning the meaning of a number of words in a foreign language; here we have a list of foreign words and their English equivalents such that the former are stimulus words and the latter response words. Or think of the task of assembling, say, an electrical instrument: the sight of each stage of the task is a stimulus, and the next step in the assembly is a response to this stimulus.

Suppose, then, that an individual has to learn two such tasks in turn, first A and then B. If the stimuli of A and B are quite different, and so are the responses in A and B, then there will be no transfer, either positive or negative. There is a proviso here: there will be no transfer of specific learning but there may be some positive transfer of general information. This was shown to be so in some studies of human subjects in early experiments reviewed by Woodworth and Schlosberg (1954); these showed some 'transfer through principles' even where the two tasks had no 'identical components'. Transfer of principles or 'learning how to learn' has also been observed in monkeys coping with simple discrimination problems (Harlow,

1949). Such *learning sets* – as this type of transfer has been called – have more recently been shown in mammals as lowly as the opossum (Friedman and Marshall, 1965).

When a person learns two tasks, A and B, the stimuli of which are different and the responses are alike, then the transfer from A to B will tend to be positive, especially in non-verbal tasks. Furthermore, the less dissimilar the stimuli, the more pronounced will be the transfer. In other words, whenever old responses have to be attached to new stimuli, transfer is positive; and this is especially so when the stimuli are similar, this situation bearing the character of stimulus generalization.

Lastly, when one learns first A and then B such that the stimuli in the two tasks are the same but the responses are different, then the transfer from A to B is negative. The second learning task disturbs an established habit of responding in a particular way, and tends to give the subject a sense of confusion. If, for example, task A consists of learning to ride a motor-cycle and task B is learning to drive a car, then there will be some positive transfer of 'road sense', but also some negative transfer owing to the fact that the same signals call in the two tasks for different manipulative responses, hand-twist acceleration in A, foot-pedal acceleration in B. Likewise, negative transfer may occur if a person has to learn first a list of English–Spanish and than a list of English–Italian words, the English words being the same both times.

The situations mentioned above are relatively simple ones. Transfer phenomena are being extensively studied in a number of fields, and in the next chapter more will be said about transfer in connexion with skills, while in Chapter 14, proaction and retroaction will be considered at some length.

Theorizing about learning

We started this chapter by wondering how much in common the various learning situations have. This problem – whether there is a central feature which characterizes all learning, whether there is basically a single kind of learning or several kinds – is one that has exercised learning theorists for some time. In particular, there have been advocates of the view that conditioning is essentially one, as well as those who have maintained that there are two different types of conditioning, classical and instrumental. This particular controversy is surveyed and the latter view is cogently argued in terms of the available experimental evidence by Rescorla and Solomon (1967).

However, this is by no means the only, or the most important, controversy in the field of learning theory. Learning theorists do not speak with one voice about the role of drives, or incentives, or rewards, and, as implied earlier, about the role of punishment in learning. And there is as much disagreement about the importance of practice and of understanding and insight in the learning process. Students of learning have striven to produce theories that are both all-embracing and fully consistent with the factual knowledge of learning phenomena. However, more than one theory appears to meet well these desiderata; and yet, all the theories cannot be equally valid.

The difficulty is that the different theories approach the problems of learning from quite different angles. An example of this is the cleavage between stimulus–response theories and cognitive theories (Hilgard and Bower, 1966). The former tend to assume that learning has to do with the chaining of responses; the latter lay stress on 'central' processes. Again, s–r theories regard learning as essentially an acquisition of habits, whereas cognitive theories are concerned with changes in 'cognitive structures'. Now we cannot choose between these approaches by referring to crucial observations or experiments. The competing theories can 'explain' all factual findings, albeit in different terms.

The classification of learning theories into s–r and cognitive ones is only one possible way of grouping them. Another, to give an example, is according to whether the theory is at all concerned with 'intermediaries', that is, with factors intermediate between stimulus and response variables, and if so, with what kind. Skinner (1950) has argued against intermediary concepts, and indeed, against broadly conceived learning theories, However, other approaches find it necessary to postulate some *intervening variables* or some *hypothetical constructs* (MacCorquodale and Meehl, 1948). Very briefly, intervening variables are constants of measurement, expressed in mathematical symbols, which relate observable phenomena but have no independent existence. Hypothetical constructs, on the other hand, are inferred intermediaries which could prove to be real. Thus, a theory might postulate certain qualities of the nervous system which facilitate learning. Only further research would then show which, if any, of such qualities are actual. It is also worth noting that the same term can sometimes be given either status. *Inhibition*, for example, is in Pavlov's sense a hypothetical construct, since it is used to denote brain processes which might be independently observed; the same term is used by Hull in a purely formal sense, to denote an intervening variable by means of which stimulus and response variables might be mathematically related.

Enough, perhaps, has been said to indicate how recondite the theoretical issues of learning can be. Theories of learning are ingenious and may be intensely interesting. They give hope of a deeper understanding of learning processes, but being largely irreconcilable, they have disillusioned many. The trend in more recent years has been to be somewhat sceptical of theories that claim a measure of completeness (Drever, 1961). On the other hand, theories with a limited scope and concerned with explaining particular learning processes, for example, discrimination learning in animals, vicarious learning in children and so on, are most valuable. They inter-relate items of knowledge and they provide guide posts for further empirical research.

Further reading
R. C. Birney and R. C. Teevan (eds.), *Reinforcement*, Van Nostrand, 1961.
R. M. Gagné, *The Conditions of Learning*, Holt, Rinehart & Winston, 1967.
E. R. Hilgard and G. H. Bower, *Theories of Learning*, Appleton-Century-Crofts, 1966.
E. R. Hilgard and D. G. Marquis, *Conditioning and Learning*, Methuen, 1961.
F. A. Logan and A. R. Wagner, *Reward and Punishment*, Allyn & Bacon, 1965.

Chapter 13
Skilled Performance

Introduction

The term 'skilled' refers to the manner in which a particular task or activity is performed. It implies both adroitness and a practised ease of execution. In everyday language, we use the word to describe performance in a variety of situations: social, intellectual, linguistic, political, artistic and so on; but in this chapter we shall restrict our attention to those types of activity generally subsumed under the heading of *sensory–motor performance*.

For reasons that we shall set out below, it is skilled sensory–motor performance of the type involved in operating a lathe or an anti-aircraft gun, flying an aeroplane or driving a car, that has attracted the greatest amount of experimental research. As a consequence, it is in this region that we have achieved our clearest understanding of the fundamental characteristics of human skill. However, as we shall see in the final section of this chapter, information obtained from the study of skilled sensory–motor performance has been useful in elucidating the basic processes involved in other types of skilled activity, particularly those involved in thought and language.

Although skilled performance has long been of interest to the psychologist (see, for example, the classic studies of Bryan and Harter, 1897, 1899), the main impetus for the study of skilled sensory–motor performance, like a great deal of contemporary psychological research, came from the military and economic pressures of the Second World War. People had to acquire new skills and acquire them quickly. Civilians were needed to take on highly skilled military activities and, on the home front, more skilled industrial labour was required to fill the vacancies created by the rapidly expanding armed forces. Moreover, it soon became apparent that our existing knowledge of sensory–motor performance based, on the one hand, upon simple reaction time studies and investigations into the formation of simple habits, and on the other hand, upon our industrial experiences with such techniques as time-and-motion study, was an inadequate basis for understanding the complex skills needed in modern warfare. Consequently, research organizations were set up in universities and government departments with the urgent task of investigating the fundamental characteristics of human skill and of devising suitable training and selection methods. A great deal of our present-day understanding of skilled behaviour is due to this wartime research, particularly to that initiated by Sir Frederic Bartlett and his associates at Cambridge.

The remainder of the chapter will be divided into four sections. The first is 'task-oriented' rather than 'operator-oriented' and is concerned with the basic characteristics of the sensory–motor task. The next two sections are devoted to skilled operation. The second section is concerned with the nature and acquisition of skill; the third section deals with some of the 'built-in' or intrinsic factors that impose limitations upon the skilled operator. In conclusion we shall briefly consider the application of this analysis to other types of skilled performance.

The nature of sensory–motor activity

In its very broadest sense, we can define sensory–motor activity as motor activity that is initiated and controlled by sensory input from the environment (exteroreceptors) and from the organism (proprioreceptors). In all sensory–motor activities there are at least four basic components, which are shown diagrammatically in Figure 50.

Receptor processes

These refer to the sense organs and the afferent sensory systems which detect and code (in terms of neural impulses) the signals which initiate and modulate the motor activity. The number of types of sense organ depends largely upon how they are classified, but it is

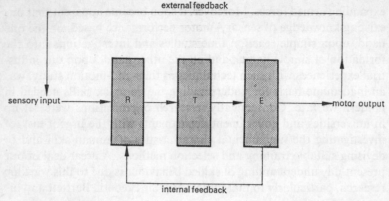

external feedback

sensory input ⟶ R ⟶ T ⟶ E ⟶ motor output

internal feedback

R = receptor processes
T = translation processes
E = effector processes

Figure 50　A simple model of sensory–motor performance

clear from the earlier chapters that there are more than the classical
five. The usual modern classification yields nine: vision, hearing, smell,
taste, touch, temperature, pain, kinaesthesis (the muscle sense) and
equilibrium (inner ear). In certain types of sensory–motor tasks
involving what are known as *man–machine systems* – i.e the pilot and
his aeroplane, the driver and his car – it is necessary to pre-synthesize
and augment some of the information that is presented to the operator's receptor processes. This information is presented symbolically
in the form of a *display*, such as the instrument panel in an aeroplane.
The display enables the operator to act upon necessary information,
such as airspeed and altitude, that is not readily available to his
senses. For the purposes of this chapter, we can consider the display
quite simply as a logical extension of the receptor processes.

Effector processes

These are involved in the *motor* aspect of sensory–motor performance.
Here we are concerned with the structures which translate neural
impulses into physical action. In the context of sensory–motor performance, the effector processes consist of the voluntary or striped

muscles and their efferent nerve supplies. Neural impulses arriving over these efferent nerve pathways end in terminal junctions within the muscles: the motor end plates. At the motor end plate, the neural activity is transformed into a synchronous contraction and relaxation of appropriate muscle fibres resulting in a movement of the muscles and the structures attached to them. In man–machine systems, it is necessary to introduce an intermediate step between an effector movement and its desired consequence. This intermediate process is *control* activity; in other words, to execute a change of direction in a car, the driver needs to turn a steering wheel. As with the receptor process and the display, we can consider the controls as a logical extension of the effector processes.

Translation processes

These are the central, decision elements of sensory–motor activity that intervene between the receptor and effector processes. The translation processes are essentially concerned with the *choice* of an action which is appropriate to the stimulation received. As Welford (1958) has pointed out, the translation process may be thought of as a *response* to sensory input and, in turn, as a *stimulus* to effector action.

In a familiar sensory–motor task, the nature of the translation process is determined by past experience; but where the task is unfamiliar, the translation process must be 'programmed' via external instructions such as 'to cancel that light you need to press this button', and so on. In many of our daily sensory–motor tasks, the rules of the translation process have become so familiar that we are rarely conscious of them. We automatically turn a water-tap in an anticlockwise direction to get water out of it. Similarly, our foot has begun to depress the brake pedal in a car while we are still considering the possibility of a future emergency. Welford (1958) has stated that,

... once a rule of translation has been built up, putting it into use can often precede the signal which would normally initiate it. When a particular signal or type of signal is expected we can often carry out the translation process and prepare responding action before it arrives so that when it does, it, as it were, triggers off a pre-formed response (p. 25).

Feedback

The term 'feedback' describes the sensory input which results from the operator's own effector activity. Thus, sensory–motor activity can be thought of as a *closed-loop system*; information generated by motor activity is fed back into the translation process, via the receptor processes, and serves to modify or direct subsequent motor actions.

In human sensory–motor performance, we can distinguish two separate but supplementary feedback loops: one existing within the operator (internal feedback) and the other existing externally (external feedback).

The internal feedback loop. The information within this internal, kinaesthetic loop is generated by sense receptors situated in the muscles, tendons and joints. This information relates to the relative position, state of tension and extent of movement of the various parts of our body and is essential to the performance of smoothly controlled actions. The effects of the loss of this internal feedback loop can be seen in patients with *tabes dorsalis* in whom the nervous pathways carrying kinaesthetic information have been damaged (Holding, 1965). A symptom of this condition is the absence of smooth co-ordinated movements together with the tendency to overshoot when reaching for objects. Similarly in cases of damage to the cerebellum, the patient shows an incapacity to regulate his movements so that they stop at the intended place. The patient with cerebellar damage is unable to make use of the fine control provided by the internal kinaesthetic loop; as a consequence his movements are 'coarse' and clumsy.

External feedback loop. In this case, information relating to the results of motor activity and to the ongoing movements themselves is fed back to the translation process generally via the visual sense modality. In the majority of sensory–motor tasks the information conveyed by the external feedback loop relates primarily to the discrepancy or 'error quantity' that exists between the operator's current performance and some desired standard. Generally, knowledge of results or external feedback is acted upon to minimize the discrepancy between the standard and current performance. However, in certain pathological conditions such as in the *intention tremor* (see Chapter 6) of disseminated sclerosis it would seem that the feedback from the perceived discrepancy operates in the wrong direction. When the patient tries to reach out and touch an object, he cannot prevent an ever-increasing oscillation of his arm the nearer his finger approaches the target.

Depending on the nature of the task, the feedback may be either of the *discrete* or *continuous* variety. In the case of shooting a rifle at a static target, knowledge of results is conveyed in a discrete parcel by the movements of the marker's disc. The marksman notes the extent and direction of the error, and makes an appropriate correction in his next aiming. However, when he tries to fire at a moving target, it is evident that he needs a continuous flow of feedback information in order to eliminate the discrepancy between his sights and the target. An important consequence of these two types of feedback is their effect upon the nature of the adjustive movements. With discrete feedback, the individual responses that go to make up the total sequence can be readily identified; but with continuous feedback the individual responses need to flow in an apparently smooth, uninterrupted succession so that they are impossible to identify individually. This continuous–discrete distinction represents a convenient way of categorizing sensory–motor tasks.

The nature of skill

Skill and habit

As we implied in our introductory section, the psychologist's understanding of skilled behaviour prior to the Second World War was, to say the least, rudimentary. A number of these early studies had assumed that acquiring a skill such as driving a car was a similar process to that of acquiring a *habit* (see Chapter 12) such as maze running or reciting a piece of verse by rote. This was part of what Bartlett (1943) called the 'unverified guess' and provided the rationale for numerous, sterile, simple task experiments using recurrent unvarying stimuli. As Oldfield (1959) has stated: 'For many years in the history of

psychology, skills were treated as if they were of the nature of habits.'
Thus it was assumed that complex skills were built up by welding
together aggregates of simple habits.

Oldfield goes on to discuss the similarities between skill and habit
which permitted these erroneous assumptions to be made. Both
habits and skills have to be learned, and 'once they have been learned,
each can be said to be *habitual* in the sense that there is economy of
action and there may be little need for close conscious attention on
the part of the performer.' There are, however, a number of fundamental differences between the nature of skill and the nature of habit
that cannot be obscured by these superficial similarities. The basic
difference (although ultimately a difference in degree rather than in
kind) lies in the nature of the adaptation to external events demanded
by the two types of activity. Once a habit has been acquired, the
component actions may be repeated on subsequent occasions with
virtually no variation; for the effective performance of a skill, on the
other hand, the actions are constantly subject to modifications originating from changes in the operator's environment. Thus it is probably true to say that skilled actions are *never* repeated in exactly the
same way. The more perfectly a habit is learned, the more independent it becomes of the environment. Once the first phase of the
habit has been initiated, the rest of the sequence tends to follow
automatically. The fact that it is sometimes difficult to remember
what letter comes after what in the middle of the alphabet unless one
runs through from the beginning illustrates this process of rigid
internalization. In skill, efficient performance demands a complete
absence of rigidity or stereotyping. The important thing in learning a
skill is not to acquire a rigid set of movements that can be activated
whenever a suitable stimulus presents itself; rather, it involves learning *how* to make actions that are appropriate to any particular
situation. A good example of the penalties of rigidity is available in a
recent account of the Crimean War. When the troopers of the Heavy
Brigade charged the Russian cavalry at Balaclava, they had some
difficulty exchanging blows with them since they were unprepared for
the Russians' less orthodox approach to mounted sword-play. The
Heavy Brigade had been rigidly trained in their sword exercises and
had been taught that each cut (specified by a number) had to be

followed by a guard. After the engagement, a surgeon was treating a trooper for a sword wound in his scalp and asked him how he came by it. 'Well, I had just cut five' (a body cut), the man replied indignantly, 'and the damned fool never guarded at all but hit me over the head' (Hibbert, 1961, p. 172).

Bartlett (1958) argued that we should only begin to apply the term 'skill' when a considerable number of receptor and effector functions are interlinked and related together in a series which possesses clear directional characteristics and moves towards an end-point or goal. He argued that two characteristics distinguished skilled from non-skilled activity. In the first place, skilled performance must all at times submit to receptor control. It must be initiated and directed by both environmental signals and those which are generated as the result of the operator's own activity: internal and external feedback. Second, throughout the performance of a skill, signals and their related actions form a *series*, not simply a succession of events. The signals have the character of a field or pattern which, although it may be highly differentiated (for example, an aircraft's instrument display), still retains its identity or 'wholeness'.

The conception of the human operator

Wartime pressures to understand the behaviour of the skilled human operator in complex weapon systems produced, as we have already noted, a considerable amount of empirical research into the nature of sensory–motor skills; but it was also responsible for more subtle development. Scientists and technologists were constantly striving to improve existing weapon systems, and the need to assess the results of their efforts by evaluating the system as a whole, rather than by considering the man and the machine separately, brought psychologists into close contact with the thought and methods of other disciplines, particularly those of the engineering sciences. Partly because it eased the communication problem, and partly because a rapidly developing technology made the exercise increasingly meaningful, psychologists began to describe and to consider the human operator in terms similar to those used by engineers to describe the function of their machines. As the result of this collaboration, a number of machine-oriented concepts found their way into the theory of the skilled operator in control systems.

Two such notions have shown themselves to be particularly useful in understanding the fundamental characteristics of human sensory–motor performance. The first was the suggestion that the human operator behaves in a very similar way to a class of self-regulating machines known as *servo-mechanisms*. The idea of using servo-mechanisms as a model for the human operator was proposed by Craik (1948) and later elaborated by Hick and Bates (1950), and has represented a considerable growing point in our knowledge of skilled sensory–motor activity. In 1948 Wiener proposed that a separate discipline – *cybernetics* – should concern itself with the study of self-regulation (feedback) in both physical and biological systems. For a useful introduction to this subject see Pask (1961).

The second important 'machine-oriented' idea to be adopted by psychologists has been termed the *single channel hypothesis*. This notion states that the human operator in a sensory–motor task can be meaningfully regarded as a single channel organizing responses from environmental signals through which one signal has to be cleared before another is dealt with: that is, a channel with a limited capacity to transmit information over a given time period. The single channel hypothesis was later elaborated by Broadbent (1958) into a more general theory relating to such activities as processing information from several sources at once, responding to infrequent and irregular signals (vigilance), as well as to the general aspects of skilled sensory–motor performance. The single channel hypothesis occupies a central position in the conceptual analysis of sensory–motor skills and will be referred to again throughout this chapter.

Processes underlying the acquisition of skill

One of the major problems in the study of skilled behaviour is to determine what changes occur within the operator between his initial fumbling attempts at a complex sensory–motor task and his final, polished performance. It is evident that this transitional area between unskilled and skilled activity must be filled with training and practice. A considerable amount of current research is being aimed at determining the optimal conditions of training and practice for various types of skilled activity. See Holding (1965) for an excellent account of these training methods. Our concern in this section is not with the methods themselves, but with the basic changes that these methods seek to achieve within the operator.

A number of investigators (see Annett and Kay, 1956) have suggested that the most important of the processes underlying the acquisition of sensory–motor skill, and the one upon which other processes depend, concerns the sensory aspect of the task. That is the gradual development of a perceptual organization which sifts and orders the incoming signals so that the maximum amount of information may pass through the limited capacity communication channel in a given time period. The basis of this organization appears to be an increasing appreciation, on the part of the trainee operator, of the *redundancy* that exists in the sensory input information. In other words, as his experience of the task increases much of the information coming in through the senses becomes redundant in that it conveys nothing new or important. Continued experience of a relatively simple sensory–motor task, for example, may allow the operator to identify certain sequences of signals that appear in a relatively fixed order at various points in the operation, i.e. that signal A is always followed by signals B, C, D, etc. When these invariant sequences have been identified, the operator learns that all the information contained in a particular series is conveyed by the first signal, the remainder being redundant. In more complex sensory–motor tasks such as driving a car or flying an aeroplane, the occurrence of these relatively invariant sequences of signals is rare; in this case, the operator has to learn to appreciate the various *sequential probabilities* of signals present in the inflow of information. Thus, instead of learning that signal A is always followed by signal B, he learns, for example, that the probability of signal A being followed by signal B is greater than the probability of its being followed by itself or by C, D, etc.

As the trainee operator becomes more aware of redundancy in the sensory input, he has more time to concentrate upon the genuinely useful cues which indicate what action is needed, guide its course, give advance warning of changing conditions, or indicate the success or failure of past actions. This greater efficiency in processing the sensory input is reflected on the motor side by an *increased economy of control action*. It is possible to illustrate this perceptually geared control efficiency by considering a fault commonly observed in pilots under training. This is the problem of 'chasing the needle' which occurs most frequently when the student pilot is being trained to fly on instruments, without external visual reference. When the only attitude information available to the student is that represented by his basic flight instruments: artificial horizon, airspeed indicator, altimeter, vertical speed indicator, turn and slip and directional indicator, he often shows a tendency to concentrate his whole attention on each individual instrument in turn and to try to maintain a particular component of his flight path, such as altitude, at the expense of other components. As he follows the fluctuations of the altimeter needle with his control column, other instruments slide rapidly away from their desired positions; when he finally notices these discrepancies he has to make large corrections to restore them. This in turn upsets his height maintenance, and so on. With further training and practice, the student pilot gradually acquires a scanning pattern; he no longer finds it necessary to concentrate on the details of each instrument, but abstracts the required information from a global impression of the whole display. When he is no longer working to capacity trying to correct his own errors, he begins to have that most precious commodity of the skilled operator: *time*. Perhaps the most distinctive feature of skilled behaviour is that the operator is able to convey the impression of 'having all the time in the world'.

The last and most important characteristic of skilled behaviour to be acquired by the trainee operator, therefore, is *accurate timing*. Bartlett (1958) stated that,

. . . timing has little or nothing to do with the absolute speed at which any component response in the skill sequence is performed. Efficiency depends, more than upon anything else, upon the regulation of the flow from component to component in such a way that nowhere in the whole series is there any appearance of hurry, and nowhere unnecessarily prolonged delay (p. 15).

Conrad (1955) has pointed out the inadequacies of earlier analyses of skilled behaviour in terms of reaction time. The reaction time approach assumed that (a) a specific stimulus preceded a specific response and (b) the interval between the stimulus and the response should be as short as possible for efficient skilled performance. Conrad argued that responses in skilled activity were *graded* in time: that is, a response is not necessarily performed hurriedly immediately after the nominal signal, but at a moment when it is most appropriate. This implies that the operator must know in advance that a response will be needed if it is to be made at the right time. When the operator is able to anticipate the appropriate responses, the basic assumption of the reaction time theorists – that the stimulus precedes the response – becomes valueless. Under these conditions, the response is just as likely to precede its nominal stimulus as it is to follow it. Frequently, the problem facing the operator will not be to produce the response in the shortest possible time but to *delay* it until the most opportune moment. Timing permits the skilled operator to manipulate the time within the inherent limits of the particular task. Good timing does not simply mean producing the fastest possible response; rather, it means that the operator should organize his activities so that the *optimal temporal conditions* are provided for each response.

Conrad (1951, 1953) has demonstrated experimentally that bodily skills inevitably have a characteristic temporal structure, and that this can become defined and smoothed through practice, so that initially long intervals between components are shortened and short intervals become lengthened. Bartlett (1950) has summarized these experiments as follows:

No single component in skilled behaviour is a function merely of that signal which immediately starts the response going. Within limits that can be experimentally determined and measured, surrounding signals and responses in both directions are contributing their shares. In the actual performance of most, and perhaps all, forms of bodily skill the temporal limits of this kind are rather narrow. It is only the near past and the near future that count. Moreover, it seems as if it is the near future – 'anticipation of what is coming next' – that plays the principal part in producing that objective smoothness of performance which is the hall-mark of a high quality of skill' (p. 15).

Timing, as we have seen, is the last characteristic of skilled performance to be acquired by the trainee operator. But it is also perhaps the most fragile and most easily disrupted feature of human skill. As we shall see in the subsequent section, timing is usually the first aspect of skilled behaviour to be lost under stressful conditions. The organization of skilled behaviour, like the trade unions, appears to follow the axiom: 'last in, first out'.

'Built-in' limitations upon the skilled operator

Limitations upon the speed of performance

Choice reaction time. One obvious limitation in skilled activity is the time taken by the operator to respond to a signal from his environment. There is a time-lag between the onset of the signal and the onset of the response which is known as the *reaction time*. Part of this time-lag is clearly due to the time needed for neural transmission; but in 1868, Donders, a Dutch physiologist, attempted to measure the additional time taken by certain mental processes such as discrimination and choice. He hoped to achieve this by superimposing these mental activities upon the simple reaction time (SRT), and then subtracting the known value of the SRT from the total reaction time to give the duration of 'mental activity'. Although Donders and, subsequently, Wundt failed in these endeavours, they did succeed in establishing the now familiar *disjunctive reaction time* experiment. This type of experiment is also commonly referred to as either the *discrimination reaction time* or the *choice reaction time*, where the latter term enjoys more frequent usage in contemporary literature.

In the choice reaction type of study, the subject's task is complicated by the fact that he is presented with different stimuli calling for different responses. In 1885, Merkel showed that the choice reaction time (CRT) increased as the possible number of stimuli and responses increased. In other words, CRT was found to be an increasing function of the number of available choices (for an account of these early findings, see Woodworth and Schlosberg, 1954). More recently there has been a revival of interest in CRT as a result of the advent of *information theory*: the conceptual and mathematical analysis of the amount of information conveyed by a signal. 'Information' in this sense can also be termed the degree of *uncertainty* (or, conversely, the degree of redundancy) in the stimulus population (E. Edwards, 1964).

Hick (1952) proposed what has come to be known as *Hick's law*: that CRT increases at a constant rate as the amount of information conveyed by a stimulus increases. The amount of information, in information-theory terms, increases as a *logarithmic* (negatively accelerated) function of the number of alternatives, each with a specific

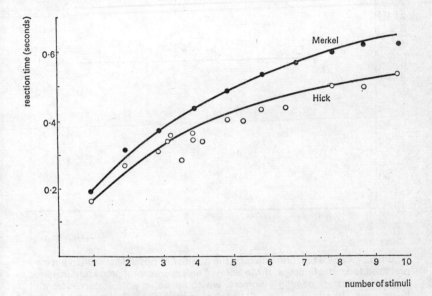

Figure 51 Choice reaction time and the number of possible stimuli : the findings of Merkel and Hick. The experimental procedure involved a motor response, pressing the appropriate key, to a visual stimulus – in Merkel's case, to a Roman or Arabic numeral presented on a screen in front of the subject, and in Hick's case, to illumination of one of ten lamps in a circular array. (Adapted from Hick, 1952, p. 15)

response requirement, which constitute the task. Thus, CRT should increase as a *logarithmic* function of the number of alternative stimuli; this is what Hick and Merkel found (see Figure 51), and essentially the same principle has been confirmed by Hyman (1953) and Brown (1960). Hick's law appears to hold good over a wide variety of situations (Adams, 1964), but only when unpractised subjects are confronted with a task in which the stimulus–response relationships are relatively unnatural or unfamiliar. When the stimulus–response relationships are familiar or subjects well practised, CRT tends to remain constant, rather than increasing, as the number of alternatives increases (Mowbray, 1960; and see Figure 52).

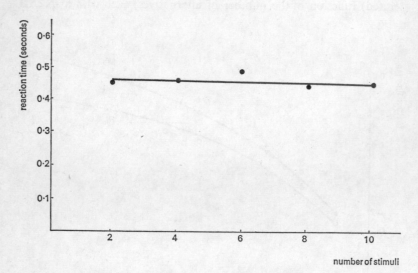

Figure 52 Choice reaction time and the number of possible stimuli in a highly practised task: the findings of Mowbray. The experimental procedure involved a vocal response – naming a numeral which appeared on a screen in front of the subject. The stimulus–response contingency was therefore a highly familiar one, and a practice period at the task was allowed before data were recorded for analysis (Adapted from Mowbray, 1960, p. 196)

Man is adaptable; faced with an unfamiliar sensory–motor task, he performs it as efficiently as he can, possibly behaving, as Welford (1960) suggested, like a computer that makes successive attempts at resolving the uncertainty in the stimulus display. As a consequence of this computer-like behaviour, he may conform to Hick's law: the greater the uncertainty (information), the greater the processing time (CRT). However, with further practice he moves out of the scope of present computer and information models. He gradually learns and adapts until, as in the case of Mowbray's experiment, his mastery of the task is complete.

The psychological refractory period. A somewhat different type of rate limitation is that imposed by the so-called *psychological refractory period* or *psychological refractoriness*. When a signal S_1 is followed by a second signal S_2 at an interval of half a second or less, the beginning of the second response is delayed. In other words, there is an increase in the reaction time to the second stimulus. The term ʹpsychological refractory periodʹ has been given to the period of time intervening between S_1 and S_2. The label has been borrowed from physiology where the term ʹrefractorinessʹ is used to describe the period of reduced responsiveness in individual nerve fibres immediately following stimulation (see Chapter 5). It must be pointed out, however, that despite the common factor of reduced responsiveness following stimulation, the physiological and psychological refractory periods are otherwise so different that it is safest to view them as analogous rather than stemming from the same neurological process.

Following the distinction made by R. Davis (1956), we can say that the evidence for a psychological refractory period is derived from three sorts of experimental situation, those requiring: (a) ʹungradedʹ responses, (b) ʹgradedʹ responses and (c) continuous tracking performance.

ʹUngradedʹ responses occur in situations in which the subject has to make a simple discrete response to a signal. The response is ungraded because it need not be continuously monitored throughout its duration. Probably the first mention of a psychological refractory period was by Telford (1931) using a simple ungraded task. Telford measured the serial reaction time to auditory stimuli. This means the reaction time when a sequence of pairs of stimuli are given at intervals – irregular intervals, in this case – and the subject has to respond as quickly as he can to each one. Telfordʹs results are summarized in Table 5.

It will be noted that the reaction time following the half-second interval is markedly longer than those reaction times following longer intervals.

Responses are said to be ʹgradedʹ when subjects are required to make a controlled movement of definite extent. An example of this type of response is found in an experiment by Vince (1948). The subject sat in front of a vertical slit in a screen, behind which a band of paper moved horizontally. On the paper was a horizontal line which made periodic vertical excursions to a new horizontal position and then returned again, vertically, to the original position. The subject's task was to follow the line with a pencil as closely as possible. The width of the slit was such that he obtained one-twentieth of a second warning of an impending change. In this way, the subject was exposed to sudden discrepancies between intention and actual performance, and his responses measured. Vince found that when the downward movement of the line followed less than half a second after the upward excursion, the second response was delayed.

Table 5
Telford's measurement of serial reaction time to auditory stimuli. (From Telford, 1931, p. 9)

Interval $S_1 - S_2$ (s)	0·5	1	2	4
Reaction time (s)	0·335	0·241	0·245	0·276

The last source of evidence is obtained from an experiment by Craik (1948) involving continuous pursuit tracking. Craik observed that the frequency of correction movements had a maximum periodicity of about two per second. The hypothesis of a psychological refractory period was advanced to explain why this rate was not exceeded.

With the exception of the studies by Vince and Craik on continuous tracking, most of the evidence has been derived from tasks involving discrete responses, and, as we stated earlier, the general conclusion has been that the reaction time to a second stimulus of a pair will be lengthened if the interstimulus interval is less than half a second. There are, however, two further observations relating to the psychological refractory period. The first of these is a limitation to the above general statement: that is that very brief interstimulus intervals cause the two stimuli to be perceived as a single entity and as a consequence are responded to as one. The second observation by Hick (1948) demonstrates that refractoriness persists in the face of considerable practice, despite specific attempts to eliminate it. This would suggest that, unlike the relationship summarized in Hick's law, psychological refractoriness is a stable aspect of the operator's performance.

There are a number of theoretical explanations of this phenomenon. All have one thing in common: they assume that refractoriness is *central* rather than peripheral in origin, that is, occurring in the cortex rather than in the receptor or effector processes. Further consideration of these theories will be omitted since they have been adequately summarized by M. C. Smith (1967).

How does refractoriness manifest itself in the skilled performance of a *continuous* sensory–motor task? Can we conclude on the basis of this phenomenon that despite the apparent visual evidence to the contrary, the skilled operator performs intermittently rather than continuously? This was the point of view advanced by Craik (1948), who stated that the human operator behaves basically like an intermittent correction servo. This so-called 'intermittency hypothesis' has enjoyed considerable support from experimentalists in this country; yet as Adams (1964) has pointed out, the relatively long periods of smooth response observed in continuous tracking performance have not, curiously enough, served as grounds for challenging this hypothesis. Craik accounts for this smoothness by the principle of inertia. Noble, Fitts and Warren (1955) explain these smooth responses by suggesting that intermittent movements are in fact occurring in accordance with the principle of the psychological refractory phase, but the subject's acquired ability to predict and prepare for the input signals has overlaid a smoothing effect. Adams, however, comes down squarely against the intermittency hypothesis and states that while 'prediction responses may well have some sort of smoothing influence, it may also be true that the intermittency hypothesis is false for continuous tracking and that relatively long smooth responses frequently occur in the absence of prediction behaviour'. The controversy continues; but it is certainly true, as we pointed out earlier, that the evidence for the psychological refractory phase has been largely derived from discrete tasks. As a consequence, its generalization to continuous tracking tasks may be limited.

Limitations upon the processing of sensory input

Sensory overloading. It has already been stated that the behaviour of the human operator is analogous to a single communication channel possessing a limited capacity. There is a maximum rate at which the human operator can process sensory information; when this rate is exceeded, i.e. when sensory overloading occurs, the channel is stressed and a breakdown in performance can ensue. The *channel capacity*, therefore, represents a fundamental limitation upon human skilled performance. J. G. Miller (1960) studied the effect of information input overload upon behaviour and observed a characteristic relationship between the rates of information input and that of the information output or responses. When the rate of information input is increased, the rate of output follows it exactly as a linear function for a period of time; then it begins to level off until it reaches the channel capacity or the maximum rate of output possible for the operator. If the information input rate increases still further, the operator will for a limited time maintain this maximum rate of output; however, if the input rate speeds up even further, the output falls drastically, sometimes to zero. The operator is 'overloaded' and can no longer transmit information.

In the course of his investigations Miller observed a number of fundamental strategies of defence that are used by living systems against the stresses of information input overloading. Some of these, relevant to the skilled operator in a sensory–motor task, can be summarized as follows:

1. *Omission* – not processing information whenever there is an extreme of overload;

2. *Error* – processing the input incorrectly and not making the necessary output adjustment;

3. *Queueing* – delaying responses during peak load periods and then catching up during lulls;

4. *Filtering* – the systematic omission of certain categories of information, according to some sort of priority scheme (see Broadbent, 1958);

5. *Approximation* – an output mechanism whereby a less precise or accurate response is given because there is no time for precision;

6. *Escape* – leaving a situation entirely or taking any other steps that effectively cut off the flow of information.

Miller observed that once individuals or groups had become familiar with all of these adjustment processes, certain characteristic choices were made depending on a particular rate of sensory flow. At medium rates, all of them were tried wherever possible; however, at high rates, filtering and particularly omission were the primary mechanisms used. At extremely rapid rates as much as 98 per cent of the total inflow was omitted rather than transmitted. This meant that the individual was able to keep operating, if only at a very low rate of information transmission.

Sensory underloading. Just as the human operator can be stressed by excessively high rates of information input, so there can also be stresses due to excessively low rates of information input: *sensory underload.* Experimental work on this problem of sensory underload has been carried out under two general headings. The first, concerned with extreme or total reductions of patterned sensory inflow, comes under the heading of *sensory* or *perceptual deprivation.* The second area of research is that related to the problem of detecting infrequent and irregular signals in monotonous surroundings, generally referred to as *vigilance performance.*

Experimental studies of sensory deprivation have been reviewed in Chapter 9. The conditions of skilled sensory–motor activity rarely reach this extreme state of sensory impoverishment; but there have been reports (A. M. H. Bennett, 1961) of aviators flying straight and level in a featureless high altitude environment who have suffered otherwise unexplained states of confusion and disorientation. Sensory underload is more commonly encountered in certain types of skilled activity, such as radar tracking, where the operator is often required to respond to infrequent and relatively indistinct (low signal–noise ratio) signals in fairly isolated and non-eventful surroundings over long periods of time. The pioneer study of vigilance performance (Mackworth, 1950) arose out of the wartime problem of detecting submarines by airborne radar. Mackworth's original experiment was a synthetic task simulating the most important features of the radar operator's job. The subject watched a pointer moving around a clock face in regular jumps at the rate of one jump per second. At infrequent and irregular intervals the pointer gave a jump of double length, to which the subject was instructed to respond by pressing a key. In the first place, subjects were required to work at this task for a period of two hours. When the half-hour periods within the session were compared, it was found that the correct detection rate in the first half-hour was significantly better than in the other three. The general nature of these results was borne out by the experience of Coastal Command in actual submarine detection which eliminated the possibility that the observed *vigilance decrement* was an artifact of the laboratory situation. Since this time, a great deal of experimental work has been done in relation to the problem of vigilance performance, and the fall-off in detection after the initial phase of the 'watch' has been well established. Comprehensive reviews of the topic have been carried out by Broadbent (1958), Frankmann and Adams (1962) and Davies and Tune (1970).

These two sources of evidence suggest that there must be a certain minimal rate of information input in order that the human operator may function efficiently. A convincing body of evidence now exists to suggest that the ascending reticular formation (see Chapters 5 and 6) has a fundamental role in responding to the quantity of information coming into the nervous system. Kleitman (1939) held that wakefulness – or arousal as it has come to be called – was maintained by a subcortical centre or centres, now believed to be the A R A S and possibly also the hypothalamus. Anatomically, as we have seen from Chapter 5, this area is situated so that nearly all afferent and efferent pathways to and from the cortex pass through it. One of the functions of the reticular system is to maintain an upward barrage of nervous impulses which exert a facilitatory influence upon cortical activities. This diffuse activity is to a large extent dependent upon the rate of informational inflow through the senses. Thus it can be seen that just as the digestive system requires a substrate of organic and inorganic materials, so the cortex needs a substrate of sensory input to maintain its efficiency.

In perceptually isolated or monotonous surroundings, such as those encountered in the vigilance situation, it has been suggested

(Broadbent, 1963) that the operator's level of arousal is lowered, rendering his performance less efficient. At the other end of the scale, when the nervous system is stressed by an excess of sensory input, the reticular system appears also to have a role in reducing this overload by selectively filtering out inputs that exceed capacity (J. G. Miller, 1961).

Limitations upon prolonged performance: fatigue

The psychological and medical literature relating to the subject of fatigue is both vast and depressing – vast, because the problem of fatigue has always been an acute one for those military and industrial organizations that sponsor human factors research; depressing, because a great number of the studies have fallen prey to the considerable methodological and conceptual dangers inherent in this type of problem. Finan, Finan and Hartson (1949), in their review of fatigue studies sponsored by the U.S.A.F., concluded that many were methodologically inadequate because of the failure to control for the influences of motivation. We have all, no doubt, witnessed or read about cases like that of the marathon runner, Jim Peters, in the 1948 Olympic Games in London, who entered the stadium in the final stages of exhaustion but managed to stay on his feet until he was a short distance from the tape. On the reverse side of this motivational coin is the familiar experience of feeling more tired when bored; a walk through dull streets is often more tiring than a walk in exciting surroundings.

The conceptual inadequacies of fatigue studies are not so easy to pin down, but perhaps part of the trouble has stemmed from the term 'fatigue' itself. 'Fatigue' suggests a unitary process, a single concept; yet it is clear that the effects of prolonged performance generally referred to by this term operate at a number of separate and diverse levels. First, there is the distinction between the subjective awareness of tiredness and the objective effects upon some measurable aspect of sensory–motor performance. It is quite clear that we cannot confine ourselves to the reports which only the operator can make about his feelings of tiredness. A number of the early scientific investigators – Mosso, Kraepelin, Rivers and Thorndike – have reported that almost any such subjective statement can be made in relation to almost any type of performance. In other words, there is virtually a zero correlation between the subjective awareness of fatigue and the objective measures of performance decrement; there may even be a negative correlation. D. R. Davis (1948), reporting on the Cambridge cockpit experiments (see below), observed that as the subjects became more fatigued they became progressively more optimistic about the quality of their performance.

In scientific terms and in the tradition of behavioural psychology, we are left with finding some objective measure of the effects of prolonged performance. But as we stated earlier, these effects are diverse and often lead to contradictory predictions, depending on the nature of the sensory–motor activity. Where the task is simple and repetitive, involving only a limited set of muscles, prolonged performance generally leads to diminished activity due perhaps to the increasing concentration within the muscle of metabolic breakdown products which may render it temporarily incapable of further work. In a complex skilled activity like piloting an aircraft simulator, however, prolonged performance may have the opposite effect: that of causing the operator to do *more* rather than less work.

Welford (1953) has gone a long way in sorting out this confusion by isolating three separate fatigue effects. The first relates to simple tasks that do not fall into the category of skilled activity. Where one aspect of performance can vary independently with other aspects, i.e. speed with accuracy, and where performance is repetitive rather than serial, then the fatigue effect may show itself as a straightforward decrement in one or more aspects of performance. For example, speed or accuracy may diminish or the ceiling of performance may be lowered. In the study of skilled activity, however, this type of effect is not really our concern; we are interested primarily in the other two effects that Welford mentions: the *disorganization* and the *cumulative disruption* of performance.

These two fatigue effects can be illustrated by reference to the findings of the Cambridge cockpit study. The experimental situation was as follows: a fully instrumented static aeroplane cockpit was constructed by Craik to simulate as closely as possible the conditions of instrument flight (i.e. flying in cloud with no external visual reference). Pilots with relatively brief wartime flying training were used as subjects. The purpose of the investigation was to study the changes that occurred in the pilot's behaviour as the result of two hours prolonged performance in the simulator. The main effects have been summarized by Bartlett (1943). Two findings are particularly relevant: first, the perceptual organization of the input information, acquired by the subject during his initial flying training, gradually broke down and fragmented as the experimental session progressed. The stimulus field (the instrument display) lost its Gestalt quality and the operator's attention seemed to 'funnel down' to unconnected instruments rather than to the display as a whole. Also peripheral signs, such as fuel state indicators, were missed. This fragmentation cut through the whole delicate fabric of flying skill: informational redundancy was lost, and the tired pilot like the trainee pilot had to do *more* work trying to 'catch up' with each instrument in turn. As a consequence, timing and anticipatory behaviour deteriorated rapidly; although until very great fatigue was reached, it was more likely that the correct rather than the incorrect response would be made.

The second significant finding of this study was that self-imposed standards or acceptable error limits deteriorated with prolonged performance. The pilot thinks he is performing more efficiently when in fact his acceptable error limits are actually getting wider. Cumulative disruption of performance occurs in this sort of task where the various components of performance, such as speed and accuracy, are dependent upon one another and where the performance is paced by events external to the operator. The size of the error to be corrected from moment to moment is a function of both the operator's current acceptable limits and the time it takes to notice that an error has exceeded these limits. In a tired man the time taken to correct an error gets longer and inevitably the errors themselves get larger. Since each component activity within skilled performance is dependent upon all the other components, the breakdown of one component snowballs to affect the total organization of the skill. The process, therefore, is a vicious circle.

These sorts of fatigue effect would appear basically to relate, as Welford suggests, to the two important limitations upon human functioning that we have discussed previously. In the first place, both the actions themselves and the translation process, intervening between the arrival of the signal and the beginning of a response, *take time*. Second, the human operator is in a number of important ways a *single-channel mechanism* – not simply in the sense that the eyes can only look in one direction at once, nor that one hand can only perform one action at a time, but also in the sense that only one signal or 'chunk' of signals can be dealt with by the central processes at any one time. Bartlett, in his discussion of the Cambridge cockpit study, asked: what do these effects of prolonged performance tell us about the central nervous system? He borrowed the notion of hierarchical levels of functioning from the neurologist Hughlings Jackson and argued that fatigue manifests itself in skilled activity as a regression down the hierarchical stages that had been built up during training. Timing is at the highest level; it is a late achievement of the brain and still very unstable, consequently it is the first to go. Receptor organization breaks down and with it goes the economy of motor action. Finally the tired man behaves very much like the unskilled operator: he is doing more work, he has to concentrate on each action and he is particularly conscious of his own body.

In this survey of limitations 'built in' to the human operator, we have emphasized those limitations which operate over a relatively short time span and have not considered the changes in performance which may occur with age. Ageing is, nevertheless, an important factor in skilled performance and has been discussed by Welford (1958) and by Welford and Birren (1965).

Conclusion

We may conclude this discussion of skilled sensory–motor activity by reiterating a basic theme of this chapter, that the human operator may be usefully regarded as a single-channel communication system, whose capacity for receiving, processing, storing and acting upon information is limited. This assumption is fundamental to our understanding of skill. The acquisition of a skill can be seen to a large extent as a process of reorganizing the input data, through the appreciation of redundancy and the selection of key cues, so that it can be handled most efficiently by the limited channel mechanism. The distinguishing features of skilled activity – accurate timing, anticipation and economy of movement – depend primarily for their existence upon this process of perceptual organization.

Again, most of the 'built-in' limitations that we discussed can be regarded as stemming in one way or another from this basic assumption of limited capacity. Choice reaction time, psychological refractoriness and sensory overloading are direct manifestations of the fact that processing information through a limited capacity single-channel system takes time. Fatigue, on the other hand, bears a more indirect relationship to this assumption. The direct effects of prolonged performance in highly skilled activity appear to be upon the delicate organization of the input data; as this breaks down, so the tired operator, like the unskilled operator, cannot process information through the limited channel at the same efficient rate as the fresh, skilled operator. As this breakdown process operates like a vicious circle, efficiency continues to deteriorate until performance breaks down completely.

One probable future development in the field of skilled performance may lie in attempts to answer the question: by what means can we increase the channel capacity of the human operator? Investigations into the effects of certain drugs represent one line of inquiry that has shown encouraging results. J. G. Miller (1961) and his associates have demonstrated that dexedrine (dextroamphetamine sulphate) definitely increases an individual's information-processing capacity and delays the point of overload. Dexedrine tends to produce undesirable side-effects, but this research does suggest that new drugs might significantly alter the nervous system's capacity for handling information.

The final question to be considered is how far the basic processes underlying skilled sensory–motor performance are characteristic of other types of skilled activity. Two attempts at generalizing our knowledge of sensory–motor skills to other spheres of human behaviour can be mentioned briefly. Bartlett (1958) proposed that thinking, at least in the first analysis, can be usefully regarded as a complex and high-level skill. He pointed out that thinking and the sensory–motor skills have a number of important common features: both possess a directional quality in that they move towards a specific goal or solution, both show some improvement with practice and both involve – either directly or indirectly – the uptake of information from the environment and its emission in the form of a response. More recently, Fitts and Posner (1967) have set out a number of ways in which the single channel hypothesis can be modified to accommodate recent research into the acquisition and nature of language skills. The reader is recommended to consult their book for an account of these modifications and also for amplification of the points raised in this chapter.

Further reading

P. M. Fitts and M. I. Posner, *Human Performance*, Brooks-Cole, 1967.
D. H. Holding, *Principles of Training*, Pergamon, 1965.
D. Legge (ed.), *Skills*, Penguin Books, 1970.
A. T. Welford, *Fundamentals of Skill*, Methuen, 1968.

Chapter 14
Remembering

The effects of early experience, and indeed the facts of learning, imply that experience is in some way retained by an organism and may be later utilized; on the other hand, much of everyday experience leads us to suppose that retention of past events is far from perfect – we learn only slowly, and we forget – and that the retention of past events varies in amount and quality, both from person to person and within the same person at different times. The obvious questions, then, with which layman and psychologist alike are concerned are: Why do we remember? Why do we forget? Why are there inter-individual and intra-individual differences in the efficiency of remembering? The word 'why' in these questions of course represents an oversimplification. More exact wording of the questions involves a statement of the kind, or kinds, of answer in which we are interested. We ask 'why' of remembering and forgetting, in the sense of seeking the *antecedent conditions* associated with the occurrence of these phenomena; we ask 'how', in the sense of seeking to analyse the processes involved, either in physiological or in psychological terms. Both the why, in this narrower sense, and the how of remembering and forgetting, and of individual differences, will be our concern.

It should be pointed out that there are many very different situations which have been studied by psychologists and which might be included under the general title 'remembering'. These range through situations involving immediate recall of single stimuli (little different from the reporting of tachistoscopically presented items), the learning of poems or connected prose, the learning of lists of items (serial learning) or of paired items (paired-associate learning), to the clinically observed phenomena of amnesia and fugues. The evidence presented here will be mainly experimental rather than clinical and will be concerned with recall of verbal material more than with recall of motor skills, which differs in certain respects from verbal memory, at least in degree (see, for example, Bilodeau, 1966; Holding, 1965; Welford, 1968). The diversity of data in this field cannot, however, be ignored. There is also considerable theoretical disunity, some stemming from actual conflicts of interpretation and some from the fact that most theories of remembering are only partial, not intended to explain all types of evidence.

The three questions posed above cannot be answered independently; what we know of the phenomena of forgetting will obviously influence our view of the nature of remembering, as will our observation of individual differences. The questions are treated separately here, as far as possible, but some overlap is unavoidable.

Why do we remember?

We can only speak of remembering, or forgetting, an item when it has once been received; reception, in the sense of impingement upon sensory receptors, we shall describe as *registration*. An item – such as a name, a picture, an event – can be said to have been remembered when, having once been registered, it can be recalled or recognized at a later time. It can be said to have been forgotten when, having been registered, it cannot later be recalled. If we wish to study the phenomena of memory, therefore, we must take care that the material which is to be remembered has been registered in the first place: that is, to distinguish memory from learning or from perception.

There are essentially two ways of effecting this distinction. One is to require a subject to learn some material to a criterion of learning, so that the learning trials themselves constitute evidence of registration, and then to examine performance at a later time to see whether the learned material has been retained. The other method is to present for retention material which is so simple that it must surely be registered – a single word or a three-digit number or a simple picture: items which can certainly be reproduced immediately after presentation. Such material has been described as *subspan* because it is said to be within the span of apprehension – the amount of a given type of material which can be taken in and immediately reproduced after a single brief presentation (see, for example, Woodworth and Schlosberg, 1954). Some experiments in remembering occupy an intermediate position in that they study characteristics of the retention of *supra*-span material, such as a ten-digit number, presented only once (Hebb, 1961; Melton, 1963). It is not clear to what extent such experiments are studying characteristics of learning as well as, or rather than, characteristics of retention; thus, although they are of undoubted importance, they will not be included for consideration in this treatment of remembering.

Experiments on remembering tend, therefore, to be of two different kinds, one involving short-term recall of simple items and the other involving longer-term recall of more complex material which has been previously learned. In everyday life one can readily encounter situations similar to these extremes. A frequently quoted example of short-term memory concerns the dialling of an unfamiliar telephone number; we can remember the number, after reading or hearing it for long enough to dial, but cannot remember it if asked a few minutes later. At the opposite extreme, our own address (a reasonably complicated series of numbers and words) is so well learned that we can reproduce it apparently without effort if required to do so. From introspective evidence, then, as well as from rather marked differences in the results obtained in experiments of the two kinds, one might suppose that different processes of remembering are involved in the two situations; and this distinction has indeed been made, both in psychological terms and in terms of the underlying processes which have been said to be involved.

One of the earliest to distinguish between *short-term* and *long-term* memory was William James (1890). He notes that 'as a rule sensations outlast for some little time the objective stimulus which occasioned them': this corresponds to the physiological after-image, and our consciousness of the after-sensation he terms elementary, or primary, memory. If a stimulus lasts for a sufficient length of time it produces a more durable image, which may pass out of consciousness but which can be recalled to it later; James termed this memory proper, or secondary, memory. It is defined as 'the knowledge of an event or fact of which meantime we have not been thinking, with the additional consciousness that we have thought or experienced it before'. Secondary memory is thus the recurrence of an image which we know belongs to the past; primary memory is of events which belong to the psychological present, which have occurred 'just now'. Primary memory fades with time; secondary memory, if it has been established at all, is at any rate much less susceptible to decay. (We shall return to the hypothesis of decay over time at later stages.)

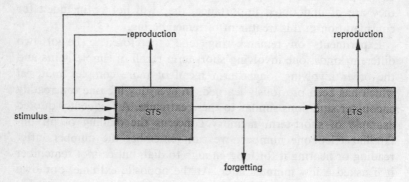

Figure 53   A simple model of memory

Later proponents of the two-process account of memory have included Broadbent (1958), Treisman (1964) and Waugh and Norman (1965), who compare memory to a storage system containing two stores. Although the accounts given by different writers vary in detail, they are sufficiently similar to provide a composite model of memory, which is shown diagrammatically in Figure 53. Any incoming stimulus, when it is registered, enters a short-term or primary memory store (which we may call STS), and may or may not pass further into a long-term or secondary memory store (LTS). If the item does not enter LTS it will soon be lost, since STS has only a limited retention capacity. A recently presented item may, then, be in STS and LTS at one and the same time, or in STS alone; a less recently presented item may be in LTS alone or may have been forgotten – that is, it may have disappeared from STS without having entered LTS. We shall not consider here whether it is possible for items to disappear from LTS; in general it is assumed here that LTS has virtually unlimited capacity. One item may be more likely than another to enter LTS because it was presented with greater intensity or for a longer period (James); because it has been rehearsed while in STS (Waugh and Norman); or because the system is 'set' to select out certain items rather than others for storage (Broadbent). We shall return to the notion of selective retention later in this chapter; it will not be our concern here, except that it must be pointed out that if such selection occurs it occurs at a stage between STS and LTS, not before STS, which is catholic in its acceptance.

A comparable model in physiological terms has been given by Hebb (1949), whose two-stage theory of memory has gained wide, though not universal, acceptance. (We have already considered the model in the context of perceptual learning in Chapter 10.) Incoming stimulation, Hebb postulates, sets up *reverberatory activity* (the *activity trace*) in the receptor and effector cells involved in the sensation; such activity would be unstable and susceptible to interference from concomitant or later activity. However, with repeated stimulation and reverberation from a specific percept, *structural changes* occur (the *structural trace*), perhaps in the form of synaptic or dendritic growths, which facilitate the relevant neural connexions, and therefore the firing of the sequence on a later occasion. This account can be compared with the older 'consolidation theory' of memory, recently reviewed by Glickman (1961). This theory, formulated in the early twentieth century, stated that the perseveration (continuation in time) of neural processes set up by incoming stimuli is necessary for the consolidation of these stimuli in memory; any other 'mental activity' occurring very soon after the registration of a stimulus will interfere with its consolidation to the extent that it involves the same neurological processes and loci.

There is certainly some evidence for a theory along these lines. Duncan (1949), for example, administered electric shock to the brains of rats (via externally applied electrodes) during a learning task. The rats received shock at a specified interval (which varied for different groups of subjects) after each learning trial; a control group of animals received no shock, and the performance of the different groups was compared over several learning trials. Electric shock would be expected to interfere with 'perseverative neural processes'; and a decrement in performance was in fact found when shock was administered after learning, the effect decreasing in magnitude as the interval increased between learning and shock. Experimental and clinical observations of human subjects undergoing a similar 'disruption' procedure (used commonly in the treatment of certain mental illnesses, when it is termed electroconvulsive therapy, or ECT) and studies manipulating other types of stress which could be considered to be disruptive of perseverative processes also support in general terms the notion of a consolidation process which is necessary for memory, although that interpretation is not always inevitable (see Glickman, 1961). We shall not be concerned primarily with consolidation theory here, since its implications for short-term memory are not entirely clear.

What, then, have been said to be the characteristics of *short-term memory* (STM) and *long-term memory* (LTM)? STM is said to involve an 'activity trace' and LTM a 'structural trace'. Autonomous decay over time occurs in STM, not in LTM. STM is a faithful mirror of events, while LTM contains only a selected proportion of events. STM has a strictly limited capacity – that is, items cannot remain in it for long – while LTM is virtually unlimited in capacity (although memories stored in LTM may prove 'unavailable' when required, for various reasons; we shall return to this point later).

Unfortunately the account of memory given here is neither as complete nor as widely accepted as it might appear. Controversy has arisen over several problems, two of which, probably the most important, will be discussed here. One concerns the limited capacity of STM; the other concerns, more basically, whether the dichotomy of STM and LTM is more apparent than real.

What limits the retention of an item in STM?

According to James, the limiting factor is *time*: a stimulus decays from primary memory as its neural after-effects decay. Although most recent workers seem to agree that the 'trace' involved in

STM cannot be equated with the sensory after-effects associated with after-images and allied phenomena, chiefly because of the very limited duration of such phenomena, the *trace-decay hypothesis* has several supporters (e.g. J. Brown, 1958; Peterson and Peterson, 1959). The evidence in support of this explanation is as follows: if a simple item is presented once and the subject is asked to recall it after a short interval, recall becomes dramatically less efficient as the interval between presentation and recall increases. Thus, a meaningless three-letter sequence such as MHZ can be recalled exactly, in most cases, after about three seconds, but is recalled inaccurately or not at all after a longer period (Peterson and Peterson, 1959). Most, though not all, experiments of this kind have employed *auditory* presentation of material.

However, to prevent subjects from rehearsing (repeating to themselves) the item which they were to recall, the experimenters had to give them some task to fill the interval; otherwise the longer intervals used would give a subject more chance to practise his response and the effects of time, if any, would be obscured. The task commonly used is counting backwards from a given number at a fixed rate. This in turn raises a problem: as the interval between presentation and recall increases, so does the amount of counting. Impaired recall after a longer interval might, therefore, be due either to 'pure decay' of memory or to the greater amount of intervening activity required of the subject. We saw in Chapter 13 that, as learning one task may influence – for better or worse – our learning of another, so intervening activity may affect our retention of previously learned material (a phenomenon termed 'retroaction'). Intervening activity may sometimes facilitate retention, but often affects it adversely; other things being equal, the amount of retroaction (which, when the effect is unfavourable, we may term simply, though less precisely, 'interference') will increase with the amount of intervening activity.

Thus, several workers have sought to explain the limitation of STM in terms of *interference* from more recent stimuli rather than in terms of 'pure decay' over time. STM may be capable of storing only a limited number of items; new items coming into STM will dislodge others, which may not have reached LTM. Waugh and

Norman (1965), who support this view, carried out an experiment in which the two factors – retention interval and amount of intervening activity – were independently varied; this was achieved by varying the rate of presentation of intervening material, so that its amount could be varied while the retention interval was held constant, and vice versa (for a more exact account of the procedure, which differed somewhat from that described earlier, see their original article). They found that when the amount of intervening material was held constant there was no relation between length of interval and efficiency of recall; when interval was held constant, on the other hand, efficiency in recall declined as the amount of intervening material increased. These results support the 'interference' explanation of earlier data rather than the 'decay' explanation. It should be noted that consolidation theory would support an interference hypothesis rather than one of decay; it would presumably hypothesize that, in the absence of interference, a recent memory would become *more* likely, rather than less likely, to be recalled as consolidation proceeded over even a short time interval.

It is probably unwise to come too readily to the conclusion that decay does not occur over time in STM; several investigators adhere to the decay theory and J. Brown (1964), for example, has argued that both factors may be of importance. There seems, however, to be little evidence that the length of time intervening between presentation of an item and its recall is important other than by varying the opportunity for rehearsal (which serves to improve recall) or for new activity (which serves to impair it). The function of practice or rehearsal could then be viewed not as the prevention of decay but as the effective replacement of items in STM by the same items rather than by different ones.

Are there adequate grounds for distinguishing STM from LTM?

The time scales over which STM has been studied vary very widely. Many experimenters have used retention periods of a few seconds only and claim that most decrement in recall occurs during this period; items retained beyond that time are presumed to be in LTM and to be relatively persistent thereafter. A celebrated experiment by Averbach and Sperling (1961) studied changes in recall over periods of half a second or less; but other experimenters have employed time intervals distinctly longer. For most experimenters it has been customary to label as STM any situation involving recall after five minutes or less; a situation involving longer recall periods is held to involve LTM. The distinction is quite arbitrary and does not in itself compel belief in the existence of different processes operating on different sides of the line thus drawn. Exactly what factors could be held to compel such a belief?

One might attempt to support the distinction between STM and LTM by pointing to the existence of two memory processes at the *physiological level*; but that two-stage model of memory, also, has been challenged. Wooldridge (1963), for example, has described *three* stages of memory: a *stimulus trace*, an *attentional trace* (which is represented by activity but which involves selective attention and rehearsal) and a structural trace. Again, some psychologists and physiologists conceptualize memory in terms of neurochemical, rather than neuroanatomical, changes. For example, several studies have been carried out in which brain material, principally RNA (ribonucleic acid), has been extracted from animals trained in a certain task and injected (or otherwise transferred) into untrained animals; such studies suggest that knowledge may be 'transferred' by this means from a trained to an untrained animal and therefore that RNA may be a vehicle for memory storage. There are often, however, considerable difficulties in the interpretation of these findings (see Dingman and Sporn, 1964).

Thus it is not clear that neurophysiological data can support the postulation of two distinct memory processes (although there is some evidence, for example, that hippocampal lesions are associated with impairment of STM but not of LTM; see Chapter 6). Even if the two-stage theory were accepted, two physiological processes of memory storage would not necessarily correspond to the two processes or 'stores' postulated by psychologists; J. Brown (1964) has argued that while LTM may depend solely upon structural changes, STM may be held to depend both upon activity traces and upon structural traces.

As far as purely *psychological considerations* are concerned, the strongest evidence for a dichotomy of STM and LTM would be that retention in the two situations obeys different laws: that a given variable is important in one situation and not in the other, or that its effect differs in the two situations. It would, for instance, be strong support for the dichotomy if it were shown beyond controversy that STM is susceptible to decay with time while LTM is not; but we have seen that the evidence for spontaneous decay in STM is very far from conclusive.

One distinction which might be made is that, while decrement in recall in both situations may be due to interference, the type of interference involved is different. In LTM, interference is usually found to be greatest when there is some semantic similarity (that is, similarity in meaning) between the items to be recalled and the interfering material (Slamecka and Ceraso, 1960). In STM, the most potent source of interference appears to be material which is structurally (for example, acoustically) but not necessarily semantically related to the items to be recalled (see Baddeley and Dale, 1966). It is not altogether clear whether this distinction is a general one or whether it reflects differences in the testing procedures commonly used in the two situations.

On the other hand, one can point to a number of similarities between STM and LTM. Both are adversely affected by the administration of *electroconvulsive shock*. Both appear to be susceptible to *proactive interference* (the interference which learning may exert upon the retention of later activity: an effect similar to transfer, but logically and operationally distinct from it). Both benefit from *repeated presentation* of an item before recall and from *rehearsal*. Evidence of these kinds has been well reviewed by Melton (1963), who concludes from it that there is an essential continuity between STM and LTM. It may be then that the distinction, while useful in the descriptive classification of experimental situations and procedures, is basically arbitrary and at times misleading. The case for either side remains unproven.

It is difficult to summarize an answer to the question: why do we remember? A few statements can be made which are at least relatively uncontroversial. Incoming stimulation sets up a memory trace; on this virtually all psychologists would agree, but as long as we avoid controversy the term 'memory trace' remains little more than metaphorical (for a discussion of the concept of the memory trace, see Gomulicki, 1953). The trace, whatever its nature, is to be distinguished from the sensory after-image, chiefly on account of the generally very brief duration of the latter, although sensory after-images may well play an important part in some experiments on STM (see, for example, J. Brown, 1964; Neisser, 1967; Sperling, 1963). The characteristics of recall differ somewhat in situations which involve different methods of presentation and retention over different time intervals; some of these differences disappear on analysis and it is not clear whether those that remain are differences of kind or of degree. There are also certain factors which are generally agreed to influence retention; some of these, such as rehearsal and interference, have been mentioned above and others will be discussed in the concluding section of this chapter. Meanwhile, however, we shall consider more specifically the nature of forgetting.

Why do we forget?

In our consideration of memory processes we have already mentioned certain ideas about forgetting. One such idea is that as time passes the traces left by outside events in the nervous system grow fainter until they can no longer be reactivated (except, of course, by a recurrence of the events which originally produced them); in other words, we forget with the passage of time. It should be noted that time is not in itself a variable which could explain changes in performance; the hypothesis is that the passage of time provides the opportunity for *trace decay*. E. L. Thorndike (1932) was the most notable of the supporters of this theory of forgetting. He suggested that one of the laws by which learning and remembering could be understood was, as he termed it, the Law of Exercise: when actions are repeatedly produced or events repeatedly experienced, they become stronger – better learned, more readily produced. When actions or events fall into disuse and are no longer practised, they become weaker and finally 'lost' from memory.

Two points implied by this account merit explicit consideration. The first is that rehearsal – or repetition to oneself – of an item appears to function in much the same way as actual repeated presentations of the stimulus itself; to a certain extent, as we saw in connexion with STM, one can give oneself, via rehearsal, additional learning trials and so increase the probability that the material will be (relatively) permanently learned. The second point is that remembrance of an item is here equated with action – the active response of recalling. Logically there is of course a distinction between *retention* – the fact that an item has been learned – and the reproduction, or *retrieval*, of a retained memory; however, we cannot distinguish operationally between the two. We can judge whether an item has been retained only by whether it can later be recalled.

The last sentence, however, requires modification. By *recall*, technically, is meant the production from memory of a given item; but this is only one of several methods of assessing retention. Another frequently used method is that of *recognition*: here the subject, after a learning task, is shown a number of items and is required to select from among them the item or items originally learned. Often the recognition method yields evidence of retention when recall does not; we know from everyday experience that even when we cannot recall, for example, the name of an acquaintance, we may recognize it instantly if it occurs in a book we are reading or in conversation. Other methods of measuring retention include the *savings* method: if a subject is asked to relearn a task which he has apparently forgotten, he may relearn it more quickly than if he were learning a new task of comparable difficulty. It is, therefore, sometimes possible to obtain evidence of retention which is independent of recall; but still the estimate of retention depends ultimately on the overt behaviour of the remembering subject.

Partly because different methods of measurement yield different estimates of retention, a simple explanation of forgetting in terms of *fading through disuse* cannot adequately account for the experimental and observational data. It appears to be more accurate to describe forgotten items as having become inaccessible, or irretrievable, rather than as having been 'lost'. The most powerful evidence for this distinction is quite simply that the same item may be remembered at one time, in one situation, and not another. For example, one may be unable to remember a fact which suddenly and apparently spontaneously emerges into consciousness later on. Clearly the memory was for some reason inaccessible at first but had not 'faded away'. In experiments on learning, it is often noted that a subject is able to recall more items from a learning task after a brief rest interval than immediately after learning. This effect is technically termed *reminiscence*; it has an analogy in the spontaneous recovery of extinguished responses in conditioning situations (see Chapter 12).

Again, one recalls some events of one's childhood and not others, even though there may seem to be nothing out of the ordinary about the recalled events. Clearly memory in this case, whether random or determined, is not a simple function of time since learning (this, of course, is not a forceful argument in the case of recalled events which have been much 'brooded over' – that is, rehearsed – in the past; but not all childhood events which are remembered appear, at least superficially, to be of this kind).

As in the special case of short-term memory, the most powerful opposition to the 'decay through disuse' theory has come from the *interference theory*, which has been and remains the most influential theory of forgetting in the field of human learning. Although some generality can be claimed for this theory, most of its argument is applied to, and supported by data from, the limited experimental situations of *transfer, proaction and retroaction*. To recapitulate and enlarge upon the definitions given in Chapter 12:

Transfer may be defined as the effect (positive or negative) of learning one task upon the learning of a second.

Proaction may be defined as the effect of learning one task upon the *retention* of a second, subsequently learned. Thus, having learned French may influence the ease with which we later learn Italian; this would be evidence of transfer. Also, having learned French may influence our retention of the Italian which we learn later, quite apart from its possible effect upon the actual learning. Proaction is therefore similar to but distinct from transfer, the practical distinction lying chiefly in the measures taken of our knowledge of the later task. A measure of transfer might be the number of learning trials required for a particular task – a vocabulary list or a declension – to be learned to a suitable criterion; a measure of proaction might be the percentage of the material, once learned to an agreed criterion, which is recalled after an interval. Of course, there may be a difference between performance at the last learning trial and performance at recall which is irrespective of any effects of previous learning: for example, reminiscence or its opposite, forgetting over time. Consequently, a control group of subjects learns and recalls the second task without having learned the first, and the difference between experimental and control subjects provides a measure of proaction. It is worth noting that the term 'task' is here used quite generally to refer to any material given to a subject to learn; it might be a language vocabulary, a list of numbers, a poem, a motor skill such as dart-throwing or car-driving. Laboratory studies, however, have generally employed verbal-learning tasks.

Retroaction is defined as the effect of interpolated learning upon the retention of a task previously learned: if we learn French and then Italian, retroaction would refer to the effect which learning Italian might have upon our retention of French. The measures used to assess retroaction are therefore measures of retention – recall, recognition, savings and so on – as in the case of proaction. Negative retroaction and negative proaction (or retroactive and proactive inhibition, as they are sometimes called) are therefore examples of forgetting and have been much used in the explanation of forgetting in terms of interference. Since proaction has been less extensively studied and with less clear-cut results, we shall be concerned chiefly with retroaction in the following discussion of interference theory. Fuller accounts of transfer and proaction may be found in McGeogh and Irion (1952) and Osgood (1953).

The typical design of experiments on retroaction is as follows: one group of subjects (the experimental group) learns task 1 either for a fixed learning time (e.g. a fixed number of trials) or until some criterion of learning is reached. These subjects then learn task 2, again for a given time or up to a given criterion; after this they are asked to recall, or sometimes to relearn, task 1. Control subjects learn task 1, and recall or relearn it after the same over-all interval as for experimental subjects; again, the difference between control and experimental subjects shows the extent to which the difference in procedure – in this case, the interpolation of task 2 between learning and recall – has influenced retention scores. This design, and designs for transfer and proaction experiments, are shown in Table 6.

Table 6
Experimental designs used to study (i) transfer, (ii) proaction and (iii) retroaction

(i) Transfer			
E group:		Learn task 1	Learn task 2
C group:		—	Learn task 2
(ii) Proaction			
E group:	Learn task 1	Learn task 2	Recall task 2
C group:	—	Learn task 2	Recall task 2
(iii) Retroaction			
E group:	Learn task 1	Learn task 2	Recall task 1
C group:	Learn task 1	—	Recall task 1

Evidence of *transfer* or of *proaction* is sought by comparing the performance of E and C groups in learning, or recalling, task 2. Evidence of *retroaction* is sought by comparing their final recall of task 1.

Naturally, the experimenter must attempt to ensure that subjects in both groups have learned task 1 (or task 2 in the case of proaction) to the same level, or at any rate must make allowances for any differences in original learning when analysing retention scores.

Many experiments using this design have furnished evidence that the interpolation of a second task influences retention of a first. The amount of retroaction, and whether it is negative or positive, is quite variable and appears to depend on several factors (for a fuller account, see Slamecka and Ceraso, 1960). One of these is the amount or degree of learning of the two tasks: in general, the better task 1 is learned the more resistant it is to negative retroaction, while the better task 2 is learned the more likely it is to cause negative retroaction (although this seems to be true only up to a point; when task 2 is very well learned it appears to be less likely to interfere with recall of task 1). The time intervals involved in the experiment – that is, the length of time elapsing between task 1 and task 2 learning, and between task 2 and recall of task 1 – may also be important, although evidence in this respect is conflicting. Probably most important is the factor of the similarity of task 2 to task 1. Clearly, if the two tasks are identical there must be positive transfer; yet it has long been held that when the tasks are not identical retroaction is usually negative and that its extent is greater when the tasks are similar than when they are dissimilar. This apparent contradiction (called, in the literature, the *similarity paradox*) is chiefly due to the fact that two kinds of similarity may be involved: *stimulus similarity* and *response similarity*. This distinction has already been discussed in Chapter 12 in connexion with *transfer* phenomena.

Often – for example, in the serial learning of a list of items, or in learning a skill – stimulus and response aspects of performance are not easily separated since the same item in a series may act both as a response (to the preceding item) and as a stimulus (to the following item). The different effects of stimulus and response similarity can most easily be seen in *paired-associate* (P-A) learning, in which the subject is presented with items in pairs, his task being to learn the second item of the pair as a response to the first. On subsequent tests the subject is presented with the first stimulus item and is asked to produce the response item. The items used in this type of learning may be verbal, such as words or nonsense syllables (a nonsense syllable consists of a three-letter unit, one vowel between two consonants, which does not form a meaningful word); they may be numbers, or nonsense or meaningful diagrams. The pairs of items may be alike or different in nature: a list for learning may, for instance, be composed of paired nonsense syllables, or of verbal stimulus terms paired with numerical responses.

When material of this kind is employed in retroaction experiments it is possible to vary the stimulus and response similarity of tasks 1 and 2 independently. In an A–B, A–C design, as it is termed, the stimuli used in the two tasks are identical and the responses different; in an A–B, C–B design the responses are identical while the stimuli differ, while both are different in an A–B, C–D design. From experiments based on material of this kind it appears that, generally speaking, when stimuli are identical but responses differ, negative retroaction occurs; response identity or close similarity, with or without stimulus similarity, produces positive retroaction. Psychologists interested in forgetting and in retroaction have generally used the A–B, A–C design. In this situation negative retroaction is typically produced, although it grows less as response similarity increases and becomes positive in effect as responses approach identity.

From these and other data the *interference* theorists (for example, Guthrie, 1935) argue that forgetting occurs because of competition among responses. In retroaction, responses from task 2 compete for production with responses from task 1: when the subject tries to remember B as a response to A, he instead remembers C, the response he learned to the same stimulus in task 2. Thus response B is not 'lost' – it has simply been supplanted by a stronger rival.

Later proponents of this type of explanation (e.g. Underwood, 1964) have pointed out that the competition involved is perhaps better described as a difficulty in *differentiating* responses from one task from responses from the other. If the two tasks have been imperfectly learned, the 'task membership' of responses cannot be readily identified and responses from the wrong task may be produced at recall. With thorough learning of the two tasks, inappropriate responses at recall will be recognized and withheld; this is why, as we have seen, very thorough learning, or overlearning, of task 2 (in the retroaction paradigm) does not produce ever greater decrement in recall of task 1 and may even reduce the decrement shown. Thus, this version of the interference theory relates not to response competition in a molecular sense but to rather global differentiations among learned material.

This interpretation of forgetting, although applicable chiefly to retroaction (and proaction) studies, can be applied to other situations also. The so-called *serial position effect* is an example. When subjects are asked to learn a list of items in their correct order, typically the first few and last few items are learned first, while the items in the middle of the list take longest to learn. The interference theorist would claim that this is because associations are formed not only between adjacent but also between more remote items; the nearer an item is to the centre of the list, the more *remote* associations (irrelevant to the task of producing items *in order*) are competing with the adjacent response which is the correct one to make and the more likely it is that an error will be made (for a fuller account of serial learning effects, see McGeogh and Irion, 1952). Interference theory has also been applied to conditioning situations. It is argued that extinction – learning not to perform a CR when it is no longer reinforced – is in fact learning to make other responses instead. A full account of this explanation is given by Guthrie (1935), Liberman (1948) and Osgood (1953). Thus, according to interference theory, a response is forgotten not because it has weakened or decayed but because some other response has taken its place.

Unfortunately, this elegant theory is not by itself adequate to explain all the experimental facts, even within the field of retroaction. The chief difficulty was pointed out by Barnes and Underwood (1959). These investigators evolved an experimental technique which they named 'modified free recall' (MFR); after learning two tasks constructed according to the A–B, A–C design, their subjects were asked, when shown each stimulus term, to produce both the responses they had learned to that stimulus, in either order. They found, as interference theory would predict, that when subjects produced both responses task 2 responses were produced first; this clearly indicates that task 2 responses were stronger. However, they also found that even when given plenty of time to produce responses subjects recalled fewer from task 1 than from task 2. Since competition between responses was no longer applicable, it seemed as though some 'unlearning' of task 1 responses must have occurred; not only are rival responses stronger, but the original response itself has weakened.

How might such unlearning occur? Underwood (1964) suggests that the process is essentially one of extinction. When the subject is learning task 2 he often thinks of responses from task 1; if he produces these responses they are treated as incorrect – that is, nonreinforced – and so become less likely to occur. They may be nonreinforced and therefore extinguished even if they are not produced overtly but are simply thought of and then rejected (for a fuller treatment of 'implicit responses' in this connexion, see Barnes and Underwood, 1959).

We are thus faced with a *two-factor theory* of forgetting. The simple 'disuse' theory is not satisfactory on its own; the interference theory, although it explains many of the data, cannot explain all, and it seems most reasonable to assume that forgetting, at least in these limited situations, may result from two factors. First, there may be competition from other responses to the same stimulus situation, which will result in the wrong item being remembered, or, when a number of responses are all of approximately equal strength, in no recall at all. Second, responses from an earlier task or situation may be unlearned during later learning because they are produced but recognized as inappropriate. It should be added that the two-factor theory may in some measure be reduced to a single-factor theory if one considers that unlearning may be simply a special case of interference. When recalling responses from task 1 the subject experiences competition between two responses: naming the correct item (the response learned during task 1 learning) and withholding the correct item (the response learned during task 2 learning). In other words, it may be just as much a 'response' to avoid giving (or to inhibit) a particular item as it is to utter it. There is no space here to discuss in more detail the various concepts of *inhibition* and the role which they may play in a theory of forgetting; see Chapter 12 for a brief account of the term, and also the accounts given by Osgood (1953), Pilkington and McKellar (1960) and Reid (1960).

Finally, two other theoretical accounts must briefly be mentioned. The first account is that of Gestalt psychology. We have already seen (Chapter 10) that the Gestalt psychologists maintained a *field theory* of cortical action; they assume that the memory trace remains subject to the same stresses as the perceptual trace. Where the trace is unstable, it may undergo modification, over time, in the direction of stability. Further, traces may by the same process be 'assimilated' to other similar traces and their individual characteristics lost (Koffka, 1935).

Many experiments have sought to show that memory for a given form may undergo *spontaneous changes* in the direction suggested by Gestalt theory. A classic early experiment was carried out by

Wulf (1922, trans. 1938), who showed his subjects diagrams such as those shown in Figure 54. Subjects were asked to reproduce the diagrams from memory, after varying intervals of time. Wulf found that changes occurred in memory, as judged from his subjects' attempts at reproduction, that the change was usually consistent in direction over several tests and that it might be either in the

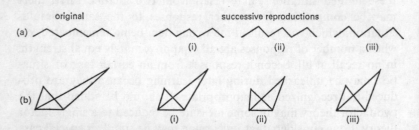

Figure 54 Successive changes in reproduction of figures from memory. Figure (a) shows a *sharpening* tendency: special characteristics and irregularities of the presented figure are emphasized in reproduction. Figure (b) shows a *levelling* effect: special characteristics and irregularities are smoothed out in reproduction and the figure tends towards symmetry.

In both cases reproductions were obtained thirty seconds (i), twenty-four hours (ii) and one week (iii) after presentation of the original. (From Wulf, 1922, trans. 1938)

direction of perfect symmetry and loss of any detail implying irregularity, or in the direction of extreme complexity in which any minor irregularity of the original figure became progressively exaggerated. These 'goals' he termed *minimal simplicity* and *maximal simplicity*, respectively, and the processes whereby the goals were approached were respectively described as *levelling* and *sharpening*. Whether in a given case levelling or sharpening occurred would depend principally upon the characteristics of the original figure (a somewhat different use of the terms 'levelling' and 'sharpening' will be mentioned later in this chapter; see also Chapter 10).

More procedurally sophisticated investigations have thrown considerable doubt on this finding. Hebb and Foord (1945), for example, pointed out that when a subject is asked to reproduce a drawing, changes may occur through inaccurate perception or imperfect drawing skills; such changes have been shown to occur even when the subject is copying a form displayed before him and therefore cannot be taken as evidence of a change in memory. Further, when the subject is tested repeatedly over a period of time, he may be influenced not only by his memory of the original stimulus but also by his memory of previous attempts at reproduction, so that a mistake occurring early in testing is likely to persist throughout all tests; thus, the consistency found in the direction of change may be purely an artifact of repeated testing. Hebb and Foord, in an experiment which controlled these factors by using a recognition test of memory and by testing different groups of subjects, rather than the same subjects, at different intervals after presentation of the stimulus forms, found no evidence of systematic or progressive change in memory over time.

The controversy did not end there. It can be argued, for instance, that the recognition method itself is not an entirely suitable measure of change in memory for form and many experiments have since been aimed at devising methods which are free from criticism. A detailed review of the methodological issues, and of the research findings, in this area has been provided by Riley (1962). In summary we can say that very little evidence has been produced to support the Gestalt view, but that the task of providing evidence whose interpretation is unambiguous has so far proved virtually impossible. It should also be pointed out that it is often extremely difficult to predict the change expected in memory, especially when memory other than for form is concerned.

The last theory of forgetting to be listed here is the Freudian theory of *repression*. Very briefly, Freud (1925) hypothesized that certain ideas and events may be forgotten because they are threatening in content: wishes, feelings or actions which in the past, maybe in childhood, have been met with punishment or the threat of punishment are 'repressed' – expelled from consciousness – and can be expressed only in distorted form or in very special circumstances, for example, during therapy. Such memories are not 'erased' but become inaccessible; this is a position similar to that of the interference and inhibition theories. It differs from the Gestalt view in that memories are held to be retained in their original form as well as in distorted form, and in that distortion occurs as a result of associated anxiety and threat rather than because of the formal instability of the memory trace. (It should, however, be pointed out in passing that other accounts of mnemonic change have considered both structural and motivational factors to be of importance; see, for example, Bartlett, 1932.)

Numerous experiments have been devised to test the notion of 'motivated forgetting' in the laboratory; a review of such work has been given by McGeogh and Irion (1952) and more recently by McKinnon and Dukes (1962). Such studies would certainly indicate, on the whole, that the affective tone of material may be reflected in its ease of reproduction at a later date; for example, memory for 'pleasant' events is better than that for 'unpleasant' events, and tasks in the laboratory which have been associated with failure and which have therefore gained unpleasant significance are less likely to be recalled than tasks which have no such connotation. There are, however, methodological difficulties with many studies and it is unclear whether the differential recall of pleasant and unpleasant material reflects differences in learning, or in rehearsal, rather than in 'purer' characteristics of retention. It is also worth noting that the orthodox Freudian bases his support for the notion of repression upon clinical evidence, rather than experimental. Reviews of such clinical evidence can be found in D. Russell Davis (1957) and Rapaport (1942).

Why are there variations in the efficiency of remembering?

Our consideration of remembering and forgetting has up till now been somewhat theoretical; in this final section we shall be concerned with a brief and empirical account of some factors which appear to influence the degree of remembering or forgetting of material. These factors are grouped here under five headings: the material to be retained, the conditions of learning, the retention interval, the remembering situation (that is, the conditions under which retention is measured) and differences among rememberers. More detailed accounts of these and other factors are given by I. L. Hunter (1964) and McGeogh and Irion (1952).

The material to be retained

It is clear that some tasks or types of material are easier than others to learn and indeed to perceive. Naturally, variations in learning and perception will be reflected in retention scores, since what is imperfectly registered cannot be perfectly retained. We are concerned here to hold learning and perception constant and to study variation in memory alone. However, there is evidence which suggests that it is unrealistic to separate out learning and retention altogether, since ease of learning, even when learning is to a constant criterion, appears to influence efficiency of memory: material which is *quickly* learned is also better remembered (Underwood, 1949). This relation is hardly surprising when one considers that learning and retention, which we consider here as being quite distinct, are far from distinct as far as measurement is concerned. We test whether learning has occurred by what is effectively a measure of immediate recall or recognition. Evidence of the relation between speed of learning and efficiency of retention may be taken to mean that people who are 'good at' immediate recall are also 'good at' delayed recall, or that material which is favoured in immediate recall will also be favoured in delayed recall (indeed, it might be taken to support the conclusion that there is no essential distinction between STM and LTM).

On the other hand, it is not altogether simple to equate the *degree of learning* of fast and slow learners. Normally, a criterion of learning is decided on, say, one perfect reproduction of the material, or perhaps an attempt at reproduction which is 80 per cent successful, and all subjects continue learning until the criterion is reached. However, a fast learner may 'overshoot' the criterion of learning; that is, he may produce a performance which on one trial is below the criterion, and on the next is well above it; if the criterion is perfect recall, the fast learner may be able to *overlearn* – that is, to practise what is already learned (a practice which also improves recall). A slow learner, on the other hand, can more accurately be stopped when the criterion is exactly reached, since he improves by a smaller amount on each trial. Thus, the better memory shown by fast learners may reflect, to some extent, a greater degree of original learning. This difficulty must be borne in mind whenever differences in the retention of different materials are considered.

Subject to this caution, there is evidence that *meaningful* material is better remembered than less meaningful materials: for example, a passage of connected prose is more easily remembered than a list of unrelated words (comparable in amount), which in turn is easier to recall than a list of nonsense syllables. Again, nonsense syllables of high associative value (that is, syllables which readily give rise to meaningful associations) are better remembered than syllables of low associative value. Similarly (and this is to some extent the same phenomenon), familiar items are more readily recalled than unfamiliar items. The effect of meaningfulness and familiarity may to some extent reflect not so much better memory as more successful guessing at the time of remembering; if part of the material is remembered, it is easier to guess at the rest if the whole is meaningfully inter-related, and familiar words or percepts are more likely to be 'tried out' in recall attempts than unfamiliar ones, simply because the subject is more likely to think of them as possibilities. The finding can be related to evidence already briefly mentioned in the section above, that 'well-organized' material is more accurately remembered than less well-organized material, and that such distortions as occur in reproduction are likely to be in the direction of organization and meaningfulness (see Bartlett, 1932).

Some experimenters have given their subjects simple tasks to perform in the laboratory and have afterwards asked for recall (simply naming) of the tasks performed. Zeigarnik (1927, trans. 1938) found that in this situation whether or not a task had been completed appeared to influence its recall; she allowed her subjects to complete some tasks while interrupting the performance of others and found that more interrupted than completed tasks were afterwards recalled. Zeigarnik argued, within the framework of Gestalt theory, that tensions are set up during performance of a task, persist if the task is uncompleted and hence facilitate recall. The effect appears to be dependent in part upon the attitude of subjects to interruption; if subjects are instructed that the tasks represent a test of their ability and that interruption represents failure, the effect is (often) reversed; more completed than uncompleted tasks are recalled (S. Rosenzweig, 1943). This finding also serves as a reminder that, as mentioned above, the affective tone of material may also influence its recall; items which are held (either *a priori*, or as a result of subjects' ratings, or because of experiences induced in the laboratory) to be unpleasant in emotional connotation tend to be less well remembered than items of neutral or pleasant connotation.

The conditions of learning

Two points here should be briefly mentioned. First, it appears that such characteristics of learning as the distribution of practice - that is, the temporal spacing of learning trials – may affect not only speed of learning but also the efficiency of remembering. Second, retention may be affected by activity prior to learning. One possible effect of this kind, proaction, has been discussed earlier. Moreover, learning activity prior to the crucial task may produce a general facilitatory effect upon remembering, termed the 'warm-up phenomenon' (Thune, 1950). This effect differs from proaction in that it is less specific to the tasks learned, and less dependent upon such factors as task similarity. It must again be stressed that it is difficult in these cases to separate out effects upon learning from effects upon remembering.

The retention interval

The clearest fact, for the layman, about retention is that the efficiency with which we remember is related to the time since learning; forgetting is a negatively accelerated function of time (although there are exceptions to this general rule; for example, reminiscence may occur, and it is a common observation that certain motor skills are very highly resistant to forgetting). The 'forgetting curve', classically demonstrated by Ebbinghaus (1885, trans. 1913), is shown in Figure 55.

We have argued that 'the passage of time' is not itself a sufficient explanation of forgetting. If time is related to forgetting, it must be because the lapse of time presents the opportunity for more basic factors to operate. Degeneration of the physiological representation of memories *may* occur over time, although the physiological basis of memory is so imperfectly understood that it is difficult to test the hypothesis. Perhaps more probable is the hypothesis that time allows interference from other memories or from new learning.

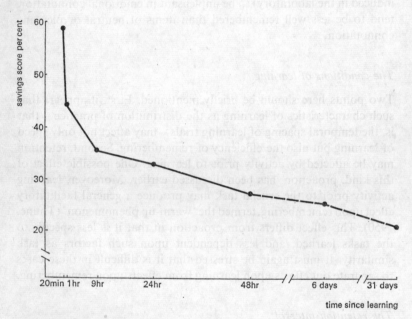

Figure 55   The rate of forgetting over time (data from Ebbinghaus, 1885). The 'savings score' represents the reduction in time needed for relearning, as opposed to original learning, of lists of nonsense syllables, expressed as a percentage of the original learning time

We have already seen that remembering may be affected by the nature of the activity intervening between learning and recall. Studies in which activity during the retention interval is drastically reduced tend to show that memory is improved under such circumstances. Jenkins and Dallenbach (1924), for example, found memory better when subjects had slept through the retention interval than when they had been awake for the same interval. There was some loss of recall even under the 'sleep' condition, which might be taken to mean either that some decay may occur spontaneously over time, or that some minimal activity continues and may interfere with retention, even during sleep – certainly a tenable assumption.

Finally, practice, as we have seen before, is extremely important. If we hold that some memories may be relatively permanent while others are lost or assimilated, it may well be, as Waugh and Norman (1965) argue, that it is the rehearsal of items which leads to their preservation. On the other hand, experimental studies of the Gestalt theory of forgetting have shown that repeated reproduction of remembered material may reveal qualitative changes in memory and that the repetition may itself accelerate such changes. It is not entirely clear, therefore, that we can describe practice as being invariably beneficial for accurate retention.

The remembering situation

Again, two points will be made here. First, the efficiency of retention demonstrated will depend very largely on the measure of retention employed. The recognition method typically is the most sensitive test of retention – that is, it most readily shows evidence of retention – and the recall method the least sensitive (for a discussion of different measures and their interrelations, see Bahrick and Bahrick, 1964, and McGeogh and Irion, 1952).

Second, remembering appears to be influenced by the general conditions in which testing is carried out. Remembering appears to be better when learning and later recall are carried out in the same room, or with the same experimenter (Abernethy, 1940). In retroaction studies, the amount of retroaction can be reduced if task 1 is both learned and recalled in the same room while the intervening task 2 is learned in a different room (Greenspoon and Ranyard, 1957).

This is not surprising if we consider that recall requires not only the reproduction of learned material but also *discrimination* between available material which is appropriate to the recall situation and available material which is inappropriate to it. Background characteristics of the situations in which learning occurs may become conditioned to the material which is learned – that is, they function as stimuli associated with the production of the learning material and not with the production of material learned under different conditions. The finding underlines the observation that even in a simple associative learning task the stimuli involved in learning may be more numerous and more diverse than is implied by the experimenter's design.

Individual differences among rememberers

The results of various studies indicate that efficiency of remembering is to some extent a function of age. For example, the memory span increases from infancy up to perhaps eighteen or twenty years of age, and declines thereafter, although the decline may not be apparent until after the age of forty or fifty. These findings, and in particular those related to old age, are rather dependent upon the techniques employed. Most studies are concerned with fairly short-term memory, while long-term memory appears to be less susceptible to age differences (useful reviews of relevant findings are given by Birren, 1964, and McGeogh and Irion, 1952). Moreover, age has been shown to affect learning speed and we are therefore faced with the often-mentioned difficulty of distinguishing between differences in acquisition and differences in recall. It is also true, at least in a general sense, that the amount of prior learning and training which the subject brings to a new task and the possibility of positive or negative proaction must vary with age.

It is often stressed in psychoanalytic writings that some individuals are more apt than others to use repression as a defence against threatening material. More generally, several workers have suggested that there are personality differences among individuals which are reflected in characteristics of memory. For example, Broadbent (1958) suggested that individuals differ in the extent to which they 'bear in mind' past events when viewing and classifying present events, and describes individuals at either extreme in this respect as *short-term or long-term samplers*. Long-term samplers commonly interpret and store incoming events against the background of previous experience; they are thus more likely to *assimilate* percepts to previous traces. The implications for memory are similar to those of the levelling/sharpening dichotomy proposed by Gardner *et al.* (1959) and already mentioned in Chapter 10.

'Levelling' and 'sharpening' are terms meant to denote differences in the characteristics of memory organization and, more specifically, the extent to which new stimuli become assimilated to the traces of earlier stimuli. Gardner *et al.* (1959) defined levellers and sharpeners operationally in these terms:

Sharpeners were characterized by small assimilation effects in a variety of situations, and their memory schemata seemed relatively differentiated. In levellers, successive perceptual impressions were assimilated to each other, so that distinctions among them were blurred. Memories of past impressions were also less available to them, presumably because of the general lack of differentiation of their memory schemata (p. 105).

It is further claimed that levelling/sharpening represents a rather general principle of cognitive functioning, related not only to memory but also to thinking and to perception. However, there are certain difficulties in the way of this interpretation. Levelling/sharpening has been demonstrated as a coherent factor (that is, as a cluster of consistently co-varying characteristics of behaviour) for women only, not for men; and several other principles of cognitive control have been hypothesized by the same authors which would appear to be independent of levelling/sharpening and of equal importance. In general, the reliability and the generality of individual differences in memory characteristics have not been unequivocally demonstrated.

Conclusions

It is impossible in any real sense to summarize the diverse data presented here, but two recurrent problems deserve final consideration. The first concerns the *generality* of findings and theories reported here.

Consider, for example, the two-factor theory which seemed to emerge as (provisionally) victorious from our discussion of forgetting. The theory was devised within the specific framework of retroaction and proaction phenomena, but it can be argued that proaction and retroaction experiments are more representative of the 'usual' forgetting situation than one might at first suppose. We acquire and retain new skills or new information against a background of more or less relevant previous learning; and skills and knowledge, once acquired, have to be retained inevitably over periods of further learning. Thus it can be said that any remembering situation possesses in some degree the characteristics of proaction and of retroaction. Hence, the two-factor theory should be applicable to a wide range of situations. In fact, it has been somewhat less than successful in this respect. The 'unlearning' factor as an explanation of forgetting is specific to the *retroaction* situation and cannot explain the decrement of recall found in *proaction* situations, even within the laboratory; the disrupting task in the proaction paradigm is learned *before* the task to be recalled and therefore cannot produce unlearning, as defined by Underwood (1964), in it (although Ceraso, 1967, has made use of an 'unlearning' factor, as well as of an interference factor which he terms 'crowding', to explain certain characteristics of proaction phenomena). Only the interference factor is therefore left as having any generality; and when precise predictions are made, on the basis of interference theory, as to the effect of specified variables upon performance in situations where interference, proactive or retroactive, is hypothesized to exist outside the experimental situation, these predictions tend not to be confirmed (e.g. Underwood and Ekstrand, 1966). On the other hand, some of the empirical relations we have mentioned (pp. 366–73) could be explained in interference theory terms.

STM situations may seem more typical of everyday experience than LTM situations; but it is, again, questionable whether the findings obtained in STM experiments would apply to the short-term recall of items in everyday life, when selective attention and rehearsal are not rigidly excluded by experimental control. It may be that the qualitative distinction between characteristics of STM and characteristics of LTM becomes even more tenuous when these controls are lacking: that, for example, recall in both situations shows selectivity, and that the factors influencing performance are more closely in correspondence.

The other problem which has been of central importance throughout this chapter concerns the notion of *loss from memory*. We have argued that the evidence for loss derives principally from two sources. First, the studies of figural variation in memory which were initiated by Gestalt hypotheses have suggested that memories may be irrevocably lost through assimilation to other memories; but, as we suggested earlier, there are considerable difficulties in the interpretation of such evidence, chiefly arising from the virtually insoluble problems of measurement. Second, some evidence, though not incontrovertible, has been produced by experiments in STM; and when we consider the characteristics of STM experiments a curious fact emerges. To ensure perfect initial registration and to exclude the necessity for response learning, many experimenters have used as stimulus materials simple and *highly familiar* items: for example, digits or letters of the alphabet, or familiar common or proper nouns. Moreover, if unfamiliar items are used (for example, nonsense syllables) they are new combinations of familiar items (for example, letters). It is therefore absurd, in many cases, to say simply that when an item is not produced in immediate recall it has been 'lost from memory', since it can almost certainly be reproduced under different circumstances – for example, under instructions to recite the alphabet, or to count to ten. What is lost is not an item but an association; presentation of material does not evoke item learning so much as *context learning*, and it is this learning – *the differentiation from other well-known items of those which are relevant to the context of the recall test* – which may be lost. (We have also seen that this kind of learning appears to be highly relevant to certain LTM situations.)

In a narrow sense, therefore, items have perhaps never (at least in the laboratory) been shown to 'disappear'. Associations, representing the relation between an item and its situational context, may be irrevocably lost; on the other hand, even the strongest evidence for loss might be interpreted to mean rather that certain items, or item–context associations, may become so deeply inaccessible that subtler measures than are available are needed to retrieve them. It seems virtually impossible to state either that all registered material is immune or that any is ever susceptible to loss.

It may be possible to argue that much if not all learning and retention beyond that of the neonate is to be explained in terms of differentiation – the discrimination of relevant from irrelevant registered material, and the problems of accessibility as well as competition involved in the discrimination. Undoubtedly, however, the notion of differentiation needs much in the way of experimental and theoretical analysis before we can hope to apply it with any generality to the diverse phenomena of remembering and forgetting.

Further reading
J. A. Adams, *Human Memory*, McGraw-Hill, 1967.
U. Neisser, *Cognitive Psychology*, Appleton-Century-Crofts, 1967.
L. Postman and G. Keppel (eds.), *Verbal Learning and Memory*, Penguin Books, 1969.
N. J. Slamecka (ed.), *Human Learning and Memory: Selected Readings*, Oxford University Press, 1967.
G. A. Talland, *Disorders of Memory and Learning*, Penguin Books, 1968.

Part Four
Symbolic Behaviour

The functions of perception, learning and memory all involve what may be termed internal representation of external events. We have seen in Part Three that internal representation is sometimes, but by no means always, an exact mirror of its external referents, and that our study of these functions has led us repeatedly to the notion of *organization*: the processes of representation impose their own characteristics upon what is recorded and utilized. In Part Four we now turn to a closer consideration of representational, or symbolic, processes. Chapter 15 is concerned with *language*, for humans the most obvious and the most important medium of symbolic behaviour, and Chapter 16 more generally with the notions of internal representation involved in the study of *thinking*. Through both chapters the definition of *symbolic behaviour* will become clearer, although it remains largely implicit; for more explicit treatments, see, for example, Creelman (1966) and Mowrer (1960b).

It is almost paradoxical that, in this book at least, the relation between man and animals should assume most prominence in a section concerned with language and thinking; for these functions are traditionally held to be exclusively human. Animals, it is commonly maintained, either do not possess such capacities or possess them only in the most rudimentary form. Moreover, thinking is private and unobservable behaviour. In the first place we know of its existence only through our own 'inner experience', and thus with the advent of early behaviourism it appeared an area of experience not appropriate to scientific investigation. Language is observable but except when it is simple 'labelling behaviour' it has reference to absent things and events, and often to those internal experiences which were themselves regarded as unsuitable for study; thus it seemed impossible in many cases to find an objective reference for language behaviour. It is only comparatively recently that language and thinking have become again topics for scientific study, with the advent of new attitudes in psychology and new methods of investigation.

In consequence, both chapters in this section will be concerned to some extent with the relation between human and animal behaviour. In both, also, the general emphasis will be rather less upon empirical findings than upon methodology and conceptual analysis.

Chapter 15
Language

Introduction

The possession of a language system, both spoken and written, is generally considered to be an exclusively human attribute, one which demarcates human beings from animals quite unequivocally. However, not all human languages have a written form; and for spoken language, too, the line of demarcation is not at first sight firmly drawn. Animals of domesticated species are able to respond appropriately to verbal commands; certain birds, for example parrots and Indian mynah birds, are able to reproduce strings of words or phrases to which they have been exposed, and anthropoid apes possess communication systems of different sounds which may appear to differ from human language only in degree. There are several 'design features' which language and vocal signalling systems of animals possess in common (see Hockett, 1960), and several of the functions of human language appear to be shared by animal communication systems. For example, sounds emitted by animals may serve to warn intruders encroaching on alien territory, to attract mates, to threaten enemies and to preserve the social structure of large groups.

Hockett suggests, however, at least four main differences. First, human beings can talk about objects or events which are remote from the speaker in terms of time or place or both. This feature of language, known as *displacement*, appears to be absent from the vocalizations of the anthropoid apes, although bee dancing, a communication which serves to inform other bees of the presence of nectar, might be said to possess it. The second major difference is that of *productivity*. Human beings are capable both of generating and of understanding utterances which have been neither heard nor spoken before. Human language is thus an 'open' system; it is capable of infinite expansion. The vocalizations of animals, on the other hand, tend to form a 'closed' system, the repertoire being fixed and finite. It is not possible for animals to coin new vocalizations by rearranging old ones. This is in part a consequence of the third and perhaps the most important difference, which Hockett calls *duality of patterning*. This term refers to the way in which a limited range of distinguishable sounds can be combined and re-combined into an enormous vocabulary. The size of the human language system is thus not limited by the number of different sounds that a human being can discriminate, especially when for the most part the discrimination has to be made under far from ideal conditions. An example of a communication system which relies on the principle of duality of patterning for its effectiveness is the Morse Code. What has to be discriminated by the Morse Code operator is a very small number of individual message elements, only two lengths of pulse and about three lengths of pause. But an infinite variety of messages can be transmitted by the rearrangement of these elementary message units. Duality of patterning does not appear to be a feature of animal communication systems and the lack of it severely restricts the efficiency and flexibility of such systems.

The fourth major difference between human and animal communication systems is that language is *transmitted* across generations through the processes of teaching and learning, whereas the communication systems used by animals appear not to be. As R. Brown (1965, p. 250) has put it:

Information that one person possesses can be delivered to others who do not have it but could use it. This kind of transmission is possible between generations as well as among contemporaries, and so, with the emergence of language, life experiences begin to be cumulative. Some animal species are able to transmit a small amount of lore across generations; chiefly knowledge of waterholes, feeding places and the habits of enemies. But most of what the aged anthropoid knows perishes with him. The young chimpanzee starts life, as he did millennia ago, from scratch.

Given these differences between human language and animal communication, do such differences represent a discontinuity or can animal communication systems be viewed as rudimentary language systems? The *continuity theory* of language development maintains that there is no essential difference between them, and that the origins of language may be found in comparative studies of animal communication. The sounds used in human language systems may be different from the acoustic signals of animals, and the number of messages which human beings can transmit may be much greater because of duality of patterning; but both these developments are considered by continuity theory to result from the increase in non-specific intelligence associated with man's position at the top of the phylogenetic scale.

The main disadvantage of this argument lies in the logical and practical difficulty of comparing 'non-specific intelligence' across species. As Lenneberg (1967, p. 229) has said, 'comparing the intelligence of different species is comparable to making *relative* measurements in *different* universes and comparing the results in *absolute* terms'.

A second type of continuity theory considers language to consist of a number of separate skills, all of which must be available before the organism is capable of developing a language system and each of which has its own unique phylogenetic history. The German zoologist Otto Koehler (accounts of his work can be found in Lenneberg, 1967, and Thorpe, 1966) has suggested that there are at least nineteen biological prerequisites of language and his experiments appear to have demonstrated, though not beyond controversy, that at least some of them are present in certain birds and animals. This second form of the continuity theory implies that, in the animals closest to man on the phylogenetic scale, the majority of these language prerequisites should be detectable, with progressively fewer of them occurring as the phylogenetic scale is descended. Little evidence is available to support such a proposition. The conclusion Lenneberg (1967) draws from a detailed consideration of these two forms of continuity theory is that the development of language in man is attributable to species-specific biological capacities, most of which are, as yet, unknown. His is, therefore, a *discontinuity* theory; he maintains that particular patterns of cognitive function are uniquely characteristic of given species, and are closely related to species-specific behaviour. One aspect of man's cognitive function is his potential for language, a characteristic not shared by any other species. The actualization of language potential is dependent both upon environmental stimulation and upon the maturation of the brain (see Chapter 4).

Our concern in the remainder of this chapter is with human language behaviour rather than animal communication. It is useful to begin with the distinction between *langue* and *parole*. The Swiss linguist, Ferdinand de Saussure, was the first to make explicit this important distinction – effectively a distinction between language and speech (de Saussure, 1915). This distinction is intended to eliminate the ambiguity revealed by a consideration of the two statements: 'He is speaking English' and 'He speaks English.' Thus, it would be quite fair to say that a mynah bird, under the appropriate circumstances, 'is speaking English' – that is, is uttering sound sequences which are acceptable as English – but it would not be appropriate to say that it 'speaks English'. Following de Saussure, it could be said that all those individuals who 'speak English' share a particular *langue* and that the utterances which they produce when they are 'speaking English' are instances of *parole*. All those who 'speak English' produce utterances when they are speaking it which, in spite of the variations between them, can be described in terms of a particular system of rules and relations: that is, in some sense, all these different utterances share the same *structural* characteristics. The utterances, which are instances of *parole*, are taken by the linguist as evidence for the construction of the underlying common structure, namely the *langue*.

The linguist is concerned with describing the *langue*, the language system. The psychologist's interest, on the other hand, is principally in *parole*, language behaviour. He may be guided either by his knowledge of findings, methods and theories in other areas of psychology – notably in the area of learning – or by a knowledge of findings, methods and theories in the area of linguistics. The first approach depends upon the assumption that language behaviour is not essentially different from other kinds of behaviour, and that all kinds are ultimately to be described in the same sorts of terms; the second approach depends upon the assumption that while linguistic concepts are not themselves appropriate as psychological descriptions they may nevertheless suggest parallel psychological concepts which will prove fruitful in the description of language behaviour.

The subject matter of the psychology of language includes the interrelated problems of *speech perception* – how speech is understood by the listener; the generation of *grammatical sentences* – how grammatical sentences are produced by the speaker; and *language acquisition* – how a child acquires the language of his community. In the last section we shall consider some empirical studies undertaken in these areas; first, however, in the next section we shall examine further the types of approach which have been made to the psychological study of language.

Approaches to the psychology of language

Learning-theory approaches

Learning-theory approaches to the psychology of language represent an extension to language behaviour of principles which were devised to account for the acquisition and modification of non-verbal (and often non-human) behaviour. In a sense the term 'learning-theory approach' is a misnomer, since theories of learning are very diverse with respect to the principles they employ; the 'learning-theory approach' to language has been almost entirely in terms of associative learning and, more narrowly, in terms of conditioning principles. The approach is most readily seen at work in the context of *verbal learning*. Verbal as well as non-verbal responses have been used in the study of learning and retention (see Chapters 12 and 14) and even in studies of instrumental conditioning (see, for example, J. H. Williams, 1964), and the same interpretative principles have been adopted whether the responses involved are verbal or non-verbal. Thus, in much verbal learning research, linguistic elements are simply vehicles for the study of learning processes. However, the 'learning-theory approach' has been applied not only to verbal responses in simple learning situations but also to integrated verbal behaviour: Skinner (1957), for example, has produced a theory of language acquisition in terms of conditioning, and writers such as Bousfield (1961), Mowrer (1960b), C. E. Noble (1963) and Osgood (Osgood, Suci and Tannenbaum, 1957) have offered accounts of meaning and meaningfulness which, while they differ considerably in detail, share a common foundation in associationist (s–r) or mediational (s–o–r) learning theory.

What sort of theoretical account can 'learning theory' give of language behaviour? We shall briefly consider two examples: first, a simple account of the acquisition of language; second, Mowrer's (1960b) account of 'the sentence as a conditioning device' whereby words may acquire meanings.

One might argue (and many have) that language learning proceeds in situations analogous to classical and instrumental conditioning. For example, a mother may bring her child a cup of milk and say the word 'milk' at the same time. The sight of the drink produces various responses such as smiling, reaching out, grasping the cup, drinking. The word which accompanies it may then become a *conditioned stimulus* eliciting a conditioned response derived from the response to the drink itself (see Chapter 12). True, the mother may vary what she says to the child when bringing milk. She may only rarely, if ever, speak the single word alone; more often, she will say 'Here's your milk' or 'Drink up your milk' or, on other occasions, 'Do you want some milk?' The child is held to be capable of generalizing from one potential cs to another on the basis of their common word 'milk'; and it is probable that the mother aids such stimulus generalization by placing selective emphasis on the crucial word when speaking. (We shall not consider here the vexed question of what sort of reinforcement, if any, might be held necessary for learning to occur; for a discussion, see Chapter 12.)

At other times, a child may utter a word-like sound, such as 'do-do'. His mother observes: 'He wants his dolly,' and gives the doll to the child. In other words, certain spontaneous vocalizations are selectively and specifically reinforced; later, when the child wants his doll, he may say 'do-do' again and will receive the doll and the *instrumental* conditioning of the response 'do-do' is strengthened. Again, if the child says 'do-do' when he is given his doll, he may gain further rewards in the form of praise, attention, perhaps a sweet. The child's correct pronunciation of the word may be effected by behaviour on the part of the mother. At first she will reward any utterance which bears some similarity to the appropriate word; later on, one might hypothesize, she becomes more selective (perhaps as a result of her acceptance of cultural norms for children's speech, perhaps because it is growing increasingly apparent that the child is improving his control over his own vocalization), and gives the doll to the child only when he produces the word 'dolly' or something close to it. This procedure is analogous to the training procedure of 'shaping' which Skinner (1938) has employed in the instrumental conditioning of animals.

Of these two situations, the first appears to describe the skill of understanding speech and the second the skill of uttering it. One can hypothesize further that there is transfer from one skill to the other. For example, in the 'classical conditioning' situation one might suppose that the child not only hears his mother say 'milk' but also imitates her; if he repeats 'milk' or some approximation to it, he is further rewarded. Again, if a mother repeats her child's utterance while also rewarding it, the stimulus word will be conditioned to the reward given. Thus the same situation can furnish the opportunity both for classical and for instrumental conditioning.

At first sight this account of language learning possesses elegance and simplicity. However, it is entirely speculative, and there are a number of difficulties in the way of its acceptance (see G. A. Miller, 1965). In the first place, the theory is less simple than it sounds; it is not clear, for example, what is the nature of the reinforcement needed for language conditioning, or whether the learning of labels is more simply a function of the repeated co-occurrence of word with referent in the child's experience, contiguity alone being needed for the association to be formed.

In the second place, it must be pointed out that the mother's teaching of her child is likely to be irregular and unsystematic. If the child is left by himself he may call for milk or for 'dolly' without being rewarded by the desired object; when he utters 'do-do' he may be given a doll when in fact he wants milk. The conditioning schedule which the mother presents is therefore likely to be one which would prove ineffective in the laboratory.

Finally, the learning techniques outlined above may account in part for the learning of words, or of sounds; but they cannot account for all aspects of language use. It has often been pointed out that humans can produce sentences which they have never heard before, and indeed it would be impossible to maintain that a child learns his repertoire of sentences in the way that he learns a vocabulary, since the range of possible sentences is far too great to render the position tenable. The simple account given here cannot furnish a model for the acquisition of grammatical rules. What these rules are will be discussed in the last part of this section.

How can an associationist theory of language explain meaning? As already indicated, even within the learning-theory approach there are several theories of meaning and we shall only quote, very briefly, one example drawn from one of them; an introductory discussion of associationist theories of meaning has been given by Carroll (1964), and a more detailed account by Creelman (1966).

Mowrer's (1960b) account of 'the sentence as a conditioning device' took as its example the now classic sentence: 'Tom is a thief.' Mowrer argued that the exchange of such a sentence between speaker and listener sets up a conditioning paradigm in the listener, which can be expressed diagrammatically as in Figure 56. The listener already knows Tom; the word 'Tom' arouses in him a complex of *mediating responses* – called here the mediating response 'Tom', or r_m (Tom) – representing total and distinctive reactions to the person. Mowrer proposes that such mediating responses can be viewed as constituting the 'meaning' of Tom for the listener. The listener also knows the meaning of the word 'thief'; that is, the word arouses a complex of mediating responses – r_m (thief) – representing distinctively, though in reduced form, 'the total reaction elicited by real thieves' (p. 144). Thus, when both words are used in the sentence: 'Tom is a thief' the r_m (thief) becomes associated with the r_m (Tom) (or, more accurately, with the *mediated stimulation*, s_m (Tom), involved in the mediation sequence; see Chapter 12). When Tom is subsequently encountered in person, his presence evokes not only r_m (Tom) but also r_m (thief). The word 'Tom' is not identical in meaning with the word 'thief' but their *meanings* (r_ms) have become associated.

While it must yet again be stressed that associationist theories – and, indeed, specifically mediational theories – of meaning vary, this example illustrates the notion which they generally share, that

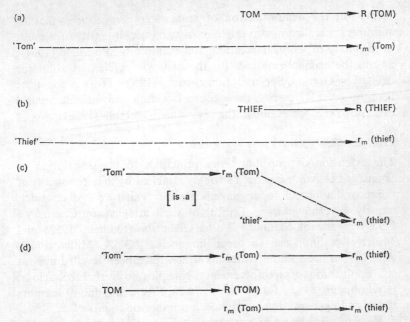

Figure 56 The sentence as a conditioning device. (After Mowrer, 1960b, pp. 144 and 146)

(a) Distinctive components of the total reaction to the real person (TOM) become conditioned to the word 'Tom'.

(b) Distinctive components of the total reaction to a real thief (THIEF) become conditioned to the word 'thief'.

(c) When – in a sentence – 'Tom' and 'thief' are experienced in conjunction, the 'thief-meaning' – r_m (thief) – becomes conditioned to the 'Tom-meaning' – r_m (Tom).

(d) When the word 'Tom' is subsequently encountered, it evokes the 'thief-meaning' – r_m (thief) – as well as, and by way of, the 'Tom-meaning' – r_m (Tom). When the person TOM is encountered, the response to TOM *includes* the 'Tom-meaning' – r_m (Tom) – which evokes the 'thief-meaning' – r_m (thief)

meaning may be held to be acquired through the interconditioning of implicit and largely verbal responses. The basic difficulties of the hypothesis are those of the learning-theory approach from which they spring. In particular, the notion of 'mediation', as we saw in Chapter 12, is speculative and almost entirely untestable, although within the context of meaning there have been attempts to test the theory: in the demonstration of *semantic generalization* – that is, stimulus generalization on the basis of semantic similarity of stimuli; in the study of word association, for example by Bousfield (1961); and in the original rationale for the *semantic differential* technique devised by Osgood, Suci and Tannenbaum (1957). There is not space here, however, to discuss these sources of data and their theoretical extension; see, for example, the review by Creelman (1966).

Learning theory versus psycholinguistics

The extension of learning-theory principles to the description of language behaviour has been strongly attacked by the proponents of the second approach to language behaviour which we shall consider, namely *psycholinguistics*. Typical of such attacks are Chomsky's (1959) review of Skinner's *Verbal Behavior* (Skinner, 1957) and Miller's 'preliminaries to psycholinguistics' (G. A. Miller, 1965). Apart from the specific criticisms which have been levelled against the application of reinforcement principles to verbal behaviour, psycholinguists have found Skinner's approach, and that of learning theorists in general, inadequate on a number of counts.

First of all they point out that a learning-theory analysis of the meaning of words in terms of discrete associative links (whether between word and thing, between word and word, or between word and feeling) fails to measure up to the full complexity of the phenomenon. This is perhaps brought out most clearly if we look at the meaning of sentences, rather than at the meaning of words.

Chomsky and Miller argue that the meaning of a sentence is not simply the sum of the meanings of the individual words that make up the sentence. Although the meanings of individual words may be acquired through discrimination learning, sentences are not understood by a process of totalling up the meanings of words, and the meanings of sentences are certainly not acquired through the same kind of learning process whereby the meanings of individual words are learned. Since the number of sentences that can be produced is unlimited, there would not be enough time for anyone to acquire, on a discrimination learning basis, the meanings of all the sentences to which he might be exposed. The meanings of words are affected by the sentences in which they occur and, as Neisser (1967) has pointed out, there is a strong link between modern psycholinguistic approaches to language and the approach to perception taken by the Gestalt psychologists (see Chapters 9 and 10). Both approaches emphasize *structure*, and just as Gestalt psychologists demonstrated the importance of structure in perception by, among other things, the use of ambiguous pictures, so modern psycholinguists have used ambiguous sentences (for example the sentence: 'They are eating apples' which will be further discussed later) to demonstrate the importance of structure in understanding the meaning of a sentence. Just as Gestalt psychologists emphasized the importance of built-in 'laws' which they believed largely determined what is perceived in a particular perceptual situation, so modern psycholinguists emphasize the importance of a built-in capacity to acquire or to conform to certain linguistic rules which largely determine how the meaning of a sentence is interpreted. Thus both Gestalt psychology and modern psycholinguistics are strongly opposed to learning-theory approaches to behaviour and they both stress a 'nativist' rather than an 'empiricist' approach to the behaviour with which they are primarily concerned. Modern psycholinguistics, as will be seen shortly, thus puts a great deal of emphasis on the importance of innate factors which are responsible for the structure of language. This, of course, contrasts with the emphasis on experience and the acquisition of discrete linguistic elements in the absence of any kind of built-in linguistic structure, which is characteristic of learning-theory approaches.

Another point of disagreement between learning-theory and psycholinguistic approaches concerns the way in which a sentence is generated by a speaker. The generation of a sentence is an example of the problem of serial order in behaviour (Lashley, 1951). Sentences must be uttered one word at a time. How, then, is each word in the sentence selected? In general, learning-theory approaches to sentence generation have been derived from approaches to serial learning, where it has been assumed that individual items in a serially presented list become 'hooked-up' to their neighbours so that simple *stimulus–response chains* are formed. For example, if a subject is learning a list of nonsense syllables such as MOG, LUN, WEF, TOZ, etc., it is assumed that MOG acts as a stimulus which elicits the response LUN; LUN in turn serves as a stimulus to elicit the response WEF and so on. This approach to serial learning has been adopted as a model for sentence generation by some learning-theory approaches (although it should be pointed out that even in the context of serial list learning there are difficulties in the way of its acceptance: see, for example, Jensen and Rohwer, 1965).

Broadly speaking, these approaches suggest that sentences are generated on a left-to-right, non-anticipatory system, each word in the sentence being selected on the basis of preceding words. Thus sentences are thought of as stimulus–response chains, with each word serving as a response to the preceding word and as a stimulus for the next. Many learning theorists are aware that an analysis of sentence production in terms of learned stimulus–response chains is inadequate. They have accordingly complicated their accounts in a variety of ways. One such development is to take account of the frequency with which letters and words occur in speech. Thus, the speaker's knowledge of the statistical structure of the language, and his appreciation of its *redundancy*, is also presumed to play a part in the generation of a sentence. In information-theory terms (see Chapter 13), messages, of which a sentence is an example, usually contain far less *information* than they could contain; to this extent they exhibit redundancy. A message contains the maximum possible amount of information if the elements comprising the message are completely independent of one another and if each of the possible elements is equally likely to occur. An example would be the successive throws of a die, where throws do not influence one another and where on each throw each of the six possibilities is equally likely to occur. Spoken or written English on the other hand is quite highly redundant. The twenty-six letters of the alphabet do not all have the same probability of occurrence (in printed English, for instance, E is the most frequent letter and J, Q and Z are the least frequent). Second, the letters are not independent of one another; for instance, U is much more likely to occur following Q than following T. What goes for letters also goes for words. It is thus possible to think of the words comprising a sentence as being 'hooked-up' into chains on the basis of the transitional probabilities between them.

This approach has some plausibility. Listeners have to interpret

sentences on a probabilistic basis and it would be biologically economical if they were to produce them in the same way. Furthermore,
the mathematics of such systems have been extensively studied under
the general topic of *Markov processes*. Thus if human beings could
be shown to operate in this way, a great deal would be known
about the level of complexity of the grammatical system underlying
their linguistic performance. However, two lines of argument suggest
that the Markovian model of a sentence generator is inadequate.
First, a sentence generator working on this basis could not generate
certain grammatical constructions such as 'nested dependencies'[1]
unless on the basis of a large and complex set of *ad hoc* rules (see
Chomsky, 1956). Second, it would be impossible to learn a language
in this way, unless one's childhood were infinitely long; and the
problem of language acquisition thus provides yet another point of
disagreement between learning theory and psycholinguistics.

It has already been indicated that learning-theory approaches
emphasize the role of experience and learning in language acquisition,
while psycholinguistic approaches argue that learning theory has
been unable to provide a satisfactory description of the kind of
learning that would enable a child to acquire his native language
within the time available to him. For this reason, and others to be
discussed in later sections, psycholinguistic approaches stress the
importance of innate factors in determining language acquisition,
attempt to give a description of these innate factors in linguistic
terms, that is, by providing a model of *linguistic competence*, and
suggest that linguistic competence embodies the speaker's knowledge
of linguistic rules, in effect, his knowledge of the *grammar* of his
language. In the next section we shall discuss these hypotheses
further.

Psycholinguistics

Psycholinguistics, as its name implies, represents a fusion of psychology and linguistics. We argued in the first section of this chapter
that linguistics is concerned with *langue* and psychology with *parole*;

1. A construction in which a single grammatical structure spans one or more
'self-contained' structures: for example, 'I must write the address that the man
who sold us the lamp gave us down.'

put in other terms, the distinction is between the study of linguistic *competence* and that of linguistic *performance*. This distinction has been well described by McNeill (1966b, p. 17):

Competence is an abstraction away from performance; it represents the knowledge a native speaker of a language must have in order to understand any of the infinitely many grammatical sentences of his language; it represents a native speaker's linguistic intuitions – his realization that *the man hit the ball* is grammatical but *the man virtued the ball* is not.[2] Performance is the expression of competence in talking or listening to speech.

Particular acts of speaking or listening are limited by such factors as sensory and motor efficiency, motivation, memory and various distractions. These are irrelevant to competence. Thus discrepancies between a speaker's knowledge of a language and his speaking or comprehension of it may frequently occur; speakers make mistakes even within their own natural linguistic domains, quite apart from the arbitrary canons of 'good' linguistic usage. Speech is not always, therefore, a reliable guide to linguistic competence. Discrepancies do not in general provide clues as to the underlying nature of language, although they may, and do, pose interesting psychological problems in their own right.

Linguists, then, are interested in building models of competence: to this end they draw on structural description of the phenomena of language, including the sound systems which are employed (*phonemics*), the sound sequences which occur (*morphemics*), the formation rules of sentences (*syntax*) and the rules for inferring what sequences of sounds mean (*semantics*). For an introduction to general linguistics the reader is referred to Robins (1964) and for a detailed account of modern linguistic theory to Lyons (1968). Psychologists, if they are interested in language, are interested in the ways in which competence is put to use in concrete situations and in the psychological and physiological mechanisms underlying linguistic performance. However, psycholinguists would argue that, in order to understand language behaviour, one must understand the rules which govern that behaviour and that the rules of language behaviour are linguistic rules. Thus, in order to obtain a model of linguistic *per-*

2. In one sense the sentence *is* grammatical. We shall discuss the definition of what is grammatical in the following pages.

formance, one must construct a model of linguistic *competence* in the form of a grammar (in the sense used by psycholinguistics a grammar includes phonemics and morphemics as well as syntax, and can be described as a theory of language). As we argued in the first section, linguistic concepts are not psychological descriptions: they refer to the analysis of a language system and do not have any necessary relation to the mechanism whereby actual speakers produce utterances. Nevertheless, it can be hypothesized that linguistic rules do have 'psychological reality'; as we shall see in the last section, several psychologists have set out explicitly to test that hypothesis.

The psycholinguistic approach, therefore, is based upon linguistic analysis, and in particular upon the study of *grammar*. Two broad kinds of grammar can be distinguished – *descriptive* and *generative*. The aim of a descriptive grammar is to classify and label linguistic units, to outline the operational criteria used for determining them and to describe a language by attaching class labels to these units. Clause analysis as taught in schools is an example of the use of a descriptive grammar. The aim of a generative grammar, on the other hand, is to outline a system of rules which would generate all those sequences of sounds which a native speaker of the language would accept as grammatical and none of those sequences which he would find ungrammatical. Thus, unlike a descriptive grammar, a generative grammar stands or falls on the acceptability of the sound sequences that its system of rules is capable of generating. Since psycholinguists have concerned themselves almost exclusively with generative grammars, these will be our sole concern here. Further, we shall confine ourselves to one example of a generative grammar, that of Chomsky (1957, 1965).

Chomsky has suggested three sorts of rules as the basis for a generative grammar: *phrase-structure' rules, classification or vocabulary rules* and *transformational rules*. The elements (words and phrases) which form sentences are assumed to be interrelated in a hierarchical fashion. Phrase-structure rules, as the name implies, govern the structural relations among the elements of a sentence, what is generally termed its *surface structure*. The structure is described in terms of constituents of the kind used in descriptive grammars and which will already be familiar from clause analysis.

A sentence such as 'Cats chase mice' could therefore be described as constituting a noun phrase (cats) and a verb phrase (chase mice), the verb phrase being further subdivided into a verb and a noun phrase. If the sentence were, say: 'The cats chase small mice,' the initial and final noun phrases would be further subdivided into, respectively, article and noun and adjective and noun. Thus phrase-structure rules determine what constituents, in what order, can be generated to form a sentence; or, putting it the other way round, the way in which a sentence can be subdivided or, as it is termed, 'rewritten'.

By way of illustration, let us take three rules. First, a sentence may be rewritten as 'noun phrase plus verb phrase'; in the notation commonly used:

$S \longrightarrow NP + VP$ (rule 1).

A noun phrase may be rewritten as 'article plus noun':

$NP \longrightarrow Art. + Noun$ (rule 2).

A verb phrase may be rewritten as 'verb plus noun phrase':

$VP \longrightarrow Verb + NP$ (rule 3).

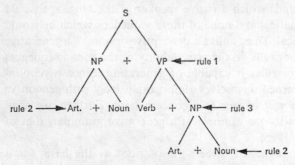

Figure 57   Phrase marker of a sentence (see text)

It will be evident even from the simple example given above that there are many alternative rules for the rewriting of constituents. A noun phrase, for example, may be rewritten not only as Art. + Noun but also as Adj. + Noun or Art. + Adj. + Noun and so on. Only one rule for the rewriting of each constituent is given here, for the sake of simplicity. Figure 57 shows how these rules might be applied in generating a sentence. Such a diagrammatic representation of the surface structure of a sentence is called a *superficial phrase marker*.

The words to be used in the sentence, when its structure is determined, are chosen according to classification or vocabulary rules. These specify the list of words which can appropriately be used as constituents of a particular kind. Let us suppose three classificatory rules, making a total of six rules altogether:

Art. $\longrightarrow$ a, the   (rule 4)

Noun $\longrightarrow$ man, ball   (rule 5)

Verb $\longrightarrow$ found, hit   (rule 6)

Given these rules a small stock of different sentences (altogether sixteen) can be generated:

The man found the ball,
The ball found the man,
The man hit the ball,
The ball hit the man,
A man hit the ball,
The ball hit a man,
A ball found a man, and so on.

Some of these sentences may strike the reader as a little odd, for example, 'A ball found a man.' The oddity resides not in the grammatical structure of the sentence but in its meaning. Chomsky has argued that the grammatical structure of a language should be specified independently of meaning, and the distinction between grammatical structure and meaning is perhaps best exemplified by his famous sentence: 'Colourless green ideas sleep furiously,' where again the sentence has a perfectly reasonable grammatical structure but its meaning, if any, is far from clear. It is therefore a matter of some dispute whether semantic considerations are a legitimate part of grammar and how they are to be accommodated within phrase-structure approaches.

Some problems of meaning, for instance the resolution of some types of ambiguity, can be dealt with by the use of phrase structure rules. For example, the sentence 'They are eating apples' can be analysed in either of two ways shown in Figure 58. Diagram (a) in Figure 58 describes what some people are doing whereas diagram (b)

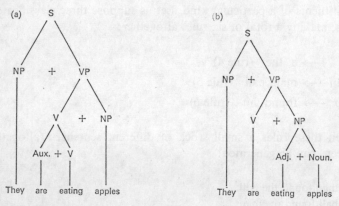

Figure 58   Two possible surface structures for an ambiguous sentence (see text). (After Neisser, 1967, p. 257)

is a description of a kind of apple. There are thus two different surface structures for this sentence. However, superficial phrase markers cannot distinguish between the two senses of each of the sentences:

Flying planes can be dangerous,
The shooting of the hunters was terrible,

or between sentences which clearly have different meanings but have similar phrase markers, for example:

The Apache are easy to kill,
The Apache are eager to kill.

Chomsky attempts to deal with these problems of meaning by, in effect, reminding us that the meaning of a sentence depends upon its relation to other sentences, that is, on some 'structure' which is 'deeper' than its surface structure. Chomsky has thus argued that there is more to sentences than a system of phrase-structure rules is capable of revealing; that, in addition, a notion of *deep structure* is necessary. The deep structure of a sentence is a representation of the sentence which reveals, in the form of a structural description (for example, subject–predicate), the semantic relationships of the constituents of the sentence much more directly than does its surface structure. Chomsky has also put forward proposals for the analysis of deep structure. We shall not discuss the analysis of deep structure in any detail here; for a recent statement of Chomsky's position the reader is referred to Chomsky (1965). It should also be briefly noted that other psycholinguists (Katz and Fodor, 1963; Katz and Postal, 1964) have attempted to parallel Chomsky's description of the rules comprising a generative grammar by describing rules governing the meanings given to words and rules governing the meanings of sentences. Katz and Fodor have been concerned with 'projection theory' which tries to show how information derived from words in isolation can be built into the meaning of a sentence. Criticisms of Katz and Fodor's theory have been advanced by Bolinger (1965).

The phrase-structure rules described above can cope more sucessfully than can Markov grammars with complex grammatical structures; but to account for sentences which are in other than a simple declarative form (often called *kernel strings*), Chomsky and others have made use of *transformational rules*. These permit the *reordering* and *re-combining*, as well as the rewriting of constituents to form different types of sentence, for example, those in negative, passive and interrogative forms and those made compound by the use of such constructions as 'and' and 'or'. Again, transformational rules permit such sentences as 'John sleeps,' 'John does sleep' and 'John is sleeping' to be made equivalent.

The postulation of transformational rules as well as those of phrase structure and vocabulary provides an answer to the recurrent problem of language learning. The acquisition of linguistic skill, apart from its intellectual demands, requires in theory a learning time which must far exceed the life span of the potential speaker. The operations of hierarchical structuring, vocabulary classification and transformation taken together render the task of generating language, and that of language acquisition, feasible. As G. A. Miller, Galanter and Pribram (1960, p. 153) have put it: 'With such a theory it should be possible to do a fairly good job of speaking English grammatically with less than 100 rules of formation, less than 100 transformations and perhaps 100,000 rules for vocabulary and pronunciation. Even a child should be able to master that much after ten or fifteen years of constant practice.'

A generative grammar thus consists of a set of rules for generating grammatical sentences, although at the same time, for reasons outlined earlier, it should not be regarded as being a model for the speaker. It is perhaps useful, therefore, to regard a generative grammar as 'a "device" that is somehow "employed" in the production of speech' (Neisser, 1967, p. 250).

The account of grammar given here, it must be stressed, is only one representative of many; Chomsky himself has modified his proposals in successive formulations, so that our account cannot be taken to represent his final position. Nevertheless, it gives some indication of the conceptual basis on which psycholinguists proceed to the study of language. One of our chief concerns in the final section of this chapter will be with the empirical investigation which has stemmed from such an approach.

Empirical studies of the psychology of language

In this section we return to the three inter-related problems mentioned at the conclusion of the first section: the problem of speech perception, that of the generation of grammatical sentences and that of language acquisition. Something has been said about each of these topics already but in this section we shall briefly discuss some of the experimental studies which have been conducted in these areas. Speech perception and production will be treated first, followed by language acquisition.

Perception and production

The input to the ear consists of a sequence of compressions and expansions of air pressure, known as *sound waves*, which can vary in *intensity* (the amplitude of the wave) and *frequency* (the spacing in time of successive waves). The auditory input can be most simply described, as Figure 59 shows, by displaying air pressure against time. The wave form in Figure 59 is called a *sinusoid* and is usually simple and regular, representing the wave form associated with a 'pure tone', like the sound of a tuning fork. However, most sounds and all speech contain more than just one frequency but, to a large extent, any complex sound can be thought of as the sum of several sinusoids and can thus be described in terms of its frequency components, together with their respective intensities. The various methods used for analysing speech into its component frequencies are discussed by Licklider and Miller (1951).

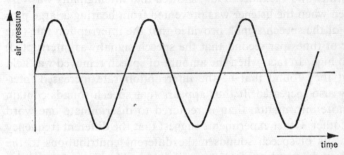

Figure 59   A sinusoidal sound wave

Many speech perception studies have examined the effects of various independent variables upon the perception of speech which has been *degraded* in some way. One of the main methods of degrading speech has been to add noise to the speech signal and to vary the ratio of speech to noise. The listener's understanding of the speech presented to him in this way is assessed by his *intelligibility score*, that is, the percentage of words he identifies correctly. This technique enables the experimenter to find out whether some kinds of verbal material are more easily perceived or recognized than others and to express this ease of recognition in quantitative terms. Thus Bruce (1956) compared intelligibility scores for a list of randomly selected words and a list of words having some common reference, either to parts of the body or to things to eat. The listener was not told that the word lists differed in any way. Bruce found that words in the two 'common reference' lists were identified significantly more easily than words in the 'random' list, although there was no significant difference in ease of identification of the two 'common reference' lists. In an experiment also concerned with the effects of context on the perception of speech, G. A. Miller, Heise and Lichten (1951) showed that it is easier to recognize words strung together to make a meaningful sentence than the same words presented in a random sequence.

Another way of degrading speech is to interrupt the speech signal periodically, thus preventing a certain amount of speech (which can be varied) from reaching the listener at all. Using this technique, G. A. Miller and Licklider (1950) showed that intelligibility was very high even when the listener was prevented from hearing a large proportion of the speech signal, provided that the interruption rate (the number of times per second that the speech signal was interrupted) was also high. In fact, when the amount of speech removed was held constant they found that as the interruption rate increased intelligibility also increased. It thus appears that speech sounds contain much more information than is required to discriminate one word from another. Other experiments suggest that the different frequency components of speech sounds make different contributions to the listener's understanding of what is said to him. The higher frequencies seem to be more important in promoting intelligibility.

Other experiments, concerned with what is known as *selective listening*, use a procedure in which speech is masked by other speech rather than by noise. Usually different verbal material is presented to the two ears of a subject who is instructed to *shadow* (that is, to repeat back what he hears as he hears it) the material coming to one of the ears. This material is known as the *attended message*, while the material coming to the other ear is known as the *unattended message*. After shadowing the attended message for a time, the subject may be required to remember as much of the unattended message as he can; this is usually very little (Moray, 1969).

The purpose of selective listening experiments is to find out how the listener is able to sort out the mass of different speech sounds from different sources and to respond to only one set of them. This situation is typically referred to as the *cocktail party problem*, the problem being that the result of all the talk going on at any one time at a cocktail party for example is, from the ear's point of view, a single very complex sound wave which, nevertheless, is 'unscrambled' by the brain so that one 'message' is responded to while the rest are rejected.

The cues used to select between competing messages seem to be of two kinds – *acoustic* and *linguistic*. Acoustic cues include voice, loudness, pitch and localization; linguistic cues include the continuity of theme and context, the constraints imposed by syntactic and semantic rules and the differing probabilities of one word rather than another following a particular spoken sequence. Thus, as Treisman (1966, p. 111) points out, 'unlikely words like *giraffe* coming after "I sang a . . ." need to be much louder than *song* and a little louder than *carol* or *ditty*, to be heard correctly'. In general, findings from selective listening experiments suggest that rejected messages are attenuated, rather than being completely blocked: it is as if the volume control on the unattended ear is turned down, rather than switched off altogether, to permit the attended message to be analysed.

The linguistic cues which play some part in enabling selection between competing messages are also important in the more general task of speech perception. But investigators who have examined the role of syntactic and semantic factors in speech perception have also been concerned, in a sense, with the assessment of the *psychological reality* of grammatical rules. Such rules may be assumed to influence not only speech perception but speech production as well – that is, the verbal behaviour of adult speakers in a variety of situations including word association, learning and recall. Perception and production are thus included here under the same heading and we shall treat them side by side in the remainder of this section.

Experiments concerned with the psychological reality of transformational rules will be considered first. In effect such experiments have tried to show that the relative difficulty of the operations involved in producing certain systematic changes in sentences is a function of their relative complexity expressed in terms of a transformational grammar. The surface structure of a sentence in the passive form, for example, differs more from its 'kernel' counterpart than does one in the negative form; thus Chomsky's transformational grammar would predict that it will take longer to transform sentences from the active to the passive form than from the affirmative to the negative. G. A. Miller, McKean and Slobin (see G. A. Miller, 1962) showed this to be so. Furthermore, transforming from the affirmative active to the negative passive took approximately the sum of the times required for the two simpler transformations.

G. A. Miller, McKean and Slobin used a paper-and-pencil method which was somewhat unsatisfactory and the experiment was later repeated using a different method which obtained even more clear-cut results (G. A. Miller and McKean, 1964). In this second version of the experiment, subjects pressed a button and were shown a sentence tachistoscopically. They had previously been instructed what transformation to apply and when they had applied it they pressed the button again and a search list consisting of eighteen sentences was then displayed. Subjects were required to find the transformed sentence in this list, to press the button and then report the sentence. Four kinds of sentences were used: *active affirmative* (AA), *active negative* (AN), *passive affirmative* (PA) and *passive negative* (PN). Two times were taken: the time between the first and second button pressings was the *transforming and reading time*, that between the second and third, the *search time*. The transforming and reading times were compared with a control condition, in which subjects were shown the same search lists as in the experimental condition but the single sentences, rather than their transformations as in the experimental condition, were identical with a sentence in the search list. By subtracting the *reading times* in the control condition from the transforming plus reading times in the experimental condition, *transformation times* could be obtained. Miller and McKean's principal results are shown in Table 6. It seems from these results that when a single transformation is applied to AA, the negative is easier to apply than the passive, and that of each of the two applications of the two transformations (negative and passive), the one involving transformations from AA is the easier (see the bottom two lines in Table 7). Finally, as in the earlier experiment there is evidence for the additivity of transformation times; that is,

$$AA \longrightarrow PN = AA \longrightarrow AN + AA \longrightarrow PA.$$

This result, and others to be discussed below, have been interpreted by Miller and his associates as suggesting that subjects re-

Table 7

The results of the Miller and McKean (1964) experiment

Sentence type	Example	Transformation time		
Active affirmative (AA)	Jane likes the old lady			
Active negative (AN)	Jane does not like the old lady	↓ 0·41 s		
Passive affirmative (PA)	The old lady is liked by Jane		↓ 0·91 s	
Passive negative (PN)	The old lady is not liked by Jane			↓ 1·53 s

PA to PN easier than AA to PA
AA to PA easier than AN to PN
AA to PN easier than AN to PA

member a kernel (an AA sentence), plus each of the transformations performed upon it, independently. Thus kernel + N + P for instance are thought to be separately stored in memory. Sentences on which many transformations have been performed are also thought to provide greater opportunity for error than simpler sentences, in learning situations for example, and they also require more time to 'decode' when subjects are required to decide the truth or falsity of a particular sentence.

In a recall situation Savin and Perchonock (1965) required subjects to listen to a sentence and, in addition, a list of unrelated words drawn from eight categories (for example, vehicle, animal, etc.) in a fixed order. Subjects had to recall the sentence first and then as many of the unrelated words as they could. Savin and Perchonock used only those trials on which the sentence was correctly recalled and on those trials took the number of subsequent words correctly recalled as an inverse measure of the amount of 'memory storage space' used up by the sentence. They then compared the 'storage space' taken up by sentences on which different transformations had been performed and found that the more transformations performed on each sentence, the fewer subsequent words recalled and hence the greater the storage space required for the sentence. Like Miller and McKean, Savin and Perchonock obtained evidence of additivity; all sentences involving one transformation took up significantly more space than AA sentences, and sentences involving two transformations took up significantly more space than those involving only one. Estimates of amount of space taken up by each transformation, passive, negative, interrogative, emphatic, and various combinations of these suggested that each transformation imposed a separate load on memory, and that two transformations (e.g. passive + negative) took up the sum of the space required by each of the transformations considered singly.

Mehler (1963) and Mehler and Miller (1964) obtained similar evidence of independence in a learning situation, concluding that subjects effectively strip down a transformed sentence to its kernel (the AA form) and then build it up again, storing separately the kernel and the transformations that must be performed to regain the original sentence. Finally, the results of McMahon (cited by G. A. Miller, 1962) and Slobin (1966), who were both concerned with the evaluation of the truth or falsity of sentences which had been transformed in various ways, although agreeing in some respects with the results already mentioned, also introduce complications. The studies mentioned so far have been concerned exclusively with syntactic variables and have virtually ignored semantic ones. McMahon found that negative sentences (for example, 13 does not precede 5) took *longer* to judge than passive (7 is preceded by 3) or AA sentences (4 precedes 15), and Slobin (1966) found that the transformation from *affirmative* to *negative* was more difficult than that from *active* to *passive* when subjects were required to decide whether a sentence was true or false on the basis of a picture describing the events referred to by the sentence.

We have already seen that the grammatical prediction that passive transformations would be easier to handle than negative ones was confirmed by Miller and McKean. The findings of McMahon and Slobin show that when meaning is introduced into the experimental situation, by requiring subjects to relate the truth value of the sentence to an actual state of affairs, the reverse result is obtained.

Semantic variables clearly interact with syntactic ones in determining the 'complexity' of a sentence; complexity is not determined by syntactic variables alone. We turn now to experiments which have examined the importance of both sets of variables for language behaviour.

First, the technique of masking speech by noise and varying the speech-to-noise ratio has been applied to sentences varying in their syntactic and semantic form by G. A. Miller and Isard (1963), in an attempt to measure the contribution of syntactic and semantic variables to speech perception. Miller and Isard used three kinds of word sequence: sentences which were both meaningful and grammatically correct, for example: 'A witness signed the official legal document'; sentences which were grammatically correct but semantically anomalous, for example: 'A witness appraised the shocking company dragon'; and ungrammatical strings, for example: 'A legal glittering the exposed picnic knight.' Miller and Isard found that in a shadowing situation, grammatical sentences were more accurately repeated back than either anomalous sentences or ungrammatical strings (in that order), and that the same order was preserved when subjects listened to the three types of sequence in noise without knowing the type of sequence they were going to hear. That is, grammatical sentences were most easily heard, followed by anomalous sentences and then by ungrammatical strings. Finally, when subjects were told what type of sequence to expect, the same order of intelligibility was obtained. Thus, both the grammatical structure of a sentence and its meaning are important determinants of its intelligibility.

An experiment performed by Marks and Miller (1964) goes some way to separating out the contribution of syntactic and semantic variables to memory. They found that both syntactic and semantic structure aided recall and that they operated to some extent independently. Furthermore, different kinds of error were associated with the recall of sentences lacking syntactic structure and with the recall of those lacking semantic structure. Order and inflectional errors were more common in the former case, while intrusion errors were more common in the latter.

Before leaving experiments concerned with transformational rules, it should be mentioned briefly that Yngve's (1960) depth hypothesis has also been applied to the problem of the complexity of a sentence (E. Martin and Roberts, 1966; P. Wright, 1969). Briefly, Yngve suggests that the 'depth' of any word in a sentence can be measured by the number of left branches leading to it in a phrase marker tree (see Figure 60) and that the mean depth of a sentence can be expressed by dividing the total sentence depth (the sum of the depths of each word in the sentence) by the number of words the sentence contains.

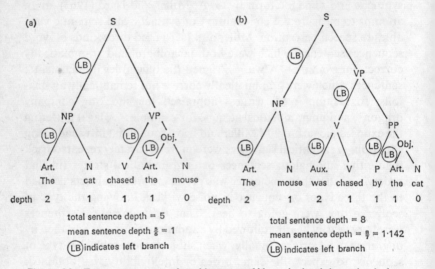

Figure 60   Two sentences analysed in terms of Yngve's depth hypothesis (see text). (a) Active affirmative: 'The cat chased the mouse.' (b) Passive affirmative: 'The mouse was chased by the cat.'

The mean depth of a sentence is an index of its complexity. Left branches are taken as an indication of depth because they reflect the constraints the speaker of a sentence has to bear in mind as he works his way through it. Yngve suggests that different memory loads are incurred with sentences of different forms because each part of the sentence commits the speaker to carry on the sentence in a particular way. For instance, the first noun produced in a sentence commits the speaker to follow it at some stage with a verb. If the verb follows immediately, the memory load is small; if, however, the noun is followed by an intervening adjectival phrase, for example, the speaker has to remember that he is committed to following the noun with a verb, and his memory load is thereby increased.

E. Martin and Roberts (1966) have argued that many experiments concerned with sentence complexity have confounded transformational complexity with 'depth' complexity and that the latter provides a better model of the difficulties encountered in the perception and recall of sentences than does transformational grammar. They were able to show that an alternative explanation of Mehler's (1963) experiment could be made in 'depth' terms and also that some data of their own, demonstrating that sentences of the same transformational type, length and word frequency were differentially recalled, could be much better explained in these terms than in terms of transformational grammar. A difficulty remains with Savin and Perchonock's (1965) experiment, where interrogative transformations, among others, were found to add to storage space although, as has later been shown, they did not differ from AA sentences in terms of their depth. However, P. Wright (1969), in a replication of Savin and Perchonock's experiment using measures of sentence depth, has shown that complexity measured in these terms also adds to storage space in memory. It remains to be seen whether a reconciliation can be effected between these two alternative, but not necessarily mutually exclusive, interpretations of sentence complexity.

Although Yngve's depth hypothesis has been included in the discussion of the psychological reality of transformational rules, it is perhaps more appropriately considered as an important, if not the most important, contribution of constituent analysis to psychology. In the discussion so far, the possibility that certain constituents of the sentence, such as phrase units, are psychologically basic has been disregarded, although there is some evidence for it (Fodor and Bever, 1965; Garrett, Bever and Fodor, 1966). Fodor and Bever adopted a technique developed by Ladefoged (see Ladefoged and Broadbent, 1960). The subjects in Ladefoged and Broadbent's experiment listened to sentences during which brief clicks were superimposed in the middle of words; subjects were subsequently asked to recall where in the sentence these clicks had occurred.

Fodor and Bever hypothesized that the constituents of a sentence revealed by phrase marker tree are the units of speech perception and it would thus be expected that a click presented during a sentence would be subsequently located at the major grammatical boundary, for example: 'That he was on form // was evident from the way he played.' Fodor and Bever showed this to be the case.

To eliminate possible confounding verbal cues, such as a longer pause, or an inflectional change, which might occur at the phrase boundary, Garrett, Bever and Fodor (1966) repeated the experiment using pairs of sentences in which the final portions were identical, but the different initial portions furnished a different grammatical structure. For instance:

1. As a direct result of their new invention's *influence the company was given an award.*

2. The retiring chairman whose methods still *influence the company was given an award.*

The italicized parts of the two sentences are the same but their grammatical structure is not, the major break occurring after 'influence' in sentence 1 and after 'company' in sentence 2. A click was presented simultaneously with the occurrence of 'c' in 'company;' it was located by subjects as occurring much earlier in sentence 1 than in sentence 2, that is, near the major grammatical separation in each case.

This result shows that phrase structure in itself is sufficient to determine where clicks are located and, presumably, how sentences are broken up by the listener. Further evidence for the hypothesis that constituent elements isolated by phrase markers are 'psychologically real' and represent the units which listeners use to process sentences, comes from experiments on learning and recall (Johnson, 1965). Johnson found that subjects required to learn and recall sentences produced *transitional errors* (going from a correct to an incorrect word) more frequently at phrase boundaries than within phrases. In addition, when errors did occur within phrases, they were more likely to occur near the stem of the phrase marker than at the periphery, that is, the larger the constituent unit between which transitions occurred, the greater the probability of making a transitional error. For instance, in the sentence: 'The black cat chased the white mouse', most errors would be expected to occur between the two phrases, that is, between 'cat' and 'chased'; but within the phrase 'chased the white mouse', transitional errors would be more likely to occur between 'chased' and 'the', than between 'the' and 'white' and more likely between 'the' and 'white' than between 'white' and 'mouse'. This result affords strong evidence for the notion that sentences are planned hierarchically in the manner suggested by phrase-structure grammar and that 'psychologically real linguistic units' are isolated by the constituent analysis such a grammar provides.

Finally, the effects of adding grammatical structure to nonsense words on the learning of such words should be mentioned. In a series of experiments, Epstein (1961, 1962) showed that if nonsense material was inserted into 'sentence frames' then it was much easier to learn. Epstein generated strings of nonsense words, for example, 'erenstan cate eleudi edom ept ledear ari' to which he added function words '*The* erenstan cate eleudi *the* edom ept *with* ledear *and* ari' and finally inflections, 'The erenstan*y* cate*s* eleudi*ed* the edom ept*ly* with ledear and ari*s*.' He found that when the complete string was presented on each trial the last sequence was learned to a criterion of perfect recall in fewer trials than the second sequence and both the second and third sequences were learned more quickly than the first. It seems that the structure provided by function words and inflections enabled subjects to group the words into phrase units much more readily and thus to learn them more easily. This is supported by the further finding that when this structure was eliminated by presenting the words one at a time at two-second intervals on a memory drum, no difference was found between the trials to criterion required for the three lists. However, the presentation interval seems to be the crucial variable in this result and sequential presentation of the material at intervals below one second seems to reproduce the original differences in the rate of learning. Presumably at faster presentation speeds the grammatical structure is no longer disrupted.

From this brief survey of experimental studies of speech perception and production it is clear that linguistic rules have important consequences for the language behaviour of adults. It is much less clear how these rules come to have the consequences they do. Both for adults and children, the importance of linguistic rules for language behaviour need not imply that these rules are consciously followed, but only that the language they use could be predicted by the rules of a generative grammar. A central question here is whether the same generative grammar can account for sentences spoken by children as well as those of adults. We turn now to experimental and observational studies concerned with the ways in which children acquire grammatical rules, and with finding out at what age and in what order they do so.

The acquisition of language

G. A. Miller and McNeill (1969) have described the child's acquisition of language as a process of 'guided invention' and have argued that a child 'formulates' the grammar of his native language. This formulation receives guidance from two major sources which interact, and the interaction between them is considered by Miller and McNeill to constitute the process of language acquisition. One source is parental influence, namely, parents' speech and their reaction to the speech of the child. The other source is the child's 'basic biological capacity for language' (p. 714).

What must a child learn in order to have learned a language? Simply put, he must learn sounds, words and grammar; and he learns them in that order. It appears to be generally agreed that the child begins to understand the utterances of others before he can produce the same words himself (McCarthy, 1954). McCarthy surveyed a number of studies of language development in children and concluded that the child first shows signs of paying attention to the sound of the human voice, for example, by altering his activity or by stopping altogether or perhaps turning round to face the speaker, at about two months of age. By the time he is six months old he seems able to discriminate between tones of voice, for instance to distinguish between a friendly and a scolding tone, although he is presumably still unable to understand the meanings of the individual words. By the age of nine months children are generally able to respond appropriately to one or two phrases when accompanied by gestures, and to show pleasure at hearing certain words rather than others. The attachment of appropriate responses to particular words increases in the tenth month and before the child is a year old he can stop when told 'no' and can follow some rudimentary commands. Between the ages of thirteen and seventeen months he understands 'Give me that' when it is accompanied by a gesture, and by the age of eighteen months he can point to his nose, eyes or hair when requested. With respect to language production, a child at first produces relatively undifferentiated vocalization; at the onset of 'babbling', at a few months of age, a very large number of sounds is produced, and not only sounds which occur in the child's own language. Over the few months of babbling, there becomes apparent a shift in the frequency of different speech sounds in the direction of cultural frequencies: that is, the sounds which 'belong' in the child's language become predominant while sounds not normal in the adult speaker drop out. At about one year of age the child produces his first word; at about eighteen months he begins to produce sentences of two or more words.

Paradoxically enough, some of the best evidence that children learn rules rather than sentences wholesale comes from cases in which children make grammatical errors. Often a child will produce a sentence such as 'I digged in the garden' or 'The sheeps runned away' – sentences which they are very unlikely to have learned from parents or other adults, and which show not an absence of grammar but rather an over-generalization of grammatical rules. The point has been further demonstrated experimentally, notably by Berko (1958). Young children about four to eight years old were asked to complete sentences which involved the grammatical modification of nonsense words; for example, a child would be shown two pictures of an imaginary animal or bird and told: 'This is a wug.' 'This is another wug.' 'Now there are two —.' Even the youngest children were able to produce the regular plural form 'wugs' in completing this sentence; they were similarly able to form regular past tenses of nonsense verbs. They showed, in fact, a strong reluctance to learn *irregular* forms; for example, when given the sequence: 'Here is a goose and there are two geese. Now there are three —,' most children especially the younger ones, would complete it with the word 'gooses'. Clearly, these young children possessed a 'productive grammar'. R. Brown and Berko (1960) were able to demonstrate further the development of grammar in six- to eight-year-old children:

for example, the increased appreciation, over this age range, of the distinction between *count nouns* such as 'dog' or 'book', which can take the plural form, and *mass nouns* such as 'water' or 'money', which cannot.

Braine (1963b) has suggested that grammar may be learned first by *position learning* – that is, learning the position which a word typically occupies in a sentence – and second by *paired-associate learning* of certain parts of speech, particularly function words. He based this conclusion upon study of children learning a 'second language' – in fact, an artificial language. Other investigations have sought more directly to observe the development of a first language in the young child. Observational studies of the language behaviour of young children present many practical problems: repeated and extensive observation is needed if a reliable picture of language production is to be obtained. A very young child does not articulate well and his (largely one-word) utterances are difficult to understand and to transcribe; an older child has too extensive and variable a repertoire of sentences for an exhaustive record to be achieved. Nevertheless, a number of studies have been carried out; recently, for example, by R. Brown and his colleagues (R. Brown, 1965; R. Brown and Fraser, 1963), by Braine (1963a) using American children and by McNeill (1966a) using Japanese children.

These investigations generally involve detailed observation of a relatively small number of children repeatedly observed in their own homes and usually in the presence of their mothers. The children are normally between two and three years old – an age at which two- and three- word utterances, as distinct from isolated words, occur, but at which the child's repertoire is still fairly limited. By means of these observations the investigators seek to construct the generative grammar of the child, that is, to discover a set of rules, as well as a set of vocabulary lists, which can predict all the sentences produced by that child.

Young children's two-word utterances can be analysed for the frequency of occurrence of different words and for the positions in the utterance that different words occupy. Another method of analysis has been the observation of 'shared contexts'. Two words in the child's repertoire are considered to belong to the same grammatical category if they appear grammatically interchangeable: if they occur in the same position in an utterance, followed or preceded by the same words and so on. The percentage of overlap in context between the words is thus taken to indicate the degree of their grammatical equivalence. The percentage value which will be accepted as evidence of equivalence has to be arbitrarily determined, and this presents some difficulty, particularly since the percentages obtained are likely to be unstable from one set of utterances to another. R. Brown and Fraser (1963) have suggested that this difficulty may well be one shared by the learning child as well as by the observing adult.

Young children's spontaneous utterances, consisting of up to four words (the first 'sentences' they produce), are greatly abbreviated compared with adult speech. Examples (from Brown) are: 'two boot', 'a gas here' and 'hear tractor'. Similarly, when young children imitate adult speech, the original word order is preserved but the sentence is shortened; sentence length is probably constrained by the immediate memory span, which is shorter in children than in adults. Words are not omitted at random; when the sentence is shortened, *function* words are dropped while *content* words are retained. The result has been described by Brown and Fraser as *telegraphic speech* because of its resemblance to the very efficient condensation of messages, retaining their essential meaning, used in telegraphic communication. This, of course, is not to say that the child consciously devises an efficient reduction process. It could be, for instance, that certain content words are more familiar than function words because they are encountered more often, or because they are more heavily accented, in the speech of adults.

The term 'telegraphic speech' does not describe the *process* of abbreviation; rather it describes the *result* of applying the rules of a simple generative grammar, which is systematically different from that of adults. Children's early two- and three-word utterances have been described by Braine (1963a) as consisting of two classes of words, *pivot* and *open*. Pivot words tend to be *modifiers*; they occupy a fixed position in the utterance, there are not many of them and the class of pivot words grows fairly slowly. There are many more open words, mainly nouns and verbs, drawn from the child's total vocabulary, at this stage, of about 250 to 300 words. Examples of pivot and open words (from Braine's study) are given in Figure 61. Each pivot word tends to occur much more frequently in the child's speech than any particular open word, and early two-word utterances seem to be of the form pivot–open or open–pivot. Open–open constructions also occur generally as the child becomes somewhat older (at perhaps twenty-four or twenty-five months of age), but pivot–pivot constructures are rarely, if ever, found. Open class words, but not pivots, can also stand alone in children's speech, resulting in one-word utterances.

In one study (R. Brown and Bellugi, 1964) it was found that there were three grammatical classes (pivot, verb and noun) present in the

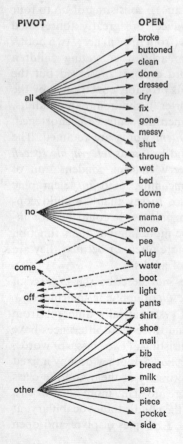

PIVOT   **OPEN**

all

no

come

off

other

broke
buttoned
clean
done
dressed
dry
fix
gone
messy
shut
through
wet
bed
down
home
mama
more
pee
plug
water
boot
light
pants
shirt
shoe
mail
bib
bread
milk
part
piece
pocket
side

Figure 61   Some two-word pivotal constructions (pivot + open and open + pivot) observed, in one child, by Braine (1963a). Arrows indicate order of utterance: e.g. 'all broke', 'other shirt', 'mama come', 'shirt off'. Note that (a) there are many more open than pivot words; (b) some open words may occur either as the first or as the second word of the utterance, but no pivot words show this flexibility; (c) many open words may occur in association with a given pivot word, but different pivot words rarely 'share' an associated open word. No three- (or more) word utterances are shown here, although a few were produced by this child, a boy aged nineteen to twenty-four months

child's speech when it was first recorded. Certain combinations of these grammatical classes into two- and three-word utterances expressed permissible grammatical relations, in terms of linguistic theory, and the child's speech was found to contain all these 'permissible' combinations and no combinations which were not 'permissible'. It seems extremely unlikely, therefore, that the child is merely producing utterances by combining grammatical classes in a random fashion. It has been suggested (G. A. Miller and McNeill, 1969) that children are actively seeking ways of expressing basic grammatical relations and that, lacking a large stock of transformations, they are forced to express these basic grammatical relations directly in their earliest grammatical constructions. In other words, they are giving direct expression to 'deep structure'.

At a later stage, differentiation of the pivot class appears to occur, and children begin to substitute phrases for the original pivot class. At this stage the rules governing the formation of a noun phrase seem to have been acquired, but the distinction between different types of noun (for instance, mass nouns, count nouns, proper nouns) has not been fully grasped and the child's utterances will thus tend to show over-generalization of this rule. The result can be utterances like 'a Tommy', 'a stories' and 'a marmalade'. Later still, further approximation to the grammar of adults takes place, and the child begins to master the use of transformations (Menyuk, 1964).

Brown and his associates have further pointed out that the mother's speech to the child exhibits certain interesting characteristics. For example, the mother speaking to her child tends to use short, simple and perfectly grammatical sentences (in contrast to much adult speech): the child's introduction to language is, therefore, as R. Brown (1965) has described it, to a 'simplified, repetitive and idealized dialect'. Again, the mother often repeats her child's utterances, rather more often indeed than the child imitates his mother; and when she repeats the utterance she lengthens it, filling in the function words which the child omits and which she judges appropriate to the sentence and to the situation to which it refers. Brown found that parents *expanded* about 30 per cent of a child's utterances in this way. For parents, expansions serve to test hypotheses about what the child is saying, on the assumption that children can understand more grammatical features than they are capable of producing. The remaining 70 per cent of children's utterances were perhaps not expanded by the parents in Brown's sample because the utterance either did not permit an hypothesis to be formed or because the hypothesis did not need testing. It should be noted that these observations are based upon a sample of intelligent middle-class parents; it is not only possible but probable that (roughly speaking) class differences are reflected in important differences in the parents' behaviour towards the language behaviour of their children (Bernstein, 1961; Irwin, 1960). Brown has suggested that expansions of the child's speech may have great importance for the acquisition process; in particular, they seem to facilitate the growth of transformations in the child's speech. It seems likely that the expansion of the child's speech – the addition of appropriate functors and qualifiers – is one means of teaching the child certain conceptions of time, number, possession, in short, something of the 'nature of reality'.

Children acquire language in spite of imperfect exposure to it and this has led some psycholinguists to argue that there must be some grammatical capacity or 'language acquisition device' (LAD) which is innate and which may be more or less specific. There appear to be at least two versions of the innate capacity notion, the 'weak' version and the 'strong' one. The weak version suggests that language is specific to human beings; there must therefore be something that human infants have and animals do not. This could be an innate ability to learn certain types of categories. Language learning would then be regarded as a special case of concept learning, not a special faculty. The weak version thus emphasizes the relation between language and the outside world. The strong version, on the other hand, argues, in effect, that the child is born with the basic grammatical rules and relations in its head.

Whichever version of the hypothesis is adopted, there seem to be good reasons for thinking that there are some innate capacities involved in language acquisition. Lenneberg (1967) has outlined five main reasons for believing that man possesses specific *biological* capacities which make language possible for man and only man. The brain mechanisms which regulate speech as well as the speech mechanisms themselves appear to be unique to the human species;

language follows an extremely regular schedule of development in all children in all cultures so far studied; language development is extremely resistant to disability or neglect; non-humans do not acquire linguistic competence, even in a rudimentary form; and it is possible to demonstrate the existence of *linguistic universals.*

One hypothesis about the internal structure of the LAD put forward by Chomsky (1965) and Katz (1966) is that it consists, in part at least, of linguistic universals, features which define the general form of human language. These guide the LAD in its development of grammatical competence from the corpus of speech to which it is exposed. A theory of grammar seeks to state what these universals are and Chomsky (1965) has argued that many (although not all) of the features of the deep structure of sentences correspond to linguistic universals. This implies that studies of the acquisition of linguistic competence by children should look for manifestations of deep structure in children's early grammatical speech, and, as already noted, these manifestations do seem to be present.

The degree to which an innate component can be said to be involved in the acquisition of language, and how specific this innate component is, are the subject of much dispute. Linguistics provides a much needed theoretical framework for investigating the language learning of children, and techniques for dissecting what has to be learned and what has been learned at different stages of development. However, some of the main problems in language learning are psychological rather than linguistic, and it remains to be seen how grammatical rules are learned, how the different types of rule interact, whether the principles involved in perception and production are the same or different and what the relationships are between syntax and semantics.

Further reading

L. A. Jacobovits and M. S. Miron (eds.), *Readings in the Psychology of Language*, Prentice-Hall, 1967.
R. C. Oldfield and J. C. Marshall (eds.), *Language*, Penguin Books, 1968.
K. Salzinger and S. Salzinger (eds.), *Research in Verbal Behavior and Some Neurophysiological Implications*, Academic Press, 1967.
F. Smith and G. A. Miller (eds), *The Genesis of Language: A Psycholinguistic Approach*, M.I.T. Press, 1966.

Chapter 16
Thinking

Introduction

The term 'thinking', as many writers have pointed out (e.g. R. Thomson, 1957), is not well defined in everyday, or indeed in technical, language; it may refer to many rather different types of activity and to a wide range of situations. Many of the questions which the layman asks about thinking are basically concerned with the legitimacy of applying the term to a particular situation or type of activity. He may ask, for example: Do animals think? Can a machine think? Are we 'thinking' when we dream? Is thinking always rational or can it be irrational? Is 'inspiration' a kind of thinking or some quite different process? Clearly, the answer to these and similar questions must depend upon our definition of the term 'thinking'.

Questions of definition

Let us as an example take the question: can animals think? Thinking has sometimes been defined simply as the internal representation of events (see Osgood, 1953). In other words, we say that thinking has occurred in any situation when behaviour is produced for which 'the relevant cues are not available in the external evironment at the time the correct response is required, but must be supplied by the organism itself' (Osgood, 1953, p. 656). While this definition clearly can be applied to many human tasks, from mental arithmetic to poetry writing, it will also cover situations in which animals behave. For example, an animal, as we have seen in Chapter 7, may be set a *delayed response* problem; in view of the animal some desired object, usually food, is placed under one of two boxes and the animal is prevented, for a short time, from approaching it, then allowed to approach. At the time at which restriction is removed the food is not visible; if the animal nevertheless goes to the box concealing the food, rather than to the other box, it must be that there is some internal representation of the earlier event – of the sight of food in association with the sight of the relevant box. Another situation in which thinking, in these terms, might be demonstrated may be called 'alternation learning'. Here a temporal maze is used; the animal may be taught to run for a specified number of times through a simple path such as the figure-of-eight shown in Figure 62, in which there is effectively only one choice point, X, and the animal is rewarded for running in a particular sequence of right or left turns. The animal may be required as it reaches X, first to turn right; then, when X is again reached, to turn left; next time, to turn right again, and so on, in a sequence R L R L R L. The animal may be temporarily halted at various points in the sequence; this constitutes a *delayed alternation* task. In more complicated sequences the animal may be rewarded for turning twice to the right, twice to the left and so on, in a *double alternation* sequence R R L L R R L L. The peculiar significance of this type of learning is that the animal must produce different responses, at different times, to the same choice point – that is, to an identical stimulus complex. Cues to the appropriate response in the sequence are not supplied by the environment, or by the position or orientation of the animal, but must be 'borne in mind' by the animal itself; the correct choice is determined by internal, representational stimuli.

If we accept such rather simple situations as appropriate to demonstrate thinking, then it is clear that animals can think. Not only primates and monkeys but also cats, dogs, rats and racoons can solve problems involving delayed response, and several of these species can also learn alternation sequences, although these, and in particular double alternation sequences, present a much more difficult task. The ability to learn such tasks varies with the position of a species on the phylogenetic scale; primates such as chimpanzees can learn quite extended double alternation sequences, while cats can learn only single R R L L sequences and rats appear to be unable to learn them. The amount of delay which can be tolerated also increases with increased phylogenetic status.

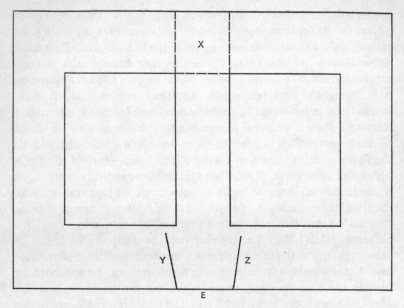

Figure 62 A figure-of-eight maze used in alternation learning (see e.g. Hunter, 1928; Karn, 1938). The animal enters the maze at E. If it correctly turns right at X, it is rewarded at Z and readmitted to the central alley; if it correctly turns left at X it is rewarded at Y. If an incorrect turn is made the animal is unrewarded at Y or Z, or is stopped before reaching Y or Z and forced to retrace its path, or is punished by administration of electric shock at some point beyond X

The objection might be made to this evidence that if thinking is defined in these terms it is no different from retention; to be regarded as anything more than synonymous with memory, thinking must be demonstrated in, and defined in terms of, more complicated situations. The construction of such situations has followed from a second definition of thinking in terms of problem-solving behaviour. Humphrey (1951) has defined thinking as 'what happens in experience when an organism, human or animal, meets, recognizes and solves a problem' (p. 311). A problem may be said to arise whenever a desired goal is not immediately accessible. Thus, the solution of a problem may be taken as evidence of thinking if it appears that the solution involves internal manipulation of elements of the situation, or the supplying 'from within' of cues which are not perceptually present. It would not be evidence of thinking if an animal solved a problem by trial and error or by repeating a well-learned response which had been rewarded in the past.

Much of the work on problem solving in animals began as an attempt to answer the question: do animals think? More precisely, the question posed was whether animals could exhibit insightful behaviour in a problem situation, as opposed to blind, mechanical trial and error. Such investigators as E. L. Thorndike (1898, 1911) argued that animals typically solve problems by a more or less random trial and elimination of possible responses until the correct response is hit upon; others, notably Köhler (1925), claimed that an animal might show a grasp of the problem situation as a whole, form hypotheses as to its solution and produce responses which were meaningful in the total context of the problem. Köhler described the process of insightful solution in this way: there is, often, a pause in activity during which the animal, literally, surveys the situation, followed by sudden and swift performance of the responses involved in the solution. Thorndike, on the other hand, described the process of solution in his animals as characterized by random and largely unrelated activity, with a gradual and irregular elimination of errors on successive attempts at solution.

The discrepancy between these accounts may be explained in various ways, not least in terms of the species of animal on which the accounts were based; Köhler's studies involved, principally, the use of primates as subjects, while Thorndike used animals lower in the phylogenetic scale (for example, cats). Generally speaking, however, it is likely that the distinction between 'insightful' and 'blind' solutions is misconceived. Thorndike's animals were tested in 'puzzle boxes', their goal being to open the door of the box and escape to food placed outside it. To open the door they had to perform one or more of a number of responses – lever pushing, pulling at strings, lifting latches – whose connexion with the door was not evident from the inside of the cage. Köhler, on the other hand, set problems for his animals in which all the cues to solution were normally present and often within the same field of vision as the 'goal object' (see Figure

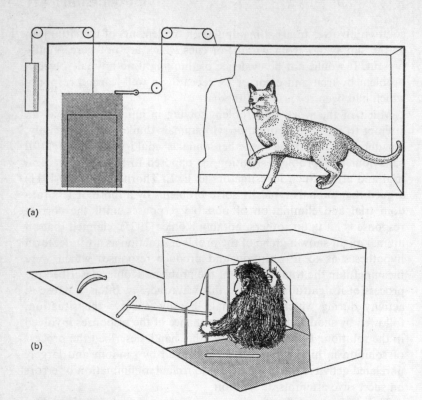

Figure 63   Problem-solving situations used by Thorndike and Köhler.
(a) A 'puzzle box' of the type used by E. L. Thorndike (1911).
To open the door of its box the cat must claw at a loop of string which, outside the box, releases the catch of the door via a pulley system. A separate
weight-and-pulley system raises and holds open the door when released.
(b) A problem situation of the type used by Köhler (1925).
The chimpanzee cannot reach its food with the short stick inside its cage; but
it can use the short stick to rake the long stick into reach, and then use the long
stick to draw in the fruit

63). It is likely that an animal faced with a problem will utilize any
cues that are available towards solution and that its performance
will vary with the number and availability of such cues. If Köhler's
animals react on the basis of visual cues they are likely to show 'insight'; if Thorndike's animals react to visual cues they will fail to

reach a solution, since the response which produces a solution is basically arbitrary. They must learn to produce an improbable response rather than the responses suggested by the (misleading) cues available.

The work done in this field has, however, proved extremely useful in a second sense: it has provided a good deal of empirical information as to the conditions which improve or impair performance at problem solving. We shall consider such information (derived from human rather than animal performance) later in this chapter; here let it suffice to say that if we define thinking in terms of the capacity to solve problems (with some auxiliary definition of what constitutes a problem), animals, or at any rate some animals, must be held to think.

These definitions are not, of course, those likely to be produced by the introspecting layman. When he asks whether animals can think, he is probably referring to some such notion as 'inner life': whether animals have self-awareness and abstract ideas. The notion that animals possess awareness, in this sense, appears to be generally and traditionally rejected, although a strong case for its reconsideration has been made by Thorpe (1966). It is in fact extraordinarily difficult to decide what would constitute evidence of such 'inner life', in the absence of its communication by speech. If it is defined narrowly as, essentially, talking to oneself in abstract terms, there is no evidence that animals possess the complex and arbitrary language system which this implies. If the criterion is taken to be the capacity for conceptual behaviour, there is certainly evidence for such behaviour in animals, at least in the sense that they are able to respond to a stimulus on the basis not of its individual characteristics but of the characteristics of the class of stimuli to which it belongs (e.g. Fields, 1932). Whether this is held to represent abstraction, whether it is described in terms of stimulus generalization or in terms of conceptual mediation is not easy to decide, and the problem has usually been solved by recourse to 'Lloyd Morgan's canon' – the principle that animal behaviour is to be explained in the simplest terms available. It is of course debatable whether accounts of animal behaviour in s–r terms are always 'simpler' than accounts which involve such notions as insight and expectancy.

The conclusion to be drawn from such considerations might well be that by a skilful use of definition well-nigh any question about thinking may receive any answer. Partly because of these uncertainties many, if not most, experimental psychologists have tended to avoid the study of cognition – notably behaviourists who sought to account for behaviour without recourse to the notion of 'internal events', which were held to be not directly observable and therefore to lead only to untestable hypotheses. If 'internal events' were incorporated into theories of behaviour, they were incorporated in the form of 'intervening variables' whose independent existence was not considered.

Nevertheless, there has in recent years been a return of interest in the analysis of what has been termed 'the central process', largely but not entirely stimulated by the growth of computer science which has focused attention on the methods by which information can be processed in machines and perhaps also in man (we shall return to the man–machine analogy implied here in a later section). Early behaviourism was described as s–r theory – the study of stimulus–response connexions. Later behaviourists expressed their approach by the formula s–o–r. Stimuli and responses must be studied; but the internal processing carried out by o, the organism, is also worthy of study. If we ignore the study of such processes our analysis is incomplete and moreover it omits, and not altogether of necessity, an area of human experience which the layman with some justification may feel to be of the greatest importance.

A provisional definition

A provisional definition of thinking might be 'the internal manipulation of symbols'. It is a poor definition for various reasons. The distinction between 'internal' and 'external' behaviour, for example, means little more than that the behaviour involved in thinking happens at present to be unobservable – and we shall see that attempts have been made to render the 'raw stuff of thinking' measurable. The term 'symbols' is also far from unambiguous, but clearly could refer to sensory images or to words. The words of the definition, in brief, sound as though they refer to non-material processes but in fact refer only to the 'light-weight' nature of the responses which comprise thinking and to the limits of our means of recording behaviour. If thinking is, then, defined as 'behaviour which happens to be unobservable', how can it be studied?

There are effectively two approaches to unobservable behaviour. One is via introspection. Thinking is not necessarily 'unobservable' to the thinker; he may be able to make his private awareness public by reporting on it. The technique of introspection – that is, of 'observing oneself think' during the performance of mental tasks and of reporting on the process to an observer – was extensively used by early investigators although with the advent of behaviourism it fell into some disrepute.

The difficulties of dealing with introspective data are considerable. Introspective data are by their nature unverifiable; they can represent only those aspects of thinking of which the thinker is readily aware and therefore can offer no clue to the existence or nature of 'unconscious' thinking; they are conveyed only by the verbal report of the thinker and this may not be sensitive enough to portray all the subtleties of experience. Further, the process of introspection involves an atypical attitude on the part of the thinker who is required not only to think but also to 'observe his thinking', and this may well lead to modification of the thinking process itself. Nevertheless, introspection has been, and is still, a valuable tool in psychological research. (For a fuller discussion of the use of introspection in the study of thinking, see Humphrey, 1951.)

The other source of evidence about 'unobserved behaviour' is, simply, that there are situations which can only be explained by postulating it. We have already referred to some of these situations – delayed-response and alternation problems in the case of animals, problem situations for both animals and humans – in which activity 'must have occurred' between stimulus and response, since the final behaviour of the subject cannot be held to derive directly from the immediate stimulus situation. In this chapter we shall base our discussion chiefly upon three related types of situation, since these are relevant to human studies and since most work in cognition has centred around them: problem solving, creativity and concept formation. It is a useful supplement to our inadequate definition of the subject matter of this chapter to consider briefly the sorts of experiment or observation which are included under these headings.

Situations used in the study of thinking

Problem solving has been defined by Gagné as 'an inferred change in human capability that results in the acquisition of a generalizable rule which is novel to the individual, which cannot have been established by direct recall, and which can manifest itself in applicability to the solution of a class of problems' (1966, p. 132). While this definition is not uncontroversial, it usefully points to the characteristics conventionally required in a demonstration of problem solving: a response complex which is novel for the individual, which requires the reorganization rather than the simple recall of previously learned responses and which is not simply a specific solution but one which can apply in principle to any of a number of problems.

The problem situations used are diverse. We have already discussed some problems employed by psychologists using animals; when humans are studied, problems have ranged from practical construction tasks (e.g. Duncker, 1945; Maier, 1945) to abstract mathematical and reasoning tasks (e.g. Duncker, 1945; Gagné, 1966; and for a survey of laboratory tasks, see Ray, 1955).

Creativity can be defined as a special case of problem solving; stressing the originality of the solution response and having usually some assessment of the *value* of the solution. Maltzman (1960) has in fact defined creativity as 'originality evaluated'. We shall not be concerned here with studies of originality *per se*, which deal with response novelty in simple situations such as word association; such studies are discussed by Maltzman in the article quoted. Our concern is with the situations more typically studied under the heading of 'creativity': that is, with scientific invention and artistic or literary production. Laboratory studies of creativity (for example, Patrick, 1935, 1937) are few, and are supplemented by introspective accounts, from 'creative' people, of their experiences and methods of work (for example, Ghiselin, 1952).

It is worth noting that several writers have pointed out a distinction between *problem solving* and *problem finding*; by the latter process is meant the creative setting up of hypotheses and formulation of questions rather than the attempt to deal with those already existent. The process of 'problem finding' has been relatively neglected by psychologists, although it is clearly central to the notion of creativity, and at least arguably of more practical importance than problem solving in that context.

Concept formation denotes the process by which stimuli come to be responded to not merely as individual and unique events but as members of a class of stimuli. When we identify a strange animal as a dog we are indicating that a concept – of 'dogs' – has been formed; and we may run away from a bull encountered in a field, not because we have previously experienced its ferocity but because we respond to its membership of a class of animals from which it is appropriate to run. The classifying, or categorizing, of stimuli can be said to be 'one of the most elementary and general forms of cognition by which man adjusts to his environment' (Bruner, Goodnow and Austin, 1956, p. 2). In so far as a distinction can usefully be made between 'categories' and 'concepts', it can be said that a *category* represents a class of events while a *concept* is a learned response to a class of events. A concept may be a verbal label which we attach to a newly encountered object to denote its class membership; it may involve a more overt response, such as running away from the stimulus, or eating it, or refraining from eating it – according to the categorical nature of the stimulus. The function of a concept is basically to relate present to previous experience, so that new situations and events may be appropriately dealt with without further learning (for further discussion, see Bruner, Goodnow and Austin, 1956; R. Thomson, 1957; Vinacke, 1952).

It follows from such definitions that concept formation has been studied experimentally by means of *sorting problems*, more often than not involving cards as stimuli. A subject is given a deck of cards, each bearing certain markings; each card is an exemplar of a certain category and the subject's task is to sort the cards into the appropriate categories – that is, to learn the concepts according to which they should be sorted. Beyond this basic condition, experimental conditions and instructions have varied widely; some subjects, for example, have been specifically told that theirs is a concept-formation task, while at the opposite extreme subjects have learnt concepts only incidentally while ostensibly performing an associative-learning task (Hull, 1920). The characteristics which determine the category to which a stimulus belongs also vary in complexity and in degree of abstractness. Further, in some experiments (for example, Goldstein and Scheerer, 1941) concept formation may be 'open ended' rather than 'closed', in the sense that there is no necessarily correct way of classifying the stimuli given; the subject's task is to devise one or more bases of classification. Performance in such tasks has been used to measure cognitive deficit in organic or functional illness. Clearly, 'closed' concept-formation tasks represent, in a sense, problem solving, while 'open-ended' concept formation might be regarded as a test of creativity. Thus all three areas of research, while operationally distinct, are in some considerable measure inter-related.

Studies of thinking

There are essentially two lines of attack in the study of thinking. The first is concerned with the conditions which affect successful thinking – that is, with the association between success and various task characteristics, experience and other subject variables. The second represents an attempt to examine more closely the nature of the 'central process' of cognition and can in turn be subdivided into attempts to measure the 'raw material' of thinking and attempts to analyse its processes and stages. The rest of this chapter will thus fall under the following three headings.

Conditions affecting successful thinking

Task variables. It is of course a tautology to say that the difficulty of the task affects the probability of successful solution; nevertheless there have been attempts to link more specific task variables to success. The *complexity* of the task, in terms of the number of response elements required in solution, has been observed (for example, by Köhler, 1925) to be negatively related to success in problem solving by animals. When humans serve as subjects, task difficulty has been more often studied in terms of the *degree of abstractness* of the learning required. A classic study by Heidbreder (1946a and b) varied the abstractness of categories in a card-sorting task; the concepts to be

Figure 64   Materials used in Heidbreder's study of concept formation. (From Heidbreder, 1946a, p. 182)

learned were either 'concrete', 'spatial' or 'abstract'. A sample of the material used in this study is shown in Figure 64. Heidbreder found that concrete concepts were most readily learned, abstract concepts least readily learned. This finding is to some extent corroborated by the observation that subjects with brain damage or with functional disorder show a greater deficit (when their performance is compared with that of control subjects) in dealing with abstract than with concrete concepts (Goldstein and Scheerer, 1941; Hanfmann and Kasanin, 1942). A related finding is that creative problem solving of the type involved, for example, in scientific innovation may be facilitated by the 'concretization' of abstract materials. Bruner (1962) has reported that applied problem solving is aided by such techniques as representing ideas pictorially and building models which can then be physically manipulated. In studies of problem solving, however, it is virtually impossible to vary the concrete or abstract nature of a problem without also varying its difficulty in other important respects, such as its demands upon immediate or delayed memory.

A consideration of the possible benefits of 'concretization' reminds us that the perceptual characteristics of the task situation may well be of importance. Where animals are concerned, problems are much more likely to be solved if all the components of the solution are readily visible: if, for example, the sticks needed for solution of a food-raking problem are left lying at the front of an ape's cage and within the same field of vision as the food. Where humans are concerned, the perceptual presence of cues to solution might be considered less important, since the human subject has greater capacity for representing to himself cues which are not present, for example by words. Nevertheless, there are studies which suggest that perceptual factors are not unimportant in problem solving by humans. A classic series of experiments by Duncker (1945) showed that the spatial arrangement of components given to subjects substantially affected the ease with which they solved construction problems. When subjects were asked to fix three lit candles against the wall, given only hammer, nails, a box and the candles, the problem was solved more readily when the box and candles were laid out separately than when the candles were presented *in* the box; the solution to this problem is to use the box not in its usual role as a container but as a shelf, which can be nailed to the wall and on which the candles can stand. The implication would seem to be that perceptual characteristics may influence a subject's grasp of the possible functions of elements of the solution; where the presentation of elements favours one functional interpretation, other functions are rendered harder to grasp.

The instructions given to the subject when the task is set are also likely to affect performance. For example, success is more likely in concept formation when subjects are specifically told to search for 'conceptual' characteristics when sorting stimuli than when they are simply instructed to learn 'the label' which belongs to each stimulus, given that some stimuli share the same label (Reed, 1946). Maier (1945) has further shown that giving a 'direction' or hint to solution increases the likelihood of solution of a practical problem, although some later studies have shown his finding to be ambiguous (Saugstad, 1957).

There may well be other factors, to a greater or lesser degree independent of those already quoted, which affect the intrinsic difficulty of a task. In concept-formation studies, Bruner, Goodnow and Austin (1956) have reported that conjunctive concepts are much more readily learnt than disjunctive concepts, even by highly intelligent and sophisticated subjects. A conjunctive concept is one for which all members of the class have one or more characteristics in common; a disjunctive concept represents a class of stimuli which qualify for membership by possession of one of several characteristics. All stimulus cards bearing a green border and a triangle would be an example of a conjunctive concept; all cards with either a green border or a triangle, or both, an example of a disjunctive concept. Thus two members of the same disjunctive category might be utterly dissimilar. Bruner *et al.* suggest that the difference in difficulty may reflect the greater frequency of conjunctive concepts in contemporary Western culture, although the opposite hypothesis could equally well be advanced that the scarcity of disjunctive concepts in 'everyday life' reflects their difficulty of formation. This interpretation points to the importance of *prior experience* in determining successful thinking.

Prior experience. A problem must by definition be a *new* one for the would-be solver; the solution must be one which he has never produced before. However, it is abundantly clear that past experience of even remotely related problems is of crucial importance in determining present success. Generally speaking, experience benefits performance in that it permits the transfer of learned principles and skills from an 'old' situation to a 'new' one; and many studies could be quoted in support of this, in both animal and human fields of study (e.g. Birch, 1945; Harlow, 1949; Maier, 1945). The significance of experience is presumably twofold: it presents the opportunity to learn the *functional characteristics* of objects and also to learn *specific skills and methods*.

However, in both respects experience can in certain circumstances lead to impaired performance when learned 'labels' and skills are transferred to inappropriate situations. This has often been termed 'functional fixation'. For example, if an object must be used in a novel way to solve a practical problem, as in the example quoted earlier (Duncker, 1945), it is less likely to be so used if the subject has already seen it used, or used it, for a different purpose; a 'neutral' block of wood is more likely to be seen as serving the purpose of a pendulum weight than is a hammer, which normally has a quite different function. Again, if a given method of problem solving has proved successful in the past, it may be applied again in situations where it is inappropriate and thus hinder solution (for further discussion, see Krech and Crutchfield, 1958).

Subject variables. We have already seen that the prior experience of subjects influences their ability to solve problems; that different species exhibit varying degrees of cognitive ability, their ability increasing as phylogenetic complexity increases; and that brain damage or functional disorder appears to reduce the capacity for abstract thinking. Other individual differences among subjects may be reflected in cognitive performance. Clearly, intelligence is one important factor; another is age. We shall not here be concerned with the development of cognitive ability in the young child or with differences in intelligence and with the relation between intelligence and creativity; such points are discussed in Chapter 18. We shall instead discuss briefly the influence of what can loosely be termed 'personality factors'. Most of the evidence here has been concerned with *creative* performance, and with the personality characteristics of creative, as opposed to non-creative, people. For this purpose creative and non-creative people can be so classified in one of two ways; on the basis of actual achievement (as rated by others in the same discipline) in some scientific, artistic or literary field, or on the basis of performance on *tests of creativity*. Such tests, and their relation to tests of intelligence, are discussed in Chapter 18.

A good deal of evidence has been collected on the personality characteristics of creative people (for example, Barron, 1965; Getzels and Jackson, 1962; Gruber, Terrell and Wertheimer, 1962; Taylor and Barron, 1963). It is unwise to draw firm conclusions from these data, since both measures of creativity and measures of personality are diverse and sometimes ill-validated, and since correlations observed between them tend to be low. In so far as a summary can be made, it appears that creative people are verbally fluent, flexible in thinking and (at any rate among actual achievers) dedicated to work, in the sense that they devote a very great deal of time and effort to it. They emerge as independent and individual in judgement and as generally unconventional, sometimes flamboyant, in manner. They have been described as self-centred and difficult to handle, and as showing more evidence of psychopathology on clinical tests; on the other hand, it is worth noting that psychoanalysts (for example, Kubie, 1958) have specifically denied that creativity is allied to neurosis or 'genius akin to madness', arguing rather that neurotic or psychotic disorder is more likely to disrupt than to facilitate productive thinking.

In connexion with personality differences it is of interest to consider the effect of ageing upon creative achievement. It is commonly held that as people grow older they become more 'rigid' in thinking and in behaviour (though Chown, 1959, has shown that the notion is at best a doubtful one), and that creativity consequently declines with advancing age. Lehman (1953) sought evidence on this point by determining from biographical and other data the age at which creative workers had produced their 'best work', as judged by others in the same field. He found that, while findings differ for different fields of activity, it is generally true that the 'best work' occurs relatively early in life – at perhaps thirty to thirty-four years of age – and that creativity, thus defined, declines thereafter. However, he also found a very wide age range, from twenty to eighty or more, over which notably creative work might be produced. There are, moreover, a number of factors which might exaggerate the decline in creativity with age: changes, for example, in the circumstances of work, and in the incidence of ill-health. Again, judges estimating creative value will perhaps tend to rate an early publication by a given author as more creative than later works which follow up and extend the notions which appeared in the first (for discussion of these points, see Bromley, 1965). It seems, then, that while some intellectual deficit – in speed of work and in capacity for abstract thinking – appears in old age, estimates of its extent, and the extent of concomitant 'creative deficit', can easily be exaggerated.

The 'raw stuff' of thinking

What is the nature of 'internal representation'? Early investigators sought the answer to this question by analysing the introspections of trained subjects during 'mental work' such as mental arithmetic, word association or complex problem solving. They were concerned in particular with the relation between thinking and sensory imagery. Many of the ancient and the empiricist philosophers had argued that thinking consists essentially of sensory imagery; and it certainly appears from introspective data that sensory images figure very largely in mental activity. Galton (1883), for example, found that even eminent mathematicians and other scientists, whose thinking might be imagined to occupy an 'abstract plane', made use of concrete imagery to aid calculation as well as invention (for a full discussion of the role of imagination in thinking, see McKellar, 1957). Might there, however, be 'pure' thought unaccompanied by sensory ideas? Different investigators produced sharply opposing results (see Humphrey, 1951) and no unequivocal answer could be produced. Indeed, it is hard to see how introspective data, for all their descriptive interest and importance, could be expected to provide a clear answer to the question.

One piece of evidence furnished by introspective data has had a marked effect upon subsequent studies of thinking. This was the frequent report, during periods of otherwise 'imageless' thought, of vague kinaesthetic sensations – an ill-defined experience of muscular tension. The finding led to the suggestion that there is motor imagery in thinking as well as, or rather than, sensory imagery. The experiments suggested by this notion, and their results, can only briefly be described. Many investigators attempted electrical recording of potential changes in the peripheral musculature of subjects during performance of mental tasks, and found some correlation between the type of task set and the pattern of activity recorded; if a subject was told to imagine hitting a nail with a hammer held in his right hand, for example, periodic bursts of activity occurred in the muscle groups of the right forearm but not in other muscle groups (Jacobsen, 1932). When subjects were asked to imagine counting or telling the time, bursts of activity occurred in the lips and tongue but not in other parts of the body. Thus there seemed to be peripheral muscular involvement in thinking which was reasonably specific in nature. It should be noted, however, that the subjects used had been trained in relaxation and were able to maintain relaxation except in the specifically reacting muscle groups. There is some evidence that in (untrained) subjects performing more obviously 'mental' rather than imaginal tasks the over-all, non-specific tension level may facilitate or impair mental work. Thus the relative importance of specific and non-specific muscular involvement is still unclear (for a summary of this type of study, see Osgood, 1953).

In the context of the 'implicit response' theory of thought, Watson (1914) suggested that thinking consists of implicit vocalization; while this is almost certainly an overstatement, the role of language in thinking is undoubtedly of great importance. Animals, by some definitions, think, although they have no true language system, but language is very likely to be a 'preferred' mode of representation when it is available, on the grounds of its economy of expression and of bodily effort. The dependence of thought upon language has been stressed by cultural anthropologists such as Sapir (1949) and Whorf (1956) who have argued that the content and logic of an individual's thinking is largely a function of the language structure which obtains in his culture (see also Hoijer, 1953). The relation between the development of language and the development of thinking has also been of enormous interest to psychologists, although we shall not consider this relation here; see, for example, Piaget (1926, 1962) and Vygotsky (1934, trans. 1962).

Against a wholesale acceptance of language as the vehicle for thought must be set the fact that, as we have seen, non-verbal imagery is often reported as facilitating problem solving, and indeed as having sometimes proved more efficient than purely verbal representation, which may hinder rather than help solution through inappropriate verbal labelling. The 'linguistic relativity hypothesis' of Whorf and Sapir has received only very limited support from the results of experimental investigation; see, for example, the summary of findings by Carroll (1964). Again, R. Brown (1965) has pointed out that 'inner speech' may be rather different in detail from speech which is directed at others; for example, it is condensed by the omission of irrelevant words and phrases much as are lecture notes taken for our own reference. Moreover, he suggests that it may not even be entirely verbal, but may rather consist of 'thought that is shaped by language and that follows linguistic rules, especially rules of syntax, but which is not necessarily consciously verbal'. Brown concludes: 'If so, then I believe we do have a great deal of inner speech. What I then wonder about is whether we have any thought that is not inner speech' (1965, p. 348).

An interesting approach to the problem of the nature of internal representation, from a somewhat different standpoint, is provided by the *mediation theory* of Osgood (1953). The notion of mediation has been discussed in an earlier chapter (Chapter 12); here it will simply be pointed out that Osgood has specified, in some detail, the nature of the representational responses said to mediate all learned associations. The responses which come to represent and mediate an overt response pattern constitute a fragmentary and reduced part of that pattern: a representation which becomes as reduced as possible while still remaining distinctively related to the total response. An eating response, for example, might be represented by salivation and by other components which identify the response pattern from which they were drawn, but which are lightweight in terms of energy expenditure and which do not interfere with the total behavioural sequence which they mediate. Thus thinking consists of mediating responses which are portions of the overt behaviour which they represent; these responses might be muscular or glandular, or in some cases 'purely neural' (Osgood, Suci and Tannenbaum, 1957). It seems likely then that internal representation of the kind involved in problem solving and other mental work includes any type of activity which is involved in overt behaviour: sensory imagery, motor imagery, subvocal speech. This versatility, and in particular the notion of 'purely neural' representation, makes Osgood's theory – and indeed virtually any enlightened hypothesis as to the raw stuff of thinking – interesting but untestable.

Analysis of the thinking process

There have been many attempts to analyse thinking which do not necessarily make any assumptions as to the 'raw stuff' of thought; such attempts may be described as 'model building'. The aim is to represent faithfully the functions involved in thinking, and their sequence, but not necessarily with reference to the organismic responses – for example, neural processes – which may be held to underlie them. (It might, however, be noted in passing that it is not always readily apparent whether a given theory of behaviour is a 'model' in this sense or whether the terms in which it is expressed are to be taken literally.)

In considering analyses of the thinking process we shall be chiefly concerned with what might be termed 'thinking to obvious purpose': cases, such as problem solving, in which the goal of thinking is clear and which have throughout this chapter been of primary interest. There are other activities to which the term 'thinking' has sometimes been applied: dreaming, hallucinatory and other imaginative activities in which the 'purpose' of thinking, and perhaps its end result, are unclear. The second part of this section will consider briefly these processes under the imprecise but useful term 'fantasy thinking'.

Thinking to obvious purpose. Among relatively early attempts to analyse thinking were the 'insight' theories of problem solving stemming essentially from the Gestalt school of psychology (see Humphrey, 1951). We have already noted Köhler's (1925) account of problem solving in animals, which comprises three distinct stages:

initial helplessness, a pause in activity and a sudden and smooth performance of the solution. In human problem solving Duncker (1945) provided a careful analysis of stages in problem solving which stressed the rational, purposive nature of the activity involved. Duncker hypothesized that, again, three stages are involved in solution. A subject at first produces a *general range* of possible means of solution, which have been described as reformulating the problem rather than offering solutions to it. When a general line of attack has been chosen, the subject begins to produce *functional solutions*, more detailed but still not entirely specific; the proposal of a functional solution – a notion as to what sort of method might be employed to achieve the goal – leads in turn to *specific solutions* which detail the exact means to be employed. If such solutions are not acceptable, another functional solution will be explored; if all functional solutions arising from a given general line of attack prove unprofitable, the subject rejects that general line and turns to another, which is then pursued in the same way. The process is thus seen to be an enlightened series of trials at solution each of which results in reorganization of the problem until the solution is achieved.

An example of behaviour thus analysed is shown in Figure 65. Duncker's subject was given this problem: given a human being with an inoperable stomach tumour, and rays that destroy organic tissue at sufficient intensity, by what procedure can one free him of the tumour by these rays and at the same time avoid destroying the healthy tissue which surrounds it? The subject's attempts at solution could be classed under three main headings: avoidance of contact between rays and tissue except at the site of the tumour; desensitization of the healthy tissue; and reduction of intensity of the rays except at the site of the tumour. Each of these aims suggested certain possibilities which in turn produced specific attempts at solution; the first, for example, might be achieved by using or creating some tissue-free path to the site of the tumour, and this led to suggestions of sending rays through the oesophagus or of operating to expose the tumour and directing rays through an inserted tube. Solutions of this kind were ruled impracticable, and others were produced on the basis of other general frames of reference; finally, the general aim of lowering intensity of rays led the subject to consider some means of

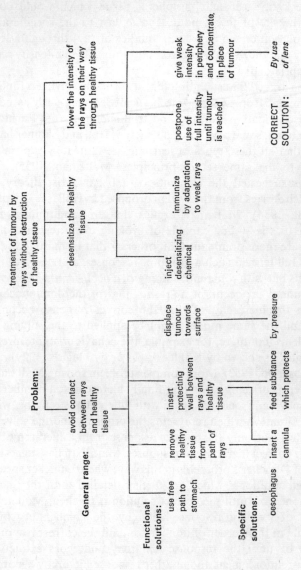

Figure 65 Duncker's (1945) analysis of problem solving. (From Duncker, 1945, p. 5)

directing weak rays through peripheral tissue which would concentrate at the site of the tumour, and at last to the specific and acceptable solution of sending weak bundles of rays through a lens in such a way that they would intersect and summate in intensity only in the appropriate area.

It was often argued that such 'intelligent' problem solving is fundamentally different from simple 'mechanical' learning such as conditioning, discrimination learning and trial-and-error rote learning. On the other hand, some psychologists such as Hull and Skinner have maintained that all these types of learning are ultimately explicable by recourse to the same set of principles. Maltzman (1955), for example, has suggested the elements of a behaviourist theory of thinking which derives from the system proposed by Hull (see Chapter 12 and Hull, 1934). Maltzman argues that in conditioning, for example, the UCS is at first capable of evoking many responses, of which some are more dominant than others – that is, more likely to be evoked; Hull termed such a group of responses, all related to the same stimulus but with differential strength, a *habit-family hierarchy*. In conditioning what occurs is a 'reshuffling' of the dominance of responses in the hierarchy so that the correct response becomes dominant; and the same model might be applied to the solving of simple problems (compare, for example, the behaviourist interpretation of 'insight' as shown by Köhler's apes or by Maier's (1929) rats reported in Osgood, 1953). More complex problem solving Maltzman explains in terms of *compound* habit-family hierarchies; a number of hierarchies may be associated, again with differential strengths, with the stimulus situation which represents the problem, and the solver's task is to select not only the correct response from a hierarchy but also, first, the correct hierarchy of responses. Maltzman has suggested an analysis of Duncker's protocols in this way; where Duncker speaks of 'functional solutions' which are further detailed until they have to be abandoned or until the correct solution is reached, Maltzman would speak of a general response hierarchy, the members of which are 'tried out' in their order of dominance until the correct response is produced or until the response hierarchy undergoes extinction through non-reinforcement and another response hierarchy becomes dominant.

While this analysis is by no means complete, it serves to illustrate that it is perfectly possible to give either a 'mechanistic' or a 'cognitive' account of the thinking process. The choice of terms for analysis depends partly upon individual preference for one level of explanation rather than another and partly upon considerations of parsimony. There is clearly the advantage of theoretical economy in explaining many different kinds of behaviour in terms of the same basic principles. On the other hand, there are the disadvantages that an estimation of complex behaviour in terms of simple behaviour may obscure real differences between them; also such an estimation may not account as adequately for the data as, and may involve a more complex system of hypotheses than, less parsimonious accounts which treat 'higher functions' in special and not easily reducible terms.

A recent development in the analysis of thinking is the 'information-processing' approach, which extends the method of analysis with the aid of computers. The general method adopted in computer simulation of thinking is as follows: the investigator first makes a provisional analysis on the basis of observations and introspections. Such a general analysis is offered by Gagné (1966), for example, who proposes roughly seven stages in the 'internal activity' of problem solving: the *statement* of the problem; the *recall* of related facts and rules; the *selection* of relevant from irrelevant data; the *combination*, or organization, of relevant data in a new way; the *production* of a provisional solution; its *verification*; and, finally, its *statement and acceptance*. Gagné also points out respects in which instructional and other task variables, as well as subject variables, may influence each of these stages in the thinking process.

When an analysis of thinking has been devised, the investigator writes a *programme*, or set of instructions, for the computer, to enable it to carry out the hypothesized process. This programme, it has been claimed, is essentially a theory of thinking, couched in computer terms (Newell, Shaw and Simon, 1958); naturally, it involves more detailed description than is provided by the analyses quoted above. The programme, or theory, is then *verified*.

In the verification of a given programme there are two questions to be asked. First, is the appropriate goal behaviour produced – for example, is the problem solved? It has been shown often that computers can in fact successfully solve practical and abstract problems and play 'intellectual' games such as chess. Second, is the 'thinking' process carried out by the machine similar to that of a human subject, in general and in detail? Basically, there are two ways of examining the similarity between the protocols produced by human and machine solvers. One of these is to lay the protocols side by side and to count up the differences between them at various stages towards solution; the other is to employ judges who are given a number of protocols and asked to sort them into those produced by machines and those produced by humans. The results of verification are on the whole encouraging (for further detail and discussion, see Reitman, 1965).

There have been objections to the use of computers in the analysis of thinking. Some are based on misapprehension of the *conceptual status* of computer simulation; it is sometimes objected, for example, that the use of computers implies that 'man is just a machine' and thinking essentially mechanical. Such an argument is made inappropriate when we remember that the computer programme is, in the narrow sense, a model which does not presuppose that humans think by processes identical with those of the machine but rather that the processes are *analogous*. The argument is therefore no more pertinent than is the view that a comparative approach to human behaviour implies that 'man is only an animal' in the pejorative sense.

A more justifiable criticism has been that 'computer thinking' is too efficient and too logical to furnish a fair analogy with human thinking; computers do not display boredom and fatigue, and do not forget. In fact it is possible to programme a computer to exhibit imperfections and, in a sense, to think 'intuitively' rather than logically. If the solution of a problem involves selection of a correct response from a set of alternatives, the computer may be made to display either *algorithmic* behaviour – in which each alternative is tried in order until the correct response is produced and verified – or *heuristic* behaviour – in which certain responses rather than others are tried out on the basis of 'hunches' and principles derived from past experience but which are not logically compelling. This criticism, then, is rather of the limitations upon versatility of programming at present than of the use of computers *per se*.

Probably the most serious criticism of computer models of thinking is that it is difficult for a model to be understood by anyone other than the programmer. To comprehend the theory, one needs to know not only the computer language but also a mass of detail regarding specific coding of the machine. The programmer-theorist must therefore 'translate' the model back into common, probably verbal, terms in order to communicate it, and this procedure is fraught with dangers and may effectively nullify the real advantages of computer simulation as a tool in analysis.

The principal advantage of computer simulation is that it necessitates *explicit* formulation of all assumptions made during analysis; in verbal expression it is easy unwittingly to omit, or leave implicit, quite basic assumptions, but if this occurs in computer simulation the programme will simply not run. Computer simulation is therefore at the very least a valuable exercise in theoretical precision. Its potential contribution to the study of thinking is great, but at present largely unrealized. Naturally, many studies of computer simulation are activated by an interest in 'artificial intelligence' in its own right, rather than in relation to human intelligence. The need would seem to be for more models of human thinking which, while they may stem in part from computer functions, are independent of them. Whether such theories will be profitable, and whether a general theory of human and computer thinking will eventually prove feasible, are still very much open questions.

Fantasy thinking. We stated earlier that there are certain phenomena of symbolic behaviour to which the account of thinking as a rational and purposive activity cannot readily be applied. A simple example concerns creative problem solving; many accounts of the problem-solving process, based upon introspection, have stressed that after a certain amount of preparatory work there is characteristically an *incubation* period, in which conscious work does not occur, and that this period may end in *illumination* – a sudden realization of the solution, which can then be tested and verified. This appears to be a solution which emerges from a period of unconscious work: some activity must have followed the preparation period in order to produce solution, but that activity is not conscious thinking of a rational kind. A similar process of illumination which does not follow immediately upon conscious work is often reported by creative writers, poets and artists (Ghiselin, 1952). In such cases, then, the nature of the thinking which is supposed to have occurred is unclear, although its end is obvious; in other cases – for example, dreaming and daydreaming activity – neither the process nor its aim is easily described. True, there is some room for doubt as to whether these types of imaginative activity should be considered instances of 'thinking'; certainly, however, our definition of thinking in this chapter would not exclude them.

Several authors have suggested, on the basis of such evidence, that there is more than one kind of thinking. McKellar (1957) argued that two kinds of thinking can be distinguished: reality-adjusted or R-thinking and autistic or A-thinking. R-thinking is logical, rational and checked against external information; A-thinking is non-rational, proceeding by the association of ideas on a non-logical basis, and independent of external correction. R-thinking is typical of purposive problem solving such as we have discussed earlier; A-thinking is most clearly seen in dreams, fantasy and some forms of psychotic thinking. McKellar further suggested that R-thinking and A-thinking may co-exist in many situations, notably in problem solving; when R-thinking has not produced a solution, A-thinking in the absence of conscious work may prove effective. In support of this notion are the many instances, quoted by McKellar, of solutions which occur in fantasy or in dreams and which prove viable on realistic verification. In such situations A-thinking can be regarded as the author, and R-thinking as the editor, of the final production.

This account of A-thinking can be compared with psychoanalytic views of autistic thinking and dreaming as wish fulfilment which is unconsciously directed and not subject to realistic assessment (Freud, 1900, trans. 1913; Murphy, 1947). On the other hand, it should be reiterated that Kubie (1958) and others have explained creative thinking in terms of preconscious, rather than unconscious, activity; so that the exact relation between A-thinking and 'unconscious thinking' is not altogether obvious (see McKellar's 1957 discussion).

Moreover, the distinction between A-thinking and R-thinking must not be equated with that between 'normal' and 'abnormal' thinking. A-thinking, as we have seen, may occur 'normally' in certain situations; and R-thinking may form a large part of the thinking of psychotic individuals.

We cannot here consider in detail analyses which have been made of the kind of thinking found in 'dream work'. Neither shall we consider analysis of the 'psychotic thinking' found in schizophrenia and other severe mental disorders. We shall simply mention in this connexion that there is always a difficulty in distinguishing between subjective experience and its communication; for example, Cameron (1944) has argued that the 'thought disorder' of the schizophrenic may reflect not a breakdown in thinking but a breakdown in the communication of thoughts to others.

Whether R-thinking and A-thinking are best viewed as separate processes or as activities differing in degree rather than in kind with regard to certain variables – notably the consideration of 'reality' in the thinking process – is far from clear if we confine our consideration to simpler phenomena associated with problem solution. Let us consider, for example, the frequent occurrence of incubation and illumination as stages in problem solution and in creative work. There are several respects in which an 'incubation period' might prove beneficial. Rest may in itself enable the thinker to grasp a solution which eluded him when he was fatigued by conscious work; or the rest period may provide time during which erroneous attempts at solution will be forgotten and therefore no longer interfere with the generation of new hypotheses. Again, if the thinker leaves a problem he may nevertheless continue to consider it, at odd moments and without devoting much effort to it; thus illumination might result from additional work, the extent of which may be underestimated by the thinker. None of these possibilities necessitates the notion of a different kind of thinking.

On the other hand, there does seem to be a good deal of anecdotal evidence that dreams may help solution of various problems: the solution itself may be dreamed, for example, and may (though by no means always) prove viable when checked after waking. From this and related evidence it seems likely that fantasy-like activity may indeed play a part in problem solution and more probably in artistic creation. But, again, is fantasy thinking really different from realistic thinking except in degree? The dream process is most obviously one of *concretization*, and we have seen that this is beneficial in purposive thinking, and indeed that it is hard to determine whether any thinking is unaccompanied by sensory imagery. Neither can it be argued that the use of language differentiates R-thinking from A-thinking, since verbal imagery seems to occur in both cases and is neither necessarily logical nor necessarily non-logical. The association and sequence of ideas are supposedly more logically based in purposive thinking; but it may be that the requirements of logical conclusion, introspection and report impose logicality upon the thinker's protocol, while the same requirements are not applicable to dream reports.

The difference between purposive and fantasy thinking, in particular the logical nature of purposive thinking, can easily be exaggerated. Confusion arises partly from the fact that 'kinds of thinking' are distinguished sometimes simply on the basis of the degree of accompanying awareness, sometimes on the basis of the processes involved and sometimes on the basis of the *situations* in which thinking may occur – for example, whether or not thinking appears to be directed towards a practical goal. It would be illuminating to write a programme for fantasy thinking and to examine the protocols obtained from computer simulation of such activity; in general, the nature of any distinction between purposive and fantasy thinking cannot be decided upon until the characteristics of each activity, and the situations which determine the occurrence of one or the other, are further analysed.

Further reading
J. B. Carroll, *Language and Thought*, Prentice-Hall, 1964.
A. J. Riopelle (ed.), *Animal Problem Solving*, Penguin Books, 1968.
P. C. Wason and P. N. Johnson-Laird (eds.), *Thinking and Reasoning*, Penguin Books, 1968.

Part Five
Individual Differences

Individual differences in task performance are regularly found in all psychological experimentation, and they are often considerable in extent. In most of the experiments discussed so far in this book, these individual differences have been regarded as sources of error and the purpose of experimental designs has been to control or randomize their influence upon the dependent variable. However, individual differences are of interest in their own right, and this part of the book will be concerned directly with their measurement and conceptualization.

The number of specific ways in which people can differ is incalculable. Fortunately the human system is such that these specific differences between people tend to be inter-related, or correlated with each other, in a manner which makes possible the specification of more general dimensions of difference. If our aim is to describe the ways in which people vary, it is obviously more economical to do this in terms of general dimensions which subsume a number of systematically related specific forms of behaviour.

At the highest level of generality, there are three respects in which people differ in behaviour: *intelligence*; what is usually called *personality*, which includes attitudes, beliefs and characteristic styles of behaving; and *psychopathology*, or deviance from normal functioning in both intelligence and personality. Chapter 18 will deal with the first of these. It consists of two parts: the first provides an introduction to the study of intelligence through tests and factor analysis, and the second offers a brief account of Piaget's work on the development of intelligence. In Chapter 19 some of the more influential theories of personality structure will be outlined and Chapter 20 will examine the concept of normality. In this last chapter, no attempt will be made to describe the various psychiatric systems of classification of behavioural disorder, nor the methods of treatment that have been evolved. For these the reader must turn to one of the standard psychiatric textbooks.

The study of individual differences is dependent upon the existence of adequate measuring devices, or tests. Chapter 17 will therefore provide an account of some of the qualities which tests must possess if they are to be satisfactory, together with a review of some of the tests which have been constructed.

Chapter 17
Assessment of Individual Differences

Introduction

What distinguishes formal assessments made by psychologists in their professional capacity from informal assessments made by both psychologists and laymen is that the former tend to be made by means of tests and in accordance with rather stringent rules. The purpose behind the rules which determine the construction and administration of tests is to ensure that the measuring process is 'objective', in the sense that it is not biased by the personal judgement of the tester. In this chapter our concern is with psychological tests of ability and personality, but the rules apply also to any kind of behavioural measurement.

If the subject's performance on a test is to be free from the influence of the tester, it is important that testers should follow the same procedure when using the test. To this end, manuals are provided which indicate precisely how the test should be administered and scored. It is of the greatest importance that testers should follow exactly the instructions given, for even small deviations can affect the subject's scores. In addition, manuals usually contain normative data, by which is meant details of the results of administering the test to large samples of subjects. The value of such data is that they enable the tester to interpret a particular individual's score in relation to specified populations of subjects.

However, the effect of the tester's personality can never be completely eliminated. This is because a testing situation is a social one, and the tester has to establish 'rapport' with his subjects: that is, he must secure the co-operation of the subjects and put them sufficiently at ease for them to produce something like their best performance. Individual testers clearly vary in the skill with which they can do this.

Assessments consist of acquiring information about an individual's behaviour in a particular test situation and using the information obtained as the basis for a decision about the testee's ability, or personality, or about his future career. The purposes for which a decision is required may be highly specific or extremely general. For example, information may be required about an individual's 'mental ability' for the selection of candidates for university training, or for deciding that a child should receive one kind of secondary education rather than another or, in industrial rehabilitation, for determining the amount and kind of retraining an individual should receive. It is unlikely that in the three examples mentioned the same test of mental ability would be given. Different tests have different advantages; a test which helps materially in making one kind of decision may be of little value in making another. Therefore, no one test of mental ability, for example, can be said to be the best; the choice of a test depends very much on the purpose for which it is required and on the kind of decision to be made.

This does not mean that there are not certain general qualities which distinguish good tests from bad. Among these are the clarity of the directions for use and how easily the test can be administered and scored. A good test has the following characteristics. First, it must be a sensitive measuring instrument which discriminates well between subjects. Second, it must have been standardized on a representative and sizeable sample of the population for which it is intended, so that any individual's score can be interpreted in relation to that of others. Third, it must be valid, in the sense of measuring what it purports to measure, and, fourth, it must be stable or reliable.

There are three main purposes for which tests might be used: selection, diagnosis and description. The first two of these, the use of tests to select subjects for jobs or for different kinds of education and their use in locating disorders such as reading disability or mental illness, will not concern us here. Our discussion of testing centres round the use of tests for descriptive purposes, that is to say, their use as measures of individual differences in a research context. In the section that follows we shall briefly examine certain basic aspects of any kind of psychological measurement, and then in the final section of this chapter, we shall describe some of the different kinds of test that have been constructed.

The use of tests

Measurement

The essence of psychological measurement is the assigning of numerical values to behavioural events such that differences in behaviour are represented by differences in score. It involves the application to subjects of a standard procedure which allows the quantification of the responses made. The systematic representation of behavioural events by numbers implies an underlying logic, or set of rules, which governs the relationship between numbers and events. The kinds of statistical transformations of the scores which are permissible depend upon the nature of this logic.

Broadly speaking, there are four different ways of quantifying a variable or four different kinds of scale that can be employed (see Stevens, 1951, for a detailed account). The most primitive is the categorization of subjects or responses into classes: for example, shots at a target can be grouped into hits and misses, or subjects given a test can be grouped into those who pass and those who fail. This kind of quantification is known as *nominal* measurement, and the data it yields are not in the form of scores but in the form of frequencies in different classes. Subjects are placed in groups, but within each group no differentiation is made. An example of nominal measurement might be the classification of subjects as neurotic and normal, or as extraverted and introverted.

The simplest form of measurement which represents each subject or response with a number is *ordinal* measurement. In this, the subjects or responses are placed in rank order with respect to the variable concerned: thus, shots at a target can be ranked according to their distance from it, or subjects could be ranked according to the number of items in a test they answer correctly.

The information conveyed by ordinal measurement, though greater than in nominal measurement, is still limited, for, since the numbers assigned to subjects or responses only represent their position in a rank order, it is impossible to tell from the numbers themselves whether or not the difference between, for example, the first and second is greater or smaller than the difference between the second and third. The form of measurement which does represent these varying differences numerically is *interval* measurement. The distinctive feature of interval measurement is that the quantifying procedure is such that any one unit difference in score represents the same amount of difference in the variable being quantified as any other unit difference in score. If the measuring procedure yields an interval scale, it means that, for example, if subject A scores 60, subject B 50 and subject C 45, then the difference between subjects A and B on the variable being measured is twice as great as the difference between subjects B and C.

If the measuring procedure, in addition to having the features of interval measurement, also has the property that a score of zero corresponds to the absence of the characteristic being measured, then it is said to yield *ratio* measurement. To use again the example of target shooting, we could measure the distance in inches of each shot from the target, so that a zero score represented a hit. Another example of ratio measurement in psychology might be the time taken for a subject to respond to a stimulus, for although it is impossible for a subject to respond in no time at all, the scale used to measure his response has a zero point.

In psychological testing of intelligence or personality, ratio measurement is in fact never attained and it is doubtful whether tests ever yield a genuine interval scale. Let us again suppose that the scores for subjects A, B and C on an intelligence test are 60, 50 and 45 respectively. We can be reasonably sure that we have ordinal measurement, that the scores tell us that A is more intelligent than B, and B than C (at least for that form of intelligence measured by the test). But it is very questionable whether we can go on to say that the difference in intelligence between A and B is twice as great as the difference between B and C. However, if the test is well constructed, we may feel that we have a form of measurement somewhat stronger than ordinal. Thus, though we cannot assert that the difference between A and B is twice the difference between B and C, we may nevertheless feel fairly confident that it is a greater difference, that $A - B > B - C$.

Let us consider further the assumptions which can be made about scores which represent interval measurement. Suppose that a group of subjects takes a test of ability for which interval measurement can be achieved; scores obtained over the group can be described in various ways, most commonly by quoting the *mean* and the *standard deviation* of the scores. The *mean* score of the group is its average score, obtained by summing all scores and dividing the sum by the number of subjects in the group. Strictly speaking the mean can only be calculated when an equal interval scale is employed. However, as a matter of expediency, an equal interval scale is often assumed for the purposes of calculating the mean. The *standard deviation* is a statistic which expresses the degree of variation in a set of scores; it can be defined as the square root of the average of the squared deviations of each score from the mean of the scores. It is, in fact, the square root of the variance, a statistic which was described in Chapter 3. The significance of the standard deviation, together with its use in the transformation of raw scores into *standard scores*, can be brought out by considering the concept of the *normal curve*.

When a large number of individuals take a test, their scores can be represented by a *frequency distribution*. The possible scores on the test are plotted along the baseline, or *abscissa*, and the number of individuals obtaining a particular score is shown along a line placed at right angles to the abscissa, the *ordinate*. Suppose that the majority of individuals taking the test obtain a score falling roughly in the middle of the abscissa, while only a few individuals obtain either very high or very low scores. The resulting frequency distribution might look like that shown in Figure 66. Such a frequency distribution would be said to approximate to a *normal distribution*.

The normal curve is a purely mathematical concept which has certain special properties:

1. By definition it describes the distribution of an *infinite* number of cases, therefore the two tails of the curve never touch the baseline.

2. It is symmetrical and there are thus an equal number of cases on either side of the mean, the central axis.

3. The mean and two other *measures of central tendency*, the *median* (that is the point on a scale of measurement both above and below which lie exactly half the total number of cases being described) and the *mode* (that value or score which occurs with the highest frequency in the group of cases considered) are all equal to one another.

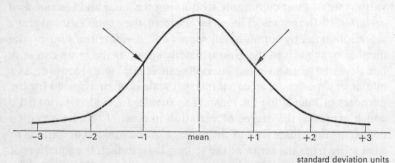

standard deviation units

Figure 66   The hypothetical 'normal curve' (see text). Arrows represent points of inflexion

A further characteristic of the normal curve is its mathematical construction. There are two points on the normal curve where it changes direction from convex to concave. These are known as points of inflexion. The distance from the mean to each point of inflexion represents one standard deviation. Using this distance on the abscissa as a standard, points two and three deviations from the mean in either direction can be found. The distance between the mean and one, two or three standard deviations away from it in either direction accounts for a progressively greater percentage of the total area under the curve, as Figure 66 shows; the two tails of the normal curve approach the abscissa so closely that the distance between plus and minus three standard deviations accounts for over 99 per cent of the total area. In principle, however, since the normal curve describes an infinite number of cases, the abscissa could be divided into an infinite number of parts, each equal to one standard deviation, and the two tails of the distribution would never reach the abscissa.

Statistical tests of significance based upon interval measurement (so-called *parametric* tests) usually assume that the scores on the measure being taken are normally distributed. Where the distribution of obtained scores grossly violates this assumption such tests cannot be applied; one usual procedure, then, is to use *non-parametric* tests which require only ordinal, or in some cases only nominal, data. For a further discussion of scaling, of statistical treatments appropriate to various levels of measurement and of the relative merits of parametric and non-parametric tests, see Siegel (1956).

We may sum up the main points that have been made in this section as follows. Measures used in most psychological tests of intelligence and personality do not fulfil the conditions necessary for ratio scale measurement, and therefore are in no sense 'absolute' measures of these traits. A psychological test of this kind can be defined as a device for scaling the *differences* between subjects on a given characteristic in such a way as to yield a frequency distribution when applied to a large sample. When the scaling procedure approximates to that of interval measurement, then it is frequently found in practice that the distributions of large samples are sufficiently close to the theoretical normal curve to justify the use of those statistical transformations of scores which are appropriate to a normal distribution. However, it is important always to remember that a score on an intelligence or personality test gains its meaning only from its position within the distribution of scores of a population.

Reliability

Given that the purpose of a psychological test is to discriminate between subjects with respect to a certain characteristic, then two of the most important questions we must ask about it are whether it is *reliable* in the sense of always discriminating in the same way, and whether it is *valid* in the sense of discriminating in the way in which it is intended to do. The issues raised by the problems of reliability and validity are central to the theory of testing, and are discussed at length in numerous textbooks (see, for example, Guilford, 1954; E. L. Kelly, 1967). For the present, we shall discuss only the meanings of these terms and the ways in which evidence relevant to their assessment is collected. In choosing a test, for whatever purpose, the psychologist needs to be confident that it is both reliable and valid, and for this reason it is the usual practice to include the relevant evidence in the test manual.

A test is reliable if, whatever it measures, it always measures the same characteristic. If we wish to replicate someone else's experiment using his tests, we need to be assured that they will measure the same thing for us as they did for him. This may seem an obvious statement, but it is in fact of great importance.

When a group of subjects takes a test, the resulting distribution of scores will be a function of both stable differences between them on the variable measured by the test (the subjects' 'true' scores on the test) and also temporary differences between them in mood, motivation, health and so on. These latter factors may be called sources of *error in measurement*, since they may be expected to fluctuate from one testing to another in a random fashion. The more the subjects' scores reflect this error, the more the test is sensitive to differences between subjects which obtain only at the time of testing, then the less reliable and stable the test is as a measure of lasting differences between subjects. To put the point another way, the more the error of measurement, the less will a subject's obtained score reflect his 'true' score on the variable the test measures.

It would follow from this that the most sensible way of checking the reliability of a test is to give it to the same subjects twice and to correlate the two sets of scores. A reliable test would be one which preserved the same relative differences between subjects on the two occasions, as shown by a high, positive correlation coefficient. Of course the actual scores of the subjects may not remain the same. For example, it would be expected that subjects would do better on the second attempt at an intelligence test than on the first. What is important for reliability is that the position of subjects relative to each other stays the same. Any factor, such as practice, which affects all subjects taking a test *in the same way*, raises questions about the validity of the test, not its reliability.

In fact, the test–retest method of estimating reliability is only one of three methods commonly used. In principle each of these methods is applicable to any test. In practice difficulties arise in using one or other method with some tests. For example, reliability based upon the test–retest method may be unduly inflated if the test is such that the subjects can remember clearly on the second testing the responses they made on the first. What is important, however, is that each of the three methods deals with a distinctive source of error. We shall briefly consider each method in turn.

Test–retest reliability. The test–retest reliability coefficient, also known as the *coefficient of stability*, is the correlation between the obtained scores of the same group of subjects taking the same test on two different occasions; the closeness of the coefficient to $+1\cdot00$ indicates the reliability of the test.

One difficulty with test–retest reliability is that the whole of the change in relative scores from one administration to another is regarded as unreliability, and this may not be an appropriate assumption. If the time interval between the two administrations of the test is very short, individuals may remember their previous responses and this may produce an unduly high reliability coefficient. If the interval is unduly long, it affords the opportunity for differential forgetting, and for different amounts and kinds of new learning, among the testees, which would be likely to affect their relative performances at retest; in consequence the reliability coefficient might underestimate the reliability of the test. Test–retest reliability coefficients, when quoted, therefore usually specify the intertest time interval used. In general, the value of the test–retest reliability coefficient falls as the interval increases, indicating the greater likelihood that 'error' variation is contributing to the differences in score.

Equivalent-form reliability. An alternative method of assessing reliability which avoids the problems of retesting is to administer equivalent forms of the same test to the same individuals at more or less the same time. Thus, the Stanford–Binet intelligence test has two forms, L and M, and the correlation between them is about $0\cdot91$ (Terman and Merrill, 1937).

This procedure involves the construction of two tests which are in fact equivalent. Strictly, two tests are equivalent or parallel only if, when administered to the same group of individuals, the means, variances and inter-item co-variances are equal. These requirements demand considerable care in the selection of items for the two forms, although in practice the test constructor may not adopt such stringent criteria.

What is meant by 'error' when the equivalent-forms method is used differs from 'error' as defined by the test–retest reliability procedure. The latter treats random *time-to-time* fluctuations in scores as error. The former includes these fluctuations, since necessarily the two forms of a test are administered at different times; but since different items are used in the two forms, fluctuations from *form to form* may also be influential. Thus the equivalent-form procedure provides a compound measure of equivalence and stability.

The types of variation that can contribute to changes in scores from one administration to another are quite diverse, but can be placed in four overlapping categories: temporary, lasting, general, specific. Following Cronbach (1964) these four sources of variation can be depicted as shown in Table 8. Random variation (that is, variation which is not uniform in its effect upon all subjects) from any of these sources will decrease the size of a correlation between administrations and thus decrease the apparent reliability of a test.

From what has been said so far, it is apparent that different measures of reliability are concerned with different sources of error. The test–retest procedure measures temporal reliability: the reliability coefficient is increased by any *lasting* determinant of scores, whether general or specific, and is decreased by temporary determinants. In other words, the test–retest procedure regards both general and specific factors as 'true' variance only if they are *lasting*. The equivalent-forms procedure, on the other hand, regards both temporary and lasting factors as 'true' variance only if they are *general*, since the specific items on the two forms are different.

A third procedure, less frequently used than the two so far described, is to interpose a similar delay to that involved in retesting between the administration of equivalent forms. In this, the *delayed-equivalence* procedure, both changes in the individual and changes in the items comprising the two forms are likely to lower the correlation and hence are included as error. Thus, in this procedure only *lasting general* factors are regarded as 'true' variance.

Different measurement procedures will therefore yield rather dif-

Table 8

Possible sources of variation in a test score. (After R. L. Thorndike, 1949, p. 73)

I. Lasting and general characteristics of the individual
 1. General skills (e.g. reading)
 2. General ability to comprehend instructions, testwiseness, techniques of taking tests
 3. Ability to solve problems of the general type presented in this test
 4. Attitudes, emotional reactions or habits generally operating in situations like the test situation (e.g. self-confidence).
II. Lasting and specific characteristics of the individual
 1. Knowledge and skills required by particular problems in the test
 2. Attitudes, emotional reactions or habits related to particular test stimuli (e.g. fear of high places brought to mind by an inquiry about such fears on a personality test).
III. Temporary and general characteristics of the individual (systematically affecting performance on various tests at a particular time)
 1. Health, fatigue and emotional strain
 2. Motivation, rapport with examiner
 3. Effects of heat, light, ventilation, etc.
 4. Level of practice on skills required by tests of this type
 5. Present attitudes, emotional reactions, or strength of habits (in so far as these are departures from the person's average or lasting characteristics – e.g. political attitudes during an election).
IV. Temporary and specific characteristics of the individual
 1. Changes in fatigue or motivation developed by this particular test (e.g. discouragement resulting from failure on a particular item)
 2. Fluctuations in attention, co-ordination or standards of judgement
 3. Fluctuations in memory for particular facts
 4. Level of practice on skills or knowledge required by this particular test (e.g. effects of special coaching)
 5. Temporary emotional states, strength of habits, etc., related to particular test stimuli (e.g. a question calls to mind a recent bad dream)
 6. Luck in the selection of answers by 'guessing'.

---

ferent estimates of the reliability of a test. If all three procedures are used in a given case, it is possible by comparing these estimates to arrive at a statement of the relative contributions of each of the sources of variation quoted – lasting general, lasting specific, temporary general, temporary specific – to the *total variance* of the scores obtained.

Split-half reliability. As we have seen, equivalent forms of a test cannot be administered to the same individuals at the same time, so that the equivalent-forms procedure does not entirely eliminate the possibility of including variation in the true score from occasion to occasion as part of the error score. The split-half method attempts to eliminate this possibility by correlating the scores of the same individuals on one half of the test with their scores on the other half, thus providing as closely as possible a measure of form-to-form fluctuation only.

Such a correlation is sometimes known as a *coefficient of equivalence*. In practice, the items comprising the two split halves are usually selected on an odd–even basis. Thus the scores obtained on the odd items are correlated with the scores obtained by the same subjects on the even items. However, since the reliability of a test is also a function of its length, for reasons which will not be considered here, a correction is needed to determine the reliability of the whole test (see Cronbach, 1964, pp. 129–33).

Split-half reliability differs from other reliability measures in that it is concerned with the homogeneity, or internal consistency, of a test rather than with its reliability from one administration to another. Thus it is more clearly a part of test *construction*, aiding the selection and comparison of test items, than are the other procedures, and is more often used for that purpose.

Validity

A test which is highly reliable, by any or all of the criteria described above, may still not be *valid*, in the sense that it might give highly reliable scores which are not in fact measures of the characteristic which the test is intended to measure. On the other hand, an entirely unreliable test logically cannot be valid; the reliability of a test must limit its validity.

Like reliability, validity is a concept capable of various definitions, based upon various methods of measurement. Three main types of validity will concern us here. The first is *content validity*, which might be said to employ criteria internal to the tests being examined; the second is *empirical validity*, which is assessed by correlation between test scores and other, 'external' criteria of the characteristic under consideration. Finally, we shall consider the notion of *construct validity*.

Content validity. This subdivides into two further types, *face validity* and *factorial validity*. Face validity refers to how appropriate a test appears to be, either to a potential user or to someone actually taking the test. For example, if a test which purports to measure mechanical aptitude consists solely of items concerned with electrical knowledge, its face validity is low. Factorial validity is a more sophisticated type of content validity which, as its name implies, involves the application of techniques of factor analysis to derive factors which different tests sample in differing degrees and to which psychological values may or may not be assigned (see Chapter 18). The factor loadings of one test can then be compared with those of another.

Empirical validity. The establishment of empirical validity involves relating performance on the test to performance on another, independent measure of the same characteristic; that is, we correlate the test with a criterion. If the criterion measure is taken some time after the test is administered, we speak of *predictive validity*; if scores on the criterion are already available at the time of testing, we speak of *concurrent validity*.

In principle, this method of validating a test is the most direct and obvious. In practice it has one major drawback which severely limits its value, at least for certain kinds of test. Before it can be used, there must be good ground for thinking that the criterion measure itself is valid.

It is only when a test is constructed solely for the purpose of predicting performance in some other, clearly defined situation, and this is usually when the test is required for selection purposes, that the problem does not arise. For example, if a test is constructed for selecting students for a degree course in French, and if the purpose is to choose those who will get good degrees, then performance in the degree examination is a completely valid criterion. Moreover, if the purpose of the test is to predict degree success, then its correlation with degree results is the only possible way of validating the test. In this context, concurrent validity would mean that the test is given to students after they have taken their degree.

A hypothetical correlation between a test and a criterion is shown in Figure 67. Let us suppose that individuals who obtain a criterion

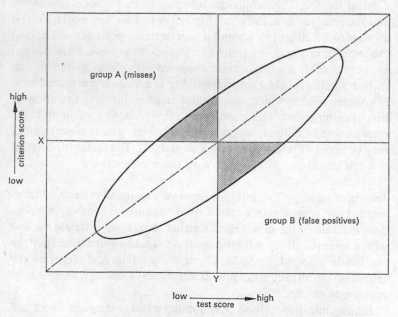

Figure 67   Hypothetical relation between a test and a criterion (see text)

score above X are satisfactory – that is, they are the individuals the selector wants to select. The problem then becomes one of finding a suitable *cutting score* on the test which will discriminate between those individuals who should be selected on the basis of their probable criterion score and those who should be rejected on the same grounds. Let us further suppose that a cutting score Y has been adopted. The two shaded areas in Figure 67 then represent incorrect selection decisions, since the cutting score has failed to select those in group A who would have obtained a satisfactory criterion score and has selected those in group B who failed to obtain a satisfactory criterion score. Those in group A are known as *misses* and those in group B as *false positives*. It can be seen that placing the cutting score at different points on the abscissa results in different proportions of misses, false positives and correct selections. The cutting score is usually determined in accordance with the risks the selector is prepared to undergo. If a large number of misses is unimportant but false positives must be avoided, the cutting score will be placed somewhere to the right of Y. If, on the other hand, misses must be avoided, even if this means that a large number of false positives will be made, the cutting score will be placed to the left of Y.

To evaluate the usefulness of a test in reaching selection decisions it is also necessary to know the *base rate*, that is, the proportion of individuals who were selected without the test being used as a selection device and who reached a satisfactory criterion score. The proportion of correct decisions made using the test for selection purposes, the *validity rate*, can then be compared with the base rate.

Of course, the construction of tests for selection faces other practical difficulties. To continue the example above, the test of ability at French can only be validated on students who have already been selected for a university course on other criteria. But for this kind of test, the logic of the validating procedure is straightforward enough.

The problems arise when we wish to use criterion validity for a test of some more general individual-difference dimension. The classic example is intelligence. The first intelligence tests to be constructed were often validated against the independent criterion of teachers' ratings for intelligence or success in school subjects. In the light of everyday usage of the term 'intelligence' it is reasonable to assume that these criteria have some validity, at least if the sample used is large and representative. But it is also certain that responsiveness to educational influence is determined by other factors than the children's intelligence, such as interest in school subjects and parental encouragement. It follows that, in a large enough sample, we should expect some positive association between performance on a test purporting to measure intelligence and success in school; a zero correlation would certainly cast doubt on the validity of the test. But at the same time, a very high positive correlation would also make us doubt that the test was measuring general intelligence alone.

The difficulty is due to the fact that intelligence is a high level construct, intended to refer to some general feature of the human system which reveals itself in so many different ways that there can be no single independent criterion. For tests designed to measure such general characteristics, correlation with a criterion can only supply modest support of their validity, and greater reliance has to be placed on other methods such as factor analysis. The most appropriate method is probably that of construct validity, discussed below; unfortunately this method requires that the characteristic to be measured be embedded in an explanatory theory, and an adequate theory of this kind does not yet exist for intelligence.

It is always essential that as much care should be taken in the construction of a criterion as in the construction of the test itself. If, for example, the test is capable of making very subtle discriminations between individuals and the criterion capable only of very gross discriminations, the validity of the test is lowered, not necessarily because the test is poor but because the test and the criterion are not sufficiently well matched for a high validity coefficient to be possible. Finally, it should be added that in practice the tendency is to validate new tests, particularly intelligence tests, by correlating them with well-established existing tests. This is not as circular as it might seem. When a test has been used a great deal in research and selection, and has consistently functioned as we should expect a good test of intelligence to do, we may justly feel more confident in its validity.

Construct validity. As noted above, construct validity is appropriate when the characteristic to be measured is a general dimension of individual difference, such as anxiety, authoritarianism, intelligence or extraversion. The establishment of construct validity is contingent upon the fact that the psychologist has an explanatory theory within which the trait to be measured features as an intervening variable or hypothetical construct, and from which it derives its definition. The validity of the test as an operational measure of a construct within the theory is then bound up with the extent to which predictions derived from the theory are confirmed by experiments using the test as one of the measures (see Cronbach and Meehl, 1955).

As a convenient example of construct validity, we can consider the personality inventory devised by Eysenck, the Maudsley Personality Inventory or M.P.I. (Eysenck, 1959b), which is designed to measure extraversion–introversion. Eysenck has developed an elaborate theory of personality, which is outlined briefly in Chapter 19. Within this theory, the personality dimension of extraversion–introversion is associated with differences in physiological functioning and in various measures of performance. Eysenck's theory of cortical inhibition suggests that individuals may differ in the rates at which they build up and dissipate reactive inhibition. Some individuals (introverts) are thought to build up inhibition slowly and to dissipate it rapidly while others (extraverts) build up inhibition rapidly and dissipate it slowly. This in turn suggests that introverts and extraverts will behave differently when tested under conditions of massed and distributed practice or that the performance of extraverts in vigilance situations will decline at a more rapid rate than will that of introverts. Now if predictions regarding the physiological and behavioural correlates of extraversion are sustained by experiments in which extraversion is defined by scores on a personality inventory, then the validity of the test as a measure of a construct within the theory is supported.

However, one of the problems attendant upon the construct validation of a test is knowing when to stop. The theory may generate many predictions, not all of which are sustained. A single negative result implies that the theory needs modification; but it is uncertain how many confirmatory results are required before the theory can be regarded as confirmed, and the test, as a measure of one of its constructs, validated.

Assessment procedures

Psychological tests may be classified in a variety of ways: (a) some have to be administered individually while others can be given to a group of subjects at the same time; (b) some contain only verbal items whereas others consist entirely of non-verbal items; (c) some are strictly timed and others have no time limit; and (d) some are highly structured in the sense that only a few possible responses are allowed to the testee, while others, in particular *projective tests* of personality, are almost completely unstructured. But perhaps the most important way in which tests may be classified is in terms of what they are designed to measure. Here the most convenient grouping, and the one to be followed in the subsequent discussion, is into tests of intelligence, tests of aptitude and achievement and tests of personality.

Intelligence tests

Compared to many other areas of psychology, the construction of intelligence tests has a long history. A major impetus to its growth came from the need, in the early years of this century, to create a method of classifying children in terms of their educational requirements. The pioneer in the measurement of individual differences was Francis Galton. But probably the most important event, historically, was the decision of the French Ministry of Public Instruction, in 1904, to appoint a committee to inquire into the education of mentally retarded children. As a consequence, Alfred Binet was asked to devise a test which would identify feeble-minded children early in their lives so that they could be given special educational treatment.

Binet's interest in mental testing had begun about twenty years earlier, and in 1905 – in collaboration with Simon – he produced the first test of intelligence. He had earlier criticized the tests of Galton on the grounds that they contained too many measures of sensory ability, and that, in any case, they were too simple to provide adequate measures of intelligence. Binet and Simon's test, therefore, consisted of a number of subtests, each with items ranging widely in difficulty, which attempted to measure such complex psychological processes as memory, imagination, comprehension and aesthetic appreciation. In a monograph translated into English after Binet's death in 1911, Binet and Simon (1916) stated 'to judge well, to comprehend well, to reason well, these are the essential activities of the intelligence' (p. 42).

This first intelligence test was standardized on a very small sample of children, but it was shortly followed by two revisions, both standardized on larger samples. The second of these, in 1911, contained five tests at each age level from three to fifteen years. Moreover, the correlations between scores on the test and external criteria such as teachers' assessments and school examinations were much improved. For a number of years this test served as a model for the construction of other intelligence tests.

Two refinements were introduced shortly after the publication of the 1911 Binet–Simon test. Burt introduced the notion of writing answers in a test booklet, as opposed to the oral question-and-answer method used by Binet, and Stern suggested the expression of test scores in the form of intelligence quotients, or I.Q.s. Stern (1912) argued that 'this quotient would show what fractional part of the intelligence normal to his age a feeble-minded child obtains' (p. 80).

In 1910 Terman, working at Stanford University, began modifying the Binet tests for administration to American children, and his Stanford Revision of the Binet scales was produced in 1916. This revision made it possible to estimate normal and superior intelligence as well as subnormal. The 1916 Stanford–Binet test was itself revised in 1937 by Terman and Merrill, who published two equivalent forms of the test, forms L and M. The most recent revision, in 1960, combined the most useful tests from the 1937 version into a single form, L–M, and has an improved scoring system.

All versions of the Binet test are scales; in other words, the test items are grouped together in terms of their difficulty and as the test proceeds the items become more and more difficult. The score a child obtains depends on how many items he can answer correctly rather than on how fast he works. However, the level of difficulty of items is also related to age, and a great deal of research has been carried out to find items of suitable difficulty for each age level. For example, an item suitable for the age level of eight years should be answered correctly by some eight-year-olds, by virtually all nine-year-olds and by hardly any seven-year-olds. But assigning values to the terms 'some', 'virtually all' and 'hardly any' has aroused controversy. For instance, does 'some' mean 50, 66 or 75 per cent? Heim (1954) has argued that the least objectionable figure is 50 per cent. The scoring system of the Binet test is expressed in terms of years and months, and the score a child obtains is his *mental age* (MA). The obtained mental age is equivalent to the chronological age (CA) at which the average child does as well as the testee does. For example, a six-year-old child who correctly answers as many items as the average eight-year-old, earns a mental age of eight years. If 'average' is also taken to mean 50 per cent, then the median mental age of a random sample of six-year-olds will be six years. This does not necessarily imply that the mean mental age will also be six years unless the mental age distribution is completely normal, when the mean will equal the median.

In practice it very rarely happens that a child answers correctly all the items as far as a particular age level and then fails to answer any more; in other words, incorrectly answered items occur at irregular points as the test proceeds. The mental age is therefore calculated by adding age credits (usually two months per test, since most forms of the Binet scale now have six tests at each age level) for each test successfully completed. Testing is normally terminated if three successive tests are failed at a particular age level.

Intelligence quotients which simply express the ratio of mental age to chronological age are known as *ratio I.Q.s*. It is a necessary feature of the ratio I.Q. that as CA increases, the *same* differences in I.Q. correspond to *increasing* differences in MA. If three children have a CA of eight years, and I.Q.s of 70, 110 and 130, then their MAs will be 5·6, 8·8 and 10·4 respectively. At age fifteen, children with the same I.Q.s will have MAs of 10·5, 16·5 and 19·5. The gap in MA between I.Q.s of 70 and 130 has widened from 4·8 years at age eight to nine years at age fifteen. As a consequence, some psychologists have interpreted MA as signifying *amount* of intelligence and I.Q. as indicating *rate of development* of intelligence.

There are, however, several considerations which must qualify these interpretations.

1. Intelligence tests are not absolute measures and hence it is very doubtful if a test score can be taken as indicating 'amount' of intelligence.

2. There is no guarantee that a test attains interval measurement,

and therefore that any one-year increase in MA is equivalent to every other.

3. As noted in the section on validity, 'intelligence' is a construct whose relationship to any single test is very much more complicated than, for instance, the relationship between a tape-measure and height. The inference from increased test score to 'development of intelligence' must remain problematic.

4. There is much evidence that improved performance with age on any test tends to reach a ceiling. On some tests, this ceiling is reached by most people by the age of fourteen or fifteen years; on other tests by the age of twenty-five years or more. This implies that *in certain of its aspects*, the growth of intelligence ceases for most people with the attainment of adulthood, and that the calculation of I.Q.s after such growth has stopped is largely meaningless.

5. I.Q.s are not, as was once thought, constant throughout development. It is true that there is fairly high stability of individual differences over a large sample through much of childhood and adolescence (see B. S. Bloom, 1964; and Chapter 4); but the scores of particular individuals may fluctuate quite widely, by as much as twenty I.Q. points or more.

These considerations, together with a number of other technical problems which cannot be discussed here, have led a growing number of psychologists to abandon the concepts of MA and ratio I.Q. Instead, greater reliance is being placed on a *deviation I.Q.* A deviation I.Q. expresses the test result as a standard score; it informs the tester how many standard deviations above or below the average of his age group the testee's score lies. This avoids the notion of mental age, and makes comparisons between different tests easier.

The conversion of test scores into standard scores implies the assumption that intelligence itself is normally distributed. This assumption is impossible to verify directly but the considerable amount of indirect evidence which has been accumulated suggests that it is at least as tenable as any other and, in addition, it confers considerable practical advantages.

However, the difficulty of intelligence test items affects the normality of the distribution, and the distributions of scores tend to be skewed on tests in which the difficulty of items is not graded in approximately equal steps. In such cases the test is not sensitive enough to spread the scores sufficiently; hence too many scores cluster at one end or the other of the distribution. Burt (1957) has shown that when a series of test items, which are selected in steps of equal difficulty and which cover the whole range of difficulty, is given to an unselected sample of testees, the distribution of scores is approximately normal. In Burt's study the items were selected using psychophysical techniques without reference to the normal curve. The relation of test-item difficulty to the distribution of test scores is clearly important in the construction of intelligence tests, although even in carefully constructed tests the distributions of scores at different ages, while normal, may differ in range.

Thus, on the 1937 Stanford–Binet, the standard deviation of ratio I.Q.s is twelve points at six years of age and about twenty points at eleven years of age. This means that a child with the same I.Q. would be placed at two different points in relation to his peers at the two different ages, which leads to confusion, although it is possible to make the standard deviations equivalent by applying appropriate computational procedures. In the 1960 revision of the Stanford–Binet, the test constructors computed the standard of mental ages for each age group and whatever mental age fell one standard deviation above the mean was converted into a deviation I.Q. of 116, while the mental age falling one standard deviation below the mean was converted to a deviation I.Q. of 84. The standard score in this case is thus based upon a mean of 100 and a standard deviation of 16. It should be emphasized that these are essentially arbitrary choices.

Psychologists have therefore tended to accept the assumption that intelligence is normally distributed on the grounds that there is no compelling evidence against it and because it is convenient from the point of view of test construction and the analysis and interpretation of test scores. This does not mean that all mental abilities are normally distributed; the distributions of special talents and attainments, such as musical aptitude or scientific creativity are much more likely to be skewed (Burt, 1943).

The Stanford–Binet test is heavily weighted on verbal abilities and the scores obtained at different ages reflect differences in these abilities. The various intelligence scales developed by Wechsler, which permit separate estimates to be made of both verbal and non-verbal abilities, provide a useful supplement to the Binet in testing children, as well as providing what is probably the best all-round test of adult intelligence. Wechsler's first test, the Wechsler–Bellevue, developed in 1939, is now no longer in use. However, it has been replaced by two separate scales, the Wechsler Intelligence Scale for Children (W.I.S.C.) which was published in 1949, and the Wechsler Adult Intelligence Scale (W.A.I.S.) for sixteen years and above, which first appeared in 1955. In addition to the introduction of a well-standardized performance scale, Wechsler made use of a deviation I.Q. which compares an individual's test score with the expected mean score of his age group, and raw scores on the test are thus differentially weighted in accordance with the individual's chronological age. The same raw score will thus be converted to different I.Q.s at different ages, in line with Wechsler's view of the growth and decline of mental abilities throughout the life-span (for further details of age changes in intelligence, see Bayley 1949, 1955; Birren, 1964; Wechsler, 1958). Cronbach (1964) gives an excellent summary of the tests which make up the Wechsler scales and of some representative research concerned with its evaluation (see also Guertin *et al.*, 1966).

Finally, it should be mentioned that there are also many group tests of intelligence, both verbal and non-verbal. A number of these, for example, the AH4 and AH5, are concerned with the measurement of superior adult intelligence. For further details of such tests the reader is referred to Cronbach (1964) and P. E. Vernon (1960).

Aptitude and achievement tests

Aptitude tests, achievement tests, and for that matter intelligence tests, rest on a similar conceptual framework and the distinction between them is largely a matter of convenience. One reason why aptitude and achievement tests are frequently considered under separate headings is a historical one; aptitudes were once thought to be innate while achievement was considered to be largely a function of learning and experience. Another is that aptitude tests are frequently used to *predict* future performance while achievement tests are used to measure the effectiveness of training procedures already administered. The training procedure may be an industrial one or it may be a school or college course. However, in some instances, achievement tests may be just as effective predictors as aptitude tests and the degree of achievement may correlate highly with aptitude test scores.

Aptitude testing can be considered from two points of view: selection and vocational guidance. When aptitude tests are used to select individuals for a particular occupation, the purpose of the test is to discover the potential which an individual possesses to perform at a certain level of competence in the occupation in question. This potential, which is a combination of innate abilities and of experience, sets a limit on the rate of acquisition of a particular skill and also on the maximum level of performance that the individual is capable of achieving. Thus in selection situations aptitude tests are used as predictors of occupational success. In vocational guidance situations, on the other hand, aptitude tests are used in an attempt to identify an individual's special talents in order to advise him on a range of occupations for which his abilities indicate that he is suitable.

Vocational guidance procedures nearly always include already established batteries of special abilities, about which a great deal of information is available. Two examples are the Differential Aptitudes Test (Bennett, Seashore and Wesman, 1959) and the General Aptitude Test Battery, both of which were developed in the U.S.A. The Differential Aptitudes Test (D.A.T.), which was developed in the 1940s, consists of subtests measuring verbal reasoning, spatial reasoning, clerical speed and accuracy, spelling and the ability to detect faults in grammar, punctuation and spelling in sentences. The General Aptitude Test Battery (G.A.T.B.) was produced by the United States Employment Service and its subtests include measures of general reasoning ability, verbal aptitude, numerical aptitude, spatial aptitude, form perception, clerical perception, motor co-ordination, finger dexterity and manual dexterity.

There seems little doubt that different occupations are associated, to some extent at least, with different patterns of ability (R. L. Thorndike and Hagen, 1959) and in both tests minimum scores in the critical aptitudes for a wide range of occupations have been laid down. It is thus possible to gain a good idea of the occupations for which the testee's ability pattern is best suited. However, possession of the appropriate ability profile does not guarantee occupational success; vocational guidance includes more than aptitude testing and information about interests, attitudes, values and attainment is highly desirable. Furthermore, vocational guidance depends for its success upon extremely close consultation with the client at each stage in the guidance process.

Selection procedures are generally used to screen applicants for a particular job and, unless the screening process is an extremely leisurely one, it is unlikely that already-established aptitude test batteries, involving a broad spectrum of abilities, will be employed. Instead, it is likely that the qualities required for the job in question will already be known, that is, a *job analysis* will have been carried out (European Productivity Agency, 1956), a test based on this analysis will have been given to employees already working at the job and the results compared with a criterion, usually supervisor's ratings. If the match between test and criterion is satisfactory, in other words, if the correlation between them is sufficiently high, the test can then be given to applicants for the job, and to further validate the test, a *follow-up study* of the job performance of the applicants selected by the test will usually be carried out. Such a test will focus on the abilities specific to the job for which it acts as a selection device (for an example of the development of an aptitude test, see Viteles, 1962).

The development of a suitable criterion against which to match test results is clearly very important in the development of an aptitude test. First of all the notion that there is a criterion for each and every job, as classified for instance in the Department of Employment and Productivity index of job classifications, may be questioned. Second, if there is such a criterion, in most jobs it is unlikely to be a single measure (Ghiselli, 1956). This suggests that the multiple criteria available should be combined into a single over-all criterion. Since, however, these various criteria are unlikely to be equally important in the determination of occupational success, they must be weighted in accordance with their relative importance. There are a number of different ways of doing this but each one is associated with certain methodological problems (Ghiselli and Brown, 1955). Furthermore, the different criteria are quite likely to be unrelated. Speed of work, for instance, is likely to correlate poorly with accuracy, yet both may be important in a particular job. This raises the question as to whether several unrelated criteria can be meaningfully combined into one multiple criterion. Third, the criterion may correlate poorly with itself at different times, that is, its reliability may be low. If this happens, then the correlation between test and criterion is also likely to be low (Ebel, 1961). Thus the low validity of a selection device may sometimes be due to the unreliability of the criterion, although it may also rise from a variety of other factors, among which should be included the quality of management (L. W. Ferguson, 1951).

Ghiselli (1966), in an extremely interesting review of occupational aptitude tests and their validity, suggests that in practice two broad types of criteria should be distinguished: first, *training criteria*, that is, criteria which are relevant to the capacity of trainees to learn a job and, second, *proficiency criteria*, criteria relevant to the job proficiency of workers who have already been trained. For further discussion of the usefulness of aptitude tests the reader is referred to Ghiselli's review.

While it is important for selection procedures to have *predictive validity*, it is more important for achievement or attainment tests to have *content validity*. Achievement tests assume importance when, for instance, the syllabuses and quality of education differ widely and where mobility within the educational system is high, since they provide virtually the only standard means of finding out how much an individual knows about a particular subject and whether his knowledge is advanced, average or retarded for his age. They are also useful as diagnostic aids when a child's achievement falls behind his intelligence.

The content of achievement tests is largely a matter of consensus, at least initially, although trial runs will probably be needed to identify test items of suitable difficulty and which also discriminate sufficiently well between different individuals. A test which does not discriminate between individuals who know a subject well and those who know it poorly is clearly of little use. For further information on achievement tests, the reader is referred to P. E. Vernon (1960) and for a discussion of intelligence and achievement tests to Wiseman (1964).

Personality tests

Personality tests have been described by Cronbach (1964) as tests of 'typical performance' as opposed to the intelligence, achievement and aptitude tests already mentioned which are tests of 'maximal performance'. The biggest problem faced by personality tests is that it is difficult to conceive of a meaningful criterion against which the test results can be checked. One way in which this problem has been solved is to use criterion groups already selected by society. For instance, if individuals already classified as mentally ill, or as criminals, produce test protocols indicating a high level of maladjustment, then this is considered to be evidence of the validity of the test.

This method of solving the criterion problem has been a popular one and its use has generated a large number of tests which emphasize negative aspects of personality. Indeed, the first personality inventory to be developed was constructed in the First World War for the purpose of identifying soldiers who were unsuited for combat on emotional grounds (Woodworth, 1920). One of the consequences of this preoccupation with maladjustment has been that it is now much easier to detect signs of instability in an apparently normal individual than it is to detect traits that both society in general and the individual himself would regard as desirable.

However, this balance has been to some extent redressed both by the use of *empirical* or *criterion keying* in tests which have sought to distinguish different occupational groups in terms of their interests and attitudes (Strong, 1955) and by the use of construct validation in the study of individual differences (Eysenck, 1957, p. 261). In addition, projective techniques have been used as part of experimental research programmes aimed at identifying the structure of needs and motives in different individuals and exploring the relation between motivation and action (see, for example, Atkinson, 1958).

The most obvious method of personality assessment might appear to be the interview. A great deal has been written on it (see Matarazzo, 1965; Richardson, Dohrenwend and Klein, 1965) and it raises too many issues to be dealt with here. Fortunately some of the main methodological problems encountered in interviewing also occur with other methods. For our present purposes, therefore, we shall consider briefly only three general approaches to the measurement of personality, namely: self-report procedures, inventories and questionnaires; rating procedures; and projective techniques. Each will be discussed in turn and we shall end with a short account of attitude scales.

Self-report procedures, inventories and questionnaires. Self-report procedures present the testee with a series of questions which he is required to answer, for convenience in scoring, by using fixed response categories such as 'yes', 'no' or 'cannot say'. The questions are usually chosen, initially at least, on the basis of their content validity, so that the resulting questionnaire looks as if it is concerned with the measurement of personality. If the responses to a personality questionnaire are taken at face value, then certain problems of interpretation arise. For instance, several factors limit the degree of trust that can be placed in the responses: subjects can easily fake their responses; they may lack insight and be unable to answer the question usefully; they may approach the test with different response sets or response styles; and finally, because of their ambiguity, test items may be interpreted in ways which the test constructor did not intend.

Test constructors have attempted to counter faking in several different ways. First, they have attempted to conceal the purpose of a test and have disguised personality tests as measures of ability (Campbell, 1957). Second, some test constructors have incorporated verification and correction keys, or lie scales, into the test, for example, by repeating the same item in two different forms. The Kuder Preference Record (Kuder, 1953) and the Minnesota Multiphasic Personality Inventory or M.M.P.I. (Hathaway and McKinley, 1942, 1943) are examples of tests which have one or other of these built-in checks against distortion.

However, one of the most important ways of meeting most of the difficulties that personality inventories face is the method of *criterion keying*. This method makes use of what has been described as actuarial validity and uses the responses gained from a questionnaire administered to already well-defined criterion groups as 'signs' which distinguish one criterion group from another. Because this method makes little or no theoretical assumptions about what the content of personality questionnaires should be, it has given rise to argument concerning the importance of test-item content (Berg, 1959; Norman, 1963). Although items may be selected initially on the basis of content validity, they are retained only if they discriminate between different criterion groups. The M.M.P.I., while not immune to criticism, is an outstanding example of a personality inventory based on the principle of criterion keying and is composed of ten scales which cover most of the various neurotic and psychotic disorders (for further details, see Dahlstrom and Welsh, 1960).

The use of criterion keying also appears to eliminate the problem of lack of insight, in that if a questionnaire can successfully discriminate between criterion groups, it matters little whether items are being answered truthfully from a full knowledge of the respondent's own personality dynamics, or whether the testee is lying or simply 'doesn't know'. However, in order to learn more about the individual personality than the criterion groups to which it belongs, other techniques, such as projective tests, are necessary.

Beginning with two papers by Cronbach (1946, 1950) the effects of *response sets* and *response styles* have been examined in considerable detail in the past twenty years, although complete agreement on the ways in which these two terms should be defined has not been reached. Response set appears to be the more general term while response style refers to the way in which a response set is expressed in a particular situation, for example, when answering a personality questionnaire. An example of a response set is *acquiescence*, which has been regarded as a basic personality trait, while an example of a response style stemming from acquiescence is the disproportionate tendency to select 'yes' as a response to items in a personality inventory. The effects of acquiescent sets and their associated response styles are reviewed by Jackson (1967) and Messick (1967).

Another important response set is the *social desirability variable* (A. L. Edwards, 1957a; 1967a and b); this response set is the tendency to agree with or endorse statements favourable to the respondent. The work of Edwards and his collaborators has demonstrated beyond much doubt that a tendency to present oneself in a favourable light when answering a self-report inventory does exist, that its effects are distinguishable from deliberate lying and that its existence has important implications for personality assessment. This tendency has been related to other personality characteristics, in particular, conformity (Crowne and Marlowe, 1964). One way of minimizing the effects of the social desirability variable is to construct personality questionnaires in accordance with the method of *forced choice keying*, in which items are matched for social desirability, or undesirability, and the respondent is required to choose between pairs of items. This approach to the construction of personality questionnaires is exemplified by the Edwards Personal Preference Schedule (A. L. Edwards, 1959).

The third major response set that has been identified is *deviance* (Adams and Butler, 1967; Berg, 1967), although the consequences of deviance – expressed in the deviation hypothesis (Berg, 1967) – extend far beyond the personality assessment situation. Deviance is expressed in personality inventories as a tendency to respond to items in an uncommon way and the deviation hypothesis is thus much more concerned with non-conformists than with conformists. Berg and his associates have shown that deviance in the personality assessment situation appears to be associated with atypical behaviour in a variety of other situations and hence that deviance can also be considered as a basic personality trait.

Response sets and response styles are considered by some investigators to be sources of error which must be minimized by more careful construction of tests and by others as important dimensions of personality in their own right (see Block, 1965). Although this controversy is far from settled, some of its effects are already apparent in the form of better-constructed self-report procedures.

Rating procedures. In addition to self-report procedures, a number of self-rating procedures have been used to assess personality characteristics, principally in personality research rather than in the clinical situation. These procedures require subjects to rate themselves in relation to various statements as part of a more complex task situation than that involved in self-report procedures. Among the more prominent of such techniques are the *Q sort* (Block, 1961; Stephenson, 1953), which has been used, *inter alia*, to evaluate the effectiveness of psychotherapy (Rogers and Dymond, 1954); the *semantic differential* (Osgood, Suci and Tannenbaum, 1957) and the *Construct Repertory Test* (Bannister and Mair, 1968; G. A. Kelly, 1955). The importance of all three tests for the assessment of personality depends, at present, perhaps more on their potential than on their performance.

Projective techniques. It has been said that the rationale underlying projective techniques is something like 'your unconscious is you, your fantasy is the key to your unconscious, your protocol is the key to your fantasy, therefore your protocol is you'. Lindzey (1961) has defined a projective technique as 'an instrument that is considered especially sensitive to covert or unconscious aspects of behavior. It permits or encourages a wide variety of subject responses, is highly multidimensional and it evokes unusually rich or profuse response data with a minimum of subject awareness concerning the purpose of the test' (p. 45).

Thus projective techniques are essentially unstructured, that is, subjects are presented with ambiguous stimuli such as pictures or incomplete sentences or stories and asked in the first case to describe what they see and in the two latter cases to complete the material with which they have been presented. The number of possible responses open to the subject is, in consequence, virtually unlimited and he is specifically told there are no right or wrong answers.

Two of the most widely used projective techniques are the Rorschach technique (see Klopfer and Kelley, 1942) and the Thematic Apperception Test, or T.A.T. (Murray, 1943; Tomkins, 1949). The Rorschach technique presents the respondent with a series of ink-blots, five in various shades of grey, two grey and red and three in several colours, and the subject is encouraged to describe what he sees in each blot. His descriptions are recorded and, together with the inquiry carried out when all ten blots have been presented, make up his test protocol. One of the principal assumptions underlying the Rorschach is that the way in which the subject structures the series of ambiguous stimuli is linked to his personality structure.

The administration, scoring and interpretation of the Rorschach is a complex matter, discussed in detail by Klopfer and Davidson (1962). The Rorschach can be considered as a psychometric test, since respondents can be assigned scores on various criteria, particularly if certain modifications are made involving an increase in the number of stimuli and the use of criterion keying (Holtzmann *et al.*, 1961), but it seems fair to say that the Rorschach, in its original form, has not coped altogether successfully with its special problems of reliability and validity.

The T.A.T. makes use of stimuli which are more highly structured than in the Rorschach. The subject is presented with a set of black and white pictures depicting various scenes and is asked to say what is happening in the picture, what led up to the events in the picture and what the outcome will be. Because Murray's original scoring system was not very specific, others have been put forward, such as those of McClelland and Eron and their respective colleagues, which emphasize quantitative methods (see Murstein, 1963). The interpretation of the T.A.T. was originally made in terms of psychoanalytic concepts (Murray, 1938), but over the years other interpretative systems have been advanced (e.g. Atkinson, 1958). The T.A.T., like the Rorschach, faces difficult problems of reliability and validity and the evidence for its general usefulness in the assessment of personality is conflicting (Harrison, 1965). Nevertheless, the experienced examiner can gain a great deal of information about the dynamics of an individual personality both from the Rorschach and from the T.A.T., information which would not be available to him from other sources.

Attitude scales. As noted above, the attitudes an individual adopts towards the various aspects of his environment form an important part of his personality. Newcomb (1966) has defined an attitude as

an individual's organization of psychological processes, as inferred from his behaviour, with respect to some aspect of the world which he distinguishes from other aspects. It represents the residue of his experience with which he approaches any subsequent situation including that aspect and, together with the contemporary influences in such a situation, determines his behaviour in it. Attitudes are enduring in the sense that such residues are carried over to new situations, but they change in so far as new residues are acquired through experience in new situations (p. 22).

Attitude scales generally consist of a series of statements with which the testee is invited to express his degree of agreement or, sometimes, merely whether he agrees with the statement or not. In some cases a hypothetical situation is described, the respondent is given a range of choices and asked about his probable course of action, which he must often indicate by a simple 'yes' or 'no'. There are three main types of attitude scale, *summated rating scales* (also known as Likert-type scales), *equal appearing interval scales* and *cumulative* or *Guttman scales*.

Summated rating scales consist of items of 'equal attitude value', which means that the scores for all items in the scale can be summed and averaged to give the individual's over-all attitude score. Such scales also allow the intensity with which an attitude is held to be expressed. This increases response variation, and enables finer discriminations to be made between individuals. A disadvantage is that this variation, on summated rating scales at least, often appears to consist mainly of variations attributable to response sets. In equal-appearing interval scales, the items are scaled, and are assigned values at equal intervals along an attitude continuum, a procedure which confers considerable statistical advantages. Cumulative scales are concerned with the measurement of one variable, which is supposed to be unidimensional. The first type of scale, using summated ratings, is probably the most widely used, since it is the easiest to work with. For further details of attitude scale construction, see A. L. Edwards (1957b).

In summary, it may be said that personality assessment has advanced considerably in the last twenty years and it is reasonable to expect even greater advances in the next two decades. One area which is attracting increasing interest is the computer simulation of personality (see Tomkins and Messick, 1963) and the use of computers in the scoring and interpretation of personality assessment procedures (see Kleinmuntz, 1967, ch. 11).

Further reading
L. J. Cronbach, *Essentials of Psychological Testing*, Harper, 2nd edn 1964.
M. Jahoda and N. Warren, *Attitudes*, Penguin Books, 1966.
D. R. Price-Williams, *Cross-Cultural Studies*, Penguin Books, 1969.
B. Semeonoff, *Personality Assessment*, Penguin Books, 2nd edn 1970.
P. Vernon, *Intelligence and Attainment Tests*, University of London Press, 1960.
P. Vernon, *Personality Assessment*, Methuen, 1964.

Chapter 18
Intelligence

This chapter will be concerned with the nature of intelligence and how it develops. There are other, related questions which can be asked about intelligence, some of which are dealt with in other chapters, and others of which are sufficiently marginal in relevance to be omitted. Thus, the problems associated with the construction of intelligence tests are examined in Chapter 17. The question, 'Is intelligence inherited?' – or, in its more precise and meaningful form, 'Is there a significant co-variance between differences in performance on intelligence tests and genotypic differences, for a given population in a given context?' – is discussed in Chapter 3. On the other hand, problems which arise in the practical application of tests, for example in education, are not relevant to a textbook of this kind.

No attempt will be made to define intelligence. The literature is replete with such definitions (see Heim, 1954; Knight, 1950); and to complicate matters further, T. R. Miles (1957) has distinguished at least six different senses in which the notion of 'definition' can be used in this context. Our interest here is in the empirical study of intellectual activities and, though the problem of definition cannot be completely ignored, there is reason to think that such study is best served by keeping our conception of intelligence elastic and imprecise, and as close to everyday usage as possible (see Heim, 1954). The justification for the concept, as ordinarily used, would seem to have its roots in two related discriminations. We customarily separate *people* into more or less intelligent, depending upon the effectiveness of their responses to certain situations; and we distinguish some *tasks* as requiring more intelligence for their successful execution than others. These are, of course, relative discriminations; there seems little point in debating whether there are tasks which do not involve intelligence at all, or whether there are totally non-intelligent organisms.

Broadly speaking, there are two lines of approach to the empirical study of intelligence. The first, which for convenience we shall call the *statistical approach*, capitalizes upon individual differences in tasks which, by general agreement, are held to require intelligence. The basic question asked by this approach concerns the *dimensionality* of intelligence. Is intelligence best conceived as a single dimension along which individuals differ, or is it a multidimensional phenomenon, such that we can only describe an individual as more intelligent than another with respect to a particular aspect of intelligence? Though primarily quantitative, this approach does involve qualitative considerations. The second, which will be arbitrarily designated the *qualitative approach*, ignores individual differences and analyses intellectual processes within the individual with a view to bringing out the factors which affect them, and how they change qualitatively in development. These two traditions of research have been pursued in independence of each other. Conceptually and methodologically they are quite different, and it is not at all clear how they could be fruitfully integrated; though some attempts are being made to bridge the gap between them (see Eysenck, 1967; Hunt, 1963; P. E. Vernon, 1955).

The statistical approach has the longer and more controversial history. A major impetus to its development has come from the demands of education, industry and the services for tests which will improve selection procedures. The claim that particular tests 'measure intelligence' has provoked the challenge that intelligence is not a single dimension, like height or weight, that can be measured by a single test. To investigate this, researchers have had recourse to the mathematical technique of factor analysis, and it is impossible to understand the subsequent controversies, and the difficulty of resolving them, without a minimal awareness of what factor analysis is. A very simple and brief introduction will be given later. One general criticism of this approach, however, is that, because it involves the testing of large numbers of individuals and the elaborate mathematical analysis of their scores, the resulting conception of intelligence is too abstract and remote from what actually goes on when people solve problems. The second, qualitative approach is certainly not open to this criticism. It includes a great deal of the research which is conventionally classified under such headings as learning, concept formation, problem solving, thinking and remembering. Since these are all being dealt with in other chapters. they will not be discussed here. Instead, the main emphasis will be upon the work of Piaget, for he has not only developed a theory of intelligence, but has also been responsible for the most comprehensive and detailed study of the development of intelligence yet made. His main aim has been to uncover the logical structures present in children's thinking and to show how these develop in complexity and mobility from birth to maturity. If the statistical approach leads to a highly general and abstract concept of intelligence, the work of Piaget leaves us with a concept almost overburdened with rich detail. Since the two are so disparate, they will be introduced separately and no attempt will be made to link them together.

The statistical approach

The empirical basis of the statistical approach is the test score. A test (or subtest) is a collection of items which samples a type of behaviour thought to involve intelligence. The items are made to vary in difficulty so that individuals differ in the number they successfully complete, and to discriminate in the same direction so that a total score has meaning. The number of possible tests is in principle unlimited, since they can vary both in the type of task sampled and in the actual items chosen to illustrate a task.

The next step in the argument is this. If two tests are given to a population sample, and are found to correlate positively, it is plausible to infer that this correlation is due to the fact that the two tests measure the same ability or abilities, at least to some extent. To put the point more cautiously, the correlation between two tests (or behavioural items) offers the best, indeed the only, operational definition for the concept of ability. Obviously the two tests must differ if this conclusion is to be informative; the closer the two tests approximate to each other, the more the argument approaches a tautology (this test measures the ability measured by this test).

Finally, if we administer to a population sample a battery of tests, all of which sample operations involving intelligence, and find that the intercorrelations between them are all positive (as in fact tends to be the case), then we can infer that all the tests measure, in varying degree, some common ability which is not unreasonably labelled as intelligence. Moreover, since these intercorrelations will vary in size, the pattern they exhibit should afford a clue to the nature and structure of intelligence. It is at this point that researchers have turned to factor analysis in order to make sense of the pattern of co-variance.

Factor analysis

It is of the greatest importance to be clear that factor analysis is a mathematical technique designed to summarize a matrix of values (in this case, intercorrelations between tests) in a small number of 'factors' such that from the factors alone the original matrix can be reproduced. Mathematically, a factor is a value which, when multiplied by another value, yields a product. Every product can be conceived in terms of the multiplication of two or more factors, and the number of possible factors for any given product is, of course, infinite. What the factor analysis of a matrix of correlation co-efficients does, then, is to reduce the matrix to a smaller set of factor values, the products of which yield the original matrix. It follows that there is an unlimited number of possible sets of factor values from which the original correlations can be calculated.

There are a number of different methods for factor analysing a matrix of correlation coefficients. Any discussion of them, and of the mathematical reasoning that underlies them, is well beyond the scope of this chapter. The reader must consult one of the many textbooks devoted to it (for example, Fruchter, 1954; Horst, 1965). However, in order to understand the controversies which have arisen in the study of intelligence, some conception of what is meant by a factor is necessary. One of the simplest ways of introducing the reader to the notion is to take up the spatial metaphor implicit in the idea of a *dimension* of intellectual difference and to represent the process of factor analysis geometrically. Again, the mathematical justification for doing this must be sought elsewhere; we are using geometrical representation here as a convenient expository device.

If two tests, A and B, are represented by lines, or vectors, of unit length on a plane surface, such that they have a common point of origin, then we can represent the correlation between the two tests by the angle between the two vectors. More accurately, the angle between the vectors must be such that its cosine equals the correlation coefficient (see Figure 68).

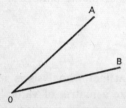

Figure 68   Geometric representation of a correlation coefficient between two tests A and B, where $r_{AB} = $ cosine AOB

To represent a correlation coefficient between two tests, then, we need a two-dimensional space. We can now draw in these two dimensions as two lines, again of unit length, and label them factor I and factor II (see Figure 69). Note that the dimensions are inde-

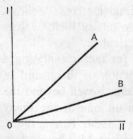

Figure 69   Geometric representation of a correlation coefficient with two factors added

pendent, and therefore drawn at right angles to each other. Moreover, their positions relative to $\angle AOB$ are arbitrary.

The next step is to draw in the projections of both tests upon the two dimensions, or factors (see Figure 70). Since the factors are of unit length, these projections will be some value between zero and one. The projection of a test vector upon a factor is called its loading on that factor.

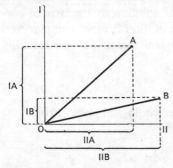

Figure 70 Geometric representation of the loadings of two tests, A and B, on factors I and II

Finally, it is now possible to calculate the correlation between tests A and B from a knowledge of their loadings on the two factors. This is done by multiplying the loadings of the two tests on factor I, doing the same for factor II and then summing the products. Thus:

$$(IA \times IB) + (IIA \times IIB) = \text{cosine} \angle AOB = r_{AB}.$$

It is possible, then, to account for the correlation between two tests in terms of their respective loadings on two factors. When only one correlation is involved there is obviously no point in doing this, for no economy in information would be achieved. But if we imagine six or seven tests, the intercorrelations between which are positive, and such that they can be represented on a single plane surface, then it would effect an economy if we could reduce the information given in the correlations to two sets of factor loadings. In practice, however, with such a number of tests, it is almost certain that more than two dimensions would be needed. But in general the usefulness of factor analysis depends upon the fact that fewer factors are needed than tests.

To return now to Figure 70, above. It is obvious that the position of factors I and II is arbitrary. Provided we retain the orthogonal relationship between them, we could rotate the factors generating an unlimited number of possible factor solutions, each of which would permit the recalculation of the original coefficient. Moreover, the factors do not necessarily have to remain orthogonal. It is possible to calculate an oblique factor solution to a matrix of correlation coefficients, though the computation is more complex and it is more difficult to assign psychological meaning to the resulting factor structure.

Table 9

Correlation coefficients between six psychological tests. (From P. E. Vernon, 1961, p. 5)

Tests	1	2	3	4	5	6
1. Vocabulary		+0·76	+0·79	+0·45	+0·41	+0·34
2. Analogies	+0·76		+0·68	+0·44	+0·35	+0·26
3. Classifications	+0·79	+0·68		+0·49	+0·39	+0·32
4. Block design	+0·45	+0·44	+0·49		+0·58	+0·44
5. Spatial	+0·41	+0·35	+0·39	+0·58		+0·55
6. Formboard	+0·34	+0·26	+0·32	+0·44	+0·55	

In order to illustrate what has been said so far, a hypothetical example of a correlation matrix is given. It is taken from the excellent introduction to the subject by P. E. Vernon (1961). Table 9 gives the correlations which might result if a battery of six tests were given to a large and varied sample of the population. Table 10 gives the results of a factor analysis of this matrix.

As can be seen, three factors are necessary to account for the correlations. All the tests have loadings on the first factor, reflecting the fact that all the correlations are positive. The remaining two factors each have positive loadings on three tests and zero loadings on three tests. From the table of factor loadings, it is possible to reconstruct the table of correlations. For example:

$$r_{34} = (0·8 \times 0·6) + (0·3 \times 0) + (0 \times 0·4) = 0·48.$$

It is true that the correlation is not precisely the same as the original; but it is near enough for the difference to be attributable to error due to the rounding of decimals.

Table 10

Completed factor analysis of six psychological tests. (From P. E. Vernon, 1961, p. 7)

Tests	Loadings			Tests	Loadings		
	g	v	k		g	v	k
1. Vocabulary	0·8	0·5		4. Block design	0·6		0·4
2. Analogies	0·7	0·4		5. Spatial	0·5		0·7
3. Classifications	0·8	0·3		6. Formboard	0·4		0·5

Factor analysis in psychology. So far we have considered only the mathematical concept of a factor. What factor analysis does is to show how many dimensions are needed to accommodate a set of intercorrelations and how the total amount of information given by them may be summarized in terms of loadings on these dimensions. Generally speaking, psychologists who have used factor analysis have not been primarily concerned with achieving economy as such. Rather they have been animated by the conviction that in discovering the dimensional structure of a correlation matrix, they were also discovering something about the structure of intelligence (Thurstone, 1940). For them, 'factor' was a psychological concept as well as a mathematical one. It is with regard to the psychological meaning of factors that all the controversy has arisen. And after years of research, it is now plain that the value of factor analysis as a technique for investigating *psychological* structure is severely limited. Some of these limitations are brought out in the following considerations:

1. Factor analysis can establish that to account for a given set of intercorrelations between tests, a certain minimal number of orthogonal factors is required. But it is possible to rotate these dimensions so that, though the number of dimensions is relatively stable, the loadings of particular tests on these factors is infinitely variable. The normal procedure for assigning psychological meaning to a factor

is to name it after what appear to be the relevant characteristics of those tests which have a high loading on it. It follows that the technique does not permit any definitive psychological description of structure. It is true, criteria have been put forward for preferring one factor solution to another. They include 'factor invariance', by which is meant that the same psychological structure can be reproduced using different subjects and tests; but mostly investigators have relied upon their own subjective judgement as to what makes the most psychologically meaningful solution. And such judgements depend upon the theories held by the investigator. A further, related problem is to know when to stop factor analysing. A complex matrix of correlations may require for its complete analysis a number of factors which have very small loadings indeed on any of the tests. Since these factors have little if any psychological value, it is customary to stop the analysis when the main factors have been extracted. This means that an element of approximation enters into the analysis.

2. The factor solutions obtained (in both the mathematical and psychological senses) depend upon the nature and number of tests used, and the sampling procedures adopted. If the tests chosen are relatively homogeneous and the subjects vary widely over the whole range of intellectual difference, then the analysis is likely to yield few factors and to give prominence to one general factor. If on the other hand the tests are very varied and the subjects relatively homogeneous, the analysis is likely to yield a large number of factors and to minimize the likelihood of there being one general factor with loadings on all tests. Plainly, the psychological meaning of the factors obtained under such differing conditions is not comparable.

3. More fundamentally we can ask what it really means to assign psychological meaning to a factor. Early factor analysis tended to assume without question that factors corresponded to abilities. The nature of an ability was determined by inspection of the tests. In the hypothetical example given above, the first factor, common to all tests, is labelled 'general cognitive ability', or *g*. The second is common to the only three tests which make extensive use of words and hence is called 'verbal ability'. The third is named 'spatial

ability', because the tests it has loadings on all involve the perception of spatial relationships. Obviously the labelling of factors is convenient. The problem lies in interpreting just what is meant when a factor is said to correspond to an ability.

There are two extreme views. On the one hand, some writers have claimed that abilities are actual entities, or circumscribable psychological functions. If a psychological function is unitary, in some sense, then this is presumably because of an underlying physiological unity of structure. Such a view appears to be assumed by Burt (1944) who argues that there are functionally unitary abilities and that these will always show up as factors in a test battery, but that not all factors found in analysis correspond to abilities. How it is possible to distinguish factors which correspond to abilities from those that do not, other than by intuition, is not clear. Spearman (1927) thought that the general factor, which he found to have loadings on all tests, corresponded to 'mental energy' which existed in varying quantities and which was measured most directly by those tests with a high loading on the general factor. This mental energy found its expression in self-consciousness, the perception of relations and the eduction of correlates.

At the other extreme is G. N. Thomson (1939), who argued that it is naïve to suppose that there are unitary abilities which could correspond to factors. It is worth quoting him at some length.

In brief, then, the author's attitude is that he does not believe in factors if any real existence is attributed to them; but that, of course, he recognizes that any set of correlated human abilities can always be described mathematically by a number of variables or 'factors', *and that in many ways*, among which no doubt some will be more useful or more elegant or more sparing of unnecessary hypotheses. But the mind is very much more complex, and also very much more an integrated whole, than any naïve interpretation of any one mathematical analysis might lead a reader to suppose. Far from being divided into 'unitary factors', the mind is a rich, comparatively undifferentiated complex of innumerable influences – on the physiological side an intricate network of possibilities of intercommunication. Factors are fluid descriptive mathematical coefficients, changing both with the tests used and with the sample of persons, unless we take refuge in sheer definition based upon psychological judgement, which definition would have to specify the particular battery of tests, and the sample of persons, as well as the method of analysis, in order to fix any factor (p. 267). In the light of the qualitative study of intellectual functioning to be discussed later, it is hard not to agree with this statement.

The conclusions to be drawn from these considerations are unambiguous. As an investigatory technique, factor analysis is meaningless unless it is related to a theory. Moreover, the technique cannot be used to *test* a theory, for to do this, it would not only have to show that a theory fitted the facts but also that alternative, logically incompatible theories are false. Since factors are 'fluid mathematical coefficients', they cannot be used to rule out alternative theories. At best, then, factor analysis will show that a given theory is tenable, and sometimes indicate that some theories are harder to maintain than others. Its main value is as an exploratory technique for shaping hypotheses rather than as a method for finding out whether the hypotheses are true.

It is hoped that by now it will be clear to the reader just why the statistical approach has led to so much unresolvable controversy. There is not space here to review the different theories that have been held, and the research which has gone into their support. This task has already been done, lucidly and comprehensively, by P. E. Vernon (1961). However, a very brief sketch of four different theories will be given to introduce the reader to the field.

1. The simplest theory is that advocated by Spearman (1927), and is usually called the *two-factor theory*. Spearman argued that individual differences in performance on any test could be accounted for by one factor which was general, and common to all tests, and one which was quite specific to that test. The former he labelled *g*, or general intelligence. Although Spearman defended this theory persuasively, the persistent finding of more than one factor common to several tests in a battery makes it the least easy to maintain.

2. The second view has been dubbed the *hierarchical theory of mental abilities*, and has been popular among British psychologists. This view maintains that individual differences can best be accounted for in terms of one general factor, common to all tests, and a series of group factors each of which has positive loadings on some tests and zero, or near zero, loadings on others. Table 10 above is an

example of a group factor solution. The number of group factors depends upon the number and variety of tests used. Among the group factors which have been found most consistently are those which have been labelled 'verbal', 'arithmetical', 'spatial' and 'mechanical'. This theory is supported by methods of factor analysis which maximize the total amount of variance due to the common factor, and is an extension of the two-factor theory. It has been defended by Burt (1955) on the grounds that it produces solutions which are closest to the way the term 'intelligence' is generally used.

3. The third theory derives from Thurstone, and is called the *multiple factor theory*. The distinctive feature of Thurstone's use of factor analysis is the criterion he adopts for selecting a factor solution. This criterion he calls 'simple structure'. By this he means a factor solution which maximizes the number of zero loadings. Ideally, each factor has high loadings on some tests and zero loadings on others. Thurstone maintains that such a solution makes the most satisfying psychological sense. Necessarily, however, it minimizes the likelihood of finding a general factor. Since tests tend in fact to correlate positively with each other, it is not easy to achieve simple structure and Thurstone has been forced to have recourse to oblique factors. This has in turn led to the generation of a 'second order' general factor to account for the correlation between the primary factors. But a theory which conceives of intelligence as a loosely related group of 'primary abilities' is tenable in terms of factor analysis. These primary abilities have been labelled: V (verbal), P (perceptual speed), I (inductive reasoning), N (number) and so on. Advocates of the group factor approach, though they accept that multiple factor analysis is logically possible, would claim that it fails to do justice to the evidence for a general factor.

4. The last theory is of a different kind. The objection which may be brought against the previous theories is that they offer a simplified concept of intelligence and fail to do justice to its richness and variety. In a series of papers and a recent book, Guilford has sought to give a comprehensive description of intellectual functioning on the basis of test measurement (see Guilford, 1967). He starts with a logical analysis of intellectual activities. First he distinguishes five

types of mental operation: thinking, remembering, divergent production (problem solving which leads to unexpected and original solutions), convergent production (problem solving which leads to the one, correct solution) and evaluating; then six types of product of these operations: units, classes, relations, systems, transformations and implications; and finally, four types of content upon which the operations are performed: figural, symbolic, semantic and behavioural. These classifications generate 120 distinguishable 'abilities', such as, for example, the ability to remember relations between symbols. Guilford then proceeds to construct test batteries designed to yield factors corresponding to these abilities. The project is still incomplete, but most of the abilities have been defined factorially. It would seem that Guilford is trying to do justice to the complex and integrated whole that Thomson described. He has not so far examined the correlations between these abilities. But it is significant that he has used a very select population of subjects in his investigations, namely men chosen to become officers in the United States Army. There is likely to be little variability in 'general intelligence' in such a population, and therefore the more qualitative aspects of intellectual functioning are more likely to be discernible.

Some later developments

The theory of fluid and crystallized intelligence. Cattell (1963b) has put forward a theory of general intelligence which presupposes that the general factor found in test batteries is really a function of two conceptually distinct but correlated factors. He labels these factors fluid and crystallized intelligence. Crystallized intelligence reveals itself in those cognitive tests which require learned habits of thinking; fluid intelligence in new situations where successful adaptation cannot be achieved by the individual's existing repertoire of cognitive skills. Cattell develops a number of predictions about these two components of general intelligence. For example, fluid intelligence is expected to have a greater association with genotypic difference than crystallized, and to have a different growth curve reaching its maximum level earlier.

A comparable theoretical distinction has been made by others, for example, Hebb (1949), whose contribution will be briefly discussed in the second half of this chapter. The distinctive feature of Cattell's approach is his use of factor analysis to support his theory. He claims that factor studies have failed to isolate definitively the nature of general intelligence because they have only used cognitive tests. To isolate intelligence, it is necessary to include personality measures in the battery. This Cattell does in his own study, and is able to extract the two correlated factors demanded by his theory.

Creativity. Conventional tests of intelligence are usually composed of items which admit of only one correct solution. They are highly structured, in the sense that sufficient information is given for the answer to be reached deductively. For some time there has been a growing suspicion that such tests do not do justice to those people who have the capacity for imaginative and original thinking. Moreover, many, if not most, of the problems which occur in real life have no single correct solution.

In the attempt to do justice to this neglected aspect of intelligence, attempts have been made to measure creativity. The tests devised have usually consisted of items in which the subject has to think of as many different but appropriate responses as possible in a given time.

Armed with tests of this kind, some investigators have attempted to show that creativity is a feature of cognitive activity which is largely independent of intelligence as conventionally measured. Getzels and Jackson (1962) compared two groups of adolescent boys, one which was very high on intelligence but relatively low on creativity measures, the other high on creativity but relatively low on intelligence. The authors found that the high creatives were equally good in academic attainment, but were less popular with teachers and tended to differ on a variety of personality measures. Though they found creativity and intelligence to be positively correlated, they claimed that this 'signifies rather that a certain amount of intelligence is required for creativity but that intelligence and creativity are by no means the same' (p. 125).

This study has come in for a good deal of criticism (see Burt, 1962; De Mille and Merrifield, 1962; Marsh, 1964). In general, it appears that tests of creativity do not correlate highly with each other and tend to be more highly correlated with intelligence than some investigators claim (see P. E. Vernon, 1964; Hasan and Butcher, 1966). Moreover, it is probably misleading to call these tests measures of creativity. Hudson (1966) argues that the term should be dropped and that we should use the term 'divergent thinking' instead. However, it is obvious that this is an important and growing field in psychology at present.

The qualitative approach

The main features of the qualitative approach are its focus upon the nature of intellectual functioning and its concern with the development of these operations through interaction between organism and environment. A major stimulus to experimental study in this field came from Hebb (1949), who observed that the effects upon intellectual performance of the removal of extensive areas of the prefrontal region of the cortex depended upon the age at which the operation occurred. Among *adults*, performance was hardly affected on tests which involved the use of words and the more or less routine deduction of answers, whereas on spatial type tests, which presented the subject with puzzles of a relatively novel kind, there was a marked deterioration. On the other hand, damage to the *infant* brain affected later performance on verbal tests as much as on the non-verbal ones.

On the basis of these findings Hebb distinguishes two meanings which the concept of intelligence can have. The first, 'intelligence A', is 'an innate potential, the capacity for development, a fully innate property that amounts to the possession of a good brain and a good neural metabolism' (Hebb, 1949, p. 294). That is to say, intelligence A is a general characteristic of nervous systems by virtue of which they are potentially able to acquire intelligent performance. The second meaning, 'intelligence B', is the actual functioning of the brain at any given time. Such functioning is due both to intelligence A and also to the memories, concepts and strategies which have been learned through interaction with the environment. Intelligence tests, of course, measure individual differences in intelligence B.

Developmentally, therefore, we need to distinguish that period during which the basic concepts and strategies of intelligent thinking are being acquired from the subsequent life of the individual in which he uses them. This not only suggests that the earlier expression of intelligence may be qualitatively different from later forms, but also that the earlier phases may be more vulnerable to the permanent adverse effects of environment than the later. In general the evidence supports this. Our concern at present, however, is with the nature of these concepts and strategies essential to intelligent thinking and how they develop. The greatest single contribution to our understanding of how these concepts and strategies evolve is certainly that of Piaget. In the course of over forty years' work, Piaget has not only accumulated a massive quantity of empirical observation and experiment, but has also developed a conceptual scheme for describing the whole process of intellectual development. It is, of course, impossible to do justice to such an achievement in the space available here (for detailed general accounts of Piaget's work, see Flavell, 1963; Hunt, 1961; Piaget, 1950[1]). Piaget's work presents certain difficulties for the student, for he has developed an individual – even idiosyncratic – terminology which takes some while to learn and which expresses a way of looking at intellectual development that contrasts with the traditional approaches within psychology. What we shall do, therefore, is first, consider those basic concepts which define Piaget's general approach, and then second, outline very briefly some of the main steps in intellectual development which he has uncovered.

The approach of Piaget

Piaget's basic orientation is biological. That is to say, he sees intelligence as an aspect or quality of *adaptation* to the environment. Adaptation, when achieved, is a state of *equilibrium* between the actions of the organism and the actions of the environment. The concept of action is very important in Piaget's system and brings out the central difference between his theoretical approach and that which has formed the main tradition in psychology. Traditionally, psychologists have tended to analyse organism–environment

1. All references to Piaget are of English translations.

interactions into a three-step sequence (see Figure 71). A given inter-action is conceived as involving three discrete events, a stimulus from the environment, a response from the organism and an internal or external consequence which is positively or negatively reinforcing. Piaget rejects this analysis as essentially mechanistic and non-

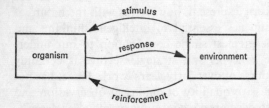

Figure 71   Three-step analysis of interaction underlying traditional S–R theory

biological. Instead he assumes that, from the point of view of the analysis of intelligence, the organism is to be considered as always active. What occurs between the organism and the environment is, at every stage, an interaction, or between-action (see Figure 72), a single event which, from the point of view of the organism, is always an action (and indeed from the point of view of the environment can

Figure 72   Piaget's single-step analysis of interaction in which what occurs between the organism and the environment is always shaped by the nature of both

always be considered an action). It follows that listening or looking are as much actions as walking or kicking. An event which can be described as the action of stimulating the organism is, from the organism's point of view, the action of perceiving an object.

Piaget's concern is not, primarily, in the content of actions but in their structure. In the development of children, the constantly changing environment on the one hand and maturational processes of a physiological kind on the other ensure that the structures of actions are constantly being modified and co-ordinated into more complex sequences. Unlike traditional learning theorists, Piaget makes no attempt to offer a mechanistic-causal explanation of these changes; that is to say, he does not try to define, through experiment, the antecedent conditions, in the environment and in the organism, which induce particular changes. Instead he concentrates upon describing that invariant, sequential ordering of the structures which constitutes the development of intelligence. Particular structural levels are evaluated in terms of their functional relevance in the service of adaptation. That is to say, in most of Piaget's empirical studies, the sole independent variable is *age itself* rather than those antecedent factors which cause age changes. In so far as Piaget offers an explanation of a given age change, it is in terms of the more effective adaptation achieved by it and in terms of its necessary place in the development from neonatal reflex behaviour to high-level, intellectual activity. Hence in describing a particular stage, Piaget contrasts it with previous and subsequent stages in order to bring out how it is an improvement in adaptation upon what has gone before, but still less effective than what is to come.

In describing the structure of actions, Piaget makes use of three basic concepts. The first and most pervasive in his writing is the *schema*. When Piaget talks about an action schema, he is referring to two observable aspects of actions: that they have a certain shape or pattern and that they tend to be repeated. But the concept is not used merely to *describe* actions. On the contrary, a schema is an inferred element of that cognitive, structural organization responsible for the shaping and recurrence of the actions of an organism. Although schemata are operationally defined in terms of the characteristics of actions, they are not so much aspects of actions as aspects of the organism which become embodied in actions. Though they manifest, as it were, conservative tendencies, they are conceived to be relatively mobile and flexible structures. This must be so, since what occurs between the organism and its environment, and which – from the organism's point of view – is called its action, is a function of both the structure of the organism and the structure of the environment, and the latter is always changing. Hence every action is strictly speaking a modification of a schema. Adaptation to a complex and changing environment presupposes schemata of great mobility.

The other concepts used to characterize the inferred organismic structure behind actions are *operation* and *grouping*. These are initially complex and difficult ideas, and the attempt to explain their meaning will be deferred to later. For the present it can be said that they refer to fully internalized and representational actions which form an inter-related whole with certain logical properties. Operational groupings are exhibited in such actions as performing complex mathematical transformations or in solving some applied scientific problem.

The embodiment of a schema in an act, then, involves both a repetition of a past action and its simultaneous modification in the face of the present environment. It is the presence of both aspects which makes an act adaptatory. The schema is a structure and an action is the functioning of that structure. In relation to environment, this functioning has a dual aspect; it involves both the incorporation of the environment into an already existing schema and the modification of the schema to fit the realities of the environment. The first aspect Piaget calls *assimilation*, and the second *accommodation*. To take a simple example. When a young child grasps a ball, he is assimilating the ball to the grasping schema; he is, as it were, turning the ball into 'something to be grasped'. At the same time he has to accommodate to it, in the sense that the grasping schema has to adjust to the size, weight, texture and position of the ball. At a more complex representational level, the student who is engaged in the action of listening to a lecture is, at one and the same time, assimilating the incoming information to existing schemata and accommodating these schemata to what is new in that information.

Thus, the development of intelligence in terms of the progressive modification, co-ordination and differentiation of schemata can be described as follows. The biological drive to adapt to environment leads the child to assimilate the objects in that environment to his existing schemata. At the same time the nature of the environmental objects forces upon the child an accommodatory adjustment of these schemata. It is thus that schemata develop. It follows that the complexity of schematic structure depends upon the variety of the environmental objects which are available for the child to assimilate and which simultaneously provoke accommodation. At a higher level, for example, when faced with a mechanical or mathematical problem, effective adaptation requires that assimilation–accommodation be so speeded up that it becomes internalized, or symbolic, and that schemata be co-ordinated with each other in the sense that they assimilate and accommodate to each other, and form complex systems.

It is evident that an organism's capacity to develop high-level intellectual skills is dependent upon the degree of schematic mobility or plasticity it possesses. Though Piaget does not develop this point, it would seem that plasticity of schema corresponds to Hebb's intelligence A, and the level of schematic complexity at any given time to his intelligence B.

Though every action involves assimilation and accommodation, the relative importance of these two aspects can vary. This can be brought out most clearly by contrasting *play* and *imitation* in the behaviour of young children. When, at play, children make use of a plank of wood as a ship or car, accommodation to the nature of the plank is minimal, and assimilation of the plank to the schemata of the game maximal. On the other hand, imitation is characterized by a predominance of accommodation over assimilation. At a higher level, the act of recognizing is mainly assimilatory, whereas, for example, rote learning is mainly accommodatory.

Finally, Piaget offers some general criteria for distinguishing more intelligent adaptations from less. First, intelligent adaptation involves a kind of homeostatic *equilibrium* between organism and environment. By this is meant that assimilation and accommodation are optimally balanced. In the example given above, symbolic play with a plank of wood is a less intelligent adaptation to the plank than, for example, would be making a model ship out of it. Second, there is the *degree of spatial-temporal distance*. At the lowest end, Piaget makes a distinction between organic and functional adaptation. At the organic level, adaptation 'involves an interpenetration between some part of the living body and some sector of the environment' (Piaget, 1950, p. 8), as in the process of assimilating and accommodating to food. Psychological life, on the other hand, begins with functional interaction: that is to say, from the point at which assimilation no longer alters the assimilated objects in a physico-chemical manner, but simply incorporates them into an action. In the very lowest forms of intelligent behaviour, the distance between the organism and environment is minimal. That is to say, the organism's behaviour is related only to the perceptual configuration of the object as it appears at a given moment. Remove this configuration, and the object ceases to exist. Indeed the configuration is not, for the organism, even an object, for to perceive a configuration as an object is to contribute more to the act of perceiving than is given in the perceived configuration. At the other end of the scale, the subject is capable of relating himself to the whole spatial-temporal universe. That is to say, at the highest level of intellectual development, the subject can have some concept of the whole universe of space and time. The third criterion is the *complexity of the routes* between the organism and the environment. The young baby has only the most limited pathways to the environment; he grasps things or sucks them. At the other extreme, the routes to the environment are highly complex and involved; the subject can relate himself to his environment through a large number of alternative operations. The last criterion, which is really another way of describing the third, is the *complexity of schematic organization*. At the lowest level, schemata are few, simple and relatively discrete. At the highest level they are vast in number and hierarchically organized in complex groupings. Indeed, the existence of the spatial-temporal world and awareness of its properties is a function of the development of schemata.

The development of intelligence

So far we have been concerned to give the reader a general idea of Piaget's approach by describing some of his key concepts. It is time to consider how intelligence actually does develop, at least as Piaget has described it. Obviously, we can only give the briefest of sketches, for Piaget has in fact written several volumes on each of the major stages of the process.

First, however, it is as well to be clear what Piaget is trying to do. It is nothing less than to provide a developmental account of how logical thinking occurs in human beings. To take a simple example, consider the following syllogism: If all As are B; and C is an A; then C is B. The first thing to be said is that this is a hypothetical, propositional argument; the conclusion holds whatever objects or concepts are substituted for A, B and C. Second, intelligent adults perceive that the conclusion necessarily follows from the premises. Piaget's concern is why it is that intelligent people perceive the conclusion as necessarily true. As he points out, there are two possible kinds of explanation. One is in terms of the logic of class relationships. But people can see that the conclusion follows without training in logic. The other is a psychological explanation, and this must, in Piaget's view, be an explanation which shows how this kind of thinking is the end term of a process of development from thinking of a much more primitive kind. In short, Piaget is attempting a developmental or historical explanation of propositional and logically necessary thinking.

The whole span of development from birth to maturity is divisible into certain major stages. Though Piaget gives age limits to these stages, he recognizes that they are only approximations and there may be considerable individual differences in rate of development. And, though there are qualitative differences between the different stages, the transition from one to the next is continuous. Piaget is sure, however, that the sequential ordering of the stages is invariant. These stages are: (1) the period of sensorimotor intelligence, from birth to one and a half years; (2) the period of pre-conceptual thought, from one and half to seven years, which is divisible into two substages, (2a) the period of symbolic thought, from one and a half to four years, and (2b) the period of intuitive thought, from four to seven years; (3) the period of concrete operations, from seven to about ten years; and (4) the period from then on which is characterized by the attainment of formal operations. Each of these main stages is in turn divided up into smaller ones, but for the full details of these, the reader must consult Piaget's works.

1. The sensorimotor stage (see Piaget, 1952a, 1954). The first actions of the infant are presumed to be a function of schemata which have matured under genetic control during the pre-natal period. At first, such actions as sucking are simply generalized so that they assimilate all appropriate objects in reach. Soon, however, there is evidence of the co-ordination of schemata. Sucking and arm-movement schemata become co-ordinated into the action of putting the thumb in the mouth and sucking it. Looking at objects and grasping them also become co-ordinated. Later, about the age of six months, there appears the first evidence of intention. The baby, having accidentally discovered that a certain action has an interesting effect, for example, if he pulls a string and finds that the canopy over his pram rattles, then proceeds to repeat the action in order to repeat the effect. This is the beginning of the differentiation between ends and means. It constitutes an anticipation of an effect and implies a primitive knowledge of reality. The first sign that objects exist for the child is when the perception of part of an object is taken as an indication of the presence of the whole of it. Towards the end of the first year, these tendencies become more pronounced. Intention is clearly evident when the child applies methods he has already learned in new situations in order to achieve his goal. If, for example, a toy the child wants is placed on a cushion out of his reach, he will now – for the first time – pull the cushion towards him in order to gain the toy. Objects have now a certain permanence, as shown when he searches for a toy which is hidden. And the child is beginning to be aware that objects are spatially related to each other, as when he anticipates the reappearance of an object which has passed behind a screen. By the end of the first year, the child is beginning to experiment. Instead of pulling the cushion towards him to get the toy, he will move the cushion about experimentally in order to see what happens to the toy. In Piaget's terms, what has happened is this: hitherto, the baby, in assimilating objects to his schemata, has had accommodation forced upon him; now he gets interested in accommodation for its own sake; in short he becomes interested in novelty.

With the close of the sensorimotor stage, we see the transition to the next stage, the beginnings of representational and reflective thought. Before considering this, it is convenient to summarize the limitations of sensorimotor intelligence. They all stem from the fact that for the first year or two of life, thinking and overt action are one and the same. Hence thinking is slow and sequential; that is to say, the child can only think one thought at a time, he cannot combine thoughts 'mentally'. Moreover, thinking is directed solely to practical ends; the child is not yet interested in knowledge as such. And the distance between child and environment is still very short. His thinking is concerned only with the actual entities in his immediate environment. Piaget suggests there are three conditions which must obtain if the child is to move on to reflective thinking. Schematic activation must be speeded up and freed from its embodiment in motor action. The child must be increasingly interested in the mechanisms whereby results are achieved, rather than in the results alone. And, of course, the distance between subject and environment must be increased.

The first signs of these developments occur about the age of eighteen months. Faced with new problems, the child can now solve them in advance of 'acting out'. This corresponds to the 'insight learning' of the Gestalt psychologists. Faced with a desired object out of reach, and a stick within reach, the child will examine the situation, then use the stick to reach the object in a single smooth action, strongly suggesting that the co-ordination of schemata into a new pattern has occurred prior to the overt behaviour. Or, when a child approaches a closed door, with both hands full, he will pause, then, in a single co-ordinated action, place the objects on the ground, open the door and then pick them up again. This kind of behaviour is taken as evidence that schemata can now be evoked and co-ordinated without necessarily being embodied in overt behaviour. In arriving at the solution before carrying it out, the child is exhibiting the first signs of interiorized action.

2a. The stage of symbolic thought (see Piaget, 1951). This period, which lasts until about the age of four years, sees the elaboration of the *symbolic function* in play and its integration with language acquisition. The capacity for representational thinking implies a differentiation of signs from significates. Piaget distinguishes two different sorts of relationship between them. The *symbol* is an object or action which comes to stand for other objects or actions by exhibiting some objective similarity to them. An example is the pebble which is used as a 'pretend' sweet in a child's game; or the action of putting a doll to bed which is symbolic of actually going to sleep. Implied in the expression of the symbolic function is an awareness in the child of the symbolic nature of the symbol; he does not eat the pebble. Words are also signs, but their relationship to significates is arbitrary and conventional. Words are social signs, and to begin with are sharply differentiated from the private symbolic thinking of the child. Progressively the two are integrated. At first language is assimilated to the private symbolisms of the child; but as the child's symbolic function is slowly weaned from its initial egocentricity, so the child's use of language becomes increasingly socialized. And the use of language in social contexts plays an important part in this weaning. But it is fundamental to Piaget's position that the symbolic function originates in independence of language.

Piaget attributes the growth of the symbolic function and the attainment of language to deferred imitation. With the speeding up and internalizing of schematic activation, the child is able to observe and to accommodate to the actions of others and defer the overt expression of these accommodations to a later time. The later manifestations of these imitatory accommodations, precisely because they are close copies of earlier actions, are primarily assimilatory in a new context.

2b. The stage of intuitive thought (see Piaget, 1926, 1952b). This period is not clearly distinguished from the previous one. Language and the symbolic function are now integrated so that the child thinks in language but, since the symbolic function is still immature, in that the internalized schemata which form its basis are not sufficiently organized in relation to each other, the child's use of language and his thinking are egocentric. Among the many ways in which this egocentricity manifests itself, we will mention two.

In one of his earliest monographs (Piaget, 1926), Piaget explored the effects of this egocentricity in linguistic communication. Since words have been assimilated to a private, even idiosyncratic symbolic function, the child is, to a considerable extent, attaching private meaning to public signs and is unaware of the fact; for his social experience is not yet rich enough for him to realize that others do not share his private meanings. Thus, when someone tells him a story, he may be completely confident he has understood, even though in fact what he understands is not what was intended in the communication. It is when he is aware of the bias of his private symbolic function that he ceases to be egocentric. But this development must await an important advance in the organization of his internalized schemata.

The second sign of the child's egocentricity is the way in which his thinking is biased by his immediate perceptions. The child's incapacity to solve certain kinds of problem is a function of the fact that he cannot yet free himself from the dominating influence of particular features of the problem. Because his view of a problem is *centred* on one particular feature of it, he cannot achieve the schematic reorganization which constitutes the attainment of a solution.

It is the decentring of thought, the freeing of it from the dominance of any particular feature of the problem, which is one of the most crucial steps in intellectual development. It occurs about the age of seven, and marks the passage from *pre-operational* thinking to *operational*. In view of its importance and in order to introduce the reader to the concept of an *operation*, or an *operational grouping*, two illustrations will be taken from the many which Piaget has provided.

The child is asked to fill two identical beakers with beads in such a way that the beakers have the same number in each, and the child acknowledges this fact. Then the experimenter pours the contents of one beaker into another which is taller and thinner while the child watches. The child under seven is likely to judge that the beakers no longer have the same number in, but that the taller one has more because it is taller. The child's perception of the problem is centred upon the relation of tallness which differentiates the beakers. If the contents of the taller beaker are then poured into an even taller and thinner one, the point may be reached when the child suddenly reverses his judgement and claims that there are now fewer beads in it because it is thinner. His perception of the problem is decentred and recentred upon another perceptual feature of the problem. It is not until the next stage, that of *concrete operations*, that the child has no difficulty with the task. And this is because he can now keep in mind simultaneously the relationships of height and thinness, and co-ordinate these relationships systematically. His thought is then, with regard to this problem, *operational*.

Another problem Piaget gave to children is as follows. A number of wooden beads are put in front of him, most of which are brown, but a few of which are white. The child acknowledges both that all the beads are wooden and that there are more brown than white ones. He is then asked whether there are more brown than wooden beads. The younger child will reply that there are, and the reason given is that there are only a few white ones. When reminded that they are all wooden and again asked, he will reply as before. Once again the older child has no difficulty because he can now hold in mind both the relationships of woodenness and colour at the same time and co-ordinate these two relationships systematically.

In relation to the succeeding stage, the pre-operational child's thought is egocentric. The child's thinking is fully representational, but the organization of schemata has not reached the stage where the relationships obtaining among objects are fully and adequately co-ordinated. The child's thinking is biased by the fact that his thinking is centred upon one relationship at a time.

3. The stage of concrete operations (see Inhelder and Piaget, 1964). The operational level of thinking is reached when the child is able to vary two or more relationships simultaneously. This implies that the schemata underlying these relationships are so organized that they form a co-ordinated system, the elements of which are highly mobile, while the system remains stable. Operational thinking is *reversible*. When the child is given, in terms of objects or quantities, the relationships $A > B$, and $B > C$, not only does he immediately know that $A > C$ but he also knows that $C < B$, $C < A$ and $B < A$. The younger child has to discover these relationships separately by examination; for the older child they are given in the original information. The relationships of 'greater than' and 'smaller than' form a stable operational system within which relationships can be reversed.

However, the operational thinking of the child is still concrete. He reaches the operational level at first only in relation to objects which form a familiar part of his experience. Piaget found, for example, that when he presented the classification problem in a more abstract form by using birds and animals rather than coloured and wooden beads, the child did not solve the problem until rather later, about the age of eight or nine years.

4. *The stage of formal operations* It is not until puberty and after that the child begins to free his operational thinking from its roots in particular experiences. The child becomes capable of general, propositional thinking; he can solve problems by hypothesizing factors and deducing consequences. For an account of this stage, the reader is referred to Inhelder and Piaget (1958).

Concluding remarks

There is not space to give a critique of Piaget's work, nor to discuss the many studies that other investigators have made in order to check his findings. There are, however, three general criticisms which will be mentioned.

1. Critics have pointed out that Piaget pays too little attention to the influence of explicit teaching and training upon intellectual development. This is probably true. But the implication made that he claims that development is primarily a function of maturation is not true. He assumes that maturation of the nervous system plays a part in intellectual development, but remains agnostic on just how great this influence is. As he says, 'the maturation of the nervous system can do no more than create the conditions for a continual expansion of the field of possibilities. The realization of these possibilities demands not only the action of the physical environment (practice and acquired experience), but also the educational influences of a favourable social environment' (Inhelder and Piaget, 1964, p. 4). It is more accurate to say that Piaget is interested in *describing* the development of intelligence rather than in uncovering the causal factors which induce this development.

2. A second criticism is that Piaget has too easily generalized from small and biased samples of subjects. There is some justice in this and Piaget seems to have accepted it, for in his later work he makes

some effort to widen his sampling of subjects. It, nevertheless, underlines the need for caution in accepting his results. However, it must be added that since Piaget's works have appeared, a large number of attempts have been made to check his results, and in general Piaget's conclusions have been vindicated. What now remains to be done is to unravel through experimental methods the conditions under which children move from one stage to another.

3. Finally, his use of the concept of stage has been criticized. Obviously, any description of qualitative developmental change must rely upon such a concept. In Chapter 4 we suggested three criteria for the use of the concept: that it be integrated into a theory, that the stages be sequentially invariant and that the limits of the stages be empirically identifiable. Piaget certainly meets the first two criteria. It is the third which is the problem. Piaget himself recognizes, and documents in detail, the fact that the borderlines between stages are blurred by intermediate steps. Moreover, a child may attain a given stage in one aspect of his thinking but not in others, and of course, older children may regress in their thinking under certain conditions. However, the concept is too convenient to be ignored, though we need to remember that its usage must always be imprecise.

Further reading
H. J. Butcher, *Human Intelligence: Its Nature and Assessment*, Methuen, 1968.
J. H. Flavell, *The Developmental Psychology of Jean Piaget*, Van Nostrand, 1963.
P. Vernon, *The Structure of Human Abilities*, Methuen, 2nd edn 1961.
S. Wiseman (ed.), *Intelligence and Ability*, Penguin Books, 1967.

Chapter 19
Personality

Introduction

The term 'personality' refers to those relatively stable and enduring aspects of the individual which distinguish him from other people and, at the same time, form the basis of our predictions concerning his future behaviour. The main emphasis of this chapter will be upon what has come to be known as the 'trait and type approach' to the study of personality. Excluded from this chapter, although coming within the scope of the above definition, will be any detailed discussion of the intellectual factors which contribute to interpersonal variation; these have already been dealt with in Chapter 18. Similarly, only passing reference will be made to the various techniques of personality measurement, since these have been dealt with in Chapter 17.

The present chapter is divided into three principal parts. The first is concerned with the description of personality, or, more specifically, with discussing some of the uses that have been made of the descriptive notions of *trait* and *type*. In the second part, we shall consider the structural and organizational aspects of personality as they have been revealed by the factor analytic studies of R. B. Cattell, in the United States, and H. J. Eysenck, in Britain. In the third and final section, we shall be examining the determinants of personality structure; in particular, the relative influences of environment and heredity upon the various components of the individual personality as they have emerged from recent experimental investigations on both sides of the Atlantic.

Before turning to an account of the 'trait and type' approach to personality, two areas of controversy must be briefly mentioned.

The first concerns the justification for using dispositional terms in describing personality, and the second arises from the claim that an individual's personality is 'unique'. In order for a science of personality to be possible, two assumptions are needed. They are: (a) that an individual's actions have sufficient consistency about them for us to say that his behaviour is to some extent characteristic of him, as well as being a function of his stimulus situation; and (b) that the idiosyncratic ways in which individuals behave can be compared and contrasted along dimensions or continua which allow individual differences to be measured. These assumptions have been challenged.

Specific habits or general disposition

The American psychologist, J. B. Watson, initiated a programme of psychological investigation whose objective was to account for all behaviour in terms of stimulus–response (s–r) sequences and patterns. Since a considerable amount of American psychology was, and to a certain extent still is, rooted in this behaviourist tradition, there has emerged from the United States a view which regards personality as a composite of specific habits built up on the basis of the individual's previous interactions with his environment. Eysenck (1953) has summarized this point of view as follows,

... there are no broad general traits of personality, no general and consistent forms of conduct which, if they existed, would make for consistency of behaviour and stability of personality, but only independent and specific s–r response bonds or habits (p. 3).

At the other extreme is the belief in general dispositional tendencies, illustrated by Jung's (1928) theory of tendencies towards introversion and extraversion, which throughout life colour all of our activities regardless of the type of situation in which we may find ourselves. As with most academic debates of this nature, the truth probably lies somewhere between these two extremes. We can illustrate this, and perhaps arrive at a compromise position, by considering the interpretations that have been placed upon the results of the well-known studies by Hartshorne and May (1928, 1929). These investigations observed the behaviour of children in a number of situations designed to test characteristics such as deceit, persistence, charitability and self-control (for a fuller account see Chapter 22). When behaviour in different situations purporting to measure the same general characteristic was scored and submitted to statistical analysis, it was found that the correlations obtained, although positive, were low. The fact that the same child revealed (for example) dishonest behaviour in some situations but not in others might be taken to make the existence of general character traits unlikely; yet in the event of their total absence one would expect zero correlations among tests, or an equal number of (low) positive and negative correlations. These findings, then, suggest the compromise conclusion, that behaviour is neither entirely specific to the stimulus situation nor very largely general and independent of it. As Eysenck (1953) has pointed out: '. . . the problem ceases to be a theoretical one, and becomes instead quantitative and empirical' (p. 9).

Unique or common characteristics

The problem here can be seen most clearly by contrasting the two approaches to personality which have been labelled *idiographic* and *nomothetic*. The former stresses the individual person, the latter differences between individuals.

The idiographic orientation stems largely from the clinical study of abnormal behaviour where the individual case is clearly the main concern of the psychotherapist. But within scientific psychology, the main exponent of this viewpoint is G. W. Allport (1937). As Hall and Lindzey (1957) put it:

He [Allport] insists that in reality no two individuals ever possess exactly the same trait. Although there may be similarities in the trait structures of different individuals, there are always unique features in the way any particular trait operates for any one person. Thus all traits are individual traits – unique and applicable only to the single individual (p. 265).

Allport has insisted that even when a trait appears to be common to many individuals, there are individual differences in quality as well as in degree. For example, each person's brand of courage or loyalty is his own, different from that of other people, and operating by idiosyncratic standards. Allport therefore has called for an approach to personality which has been termed 'the psychology of the individual'. He feels that the study of common traits can be helpful only so long as the investigator does not blind himself to the fact that these concepts do not accurately represent the individual.

Allport's theoretical contribution to the study of personality, although considered reactionary and isolated from the mainstream of scientific personality investigation, has been valuable in that it has compelled others to re-evaluate the nomothetic or 'statistical' orientation. In terms of methodology, the idiographic approach means the intensive and extensive study of one person at a time. The nomothetic approach calls for the study of many individuals at a less extensive level. In the former case, a few individuals are likely to be studied with reference to many traits, where the major interest is the pattern of traits presented by each person. In the latter case, there are likely to be a large number of individuals involved, but only relatively few traits under investigation. For any trait, the main reference point will be the average trait position of the population concerned in the study.

It is important to be clear that we cannot describe any person except in contrast to others. The nomothetic approach assumes that there are numerous dimensions along which individuals can differ. Each individual will have a unique *profile* on these dimensions; that is to say, no one else will have exactly the same pattern of positions on these dimensions. What Allport appears to be claiming in addition is that each profile has properties which cannot themselves be placed upon any dimensions of comparison, for they are unique to that configuration. In making this claim Allport is giving expression to the common feeling that, although people can be compared in many ways, there is yet something irreducibly unique about each one. The controversy has arisen because it is claimed that unique properties cannot be the object of scientific study.

In his discussion of this problem, Guilford (1959) uses the terms 'personal' and 'impersonal' to correspond roughly to the idiographic and nomothetic approaches. His resolution of the problem is as follows:

... the impersonal view and the nomothetic approach belong to basic science; the personal view and the idiographic approach belong to technology. In every science, the individual case is properly regarded as merely an opportunity for making another observation. The single case belongs to history, not to science. In approaching a final goal, science aims at generalizations that apply to *classes* of phenomena, not as descriptions of particular events (p. 24).

This is the point of view adopted within the present chapter which, from henceforth, will deal exclusively with the nomothetic approach to the study of personality. That is, the communality of traits, rather than their unique aspects, will be stressed.

To offset this quantitative bias the reader is recommended to consult the numerous textbooks devoted to this topic, in particular, those by Allport (1937) and Hall and Lindzey (1957; Lindzey and Hall, 1965). The latter are especially valuable in that they present a concise and evaluative review of the major theories of personality and their experimental or clinical foundations.

The description of personality

When asked the question: 'What is so-and-so like as a person?' we usually resort, in the first place, to a description in terms of *traits* or *types*. We may say that the person is highly sociable, active, impulsive and talkative, thus describing him by reference to his salient traits; or we may simply attach a type label and call him an extravert. These two kinds of description are also relevant to the scientific study of personality; we shall first consider each in turn, and then the distinction between them.

Traits

We identify traits by observing individuals behaving *consistently* in response to a variety of environmental conditions. To identify a specific trait, we must observe a characteristic *modus operandi*, or style of behaviour, that is evident in a large number of widely differing circumstances. It is the extent to which this pattern of response occurs independently of any particular immediate stimulus configuration that defines the existence of a trait.

Carr and Kingsbury (1938) suggested that there are three related steps involved in the identification and naming of a trait. First, we observe certain *adverbial* characteristics of the individual's behaviour: we see, for instance, that he acts aggressively and persistently in his endeavours. The next step is to transfer these qualities from the action to the actor; they now come to describe the person whose actions are coloured by them. Thus, we define the reactive nature of the individual by using *adjectival* terms: we refer to him as a persistent and aggressive person. Finally, having decided that these qualities belong to the individual rather than his actions, we then abstract them and refer to these qualities as things. In other words, they become *nouns*, and we say that a person has a trait of aggression, and a trait of persistence. This process illustrates the important point that traits are essentially abstractions; they do not *necessarily* relate to any structural aspect of the individual.

How many traits, and of what kind, are required to make an adequate description of the personality? The initial difficulty is that there are so many possible trait terms. An investigation by Allport and Odbert (1936) showed that the languages of civilized peoples typically carry from 3000 to 5000 words defining traits. Obviously this is too large a number to be of use in scientific measurement. The aim in all such measurement is to have as much information as possible contained in the smallest number of measurements.

It is apparent from an inspection of a list of English trait words that there is likely to be a considerable degree of overlap between their different meanings. The likelihood is that many of these terms will be related together as manifestations of a smaller number of more fundamental underlying trait structures. The goal of the scientific investigator in this field is to identify these basic trait structures and thus account for the variation among these lesser traits or *trait-elements* in terms of a relatively few important *source traits* or *dimensions* of personality.

In general, two main methods have been used to determine which dimensions of measurement to use in personality description. Some psychologists, like Allport (1937), have selected dimensions named in everyday speech which seem, on the face of it, to be the most important personality variables. Others, however, have preferred to select their dimensions of measurement by employing the considerably more objective procedure of factor analysing the scores obtained from a large number of tests relating to the individual trait elements. The purpose of factor analysis (previously outlined in Chapter 18), in this context, is to determine which factors or dimensions provide the greatest information about the ways in which individual personalities differ. There is no guarantee that the factors arrived at by this mathematical technique will correspond directly to something which has a name in common speech. Hence the factor analyst is frequently forced to invent new names for his factors. Cattell, for instance, uses both letters and rather cumbersome coined names, such as Threctia, Surgency, Autia-praxernia, etc., to identify his factors in order to avoid the trap of attributing additional meaning by using more familiar terms. Frequently, as with some of Eysenck's work, the two methods are combined by the investigator who obtains independent and informative dimensions of measurement by factor analysis, and then rotates the axes he has obtained until they coincide with traits distinguished in common speech or with some other external criterion such as diagnostic classification.

Types

In everyday life, type descriptions of personality are characterized by the technique of picking some salient feature of the individual and then using this as a label for his total personality. Within psychology, type notions have been erected on a variety of foundations. We will consider some of these notions under three broad headings: typologies based upon physical characteristics; typologies based upon mental function; and typologies based upon experience patterns.

Typologies based upon physical characteristics. Perhaps the earliest of these constitutional typologies was the four-way classification due, initially, to Hippocrates and later used by Galen, Kant and Wundt. Individual temperaments were categorized on the basis of the relative preponderance of one or other of the four bodily humours: blood, phlegm, black and yellow bile. *Sanguine* individuals, characterized by a preponderance of blood, tended to be habitually hopeful, confident and optimistic. In antithesis to this was the *melancholic* type, characterized by an excess of black bile, who tended towards depression and ill-grounded fears. Individuals with a preponderance of phlegm, or *phlegmatic* types, tended to be sluggish and apathetic; while those with an excess of yellow bile, the *choleric* types, tended to be active and irascible. These terms have persisted in our everyday speech, and have done much to influence later typologists (see Eysenck, 1953).

However, it was not until comparatively recently that systematic attempts were made to classify physical types on the basis of controlled observation and measurement (for example, by Viola, 1909) and to relate physical type with personality type (for example, by Kretschmer, 1925). Probably the most well-known constitutional typology is that developed by Sheldon (1942), which owes much to the typology of Kretschmer but is conceptually and technically more sophisticated. Sheldon based his inquiry on the assumption that body build reflected the relative influences of the three primitive embryonic layers, the endoderm, the mesoderm and the ectoderm. Working from roughly 4000 photographs of male college students, Sheldon identified three physical types:

1. *Endomorphs*, in whom the endoderm was prominent, showed massive and highly developed viscera, and a predominance of soft roundness throughout the various regions of the body. It should be noted that this type has much in common with Kretschmer's pyknic.

2. *Mesomorphs*, in whom the mesoderm was prominent, were distinguished by the relative predominance of muscle, bone and connective tissue. These correspond roughly to Kretschmer's athletic types. The extreme mesomorph is typically broad-shouldered, slender-waisted, and with developed muscles.

3. *Ectomorphs*, in whom the ectodermal layers were prominent, were characterized by the relative predominance of linearity and fragility. These are similar to Kretschmer's asthenic or leptosomatic types. The typical ectomorph is narrow shouldered and has stringy muscles.

It is important to emphasize that these type labels were appropriate to only a few individuals who showed these physical characteristics to an extreme degree. It follows from the assumption of normality that the majority of individuals will show an intermediate degree of these three components. Thus, every individual can be described by three digits, each one representing a position on the seven-point scales of endomorphy, mesomorphy and ectomorphy. These three ratings were said to define the individual's *somatotype*.

Parallel to these three physical components, Sheldon identified three primary components of temperament: *viscerotonia*, *somatotonia* and *cerebrotonia*. Extreme viscerotonia was characterized by general bodily relaxation, love of comfort, sociability and affection. The somatotonic temperament was characterized by activity and energy, assertiveness and noisy aggressiveness, a concern with the here and now, and a tendency to meet problems with some form of action. The cerebrotonic temperament was associated with excessive restraint, inhibition of action and a withdrawal from social contact.

In 1942 Sheldon reported an investigation of the association between the somatotype, or physical type, and temperament. A correlation of $+0.79$ was found between endomorphy and viscerotonia, $+0.82$ between mesomorphy and somatotonia, and $+0.83$ between ectomorphy and cerebrotonia.

Sheldon's work is generally considered to be markedly superior to that of previous typologists in terms of its theoretical and empirical foundations. However, a number of serious criticisms have been levelled at his methodological and statistical procedures. For a detailed account of these criticisms, the reader is recommended to consult the paper by Humphreys (1957), and the relevant chapter in Hall and Lindzey's (1957) textbook.

Typologies based upon mental function. A number of psychologists have erected typologies on purely psychological foundations without going beyond these to seek connexions with physical make-up. The most influential of these psychological-type notions have been those which have focused upon the direction of interest and attention exhibited by the individual, either inwards upon the self or outwards upon the environment. Among these are the typologies of Stern, James and Rorschach, but the best known, and the only one to be considered here, is the extraversion–introversion distinction made by Jung. Complete accounts of this typology are given by Jung (1928) and Fordham (1953).

Jung's extraversion–introversion typology is based upon the notion of relatively stable collections of temperamentally determined attitudes within the individual. The Jungian introvert is the person to whom the inner, subjective world is more important than the world of external reality. Thus, he adapts himself by internalized actions, or thought constructions, rather than by overt action; he tends towards the philosophical rather than the scientific. Although the introvert must take account of external conditions, it is generally the subjective determinants which are the most decisive. In the extravert, on the other hand, the consciousness is directed outwards. To him, the external objective determinants are the more important. He adapts himself by feeling rather than thought; by action rather than fantasy. His interests are apt to be scientific rather than philosophical.

Jung further distinguished the introvert and the extravert by the main classes of neurotic disorder to which they are prone. He believed that introverts, in the case of neurotic breakdown, are predisposed to the condition of psychasthenia, what is nowadays termed 'an anxiety state' or 'reactive' depression. When the extravert is affected by a neurosis, Jung believed that he would be more likely to present the symptoms of hysteria.

The distinction between introverts and extraverts – upon which other classifications may be superimposed – has been adopted, often in somewhat different senses, by other workers; an account of different uses of the terms, the measures adopted and their interrelations has been given by Carrigan (1960). Notable among those who have adopted the terms is Eysenck, whose scheme of personality will be discussed in some detail in further sections of this chapter.

Typologies based on experience patterns. Implicit within the type concept is the notion of personality structure as being tightly organized and relatively unchanging. Following this idea of permanence and stability back in time, we logically arrive at a theory of innate determination, even when this is not made explicit within the original type system. There are a few writers, however, who have put forward type notions which are based explicitly on the effects of past experience. The most important of these, and the only one to be discussed here, is the psychoanalytic.

The theory of personality developed by Freud and his followers places considerable emphasis upon the influence of events experienced in childhood. Thus the child is thought to be 'father to the man'. The development of a 'normal' personality involves the successful negotiation of a series of developmental phases which relate to the disposition of so-called *erotogenic zones*, principally the oral, the anal and the genital zones. The psychoanalytic typology is based upon the belief that an individual may become fixated at one or other of these developmental stages, and the residual elements of this fixation manifest themselves in the adult personality and thus distinguish him as a type. Basically, three psychoanalytic types have been identified:

Oral. There are two distinct oral erotic types: the passive or 'sucking' type and the sadistic or 'biting' type. The former is the dependent, optimistic, immature individual who longs to continue within the comfortable aura of parental care and security. These characteristics are thought to result from a fixation at the nursing, sucking stage of infancy. Fixation is said to occur as a result of either excessive gratification or excessive frustration, and whether or not the character is of the 'sucking' or 'biting' type depends upon the kind of oral experience in which the child is fixated.

The basic outlook of the oral-sadistic individual is one of pessimism and the anticipation of malice. Like the oral-passive type, he feels that the world owes him a living, but unlike the passive type, he suspects that he will not get it. He is likely to be caustic and sarcastic in conversation, if not actively sadistic in his treatment of others. These characteristics are thought to stem from a frustration of nursing activity, and a libidinal fixation upon the nursing, sucking activities of infancy.

Anal. Freud (1924) noted a triad of characteristics, orderliness, parsimony and obstinacy, and designated them as making up the 'obsessional character'. On examining several cases who exhibited these qualities in the extreme, he came to the conclusion that the underlying phenomenon was the fixation of the libidinal energy (i.e. basic motivation) upon anal mechanisms. In general, it is believed that the 'anal' character develops as the result of an experience such as severe toilet training in which the child finds that he can obtain special satisfactions from the control of his bowel movements.

Phallic. If the child succeeds in negotiating the oral and anal phases, he may become fixated at the phallic stage instead of progressing to the normal 'genital' level of mature adjustment. The phallic type is characterized by narcissism and excessive ambition; he is also an exhibitionist and a braggart.

Fuller accounts of these character types have been given by Fenichel (1946). It should be pointed out that, as with other typologies, 'pure types' occur very rarely; they are extremes which are more moderately represented, and represented in 'mixtures', by most individuals. The typology is based upon clinical data; experimental investigations may be said to have yielded ambiguous support for it (Sears, 1944).

A comparison of trait and type descriptions

It has probably become clear that the distinction between trait and type is not self-evident. One difference often pointed out is that while traits are reflected in the enduring features of an *individual's* behaviour, the notion of type depends upon consistently similar features within the behaviour of a *group of individuals*. As Allport (1937) has put it: 'Unlike traits, types always have a biosocial reference. A man can be said to *have* a trait, but he cannot be said to *have* a type. Rather he fits a type' (p. 295).

It follows from such a distinction that Allport's sympathy, and indeed that of many others, has been with a trait approach. A further quotation from Allport (1937) makes clearer the objection to typologies which is involved.

Whatever the kind, a typology is always a device for exalting its author's special interest at the expense of the individuality of life which he ruthlessly dismembers. Every typology is based on the abstraction of some segment from the total personality, and the forcing of this segment to unnatural prominence. All typologies place boundaries where boundaries do not belong. They are artificial categories (p. 296).

Individuals, it is argued, cannot be forced into a limited number of type categories without remainder. The variability between people, these critics argue, is far too rich and complex to submit to the 'pigeon-holing' that is assumed to be a necessary part of any type schema. However, as Eysenck (1953) is at pains to point out, this is an incorrect assumption. The influential typologists, such as Jung, Kretschmer and Sheldon, all postulated a dimensional rather than a categorical system of personality types. The dimensional approach implies a continuous rather than discontinuous distribution of graded, quantitatively estimated variations along a continuum, the extremes of which, and only the extremes, are identified by type labels. Thus, the terms introvert and extravert, for instance, define the ends of the personality dimension of introversion–extraversion. Since the possession of extraverted or introverted qualities is assumed to follow a normal distribution within the population, the majority of individuals may be expected to occupy intermediate rather than extreme positions along this continuum. In these terms a typology is indistinguishable from a trait description which quotes extreme examples of the dimensions under consideration.

The main distinction which can be made between trait and type is one of *generality*: as a rule, the dimensions of personality employed in typologies are wider and more inclusive than those employed in trait description (although this is not always the case; consider, for example, Allport's (1937) concept of the *cardinal trait*). Eysenck's scheme of personality employs this distinction, which involves treating trait and type as complementary rather than as opposed concepts. They are distinguished only by the fact that they occupy different levels within his hierarchical scheme of personality organization. Thus, a trait is defined as a group of correlated behavioural acts or action tendencies, while a type is defined simply as a group of correlated traits. Within the format of factor analysis, these constitute workable operational definitions, relating to a specific process of measurement. This hierarchical view offers a convenient resolution to the earlier disputes between trait and type psychologists. As Eysenck (1953) says: '. . . the difference between the concepts of trait and type lies not in the continuity or lack of continuity of the hypothesized variable, nor in its form of distribution, but in the greater inclusiveness of the type concept' (p. 13). We shall be examining the inter-relationship between these two notions in the next section in which we consider the structural aspects of personality as they have emerged from factorial investigations.

The structure of personality

As mentioned in the introductory section, this part of the chapter will be devoted to a consideration of the structural models of personality developed by Cattell and Eysenck on the basis of treating empirical data by the technique of factor analysis. The reason for restricting our attention to the work of these men and their collaborators is twofold. First, both are generally regarded as the principal exponents of the quantitative and objective approach to the study of personality. Second, presenting the work of a contemporary trait psychologist (Cattell) and a contemporary typologist (Eysenck) will serve to endorse the moral of the preceding section that trait and type notions of personality are supplementary rather than conflicting.

Initially, the structural models of personality arrived at by Cattell and Eysenck will be presented separately. Afterwards, we will examine their notions comparatively and consider the main points of difference and agreement between their respective views.

Cattell's group factor theory

The most important concept within Cattell's structural model of personality is the trait. For him the trait is a 'mental structure', an inference made from observed behaviour to account for its regularity and consistency. Cattell's extensive empirical work can be regarded as a search for the definitive list of *source traits* which comprise the fundamental structures of the total personality.

The source trait is an underlying variable which largely determines the clusters of manifest or overt variables that seem, to the observer, to go together. In this respect it is closely similar to the concept of *ability* discussed in the previous chapter. These apparent clusters of observable trait elements are termed *surface* traits. They are thought to be produced by the interaction of source traits with the stimulus situation and hence are likely to be less stable and more situationally determined than the source traits themselves. In everyday life, for example, there might be a cluster of surface traits including such things as the possession of a large vocabulary, an understanding of mathematics, a knowledge of history and so on. These surface traits are likely to be a function of at least three relatively independent source traits, namely education, intelligence and a studious temperament.

Only by factor analysis, Cattell argues, can we avoid the pitfalls of falsely identifying surface traits as the basic structural components of personality. Only factor analysis allows the investigator to identify (correctly) the source traits. In a considerable number of factor analyses, using measurements derived from real life, from clinical and from objective test situations, Cattell has isolated some sixteen to twenty-one source traits, otherwise called *primary* or *group* factors. The best known of these source traits are the sixteen which go to form the basis of the Sixteen Personality Factor Questionnaire (the 16 P.F. Test). A brief description of these factors, together with their identifying names and letters, is given in Table 11.

These sixteen factors or dimensions are relatively independent or uncorrelated. Thus, up to a certain point, the position occupied by a given individual along one of these dimensions does not affect his position on any other dimension. However, since these dimensions tend to be correlated to a small extent, they can themselves be submitted to further factor analysis in the same way as the original specific behaviour measures. When this is done, second- or higher-order factors are obtained. Cattell (1965) describes their role within the total structure as follows:

These (second-order) factors are typical 'organizers of primary factors' just as primary factors are in turn organizers of specific pieces of behaviour. Naturally, these second- or higher-order factors are broader in their

Table 11
Cattell's sixteen primary factors (Cattell, 1963a)

High-score description	Factor	Low-score description
Outgoing, warmhearted, easy-going, participating (Cyclothymia)	A	*Reserved*, detached, critical, cool (Schizothymia)
More intelligent, abstract thinking, bright (Higher scholastic mental capacity)	B	*Less intelligent*, concrete thinking (Lower scholastic mental capacity)
Emotionally stable, faces reality, calm (Higher ego strength)	C	*Affected by feelings*, emotionally less stable, easily upset (Lower ego strength)
Assertive, independent, aggressive, stubborn (Dominance)	E	*Humble*, mild, obedient, conforming (Submissiveness)
Happy-go-lucky, heedless, gay, enthusiastic (Surgency)	F	*Sober*, prudent, serious, taciturn (Desurgency)
Conscientious, persevering, staid, rule-bound (Stronger superego strength)	G	*Expedient*, a law to himself, by-passes obligations (Weaker superego strength)
Venturesome, socially bold, uninhibited, spontaneous (Parmia)	H	*Shy*, restrained diffident, timid (Threctia)
Tender-minded, dependent, over-protected, sensitive (Premsia)	I	*Tough-minded*, self-reliant, realistic, no-nonsense (Harria)
Suspicious, self-opinionated, hard to fool (Protension)	L	*Trusting*, adaptable, free of jealousy, easy to get on with (Alaxia)
Imaginative, wrapped up in inner urgencies, careless of practical matters, bohemian (Autia)	M	*Practical*, careful, conventional, regulated by external realities, proper (Praxernia)
Shrewd, calculating, worldly, penetrating (Shrewdness)	N	*Forthright*, natural, artless, sentimental (Artlessness)

Table 11–*Continued*

High-score description	Factor	Low-score description
Apprehensive, worrying, depressive, troubled (Guilt proneness)	O	*Placid*, self-assured, confident, serene (Untroubled adequacy)
Experimenting, critical, liberal, analytical, free-thinking (Radicalism)	Q_1	*Conservative*, respecting established ideas, tolerant of traditional difficulties (Conservatism)
Self-sufficient, prefers own decisions, resourceful (Self-sufficiency)	Q_2	*Group-dependent*, a 'joiner' and sound follower (Group adherence)
Controlled, socially precise, self-disciplined, compulsive (High self-concept control)	Q_3	*Casual*, careless of protocol, untidy, follows own urges (Low integration)
Tense, driven, overwrought, fretful (High ergic tension)	Q_4	*Relaxed*, tranquil, torpid, unfrustrated (Low ergic tension)

influence than primary factors. They are analogues to higher executives in a hierarchy in that they do not have immediate, intimate, effect on the lowest operators but act on them indirectly only through their direct influence on the intermediate controllers (i.e. the primary factors) (p. 117).

Cattell and his collaborators have carried out further analyses of these primary factors, obtained in the first place from administering the 16 P.F. Test to normal adults. Some six second-order factors were found to be operating among the sixteen primaries, of which the two most important were labelled extraversion (exvia–invia and anxiety). The second-order anxiety factor was found, in numerous analyses, to have a negative loading on C (ego weakness) and H (shyness, timidity), and a positive loading on O (guilt proneness), L (suspiciousness), Q_3 (controlled, compulsive) and Q_4 (high ergic tension).

The exvia (extraversion) second-order factor was found to have positive loadings on A (cyclothymia), F (surgency), H (parmia, or adventurous boldness) and Q_2 (group-dependency). It was also found to have some correlation with E (dominance) and with L (freedom from paranoid suspicion). The hierarchical inter-relationships between these first- and second-order factors have been summarized diagrammatically in Figure 73.

Although second-order and even third-order factors (see Pawlik and Cattell, 1964) have been isolated, Cattell (1964) prefers to place greatest importance on the predictive value of the first-order or primary factors:

... the general statistical principle holds that one can get better prediction in regard to absolutely any criterion from using several primaries instead of a few secondaries. ... However, even apart from the statistical argument, there is the psychological argument that the primary factors which commonly cohere in a second-order factor may, in respect to particular concrete criteria, even operate in opposite directions (p. 72).

To support this statement, Cattell (1964) cites the example of the typical 16 P.F. profile obtained from leading researchers in physics and other scientific fields. In this, the four main first-order factors that comprise the second-order factor of extraversion–introversion differ in direction. Thus these scientists are low on the A and F factors, marking them off as introverts, while, at the same time, they are high on the H factor, i.e. tending towards social boldness, which suggests that they are extraverted. Cattell (1964) draws the moral from this example that 'in vocational selection one would be making a serious blunder by predicting from a single score on the composite defining the second-order introversion–extraversion factor' (p. 72).

Eysenck's dimensional theory

The contemporary British approach to the organization of abilities and traits differs from that typical of American psychologists in that it is essentially multilevel or hierarchical. As was pointed out in the previous chapter, British factor analysts, following in the tradition of Thomson, Spearman and Burt, tend to place greatest emphasis on the isolation of general or *g* factors rather than upon the group (or primary) factors favoured by Americans working in the Thurstone tradition. Thus, the variance observed in numerous tests of intel-

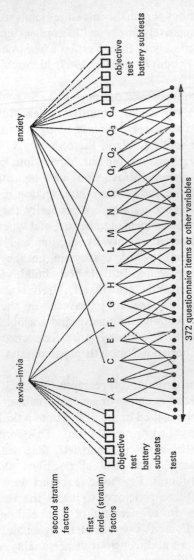

Figure 73 Diagram showing hierarchical arrangement of Cattell's first- and second-order factors. (After Cattell, 1965, p. 118)

lectual ability and various personality measures tends to be accounted for on the basis of a relatively few broad factors or dimensions. This is clearly demonstrated in both P. E. Vernon's hierarchical theory of human abilities (1961) and Eysenck's (1963) hierarchical model of personality structure.

In his first major study, carried out during the Second World War, Eysenck (1947) administered a large number of behavioural, physical and clinical measures to a total sample of approximately 10,000 normal and neurotic soldiers. When these data were submitted to factor analysis, two orthogonal, bipolar, dimensions of personality were isolated: extraversion(–introversion) and neuroticism(–stability). The isolation of the extraversion–introversion dimension was seen by Eysenck as providing support primarily for the Jungian typology but also for Kretschmer's temperamental types. Eysenckian introverts are characterized mainly by caution and unsociability. When neurotic, they tend towards dysthymia, i.e. they show symptoms of anxiety and depression. In their body build, vertical growth predominates over horizontal growth (cf. Kretschmer's asthenics, Sheldon's ectomorphs). Eysenckian extraverts, on the other hand, are characteristically outgoing, impulsive and sociable. In neurosis they show a tendency to develop hysterical conversion symptoms. In their body build, horizontal growth predominates over vertical growth.

In a subsequent programme of research, Eysenck (1952) conducted a number of studies employing normal subjects and mental hospital patients which resulted in the isolation of a third personality dimension, which he called 'psychoticism'. This seriously undermined the view, held by many psychiatrists, that neuroticism and psychoticism were simply two distinct positions along a single continuum of mental illness. Psychotic reactions were found to be sufficiently dissimilar to neurotic ones to justify the assumption that the psychotic dimension of personality was orthogonal to the neurotic dimension. Eysenck's factorial analyses thus led to the isolation of three structural dimensions of personality: extraversion, neuroticism and psychoticism.

These three dimensions of personality constitute the highest levels in Eysenck's hierarchical model of personality structure. The different

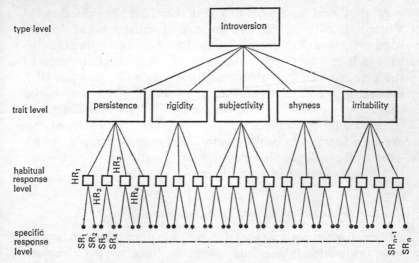

Figure 74   Eysenck's hierarchical model of personality structure as it relates to the introversion dimension. (From Eysenck, 1953, p. 13)

levels of this model as they relate, for example, to introversion have been displayed diagrammatically in Figure 74.

At the apex is the type level relating to the three dimensions of personality discussed earlier. Immediately below this comes the trait level. As we see in the diagram, one type dimension, in this case introversion, breaks down into the subordinate traits of persistence, rigidity, subjectivity, etc. Below the trait level comes the 'habitual response' level. This level relates to responses that tend to recur under similar circumstances, i.e. if a test is repeated, a similar response is given, or if a real-life situation recurs, the individual reacts in a similar fashion. This is the lowest level of organization *per se*. Roughly speaking, the amount of organization present at this level is indicated by the reliability coefficient obtained in a test–retest situation. The fourth and lowest level is that of specific responses. Eysenck (1953) describes these as 'acts such as responses to an experimental test, or to experiences in everyday life, which are observed once, and may or may not be characteristic of the individual' (p. 13).

As mentioned earlier, it is clear that within this hierarchical model the notions of trait and type are complementary rather than inconsistent terms. The question of continuity or distribution is irrelevant to the distinction between them, which is merely in terms of the level at which they occur within the personality structure. It is interesting to note that Guilford, who is principally known in this field as a group factor analyst, advocates a similar hierarchical model of personality structure (Guilford, 1959). This would suggest that despite differences in background there is some agreement on both sides of the Atlantic that this type of formulation of personality structure is a useful and workable one.

Comparing the structural models of Cattell and Eysenck

At a relatively superficial level, the most apparent difference between these two models is that, from essentially similar types of measurement, Cattell has isolated some sixteen to twenty-one factors, while Eysenck has isolated only three. However, as Anastasi (1958) points out:

That different investigators may arrive at dissimilar schemes of trait organization becomes less perplexing when we recognize that the traits identified through factor analysis are simply an expression of correlation among behavior measures. They are not underlying entities or causal factors, but *descriptive* categories. Hence, it is conceivable that different principles of classification may be applicable to the same data (p. 329).

As with the sausage machine, what emerges at the end of factor analysis depends upon what went in at the beginning and what happens to it in between. Thus the differences in the factor structures of Cattell and Eysenck are principally due to technical differences in both the type of population investigated and the type of factor analysis to which the measures were submitted. In relation to the type of population, Eysenck and his collaborators have made greater use of neurotic and pathological groups, whereas Cattell has tended to work with normal groups. Second, in determining the nature of personality structure, Cattell has used the factor-analytic technique which results in oblique or correlated factors, and Eysenck has depended more on techniques which yield orthogonal or uncorrelated factors. The first technical difference, i.e. in types of population, accounts partly for the differences in type or identity of the factors isolated, while differences in factor-analytic technique partially explain the disparity in the number of factors isolated. In fact, this apparent difference in the number of factors is primarily one of the final levels of analysis adopted by the investigator. Eysenck's two most important dimensions, extraversion and neuroticism, actually correspond both in level and in kind to the second-order factors (extraversion and anxiety) emerging from Cattell's analyses of questionnaire data.

In pointing out that the different factor structures of Cattell and Eysenck depend primarily upon technical rather than upon substantive differences, it is important that we do not gloss over the very real differences in the approach of these two investigators that are reflected in these different technical preferences. As we noted earlier Cattell bases his structural model on the trait level of group- or first-order factors because he believes that they improve prediction to most real-life criteria. Eysenck, on the other hand, prefers to deal in second-order factors, at the type level, because he believes that while first-order factors may provide a better prediction to concrete criteria, higher-order factors contribute more to the theory of personality structure.

This divergence of approach is also reflected in the type of measuring device that has been developed by these two investigators. Cattell has developed, among others, the 16 P.F. Test which measures personality along sixteen different source traits; while Eysenck and his collaborators have developed the Maudsley Personality Inventory (M.P.I.), and later the Eysenck Personality Inventory (E.P.I.), which measure personality differences along the two principal dimensions of neuroticism and extraversion. The fact that both tests appear to be measuring the same things will be discussed at a later point in this section.

Turning to the points of similarity between Cattell and Eysenck, it is clear that both are agreed that whatever differences exist between them, they are little more than family squabbles compared to the extent to which they are in accord with each other (see Cattell, 1964; Eysenck, 1961). It is these points of agreement that need to be stressed in a test of this nature, since they represent small oases of achievement in the fairly barren desert of personality research.

Both Cattell and Eysenck share the 'reasoned conviction' that the only valid theory of personality is one which begins with, and is based upon, the use of sophisticated multivariate factorial methods to map the salient features of personality structure. Both emphatically reject any approach that begins with 'armchair theorizing'. They both believe that 'a body of clinical theory is now arising *directly* from these [their] experiments which has a greater future than concepts borrowed from the decaying structure of psychoanalysis' (Cattell, 1964, p. 84).

At a more tangible level, there is, as we have seen, a convergence of empirical findings, definitions and measurement on such factors as neuroticism, anxiety and extraversion. It is in this latter area, of the second-order factor of extraversion–introversion, that this convergence is most marked. The fact that the extraversion–introversion concepts of Eysenck and Cattell are in close agreement is indicated by the fact that the 'extraversion' scale of the M.P.I., and the extraversion score obtained from the appropriate first-order factor complex on the 16 P.F. Test (the I.P.A.T. extraversion scale) correlate together in the region of 0·70. When the error implicit in this questionnaire type of measurement is taken into account, this order of correlation clearly indicates the possibility of complete identity between these two factors.

The determinants of personality

The personality scales developed by Cattell and Eysenck are, like all such scales, phenotypic instruments. They serve a descriptive function, but they do not in themselves offer any explanation concerning causality. Having considered the means whereby we can describe the unique personality in terms of its relative position along a number of structural dimensions or factors, we now turn to the problem of discovering what it is that determines an individual's particular location in factor space.

Personality is a complex function of the interaction of genotypic and environmental factors. Both Cattell and Eysenck have sought to differentiate the influence of these two kinds of determinant. In Chapter 3, the use of twins in genetic studies was discussed, and the results were reported of experiments by Eysenck and others, in which twins were used to establish that genetic differences are associated with differences in extraversion and neuroticism. Brief mention was also made of Cattell's more general approach to the problem through what he calls Multiple Abstract Variance Analysis, or M.A.V.A. for short. In this section we shall give some further detail of Cattell's study of the genetic influences upon personality, together with an account of another study in which the effects of cultural influences were demonstrated. This will be followed by an exposition of Eysenck's theory of the biological determinants of personality. What Eysenck is doing is trying to locate those physiological factors which intervene between the primary gene effect on the one hand and overt behaviour on the other (see Chapter 3).

Cattell's investigations into the formation of personality by heredity and environment

Cattell (1965) describes the multiple analysis of variance technique as follows:

The M.A.V.A. method tells us *how much* of the environmental influence on a trait is typically due to differences in treatment within the family, and how much to social differences between families. Similarly, it tells us the typical magnitude of the hereditary differences within families and between families (p. 36).

Using this technique, Cattell, Blewett and Beloff (1955) obtained scores from a large number of children of varied hereditary and environmental similarity (i.e. identical twins, fraternal twins, siblings reared together, unrelated children reared together and children randomly selected from the general population) on twelve personality factors which earlier research (see Cattell and Beloff, 1953) had established as significant. The main findings of this study are summarized below:

1. In five factors (tender-mindedness, general neuroticism, surgency–desurgency, will control and somatic anxiety) environmental factors appear to play the dominant role. In the case of two of

these factors (general neuroticism and somatic anxiety), however, hereditary influences appear to be quite important in determining between-family differences, whereas the within-family differences seem to be largely controlled by environmental influences.

2. Four factors (energetic conformity, dominance, socialized morale and impatient dominance) seem to be equally influenced by both heredity and environment. Although, as above, heredity is more important in determining differences between-families than within-families.

3. In three factors (cyclothymia–schizothymia, adventurous cyclothymia versus submissiveness and general intelligence) the role of hereditary factors is clearly the most important.

The second study that we shall consider concerns the influence of differing cultural environments (i.e. the American and the British) upon the second-order personality dimensions of extraversion and anxiety. Cattell and Warburton (1961) compared the scores of 604 American university students with those obtained from a group of 112 British undergraduates, and ninety-two British students from a college of advanced technology (as it then was) on the first- and second-order dimensions of the 16 P.F. Test. They found that the forms of the second-order anxiety and extraversion factor patterns were sufficiently similar to justify using the same concepts – anxiety and extraversion – in relation to both American and British students. But there were a number of interesting 'species' differences within this common genus. The most obvious was that American university students showed a significantly higher level of anxiety than either of the two British student groups and they were also significantly more extraverted than the British undergraduate group. On examining the differences in structure among the first-order factors the authors hypothesized that the higher level of anxiety among the American university students was the result of a greater ergic tension and a greater guilt proneness. The greater degree of extraversion shown by the Americans appeared to be primarily due to the fact that they showed a higher level of surgency than the British students.

Apart from these differences in anxiety and extraversion, the British group, as a whole, showed a significantly higher ego strength

(C factor) and self-sentiment development (Q_3 factor), while the American group showed a higher superego development, in terms of both guilt proneness (O factor) and the strength of the learned sociomoral pattern (G factor). This difference, the authors suggested, may have been due to the greater development of a rationalist moral outlook in Britain and a more fundamentalist religious moral outlook in America. A British education stresses the polish of a gentleman, while an American education, the authors argued, is strongly influenced by the 'rigid convictions which the society of saints planted in New England'.

Finally there were also indications that British undergraduates were, in terms of second-order factors, more emotionally sensitive and more radical than American students. Thus we can summarize the important differences between the two cultural groups by stating that British students were less anxious, more introverted, more sensitive and more radical; the American students were more anxious, more extraverted, less sensitive and more conservative.

Although these two studies represent only a small part of Cattell's total experimental onslaught on the problems of personality, they serve to illustrate the breadth and the technical sophistication of his work.

Eysenck's biological determinants of personality

The greater part of Eysenck's work within the last decade has been concerned with developing and testing causal theories that serve to explain those relationships between the descriptive elements of personality which were revealed in his earlier dimensional studies.

Characteristic individual differences in behaviour are seen to derive from inherited determinants operating within the basic neural structures of the body. An individual's position along the neuroticism dimension is thought to depend upon the relative lability or excitability of the autonomic nervous system. Position along the extraversion dimension, however, is thought to be based upon characteristic properties of the central nervous system, i.e. the balance between excitatory and inhibitory processes within the cortex. Since the greater part of Eysenck's recent theorizing has been concerned with the determinants of extraversion–introversion, and since this dimension was seen, in the preceding section, to represent the point of greatest descriptive agreement between Eysenck and Cattell, we will restrict ourselves, in the remainder of this section, to presenting Eysenck's cortical inhibition theory of extraversion.

The neural aspects of this theory have their origin in the postulation by learning theorists, principally Pavlov and Hull, of the importance of excitatory and inhibitory potentials in accounting for a large number of laboratory phenomena. Excitation is the 'connexion-forming activity' (see Eysenck, 1959a) involved in the transmission of neural impulses between different regions of the cortex, while inhibition is a fatigue-like process which develops as a consequence of excitation, and acts to impede the further passage of the excitatory neural impulses. Within this conception, performance is seen as the end-product of an 'interplay between excitation and inhibition, being proportional to the total amount of excitatory potential *minus* the total amount of inhibitory potential' (Eysenck, 1959a, p. 137).

The link connecting the notions of excitation and inhibition, and the personality dimension of extraversion–introversion, is provided by Jung's observation that neurotic extraverts show symptoms of hysteria, while neurotic introverts tend to present symptoms of a dysthymic nature (i.e. psychasthenia). This ties in with Pavlov's observation that the hysteric patient shows symptoms analogous to the behaviour patterns of his *inhibitory* type of dog (i.e. those animals which were hard to condition and quick to extinguish, a condition which Pavlov postulated was characterized by excessive cortical inhibition). Pavlov also noticed that the dysthymic patient shows symptoms similar to the behaviour patterns he observed in dogs characterized by a predominance of cortical excitation (i.e. easy to condition, slow to extinguish). These two sets of observations, together with their empirical verification by Eysenck and his colleagues (see Eysenck, 1953), form the basis of Eysenck's 'typological postulate'. This is stated as follows:

1. Whenever any stimulus–response connexion is made in an organism (excitation), there also occurs simultaneously a reaction in the nervous

structures mediating this connexion which opposes its recurrence (reactive inhibition).

2. Human beings differ with respect to the speed with which reactive inhibition is produced, the strength of the reactive inhibition and the speed with which it is dissipated. The differences themselves are properties of the physical structures involved in the evocation of responses.

3. Individuals in whom reactive inhibition is generated quickly, and in whom it is dissipated slowly, are predisposed to develop extraverted patterns of behaviour (Eysenck, 1955).

Eysenck's total cortical inhibition theory, linking the constructs of excitation and inhibition with the behaviour patterns relating to introversion and extraversion, is shown in diagrammatic form in Figure 75.

It can be seen from this diagram that Eysenck's theory exists at four different levels. The first, at the bottom, is the neural level which is assumed to be constitutionally determined. As we have seen from the 'typological postulate', a particular person may be predisposed to develop strong excitatory and weak inhibitory potentials (introvert), or he may develop weak excitatory and strong inhibitory potentials (extravert). This, then, is the theoretical construct level, L_1. From this one can predict to the second level of observable laboratory behaviour, L_2. On the basis of the typological postulate, extraverts should condition less well, and extinguish more rapidly, show greater reminiscence and figural after-effects, report shorter-motion after-effects, and perform less efficiently on vigilance tasks (i.e. tasks involving the detection of weak signals at infrequent and irregular intervals). For an account of the arguments underlying these predictions, and a summary of their experimental verification, the reader is recommended to consult Eysenck's book, *The Dynamics of Anxiety and Hysteria* (Eysenck, 1957).

The relationship between L_2 and L_3, that is between observable experimental phenomena and observable behavioural phenomena, is a complex one, and one that is crucial to the total theoretical structure. Primarily, this linkage is based on the assumption that the process of early socialization is mediated by Pavlovian or 'Type I' conditioning. If introverts are easy to condition by virtue of their high excitatory and low inhibitory cortical potentials, they will

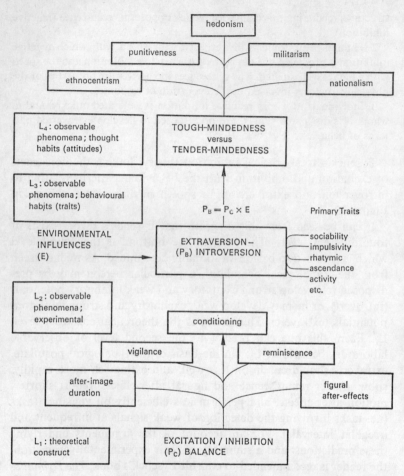

Figure 75   Eysenck's diagrammatic representation of his theory of personality. (From Eysenck, 1963, p. 1033)

respond more readily to socialization practices in childhood to the extent of becoming oversocialized. The introvert is the person who has learned the lessons of socialization too well, so that he tends to prefer thought to action, and turns inwards for his satisfactions. The converse applies to the extravert, who by virtue of his low excitatory and high inhibitory potential has only inadequately absorbed the lessons of socialization. As a result he prefers the immediate satisfaction of his impulses through action rather than thought. At this level, therefore, differences in cortical make-up express themselves in dissimilar behaviour patterns. It is important to note that the logical link between L_2 and L_3 is provided by the environmental process of socialization.

Thus, the third level, L_3, represents traits or behavioural habits of the sort usually called 'personality'. Variations in sociability, impulsiveness, activity and so on, can be sampled by scores obtained from the extraversion scale of the M.P.I.

At the fourth level, L_4, are attitudes or habits of thought: tough-mindedness versus tender-mindedness, punitiveness, ethnocentrism, etc. These are more environmentally determined than any of the previous three levels. It will be noted that as one moves from L_1 to L_4, one encounters increasing environmental modifications of the original neural determinants.

Eysenck's recent work has been increasingly diversified. He has explored the implications of his cortical inhibition theory in relation to drugs, behaviour therapy, smoking habits, political beliefs. There is not space to consider these ramifications in the present chapter. In recent years an enormous number of experimental reports have appeared which stem either directly or indirectly from Eysenck's theoretical and experimental contributions to the study of personality. While the volume of related work does not necessarily reflect on the accuracy or truth of these contributions, it certainly testifies to their considerable influence upon other researchers.

Further reading
G. W. Allport, *Pattern and Growth in Personality*, Holt, Rinehart & Winston, 1961.
R. B. Cattell, *The Scientific Analysis of Personality*, Penguin Books, 1965.
H. J. Eysenck, *The Structure of Human Personality*, Methuen, 2nd edn 1960.
C. S. Hall and G. Lindzey, *Theories of Personality*, Wiley, 1957.
R. S. Lazarus and E. M. Opton (eds.), *Personality*, Penguin Books, 1967.

Chapter 20
Normality and Abnormality

'Normality' is a very common word in psychological literature and discourse. The layman is likely, when faced with any action by another person which is not part of his own usual repertoire of behaviour, or which he dislikes or disapproves of, to label it as 'abnormal'. Psychology is not well served by such subjective and ill-defined usages. Nevertheless, the distinction between 'normal' and 'abnormal', or one like it, has often to be made in practice. In the present chapter we are concerned with the distinction as it applies in the field of mental health, although the issues raised have much wider implications. In this context, 'abnormal' is more or less equivalent to 'mentally ill'; and therefore to classify someone as abnormal is to say he needs treatment. The problem at issue here is to decide the criteria we are to use in making this classification.

Within the field of psychology, and of its related discipline, psychiatry, two main attempts to give adequate meaning to the word 'normal' may be distinguished. The first of these is an extension of the lay word 'usual' and is, in essence, based on a statistical approach. This is perfectly legitimate where samples of the behaviour in question are large and where some kind of statistically normal distribution for the characteristic has been shown. Here the investigator or clinician is entitled, arbitrarily, to say in effect: 'Any behaviour which falls more than, say, one standard deviation from the mean of my samples of this behaviour I will regard as "abnormal".' An example is the definition of mental subnormality. Since the statistical distribution of I.Q.s is known, it is convenient to define as 'mentally subnormal' those whose I.Q.s fall below a certain point (usually 70). It is essentially an operational procedure and, within its intrinsic limits, legitimate. But it is seldom used in practice for, first, the behaviour of the human race is not well documented enough for adequate statistics to be computed; second, it is very difficult to limit specific acts for study – compound interactions of areas of behaviour are the rule; third, any type of behaviour may not be normally distributed in a population – there may not be a graded series of people, with the particular action varying in intensity or frequency through all of them. The question may simply be of a 'yes' or 'no' kind – 'Does the person do this or does he not?' Fourth, though it may have value for research purposes, it is too inflexible a basis for making the decision to give someone treatment.

Lee (1961), investigating a syndrome of screaming among the Zulu in which the victim might yelp for hours, days or even weeks, found from two large random samples (416 and 200 women respectively), that in each case almost 50 per cent of the sample reported a history of such screaming. Now here we have behaviour that is, by Western standards, grossly abnormal. But among the Zulu women it was as usual to be a screamer as not to exhibit this behaviour. Here we have a bimodal distribution and conclusions based upon a hypothetical normal curve of distribution for the screaming would be valueless. Similarly, in the same investigation it emerged that some 30 per cent of Zulu women suffered visual and auditory hallucinations of 'angels', 'babies', 'little short hairy men', etc. In the West this would be regarded as grossly abnormal. Yet few of these women showed any other signs of mental disorder and, within the limits of their culture, their hallucinations were reasonably legitimate.

So we must have recourse to our second main type of definition based upon qualitative distinctions. These are usually couched in terms of 'health' or 'efficiency' as opposed to 'sickness', 'pathology' or 'inefficiency'. We are often speaking, here, of some kind of 'ideal' normality, namely perfect functioning by the person, though, if we conceive, in ordinary lay language, the idea of a 'normally' healthy person we do not, necessarily, think of him as continually possessing perfect health. Here, too, quantitative criteria enter: for example, a person's efficiency or happiness is apt to be judged against the imagined average of these qualities among his peers. Essentially, however, this type of concept is probably most readily exemplified in medical ideas of health and disease. A person is gravely ill ('in a very abnormal state of health') when death is likely to supervene if he does not receive treatment. Although this judgement is based on the past histories and prognoses of many cases of a similar nature, there is also here a qualitative aspect, and the patient's own pattern of signs and symptoms, unique to himself, may influence the diagnosis. Now medicine has this distinctive base-line of possible death to work against in the assessment of clinical abnormality. Very few people, however, die as the direct result of psychological disturbance, and so we are forced to look for other criteria bearing on the human condition and these are not nearly as clear-cut or easy to establish. To cite Jahoda (1958):

At the present state of our knowledge, mental disease in many cases cannot be inferred from physiological changes in the functioning of the organism. When psychiatrists agree among themselves that they are dealing with a mentally sick person, they use as a basis for inference highly complex behavior patterns whose physiological correlates are usually not known (pp. 10–11).

From the qualitative point of view, the terms 'normal' and 'abnormal' are evaluative in connotation and, as we have suggested, their application must take account of the cultural context. Psychiatrists, in assessing whether a potential patient is abnormal, are applying those qualitative criteria which are generally thought relevant in their society.

Let us, then, critically consider some of the most commonly used 'qualitative' criteria for normality; some of the 'highly complex behaviour patterns' mentioned above. These are (not necessarily in order of usefulness or importance): happiness, efficiency, lack of anxiety, lack of guilt, maturity, adjustment (often the ability to fit into the *mores* of a society), self-fulfilment, autonomy (often associated with self-fulfilment), self-confidence, adaptability, the ability to establish adequate emotional bonds with others – 'love', and contact with reality.

As will become clear, there is considerable overlap among these criteria; moreover, while they are not ostensibly based on a statistical norm, statistical assumptions are apt to permeate their use.

In addition to these criteria for normality, a commonly used mark of identification for abnormality is the simple fact of the person in question being under psychiatric treatment. It is probably as well, before returning to the indicators above, to deal with the deficiencies of this last type of classification first. Any findings based on the study of, say, comparative rates in different populations are likely to be invalid, in that such factors operate as the number of psychiatrists in an area, the availability of in-patient care (often hospitalization is the criterion) or even the presence of an idiosyncratic psychiatrist! Essentially, this kind of classification is circular and begs the questions of whether all inmates of mental hospitals should be there or whether there are many others, equally abnormal, in the unscreened population that have not come to the notice of the psychologist or psychiatrist.

Happiness

This criterion is normally based upon the subjective report of the person himself, although a marked appearance of unhappiness with or without verbal report may also encourage the diagnosis of 'abnormality'. Generally speaking, there is a high correlation between subjective feelings of unhappiness and other evidence of mental disorder; unhappiness is often the presenting symptom, and the gravity of the disorder is to a large extent assessed in terms of the unhappiness it causes in the sufferer.

However, there are clear limitations to the usefulness of this criterion. It is characteristic of certain mental disorders that the patient may report a personal sense of well-being or contentment with his lot which seems, at any rate to the outside observer, to be entirely unjustified by the patient's state and circumstances. Examples of such disorders are *cyclothymia*, which is characterized by fluctuations in mood between the extremes of profound depression and manic gaiety, and the hysterical symptom termed *la belle indifférence* in which adverse circumstances are not accompanied by what most people would regard as appropriate affect. Further, as Ernest Jones (1948) has pointed out:

With the milder forms of cyclothymia we may often make the interesting observation that the patient in his depressed mood has a vivid sense of now being more normal, of perceiving life as it really is, and of recognizing that in his gayer mood he was really being influenced by various illusions that distorted his perceptions of reality (p. 205).

It is clear that, in using happiness as a criterion, consideration of the patient's actual circumstances cannot be neglected; unhappiness is often a necessary and acceptable emotional response – for example, in justifiable grief and sympathy for others. But it is still a useful criterion in many situations, particularly so as the emotional state is common to all men – the subjective unhappiness of a Bushman is comparable with that of an Eskimo or with that of an American.

Efficiency

Maher (1966) is concerned with a basic meaning of the term:

Efficiency, when applied to a machine, is a function of the amount of work done by the machine in relation to the energy put into it. Depending upon the design of the machine, more or less energy is lost in non-productive effort, e.g. in overcoming friction, etc. Thus efficiency is also an inverse function of the amount of energy wasted by the system. Biological systems might be assessed for efficiency in terms of the amount of effort expended by the system to achieve a given goal or end product. Such assessment requires, of course, that we know what the intended goal is (p. 11).

In this last sentence lies the rub. Here either behavioural criteria *or* the degree to which the person considers himself efficient may be used, and, indeed, these may often clash. Different levels of judgement present themselves. The successful ('efficient') business executive who manages his work with great outward efficiency may be grossly inefficient at more inward levels and be suffering from such ills as obsessional neurosis, gastric ulcers, or hypertension, and may be very unhappy. The central difficulty in all assessment of normality is the fact that the clinical psychologist is always judging behaviour from the *outside*; he cannot step into the skin of his patient and make an adequate statement of the true 'intended goal' of any behaviour. Even the patient may be unaware of his true motives, but if we make the imaginative step into his inner world, all his behaviour is, in one sense, consistent, and all of it an attempt at maximum efficiency in a highly complex situation, even though to the outside judge it appears grossly inefficient and thus pathological. Again, in a stress situation the increased activity of the sympathetic division of the autonomic nervous system, although biologically useful to man both now and throughout his evolution as an alerting, arousing device, may, through hyperactivity, lead to physiological deterioration of a permanent nature (Alexander, 1950; Wolf and Wolff, 1942). One system, whether physiological or psychological, is apt to be efficient at the expense of another. If man were a simple machine our problem would be easier.

Within the constructs of depth psychology, the idea of efficiency coincides fairly closely with the Freudian idea of ego-strength. Briefly, Freud's model of human functioning is hydraulic in type. Each person is equipped with a reservoir of a relatively fixed amount of energy, and in a 'wasteful' system too much of this energy is devoted by the ego to coping with internal friction and not enough to its central tasks of securing instinctual gratification while maintaining contact with reality.

One way in which the concept of efficiency can be more rigorously used is by comparing the present performance of the subject, *in a stated and demarcated area of behaviour*, with his performance on previous occasions. In this way deterioration, whether physical or mental, may be measured fairly accurately within strict limits. Such deterioration may be rapid and temporary, as under conditions of experimental sensory deprivation, or long drawn out and permanent, as in the process of ageing. Here it is feasible to say that the subject *judged by his own past standards* is better or worse in some capacity than he used to be. In practice, a great difficulty arises here in that records of previous performance are often lacking or, if present, fragmentary.

Lack of anxiety

Anxiety is probably the chief common component of a wide range of mental disorders, particularly the neuroses, and is a useful criterion of mental malfunction in that it is usually accompanied by certain well-marked physical signs. These include undue sweating of the hands and feet, pre-cordial pain and vasomotor disturbances. The skin resistance response (see Chapter 7) is an example of a physiological measure that may show changes concomitant with feelings of anxiety. Furthermore, the cardiovascular system shows heightened tone and lability.

Anxiety has been both compared with and contrasted to fear. Both are reactions to 'danger' situations, but in the case of fear the response is to the immediate threat; in anxiety the state is essentially anticipatory in nature, an attempt to cope with the future, however ineffectively. Also, fear is the more likely to refer to some specific object or situation, whereas anxiety may, as Freud claimed, be 'free-floating': the sufferer may be unaware of the cause of his anxiety which may attach itself to any objects that have the suitable character of subjective harmfulness. Not all anxiety is free-floating, however, and much anxiety is relatively justified and legitimate – for example, examination anxiety in students. Anxiety has been described as 'fear spread thin', and this again emphasizes its more diffuse nature.

Fear and anxiety may also be distinguished at the level of physiological function. Wolf and Wolff (1942) investigated human gastric functioning by studying the reactions induced in the stomach mucosa of a subject, part of whose gastric system was exposed through a permanent gastric fistula. Records of stomach contractions and chemical and colour changes were kept, and correlated with the subject's moods and preoccupations. They conclude: 'Emotions such as fear and sadness, which involved a feeling of withdrawal, were accompanied by pallor of the gastric mucosa and by inhibition of acid secretion and contractions. . . . Emotional conflict involving anxiety, hostility and resentment was accompanied by accelerated acid secretion, hypermotility, hyperemia and engorgement of the gastric mucosa' (p. 675).

Of all animals man is the most prone to anxiety because of his greater capacity to anticipate events. The anxiety which inevitably accompanies this capacity is part of everyday life, and people would be handicapped without it. Jahoda (1958) cites Janis (1958) in stating: 'Not only does the mentally healthy person tolerate anxiety without disintegration, but, he suggests (at least by implication), the healthy person must be able to produce and experience anticipatory anxiety in order to cope better with subsequent danger' (pp. 42–3).

It seems probable that anxiety is related to human performance (or efficiency) in very much the same way that Gray (1964) has described when plotting arousal level against performance: both very weak and very intense anxiety are associated with poor performance. Only when anxiety is too severe (judged by disruption of performance, and here we have the efficiency criterion appearing again), or lacking, is the person to be considered as abnormal. So that, probably, the criterion is best expressed as *relative freedom from anxiety*. But here, too, we face the difficulty of assessing the word 'relative' and we are forced back to our original statistical considerations and difficulties.

Since pathological anxiety is a major cause of human misery, the anxiety and happiness criteria necessarily overlap and, taken together, the two form a very useful multiple criterion for the differentiation of normal from abnormal (except in certain disorders). Also, the physical components of anxiety states are found to be universal and this fact enables us to bridge the pitfalls of cultural relativism. What differs between cultures is not anxiety, whose physiological manifestations are everywhere very much the same, but the stimuli which give rise to anxiety and to anxious behaviour.

Lack of guilt

As Ernest Jones (1948), from the standpoint of psychoanalysis, has pointed out: 'Guilt is a shorthand expression for unconscious feelings of guiltiness that give rise to the need for self-punishment' (p. 213). But here we are in the realms of depth psychology and have the great difficulty of trying to assess unconscious factors in the personality of the subject. Without recourse to the beliefs and methods of psychoanalysis this is virtually impossible to do, if then. Conscious guilt, however, is another matter; it can be assessed from the subject's own statements, and, in common-sense terms, we have little doubt that it frequently is the cause of great unhappiness.

The psychological study of guilt will be dealt with in some detail in Chapter 22. In that chapter we shall examine the two main definitions of guilt that have been advanced (in terms of self-punishment and anxiety respectively), the operations devised for measuring it, and its correlates and antecedents. The point here is that people vary widely in the frequency and intensity of their guilt feelings. At one extreme are those whose feelings of guilt are far in excess of what appears reasonable in the light of their actual transgression and who are thereby both unhappy and crippled in their efforts to adjust efficiently to the demands of work and social life. Such people are usually judged abnormal and in need of treatment. Equally abnormal and in need of treatment are those who appear incapable of guilt responses. One of the distinguishing features of the *psychopath* is his inability to express or feel 'adequate guilt' for his antisocial behaviour. This may well be linked with other common attributes of psychopaths; their inability to establish adequate emotional ties with other people, and their relative inability to envisage the future consequences of their present actions. To cite Maher (1966):

Turning for the moment from the questions of learning differences between psychopaths and other individuals, we may consider the idea that the seeming inability of the former to adapt their behavior to its probable future consequences reflects some difficulty in behaving in terms of the future at all. Thus the problem may be not only that the patient does not respond to the threat of punishment, but that he does not respond to *future* consequences of any kind – preferring immediate gratifications to future gratifications (p. 221).

The relevance of this formulation to the problems of both guilt and shame is obvious and delinquents have been shown, experimentally, to have poor time judgement and shorter future 'time perspectives' (Siegman, 1961).

However, in calling these extremes abnormal, we cannot ignore cultural differences. Benedict (1935) and Hsu (1949) discriminate between guilt and shame cultures. The former are those which, in order to maintain social stability, rely heavily upon developing internalized controls in people, so that they blame themselves when they transgress, whether they are found out or not. In a shame culture, any person breaking the rules would not suffer discomfort unless his transgression were public knowledge. Social control is achieved by developing in people a strong motivation to do what others expect them to do and an associated anxiety over being found to have deviated from these expectations. But it is possible that in *all* cultures individuals may be different in their own 'guilt' and 'shame' components. This view is essentially similar to that of Riesman (1950), who uses the terms 'inner-directed' and 'outer-directed' to describe the mainsprings of American behaviour. The 'inner-directed' person relies on his own built-in standards as his guide – the presumption being that these have been incorporated within him during the early formative years of his life. He will be 'lonely' and rather specifically anxious. The 'outer-directed' person will, on the other hand, pay much greater attention to the standards of his immediate community and will thus be liable to more diffuse anxiety. Riesman's essentially anecdotal account is based on acute social observation and more controlled efforts to validate his views, by psychologists, might prove very valuable.

Finally, the close overlap between guilt and anxiety, adjustment, self-fulfilment, autonomy and adaptability as criteria for mental health must be emphasized. It is very doubtful whether guilt can stand on its own as a usable criterion for our purposes.

Maturity

Frequently, 'immature behaviour' will be stigmatized as 'abnormal'. And so, sometimes, it should be; but immaturity can be considered in several ways:

1. Quantitatively (essentially statistically), and here the judgement is made against the typical behaviour of people of the same chronological age as the subject or, quite often and most erroneously, comparison is made with the customary behaviour of the clinicians' own age group.

2. Qualitatively, in terms of the subject's own past performance, using such subcriteria as disorganization, ineffectiveness or lack of constructiveness.

3. Against some mythical and ideal 'norm', in the mind of the clinician, for 'mature behaviour'.

With all these, the same difficulties apply that we have already discussed under other similar categories. It is still as impossible to enter the inner world of the person. But a useful example of a definable kind of immature behaviour is provided by the classic experiment by Barker, Dembo and Lewin (1943).

In children, constructiveness of play was found to correlate highly with chronological age and a 'play age' scale, analogous to 'mental age' scales, was constructed. Thirty pre-school children were then put through the following procedure. Each child was allowed to play alone with some toys for half an hour. The next day he was returned to the same room, but on this occasion a far more interesting set of toys was placed at the other end of the room. He was allowed to play with these for a quarter of an hour and then, without explanation, was returned to the original toys of the day before and left to play with these for thirty minutes. On his leaving the better toys they were shut off from him by a locked open-mesh wire screen. His play was observed throughout the whole procedure.

Over all (though this and later studies showed wide individual differences between the children) the result was a deterioration in the 'standard' of the children's play and a considerable display of aggression, the average decrement being 17·3 months of 'play age'. The childrens' ages varied from twenty-eight to sixty-one months so that the mean loss, contributed to mostly, of course, by the older children, was proportionately considerable. Here we have an interesting example of immature behaviour induced in the laboratory, the whole process probably best described by the word 'primitivation' ('regression' has similar but much more specific meaning – see below), with the immaturity brought on by a very frustrating situation.

The terms 'regression' and 'frustration' require further explanation.

Regression

In the Freudian canon, this is shown by the tendency of the person to return to earlier modes of gratification (pleasurable and thus, within Freud's definition, sexual) which were appropriate at an infantile stage of development. Thus, excessive dependence and immaturity in the adult (the 'sucking type' – see Chapter 19) would be a sign of an 'abnormal' regression to the oral stage of psychosexual development, shortly after birth, when pleasure was gained from the contact of the mouth with the breast of the mother. Like so many of Freud's insights this hypothesized sequence of events is not, except in remote experimental analogues, readily testable in the laboratory; but it seems likely that the adult, foiled in the present, may act in an immature fashion reminiscent of his childhood behaviour.

Frustration

Here we have a more easily manipulable condition and Rosenzweig (1944) has probably done more than anyone to explore it within the field of human psychology. Briefly, he defines frustration as occurring when an organism meets a more or less insurmountable obstacle in its route to the satisfaction of any need. Aggression will often result and a human being, faced with such an obstacle, may blame himself (intropunitive response), others (extrapunitive response) or no one (impunitive response – an attempt being made to gloss over the harmful aspects of the situation). Biologically, all these modes of response are adjustive in aim but, judged from the outside, they *can* be inefficient and may often appear regressive in character.

But frustration is not an unmixed evil and much human learning is dependent upon its presence – the individual indulges in trial-and-error behaviour to secure his ends and optimally a balance should be struck between persistence and variation in such behaviour. Too long a persistence with some unsuccessful strategy would imply pathological rigidity while the reverse would indicate too great a degree of lability or even disorganization of behaviour. This leads us to the concept of 'frustration tolerance', the absence of which is often taken as an indicator of immaturity. The younger the child the stronger its demands for the immediate gratification of all its wants; the adult should be able to delay his responses for a longer period and withstand frustration without psychological disorganization – shown in useless modes of reaction. The discussion here has only glanced at the topic of frustration; for a very adequate discussion Rosenzweig (1944) should be consulted.

It will be seen that immaturity overlaps with the efficiency criterion but has its own distinct nature. Used within the context of the individual's own performances, over time it can be a useful criterion of normality.

Adjustment, adaptability, autonomy, self-fulfilment, self-confidence

Hush little sibling, don't you cry
You'll be adjusted by and by.

This quotation is from a satirical song of the 1950s, and has implications for the relationship between the individual and his environment, particularly his social environment. The criteria above have been grouped as they interact and overlap, in both meaning and application, to such an extent that to attempt to write of them separately would be nugatory. All of them relate to the person's relationship, in his acts, to the wider society of which he is a member.

Adjustment is often taken as a fitting in with society, not breaking its laws, not overstepping the bounds of customary behaviour nor setting oneself up against the ideals of one's group. Occasionally the word adaptability will be loosely used to convey an identical meaning, but there is another usage of this latter term which is very different, relating to the individual's capacity to solve *new* problems in his life, showing a pertinent flexibility.

This latter aspect brings adaptability very close to the next criterion, autonomy, which normally embraces the capacity for independent action such as the maturity involved in being relatively independent of parental bonds built up in childhood. Self-confidence is apt to be the subjective aspect or 'compound result' of many of these qualities, and is often linked with the efficiency criterion and with the idea of self-fulfilment. This may not be so – a person may be, outwardly, very successful and still feel himself inadequate. Again, as with happiness, the person may be in a state of euphoria, out of contact with reality (see reality criterion below), and very confident without adequate justification.

Let us deal with *adjustment* and *adaptability* first. Adaptation, both by the individual and his group, is essential biologically, and group behaviour will change with changing circumstances. But no man is exactly like any other and so there must be some *individual* component in his new acts. Often, he will do well to conform with group adaptations; on occasion he would do better to act alone. A compromise must be struck between his tendencies to conformity and his individuality. Various writers have emphasized different weightings as desirable. To Freud the pressures of society seemed to cut directly across man's built-in, pleasure-seeking instincts that were the mainsprings of his behaviour and thus man, biologically anti-social, was continuously being thwarted by the rules of society. There is some truth in this and any society which conflicts with individual motivation very strongly is apt to have many sick people among its members (cf. J. Halliday, 1948). Linton's (1945) view, however, is probably the more satisfactory, in which the individual is regarded as both gaining and losing by his membership of a group, and much of his gratification is social gratification. But he pushes his argument to considerable lengths:

The tests of absolute normalcy are the individual's ability to apprehend reality, as understood by his society, to act in terms of this reality and to be effectively shaped by his society during his developmental period. The test of relative normalcy is the extent to which the individual's experience has given him a personality conforming to the basic personality of his society (Linton, 1956, p. 63).

W. A. Scott (1958) succinctly defines the central problem:

The criterion of mental health based on adjustment clearly implies that conformity to the social situation in which the individual is permanently embedded is a healthy response. . . . If the stability of the larger social system be regarded as the final good, or if human development be seen as demanding harmony in relation to that social system, then such an assumption would appear basic and defensible. But one is still compelled to consider the possibility that the social system, or even an entire society, may be sick, and conformity to its norms would constitute mental illness, in some more absolute sense (p. 41).

Indeed, the idea of a sick society is probably as valid as, if more complex than, the idea of a sick individual. In our own time we may well consider the Congo (in the months following independence) or Nazi Germany as 'sick' societies, differing in type of disorder. The first is a clear illustration of a disintegrated society, classically handled by Durkheim (1963), in terms of *anomie*, and by J. Halliday (1948). Both these writers lay stress on disruption of coherent patterns as being the sign of 'ill health' in a society, individual members of which, denied a stable and relevant framework of social expectation, will be liable to breakdown.

Nazi Germany, on the other hand, had a rigidly controlled social pattern, with very fixed roles for its members; it was highly organized and often efficient. Here it is difficult to pinpoint the reasons for its possible 'sickness', though in his *Fear of Freedom* (1942) Erich Fromm has made a notable attempt, pointing to causes and effects within the individual members of the society. It is a rewarding exercise to seek to apply to societies the criteria for individual normality discussed in this chapter and to decide on their pertinence in any single case. Possibly, the crucial test of any social system is its ability to survive.

Jahoda (1958), in a neat and comprehensive discussion of *autonomy*, considers two main usages for the term: (a) independence, where the emphasis is on self-direction, self-control and self-sufficiency and the autonomous person is regarded as having a built-in armour against fate or social pressures and vicissitudes; and (b) the ability to *choose* whether 'to go along with the world' or to oppose it. To Angyal (1952) this last characteristic would essentially involve the person's balance between *self-determination* and *self-surrender*, two tendencies present in all men. Jahoda suggests various further refinements of meaning, beyond the scope of this chapter. The problems that arise over the choice of autonomy as a criterion of normality are essentially of the same nature as those discussed earlier. It is probable that some capacity for independent action is essential for the solution of new problems arising in the life-span of every individual.

Self-fulfilment is slightly different from the other criteria discussed in this section in that, on a subjective plane, a deliberate act of comparison is made between the potentialities of the individual and his actual achievement. Great difficulty may be encountered in establishing either, or both, of these.

In psychoanalysis, the general assumption is often made that therapy will make available to the patient, for the handling of reality, psychic energy which has hitherto been used up in inner conflict. Ernest Jones (1948) has claimed that the result of therapy is 'a general freeing of the personality in addition to relief from the actual symptoms' (p. 206). This claim is very sweeping and the value of his 'proof' is slight. Even Jones, later in the same article, concedes: 'An impartial observer cannot fail to be struck by the disconcerting fact that analysed people, including psychoanalysts, differ surprisingly little from unanalysed people in the use made of their intelligence' (p. 207). In this last paragraph we have found ourselves back at the criterion of efficiency again and, as we have seen, this efficiency can be at many different levels and of many different kinds.

Nevertheless, under controlled conditions, many attempts have been made to measure, by the use of questionnaires and rating scales, discrepancies between the 'ideal self' or 'ego-ideal' (the latter an integral part of the superego, according to Freud) and ratings by the subject of his actual level of performance. Any great discrepancy is regarded as some reflection of self-dissatisfaction – a subjective feeling that the individual is not measuring up to his own standards. In this field a useful study by Silber and Tippett (1965) discusses various possible measures and then empirically examines their intercorrelations. Three 'levels' exist in the mind of the person: perfection in any particular attribute, the level that he thinks he might himself obtain and the level he thinks he has reached. Experimental control is difficult as previous answers at one level are apt to contaminate later responses. The other scales are apt to shift when any one has been considered. Generally, the results are not yet reliable enough for use in the single case.

But self-fulfilment is probably a legitimate idiographic criterion of normality, particularly when longitudinal research or therapy on an individual is being undertaken.

All criteria in this section suffer from being extremely complex, rather nebulous and unaccompanied by definite physiological change, or for that matter, accurately measurable psychological change. They are relativistic and strongly culture-bound.

The ability to establish adequate emotional bonds with others

While many clinicians would agree that the emotionally isolated subject is often suffering from mental ill health, it is necessary to draw a distinction between people who *cannot* establish such contact and those who *do not*. Further, the excessively friendly person may well be compensating for serious psychological deficiencies. These considerations make it difficult, if not impossible, to measure 'capacity for love' in any very accurate fashion.

The position is further complicated by the hypotheses of many investigators that social isolation is a cause of mental breakdown, and not merely a sign of its presence (see, for example, Durkheim, 1963; Ellis, 1952; Faris, 1944). Causal factors are notoriously difficult to establish in any study of behaviour and this criterion, increasingly stressed in modern Western societies, is very difficult to apply in the individual case, except where the isolation of the individual from his fellows is extreme or where inability to establish emotional attachments to specific persons is the presenting symptom.

This is one of the most important concomitants of adequate mental functioning and provides an important criterion for making one of the most pervasive distinctions in the classification of mental disorder – that between neurosis and psychosis. Usually the neurotic patient is still capable of distinguishing between fantasy and reality. He is aware that he is suffering and, while he may go to great lengths to justify what appear to the clinician as irrational acts such as continual compulsive handwashing or rituals which allay his anxiety, his account of his motives and feelings will readily be apprehended by the listener. It will be neither bizarre nor expressed in language whose meanings are peculiar to the patient himself.

The psychotic, on the other hand, may appear completely withdrawn – 'just not in the same world as the clinician' – his thinking expressed in bizarre speech filled with illogical 'jumps'; he may even coin unique terms (neologisms) carrying meaning only for him. All these symptoms occur frequently in schizophrenia, the commonest of the psychoses, and are distributed throughout the world.

Generally, the experiences of the patient, and hence his 'psychology', are regarded as being of greater aetiological significance in the neuroses; his genetic endowment and, possibly, his bodily chemistry, are seen to have greater importance in the development of a psychosis. But while organic impairment is found in some psychoses, for example Korsakow's psychosis, in which discernible brain damage has followed excessive intake of alcohol over a long period, in others such as schizophrenia and cyclothymia the search for physical agents, toxic or otherwise, has been less successful.

From these two emphases, however, the debate has arisen whether neurosis and psychosis are essentially different types of disorder, or whether they should be regarded as lying along the same continuum. If such a disagreement can be resolved at all by an appeal to empirical evidence, then such evidence is probably in favour of the former hypothesis (Maher, 1966). Whatever the truth in this controversy, what can be said with certainty is that psychoses carry the graver prognoses, and that the thinking of the psychotic is much more divorced from reality than is that of the neurotic.

The major disadvantage of this criterion lies in the definition of reality. As we have seen earlier, among Zulu women auditory and visual hallucinations may have to be considered as, statistically, fairly 'normal' and thus as carrying no grave prognosis in that culture – unlike our own society, where such claims by the patient would probably lead to immediate admission to a mental hospital. Why are these disorders of 'reality testing' to be considered significant on one occasion and not on another?

The answer lies, basically, in the way that the human being checks on the world about him. Suppose, for example, that he sees what he takes to be a rose. Usually he will take the evidence of his senses at their face value but, should he wish to check on his first impression, he has two major means open to him. Firstly, he can increase the probability of the object's being a rose by further 'sampling' of its characteristics, using senses other than vision. He can touch it, smell it or even listen to it. When all his tests have consonant results he will be 'certain' that it is a rose. More commonly, however, he will adopt an easier and less time-consuming strategy and simply ask someone else or, preferably, several other people. If they agree that it is a rose he will be satisfied, *and so will they*. They will regard him as a sensible chap who knows a rose when he sees one. But their agreement on the naming of the object stems solely from their culture, which includes both horticulture and their language. So that in cultures where angels, familiars or other non-material objects are expected to be seen by many people, and this expectation has been fostered in each individual from birth onwards, these are indeed legitimate – each apparition having a valid 'reality'.

So that the concept of reality is inextricably bound up with social variations. There are exceptions to this rule: two plus two does not equal seventeen anywhere in the world and here we have a means of testing the thinking that has been classified under the term 'thought disorder' and applied, successfully, to the study of schizophrenia (K. Goldstein, 1943). Additional aid is given us, too, in that individuals *are* members of their cultures, and may legitimately be judged against local standards and acceptances. The individual can be expected, if 'normal', to cope adequately with the 'realities' of his group.

Conclusion

It is obvious that no one criterion is, by itself, adequate for our task. A multiple criterion approach is essential. Wherever possible, measurement of the relevant variables should be attempted. (Within limits, it is possible to get a clear idea of the cognitive capabilities of the person at any one time and his position on some kind of scale determined. His degree of *sub*normality, a statistical use, can be assessed.) Where measurement is not possible, value judgements and gross individual biases on the part of the clinician may still be tempered by a sensible 'balancing act' between the various criteria discussed above.

This is particularly necessary when we are not paying attention to any statistical considerations. The person's behaviour is a compromise of adaptive reactions, always 'purposive' (even if ineffectual) in evolutionary and individual terms, mediated by both conscious and unconscious thinking, sometimes in the company of others, sometimes alone – always altering. In the end, we can only agree with Ernest Jones (1948):

Is there any reason to suppose that a mind could be ideally normal in the absolute sense? As we do not meet absolute perfection elsewhere in the universe, even in Newton's Laws of Motion, it would be astonishing ever to find it in such a wry locality as the mind of man (p. 216).

Further reading

M. Hamilton (ed.), *Abnormal Psychology*, Penguin Books, 1967.

M. Jahoda, *Current Concepts of Positive Mental Health*, Basic Books, 1958.

E. Jones, 'The concept of a normal mind', in *Papers on Psychoanalysis*, Baillière, Tindall & Cox, 5th edn 1948.

Part Six
Social Influence

Social psychology has a history as long as that of any other branch
of psychology, but it has been slower than most in abandoning
armchair speculation for the experimental method. Until about
thirty years ago, experiments were comparatively rare in this field.
Since then the increase in experimental research has been very
rapid indeed. However, the adoption of the experimental method
for the investigation of human social behaviour generates a major
problem. When social situations are reconstructed under controlled
laboratory conditions they are apt to become highly artificial. An
experiment is itself a structured social situation, in which subjects
recognize that certain things are expected of them and respond
accordingly. They are passively obedient to the experimenter and
accept as normal in the laboratory tasks which would be judged
to be very odd outside it. The psychologist who wishes to study
some aspect of social life by taking it into the laboratory
necessarily distorts the thing he is studying by imposing upon it the
social structure of the experimental situation. Whereas this is in
some degree true of most psychological experiments, the problem
is especially acute when it is social behaviour that is being studied.
It is true that experiments have been conducted under 'real life'
conditions in which the subjects did not know that an experiment
was taking place. But such experiments take much time and
organization, and it is difficult to control the situation sufficiently
to allow firm conclusions to be drawn. The resolution to the
problem lies in complementing laboratory experimentation with
field observation, and in studying the social structure of the
experimental situation itself so that its distorting effect is more
precisely known.

In keeping with the general policy adopted in this book, our account of social influence will be based upon the experimental approach. Since these experiments have mostly been conducted under laboratory conditions, it follows that extrapolation to 'real-life' social situations must be cautious and tentative. The first of the three chapters in this Part deals with the two-person situation, and examines some of the ways in which the behaviour of one person can determine the behaviour of another. The second deals with one aspect of socialization, namely the long-term effects of adult influence upon the internalization of prohibitions and values in children. In the final chapter we shall consider the way attitudes and beliefs can be modified by persuasive communications and the processes that occur in small groups.

Chapter 21
Social Learning

Efforts to define the major areas of study within psychology, such that clear demarcation lines can be drawn between them, have generally failed, and in any case would probably be of little use if achieved. This is especially true of the area labelled 'social psychology'. Social psychology is usually defined as the branch of general psychology which investigates the determining influence upon the behaviour of an organism of other members of the same species. Such a definition would include much of the content of most of the chapters of this book; consider, for example, the experiments on the naming of emotions by Schachter and Singer described in Chapter 7, the discussion of aggression in Chapter 8 and the descriptions of the effects of early experience in Chapter 11. But if social psychology is at one end imperceptibly merged with general psychology, it has at the other a distinctive contribution to make. This contribution does not lie in any special method, for the logic of an experimental design remains the same whatever the problem, nor in the general nature of the data, for this is still the behavioural responses of individual subjects; it lies in the nature of the concepts used.

As Stotland (1965) has said, there are two levels of discourse to be found within social psychology. The first, the 'individual-social' level, is continuous with general psychology in that individual responses are used as indices of the characteristics of individual subjects. In the second, the 'group' level, individual responses are used as measures of the *relationships* between subjects. That is to say, the concepts employed refer to relationships though the operations used in measurement are applied to individuals. Thus the social psychologist may investigate the factors which determine the cohesiveness of a group, where cohesiveness is *defined* in terms of the relationships between members but measured by recording the responses of each one. In other words, the system taken as basic is not the single person but a group of people interacting with each other; the dependent variable is some feature of this system such as its role structure or interaction pattern, and the independent variable a condition which influences the system as a whole, such as the nature of the task before the group or competition with other groups.

In this part of the book we propose to sample both levels of discourse. The study of group functioning will be postponed until Chapter 23. In the present chapter we shall concentrate upon the two-person situation, and look at some of the ways in which the behaviour of one person (the Subject) can be influenced by the behaviour of another (here called the Other, or sometimes the Model). The behaviour of the other constitutes the independent variable, the behaviour of the subject the dependent variable.

Personal influence can be analysed into a number of elements or processes and shortage of space necessarily precludes discussion of many of them. For example, the area of study usually labelled 'person perception', which deals with the factors that determine one person's impression or concept of another, will be omitted (for an introduction, see Secord and Backman, 1964). Then there is the study of the strategies and manipulative techniques which subject and other adopt when they interact in conversation. Recent approaches have analysed personal interaction in terms of skill, and have examined, for instance, the way 'eye-contacts' serve as cues controlling the interaction. For an introduction to this work the reader is referred to Argyle (1967).

Most social influence among human beings is mediated by language. An important step in the socialization of the child is when the parents can substitute linguistic for physical control over his behaviour (see Luria, 1961, for an experimental study of this). Certain aspects of the linguistic control of one person by another will be discussed; later in this chapter we shall deal with the effects of the other's positive and negative evaluations upon the subject's behaviour, and in Chapter 23 we shall consider some of the experiments on the way persuasive communications from one person can change the attitudes and opinions of another. But much will have to be left out, such as the conditions under which commands and requests are obeyed, or the way the subject can learn from the factual statements of the other.

Within traditional learning theory there are essentially two roles which can be assigned to the other in a two-person situation: he can be a source of information, in the sense that he provides stimulation which directs the subject's behaviour, and he can be a source of reinforcement in the sense that his presence, or certain of his responses, are actively sought or avoided by the subject and thus serve as rewards or punishments. It is a matter of dispute whether these two roles can be effectively differentiated; but in so far as they can it is to be expected that their salience will vary from one situation to another. What we intend to do is to select several situations in which these roles appear, superficially, to vary, and examine some of the relevant experimental findings. This work is mostly of recent date and it has given rise to the suggestion that learning in social situations involves rather different principles from those which have been found to apply in non-social learning. However, the existence of other principles has not yet been demonstrated beyond question and it may be more parsimonious to assume that they are not required. For a discussion of the general question of social learning, see Bandura and Walters (1963) and Bandura (1965a).

Broadly speaking, three situations will be studied. They are:

Audience and co-action. In this, the subject engages in a task in the presence of the other who watches or engages in the same task.
Social reinforcement. This is the situation in which the subject, engaged upon a task, is periodically reinforced by the other's expressions of pleasure or displeasure at his performance.
Imitation. In this situation the subject observes the other, or model, who is occupied in a task and interest centres upon the effects of the model's behaviour upon the subject, either while he is watching or afterwards when he is faced with the same task.

Audience and co-action

In the interests of clarity we must avoid confusing the effects of audience and co-action with those of competition and collaboration.

In the audience situation (see Figure 76) the other is passively watching and is not a source of task-relevant information, and in co-action (see Figure 77) the subject and the other are occupied with the same task in each other's presence but not communicating nor, in theory anyway, competing. Competition will not be discussed in detail and collaboration will receive some mention in Chapter 23.

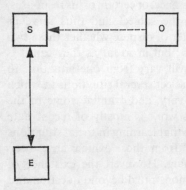

Figure 76   Audience situation. Other watches while subject interacts with his environment

The results of experiments on the effects of audience and co-action have been reviewed in detail by Zajonc (1965, 1966). They present a fairly consistent picture. When the subject is engaged in a relatively simple, well-learned task, his performance is improved by having someone watching him. For example, Bergum and Lehr (1963) used a vigilance task in which subjects had to respond to a signal that appeared at irregular intervals and found that performance was better with an audience than without one. A similar result has been found with other simple tasks. It is likely that the improved performance with an audience would depend upon such variables as the status and familiarity of the other, but so far this has not been systematically explored.

If, however, the subject is learning something new, then the presence of a spectator may impair learning. For example, it was found that subjects needed more trials to learn a finger maze with an audience than when alone. In short, 'an audience impairs the acquisition of new responses and facilitates the emission of well-learned responses' (Zajonc, 1966, p. 13). As Zajonc adds, an alternative way of putting it is to say that an audience enhances the emission of dominant responses. In the early stages of learning a new task, the correct responses are not dominant and incorrect ones often are. Zajonc explains this enhancement of dominant responses by supposing that an audience raises the subject's general level of arousal, and he quotes some physiological evidence in support of this.

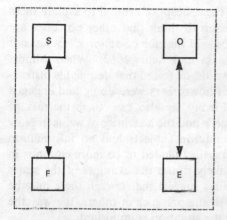

Figure 77   Co-action. Other and subject both engage in the same task in each other's presence without interacting

It is regularly found that there are wide individual differences in susceptibility to the audience effect. A number of experiments (reviewed by Paivio, 1965) have been directed towards defining these individual differences using a more naturalistic audience setting. An Audience Anxiety Scale for use with children has been constructed, which is predictive of behaviour in the audience situation. The evidence so far suggests that high audience anxiety in children is associated with past experience of negative evaluation of performance by the audience.

The experimental study of co-action has led to a similar conclusion. In an early series of experiments, F. H. Allport (1924) obtained results which have been largely substantiated by subsequent research.

Subjects performed simple mechanical tasks, like crossing out vowels in a passage of prose, or more complex ones, like finding the logical flaws in arguments, either alone or in the presence of others doing the same task. Allport did his best to exclude competition through his initial instructions and ensured that collaboration did not occur. On the simple tasks subjects did best when co-acting; on the logical reasoning task co-acting subjects actually wrote more words but the quality of their thinking was judged to be inferior by independent assessors.

Zajonc again makes use of the concept of arousal to explain these results. However, there is reason to think that other processes are at work. First of all, it must be said that the co-action effect has not always been found (see Bergum and Lehr, 1962). When Allport interviewed his subjects afterwards, he found that despite his instructions many of them wondered how others were doing and engaged in speculative comparisons. Finally, he also gave them the task of judging the pleasantness of smells and the heaviness of weights. Now although in the co-action condition subjects had no information about the judgement of others, they tended to be more cautious in their judgements, being less likely to use the extremes of the scales than when alone. These findings suggest that though there may be a primary arousal effect due to the presence of others, the way the subject cognitively structures the situation is important.

There is little doubt that the explicit introduction of competition between subjects strengthens the co-action effect. This is most clearly seen in athletics; individuals perform much better in competition than when practising on their own. But it has also been demonstrated for such things as pain tolerance. Lambert, Libman and Poser (1960) found that Jews raised their threshold for pain tolerance when told that in general Christians had a higher threshold than Jews.

Social reinforcement

One person can reinforce another either by being a source of such 'non-personal' rewards and punishments as money or imprisonment, or by direct, personal expressions of approval and disapproval such as nods, smiles, frowns and evaluative verbalizations (see Figure 78).

Of course in practice the two are related, for material gifts and sanctions come to signify personal approval or disapproval; but in the present chapter we are only interested in the reinforcing effects of the directly expressive responses of the other. In ordinary life, people are constantly shaping each other's behaviour through their deliberate or spontaneous reactions of pleasure or displeasure, attention or inattention, and it is hardly surprising that many experiments have been performed to investigate the phenomenon.

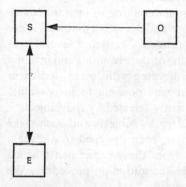

Figure 78   Social reinforcement. Other expresses approval or disapproval on subject's performance in a task

The simplest way of demonstrating the effect of positive social reinforcement is through an operant conditioning procedure in which one from a number of responses in the subject's repertoire is reinforced by approval and the probability of its occurrence in the situation increased thereby.

With child subjects, a frequently used task has been marble sorting. The child is given a large number of marbles and is required to insert them into a box through one of two holes. A baseline measure is taken by allowing the child to select either hole as he pleases without any response from the experimenter. Then the experimenter selects the least used hole and systematically reinforces the child by saying 'good' when he uses it. In this way the experimenter can increase the frequency with which that hole is chosen (see Stevenson and Hill, 1966).

With adult subjects the most favoured procedure has been to use verbal responses, and to show that if the experimenter responds with 'Mmhmm' when the subject emits a verbal response of a certain class, then the frequency with which this class of response is emitted increases. For example, Greenspoon (1955) reinforced plural nouns in this way and showed that their frequency increased. It should be added that it is questionable whether this procedure should properly be labelled 'operant conditioning', since it is not a specific response that is reinforced but a class of responses defined logically or grammatically. Somewhat closer to the usual definition of operant conditioning is the procedure devised by Taffel (1955). Subjects were presented with cards on which were printed a verb and several pronouns. They were required to select one of the pronouns and invent a sentence using the verb given. By reinforcing with 'good' sentences involving one particular pronoun, it was possible to increase the frequency with which it was subsequently selected by the subject.

In general, experiments using children as subjects and such tasks as marble sorting or lever pulling have been designed to answer a somewhat different set of questions from those experiments which have used adult subjects and a verbal conditioning procedure. We shall therefore deal with them separately.

One of the earliest questions to be studied with children was how the effect of positive social reinforcement should be explained. Gewirtz and Baer (1958a and b) postulated a social drive for approval which functions like other drives in that its strength is increased by antecedent deprivation and reduced by antecedent satiation. They tested this and found that twenty minutes' social isolation increased the social reinforcement effect whereas twenty minutes of satisfying social interaction depressed it. Lewis (1965) was able to show that for periods up to twelve minutes, social isolation was curvilinearly related to the social reinforcement effect. For boys, periods of three and twelve minutes' isolation increased the social reinforcement effect whereas intervening periods did not. Walters and his associates (Walters and Karal, 1960; Walters and Parke, 1964; Walters and Ray, 1960) also found that social deprivation increased susceptibility to social reinforcement but offered evidence for an interpretation in terms of anxiety rather than a social drive. Probably the most plausible interpretation is that some stimulus-seeking motive which has been shaped by previous learning is at work (see Stevenson, 1965).

A number of studies have looked at the developmental aspects of the positive social reinforcement effect. There is no stable evidence that age by itself is a related factor, though there is a possibility that the effect is weaker with older subjects. However, there is ground for thinking that age interacts with other variables. Several studies have found that after the age of about five years, a cross-sex effect appears, girls being more susceptible to male than to female reinforcers, and the converse for boys (for example, Stevenson, 1961). It has also been found that after this age, children are more influenced by an adult stranger than by parents (Stevenson, Keen and Knights, 1963). Comparing four- and five-year-old children, Hartup (1964) found that disliked peers were more effective reinforcers than liked peers for the older group.

It is plain from experiments in which a number of adults have acted as reinforcers that some are more effective than others. In a recent study, Stevenson and Allan (1967), using students as subjects and a marble sorting task, correlated the effectiveness of a reinforcer with the subjects' conception of him. They found that successful reinforcers were more likely than unsuccessful ones to be judged warm, gentle, thoughtful, calming and attentive. In a second experiment they trained the reinforcers to act one of two roles, a 'cold' role in which there was no smiling and little eye contact and reinforcements were administered in a flat tone of voice, and a 'warm' role in which there was frequent eye contact and smiling and reinforcements were given in an enthusiastic tone of voice. Reinforcers were consistently more effective in the 'warm' role.

Many of the experiments on verbal conditioning in adults have focused on the question whether the subject's awareness that certain of his responses are being reinforced is an important variable. At first it was assumed that conditioning could occur without awareness on the part of the subject. In the experiment by Greenspoon mentioned above, subjects who became aware were excluded from the analysis. However, the method employed for finding out whether the subject was aware or not consisted in asking a few questions.

Subsequent work, however, in which more extensive interviews were employed (for example, Spielberger, 1962; 1965) strongly suggests that there are levels of awareness in this situation, and it is likely that a minimal level is needed for successful conditioning.

Other studies have sought to define the personality variables associated with conditionability in this situation. Williams (1964) has reviewed them and although there is some evidence, for example, that hypnotizability is positively related and measures of 'achievement through independence' are negatively related, no clear picture emerges.

So far the discussion has been limited to the effects of positive social reinforcement in a situation in which reinforcement is contingent upon the occurrence of a particular response and in which the effect of reinforcement is to increase the frequency or intensity of that response relative to the other responses that the situation evokes. We must turn now to those studies that have contrasted positive and negative social reinforcement. Broadly speaking, there are two contexts to be examined: that in which social reinforcement is not contingent upon particular responses but offered as a general incentive for improving performance; and that in which social reinforcements are contingent upon particular responses, not in order to accentuate an already learned response but so that the subject will learn a new sequence of responses.

In experiments on the incentive values of praise and blame, subjects are given a task of some kind, after which the experimenter administers generalized approval or criticism. The subjects then perform the same task again, or a similar one, and the degree of improvement is recorded. In a review of these studies, Kennedy and Willcutt (1964) conclude that praise has a generally facilitative effect upon performance, whereas criticism tends to inhibit it. There are certain exceptions: severe under-achievers tend to be inhibited by praise, presumably because they do not find it credible in the light of their own assessment of their performance; and intelligent adolescents tend to improve their performance more under the stimulus of criticism than under the stimulus of praise. In a recent study, S. A. Allen (1966) found that kindergarten boys were more responsive to praise and adolescent boys to blame, and that the more difficult the task, the less the effect of any kind of social reinforcement at both ages.

It is clear from the results of these and other experiments that future research must take account of the reinforcement histories of the subjects. Baron (1966) has put forward a conceptual scheme for accommodating this variable. He assumes first of all that the expressive responses of the other person can be placed on a continuum from extreme favour at one end, through a neutral point, to extreme disfavour at the other. He then proposes that, as a consequence of his reinforcement history, the subject develops a 'social reinforcement standard'. By this he means, not a neutral point from which to judge the favourableness of the other's response, but that region on the continuum which he has come to prefer, with which he feels most happy and secure and which he actively seeks to evoke in the other. Finally, large discrepancies in either direction are felt as negative, and the subject engages in actions designed to avoid them and to restore the standard.

As yet there is no systematic experimentation based upon this scheme, and, of course, there are problems attached to the definition of a dimension of favourableness. But it does draw attention to the fact that what is overpraise or blame for one person may not be so for another. And it contains the implication that, for people whose reinforcement history is mainly negative, the desired region could conceivably be towards the disfavour end of the continuum. For them, all praise would induce discomfort.

Studies of the effects of social reinforcement upon more complex learning have been mainly concerned with one question: in the learning of a new sequence of responses, which is more facilitative of learning, positive reinforcement of correct responses or negative reinforcement of incorrect responses? This problem has a long history, but early experiments were inconclusive, often because the amount of task-relevant information conveyed by the two kinds of social reinforcement was not held constant. Recent experiments have been better controlled and they yield a fairly consistent picture: social reinforcement is in general better than intrinsic feedback from the task among children, though less clearly so among older subjects; and negative reinforcement of incorrect responses is more effective than positive reinforcement of correct responses, though learning is best when both are used. These results have been found for paired associates learning (for example, Travers *et al*., 1964), simple discrimination learning (for example, Terrell and Kennedy, 1957), concept learning (for example, Meyer and Seidman, 1960) and maze learning (Wright, 1968). A general review is provided by Marshall (1965).

Imitation

The phenomenon of deliberate or unconscious imitation is familiar to everyone. Efforts to define the term precisely, however, run into difficulties because several distinguishable processes are commonly subsumed under the label. The subject observes the model interacting with his environment in some task (see Figure 79). Imitation occurs when this experience shapes the subject's own behaviour in the

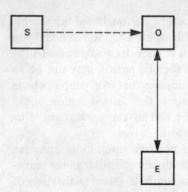

Figure 79   Imitation. Subject watches while other (model) interacts with his environment

direction of greater similarity to that of the model. But the conditions under which the subject's matching responses occur can vary. They can take place while the subject is actually watching or afterwards, in the presence of the model or when the subject is alone, and in the same situation as that in which the model was or in other situations. It is likely that the full explanation of imitation will have to take account of these different conditions. Furthermore, we can distinguish between imitation which involves the learning of a new sequence of responses and imitation in which no learning occurs, and between spontaneous imitation and deliberate copying.

In the present context, imitation will be taken as the generic term for all matching behaviour, whatever the conditions under which it occurs. We shall therefore use other labels for the various subclasses of imitation. The first kind of imitation we shall discuss is that in which the subject produces the matching responses while he is watching the model. The convenient term for this is *empathy*, though it must be emphasized that we are considerably narrowing the usual meaning of this term. The second kind, that in which the subject's matching responses immediately follow observation of the model and are made in his presence, has no obvious label and will be arbitrarily called *behavioural induction*. There are obvious affinities between this situation and that used in the experiments on group pressure and conformity which will be discussed in Chapter 23. The third situation, in which the subject's matching responses occur when he is faced with the same task as the other but afterwards and alone, corresponds to what most psychologists would consider to be the central meaning of the word 'imitation'. To distinguish it from the more generic term, it will here be called *internalized imitation*, though 'internalization' is usually used in a stronger sense than is implied here. Finally, there is matching behaviour which is generalized beyond the situation in which the other was originally observed. This more pervasive and long-lasting influence of the other will be discussed separately under the heading of *identification*.

Empathy

The subject is said to be empathically imitating the other if he emits matching responses while passively watching the other engaged in a task. Since the subject is not faced with the same stimulus situation as the other, his matching responses will be limited to implicit motor responses and muscle tension, and expressive emotional responses. Such imitation is presumed to be spontaneous in the sense that the subject does not deliberately try to match the other.

The experimental study of empathic motor responses in human beings has been somewhat neglected, though the phenomenon has been shown to occur. Rather more attention has been given to empathic emotional responses. The familiar experience of vicarious emotional involvement in the fate of a hero of a film has been studied by Lazarus *et al.* (1962). These investigators, using various physiological measures, showed that subjects watching a film exhibited stress reactions when the actors did. Alfert (1966) found that the pattern of autonomic reaction under vicarious stress was closely similar to the reaction to direct stress.

There are at least three factors which may be involved in the spontaneous matching of emotional responses in adult human beings. First, certain emotional responses may serve as 'innate releasers' in evoking matching responses in the observer. An example might be a scream of fear which induces a feeling of fear in the listener. Then it is probable that many matching responses are learned through conditioning. If two people face a common emotion-inducing situation, the stimuli provided by the emotional reactions of one of them will become associated with the emotional responses of the other and subsequently capable of eliciting them.

The third factor is the subject's cognitive structuring of the situation. This was brought out in a series of experiments by Berger (1962). In these experiments the subject watched a model engaged in a task during which from time to time he acted as if he had received an electric shock. The subject's galvanic skin responses were recorded throughout, and it was found that he responded with 'anxiety' at times when the shock was apparently being administered. However, if the subject was told that the model was pretending, his autonomic responses were much reduced. The stimulus situation remained constant, but its meaning to the subject was varied and this variation clearly affected his empathic responsiveness.

Berger went on to demonstrate that if a buzzer was sounded as the model was apparently shocked, the subject could be conditioned to respond autonomically to it. Bandura, Grusec and Menlove (1965) showed that dog phobia in subjects could be reduced by watching others behaving towards dogs in a non-anxious way. It has been suggested that this 'vicarious emotional conditioning' can occur symbolically, through language, and that the transmission of attitudes from parents to children is brought about in this way (see Bandura, 1965b).

Behavioural induction

Behavioural induction refers to the following sequence of events: the subject observes the model responding to his own stimulus field; he then responds to the same stimulus field with matching responses in the presence of the model. This situation can be analysed further by distinguishing between (a) occasions when the stimulus field itself evokes the subject's response but observation of the model determines its shape or pattern, (b) occasions when the model's behaviour also serves as an eliciting stimulus for the matching response in the subject and (c) occasions when observation of the model disinhibits the subject by weakening the restraints which prevent him from responding.

A neat demonstration of the shaping, rather than eliciting, effect of a model was given in an early experiment by Starch (1911). Adult subjects were required to copy out several handwritten prose passages, and it was found that their own handwriting was systematically influenced in the direction of closer similarity to the handwriting of the passages they were copying. Recently, Bandura and Kupers (1964) gave children a game to play in which they were given complete freedom to reward themselves with sweets whenever they thought they merited it. It was emphasized that there was no restraint upon the frequency with which they could reward themselves. All subjects watched a model demonstrate the game first. There were two conditions: under one, the model set himself stringent standards, rewarding himself only for a high score, and under the other the model set himself low standards. As was predicted, subjects who watched a model set high standards did so themselves.

What these experiments show is that when the subject is deliberately copying the task-relevant behaviour of the model, his behaviour is also shaped by the task-irrelevant aspects of the model's behaviour. A study by Bandura and Huston (1961) showed that, at least among children, this tendency is strengthened if the subject has a warm and friendly relationship with the model.

The eliciting effect of a model's behaviour is most clearly illustrated in the phenomenon of 'social facilitation' or behavioural contagion in animals (see Thorpe, 1963). Social facilitation occurs when the actions of one animal induce the same actions in another; for example, the sight of one bird eating may induce eating in another even though the other is not hungry. A parallel phenomenon among human beings might be the contagious effect of yawning. The explanation of these phenomena presumably lies in previous learning or in some 'innate releasing mechanism'.

These explanations do not seem sufficient for those eliciting effects of a model in which complex cognitive and decision processes are involved. A number of experiments have examined the effect upon the subject's choosing of watching the model make his choice first. Helson, Blake and Mouton (1958a) conducted an experiment in which signatures were canvassed for two petitions among university students. In a control condition it was established that one petition was popular since 96 per cent signed when approached by themselves and the other unpopular since only 15 per cent signed when alone. In the experimental condition, subjects were invited to sign after they had witnessed a confederate of the experimenter sign first or refuse to sign. The proportion who signed the popular petition after watching a model refuse dropped to 30 per cent, and the proportion who signed the unpopular petition after watching a model sign rose to 33 per cent.

Blake (1958) has reviewed a number of such studies. It is clear, for instance, that subjects are more likely to volunteer to take part in a psychological experiment if they watch someone else volunteer first, and that both the frequency and size of the financial contributions made to a cause can be influenced by evidence of other people's contributions.

The disinhibitory effects of a model have been shown in several experiments in which the subject is faced with a prohibition of some kind. Subjects are more likely to violate a traffic sign (Lefkowitz, Blake and Mouton, 1955) and a sign prohibiting the use of a convenient door (Freed et al., 1955), if they see a model violate the prohibitions first. It has also been shown that the strength of the prohibition and the status of the model are important factors in the situation. Other experiments have shown that subjects are more likely to look at sexually significant stimuli if they are given evidence that a model has looked at them first than if they are given evidence that the model has avoided looking at them (Walters and Amoroso, 1967; Walters, Bowen and Parke, 1964).

Internalized imitation

Unlike the forms of imitation outlined so far, internalized imitation requires that the matching responses occur in the absence of the model and at least a short time after observation. This suggests that there are two components to the total process, each with its own conditions; there is observational learning whereby the subject is able to remember the model's behaviour and there is the subject's performance of the matching responses.

That these two components are empirically discriminable is brought out in an experiment by Bandura (1965b). The subjects, who were young children, watched a film in which a model engaged in aggressive acts of an unusual kind towards a doll. There were three conditions: the model was rewarded for his aggression by an adult, or punished, or, in the control condition, no adult appeared on the film at all. Subjects were then placed in a room with the doll, and their matching responses recorded. Those who saw the model rewarded engaged in significantly more imitative acts than those who saw the model punished. In the final stages of the experiment, all subjects were offered rewards if they could imitate the model, and the differences between the experimental groups disappeared. This result implies that though the reinforcing consequences to the model helped to determine whether matching responses occurred, they did not affect the amount of learning that went on.

A series of experiments reported by Lumsdaine (1961) show that subjects can learn a new sequence of responses by simply observing a model when there is no obvious reinforcement either to the model or to the subject at the time the learning is taking place. In these experiments, subjects watched a film in which a model assembled pieces of machinery. Subsequently, they were presented with the same array of components and required to assemble them. It was plain that from observing one demonstration subjects were able to learn a great deal and, indeed, the main concern of these experiments was to determine how much subjects could take in through observation before they needed practice. The implications of these experiments are that observational learning is at its best when the subject is deliberately set to imitate and that there is an optimal 'span of observational learning' which is a function of both the subject and the kind of task.

When the reinforcement the model receives is contingent upon particular responses, as in operant conditioning, then it may facilitate learning in the subject. In a series of experiments on verbal conditioning, Kanfer and Marston (1963) and Marston and Kanfer (1963) found that reinforcement to a model was as effective as direct reinforcement to the subject in producing learning. It was also found that subjects who observed a model being verbally conditioned were more likely to become aware of the relationship between response and reinforcement than the model (see Kanfer, 1965).

It is clear from the experiment by Bandura quoted above that when the subject is not explicitly set to copy the model, the reinforcement consequences to the model determine whether the subject will engage in matching behaviour. Punishment to the model reduces and reward increases the amount of imitation shown by the subject. It has also been shown that the timing of the punishment of the model is important (Walters, Parke and Cane, 1965); if a model is punished just before touching a forbidden toy, the subject is subsequently less likely to touch it than if the model is punished after he has touched it.

The careful, experimental study of internalized imitation has only just begun and much more work is needed before we can be confident of the conditions which control it. What is needed, too, is a precise analysis of the processes involved. Such an analysis will need to preserve certain distinctions – for example, those between observational learning and overt and implicit performance, between situations in which the subject is set to imitate, where his explicit task is to copy, and situations in which imitation is incidental and 'unconscious', and between reinforcement to the model which is response-specific and reinforcement which is general. Then there is the question whether the reinforcement the model receives is to be conceived as directly reinforcing the subject through his empathic response to the model, or whether the model's reinforcement is to be construed as a further piece of information learned by the subject. Whatever the outcome, it is surely true that the phenomena of imitation are of great importance for the understanding of human socialization and of social influence between people.

Identification

The concept of identification and the kind of research associated with its use differ in important respects from the concepts and research described so far. Like imitation, identification refers to the process or processes whereby one person models himself upon another. It differs from the concept of imitation in two main ways. First, it implies a relatively long-lasting relationship between subject and model and draws attention to the fact that some models exert more influence over the subject than others. A subject is said to be identified with a model if he is more likely to match that model's behaviour than other models' behaviour. Second, the matching behaviour is more extensive than that implied in the notion of imitation. The subject behaves *as if* he were the model, both in situations other than those in which he has seen the model and in a relatively thorough-going way. That is to say, he adopts the model's values, beliefs, attitudes and style of life, as well as matching particular forms of behaviour.

Identification is therefore a more inclusive and less precise term than imitation. This is largely because it originated in psychoanalysis rather than in the laboratory, and its field of application has been mainly, though not exclusively, in those areas of developmental psychology concerned with the continuous and pervasive influences of parents upon children. Critics of the term, who argue that it is in reality another word for imitation and therefore redundant, have mostly based their case upon short-term laboratory experiments in which the subjects have usually not seen the model before. In that context, it is true that the concept is unnecessary. But students of socialization or social influence, who endeavour to locate the effects of relationships which may last over several years, still find the idea useful.

Since Freud was originally responsible for putting the concept into circulation, a brief summary of his view on the topic will be given. His classic statement (Freud, 1922) was to the effect that in object relationships the child desires to *have* the other person, in identification he wants to *be* the other person. He distinguishes two forms, *anaclitic identification* and *identification with the aggressor*. The mechanism said to be behind the former is as follows. The child has a limited capacity for love. The more he loves a parent, the less he loves himself. Depleted self-love is felt as unpleasant. The child restores his self-love by imagining or pretending that in some sense he is the parent. The ego, 'by identifying itself with the object, recommends itself to the id in place of the object and seeks to attract the libido to itself' (Freud, 1933, p. 102). Aspects of the parent are incorporated into the child's sense of himself and this restores self-esteem.

Identification with the aggressor occurs under a different set of conditions. The child meets aggression from a powerful adult but cannot express his own aggression back or effectively displace it. He is again faced by loss of self-esteem but this time because of a direct assault upon it, and he cannot regain self-esteem by attacking the aggressor. The child resolves the problem by identifying with the aggressor; that is, he restores his self-esteem by acting as if he were the aggressor and adopting towards himself the same punitive attitude that the aggressor displayed towards him.

It is to be presumed that in the course of normal upbringing, the two forms of identification occur together, since the punitive parent is also the loved parent. But within psychoanalytic theory, anaclitic identification is held to be mainly responsible for the formation of the 'ego-ideal', or the individual's personal goals, and identification with the aggressor mainly responsible for the development of conscience, or the inhibition of behaviour (see also Chapter 22).

Since Freud, many psychologists have offered their own theoretical analyses of identification, too many for them to be discussed here. However, three general comments seem justified. First, attempts to translate the psychoanalytic concept into orthodox learning theory (for example, Lazowick, 1955; Mowrer, 1950; Sears, 1957) effectively reduce it to imitation. Second, theorists have tended – in one form or another – to preserve the distinction between the two forms of identification. Thus Kagan (1958), for example, argues that identification is maintained by the motive to command or experience desired goal states of the model and these goal states are either mastery of the environment or love. Third, the psychoanalytic view that the root of the process is the effort to maintain or restore self-esteem can usually be traced in most reformulations.

Instead of concentrating upon the conditions affecting behavioural matching in the laboratory, most studies of identification have been concerned with one or more of three problems: measuring identification directly, and establishing relationships between these direct measures and both characteristics of the model, such as his nurturance towards the subject or his power and prestige, and forms of behavioural matching. However, many other studies have not used a direct measure of identification, but have related parental nurturance or dominance to behavioural similarity in the children and have conceptualized the results in terms of identification. This is especially true of those studies of sex typing in children where, for example, attitudes of the father towards the son are related to 'masculinity' in the son, and the effects said to be mediated by identification. Nearly all these studies have been of a correlational kind in which inferences about the directions of cause and effect are speculative and inconclusive.

The direct measure of identification most often used is the degree of similarity between the subject's concept of himself and his concept of the model. The subject rates himself and the model on some personality measure and if the two ratings are similar the subject is said to be identified with the model. There are variants on this procedure, such as taking the similarity between the subject's concept of himself and the model's concept of himself. A detailed critique of these methods has been given by Bronfenbrenner (1958). The general problem they raise is just how the measure should be interpreted and whether it is really measuring identification as theoretically defined. It should be added that Heilbrun (1965) has attempted to produce a measure which meets these criticisms.

The empirical results of the many studies which have been done present a somewhat confusing picture and there is not space to document this confusion here. What follows is intended as a very brief illustration of the kind of results that have been found.

In a series of experiments (Mussen and Distler, 1959, 1960; Payne and Mussen, 1956) it was found that boys were more likely to identify with their fathers, in the sense of seeing them as similar or in the sense that they themselves were 'masculine', if their fathers were warm, affectionate and rewarding to them and, less clearly, if they were also somewhat strict. Cooper and Blair (1959) found that children who valued their parents highly were more likely to share their ideologies. Heilbrun and Fromme (1965) found that perceived similarity to fathers was related to good psychological adjustment in male students.

Hetherington and Frankie (1967), in an experiment with young children, obtained measures of parental dominance and warmth, and of the child's imitation of the parents in a controlled experimental setting. Whereas there was some general tendency for boys to imitate their fathers most, and girls their mothers, the warmth and dominance of the parents were important factors. The more dominant or warm the parent, the more he was imitated. There was some evidence, however, that dominance was rather more important for boys and warmth for girls.

Kagan and Phillips (1964) showed that for children empathic responses while watching the mother were greater than empathic responses while watching a stranger. In an experiment in which perceived similarity was the measure of identification, De Wolfe (1967) showed that student nurses working in a tuberculosis ward who identified with experienced members of staff lost their fear of tuberculosis more quickly than nurses who did not identify with the staff.

The results of studies like these can usually be interpreted in other ways than through the idea of identification. This, together with the general imprecision of the term, has persuaded some psychologists to abandon it. It is not yet clear whether the concept has a future in psychology; but the fact that some such concept is needed in describing the developmental influence of parents, and others, suggests that it is premature to reject it now.

Further reading
A. Bandura and R. H. Walters, *Social Learning and Personality Development*, Holt, Rinehart & Winston, 1963.
E. C. Simmel, R. A. Hoppe and G. A. Milton (eds.), *Social Facilitation and Imitative Behaviour*, Allyn & Bacon, 1968.
R. B. Zajonc, *Social Psychology: An Experimental Approach*, Wadsworth, 1966.

Chapter 22
Moral Development

The survival of many species depends upon the development among their members of co-operative and 'altruistic' forms of behaviour, as, for example, when the young have to be cared for and protected by adult animals, or when defence against predators necessitates the formation of large social units. This basic interdependence of members of a species leads to the evolution of forms of social control. In lower species, the mechanism of social control would seem to be a system of innately determined behavioural patterns which serve as sign stimuli, or releasers, and which evoke complementary responses in other animals.

The human species is unique in that the main mechanism of social regulation is a system of conceptually formulated rules, conventions and values. These norms of conduct are not innately determined, and vary widely across different cultures. Individuals have to be inducted into the codes of their society by a long and complex process of learning, or socialization. The essentially asocial baby is required to develop – through interaction with caretaking adults – into a mature person who accepts the norms of his society, who acts upon them without continual supervision, who in turn transmits these norms to his own children, and who is able to contribute to the modification and development of these norms from a position of understanding and insight into their function. Such a transformation is hard enough to achieve in a static society; when social structures and norms are themselves changing, the task becomes doubly difficult. It is not surprising, therefore, that one of the main sources of impetus for the study of socialization has been society's growing awareness of its failure in this respect.

In the present chapter we shall examine in some detail only one product of the socialization process, namely moral behaviour. This involves a certain narrowing of the field, at least as it is customarily treated in textbooks. For socialization involves many aspects of personality change which are not obviously matters of moral concern, such as the acquisition of socially acceptable habits of dressing and eating, the adoption of the socially prescribed sex role and the acceptance of political and religious beliefs which fall within the culturally permitted range. Of course, these too may become the subject of moral evaluation. The point is that there are other aspects of human behaviour, such as honesty and respect for the ownership of property, which are more central to the continuing existence of society, and it is with these that we shall be primarily concerned.

There are broadly two ways of investigating moral behaviour – the field study and the laboratory experiment. The former is essentially correlational, in that the investigator attempts to find out what factors in personality and upbringing are significantly associated with a measure of moral behaviour; in the latter, attempts are made to vary antecedent conditions and to record the consequences upon a moral variable. The two approaches are complementary. But it is only recently that problems of moral behaviour have been taken into the laboratory; most studies have been of the field variety. As yet, the results of these studies present a somewhat confusing picture; but if existing evidence answers few questions, at least the problems are better understood. For convenience, the discussion will be structured around the following basic questions: How is moral behaviour measured? How do the various measures of moral behaviour relate to each other? What are the correlates and antecedents of moral behaviour? What sorts of theory have been offered to account for its development?

The measurement of moral behaviour

Common-sense analysis would suggest that there are at least five conceptually distinct aspects of moral behaviour, or five dimensions along which people's moral behaviour can vary. These are: (a) resistance to temptation or the capacity to inhibit behaviour which violates a moral norm when motivated to engage in it; (b) the active pursuit of morally praiseworthy goals; (c) post-transgressional responses, such as guilt; (d) cognitive insight into the structure and functioning of moral rules; and (e) the content and strength of moral beliefs. Each of these has been measured in several different ways. Our first task is to examine these measuring techniques.

Resistance to temptation

Society requires that those forms of behaviour which are destructive of social harmony be inhibited. Examples are lying, stealing and aggressive assault on others. The mechanisms which control or inhibit the individual's behaviour can be crudely classified into those which are internal and constitute his conscience, and those which are external and reside in the social context. By the latter we mean those processes of social pressure which induce conformity to the expectations of others, and that system of social rewards and punishments which creates in people the desire to please others and the fear of displeasing them. People differ both in the strength of their consciences and in their susceptibility to social pressures. The assumption is that internalized control – or conscience – will lead to the inhibition of morally unacceptable behaviour even when there is virtually no likelihood of the individual being found out if he transgresses. Social mechanisms of control, on the other hand, are presumed to inhibit only socially visible behaviour and to be powerless if there is little possibility of the individual being found out.

In this chapter our concern is with conscience; the topic of social control will receive attention in the next chapter. However, though it is easy enough to draw a conceptual distinction between the two forms of control, the measurement of internalized control, or 'resistance to temptation in private', is difficult and beset with problems of interpretation.

In general, three different kinds of measure have been used. The first is the direct, experimental testing of resistance to temptation in private; the second is society's classification of individuals into delinquent and non-delinquent; and the third is through questionnaires and interviews in which subjects are invited to disclose whether or not they have transgressed particular moral injunctions. They will be dealt with in that order.

A variety of techniques has been devised for measuring resistance to temptation in private. They have this in common, that subjects are given motive and opportunity to transgress a moral injunction in situations in which it would be reasonable for them to suppose that they would not be found out. Of course, through various subterfuges, the experimenter can find out. The transgressions most commonly sampled in this way have been cheating, lying, stealing and disobedience. An example is the ray-gun game devised by Grinder (1961). This is a target-shooting game in which subjects are motivated by the promise of rewards if they achieve a certain score. However, the gun is so programmed that it is impossible to succeed without cheating. At a crucial moment in the test, the subject is left to score his performance by himself. If the subject gives himself a score above a certain value, the experimenter knows that he has cheated.

Measures of this kind have been frequently used and they have the virtue that they approximate to real-life temptation situations. However, they raise problems of interpretation that are as yet unresolved. Presumably, a subject's behaviour in the test situation is the result of two conflicting factors, strength of inhibition or self-control and strength of temptation to transgress. The test is intended to discriminate the strength of the subject's conscience. But to do this, motivation to transgress must be held constant over all subjects. Not only is this not done, but it is difficult to see how it could be done and even what it means to say that two people are equally tempted. The problem does not arise in those experiments in which subjects are randomly assigned to different groups before being given the test, since motivational differences between groups can then be attributed to chance. The more usual procedure, however, has been to categorize subjects as, for example, 'cheaters' and 'non-cheaters', on the basis of the test and then to compare them in other ways. In such a design we cannot be sure that it is strength of conscience which differentiates the groups. Some investigators have tried to get round the problem by trying to induce maximum motivation in all subjects, or by using large numbers and hoping that individual differences in motivation will somehow cancel themselves out. Neither move is satisfactory. And the problem becomes acute when the sexes or different age groups are being compared.

A further point which makes interpretation difficult is that we do not usually know how the subjects assess their chances of being found out, and how much they are deterred by their assessments. Though the experimenter does his best to ensure that detection appears highly unlikely, he cannot control the subjective evaluation of the detection risk on the part of the subject.

With these cautions in mind, we can proceed to ask whether people who resist temptation in one experimental situation are likely to do so in another. Is honesty a general trait, or is it specific to particular situations? Hartshorne and May (1928) gave a battery of such measures to children between the ages of eleven and sixteen. Some 12,000 subjects were involved. They found only very small correlations between performance on the different tests and concluded that resistance to temptation was much more a function of situational factors than of a general character trait. However, their correlations were nearly all positive, and in a re-analysis of some of their data, Burton (1963) was able to show that there was a significant, if small, tendency for children who were honest on one test to be so on others. Brogden (1940) analysed a large battery of character tests and found that measures of honesty tended to form a single dimension. Sears, Rau and Alpert (1966) obtained six measures of resistance to temptation from five-year-old children and found them to be positively associated with each other. We may conclude, therefore, that existing evidence does support the assumption that the capacity to resist temptation in private is a personality trait of some generality; but it is also clear that situational factors exert a powerful influence upon it.

The second measure is society's classification of individuals into delinquent and non-delinquent. The usual procedure is to compare a sample of delinquents with a sample of non-delinquents matched for age, intelligence, socio-economic level and subculture. The assumption is that delinquents have weaker internalized controls and that, therefore, those factors of home background, physique and temperament which differentiate the groups serve as direct or indirect causal influences in the development of conscience.

The measure is obviously a crude one. Among the many reservations that have to be made, the most relevant one here is that a large proportion of delinquent acts, though they may be committed in the expectation of escaping detection by authority, are not done in private but in the presence of other members of a gang. Characteristically, delinquents belong to peer groups, the norms of which make permissible – and even obligatory – acts which the rest of society condemns as wrong. It is well known that groups exercise a powerful influence over the socially visible actions of their members through the norms they evolve and the sanctions they apply to deviant members (see Chapter 23).

We cannot therefore assume that because an individual is classified as a delinquent he necessarily has a weak 'conscience'. From the point of view of moral development, we can speculatively distinguish four subgroups of delinquent: (a) those with weak internalized standards who belong to delinquent groups and who follow the norms of such groups without conflict; (b) those with strong internalized standards who value their membership of delinquent groups so much that they follow the norms of such groups but feel guilt and conflict over doing so; (c) those with strong internalized standards, but whose standards are deviant from the point of view of society as a whole; and (d) those who might be described as neurotic delinquents, who have developed consciences but who are subject to uncontrollable impulses and who, we may suspect, are somewhat less likely to be members of a delinquent group. Distinctions of this kind appear to be needed to account for such findings as that delinquents are less likely to be members of church groups than matched non-delinquents (Ferguson, 1952; Glueck and Glueck, 1950), but that members of church groups are no different from non-members on measures of resistance to temptation in private (Hartshorne and May, 1928).

The relevance of delinquency studies in this context depends upon the assumption that, though delinquents may vary among themselves, yet nevertheless they are in general more likely than non-delinquents to have weak internalized controls. There is some reason to think this assumption is justified. Thus, Bandura and Walters (1959) found that delinquents were more likely to engage in socially disapproved forms of sexual behaviour, and Glueck and Glueck (1950) present an over-all picture of the typical delinquent as one in whom there is a general lack of self-control.

The third measure of resistance to temptation which has been used involves some kind of verbal report. One variant is to ask subjects, in interviews or questionnaires, to report whether, and how often, they have transgressed some moral norm. The relation between such verbal report and actual behaviour is largely unknown and it might be expected to vary with factors in the situation in which the questions are asked. The matter is complicated by the fact that to invite verbal report on moral behaviour is to tempt the subject to lie. Brogden (1940) did find, however, that the subject's report on how he thought he would behave when tempted to cheat was related to his actual behaviour on a cheating test; and it is not implausible to think that, when subjects are given every inducement to be honest and when anonymity is guaranteed, their verbal reports will bear some relation to their actual behaviour. A second variant is to use the reports of others. Some investigators have used moral reputation as their measure (e.g. Havighurst and Taba, 1949). This measure is restricted to socially visible behaviour, and is so susceptible to the 'halo' effect as to be of little use. Sears, Maccoby and Levin (1957) made use of the report of mothers to gain a general measure of conscience development in five-year-old children. Though this measure is perhaps better thought of as a measure of guilt, Sears, Rau and Alpert (1966) found no relation between it and tests of resistance to temptation in private. Finally, a third variant is to use the projective story completion technique. The subject is required to complete a story about a hero, similar to himself, who is faced with temptation. The assumption is that the way the subject completes the story will in some degree reflect his own capacity to resist temptation. This assumption still awaits adequate testing. Meanwhile, though we may agree that the technique does tap differences in moral attitudes, it seems unwise to attempt any more precise interpretation.

The active pursuit of praiseworthy goals

This aspect of moral behaviour has been somewhat neglected, though its measurement is not difficult. Hartshorne and May (1929) devised a number of tests of helpfulness and service, in which, for example, children were asked to collect toys for other children in hospitals, or faced with the choice of sending money to a charity or spending it on themselves. Ugural-Semin (1952) measured generosity by requiring children to share five sweets with another child. If the subject only kept two sweets for himself, he was judged to be generous. In view of the high social visibility of this form of moral behaviour, it is to be expected that the individual's actions will be considerably influenced by the norms of the groups of which he is a member, and Hartshorne and May found clear evidence of this. They also found that altruistic behaviour on one test tended to go with similar behaviour on others.

Reactions to transgression

It has generally been assumed that the way an individual behaves after he has transgressed is also a measure of the strength of his 'conscience'. A strong conscience, it is said, shows itself not only in resistance to temptation but also in the intensity of guilt experienced after transgression. Writers have also distinguished guilt from shame. The former is the discomfort and loss of self-esteem induced by a failure to live up to internalized standards; the latter is the anxiety evoked by actual or anticipated disapproval of others. The distinction parallels that between social and self-control mentioned earlier. Unequivocal evidence of guilt would require that the individual exhibit emotional upset even though he is entirely immune from discovery. Though in some ways this is a useful distinction, it is not easy to maintain upon closer analysis. First of all it implies that guilt and shame are somewhat different subjective experiences which can only be indexed by the labels the subject himself uses. Then second, many of the behavioural expressions of guilt, such as confession, are socially orientated and can be construed as seeking for social acceptance. Finally, it is hard to assess just how real the possibility of being found out is to the subject. It may be the case that those who show most guilt are also those who are most likely to believe that 'you always get found out in the end'. It seems wiser therefore not to put too much emphasis upon this distinction at the psychological level, but instead to examine the influence upon post-transgressional responses of all relevant factors, including social disapproval. These responses include on the one hand emotional disturbance, and on the other such specific actions as confession, self-criticism, apology, reparation, self-punishment and the blaming of others.

In general, three types of measure have been used. In the first, the subject simply rates his own guilt feeling after transgression. The second is projective. The commonest method is to give the subject an incomplete story in which the hero has transgressed and to ask him to complete it. The assumption is that he is most likely to give the hero the kind of responses he himself would display in a similar situation. The third method is observational. The experimenter records how a subject behaves, either when he is on his own (viewed through a one-way screen) or in a social situation, after he has transgressed.

From these different measures it is possible to discriminate individuals according to their readiness to experience emotional disturbance after transgression and according to the kind of post-transgressional actions they engage in. There is general agreement that they are all measures of guilt response, but there is some divergence of opinion over how the notion of guilt should be understood. Two main interpretations have been advanced. According to the first, guilt is a form of self-punishment in which the individual adopts towards himself the disapproving and aggressive attitudes which adult caretakers adopted towards him when he misbehaved in early childhood. This view has its roots in psychoanalytic theory. According to the second, guilt feeling is defined as anxiety which, through training procedures, has been conditioned to the knowledge that an offence has been committed. The knowledge that a moral rule has been broken evokes anxiety and the specific post-transgressional responses such as confession are learned instrumental techniques for reducing this anxiety.

Some support for the first interpretation can be found in Mackinnon's (1938) study where it was observed that those subjects who resisted temptation and reported a high level of guilt feeling also engaged in more aggressive actions directed towards themselves in the test situation. On the other hand, it is difficult to see how many of the specific forms of post-transgression behaviour can be interpreted as self-punitive. Confession and reparation can as easily be construed as attempts to avoid punishment as being themselves self-punitive. Certainly they can occur without other evidence of self-blame. The most obvious candidate for the title of self-punitive is verbal self-criticism or self-devaluation. But Aronfreed has shown (Aronfreed, 1961, 1964; Aronfreed, Cutick and Fagen, 1963) that self-criticism is not normally a frequent response and that its occurrence is contingent upon the extent to which it has been reinforced in the past by, for example, forestalling punishment.

A recent experiment by Wallace and Sadalla (1966) has directly examined this question. Subjects were assigned to three conditions. In the two experimental conditions they were induced to transgress; in the control condition they were not. Under one experimental condition, the experimenter 'found out'; in the other he did not. After transgression, subjects were invited to volunteer for another experiment in which they would receive a number of painful electric shocks. The transgressors who were not found out volunteered more than the controls, but the difference was not statistically significant. The experimental subjects who were found out did volunteer significantly more than the controls. The suggestion from this experiment is that though transgression does generate some self-punitive tendencies, these are considerably strengthened when they also serve an instrumental function, for instance, by effecting reconciliation with others. As Kohlberg concluded in his excellent review of the evidence (Kohlberg, 1963), neither interpretation of the guilt response is wholly adequate.

But in either case, whether guilt is defined in terms of self-punishment or anxiety, we would expect some measure of emotional disturbance to accompany the specific responses made. Sears, Rau and Alpert (1966) found that emotional upset and confession were positively associated. However, they also found that 'fixing', or reparation, was negatively associated with emotional disturbance. It would seem, therefore, that some responses to transgression can be described as neither self-punitive nor as anxiety-reducing.

Finally, if the capacity for guilt, however defined, is a general trait, we should expect that those who exhibit high guilt for one sort of transgression would do so for others. The evidence is slender. Bandura and Walters (1959) found that guilt over aggressive acts was positively associated with guilt over violation of sexual norms. On the other hand, Allinsmith (1960), using the story completion method, found that guilt over the wish for another's death was independent of guilt over theft and disobedience.

Moral insight

Moral behaviour involves thinking. An important aspect of an individual's morality is the nature of his moral concepts and the logic of his moral thinking. A great deal of the work in this area has its source of inspiration in a monograph by Piaget (1932) on the development of moral judgement in children. Most investigators have worked within Piaget's theoretical system and have used essentially the same methods.

Piaget described two different kinds of morality. One characterized the young child of between five and eight years; the other was manifested by children of about ten years and above. Since the later morality is thought by Piaget to be a natural consequence of greater age and richer experience it is labelled 'mature' and the earlier one 'immature'. The differences between these moralities can be brought out in relation to the main groups of variable Piaget studied.

The nature of rules. The immature conception of rules is that they are absolute, fixed and unchangeable, and derive from authorities of a semi-mystical kind; the mature conception holds that rules serve the purpose of facilitating social intercourse, can be changed if all agree and, far from being derived from authority, become themselves the basis for evaluating authorities. Piaget also noted that the mature understanding of rules went with an ability to keep them.

The nature of wrong acts. The immature child takes no account of motive and intention in evaluating the wrongness of actions. His criteria are the literal deviation from the rule, the amount of damage done, the degree of disobedience of authority involved and the seriousness of the punishments normally decreed for the action by authorities. Mature children make motive and intention a critical factor in their judgement of a misdeed; they do not see disobedience of authority as necessarily wrong and are much less influenced in their judgements by the sanctions that authorities have ordained.

The nature of punishment and justice. Immature children see the function of punishment as essentially retributive; misdeeds must be balanced by punishment no matter what form it takes, though they also tended to think that the severer the punishment, the better. They see no injustice when a group is punished for the misdeeds of an individual (collective responsibility) and they interpret accidental mishaps which follow wrong-doing as punishment for it (immanent justice). For the mature child, the point of punishment is to bring home to the offender the fact that his behaviour is destructive of social harmony; it must therefore fit the offence and the offender. The attribution of responsibility to the collective for the offences of the individual is no longer accepted without question; nor are accidental events any longer seen as punitive.

In general, Piaget has described a movement from what he calls 'moral realism', a condition in which morality is essentially based upon authority and external to the child, to an internalized form of morality, a 'morality of co-operation'. He conceived this development to be an inevitable consequence of growing up, due on the one hand to a maturation of the intellectual functions and on the other to increased experience of mutual respect among peers, as contrasted with the unilateral respect for adults which prevails in the early years.

In measuring these variables, Piaget used his own method of clinical interrogation. His technique consisted in engaging the child in conversation, then leading him on by sensitive questioning until he was posing the child problems he had never had to face and for which he had no prepared answers. In this way Piaget hoped to tap the spontaneous thinking of the child, and to be able to describe its structure. Such interrogations were supplemented by short stories which the child was asked to evaluate. For instance, the child would be presented with two stories, one in which a well-intentioned but clumsy act resulted in a lot of damage, and another in which an act – motivated by the intention to deceive – resulted in little damage, and then asked whether one was more morally reprehensible than the other, and if so, why. Piaget, in this way, could discover whether or not the child took account of motive in his judgements.

Since Piaget's study was exploratory, he did not try to standardize his interviews in any rigorous way and he did not concern himself with questions of adequate sampling; these tasks he left to future investigators. But he was very much concerned with the more fundamental problem of how a young child's answer to a question should be evaluated. It is obvious that if a child's response is a formula taken over from an adult, or if it is situationally determined in the sense that the child is giving back to the adult what he thinks the adult wants, or if, indeed, his response is just an expression of a desperate need to say something, no matter what, then it has little value as an index of the child's own, serious thinking. Piaget (1929) has given his own analysis of the types of response that children give, and has given criteria for distinguishing those which provide evidence of genuine thinking. He also took trouble to frame his questions within the vocabulary and idiom of the child. It follows that successful interrogation of children is a delicate art. Without doubt, subsequent experimenters, in the effort to standardize Piaget's technique and to make results amenable to statistical treatment and generalization, have had to sacrifice much of the sensitivity of his original approach.

It is basic to Piaget's theory that the immature forms of moral insight are functionally related, for they are all a consequence of undeveloped intelligence and a pattern of social relationships which inevitably follows from the child's dependence upon adults. We would expect, therefore, that children who are immature on one measure would be so on others. The most comprehensive attempt to test this was made by Johnson (1962). Some 800 children were given a battery of measures which included most of the variables used by Piaget. Of the 760 intercorrelations, 294 were statistically significant in the predicted direction, and this is many more than would be expected by chance. However, seventy-nine were significant in a negative direction and this, too, is more than would be expected by chance. The results clearly showed that there were areas of moral judgement within which responses were related to each other, but that these areas were only slightly, if at all, related to each other. A somewhat similar conclusion is reported by MacRae (1954). There is also evidence, notable for the concepts of immanent justice and punishment, that the child's response is specific to the kind of situation he is asked to evaluate (Durkin, 1961; Medinnus, 1959); subjects who give the immanent justice response on one story do not necessarily do so on a different one.

In conclusion, Piaget's monograph has had a stimulating influence, but subsequent work has revealed both the need to revise his original position and the need for greater analytic precision in the formulation of variables (see Bloom, 1959, for a useful critique). It is also apparent that there are further developments in moral insight through adolescence which he did not investigate (Kohlberg, 1963).

The content and strength of moral beliefs

People vary in the forms of behaviour they consider wrong, in the degree of conviction with which they hold these beliefs and in the strength of their condemnation of misbehaviour. Because these variables can be relatively easily measured, by interviews, questionnaires and rating scales, there are numerous studies of this aspect of morality. Most have been concerned with the social and personality correlates of moral belief. It would appear, for example, that an uncompromising rigidity in moral belief not only tends to be general across different moral issues, but is also related to rigidity in other types of belief (Adorno *et al.*, 1950; Rokeach, 1960), and moral beliefs vary across class, culture and sex.

It would seem likely that moral beliefs, as measured by verbal report, serve various social – and individual – functions in addition to that of guiding individual behaviour; for example, in certain circumstances the expression of moral belief can be a means of gaining social approval.

The relationships between moral variables

So far we have considered each of the five main dimensions of moral behaviour separately. It is time now to consider how they relate to each other. Our concern is with the empirical question whether positive associations exist between them. As yet the evidence is scanty, for the problem has seldom been directly studied.

Perhaps the most important relationship is that between resistance to temptation and guilt responses, for there is a point of view which holds that these are functionally equivalent indices of strength of conscience. Mackinnon (1938) found that resistance to temptation was positively related to self-reported guilt feelings in college students. Bandura and Walters (1959) report that aggressive, delinquent boys showed significantly less guilt on a number of indices than matched controls, and Glueck and Glueck (1950) present a picture of the typical delinquent as relatively guilt-free. Allinsmith (1960) found no general relationship between resistance to temptation and post-transgressional response when both were measured by the story completion technique, though he did find that those who resisted temptation were more likely to use confession, and those who used externalization, or blaming others, in response to transgression were less likely to resist temptation. Rebelsky, Allinsmith and Grinder (1963) found that non-cheaters in the ray-gun game were more likely to use confession in the story completion measure. A similar finding was reported by Grinder and McMichael (1963). Burton, Maccoby and Allinsmith (1961) found a small negative association between resistance to temptation and a measure of guilt based on parental report, though Grinder (1964) found that a similar measure of guilt taken at age five years was positively related to resistance to temptation at age eleven. Using observational measures, Sears, Rau and Alpert (1966) found a small positive association between resistance to temptation and post-transgressional emotional upset and the use of confession in boys, but not in girls. These investigators also found that another category of post-transgressional response, labelled 'fixing', and which consisted in helping to put things right again, was negatively associated with resistance to temptation.

It is obvious that we need to analyse these studies more closely, taking account of the age of subjects and the type of measure used. In general, the weight of evidence does tend to support the belief that resistance to temptation and reactions to transgression are related. But it is also plain that this relationship is neither as simple nor as strong as is implied in the assumption of functional equivalence. A possible way of integrating the findings is suggested by some recent experiments on puppies performed by Solomon (reported in Mowrer, 1960a). Solomon compared puppies who were punished as they approached forbidden food with others who were punished after they had already eaten much of it. The former resisted temptation longer in a test situation but showed little sign of 'guilt' once they had succumbed; the latter gave way to temptation sooner but showed stronger evidence of 'guilt' afterwards. In an ingenious series of experiments (Aronfreed, 1964; Aronfreed and Reber, 1965), essentially similar findings have been found with children. It would seem from these experiments that the same anxiety-inducing sanctions can produce resistance to temptation or post-transgressional guilt responses depending upon the timing of their administration. In the normal course of upbringing, we would expect the timing of punishments to vary widely, both for each child and between children.

Very few studies provide evidence bearing upon the remaining relationships. Hartshorne and May (1929) found a small, positive association ($r = 0.33$) between over-all measures of helpfulness and honesty. One of Piaget's original observations was that children who were mature in their conception of the function of rules were also better at keeping them, and he certainly thought that insight and behaviour were closely related. Grinder (1964) gave his subjects measures of moral realism and immanent justice, and also tested them in a cheating situation. Among boys he found no relationship at all between the insight measures and resistance to temptation. Among girls there was a small positive association between maturity on the moral realism measures and resistance to temptation, but no relation for the immanent justice measures. Medinnus (1966a) found no relationship at all between insight and resistance to temptation for either sex. On the other hand, Kohlberg (1963) reports that an experimental measure of cheating was positively related to maturity of moral judgement, but his measure of moral judgement was not the same as that used by Piaget. Attempts to show that measures of moral belief are predictive of actual behaviour have largely failed (see the review by Pettel and Mendlesohn, 1966), though strong verbal endorsement of moral belief is negatively related to verbally reported transgression of those beliefs (Middleton and Putney, 1962).

It will now be evident to the reader how much more research is needed before the dimensions of moral behaviour are precisely defined and the relationships between them understood. One thing, however, is clear. The number and relative independence of the variables involved are such that a wide variety of individual profiles on these dimensions is possible. In order to bring some preliminary structure to this confusion of possibilities, some writers have developed character typologies (see, for example, Bronfenbrenner, 1962; McCord and McCord, 1960; Peck and Havighurst, 1960). These typologies are speculative and idealized conceptual schemas. They tend to be loosely formulated and they differ from each other in the number of types described, the labels used and the kinds of distinction made. But they have some value. And though they differ from each other, examination suggests that they are all refinements and elaborations upon four basic types. To conclude this section a very brief sketch will be given of these four.

The first is the morally undeveloped character, with weak attachments to and weak sympathy for other people. Behaviour is controlled, if at all, by its pleasurable and painful consequences to the individual, and allegiance to moral principles is nominal. The extreme form of this type is the psychopath. The second is the socially dependent character, whose primary aim is to maintain acceptance in his social milieu and to avoid social disapproval. His socially visible behaviour and beliefs are determined by the norms of the groups to which he belongs, and both change as group membership changes. Lacking internalized morality, he is poor at resisting temptation in private and his post-transgressional responses are socially orientated. It is assumed that such a character is the product of an upbringing in which the main socializing agent has been the peer group rather than adults. The third is the highly internalized and rigid character, for whom the main socializing agents have been adults and who therefore has a morality rooted in unilateral respect for authority. Such a character has high resistance to temptation in private and strongly self-punitive reactions to transgression. His moral principles are inflexible and obsessionally followed, regardless of the consequences to himself and others. Attachment to principles takes precedence over attachment to people. Finally, there is the autonomous moral character, who, because of some optimum balance of adult and peer influences in socialization, has achieved a measure of independence of both. His morality is internalized, individual and flexible, so that he is neither so dependent upon social support that he cannot go against group norms when he thinks these norms are wrong, nor so committed to rigid principles that he cannot modify them in the light of actual social situations.

Some correlates of moral behaviour

Besides their intrinsic interest, an examination of the correlates of the various moral behaviour variables helps to throw light upon the inter-relationships between them. Only three factors will be discussed here; namely, sex differences, age and intelligence. Other factors for which some evidence exists are socio-economic level, cultural difference and genetic difference.

Sex differences

Most studies have been unable to find any stable difference between the sexes on measures of resistance to temptation in private (Burton, Allinsmith and Maccoby, 1966; Grinder, 1962, 1964; Medinnus, 1966b; Rebelsky, Allinsmith and Grinder, 1963). Hartshorne and May (1928) found no over-all difference, but on some measures girls cheated more. Sears, Rau and Alpert (1966) found a slight tendency for girls to resist temptation more, but since the subjects in this study were very young, this could be attributed to the tendency for girls to develop more quickly than boys. Girls are much less often delinquent than boys but there are many possible explanations of this. As for socially visible, virtuous actions, Hartshorne and May (1929) found that girls tended to score higher on their measures of helpfulness, though Ugural-Semin (1952) found no difference on his measure of generosity. It would seem that girls have a greater reputation for virtue among their mothers (Sears, Maccoby and Levin, 1957) and at school (Hartshorne and May, 1930). They are also somewhat less likely to report transgressions on questionnaires (Dentler and Monroe, 1961; Middleton and Putney, 1962). On measures of reaction to transgression, the picture is not clear. Some studies have found no difference (e.g. Luria, Goldwasser and Goldwasser, 1963). In others, girls have reported more guilt feeling (London, Schulman and Black, 1964) and exhibited more emotional upset (Sears, Rau and Alpert, 1966). A somewhat more stable finding is that girls make more use of confession (Rebelsky, 1963; Rebelsky, Allinsmith and Grinder, 1963), though the presence of this difference appears to be culturally dependent. No stable difference between the sexes has been found for measures of moral insight, though there is some slight tendency for girls to mature earlier (Whiteman and Kosier, 1964). On the other hand, girls did consistently better than boys on measures of moral knowledge (Hartshorne and May, 1930) and they tend to express stronger commitment to moral beliefs and to be more severely condemnatory of immoral behaviour (Middleton and Putney, 1962; Rettig and Pasamanick, 1959). The pattern of these results is generally consistent with the hypothesis that, because of the socialization pressures to which they are subjected, girls in Western, English-speaking cultures are more strongly motivated than boys to maintain a reputation for virtue.

Age

No relationship has been found between age and resistance to temptation in private, at least between the ages of eleven and sixteen years (Hartshorne and May, 1928) and seven and eleven years (Grinder, 1964; Medinnus, 1966b). There is evidence that delinquents first show antisocial behaviour at an early age, by age eight (Glueck and Glueck, 1950), though it also appears that a large number of delinquents have 'grown out' of their delinquency by their middle twenties. Though this evidence points to the conclusion that the internal, inhibitory aspect of morality is largely fixed by an early age, we must remember that both types of measure used are affected by a number of other factors. Hartshorne and May (1929) found virtually no relation between age and helpfulness, though Ugural-Semin (1952) found that generosity increased with age. The more cognitive aspects of morality are related to age, however. Moral knowledge increases (Hartshorne and May, 1930) and the content of moral beliefs changes (Hurlock, 1964). Nearly all Piaget's indices of moral insight have repeatedly been found to be associated with age in the manner predicted by Piaget. These results suggest that the cognitive and inhibitory aspects of morality are functionally distinct; but in view of the problems of interpreting some of the measures, it would be wiser to reserve judgement at present.

Intelligence

Hartshorne and May (1928) found a clear correlation between resistance to temptation and intelligence and Terman and Odin (1947) discovered that intellectually gifted children tended to be more moral than average controls. On the other hand, Brogden found intelligence to be largely independent of his measures of character. There is an obvious need for caution in interpreting evidence that virtue is associated with intelligence, since the intelligent child may have less need to cheat or lie, or he may more readily suspect a trap in the experimental testing situations. It has been shown that the subjective estimate of the chance of being found out is an important factor in resisting temptation (Rettig and Pasamanick, 1964). Intelligence was slightly related to helpfulness (Hartshorne and May, 1929) and strongly related to moral reputation (Terman and Odin, 1947). Allinsmith (1960) and Aronfreed (1961) found no relation between guilt responses and intelligence. Measures of moral insight have frequently been found to be related to mental age; the exception is those aspects which concern the concept of justice, where the relation to intelligence is not yet clear (Durkin, 1959a; Johnson, 1962).

Child-rearing antecedents of moral response

It has been assumed for some time now that a child's moral development is to a considerable extent determined by his early experience within the family. This is especially so for the resistance to temptation and guilt variables, and the failure to find age changes on these variables tends to support this. However, direct evidence for the influence of child-rearing variables is not yet extensive enough to allow unqualified statements to be made. Moreover, it is sometimes conflicting and hard to interpret. There are several reasons for this. First, if child-rearing factors are important, it must be because they produce stable differences between people which show up in spite of situational variability. From the discussion above, it is evident that most of the measures of moral response, though they probably do tap enduring personality differences, are also very susceptible to the influence of situational factors. Second, the measurement of child-rearing conditions is usually based upon intensive interviews with parents or children, the results of which are rated for such global variables as 'maternal warmth', or 'consistency of discipline'. Though we may have a modest confidence that the resulting scores bear some relation to actual differences between parents, we do not know how closely the two correspond, nor precisely what is being measured. Third, the design of many of the studies is not such as to permit very firm conclusions to be drawn. The most common procedure is to compare high and low scorers on some moral variable for such things as frequency of physical punishment in childhood. If the two are related, we cannot conclude that physical punishment is causally related to performance on the moral test. The functional link may be some other factor, such as genetic similarity, to which both the tendency to resort to physical punishment and performance on the moral test are independently related. With these reservations in mind, we can turn to the evidence.

There is a large measure of agreement among those studies which have compared delinquents with matched non-delinquents for family conditions (see, for example, Bandura and Walters, 1959; Bennett, 1960; Glueck and Glueck, 1950; McCord, McCord and Zola, 1957). On the basis of these studies, the conditions conducive to the development of internalized forms of moral behaviour appear to be these: strong affectional ties between parents and children; firm moral demands made by parents upon the children; the *consistent* use of sanctions; techniques of punishment that are psychological rather than physical, that is, techniques which signify or threaten withdrawal of love; and a high use of reasoning and explanation. When the affectional ties are very close and exclusive, and when parental demands are impossibly high and withdrawal of love the sanction always used, there is a danger that the child will be neurotically 'guilt-ridden'. This is especially the case when relations between the parents are strained. By contrast, delinquents tend to come from homes where affectional ties are weak, where parents are erratic and inconsistent (lax one moment and over-strict the next), where punishment tends to take the form of aggressive physical or verbal assault and where little attempt at explanation is made. The relative importance of the roles of mother and father is still unclear; but the evidence suggests that, though the paternal role is important (Andry, 1960; Glueck and Glueck, 1950), the maternal role is the more fundamental (McCord, McCord and Zola, 1957).

This reasonably coherent picture has not been supported by studies using an experimental measure of resistance to temptation. Maternal affection has not been found to be related to this variable (Burton, Maccoby and Allinsmith, 1961; Grinder, 1962; Sears, Rau and Alpert, 1966). Though Mackinnon (1938) found that students who cheated were more likely to report that their parents used physical punishment, other studies have failed to find such a relationship, and one study has found a small relationship in the other direction (Burton, Maccoby and Allinsmith, 1961). In an experiment, Burton, Allinsmith and Maccoby (1966) found no relation between withdrawal of nurturant attention and resistance to temptation. On the other hand, there is evidence that parental setting of standards and the use of reasoning are related to measures of resistance to temptation (Burton, Maccoby and Allinsmith, 1961; Sears, Rau and Alpert, 1966).

The reasons for this inconsistency between studies using delinquents and studies based upon experimental measures are not known. But there are several obvious considerations. First, there is the ambiguity in interpreting both the delinquency and experimental measures, and the uncertainty over the extent to which they are measuring the same traits. Second, the situational factors which determine responses in experimental tests may so reduce the usefulness of these measures as indices of stable character traits that long-term antecedent conditions cannot register on them. Third, studies using experimental methods have mostly been limited to small samples of middle-class children, in contrast to delinquency studies which have tended to use large, working-class samples. It is possible that among middle-class parents there is less variability in child-rearing attitudes and practices, so that such differences as do exist are not great enough to show through the situational factors which influence responses in the test. Only further research can clarify the problem.

.Studies of the antecedents of guilt responses have yielded results more consistent with those of delinquency studies. When parental interviews are the source of measures of guilt as well as of parent–child interaction, high guilt is found to be related to maternal warmth and the use of psychological techniques of discipline, and negatively related to the use of physical punishment (Burton, Maccoby and Allinsmith, 1961; Sears, Maccoby and Levin, 1957; Sears, Rau and Alpert, 1966). Similar findings are reported in studies using projective measures of guilt (Allinsmith, 1960; Allinsmith and Greening, 1955). Less directly supportive is the evidence from cross-cultural studies. If the antecedents of guilt are similar to those for delinquency, we should expect that family structures which encourage strong attachments to a few adults would produce stronger guilt responses in children than family structures which encourage attachments to a number of adults. Rabin and Goldman (1966) found less evidence of guilt in children raised in an Israeli kibbutz than in matched controls; though, interestingly, it has also been found that kibbutz children tend to make greater use of confession (Luria, Goldwasser and Goldwasser, 1963). Whiting (1959) found that societies with monogamous nuclear families exhibited more self-blame as measured by their accounts of the origin of illness than societies with more extended family units. A somewhat different pattern of antecedents was found when the measure of guilt was observed emotional upset. Among boys, Sears, Rau and Alpert (1966) found that those with high guilt were more likely to have parents who were anxious and non-permissive over sexual behaviour. Girls with high guilt tended to have close and sexually tinged relationships with their fathers, and to have mothers who lacked anxiety over sexual behaviour.

The other dimension of morality for which parent–child relationships are thought to be important antecedents is moral insight. Though the number of studies of moral insight, in Piaget's sense, is considerable, few have been concerned with its relationship to family variables. Immature insight, in Piaget's theory, is said to follow from relationships of high dependence upon parents who control and dominate. More mature judgement is held to be a function of relations of reciprocity, of give and take and mutual respect among peers. It would follow that the more controlling and dominating the parents, the less likely the child is to be mature in his judgement. Johnson (1962) gave parents a questionnaire measure of their attitudes towards their children and found some evidence consistent with this prediction. MacRae (1954) also found some slight evidence of a relationship between parental control and immaturity of judgement. Children brought up in institutions were less mature than controls brought up at home (Abel, 1941). On the other hand, it is not clear yet that membership of peer groups leads to maturity of judgement in the way Piaget thought (Durkin, 1959a and b).

Theory

So far in this chapter we have focused upon the results of empirical investigations. It is time to turn to the theories which have been offered to account for these results and which have guided the studies themselves. There are broadly three kinds of theoretical orientation which have dominated the field. They are psychoanalytic theory, learning theory and social learning theory; an introductory outline of them follows.

Psychoanalytic theory

Freud attributed the moral control of behaviour to a system or agency within the personality, the superego, which is relatively autonomous and independent of the ego (hence the subjectively felt distinction between 'I want' and 'I ought'), and which constitutes the voice of society within the individual. The superego is thought to have two components: the conscience, which is largely unconscious and which causes people to resist temptation or, if they yield, feel self-punitive guilt, and the ego-ideal which consists of consciously held values and aspirations and which accounts for striving after good. These components can vary independently and can, therefore, be considered separately.

The dynamic of conscience is provided by aggressive energy which has been more or less permanently directed inwards. Since the only source of energy in the personality is the id, or the unconscious instincts, internalized control of the id can only come about when part of it is given the task of inhibiting the rest. The cognitive aspect of conscience is provided by the rules and demands of parents which are introjected at the time at which the conscience is being formed. The introjection of parental demands and the inturning of aggression occur about the age of five years as a consequence of an emotional crisis. Three factors contribute to this crisis. First, there is the ambivalence of the parent–child relationship. The child learns to love, or invest in, his parents. These parents frustrate him, particularly when they make their own affection contingent upon conformity to their demands. This frustration generates hostility towards them. With the development of cognition, the child comes to realize that the parent he hates and the parent he loves are one and the same. Second, in relation to the agent of discipline, the child finds himself trapped. Parental sanctions for misbehaviour produce aggression, which, when expressed towards its cause, provokes even severer sanctions. Third, both these sources of conflict are heightened by the sexual rivalry which is presumed to occur when the child sexually desires the parent of the other sex and finds himself an impotent rival of the parent of the same sex. The love–hate tension resulting from these sources of conflict is resolved by the child's directing his aggression upon himself and by his adopting towards himself those attitudes and demands which his parents express towards him.

The origins of the ego-ideal are less conflictful. The child comes to invest strongly in an adult. Since, according to the theory, the child's capacity to invest is limited, this results in a depletion of self-love. Self-love is then restored by identifying with the other person, that is, by pretending to be him. With increased awareness of reality and therefore of the differences between the self and the other, this 'pretending to be the other' becomes difficult, and the child compromises by adopting the other as his ideal, as the kind of person he wants to become. Unlike the conscience, the ego-ideal continues to develop at least through the first half of life, and it develops through successive identifications with other people (see also Chapter 21).

This outline is enough to show that in some respects the theory is congruent with the evidence reported above, for example, in its emphasis upon the affection between parent and child, and in the importance it gives to parental discipline. Moreover, on this view, the strength of conscience is not likely to change much after early childhood. However, it also interprets guilt responses as self-punitive and predicts that guilt and resistance to temptation will be closely associated. Neither of these is well supported by the evidence.

Learning theory

Instead of postulating inner moral agents to account for moral behaviour, learning theorists base their approach upon the assumption that there is nothing about moral learning to distinguish it qualitatively from other forms of learning, such as learning not to touch electric fires or learning to read. Hence it can be adequately explained in terms of the principles which derive from the study of anxiety conditioning on the one hand and instrumental learning on the other.

Resistance to temptation is explained as follows. The young child, when about to engage in a forbidden action, is punished in some way. The anxiety evoked by punishment becomes associated with the configuration of external and internal stimuli present at the time.

Anxiety is a powerful response which inhibits other responses and, once learned, is hard to unlearn. In similar situations on future occasions this learned anxiety will be evoked and will inhibit behaviour. However, the internal and external stimuli present in a situation are often virtually the same for both forbidden and permitted behaviour (compare, for example, stealing a book from the library shelves and borrowing one). The difference lies in the way the situations are cognitively structured. Hence effective moral training requires that when the young child is punished for incipient misbehaviour, the situation be verbally labelled and cognitively structured for him. The labels, and later concepts, themselves become capable of evoking the anxiety response. Eventually, through the mechanisms of generalization and discrimination, the concept itself becomes the major anxiety-evoking agent, so that, on later occasions, the way the individual cognitively structures the situation will determine whether or not the inhibiting anxiety is evoked.

In a similar way, guilt is interpreted as anxiety which has been conditioned to the post-transgressional situation, which includes the way it has been cognitively structured. Guilt responses such as confession, self-criticism and apology, are treated as learned behaviours which have been found to be instrumental in reducing post-transgressional anxiety. The pursuit of virtue is explained in terms of instrumental learning. Because honesty and helpfulness have in the past been rewarded by parents, they become established habits; and since the concepts which structure such behaviour have also been associated with positively reinforcing experiences, the individual's recognition of his own honesty becomes rewarding. And, of course, strong habits of 'good' behaviour themselves have an inhibitory effect upon the corresponding but incompatible 'bad' behaviour. (For detailed accounts of this approach, see Aronfreed, 1964; Eysenck, 1964a; Kohlberg, 1963; Mowrer, 1960a and b.)

This theoretical approach has certain advantages over the psychoanalytic one in that it is more consistent with the evidence, it is based upon principles which have been well established in other contexts and it leads to more precisely formulated predictions. Its major weakness is that it does not account sufficiently for the fact that moral behaviour develops exclusively in a two-person situation.

Within the theory, there is no basis for differentiating punishment and reward mediated by human agents from those which are the impersonal consequences of behaviour. Yet it appears that the nature of the reinforcing agent, and of the individual's relationship to this agent, are crucial factors.

Social learning theory

The distinctive viewpoint of those who will here be called 'social learning theorists' is that, although they share the basic orientation of general learning theory, they recognize that certain extensions and modifications of that theory are needed to account for social influence, or learning, in a two-person situation. Thus, in addition to the concepts of conditioning and instrumental learning, the social learning theorist finds it necessary to develop concepts of empathy, imitation, identification and introjection (Argyle, 1964). Since many of these are discussed in the previous chapter, nothing further will be said about them here. The value of such concepts is that they draw attention to the importance of personal relationships in socialization.

Finally, none of the theoretical positions just described seems quite adequate to account for those developed forms of moral behaviour in which all aspects of moral response are integrated under cortical, or conceptual, control. Maturity in moral behaviour presumably involves some kind of creative autonomy, in which the individual modifies his own moral responses in the light of ideas and reasons. Although in other fields such as motivation and problem solving, psychologists have found it necessary to postulate autonomous processes inherent in the functioning of the central nervous system, the relevance of this for the understanding of moral development has not yet been adequately recognized.

Further reading
H. J. Eysenck, *Crime and Personality*, Routledge & Kegan Paul, 1964.
L. Kohlberg, 'Moral development and identification', in H. W. Stevenson (ed.), *Child Psychology*, University of Chicago Press, 1963.
L. Kohlberg, 'Development of moral character and moral ideology', in M. L. Hoffman and L. W. Hoffman (eds.), *Review of Child Development Research*, Russell Sage Foundation, 1964.

Chapter 23
Persuasive Communications and Small Group Processes

Most of the problems dealt with in the previous two chapters have only claimed the attention of psychologists, to any widespread extent, in the last few years. Moreover, there is still much work waiting to be done on them. By contrast, the two main topics of this chapter have been prominent areas of research for more than two decades. Most of the obvious questions have been asked, and the answers tidily summarized in numerous review articles and textbooks. Many findings have been replicated sufficiently often for them to be accepted as established, and a variety of theoretical systems have been advanced to account for them.

In the study of *persuasive communications*, the subject receives a communication from some source, and interest lies in the extent to which his attitudes, beliefs and opinions are thereby modified. Essentially, this is the situation which obtains in the mass media, in written communications and in political speeches. The study of the effects of persuasive communications received its initial impetus during the last war, when there was an immediate need to devise effective techniques for maintaining morale and changing attitudes and behaviour in large numbers of people. Since then, the crucial role of mass communications in highly developed societies has confirmed and strengthened this interest.

In the *small group*, individuals influence each other through face-to-face interaction. The experimental study of social influence in this kind of situation has been stimulated on the one hand by the fact that in society a great deal of work and decision making is done in a group setting, and on the other by the suspicion that within a group, factors are at work determining individual behaviour which are unique to that setting.

Though there are respects in which these two areas of research complement and support each other, they will be treated separately. A sample of the main findings will be given, and these will be limited to experiments conducted under laboratory conditions and to a few which took place in conditions closer to real life. We shall not, for instance, discuss the sociological aspects of mass communications, nor the clinical study of small groups.

Persuasive communications

The situation we shall examine is one in which a communication designed to modify opinion and attitude in a particular direction is given to a number of subjects, usually at the same time. Two experimental designs are commonly used. In the first, the before–after design, the attitudes of the subjects are measured before they receive the communication and then again afterwards so that changes can be recorded. In the second, the after–after design, the attitudes of subjects are not measured before they receive the communication. Instead, their attitudes after receiving the communication are compared with those of a control group which does not receive it. Normally, it is important that the subjects, even though they may know they are taking part in an experiment, do not know what is being studied.

There are three groups of variables which can be related to attitude change, those pertaining to the communicator, to the communication and to the subjects. In any experiment, one or more of these is varied systematically and the remainder held constant or, in the case of subject variables, randomized. These variables are set out schematically in Figure 80. Those listed by no means exhaust the variables which have been studied, but they are the main ones selected for discussion here. In addition, there are the variables associated with the situation in which the communication is given, but these will not be discussed in any detail.

It should be added that the account which follows is oversimplified. In considering the influence of these variables we shall be compelled to ignore to a large extent the interactions between them. In general, earlier experiments took one independent variable at a time, whereas later ones have taken several and shown that there are interactions between them. These interactions present too complex a picture to be described in detail here.

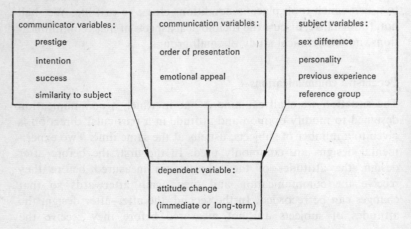

Figure 80　Communication variables

Communicator variables

It may seem obvious to say that the success of a persuasive communication in effecting opinion change is partly a function of the way in which the subjects evaluate the source of the communication. Nevertheless, the experimental checking of the obvious is apt to bring to light aspects of the problem which are less obvious. In the experiments to be described, the design consisted in presenting the same communication to randomly divided subjects and systematically varying certain aspects of the source.

The common-sense expectation that subjects are more influenced by a communication from a source they judge to be credible or reliable was tested by Hovland and Weiss (1951). Two groups of subjects were given the same four communications on four different topics. For one group the sources were presented as highly credible, for example, Dr Robert Oppenheimer, or the *Journal of Biology*, and for the other the sources were of low credibility, for example, a glossy magazine or *Pravda*. The authors checked that these sources did in fact differ in credibility for the subjects. They found significantly greater opinion change when the source of credibility was high.

In an earlier study, Ewing (1942) examined the effects of varying the declared bias of the communicator. Having ascertained that the subjects had a generally favourable attitude towards Henry Ford, he gave them a communication recommending a less favourable attitude. Under one condition, the communicator announced that he was biased in favour of Henry Ford, in the other that he was biased against him. The former condition was distinctly more effective. By saying that he was in favour of Henry Ford, the communicator was better able to change the subjects' opinions to a less favourable position. As Ewing points out, it is important that the subjects do not notice the discrepancy between the declared bias and the actual communication.

It appears that a communication is more effective if it is seen as running counter to the self-interest of the communicator. Walster, Aronson and Abrahams (1966) gave subjects communications which advocated either more or less power for the courts and which purported to come from either a criminal or a prosecuting attorney. The criminal was less effective than the prosecutor when advocating less power for the courts but more effective when advocating more power. On the other hand, when the communicator is perceived as trying to persuade the subjects, counter-arguments are provoked in the subject to a greater extent than if the communicator is not seen as obviously intending to persuade (Brock, 1967). The more the subjects engage in counter-argument, the less effective the communication. Allyn and Festinger (1961) used two conditions in an experiment to test this. In one condition, the subjects were set to listen carefully, and informed beforehand that the communicator was going to try to convince them of a point of view that ran counter to their strongly held beliefs. Under the other condition, subjects were not forewarned and were distracted from counter-argument while listening to the communication by being required to assess the speaker's personality. Opinion change was much greater under the second condition (see also Festinger and Maccoby, 1964). There is also some evidence that an 'overheard' communication is more effective than one explicitly directed to the subject, at least when the subject is initially somewhat favourably disposed towards the position advocated in the communication (Brock and Becker, 1965).

Burnstein, Stotland and Zander (1961) examined the effects upon opinion change of the perceived similarity and success of the communicator. An adult, purporting to be a deep-sea diver, gave a standard talk to groups of boys. The independent variable was the way he introduced himself. He presented himself as either successful or unsuccessful and as either similar or dissimilar in background to the subjects. Adoption of the diver's opinions was greatest under the high success and high similarity conditions. In another experiment, Berscheid (1966) found that perceived similarities between subject and communicator that were relevant to the communication were much more influential in producing opinion change in the direction of the communication than perceived similarities which were not relevant. It was also found that relevant, perceived dissimilarities tended to have a 'boomerang' effect in pushing the subject's opinions further away from those advocated in the communication.

These and many other experiments demonstrate the importance of the attributes of the communicator in determining the effectiveness of a persuasive communication. Attempts have been made to explain these effects. As for the first experiment, by Hovland and Weiss, it might well be said that there is no need for a psychological explanation, since it is reasonable to give more credence to statements by people we judge to be expert. But the effects of perceived similarity of background, for example, can hardly be justified so well on rational grounds. Burnstein, Stotland and Zander offer their own theory of identification to account for this effect. This theory hypothesizes that there is a tendency for subjects, when they initially perceive similarities between themselves and others, to increase these similarities, and that this process may function to enhance self-esteem.

However, experiments have, in general, failed to show that communicator effects are very long-lasting. It would appear that, once the immediate situational impact has passed, the effects of the content of the communication continue, so that differences due to communicator variables reduce with time.

Communication variables

In constructing a persuasive communication, a number of decisions have to be made. For example, do we save our strongest argument to the end? Do we include counter-arguments? And to what extent should we seek to arouse emotion? A number of experiments have been designed to answer these questions and we will simply summarize the main conclusions (see Hovland, Janis and Kelley, 1953; Hovland, 1957). In a one-sided presentation, putting the strongest argument first is an advantage only if the audience is initially uninterested in the topic. If both sides are presented by different people there is no necessary advantage in being first. The inclusion of counter-arguments is more effective if the audience initially disagrees with the communication or if it is highly educated. A two-sided argument is also better if the subjects are already familiar with the topic (Chu, 1967). It seems that when subjects are likely to counter-argue to themselves, if the communicator recognizes the counter-argument in his communication, he is more likely to win them over to his point of view.

Another advantage to the communicator of including counter-arguments is that the subjects become to some extent inoculated against them. In several experiments (for example, McGuire and Papageorgis, 1961; Papageorgis and McGuire, 1961) it was found that by exposing subjects to weakened forms of a counter-argument they were subsequently immunized against the same counter-arguments in a stronger form. Resistance to a counter-communication can also be strengthened by inducing subjects to declare publicly their position beforehand.

An important question when constructing a persuasive communication is to decide upon that degree of discrepancy between the subject's position and that recommended in the communication which is likely to produce most attitude change. Will the subject's attitude shift more if the position advocated is very different from his own than if it is only moderately different? There are two main possibilities: either the relationship between discrepancy and attitude shift is linear, so that attitude shift is always greater the greater the discrepancy, or it is curvilinear, in that with extreme discrepancies other mechanisms are evoked, such as disparagement of the source, which reduce attitude shift. The experimental results are equivocal. Most studies have found the relationship between discrepancy and attitude change linear (for example, Helson, Blake and Mouton, 1958b); but some have found a curvilinear relationship (for example, Freedman, 1964).

There seem to be at least two possible reasons for this lack of agreement. First, discrepancy may be interacting with other variables in the situation; and second, it is often difficult to be sure whether the extremes of discrepancy have been properly sampled. Bochner and Insko (1966) attempted to deal with these two possibilities. They interacted discrepancy with source credibility and used an issue which would permit the sampling of all degrees of discrepancy. They presented subjects with a communication arguing that people sleep too much at night for optimal health. The number of hours of sleep recommended varied from eight to nought. Two levels of source credibility were used, 'Sir John Eccles, Nobel prize-winning physiologist' and 'Mr Harry J. Olson, director of the Fort Worth Y.M.C.A.' Amount of attitude shift was linearly related to discrepancy for the high-credibility source, except for the nought-hour recommendation when opinion change dropped, and curvilinearly related for the low-credibility source. This suggests that, if the source has high credibility and the position advanced is not so extreme as to be entirely absurd, discrepancy and attitude change are linearly related.

One of the criticisms that has been levelled against research in this field is that it employs communications on topics of a trivial nature which are of little consequence to the subjects. This criticism is not entirely fair, since a wide range of topics has been used. But inevitably, when the effects of ordering of arguments or source credibility are being studied, it is desirable to reduce variability due to other factors, and hence topics have usually been chosen that are relatively unfamiliar to the subjects. However, the effects of personal involvement have been examined. N. Miller (1965) found that subjects who were personally committed and dogmatic were much less affected by the communication. In fact, some of them shifted their attitudes even further away from the position advocated in the communication. Other studies (for example, Freedman, 1964) have come up with similar findings.

Finally, there is the question of emotional arousal. In an interesting experiment, Janis and Feshback (1953) presented a communication on dental hygiene under several degrees of fear arousal. Fear was induced by the way descriptions were phrased and by the use of visual aids. They found that opinion change was curvilinearly related to arousal, with the maximum change occurring under minimal or moderate arousal. It would seem that maximum arousal induced a defensive reaction in subjects, the feeling of being 'got at'. Though subsequent studies have confirmed this finding, they have also revealed some important qualifications. Thus, strong fear arousal is more effective if the subjects are given at the same time some reassuring recommendations as to how the threat can be averted (De Wolfe and Governdale, 1964). And though it has been shown that moderate arousal is more effective in changing the opinions of smokers against smoking, strong fear arousal is more effective in strengthening the resolve of non-smokers never to smoke (Insko, Arkoff and Insko, 1965). When the topic holds little interest for the subjects, high fear arousal may be no different in its effects from low fear arousal (Berkowitz and Cottingham, 1960).

Of course, results of this kind cannot be generalized beyond the population of subjects used and the topic chosen; but the suggestion is that fear arousal brings diminishing returns when it induces too much conflict in the subject, either between the degree of arousal and the perceived seriousness of the topic or between arousal and existing behaviour and attitude.

Subject variables

In every experiment on persuasion, wide individual differences are found in susceptibility to the influence of a communication. It would seem obvious that the relation between subject variables and opinion change is a complex one. Some people may be relatively more affected by the communicator than by the communication, or by one sort of content or style of argument than another. The dangers attendant upon generalizing from one topic or communicator to another, or one age group or social class to another, are indeed great. But it may nevertheless be the case that there is a tendency for some people to be more persuasible than others and it is to this question that we must now turn. Studies which examine the personality correlates of opinion change in a small group setting are also relevant and these will be discussed later.

There are two sorts of evidence relevant to the question of general persuasibility. The first comes from those studies which demonstrate that individual differences in opinion change remain to some extent stable across different topics and communicators. The second kind of evidence is the repeated findings by different investigators that a given personality variable is related to opinion change even though the content of the communication and the nature of the communication have varied widely.

As for the first type of study, a definitive answer to the question of stable individual differences in persuasibility would require an adequate sampling of subject, topic, type of appeal and communicator, and such a study has not been done. There is, however, some more limited evidence. Hovland and Janis (1959) have reviewed a number of studies which reveal a positive association between persuasibility for different topics and communicators. They themselves have devised a measure of general persuasibility based upon opinion change produced by five communications varying widely in content. But the range of content difference is limited and the correlations are small.

More interesting is the repeated finding of an association with a subject variable in studies using different kinds of communication. One of the most stable findings is that females are more susceptible to persuasive influence than males, at least among adolescents and young adults. Whittaker and Meade (1967) found that this tendency for females to be more persuasible than males held across several different cultures. These authors also found that there was a decline in persuasibility over the ages from fourteen to thirty-two years.

It has also been found in a number of studies that, among males, persuasibility is related to low self-esteem, as measured by questionnaires. The lack of such an association among females is puzzling. However, in a recent study, Cox and Bauer (1964) did find an association between self-esteem and persuasibility among women, but a curvilinear one. Those with medium self-esteem were most affected by a persuasive communication. Those with the lowest self-esteem tended to react against the communication and shift their opinions further away from it, whereas those with high self-esteem were not affected at all. The authors interpret the change in the low-esteem group as defensive or self-protective.

Cox and Bauer also point out the need to distinguish a general lack of confidence in making judgements from a specific lack of confidence in judging a particular issue. Whereas the former may be a general personality trait, the latter may be due to ignorance of the specific issue. They found that subjects with high general confidence were persuasible if their confidence on the particular issue was low; and conversely, high specific confidence compensated for low general confidence and reduced persuasibility for that particular topic.

There is some evidence of a relationship between persuasibility and emotional disorder. Subjects characterized as timid, guilt-ridden and socially passive were more persuasible, those with relatively aggressive, antisocial tendencies less persuasible, than normal controls. Salience of group membership is also a relevant variable. Catholics who were reminded of their religious affiliations were less affected by an anti-Catholic communication than Catholics who were not so reminded.

A number of studies have examined the effect of various situational factors upon opinion change. For example, it has been shown several times that counter-attitudinal role-playing is a potent determinant of change. Janis and King (1954) required subjects to play the role of the communicator. They were given an outline of an argument which advocated a position discordant with their own and then made to present this argument to others. Their attitudes changed significantly more than control subjects who listened passively. In a later study (King and Janis, 1956) they showed that improvising a communication was more effective than reading it aloud or silently. Recently,

Janis and Mann (1965) required subjects to play the role of patients who had just been told that they had lung cancer. The procedure was elaborate and convincing. Not only were their attitudes towards smoking modified to a greater extent but they also changed their actual smoking habits more than subjects who simply heard the procedure recorded on tape.

There are many other important questions which cannot be discussed here. They include, for example, the effect of initial certainty of belief upon subsequent change, the factors determining the permanence of change, the effects of public declaration of opinion upon future attitudes and the relationship between attitudinal and behavioural change. But before leaving this section, something must be said about the theories which have been advanced to explain various of the findings described above.

Broadly speaking, these theories fall into two groups, those which focus upon the nature of attitude and belief, and formulate principles to account for change, and those that focus upon the social situation, and explain opinion change in terms of interpersonal relationships. Among the more important of the first kind are Festinger's theory of cognitive dissonance (Festinger, 1957), Osgood's congruity model of attitude change (Osgood and Tannenbaum, 1955), the 'cognitive balancing' theory of Rosenberg and Adelson (see Rosenberg and Hovland, 1960) and Rokeach's theory of belief congruence (Rokeach, 1960). An excellent account of these and other theories will be found in Insko (1967). These theories vary in scope, content and precision; but they tend to have in common the implication that attitude change is, in the loose sense of the word, a homeostatic mechanism for reducing that dissonance, incongruity or imbalance which occurs when an individual is faced with a persuasive communication which conflicts with his existing attitudes, beliefs and behaviour.

The second type of theory fastens upon the relationships between subject and communicator, and attempts to characterize the nature of these relationships and their influence upon opinion change. Most of these theories use such concepts as *identification* or *imitation* and have been developed mainly in the study of socialization. An example of the extension of this kind of theory into the field of communication research is the theory put forward by Kelman (1961). Kelman distinguishes three processes of opinion change: *compliance*, in which the subject adopts the beliefs of another, not because the issue matters to him but because in doing so he produces a satisfying social effect; *identification*, in which attitude change is instrumental to the maintenance of a satisfying, self-defining relationship to the communicator so that agreement enhances self-esteem; and *internalization*, in which opinion change occurs because of the perceived plausibility of the communication, and its congruence with existing values and beliefs. Although these processes are not mutually exclusive, Kelman distinguishes different antecedents and consequents for them. Compliance will occur when the communicator has the power to reward the subject and it will continue just so long as these rewards are forthcoming. Moreover, it implies only public agreement. Identification occurs when the communicator has prestige and when agreement with him is important for the subject in establishing his sense of identity (as, for example, when someone who wants to think of himself as a Socialist listens to a distinguished Socialist speaker). The influence will last so long as the relationship remains important and will affect both public and private attitudes. Internalization is essentially independent of the communicator and primarily a function of the communication. It would be expected to influence both public and private belief and to be more or less permanent.

The former kind of theory is concerned primarily with what happens *within* the individual, the latter with what happens *between* individuals. The latter type of theory takes the two-person situation as basic. Whether or not this type of theory is wholly reducible to the former kind is a matter for debate.

Small groups

It is not easy to give a precise and unequivocal definition of a small group in the sense in which the term is used here. For practical purposes it can be thought of as a number of people, usually between two and about twenty, who meet for some common purpose which requires them to interact with each other over a period of time. But it is obviously an arbitrary matter when we say that a collection of people is not a group, or that a group is no longer small.

Four kinds of group have been studied: the 'real life' group such as a board of management, a delinquent gang or a family; the therapeutic group, where the group experience is used as an instrument for helping neurotic people; the training group, which has as its aim the creation of insight into group functioning among its members; and the laboratory group. Though efforts are being made to apply the experimental method to the first three kinds of group, the difficulties are considerable, and for the detailed experimental study of group processes we have no alternative at present but to rely heavily upon the work done with laboratory groups.

This necessarily limits the generality of the conclusions that can be drawn. Laboratory groups differ from the others in a number of ways. Their members have not usually met before the group is formed, the 'life' of the group is short, the task before it is often one that is never encountered outside the laboratory and which is not important to the members, and the members know that, superimposed upon this specific task, is the more general one of helping an experimenter. Moreover, many experiments have used procedures which are highly artificial, such as preventing members from seeing each other and compelling them to communicate with each other by signals.

These limitations do not mean that the study of laboratory groups has been wasted. A functional relationship between two variables which is discovered in the laboratory, and which can usually only be discovered there, still tells us something about the way groups function. What we cannot assess on the basis of laboratory groups alone is how important this relationship is for understanding group functioning outside the laboratory, where many other variables are systematically influencing it at the same time.

There is a sense in which an individual's behaviour in a group setting becomes a function of the group. By this is meant that his behaviour has the appearance of being controlled by features of the group as a whole, as well as by the characteristics of the other individuals. Members may consciously recognize an obligation to the group which takes precedence over their obligations to any other particular member. Formal groups, such as committees, and even to some extent informal groups, have an identity which persists even though individual members may change. It is considerations of this kind which suggest that a group is a kind of pseudo-organism, of which the individual is a functioning organ. Though a moment's thought will show that the analogy cannot be sustained, there is enough point in it to justify the experimenter in taking the group as his basic unit, even though his measures of group behaviour involve observing and measuring individual actions.

Groups form, develop and break up, and some of the main variables involved in this process are presented schematically in Figure 81. A group is formed when a number of people meet for a purpose they propose to achieve together. There are two sorts of problem which a group faces. The first is the *task*, which may be the solving of a problem, the making of a decision or simply having a good time. The second is the *socio-emotional problem*, by which is meant the problem of establishing friendly and harmonious relationships between members. It is possible to classify the actions of individuals within the group on the basis of their relevance to the solution of these two kinds of problem.

After interaction has continued for a while, three processes usually become discernible. First, individual members begin to specialize in aspects of interaction. Not only do some people contribute more than others but people also begin to specialize in the kind of contribution they make. Some may concentrate on socio-emotional problems, others on the task. In short, *role structure* emerges. In formal groups, this role structure may be imposed from without, though, even then, an informal role differentiation is likely to occur as well. Second, there is a tendency for the opinions of members to converge upon agreement. The mere fact of being a member of a group means that the individual is subject to pressures to conform to the expectations of others. In other words, groups develop *norms* in relation to both the socio-emotional and the task problems. Third, groups develop *cohesion* – a tendency to stay together because members have come to like each other.

Role structure, norm formation and cohesion can be thought of as conditions instrumental to the achievement of the task, to lasting changes in belief and attitude among members and to the members' satisfaction with the group. Under some conditions, of course, they may impede the achievement of these ends, but their function is best evaluated in relation to them.

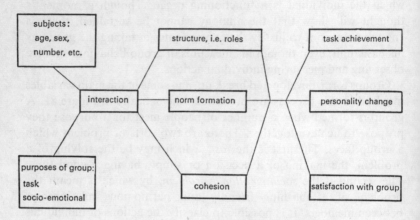

Figure 81   Group variables

Typically, experiments in this field take the group as the basic unit. Groups are assigned to different experimental conditions, such as different types of task or pattern of interaction, and the effects of such manipulation upon some general feature of the group such as its cohesion or task success are measured. The number and variety of the experiments that have been done are considerable. In the brief outline to be given here, we shall begin with the process of interaction itself, then examine role structure, norm formation and cohesion and end with some discussion of the factors associated with task success. For a detailed survey of the field, the reader is referred to Hare (1962).

Group interaction

The process of interaction within a group can be examined in two ways. We can consider only the nature and frequency of communicatory acts, such as utterances and gestures; or we can examine the direction that communications take within the group and plot its communication network.

Of the systems developed for classifying and recording communicatory acts, the most influential has been that of Bales (1951). Within this system an act is defined as a unit of behaviour, usually a sentence, which can elicit a meaningful response from others. Trained observers watch groups at work and record actions made by members using the system given in Table 12. It will be seen that the system allows

Table 12

The system of categories used in observation and their relation to major frames of reference. (Adapted from Bales, 1950, p. 258)

A. Socio-emotional area: positive reactions	1 *Shows solidarity*, raises others' status, gives help, reward 2 *Shows tension release*, jokes, laughs, shows satisfaction 3 *Agrees*, shows passive acceptance, understands, concurs, complies
B. Task area: attempted answers	4 *Gives suggestion*, direction, implying autonomy for others 5 *Gives opinion*, evaluation, analysis, expresses feeling, wish 6 *Gives orientation*, information, repeats, clarifies, confirms
C. Task area: questions	7 *Asks for orientation*, information, repetition, confirmation. 8 *Asks for opinion*, evaluation, analysis, expression of feeling 9 *Asks for suggestion*, direction, possible ways of action
D. Socio-emotional area: negative reactions	10 *Disagrees*, shows passive rejection, formality, withholds help 11 *Shows tension*, asks for help, withdraws out of field 12 *Shows antagonism*, deflates others' status, defends or asserts self

twelve categories, half of which fall in the task and half in the socio-emotional area. Each communicatory act made by a member is placed into one of these categories. It is then possible to contrast both individuals and groups in their characteristic action profiles.

This system has been used to investigate the developmental changes which occur throughout the life of a group, and the effects upon type of action of different tasks and different kinds of subject. Thus, in the development of problem-solving groups, acts of giving information steadily decrease, the making of suggestions increases, and negative emotional reactions initially increase and thereafter decrease (Bales and Strodtbeck, 1951). Psychiatric interviews and therapeutic groups have been shown to differ systematically from laboratory groups in the type of action which predominates. In a study of mock juries, clear differences between the sexes were found in the type of communicatory acts made. Men were more likely to give suggestions, opinions and information, and to show more antagonism; women showed more agreement and tension release, and more often asked for information (Strodtbeck and Mann, 1956).

Besides specializing in particular types of action, individuals in a group tend to differ in the extent to which they initiate and receive communications. The consequence of such differentiation is the spontaneous emergence of a network of communication within the group, such that members tend to address more remarks to some individuals than others. Of course, in informal groups, it cannot be expected that the communication network will remain stable. But attempts have been made to investigate the consequences of different kinds of network by experimentally manipulating them. This is usually done by using a simulated group situation in which subjects are in cubicles, unable to see other members but able to communicate by signals, messages or telephone. In such a situation, the experimenter can control the pattern of communication. Examples of patterns which have been used are the *circle*, in which each member can communicate to one other and is the recipient of communications from one other, and the *wheel*, in which members interact only with a central person. Experiments have shown that the nature of the communication net influences the total activity of the group, the emergence of a leader, the satisfaction of members with the group and the success of the group in achieving its task (see, for example, Leavitt, 1951).

Group structure

One of the major characteristics differentiating a group from a collection of people is that a group has structure. Because there is a tendency for certain communication nets to predominate and because individuals tend to specialize in certain kinds of act, it is possible to talk about the *position* of members and their *roles*. By position we mean an individual's location in the communication net and by role we mean those behaviours which other members expect from the occupant of a particular position. The best illustration is the highly formalized group where both position and role are defined by rules. In a committee, for example, the chairman's position in the communication net is rigidly fixed and there are compelling expectations governing the kind of contribution he can make. The same applies to the other officers and members. But even in informal groups it may be possible to specify such roles as leader or policy maker, most popular person, organizer, scapegoat, wit and so on.

The roles which have received the greatest attention from experimenters are the leader and the most popular person. In deciding whether an individual is the leader of a group or not, investigators have made use of three main methods: they have used the ratings of observers, the ratings of group members and formal election to office within the group. Popularity has been measured by members' ratings for likeableness or choice as a friend. In practice, leadership and popularity tend to go together (see, for example, Harvey and Rutherford, 1960) but there is no necessary association between the two. Moreover, the leadership role tends to bifurcate into a task and a socio-emotional leader, and popularity may be more closely associated with the latter. It has been suggested that the most satisfactory family structure is one in which the father takes the task leadership role and the mother becomes the socio-emotional leader.

The question concerning leadership which has excited most

interest is whether it is a general personality trait. Do some individuals naturally become leaders whatever the context and, if so, what sort of person is a leader? The evidence is equivocal. There is some tendency for leadership to be a general trait but there is also evidence that such situational factors as the task, the communication pattern, the degree of formalization of the group and the personalities of members help to determine who will emerge as leader. It cannot therefore be expected that the many attempts to demonstrate an association between leadership and personality will yield consistent results. Mann (1959) has provided a thorough review of the studies done. It is clear that there is no result which is not contradicted by others. From the accumulated evidence, however, some trends do emerge. For example, of the 196 results relating intelligence to leadership, ninety-one are positive and significant and a further eighty-two are positive but not significant, whereas there is only one result which is negative and significant. Other, though weaker, trends are for personal adjustment, extraversion, dominance, masculinity and interpersonal sensitivity to be positively related, and conservatism to be negatively related to leadership. The personality correlates of popularity are less clear, though with one exception they are similar in direction to those for leadership. Popularity tends to be positively related to intelligence, extroversion and adjustment, but also positively related to conservatism.

Norm formation and conformity

More than twenty years ago, two series of experiments were conducted which have had a considerable influence upon subsequent research on small groups. The first of these was performed by Sherif (see Sherif and Sherif, 1956). Subjects were placed in a darkened room with a single point of light visible. Normally, in this situation, the light appears to move (the autokinetic effect). Subjects were required to estimate the amount of apparent movement. Sherif found that if subjects made their estimates alone, they exhibited a much greater variability than if they made them in a group situation where they could hear the judgements of others. In the group, there was a tendency for judgements to converge upon a common *norm.* These results suggested the hypothesis that in a group situation, there is generated a tendency for those judgements and opinions of members which are relevant to the task to shift in the direction of closer agreement.

The second series of experiments was directed by Asch (see Asch, 1952). In these experiments subjects were required to judge which of three lengths of line was the same as a standard line. The differences were such that, when alone, subjects rarely, if ever, made a mistake. Asch, however, placed the subjects in a group situation, in which, unknown to the subject, all other members has been primed by the experimenter beforehand. On each trial, every member called out in turn the line which he judged to correspond to the standard. On the critical trials, it was prearranged that the subject should be the last to call out and that all the other members would call out a wrong line, one which plainly was not the same length as the standard. It was found that a surprisingly high proportion of the subjects sided at one time or another, with the majority against the evidence of their senses. For example, in one experiment with thirty-one subjects and a number of trials, 33·2 per cent of the critical judgements coincided with the incorrect judgements of the majority. There were wide individual differences. Some subjects resisted, others succumbed on every critical trial. Few failed to show signs of tension and discomfort.

These two experiments obviously differ in important respects. Sherif's situation involves a highly ambiguous stimulus and there is no objectively correct judgement the subject can make; moreover, it has been found that subjects are often unaware of the social influence operating and feel no conflict. In the Asch experiment, on the other hand, there is no ambiguity about the true answer for it is plainly visible and the subject is in no doubt about the existence of social pressure for he has to meet it directly and hence suffers considerable conflict. These differences suggest that the experiments may not be dealing with quite the same process.

In an experiment by Deutsch and Gerard (1955) it was found that if subjects were allowed to make their judgements secretly in the Asch situation, they were not influenced by group pressure. This led the authors to distinguish two kinds of group influence, *normative social influence*, which is the immediate, situational pressure to conform to the expectations of others, and *informational influence*, which is the pressure to accept information from others as evidence of reality when the subject is himself unsure. Other experiments offer support for this distinction. For example, Snyder, Mischel and Lott (1960) gave groups the task of judging pictures. It seems likely that both sorts of group influence would be at work in this situation. The results showed that conformity was reduced by two conditions, high involvement in the problem which presumably reduces normative influences, and high knowledge about the problem which reduces informational influence, and the effects of these two variables were quite independent of each other.

Whether or not the distinction will prove permanently useful, it has some value when we compare the experiments of Asch and Sherif. For the former would seem to involve primarily normative influences and the latter informational. The results of other experiments using the Asch and Sherif situations are consistent with this. In the Asch situation, conformity does not carry over to judgements of the same material made afterwards without group pressure (Luchins and Luchins, 1955); while under group pressure subjects will still conform to some extent, even though they are aware that a deception is being imposed on them and that the other members of the group are obeying the experimenter (V. L. Allen, 1966). Social influence in the autokinetic situation, on the other hand, persists after the experiment is over, even as long as a year later, and the influence disappears when subjects are told that the light is in fact motionless and that the impression of movement is entirely subjective (V. L. Allen, 1965). These experiments clearly show that the effects of normative social pressure are indeed confined to the immediate situation whereas informational social influence may persist for a long time.

The original experiments by Asch and Sherif stimulated a line of research which has now grown to considerable proportions. Since most of these studies have involved judging objective issues which have a fairly high degree of ambiguity, we may suppose that they involve both types of influence in more or less equal degree. For a full discussion of the issues raised by this research, the reader is referred to Berg and Bass (1961). In what follows we shall discuss briefly only the relationship of conformity to subject variables and leadership.

As with the effects of persuasive communications, the question whether there are stable associations between subject variables and conformity also involves the question whether there are stable individual differences in conformity across different tasks. Few studies have directly examined this, but the evidence does offer some support for the view that conformity is a general trait. For example, Blake, Helson and Mouton (1956) found stability in conforming behaviour across such tasks as estimating the number of metronome clicks in a given time, expressing opinions and solving arithmetical problems. A great many studies have correlated subject variables with conformity in different situations and, though many of the results are contradictory and confusing, trends do emerge. As with persuasion, females conform more than males and there is some association between conformity and low self-esteem. Developmentally, susceptibility to peer-group pressure increases up to about the age of fifteen years and thereafter declines. The studies using various personality measures have been reviewed by Mann (1959). When the measures used are personality inventories or ratings by others, there are clear trends for conforming people to be less well adjusted, lacking in dominance and conservative in the sense of being conventional and authoritarian. When the measures are self-ratings by the subjects, conformity is related to good adjustment and extraversion. This is presumably because conforming people, in describing themselves, try to conform to an image they consider socially desirable. There is some evidence of a negative relationship to intelligence (Crutchfield, 1955).

Though this evidence does support the notion that there is a conforming personality, it seems clear that future research will be more fruitful if it distinguishes between different forms of social influence, in particular between normative and informational influences. Steiner and Vannoy (1966) found marked personality differences, not between conformers and non-conformers but between conformers who continued to maintain their new position after the experiment and those who did not.

A number of studies have examined whether leadership or popularity status is related to conformity (see V. L. Allen, 1965). It can be argued both that the high-status person will conform more because his status depends upon conformity and that the high-status person will conform less because his status allows him greater latitude. The results are not clear. There is, however, a suggestion that the relationship may be curvilinear and that those in the middle of the status hierarchy are likely to conform most.

Of all aspects of group functioning, it is norm formation which has excited most theoretical interest. A number of attempts have been made to develop formal theories which will permit the derivation of empirical predictions from a few basic hypotheses. Examples of such theories are those of Festinger (1954) and Zetterberg (1957). Festinger's theory of social comparison processes can be generalized beyond the small group setting and appears to be primarily concerned with informational influences. The theory is elaborate, but the central postulate is that individuals have a drive to evaluate their opinions and abilities by comparison with others. Zetterberg's theory of compliant actions, on the other hand, is more limited to the small group situation and focuses upon normative influences. It is a more precise and tightly organized theory but its central postulate is a simple one. Man has a need to maximize the occurrence of evaluations of himself that are favourable, and compliant action is instrumental to this end.

These, and other, theories (see Hollander and Hunt, 1963; Jones, 1965) are useful in that they give coherent shape to the evidence and generate testable predictions. Many students of the subject, however, are repelled by the postulation of imprecisely defined social 'needs' and prefer a more analytic and reductive approach. Campbell (1961) interprets conformity as a result of a conflict between those nonsocial and social mechanisms of learning which have been experimentally isolated in contexts other than that of the small group.

Cohesion

The widest definition of cohesion is that it is a general property of a group inferred from evidence that the group attracts its members.

A highly cohesive group would be one in which members have a considerable investment in their membership, are drawn to the group and make sacrifices to maintain its existence. A number of factors influence the attractiveness of a group, such as the extent to which the personal and private goals of the members coincide with the goals of the group. One of these factors, however, is of such central importance that it has become the substance of a more limited definition of cohesion and one which has proved more popular among experimenters. According to this narrower definition, the cohesiveness of a group is the extent to which members like each other. It is measured by finding out the extent to which members choose as friends other members rather than non-members, or by getting members to rate each other for mutual liking. It is this narrower definition which will be adopted here. A number of variables have been related to interpersonal attraction within groups and a detailed review has been given by Lott and Lott (1965). We shall only mention some of the more stable findings here.

First it would appear that interpersonal attraction is a positive function of interaction (for example, Bieri, 1953). The mere fact of people being together tends to result in their liking each other and this liking increases the longer interaction continues (see Bovard, 1956). The tendency is weakened if in the first instance people are forced to be together against their choice, and it is strengthened if they are provided with a task which requires them to co-operate rather than to compete with each other. Cohesion is further strengthened, at least initially, when co-operative groups are subjected to stress from an external source. People are more likely to value a group if their initiation into it has been difficult (Aronson and Mills, 1959).

Studies concerned with the relation between subject variables and cohesion have mostly concentrated upon the similarity or compatibility (i.e. non-conflictful difference) between members. There is good evidence of a correlation between perceiving others as similar to the self and liking them, but it is usually unclear which, if either, of these variables is antecedent. Studies using personality inventories and attitude scales have usually found that mutual liking goes with similarity. It seems probable, however, that it is task relevant similarity and compatibility which matters and hence the personality dimensions upon which similarity and compatibility are based will vary from one situation to another.

The effects of different kinds of leadership style upon group life have received some attention. The pioneer work was initiated by Lewin in a series of studies which have since become classics (for an introduction, see Hare, 1962; Lippitt and White, 1958). In these experiments, groups of boys were given three types of adult leadership: authoritarian, democratic and *laissez-faire*. In the first condition the leader gave many orders and made most of the decisions; in the second he gave few orders and made few decisions but was very active in influencing group opinion; and in the third the leader functioned mainly as an observer. The behaviour of the groups was closely observed.

In general, boys in democratic groups showed greater friendliness towards each other, praised each other more and had higher morale. Later studies have shown a positive relationship between leader permissiveness and cohesion. However, close examination of these studies suggests that the relationship between democratic group structure and cohesion is complex and not enough is yet known for firm generalizations to be made.

The relationship between cohesion and conformity appears to depend upon the nature of the task (see V. L. Allen, 1965; Lott and Lott, 1965). We might expect cohesion to accentuate normative pressures upon conformity but, in fact, experiments using the Asch situation have found no such effect. Nor has cohesion been found to influence conformity in judging the autokinetic effect. On the other hand, when the task used is the expressing of attitudes and opinions on matters of general interest, the results are fairly consistent in showing that greater cohesion is associated with greater conformity. The puzzle presented by these conflicting results is as yet unresolved. A possible way through the problem is to view conformity as instrumental to the achievement of cohesion. This way of conceiving the relationship is implied in some of the theories of conformity discussed above. People conform in order to be liked and when they feel assured of this liking they are free to deviate. Such an interpretation finds some support from those results which show a curvilinear relationship between popularity and conformity.

The task

The relation between task and group process is complex. The nature of the task is a determinant of group process; the achievement of the task, its consequence. Group processes are the intervening variables between the task and its achievement. Tasks vary widely, and in many different ways. It is to be expected that, for each kind of task, there will be some group processes which are optimal for its achievement. Obviously we cannot make generalizations relating group processes to achievement which hold for all tasks unless we have first classified and studied all possible kinds of task, and also examined possible interactions between task and subject variables. Neither of these has yet been done. At best, therefore, the existing literature can suggest hypotheses which have been consistent sufficiently often to merit further testing.

First of all, there is some evidence that the way a task is initially structured for the group influences its achievement. Raven and Rietsema (1957) have shown that, in the simple task of cutting out geometrical shapes, performance was better if subjects clearly understood the group goal. Lewin (1948) reports evidence that the perceived attainability of the goal significantly influenced production among trainee sewing-machine workers. Those who were just told the final standard they were expected to achieve by the end of training – a standard which appeared impossibly high in relation to their initial performance – improved more slowly and achieved a lower standard at the end than those who were given a succession of intermediate but more realistic goals.

In relation to the task, the structure of a group, or its network of communication channels, can be studied either as an independent variable influencing task achievement, or as a dependent variable functionally related to the nature of the task. The former type of experiment requires the experimental control of the communication network through a simulated group situation. Studies of this kind have repeatedly demonstrated that particular tasks are more effectively achieved by one network than by another. But the total picture presented is confusing and no generalizations emerge, except possibly the suggestion that a more centralized network is better for simple tasks, a less centralized network for more complex tasks (see Glanzer and Glaser, 1961). A more promising approach is to treat communication network and group performance as dependent variables and to see how they vary as a function of the nature of the task. In a recent study, Faucheux and Mackenzie (1966) did just that. They used two tasks, one which was routine and deductive, and the other relatively unusual, involving creative inferences. Both tasks required members to share information and ideas. The results clearly showed that the first task led to the emergence of a more centralized structure, and among groups in this condition, the more centralized the structure, the better the performance.

The effects of leadership style upon group productivity were examined in the experiments, mentioned above, which compared authoritarian and democratic groups. In general, the authoritarian groups were more productive quantitatively but democratic groups were better qualitatively. Further differences were noted. When authoritarian groups were left leaderless for a time, productivity dropped at once, whereas in democratic groups productivity was not affected by the departure of the leader.

Norm formation and conformity can relate to task achievement in two ways. In the first place, it may be intrinsic to the task in the sense that part of the task is for members to arrive at agreement. An example would be a jury. In the second place there are aspects of norm formation which may be relevant to any task. It is reasonable to suppose that groups will be more productive and efficient, whatever the task, if the norms are that members should work hard and not waste time. S. Schachter *et al.* (1951) confirmed this in an experiment in which they used a simulated group situation and experimentally manipulated the norms by controlling the content of the communications between members. Subjects were given messages purporting to come from other members which recommended either working hard or taking it easy. Productivity was greater under the former condition.

In general, studies using a variety of tasks tend to support the proposition that the more cohesive the group, the more effective its task achievement. This is to be expected if cohesion implies that some of the socio-emotional problems of the group are solved and that social interaction is more harmonious. Van Zelst (1952) found that when building labourers were allowed to choose the men they worked with, production improved. S. Schachter *et al.* (1951) varied cohesiveness and found greater task achievement in the high-cohesive groups. Deutsch (1949) compared co-operative, and there-fore more cohesive, groups with groups in which members were competing with each other. He found that the former were better, both quantitatively and qualitatively, at solving problems of different kinds. But if cohesion tends to improve task relevant activity, it can under some circumstances impede it. When groups get too friendly they incline to engage in more task irrelevant social interaction and task achievement may suffer.

The attempt has been made to present a swift outline of a complex area of research. Inevitably, justice has not been done to it. For a detailed review of the empirical findings, the reader is recommended to consult Hare (1962). In addition to theories which have been developed to explain particular aspects of group process, a number of more general conceptual orientations have been worked out. Notable among them are the theories of Cartwright and Zander (1960), Homans (1961) and Thibaut and Kelley (1961). An intro-duction to the application of mathematical concepts to group functioning will be found in Coleman (1960).

Further reading
A. P. Hare, *Handbook of Small Group Research*, Free Press of Glencoe, 1962.
C. I. Hovland, I. L. Janis and H. H. Kelley, *Communication and Persuasion*, Yale University Press, 1953.
C. A. Insko, *Theories of Attitude Change*, Appleton-Century-Croft, 1967.
W. H. J. Sprott, *Human Groups*, Penguin Books, 1958.

References

Some of the following entries have been included as papers in the Penguin Modern Psychology Readings series. The name in square brackets after some entries denotes the editor of the volume in which that entry appears. An asterisk denotes that only an excerpted or abridged version appears in that volume. A full list of Penguin Modern Psychology Readings appears at the end of this list.

Page

611   ABEL, T. M. (1941), 'Moral judgements among subnormals', *J. abnorm. soc. Psychol.*, vol. 36, pp. 378–92.

371   ABERNETHY, E. M. (1940), 'The effect of changed environmental conditions upon the results of college examinations', *J. Psychol.*, vol. 10, pp. 293–301.

478   ADAMS, H. E., and BUTLER, J. R. (1967), 'The deviation hypothesis: a review of the evidence', in I. A. Berg (ed.), *Response Set in Personality Assessment*, Aldine.

331, 335   ADAMS, J. A. (1964), 'Motor skills', *Ann. Rev. Psychol.*, vol. 15, pp. 181–202.

601   ADORNO, T. W., *et al.* (1950), *The Authoritarian Personality*, Harper.

287   AINSWORTH, M. D., *et al.* (1962), *Deprivation of Maternal Care: A Reassessment of its Results*, World Health Organisation.

152   AKERT, K., *et al.* (1961), 'Klüver–Bucy syndrome in monkeys with neocortical ablations of temporal lobe', *Brain*, vol. 84, pp. 480–98.

547   ALEXANDER, F. (1950), *Psychosomatic Medicine*, Norton.

Page

578   ALFERT, E. (1966), 'Comparison of responses to a vicarious and a direct threat', *J. exp. Res. Personal.*, vol. 1, pp. 179–86.

233   ALLEN, C. H., FRINGS, H., and RUDNICK, I. (1948), 'Some biological effects of intense high frequency airborne sound', *J. Acoust. Soc. Amer.*, vol. 20, pp. 62–5.

574   ALLEN, S. A. (1966), 'The effects of verbal reinforcement on children's behavior as a function of the type of task', *J. exp. child Psychol.*, vol. 3, pp. 57–73.

636, 638, 640   ALLEN, V. L. (1965), 'Situational factors in conformity', in L. Berkowitz (ed.), *Advances in Experimental Social Psychology*, vol. 2, Academic Press.

636   ALLEN, V. L. (1966), 'Effect of knowledge of deception on conformity', *J. soc. Psychol.*, vol. 69, pp. 101–6.

598, 602, 607, 610   ALLINSMITH, W. (1960), 'The learning of moral standards', in D. R. Miller and G. Swanson (eds.), *Inner Conflict and Defense*, Holt.

610   ALLINSMITH, W., and GREENING, T. C. (1955), 'Guilt over anger as predicted from parental discipline', *Amer. Psychol.*, vol. 10, p. 320 (abstract).

569   ALLPORT, F. H. (1924), *Social Psychology*, Houghton Mifflin.

243, 249, 254, 269   ALLPORT, F. H. (1955), *Theories of Perception and the Concept of Structure*, Wiley.

513, 515, 516, 522, 523   ALLPORT, G. W. (1937), *Personality: A Psychological Interpretation*, Holt. [Lazarus and Opton*]

17, 32, 33   ALLPORT, G. W. (1947), *The Use of Personal Documents in Psychological Science*, Social Science Research Council, New York.

82   ALLPORT, G. W. (1961), *Pattern and Growth in Personality*, Holt, Rinehart & Winston. [Semeonoff*]

516   ALLPORT, G. W., and ODBERT, H. S. (1936), 'Trait names: A psycho-lexical study', *Psychol. Monogr.*, vol. 47, no. 211, pp. 1–171.

266   ALLPORT, G. W., and PETTIGREW, T. F. (1957), 'Cultural influence on the perception of

Page

movement: the trapezoidal illusion among
Zulus', *J. abnorm. soc. Psychol.*, vol. 55, pp.
104–13.

619   ALLYN, J., and FESTINGER, L. (1961), 'The
effectiveness of unanticipated persuasive
communications', *J. abnorm. soc. Psychol.*, vol.
62, pp. 35–40.

248   AMES, A., JR (1951), 'Visual perception and the
rotating trapezoidal window', *Psychol. Monogr.*,
vol. 65, no. 7.

139, 140   ANAND, B. D., and BROBECK, J. R. (1951),
'Hypothalamic control of food intake', *Yale J.
biol. Med.*, vol. 24, pp. 123–40.

46, 532   ANASTASI, A. (1958), *Differential Psychology*,
Macmillan, 3rd edn.

143   ANDERSSON, B. (1953), 'The effect of injections
of hypertonic NaCl-solutions into different parts
of the hypothalamus of goats', *Acta Physiol.
Scand.*, vol. 28, pp. 188–201. [Pribram, vol. 1]

609   ANDRY, R. G. (1960), *Delinquency and Parental
Pathology*, Methuen.

556   ANGYAL, A. (1952), 'A theoretical model for
personality studies', in D. Krech and G. S.
Klein (eds.), *Theoretical Models and Personality
Theory*, Duke University Press.

327   ANNETT, J., and KAY, H. (1956), 'Skilled
performance', *Occup. Psychol.*, vol. 30, pp. 112–17.

266   ARDIS, J. A., and FRASER, E. (1957),
'Personality and perception: the constancy effect
and introversion', *Brit. J. Psychol.*, vol. 48, pp.
48–54.

615   ARGYLE, M. (1964), 'Introjection: a form of
social learning', *Brit. J. Psychol.*, vol. 55, pp.
391–402.

566   ARGYLE, M. (1967), *The Psychology of
Interpersonal Behaviour*, Penguin Books.

184   ARNOLD, M. B. (1960), *Emotion and Personality,
Volume II, Neurological and Physiological
Aspects*, Columbia University Press.

597, 607   ARONFREED, J. (1961), 'The nature, variety and
social patterning of moral responses to
transgression', *J. abnorm. soc. Psychol.*, vol. 63,
pp. 223–40.

Page

597, 603   ARONFREED, J. (1964), 'The origins of self-criticism', *Psychol. Rev.*, vol. 71, pp. 193–218.

614, 597   ARONFREED, J., CUTICK, R. A., and FAGEN, S. A. (1963), 'Cognitive structure, punishment, and nurturance in the experimental induction of self-criticism', *Child Devel.*, vol. 34, pp. 281–94.

603   ARONFREED, J., and REBER, A. (1965), 'Internalized behavioral suppression and the timing of social punishment', *J. Pers. soc. Psychol.*, vol. 1, pp. 2–17.

639   ARONSON, E., and MILLS, J. (1959), 'The effect of severity of initiation on liking for a group', *J. abnorm. soc. Psychol.*, vol. 59, pp. 177–81.

635   ASCH, S. E. (1952), *Social Psychology*, Prentice-Hall. [Jahoda and Warren *]

132   ASERINSKY, E., and KLEITMAN, N. (1955), 'Two types of ocular motility occurring in sleep', *J. appl. Physiol.*, vol. 8, pp. 1–10.

475, 480   ATKINSON, J. W. (ed.), (1958), *Motives in Fantasy, Action and Society*, Van Nostrand.

68, 70   AUSUBEL, D. P. (1958), *Theory and Problems of Child Development*, Grune & Stratton.

353   AVERBACH, E., and SPERLING, G. (1961), 'Short-term storage of information in vision', in C. Cherry (ed.), *Proceedings of the Fourth London Symposium on Information Theory*, Butterworth.

191   AX, A. F. (1953), 'The physiological differentiation between fear and anger in humans', *Psychosom. Med.*, vol. 15, pp. 433–42.

354   BADDELEY, A. D., and DALE, H. C. A. (1966), 'The effect of semantic similarity on retroactive interference in long- and short-term memory', *J. verb. Learn. verb. Behav.*, vol. 5, pp. 417–20.

371   BAHRICK, H. P., and BAHRICK, P. O. (1964), 'A re-examination of the interrelations among measures of retention', *Quart. J. exp. Psychol.*, vol. 16, pp. 318–24.

631   BALES, R. F. (1950), 'A set of categories for the analysis of small group interaction', *Amer. sociol. Rev.*, vol. 15, pp. 257–63.

631   BALES, R. F. (1951), *Interaction Process-Analysis*. Addison-Wesley.

Page

632   BALES, R. F., and STRODTBECK, F. L. (1951),
           'Phases in group problem solving', *J. abnorm.
           soc. Psychol.*, vol. 46, pp. 485–95.

303   BANDURA, A. (1962), 'Social learning through
           imitation', in M. R. Jones (ed.), *Nebraska
           Symposium on Motivation*, University of
           Nebraska Press.

576   BANDURA, A. (1965a), 'Vicarious processes: a
           case of no-trial learning', in L. Berkowitz (ed.),
           Advances in Experimental Social Psychology,
           vol. 2, Academic Press.

579, 581   BANDURA, A. (1965b), 'Influences of model's
           reinforcement contingencies on the acquisition of
           imitative responses', *J. Pers. soc. Psychol.*, vol. 1,
           pp. 589–95.

578   BANDURA, A., GRUSEC, J. E., and MENLOVE,
           F. L. (1965), 'Vicarious extinction of avoidance
           responses', unpublished MS.

579   BANDURA, A., and HUSTON, A. C. (1961),
           'Identification as a process of incidental
           learning', *J. abnorm. soc. Psychol.*, vol. 63,
           pp. 311–18.

579   BANDURA, A., and KUPERS, C. J. (1964),
           'Transmission of patterns of self-reinforcement
           through modeling', *J. abnorm. soc. Psychol.*,
           vol. 69, pp. 1–9.

223, 593, 598, 602, 608   BANDURA, A., and WALTERS, R. H. (1959),
           Adolescent Aggression, Ronald Press.

567   BANDURA, A., and WALTERS, R. H. (1963),
           Social Learning and Personality Development,
           Holt, Rinehart & Winston.

579   BANNISTER, D., and MAIR, J. M. M. (1968),
           The Evaluation of Personal Constructs, Academic
           Press.

223, 552   BARKER, R., DEMBO, T., and LEWIN, K.
           (1943), 'Frustration and regression: an
           experiment with young children', in R. Barker *et
           al.* (eds.), *Child Behavior and Development*,
           McGraw-Hill.

362, 363   BARNES, J. M., and UNDERWOOD, B. J. (1959),
           ' "Fate" of first-list associations in transfer
           theory', *J. exp. Psychol.*, vol. 58, pp. 95–105.

575   BARON, R. M. (1966), 'Social reinforcement

Page

effects as a function of social reinforcement history', *Psychol. Rev.*, vol. 73, pp. 527–39.

433   BARRON, F. (1965), 'The psychology of creativity', in *New Directions in Psychology*, vol. 2, Holt, Rinehart & Winston.

366, 368   BARTLETT, F. C. (1932), *Remembering: A Study in Experimental and Social Psychology*, Cambridge University Press.

323, 341   BARTLETT, F. C. (1943), 'Fatigue following highly skilled work', *Proc. Roy. Soc. (Series B)*, vol. 131, pp. 247–57. [Legge *]

325, 328, 329, 343   BARTLETT, F. C. (1958), *Thinking: An Experimental and Social Study*, Allen & Unwin. [P. E. Vernon *; Wason and Johnson-Laird *]

281   BATESON, P. P. G. (1966), 'The characteristics and context of imprinting', *Biol. Rev.*, vol. 41, pp. 177–200.

79, 471   BAYLEY, N. (1949), 'Consistency and variability in the growth of intelligence from birth to eighteen', *J. genet. Psychol.*, vol. 75, pp. 165–96.

68, 70, 85   BAYLEY, N. (1951), 'Development and maturation', in H. Helson (ed.), *Theoretical Foundations of Psychology*, Van Nostrand.

81, 471   BAYLEY, N. (1955), 'On the growth of intelligence', *Amer. Psychologist*, vol. 10, pp. 805–18.

212   BEACH, F. A. (1947), 'Evolutionary changes in the physiological control of mating behavior in mammals', *Psychol. Rev.*, vol. 54, pp. 297–315.

143   BEACH, F. A. (1948), *Hormones and Behavior*, Hoeber.

143   BEACH, F. A. (1965), 'Experimental studies of mating behaviour in animals', in J. Money (ed.), *Sex Research*, Holt, Rinehart & Winston.

262   BEACH, F. A., and JAYNES, J. (1955), 'Effects of early experience upon the behavior of animals', *Psychol. Bull.*, vol. 51, pp. 239–63.

550   BENEDICT, R. (1935), *Patterns of Culture*, Routledge.

183   BENJAMIN, L. S. (1963), 'Statistical treatment of the law of initial values (LIV) in autonomic research: a review and recommendation', *Psychosom. Med.*, vol. 25, pp. 556–66.

Page

231, 337   BENNETT, A. M. H. (1961), 'Sensory deprivation in aviation', in P. Solomon *et al.* (eds.), *Sensory Deprivation*, Harvard University Press.

58   BENNETT, E. L., *et al.* (1964), 'Chemical and anatomical plasticity of the brain', *Science*, vol. 146, pp. 610–19.

472   BENNETT, G. K., SEASHORE, H. G., and WESMAN, A. G. (1959), *Manual for the Differential Aptitude Tests*, Psychological Corporation, 3rd edn.

608   BENNETT, I. (1960), *Delinquent and Neurotic Children*, Tavistock Publications.

477   BERG, I. A. (1959), 'The unimportance of test-item content', in B. M. Bass and I. A. Berg (eds.), *Objective Approaches to Personality Assessment*, Van Nostrand.

478   BERG, I. A. (1967), 'The deviation hypothesis: a broad statement of its assumptions and postulates', in I. A. Berg (ed.), *Response Set in Personality Assessment*, Aldine.

637   BERG, I. A., and BASS, B. M. (1961), *Conformity and Deviation*, Harper.

578   BERGER, S. M. (1962), 'Conditioning through vicarious instigation', *Psychol. Rev.*, vol. 59, pp. 450–66.

570   BERGUM, B., and LEHR, D. J. (1962), 'Vigilance performance as a function of paired monitoring', *J. appl. Psychol.*, vol. 46, pp. 341–3.

568   BERGUM, B., and LEHR, D. J. (1963), 'Effects of authoritarianism on vigilance performance', *J. appl. Psychol.*, vol. 47, pp. 75–7.

411   BERKO, J. (1958), 'The child's learning of English morphology', *Word*, vol. 14, pp. 150–77.

223   BERKOWITZ, L. (1962), *Aggression: A Social Psychological Analysis*, McGraw-Hill.

623   BERKOWITZ, L., and COTTINGHAM, D. (1960), 'The interest value and relevance of fear-arousing communications', *J. abnorm. soc. Psychol.*, vol. 60, pp. 37–43.

215   BERLYNE, D. E. (1960), *Conflict, Arousal and Curiosity*, McGraw-Hill.

416   BERNSTEIN, B. (1961), 'Social class and

Page

linguistic development: a theory of social learning', in A. H. Halsey, J. Floud and A. Anderson (eds.), *Education, Economy and Society*, Free Press of Glencoe.

620   BERSCHEID, E. (1966), 'Opinion change and communicator–communicatee similarity and dissimilarity', *J. Pers. soc. Psychol.*, vol. 4, pp. 670–80.

233   BEVAN, W. (1955), 'Sound-precipitated convulsions: 1947 to 1954', *Psychol. Bull.*, vol. 52, pp. 473–504.

265   BEVERIDGE, W. M. (1935), 'Racial differences in phenomenal regression', *Brit. J. Psychol.*, vol. 26, pp. 59–62.

265   BEVERIDGE, W. M. (1939), 'Some racial differences in perception', *Brit. J. Psychol.*, vol. 30, pp. 57–64.

639   BIERI, J. (1953), 'Changes in interpersonal perceptions following social interaction', *J. abnorm. soc. Psychol.*, vol. 48, pp. 61–6.

346   BILODEAU, E. A. (1966), *Acquisition of Skill*, Academic Press.

197   BINDRA, D. (1955), 'Organization in emotional and motivated behaviour', *Canad. J. Psychol.*, vol. 9, pp. 161–7.

223   BINDRA, D. (1959), *Motivation: A Systematic Reinterpretation*, Ronald Press. [Bindra and Stewart *]

466   BINET, A., and SIMON, T. (1916), *The Development of Intelligence in Children*, translated by Elizabeth S. Kite, Williams & Wilkins.

432   BIRCH, H. G. (1945), 'The relation of previous experience to insightful problem-solving', *J. comp. Psychol.*, vol. 38, pp. 367–83. [Riopelle]

471, 472   BIRREN, J. E. (1964), *The Psychology of Aging*, Prentice-Hall.

155   BITTERMAN, M. E. (1965), 'The evolution of intelligence', *Scient. Amer.*, vol. 212, no. 1, pp. 92–101.

155   BITTERMAN, M. E., WODINSKY, J., and CANDLAND, D. K. (1958), 'Some comparative psychology', *Amer. J. Psychol.*, vol. 71, pp. 94–110.

Page

201   BLAKE, M. J. F. (1965), 'Physiological and
          temperamental correlates of performance at
          different times of day', *Ergonomics*, vol. 8, pp.
          375–6 (abstract).

480   BLAKE, R. R. (1958), 'The other person in the
          situation', in R. Tagiuri and L. Petrullo (eds.),
          Person Perception and Interpersonal Behavior,
          Stanford University Press.

437   BLAKE, R. R., HELSON, H., and MOUTON, J. S.
          (1956), 'The generality of conformity behavior as
          a function of factual anchorage, difficulty of task
          and amount of social pressure', *J. Pers.*, vol. 25,
          pp. 294–305.

479   BLOCK, J. A. (1961), *The Q–Sort Method in
          Personality Assessment and Psychiatric Research*,
          Charles C. Thomas.

478   BLOCK, J. A. (1965), *The Challenge of Response
          Sets: Unconfounding Meaning, Acquiescence and
          Social Desirability in the M.M.P.I.*,
          Appleton-Century-Crofts.

302   BLODGETT, H. C. (1929), 'The effect of the
          introduction of reward upon the maze
          performance of rats', *Univ. Calif. Publ. Psychol.*,
          vol. 4, pp. 113–34.

78, 469   BLOOM, B. S. (1964), *Stability and Change in
          Human Characteristics*, Wiley.

601   BLOOM, L. (1959), 'A reappraisal of Piaget's
          theory of moral judgment', *J. genet. Psychol.*,
          vol. 95, pp. 3–12. [Jahoda and Warren *]

622   BOCHNER, S., and INSKO, C. A. (1966),
          'Communicator discrepancy, source credibility,
          and opinion change', *J. Pers. soc. Psychol.*, vol.
          4, pp. 614–21.

397   BOLINGER, D. (1965), 'The atomization of
          meaning', *Language*, vol. 41, pp. 555–73.

229   BORING, E. G. (1942), *Sensation and Perception
          in the History of Experimental Psychology*,
          Appleton-Century-Crofts.

383, 388 BOUSFIELD, W. A. (1961), 'The problem of
          meaning in verbal learning', in C. N. Cofer (ed.),
          Verbal Learning and Verbal Behavior,
          McGraw-Hill.

639   BOVARD, E. W. (1956), 'Interaction and

Page

attraction to the group', *Hum. Rel.*, vol. 9, pp. 481-9.

286, 287   BOWLBY, J. (1944), 'Forty-four juvenile thieves: their characters and home life', *Int. J. Psychoanal.*, vol. 25, pp. 19-52, 107-27.

286   BOWLBY, J., *et al.* (1956), 'The effects of mother-child separation: a follow-up study', *Brit. J. med. Psychol.*, vol. 29, pp. 211-47.

88, 109   BOWSHER, D. (1961), *Introduction to Neuroanatomy*, Blackwell.

132   BRADLEY, P., and KEY, B. J. (1958), 'The effect of drugs on arousal responses produced by electrical stimulation of the reticular formation of the brain', *EEG and clin. Neurophysiol.*, vol. 10, pp. 97-110.

151   BRADY, J. V., and NAUTA, W. J. H. (1953), 'Subcortical mechanisms in emotional behavior: affective changes following septal forebrain lesions in the albino rat', *J. comp. physiol. Psychol.*, vol. 46, pp. 339-46.

412, 413, 414   BRAINE, M. D. S. (1963a), 'The ontogeny of English phrase structure: the first phase', *Language*, vol. 39, pp. 1-13.

412   BRAINE, M. D. S. (1963b), 'On learning the grammatical order of words', *Psychol. Rev.*, vol. 70, pp. 323-48.

133   BREMER, F. (1935), 'Cerveau isolé et physiologie du sommeil', *Compte Rendu de la Société de Biologie (Paris)*, vol. 118, pp. 1235-41.

133   BREMER, F. (1954), 'The neurophysiological problem of sleep', in E. D. Adrian *et al.* (eds.), *Brain Mechanisms and Consciousness*, Blackwell.

180, 181   BRENER, J. (1967), 'Heart rate', in P. H. Venables and I. Martin (eds.), *A Manual of Psychophysiological Methods*, North-Holland.

81   BRIDGES, K. M. B. (1932), 'Emotional development in early infancy', *Child Devel.*, vol. 3, pp. 324-41

204   BROADBENT, D. E. (1953), 'Noise, paced performance and vigilance tasks', *Brit. J. Psychol.*, vol. 44, pp. 295-303.

232   BROADBENT, D. E. (1957a), 'Effects of noise on behavior', in C. M. Harris (ed.), *Handbook of*

Page

Noise Control, McGraw-Hill. [Holding*]

136   BROADBENT, D. E. (1957b), 'A mechanical model for human attention and immediate memory', *Psychol. Rev.*, vol. 64, pp. 205–15.

136, 326, 336, 338, 348, 372   BROADBENT, D. E. (1958), *Perception and Communication*, Pergamon.

203, 232, 339   BROADBENT, D. E. (1963), 'Possibilities and difficulties in the concept of arousal', in D. N. Buckner and J. J. McGrath (eds.), *Vigilance: A Symposium*, McGraw-Hill.

274   BROADBENT, D. E., and GREGORY, M. (1967), 'Perception of emotionally toned words', *Nature*, vol. 215, pp. 581–4.

53   BROADHURST, P. L. (1960), 'Experiments in psychogenetics', in H. J. Eysenck (ed.), *Experiments in Personality*, vol. 1, Routledge & Kegan Paul.

54, 66   BROADHURST, P. L. (1963), *The Science of Animal Behaviour*, Penguin Books.

106   BROCA, P. (1878), 'Anatomie comparée des circonvolutions cérébrales. Le grand lobe limbique et la scissure limbique dans la série des mammifère', *Rev. Anthropol.*, vol. 1, pp. 385–498.

619   BROCK, T. C. (1967), 'Communication discrepancy and intent to persuade as determinants of counter-argument production', *J. exp. soc. Psychol.*, vol. 3, pp. 296–309.

620   BROCK, T. C., and BECKER, L. A. (1965), 'Ineffectiveness of "overhead" counterpropaganda', *J. Pers. soc. Psychol.*, vol. 2, pp. 654–60.

157   BRODMAN, K. (1914), 'Physiologie des Gehirns', in *Die allgemeine Chirurgie*, vol. 2, Enke.

592, 594   BROGDEN, A. E. (1940), 'A factor analysis of forty character tests', *Psychol. Monogr.*, vol. 52, no. 3.

434   BROMLEY, D. (1965), *The Psychology of Human Ageing*, Penguin Books.

585   BRONFENBRENNER, U. (1958), 'The study of identification through interpersonal perception', in R. Tagiuri and L. Petrullo (eds.), *Person*

Page

Perception and Interpersonal Behavior, Stanford
University Press.

604 BRONFENBRENNER, U. (1962), 'Soviet methods
of character education: some implications for
research', *Relig. Educ.*, vol. 57 (res. suppl.).

331 BROWN, I. D. (1960), 'Many messages from few
sources', *Ergonomics*, vol. 3, pp. 159–68.

351 BROWN, J. (1958), 'Some tests of the decay
theory of immediate memory', *Quart. J. exp.
Psychol.*, vol. 10, pp. 12–21. [Postman and
Keppel]

236 BROWN, J. (1960), 'Evidence for a selective
process during perception of tachistoscopically
presented stimuli', *J. exp. Psychol.*, vol. 59,
pp. 176–81.

352, 353 BROWN, J. (1964), 'Short-term memory', *Brit.
med. Bull.*, vol. 20, no. 1, pp. 8–11.

355 BROWN, J. F., and VOTH, A. C. (1937), 'The
path of seen movement as a function of the
vector-field', *Amer. J. Psychol.*, vol. 49, pp.
543–63.

380, 412, 415, 436 BROWN, R. (1965), *Social Psychology*, Free Press
of Glencoe and Collier-Macmillan of Glencoe.

414 BROWN, R., and BELLUGI, U. (1964), 'Three
processes in the child's acquisition of syntax',
Harv. educ. Rev., vol. 34, pp. 133–51.

411 BROWN, R., and BERKO, J. (1960), 'Word
association and the acquisition of grammar',
Child Devel., vol. 31, pp. 1–14.

412, 413 BROWN, R., and FRASER, C. (1963), 'The
acquisition of syntax', in C. N. Cofer and
B. S. Musgrave (eds.), *Verbal Behavior and
Learning*, McGraw-Hill.

144 BROWN, S., and SCHAEFER, E. A. (1888), 'An
investigation into the functions of the occipital
and temporal lobes of the monkey's brain', *Phil.
Trans. Roy. Soc.* (London), vol. 179, pp. 303–27.
[Pribram, vol. 2*]

271 BROWN, W. P. (1961), 'Conceptions of
perceptual defence', *Brit. J. Psychol. Monogr.
Supp.*, no. 35, Cambridge University Press.

214 BROWNFIELD, C. A. (1965), *Isolation: Clinical
and Experimental Approaches*, Random House.

Page

399   BRUCE, D. (1956), 'Effects of context upon the intelligibility of heard speech', in C. Cherry (ed.), *Information Theory*, Butterworth.

430   BRUNER, J. S. (1962), 'The conditions of creativity', in H. E. Gruber, G. Terrell and M. Wertheimer (eds.), *Contemporary Approaches to Creative Thinking*, Atherton.

427, 431   BRUNER, J. S., GOODNOW, J. S., and AUSTIN, G. A. (1956), *A Study of Thinking*, Wiley.

272, 427, 431   BRUNER, J. S., and POSTMAN, L. (1949), 'On the perception of incongruity: a paradigm', *J. Personal.*, vol. 18, pp. 206–23. [M. D. Vernon*]

248   BRUNSWIK, E. (1956), *Perception and the Representative Design of Psychological Experiments*, University of California Press.

318   BRYAN, W. L., and HARTER, N. (1897), 'Studies in the physiology and psychology of the telegraphic language', *Psychol. Rev.*, vol. 4, pp. 27–53.

318   BRYAN, W. L., and HARTER, N. (1899), 'Studies on the telegraphic language: the acquisition of a hierarchy of habits', *Psychol. Rev.*, vol. 6, pp. 345–75.

131   BURNS, B. D. (1958), *The Mammalian Cerebral Cortex*, Arnold.

620   BURNSTEIN, E., STOTLAND, E., and ZANDER, A. (1961), 'Similarity to a model and self-evaluation', *J. abnorm. soc. Psychol.*, vol. 62, pp. 257–64.

470   BURT, C. (1943), 'Ability and income', *Brit. J. educ. Psychol.*, vol. 13, pp. 83–98.

491   BURT, C. (1944), 'Mental abilities and mental factors', *Brit. J. educ. Psychol.*, vol. 14, pp. 85–94.

81   BURT, C. (1954), 'The differentiation of intellectual ability', *Brit. J. educ. Psychol.*, vol. 24, pp. 76–90.

493   BURT, C. (1955), 'The evidence for the concept of intelligence', *Brit. J. educ. Psychol.*, vol. 25, pp. 158–77. [Wiseman*]

470   BURT, C. (1957), 'The distributions of intelligence', *Brit. J. Psychol.*, vol. 48, pp. 161–74.

Page

64   BURT, C. (1958), 'The inheritance of mental abilities', *Amer. Psychol.*, vol. 13, pp. 1–15.

495   BURT, C. (1962), 'Critical notice of *Creativity and Intelligence* by Getzels and Jackson: the psychology of creative ability', *Brit. J. educ. Psychol.*, vol. 32, pp. 292–8. [P. E. Vernon]

65   BURT, C., and HOWARD, M. (1956), 'The multifactorial theory of inheritance and its application to intelligence', *Brit. J. stat. Psychol.*, vol. 9, pp. 95–131.

592   BURTON, R. V. (1963), 'Generality of honesty reconsidered', *Psychol. Rev.*, vol. 70, pp. 481–99.

609   BURTON, R. V., ALLINSMITH, W., and MACCOBY, E. (1966), 'Resistance to temptation in relation to sex of child, sex of experimenter, and withdrawal of attention', *J. Pers. soc. Psychol.*, vol. 3, pp. 253–8.

609   BURTON, R. V., MACCOBY, E., and
610   ALLINSMITH, W. (1961), 'Antecedents of resistance to temptation in four-year-old children', *Child Devel.*, vol. 32, pp. 689–710.

309   BUSS, A. H., and BUSS, E. H. (1956), 'The effect of verbal reinforcement combinations on conceptual learning', *J. exp. Psychol.*, vol. 52, pp. 283–7.

217   BUTLER, R. A. (1953), 'Discrimination learning in rhesus monkeys to visual exploration motivation', *J. comp. physiol. Psychol.*, vol. 46, pp. 95–8.

217   BUTLER, R. A. (1954), 'Incentive conditions which influence visual exploration', *J. exp. Psychol.*, vol. 48, pp. 19–23.

445   CAMERON, N. (1944), 'The functional psychoses', in J. McV. Hunt (ed.), *Personality and the Behavior Disorders*, Ronald Press.

476   CAMPBELL, D. T. (1957), 'A typology of tests, projective and otherwise', *J. consult. Psychol.*, vol. 21, pp. 207–10.

638   CAMPBELL, D. T. (1961), 'Conformity in psychology's theories of acquired behavioral dispositions', in I. A. Berg and B. M. Bass (eds.), *Conformity and Deviation*, Harper.

189, 190   CANNON, W. B. (1927), 'The James–Lange

Page

theory of emotions: a critical examination and an alternative theory', *Amer. J. Psychol.*, vol. 39, pp. 106–24. [Arnold*; Pribram, vol. 4]

189   CANNON, W. B. (1931), 'Again the James–Lange and the thalamic theories of emotions', *Psychol. Rev.*, vol. 38, pp. 281–95.

183   CANNON, W. B. (1932), *The Wisdom of the Body*, Norton.

183   CANNON, W. B. (1936), *Bodily Changes in Pain, Hunger, Fear and Rage*, Appleton-Century-Crofts, 2nd edn.

76   CARMICHAEL, L. (1926), 'The development of behavior in vertebrates experimentally removed from the influence of external stimulation', *Psychol. Rev.*, vol. 33, pp. 51–8.

76   CARMICHAEL, L. (1927), 'A further study of the development of behavior in vertebrates experimentally removed from the influence of external stimulation', *Psychol. Rev.*, vol. 34, pp. 34–47.

73, 85   CARMICHAEL, L. (1954), 'The onset and early development of behavior', in L. Carmichael (ed.), *Manual of Child Psychology*, Wiley, 2nd edn.

516   CARR, H. A., and KINGSBURY, F. A. (1938), 'The concept of traits', *Psychol. Rev.*, vol. 45, pp. 497–524.

520   CARRIGAN, P. M. (1960), 'Extraversion–introversion as a dimension of personality: a reappraisal', *Psychol. Bull.*, vol. 57, pp. 329–60.

386, 436   CARROLL, J. B. (1964), *Language and Thought*, Prentice-Hall.

643   CARTWRIGHT, D., and ZANDER, A. (1960), *Group Dynamics: Research and Theory*, Row, Peterson, 2nd edn. [Smith*]

526   CATTELL, R. B. (1963a), *The Sixteen Personality Factor Questionnaire (The 16 PF)*, Institute for Personality and Ability Testing, Illinois.

494   CATTELL, R. B. (1963b), 'Theory of fluid and crystallized intelligence: a critical experiment', *J. educ. Psychol.*, vol. 54, pp. 1–22.

528, 533, 534   CATTELL, R. B. (1964), 'Objective personality tests: a reply to Dr Eysenck', *Occup. Psychol.*, vol. 38, pp. 69–86.

Page

525, 529, 535   CATTELL, R. B. (1965), *The Scientific Analysis of Personality*, Penguin Books. [Lazarus and Opton*]

535   CATTELL, R. B., and BELOFF, J. R. (1953), 'Research origins and construction of the IPAT Junior Personality Quiz', *J. consult. Psychol.*, vol. 17, pp. 436–42.

65   CATTELL, R. B., BLEWETT, D. B., and BELOFF, J. R. (1955), 'The inheritance of personality: a multiple variance analysis determination of approximate nature–nurture ratios for primary personality factors in Q-data', *Amer. J. hum. Genet.*, vol. 7, pp. 122–46.

536   CATTELL, R. B., and WARBURTON, F. W. (1961), 'A cross-cultural comparison of patterns of extraversion and anxiety', *Brit. J. Psychol.*, vol. 52, pp. 3–15.

374   CERASO, J. (1967), 'The interference theory of forgetting', *Scient. Amer.*, vol. 217, no. 4, pp. 117–24.

125   CHANG, H.-T. (1959), 'The evoked potentials', in J. Field, H. W. Magoun and V. E. Hall (eds.), *Handbook of Physiology*, sect. 1, vol. 1, American Physiological Society.

391   CHOMSKY, N. (1956), 'Three models for the description of language', *I.R.E. Transactions on Information Theory*, vol. IT-2, no. 3, pp. 113–24.

393   CHOMSKY, N. (1957), *Syntactic Structures*, Mouton.

388   CHOMSKY, N. (1959), 'Review of Skinner's *Verbal Behavior*', *Language*, vol. 35, pp. 26–58.

393, 397, 417   CHOMSKY, N. (1965), *Aspects of the Theory of Syntax*, M.I.T. Press.

153   CHOW, K. L. (1954), 'Effects of temporal neocortical ablation on visual discrimination learning sets in monkeys', *J. comp. physiol. Psychol.*, vol. 47, pp. 194 8.

433   CHOWN, S. M. (1959), 'Rigidity – a flexible concept', *Psychol. Bull.*, vol. 56, pp. 195–223.

621   CHU, G. C. (1967), 'Prior familiarity, perceived bias, and one-sided versus two-sided communications', *J. exp. soc. Psychol.*, vol. 3, pp. 243–54.

Page

310 CHURCH, R. M. (1963), 'The varied effects of punishment on behavior', *Psychol. Rev.*, vol. 70, pp. 369–402.

231 CLARK, B., and GRAYBIEL, A. (1957), 'The break-off phenomenon: a feeling of separation from the earth experienced by pilots at high altitude', *J. aviat. Med.*, vol. 28, pp. 121–6.

158 COBB, S. (1941), *Foundations of Psychiatry*, Williams & Wilkins.

73, 80 COGHILL, G. E. (1929), *Anatomy and the Problem of Behaviour*, Cambridge University Press. [Pribram, vol. 2 *]

161 COHEN, L. (1959), 'Perception of reversible figures after brain injury', *Arch. Neurol. Psychiat.*, vol. 81, pp. 765–75.

232 COHEN, W. (1957), 'Spatial and textural characteristics of the *Ganzfeld*', *Amer. J. Psychol.*, vol. 70, pp. 403–10. [M. D. Vernon]

643 COLEMAN, J. S. (1960), 'The mathematical study of small groups', in H. Solomon (ed.), *Mathematical Thinking in the Measurement of Behaviour*, Free Press of Glencoe.

281 COLLINS, T. B. (1965), 'Strength of the following response in the chick in relation to degree of "parent" contact', *J. comp. physiol. Psychol.*, vol. 60, pp. 192–5.

201 COLQUHOUN, W. P., and CORCORAN, D. W. J. (1964), 'The effect of time of day and social isolation on the relation between temperament and performance', *Brit. J. soc. and clin. Psychol.*, vol. 3, pp. 226–31.

166 CONRAD, K. (1954), 'New problems of aphasia', *Brain*, vol. 77, pp. 491–509.

329 CONRAD, R. (1951), 'Speed and load stress in a sensori-motor skill', *Brit. J. industr. Med.*, vol. 8, pp. 1–7.

329 CONRAD, R. (1953), 'Timing', *MRC Appl. Res. Unit. Rep.*, no. 188.

328 CONRAD, R. (1955), 'Timing', *Occup. Psychol.*, vol. 29, pp. 173–81.

586 COOPER, J. B., and BLAIR, H. A. (1959), 'Parent evaluation as a determiner of ideology' *J. genet. Psychol.*, vol. 94, pp. 93–100.

Page

58
COOPER, R. M., and ZUBEK, J. P. (1958),
'Effects of enriched and restricted early
environment on the learning ability of "bright"
and "dull" rats', *Canad. J. Psychol.*, vol. 12,
pp. 159–64.

203
CORCORAN, D. W. J. (1962), 'Noise and loss of
sleep', *Quart. J. exp. Psychol.*, vol. 14, pp.
178–82.

205
CORCORAN, D. W. J. (1964), 'Changes in heart
rate and performance as a result of loss of
sleep', *Brit. J. Psychol.*, vol. 55, pp. 307–14.

204
COURTS, F. A. (1942), 'Relations between
muscular tension and performance', *Psychol.
Bull.*, vol. 39, pp. 347–67.

625
COX, D. F., and BAUER, R. A. (1964),
'Self-confidence and persuasibility in women',
Publ. Opin. Quart., vol. 28, pp. 453–66.

326, 334, 335
CRAIK, K. (1948), 'Theory of the human
operator in control systems', *Brit. J. Psychol.*,
vol. 38, pp. 56–61, 142–8.

377, 386, 388
CREELMAN, M. B. (1966), *The Experimental
Investigation of Meaning*, Springer.

477
CRONBACH, L. J. (1946), 'Response sets and
test validity', *Educ. psychol. Measmt*, vol. 6,
pp. 475–94.

477
CRONBACH, L. J. (1950), 'Further evidence on
response sets and test design', *Educ. psychol.
Measmt*, vol. 10, pp. 3–31.

458, 460, 471, 475
CRONBACH, L. J. (1964), *Essentials of
Psychological Testing*, Harper & Row
International Student Reprint, 2nd edn.

465
CRONBACH, L. J., and MEEHL, P. E. (1955),
'Construct validity in psychological tests',
Psychol. Bull., vol. 52, pp. 281–302.

478
CROWNE, D. P., and MARLOWE, D. (1964),
*The Approval Motive: Studies in Evaluative
Dependence*, Wiley.

637
CRUTCHFIELD, R. S. (1955), 'Conformity and
character', *Amer. Psychol.*, vol. 10, pp. 191–8.

477
DAHLSTROM, W. G., and WELSH, G. S. (1960),
*An M.M.P.I. Handbook: A Guide to Use in
Clinical Practice and Research*, University of
Minnesota Press.

Page

190   DANA, C. I. (1921), 'The anatomic seat of the
            emotions: a discussion of the James–Lange
            theory', *Arch. Neurol. Psychiat.*, vol. 6, pp.
            634–9.

204   DAVIES, D. R., and HOCKEY, G. R. J. (1966),
            'The effects of noise and doubling the signal
            frequency on individual differences in visual
            vigilance performance', *Brit. J. Psychol.*, vol. 57,
            pp. 381–9.

338   DAVIES, D. R., and TUNE, G. S. (1970),
            Human Vigilance Performance, Staples Press.

212   DAVIS, C. M. (1928), 'Self-selection of diet by
            newly weaned infants', *Amer. J. Dis. Child*, vol.
            36, pp. 651–79.

340   DAVIS, D. R. (1948), 'Pilot error', *Air Publication
            3139a*, H.M.S.O.

366   DAVIS, D. RUSSELL (1957), *An Introduction to
            Psychopathology*, Oxford University Press.

333   DAVIS, R. (1956), 'The limits of the
            "psychological refractory period"', *Quart. J.
            exp. Psychol.*, vol. 8, pp. 24–38.

186, 187   DAVIS, R. C. (1957), 'Response patterns', *Trans.
            New York Acad. Sci.*, vol. 19, pp. 731–9.

186   DAVIS, R. C., BUCHWALD, A. M., and
            FRANKMAN, R. W. (1955), 'Autonomic and
            muscular responses and their relation to simple
            stimuli', *Psychol. Monogr*, vol. 69, pp. 1–71,
            whole no. 405.

139   DELGADO, J. M. R., and ANAND, B. K. (1953),
            'Increased food intake induced by electrical
            stimulation of the lateral hypothalamus', *Amer.
            J. Physiol.*, vol. 172, pp. 162–8.

306   DELGADO, J. M. R., ROBERTS, W. W., and
            MILLER, N. E. (1954), 'Learning motivated by
            electrical stimulation of the brain', *Amer. J.
            Physiol.*, vol. 179, pp. 587–93.

267, 271, 275   DEMBER, W. (1961), *The Psychology of
            Perception*, Holt, Rinehart & Winston.

131, 132   DEMENT, W. C., and KLEITMAN, N. (1957),
            'Cyclic variations of EEG during sleep and
            their relation to eye movements, body motility
            and dreaming', *EEG clin. Neurophysiol.*, vol. 9,
            pp. 673–90.

Page

495   DE MILLE, R., and MERRIFIELD, P. R. (1962), 'Review of *Creativity and Intelligence* by Getzels and Jackson', *Educ. psychol. Measmt*, vol. 22, pp. 803–8.

278   DENENBERG, V. (1959), 'The interactive effects of infantile and adult shock levels upon learning', *Psychol. Rep.*, vol. 5, pp. 357–64.

277   DENENBERG, V. (1963), 'Early experience and emotional development', *Scient. Amer.*, vol. 208, pp. 138–46.

280   DENNIS, W. (1960), 'Causes of retardation among institutional children: Iran', *J. genet. Psychol.*, vol. 96, pp. 47–59.

75   DENNIS, W., and DENNIS, M. G. (1940), 'The effect of cradling practices upon the onset of walking in Hopi children', *J. genet. Psychol.*, vol. 56, pp. 77–86.

606   DENTLER, R. A., and MONROE, L. (1961), 'Social correlates of early adolescent theft', *Amer. soc. Rev.*, vol. 25, pp. 733–43.

17, 308   DEUTSCH, J. A. (1960), *The Structural Basis of Behaviour*, Cambridge University Press.

211   DEUTSCH, J. A., and DEUTSCH, D. (1966), *Physiological Psychology*, Dorsey Press.

643   DEUTSCH, M. (1949), 'An experimental study of the effects of cooperation and competition upon group process', *Hum. Rel.*, vol. 2, pp. 199–231.

635   DEUTSCH, M., and GERARD, H. (1955), 'A study of normative and informational social influences upon individual judgment', *J. abnorm. soc. Psychol.*, vol. 51, pp. 629–36.

586   DE WOLFE, A. S. (1967), 'Identification and fear decrease', *J. consult. Psychol.*, vol. 31, pp. 259–63.

623   DE WOLFE, A. S., and GOVERNDALE, C. (1964), 'Fear and attitude change', *J. abnorm. soc. Psychol.*, vol. 69, pp. 119–23.

157   DIAMOND, I. T., and NEFF, W. D. (1957), 'Ablation of temporal cortex and discrimination of auditory patterns', *J. Neurophysiol.*, vol. 20, pp. 300–315.

353   DINGMAN, W., and SPORN, M. B. (1964), 'Molecular theories of memory', *Science*, vol. 144, pp. 26–9.

Page

222   DOLLARD, J., *et al.* (1939), *Frustration and Aggression*, Yale University Press.

156   DOTY, R. W. (1961a), 'Functional significance of the topographical aspects of the retino-cortical projection', in R. Jung and H. Kornhuber (eds.), *The Visual System: Neurophysiology and Psychophysics*, Springer Verlag, Berlin.

160   DOTY, R. W. (1961b), 'Conditioned reflexes formed and evoked by brain stimulation', in D. E. Steer (ed.), *Electrical Stimulation of the Brain,* University of Texas Press. [Pribram, vol. 3]

148   DOUGLAS, R. J. (1967), 'The hippocampus and behavior', *Psychol. Bull.*, vol. 67, pp. 416–42.

152   DOWNER, J. L. DE C. (1961), 'Changes in visual gnostic functions and emotional behaviour following unilateral temporal pole damage in the "split brain" monkey', *Nature*, vol. 191, pp. 50–51.

317   DREVER, J. (1961), 'Perception and action', *Bull. Brit. Psychol. Soc.*, vol. 45, pp. 1–9.

189
199   DUFFY, E. (1941), 'An explanation of "emotional" phenomena without the use of the concept "emotion"', *J. gen. Psychol.*, vol. 25, pp. 283–93.

200   DUFFY, E. (1957), 'The psychological significance of the concept of "arousal" or "activation"', *Psychol. Rev.*, vol. 64, pp. 265–75.

184, 200, 205   DUFFY, E. (1962), *Activation and Behavior*, Wiley.

349   DUNCAN, C. P. (1949), 'The retroactive effect of electro-shock on learning', *J. comp. physiol. Psychol.*, vol. 42, pp. 32–44.

426, 430, 432, 438, 439   DUNCKER, K. (1945), 'On problem solving' (translated by L. S. Lees from the 1935 original), *Psychol. Monogr.*, vol. 58, no. 270. [Wason and Johnson-Laird *]

556, 558   DURKHEIM, E. (1963), *Suicide*, Routledge & Kegan Paul.

607, 611   DURKIN, D. (1959a), 'Children's concepts of justice: a comparison with Piaget's data', *Child Devel.*, vol. 30, pp. 59–67.

Page

611   DURKIN, D. (1959b), 'Children's acceptance of reciprocity as a justice principle', *Child Devel.*, vol. 30, pp. 289–96.

601   DURKIN, D. (1961), 'The specificity of children's moral judgments', *J. genet. Psychol.*, vol. 98, pp. 3–13.

369, 370   EBBINGHAUS, H. (1885), *Memory: A Contribution to Experimental Psychology* (translated 1913 by H. A. Ruger and C. E. Busserinus), Teachers College, Columbia University.

474   EBEL, R. L. (1961), 'Must all tests be valid?', *Amer. Psychol.*, vol. 16, pp. 640–47.

477   EDWARDS, A. L. (1957a), *The Social Desirability Variable in Personality Assessment and Research*, Dryden Press.

481   EDWARDS, A. L. (1957b), *Techniques of Attitude Scale Construction*, Appleton-Century-Crofts.

478   EDWARDS, A. L. (1959), *Edwards Personal Preference Schedule*, Psychological Corporation, New York.

42   EDWARDS, A. L. (1960), *Experimental Design in Psychological Research*, Holt, Rinehart & Winston.

477   EDWARDS, A. L. (1967a), 'The social desirability variable: a broad statement', in I. A. Berg (ed.), *Response Set in Personality Assessment*, Aldine.

477   EDWARDS, A. L. (1967b), 'The social desirability variable: a review of the evidence', in I. A. Berg (ed.), *Response Set in Personality Assessment*, Aldine.

51   EDWARDS, A. L. (1967c), *Statistical Methods*, Holt, Rinehart & Winston, 2nd edn.

330   EDWARDS, E. (1964), *Information Transmission*, Chapman & Hall.

140   EHRLICH, A. (1964), 'Neural control of feeding behavior', *Psychol. Bull.*, vol. 61, pp. 100–114.

221   EIBL-EIBESFELDT, I. (1961), 'The fighting behavior of animals', *Scient. Amer.*, vol. 205, pp. 112–22.

558   ELLIS, E. (1952), 'Social psychological correlates of upward social mobility among unmarried

Page

career women', *Amer. sociol. Rev.*, vol. 17, pp. 558–63.

188   ENGEL, B. (1960), 'Stimulus–response and individual–response specificity', *Arch. gen. Psychiat.*, vol. 2, pp. 305–13.

188   ENGEL, B., and BICKFORD, A. F. (1961), 'Response-specificity: Stimulus–response and individual–response specificity in essential hypertensives', *Arch. gen. Psychiat.*, vol. 5, pp. 478–89.

409   EPSTEIN, W. (1961), 'The influence of syntactical structure on learning', *Amer. J. Psychol.*, vol. 74, pp. 80–85.

409   EPSTEIN, W. (1962), 'A further study of the influence of syntactical structure on learning', *Amer. J. Psychol.*, vol. 75, pp. 121–6.

271   ERIKSEN, C. W. (1954), 'The case for perceptual defense', *Psychol. Rev.*, vol. 61, pp. 175–82.

273   ERIKSEN, C. W. (1960), 'Discrimination and learning without awareness: a methodological survey and evaluation', *Psychol. Rev.*, vol. 67, pp. 279–300.

61   ERLENMEYER-KIMLING, L., and JARVIK, L. F. (1963), 'Genetics and intelligence: a review', *Science*, vol. 142, pp. 1477–9. [Wiseman]

309   ESTES, W. K. (1944), 'An experimental study of punishment', *Psychol. Monogr.*, vol. 54, no. 263.

304   ESTES, W. K. (1950), 'Toward a statistical theory of learning', *Psychol. Rev.*, vol. 57, pp. 94–107.

473   EUROPEAN PRODUCTIVITY AGENCY (1956), *Job Analysis: A Tool of Productivity*, E.P.A.

619   EWING, T. N. (1942), 'A study of certain factors involved in changes of opinion', *J. soc. Psychol.*, vol. 16, pp. 63–8.

530   EYSENCK, H. J. (1947), *Dimensions of Personality*, Routledge & Kegan Paul.

530   EYSENCK, H. J. (1952), *The Scientific Study of Personality*, Routledge & Kegan Paul.

512, 513, 518, 523, 524, 538   EYSENCK, H. J. (1953), *The Structure of Human Personality*, Methuen.

Page

539   EYSENCK, H. J. (1955), 'Cortical inhibition, figural after-effect and theory of personality', *J. abnorm. soc. Psychol.*, vol. 51, pp. 94–106.

62   EYSENCK, H. J. (1956), 'The inheritance of extraversion–introversion', *Acta Psychol.*, vol. 12, pp. 95–110.

539, 575   EYSENCK, H. J. (1957), *The Dynamics of Anxiety and Hysteria*, Routledge & Kegan Paul.

338   EYSENCK, H. J. (1959a), 'Inheritance and nature of extraversion', in P. Halmos and A. Iliffe (eds.), *Readings in General Psychology*, Routledge & Kegan Paul.

465   EYSENCK, H. J. (1959b), *The Maudsley Personality Inventory*, University of London Press.

533   EYSENCK, H. J. (1961), 'Review of Cattell and Scheier's book, *The Meaning and Measurement of Neuroticism and Anxiety*', *Occup. Psychol.*, vol. 35, pp. 253–6.

530, 540   EYSENCK, H. J. (1963), 'Biological basis of personality', *Nature*, vol. 199, pp. 1031–4.

296, 614   EYSENCK, H. J. (1964a), *Crime and Personality*, Routledge & Kegan Paul.

57   EYSENCK, H. J. (ed.) (1964b), *Experiments in Motivation*, Pergamon.

483   EYSENCK, H. J. (1967), 'Intelligence assessment: a theoretical and experimental approach', *Brit. J. educ. Psychol.*, vol. 37, pp. 81–98.

62   EYSENCK, H. J., and PRELL, D. B. (1951), 'The inheritance of neuroticism: an experimental study', *J. ment. Sci.*, vol. 97, pp. 441–65.

296   EYSENCK, H. J., and RACHMAN, S. (1965), *The Causes and Cures of Neurosis*, Routledge & Kegan Paul. [Semeonoff *]

41, 261, 262   FANTZ, R. L. (1961), 'The origin of form perception', *Scient. Amer.*, vol. 204, no. 5, pp. 66–72.

558   FARIS, R. E. L. (1944), 'Ecological factors in human behavior', in J. McV. Hunt (ed.), *Personality and the Behavior Disorders*, vol. 2, Ronald Press.

642   FAUCHEUX, C., and MACKENZIE, K. D. (1966), 'Task dependency of organizational

668   References

Page

centrality: its behavioral consequences', *J. exp. soc. Psychol.*, vol. 2, pp. 361–75.

135   FELDMAN, S. M., and WALLER, H. J. (1962), 'Dissociation of electrocortical activation and behavioural arousal', *Nature*, vol. 196, pp. 1320–22.

522   FENICHEL, O. (1946), *The Psychoanalytic Theory of Neurosis*, Routledge.

474   FERGUSON, L. W. (1951), 'Management quality and its effects on selection test validity', *Pers. Psychol.*, vol. 4, pp. 141–50.

593   FERGUSON, T. (1952), *The Young Delinquent in his Social Setting*, Oxford University Press.

298   FERSTER, B. C., and SKINNER, B. F. (1957), *Schedules of Reinforcement*, Appleton-Century-Crofts.

638   FESTINGER, L. (1954), 'A theory of social comparison processes', *Hum. Rel.*, vol. 7, pp. 117–40.

626   FESTINGER, L. (1957), *A Theory of Cognitive Dissonance*, Row, Peterson.

620   FESTINGER, L., and MACCOBY, N. (1964), 'On resistance to persuasive communications', *J. abnorm. soc. Psychol.*, vol. 68, pp. 359–66.

88   FIELD, J., MAGOUN, H. W., and HALL, V. E. (1959), *Handbook of Physiology*, sect. 1, vol. 1 (vols. 2 and 3, 1960), American Physiological Society.

423   FIELDS, P. E. (1932), 'Studies in concept formation: I. The development of the concept of triangularity by the white rat', *Comp. Physiol. Monogr.*, vol. 9, no. 2.

163   FINAN, J. L. (1939), 'Effects of frontal lobe lesions on temporally organized behavior in monkeys', *J. Neurophysiol.*, vol. 2, pp. 208–26.

339   FINAN, J. L., FINAN, S. C., and HARTSON, L. D. (1949), 'A review of representative tests used for the quantitative measurements of behaviour-decrement under conditions related to aircraft flight', *USAF Technical Report*, no. 5830, Air Materiel Command, Dayton, Ohio.

221   FISHER, J. (1964), 'Interspecific aggression', in J. D. Carthy and F. J. Ebling (eds.), *The*

Page

Natural History of Aggression, Academic Press.

344   FITTS, P. M., and POSNER, M. I. (1967), *Human Performance,* Brooks/Cole. [Legge*]

85, 497   FLAVELL, J. H. (1963), *The Developmental Psychology of Jean Piaget,* Van Nostrand.

407   FODOR, J. A., and BEVER, T. G. (1965), 'The psychological reality of linguistic segments', *J. verb. Learn. verb. Behav.,* vol. 4, pp. 414–20.

520   FORDHAM, F. (1953), *An Introduction to Jung's Psychology,* Penguin Books.

132   FOULKES, D. (1964), 'Theories of dream formation and recent studies of sleep consciousness', *Psychol. Bull.,* vol. 62, pp. 236–47.

132   FOULKES, D. (1966), *The Psychology of Sleep,* Scribner.

125   FRANK, K. (1959), 'Identification and analysis of single unit activity in the central nervous system', in J. Field, H. W. Magoun and V. E. Hall (eds.), *Handbook of Physiology,* sect. 1, vol. 1, American Physiological Society.

338   FRANKMANN, J. P., and ADAMS, J. A. (1962), 'Theories of vigilance', *Psychol. Bull.,* vol. 59, pp. 257–72.

580   FREED, A., *et al.* (1955), 'Stimulus and background factors in sign violation', *J. Pers.,* vol. 23, p. 499.

76   FREEDMAN, D. G., and KELLER, B. (1963), 'Inheritance of behaviour in infants', *Science,* vol. 140, pp. 196–8.

623   FREEDMAN, J. L. (1964), 'Involvement, discrepancy and change', *J. abnorm. soc. Psychol.,* vol. 69, pp. 290–95.

137   FRENCH, J. D. (1957), 'The reticular formation', *Scient. Amer.,* vol. 196, no. 6, pp. 54–60.

444   FREUD, S. (1900), *The Interpretation of Dreams,* translated 1913, Macmillan.

83   FREUD, S. (1905), *Three Essays on the Theory of Sexuality,* translated by J. Strachey, 1949, Imago Publishing.

584   FREUD, S. (1922), *Group Psychology and the Analysis of the Ego,* International Psychoanalytic Press.

Page

521   FREUD, S. (1924), 'Character and anal erotism', in *Collected Papers*, vol. 2, Hogarth Press.

365   FREUD, S. (1925), 'Repression', in *Collected Papers*, vol. 4, Hogarth Press.

584   FREUD, S. (1933), *New Introductory Lectures on Psychoanalysis*, translated by W. J. H. Sprott, Hogarth Press.

315   FRIEDMAN, H., and MARSHALL, D. A. (1965), 'Position reversal training in the Virginia opossum: evidence for the acquisition of a learning set', *Quart. J. exper. Psychol.*, vol. 17, pp. 250–54.

556   FROMM, E. (1942), *Fear of Freedom*, Routledge.

76   FROMME, A. (1941), 'An experimental study of the factors of maturation and practice in the behavioral development of the embryo of the frog, *Rana pipiens*', *Genet. Psychol. Monogr.*, vol. 24, pp. 219–56.

485   FRUCHTER, B. (1954), *Introduction to Factor Analysis*, Van Nostrand.

289   FULLER, J. L., and CLARKE, L. D. (1966), 'Genetic and treatment factors modifying the post-isolation syndrome in dogs', *J. comp. physiol. Psychol.*, vol. 61, pp. 251–7.

56, 64, 66   FULLER, J. L., and THOMPSON, W. R. (1960), *Behavior Genetics*, Wiley.

191   FUNKENSTEIN, D. H., KING, S. H., and DROLETTE, M. E. (1957), *Mastery of Stress*, Harvard University Press.

136   FUSTER, J. M. (1958), 'Effects of stimulation of brain stem on tachistoscopic perception', *Science*, vol. 127, p. 150.

426, 441   GAGNÉ, R. M. (1966), 'Human problem solving: internal and external events', in B. Kleinmuntz (ed.), *Problem Solving: Research, Method and Theory*, Wiley.

293   GAGNÉ, R. M. (1967), *The Conditions of Learning*, Holt, Rinehart & Winston.

308   GALLISTEL, C. R. (1964), 'Electrical self-stimulation and its theoretical implications', *Psychol. Bull.*, vol. 61, pp. 23–34.

60   GALTON, F. (1869), *Hereditary Genius*, Macmillan. [Wiseman *; P. E. Vernon *]

Page

434   GALTON, F. (1883), *Inquiry into Human Faculty and its Development*, Macmillan.

88   GARDNER, E. (1963), *Fundamentals of Neurology*, Saunders, 4th edn.

372, 373   GARDNER, R. W., *et al.* (1959), 'Cognitive controls: a study of individual consistencies in cognitive behavior', *Psychol. Issues*, vol. 1, no. 4.

407, 408   GARRETT, M., BEVER, T. G., and FODOR, J. A. (1966), 'The active use of grammar in speech perception', *Percept. Psychophys.*, vol. 1, pp. 30–32.

234   GELDARD, F. A. (1953), *The Human Senses*, Wiley and Chapman & Hall.

70   GESELL, A. (1929), 'Maturation and infant behavior patterns', *Psychol. Rev.*, vol. 36, pp. 307–19.

74   GESELL, A. (1954), 'The ontogenesis of infant
81   behavior', in L. Carmichael (ed.), *Handbook of Child Psychology*, Wiley, 2nd edn.

84   GESELL, A., and ILG, F. L. (1949), *Child Development*, Harper.

77   GESELL, A., and THOMPSON, H. (1929), 'Learning and growth in identical twins', *Genet. Psychol. Monogr.*, vol. 6, pp. 1–124.

75   GESELL, A., and THOMPSON, H. (1941), 'Twins T and C from infancy to adolescence: a biogenetic study of individual differences by the method of co-twin control', *Genet. Psychol. Monogr.*, vol. 24, pp. 3–121.

433, 495   GETZELS, J. W., and JACKSON, P. O. (1962), *Creativity and Intelligence*, Wiley.

572   GEWIRTZ, J. L., and BAER, D. M. (1958a), 'The effect of brief social deprivation on behavior for a social reinforcer', *J. abnorm. soc. Psychol.*, vol. 56, pp. 49–56.

572   GEWIRTZ, J. L., and BAER, D. M. (1958b), 'Deprivation and satiation of social reinforcers as drive conditions', *J. abnorm. soc. Psychol.*, vol. 57, pp. 165–72.

426, 444   GHISELIN, B. (1952), *The Creative Process: A Symposium*, University of California Press. [P. E. Vernon*]

Page

473   GHISELLI, E. E. (1956), 'Dimensional problems of criteria', *J. appl. Psychol.*, vol. 40, pp. 1–4.

474   GHISELLI, E. E. (1966), *The Validity of Occupational Aptitude Tests*, Wiley.

474   GHISELLI, E. E., and BROWN, C. W. (1955), *Personnel and Industrial Psychology*, McGraw-Hill.

244, 249   GIBSON, J. J. (1950), *The Perception of the Visual World*, Houghton Mifflin.

642   GLANZER, M., and GLASER, R. (1961), 'Techniques for the study of group structure and behavior: II. Empirical studies of the effects of structure in small groups', *Psychol. Bull.*, vol. 58, pp. 1–27.

349, 350   GLICKMAN, S. (1961), 'Perseverative neural processes and consolidation of the memory trace', *Psychol. Bull.*, vol. 58, pp. 218–33.

593, 594, 602, 608, 609   GLUECK, S., and GLUECK, E. (1950), *Unraveling Juvenile Delinquency*, Commonwealth Fund, Harper.

149, 150   GODDARD, G. V. (1964), 'Functions of the amygdala', *Psychol. Bull.*, vol. 62, pp. 89–109.

157   GOLDBERG, M. M., and NEFF, W. D. (1961), 'Frequency discrimination after bilateral section of the brachium of the inferior colliculus', *J. comp. Neurol.*, vol. 113, pp. 265–82.

230   GOLDBERGER, L., and HOLT, R. R. (1961), 'Experimental interference with reality contact: Individual differences', in P. Solomon *et al.* (eds.), *Sensory Deprivation*, Harvard University Press.

286   GOLDFARB, W. (1943), 'Effects of institutional care on adolescent personality', *J. exp. Educ.*, vol. 12, pp. 106–29.

274   GOLDIAMOND, I. (1958), 'Indicators of perception: I. Subliminal perception, subception, unconscious perception: an analysis in terms of psychophysical indicator methodology', *Psychol. Bull.*, vol. 55, pp. 373–412.

274   GOLDIAMOND, I., and HAWKINS, W. F. (1958), 'Vexierversuch: the log relationship between word frequency and recognition obtained in the

Page

absence of stimulus words', *J. exp. Psychol.*, vol. 56, pp. 457–63.

274   GOLDSTEIN, K. (1943), 'The significance of psychological research in schizophrenia', *J. nerv. ment. Dis.*, vol. 97, pp. 261–79.

260   GOLDSTEIN, K., and SCHEERER, M. (1941), 'Abstract and concrete behavior; an experimental study with special tests', *Psychol. Monogr.*, vol. 53, no. 2

428, 430   GOLDSTEIN, M. (1962), 'A test of the response probability theory of perceptual defense', *J. exp. Psychol.*, vol. 63, pp. 23–8.

355   GOMULICKI, B. R. (1953), 'The development and present status of the trace theory of memory', *Brit. J. Psychol. Monogr. Supp.*, no. 29.

62   GOTTESMAN, I. I. (1963), 'Heritability and personality', *Psychol. Monogr.*, vol. 77, no. 9.

131   GRANIT, R. (1955), *Receptors and Sensory Perception*, Yale University Press.

200, 549   GRAY, J. A. (1964), *Pavlov's Typology*, Pergamon.

234   GREEN, D. M., and SWETS, J. A. (1966), *Signal Detection Theory and Psychophysics*, Wiley.

148   GREEN, J. D., CLEMENTE, C. D., and DE GROOT, J. (1957), 'Rhinencephalic lesions and behavior in cats', *J. comp. Neurol.*, vol. 108, pp. 505–46.

219   GREEN, R., CARR, W. J., and GREEN, M. (1968), 'The hawk–goose phenomenon: further confirmation and a search for the releaser', *J. Psychol.*, vol. 69, pp. 271–6.

371   GREENSPOON, J., and RANYARD, R. (1957), 'Stimulus conditions and retroactive inhibition', *J. exp. Psychol.*, vol. 53, pp. 55–9.

572   GREENSPOON, T. (1955), 'The reinforcing effect of two spoken sounds on the frequency of two responses', *Amer. J. Psychol.*, vol. 68, pp. 409–16.

266   GREGOR, A. J., and MCPHERSON, D. A. (1965), 'A study of susceptibility to geometric illusion among cultural subgroups of Australian aborigines', *Psychol. Afric.*, vol. 11, pp. 1–13.

Page

238, 252   GREGORY, R. (1966), *Eye and Brain: the Psychology of Seeing*, Weidenfeld & Nicolson.

265   GREGORY, R. L., and WALLACE, J. G. (1963), 'Recovery from early blindness: a case study', *Exp. Psychol. Soc. Monogr.*, no. 2.

591   GRINDER, R. E. (1961), 'New techniques for research in children's temptation behavior', *Child Devel.*, vol. 32, pp. 679–88.

605, 609   GRINDER, R. E. (1962), 'Parental child-rearing practices, conscience and resistance to temptation of sixth-grade children', *Child Devel.*, vol. 33, pp. 803–20.

602, 603, 605, 606   GRINDER, R. E. (1964), 'Relations between behavioral and cognitive dimensions of conscience in middle childhood', *Child Devel.*, vol. 35, pp. 881–91.

602   GRINDER, R. E., and McMICHAEL, R. (1963), 'Cultural influences on conscience development', *J. abnorm. soc. Psychol.*, vol. 66, pp. 503–7.

170   GROSSMAN, S. P. (1960), 'Eating or drinking elicited by direct adrenergic or cholinergic stimulation of hypothalamus', *Science*, vol. 132, pp. 301–2.

120, 139, 170, 211   GROSSMAN, S. P. (1967), *A Textbook of Physiological Psychology*, Wiley.

433   GRUBER, H. E., TERRELL, G., and WERTHEIMER, M. (eds.) (1962), *Contemporary Approaches to Creative Thinking*, Atherton.

471   GUERTIN, W. H., et al. (1966), 'Research with the Wechsler Intelligence Scales for adults: 1960–1965', *Psychol. Bull.*, vol. 66, pp. 385–409.

455   GUILFORD, J. P. (1954), *Psychometric Methods*, McGraw-Hill, 2nd edn.

514, 532   GUILFORD, J. P. (1959), *Personality*, McGraw-Hill.

493   GUILFORD, J. P. (1967), *The Nature of Human Intelligence*, McGraw-Hill.

288   GUITON, P. (1959), 'Socialisation and imprinting in Brown Leghorn chicks', *Anim. Behav.*, vol. 7, pp. 26–34.

361, 362   GUTHRIE, E. R. (1935), *The Psychology of Learning*, Harper.

53   HALL, C. S. (1951), 'The genetics of behavior',

Page

in S. S. Stevens (ed.), *Handbook of Experimental Psychology*, Wiley.

290 HALL, C. S. (1954), *A Primer of Freudian Psychology*, World Publishing Co.

513, 515, 519 HALL, C. S., and LINDZEY, G. (1957), *Theories of Personality*, Wiley.

303 HALL, K. R. L. (1963), 'Observational learning in monkeys and apes', *Brit. J. Psychol.*, vol. 54, pp. 201-26. [Riopelle]

555, 556 HALLIDAY, J. (1948), *Psychosocial Medicine*, Heinemann.

218 HALLIDAY, M. S. (1966), 'Effect of previous exploratory activity on the exploration of a simple maze', *Nature*, vol. 209, pp. 432-3.

161 HALSTEAD, W. C. (1947), *Brain and Intelligence: A Quantitative Study of the Frontal Lobes*, University of Chicago Press.

430 HANFMANN, E., and KASANIN, J. (1942), 'Conceptual thinking in schizophrenia', *Nerv. ment. Dis. Monogr.*, no. 67.

630, 640, 643 HARE, A. P. (1962), *Handbook of Small Group Research*, Free Press of Glencoe.

315 ,432 HARLOW, H. F. (1949), 'The formation of learning sets', *Psychol. Rev.*, vol. 56, pp. 51-65. [Riopelle]

217 HARLOW, H. F. (1953), 'Mice, monkeys, men and motives', *Psychol. Rev.*, vol. 60, pp. 23-62.

163 HARLOW, H. F. (1959a), 'The development of learning in the rhesus monkey', *Amer. Scient.*, vol. 47, pp. 459-79.

284 HARLOW, H. F. (1959b), 'Love in infant monkeys', *Scient. Amer.*, vol. 200, pp. 68-74.

126, 163, 165 HARLOW, H. F., AKERT, K., and SCHILTZ, K. A. (1964), 'The effects of bilateral prefrontal lesions on learned behavior of neonatal infant and preadolescent monkeys', in J. M. Warren and K. Akert (eds.), *The Frontal Granular Cortex and Behavior*, McGraw-Hill.

128 HARLOW, H. F., *et al.* (1952), 'Analysis of frontal and posterior association syndromes in brain-damaged monkeys', *J. comp. physiol. Psychol.*, vol. 45, pp. 419-29.

285 HARLOW, H. F., and HARLOW, M. K. (1962),

Page

'Social deprivation in monkeys', *Scient. Amer.*, vol. 207, pp. 137–46.

217 HARLOW, H. F., HARLOW, M. K., and MEYER, D. R. (1950), 'Learning motivated by a manipulation drive', *J. exp. Psychol.*, vol. 40, pp. 228–34.

215, 284 HARLOW, H. F., and ZIMMERMANN, R. R. (1959), 'Affectional responses in the infant monkey', *Science*, vol. 130, pp. 421–32.

255, 256 HARRIS, C. S. (1965), 'Perceptual adaptation to inverted, reversed, and displaced vision', *Psychol. Rev.*, vol. 72, pp. 419–44.

68, 85 HARRIS, D. B. (ed.) (1957), *The Concept of Development*, Minneapolis University Press.

480 HARRISON, R. (1965), 'Thematic apperceptive methods', in B. B. Wolman (ed.), *Handbook of Clinical Psychology*, McGraw-Hill.

592, 593, 605, 606, 607 HARTSHORNE, H., and MAY, M. (1928), *Studies in the Nature of Character*, vol. 1, Macmillan.

606, 607 HARTSHORNE, H., and MAY, M. (1929), *Studies in the Nature of Character*, vol. 2, Macmillan.

573 HARTSHORNE, H., and MAY, M. (1930), *Studies in the Nature of Character*, vol. 3, Macmillan.

633 HARTUP, W. W. (1964), 'Friendship status and the effectiveness of peers as reinforcing agents', *J. exp. Child Psychol.*, vol. 1, pp. 154–62.

496 HARVEY, O. J., and RUTHERFORD, J. (1960), 'Status in the informal group: influence and influencibility at differing age levels', *Child Devel.*, vol. 31, pp. 377–85.

476 HASAN, P., and BUTCHER, H. J. (1966), 'Creativity and intelligence: a partial replication with Scottish children of Getzels' and Jackson's study', *Brit. J. Psychol.*, vol. 57, pp. 129–35.

476 HATHAWAY, S. R., and MCKINLEY, J. C. (1942), *Minnesota Multiphasic Personality Inventory*, University of Minnesota Press. [Semeonoff *]

476 HATHAWAY, S. R., and MCKINLEY, J. C. (1943), *Manual for the Minnesota*

Page

Multiphasic Personality Inventory, Psychological Corporation, New York.

594   HAVIGHURST, R., and TABA, H. (1949), *Adolescent Character and Personality*, Wiley.

306   HEATH, R. G. (1955), 'Correlations between levels of psychological awareness and physiological activity in the central nervous system', *Psychosom. Med.*, vol. 17, pp. 383–95.

161, 162   HEBB, D. O. (1942), 'The effect of early and late brain injury upon test scores, and the nature of normal adult intelligence', *Proc. Amer. Philos. Soc.*, vol. 85, pp. 275–92.

161   HEBB, D. O. (1945), 'Man's frontal lobes', *Arch. Neurol. Psychiat.*, vol. 54, pp. 10–24.

190   HEBB, D. O. (1946a), 'Emotion in man and animal: an analysis of the intuitive processes of recognition', *Psychol. Rev.*, vol. 53, pp. 88–106.

220, 285   HEBB, D. O. (1946b), 'On the nature of fear', *Psychol. Rev.*, vol. 53, pp. 250–75.

190, 247, 248, 254, 269 349, 494, 496   HEBB, D. O. (1949), *The Organization of Behavior*, Wiley. [Dodwell *; Wiseman *]

202   HEBB, D. O. (1955), 'Drives and the C.N.S. (conceptual nervous system)', *Psychol. Rev.*, vol. 62, pp. 243–54. [Bindra and Stewart; Pribram, vol. 4]

97, 111   HEBB, D. O. (1958), *A Textbook of Psychology*, Saunders, 1st edn.

347   HEBB, D. O. (1961), 'Distinctive features of learning in the higher animals', in J. Delafresnaye (ed.), *Brain Mechanisms in Learning*, Oxford University Press.

21, 68, 70, 247   HEBB, D. O. (1966), *A Textbook of Psychology*, Saunders, 2nd edn.

364   HEBB, D. O., and FOORD, E. N. (1945), 'Errors of visual recognition and the nature of the trace', *J. exp. Psychol.*, vol. 35, pp. 335–48.

429   HEIDBREDER, E. (1946a), 'The attainment of concepts: I. Terminology and methodology', *J. genet. Psychol.*, vol. 35, pp. 173–89.

429   HEIDBREDER, E. (1946b), 'The attainment of concepts: II. The problem', *J. genet. Psychol.*, vol. 35, pp. 191–223.

Page

585   HEILBRUN, A. B. (1965), 'The measurement of
       identification', *Child Devel.*, vol. 36, pp. 111–27.

586   HEILBRUN, A. B., and FROMME, D. K. (1965),
       'Parental identification of late adolescents and
       level of adjustment: the importance of parent-
       model attributes, ordinal position, and sex of the
       child', *J. genet. Psychol.*, vol. 107, pp. 49–59.

467, 482   HEIM, A. W. (1954), *The Appraisal of
           Intelligence*, Methuen.

263, 264   HELD, R., and HEIN, A. (1963),
           'Movement-produced stimulation in the
           development of visually guided behavior',
           J. comp. physiol. Psychol., vol. 56, pp. 607–13.
           [Dodwell]

580   HELSON, H., BLAKE, R. R., and MOUTON,
       J. S. (1958a), 'Petition-signing as adjustment to
       situational and personal factors', *J. soc.
       Psychol.*, vol. 48, pp. 3–10.

622   HELSON, H., BLAKE, R. R., and MOUTON,
       J. S. (1958b), 'An experimental investigation of
       the effectiveness of the "big lie" in shifting
       attitudes', *J. soc. Psychol.*, vol. 48, pp. 51–60.

136   HERNÁNDEZ-PEÓN, R. (1961), 'Reticular
       mechanisms of sensory control', in W. A.
       Rosenblith (ed.), *Sensory Communication*,
       M.I.T. Press.

57   HERON, W. T. (1935), 'The inheritance of maze
       learning ability in rats', *J. comp. Psychol.*, vol.
       19, pp. 77–89.

57   HERON, W. T. (1941), 'The inheritance of
       brightness and dullness in maze learning ability
       in the rat', *J. genet. Psychol.*, vol. 59, pp. 41–9.

144   HERRICK, C. J. (1933), 'The functions of
       olfactory parts of the cortex', *Proc. Nat. Acad.
       Sci. (Washington)*, vol. 19, pp. 7–14. (Pribram,
       vol. 1]

281   HESS, E. H. (1959), 'Imprinting', *Science*, vol.
       130, pp. 133–41.

138, 174   HESS, W. R. (1954), *Diencephalon: Autonomic
           and Extrapyramidal Functions*, Grune &
           Stratton.

139   HETHERINGTON, A. W., and RANSON, S. W.
       (1942), 'The spontaneous activity and food intake

Page

of rats with hypothalamic lesions', *Amer. J. Physiol.*, vol. 136, pp. 609–17.

586   HETHERINGTON, E. M., and FRANKIE, G. (1967), 'Effects of parental dominance, warmth, and conflict on imitation in children', *J. Pers. soc. Psychol.*, vol. 6, pp. 119–25.

325   HIBBERT, C. (1961), *The Destruction of Lord Raglan*, Penguin Books.

334   HICK, W. E. (1948), 'The discontinuous functioning of the human operator in pursuit tasks', *Quart. J. exp. Psychol.*, vol. 1, pp. 36–51.

331   HICK, W. E. (1952), 'On the rate of gain of information', *Quart. J. exp. Psychol.*, vol. 4, pp. 11–24.

326   HICK, W. E., and BATES, J. A. V. (1950), 'The human operator of control mechanisms', *Permanent Records of Research and Development*, no. 17.204, Ministry of Supply, H.M.S.O.

316, 317   HILGARD, E. R., and BOWER, G. H. (1966), *Theories of Learning*, Appleton-Century-Crofts.

298, 301   HILGARD, E. R., and MARQUIS, D. G. (1961), *Conditioning and Learning*, Methuen.

123   HILL, D., and PARR, G. (eds.) (1950), *Electroencephalography*, Macdonald, rev. edn 1963.

304, 305, 311, 313   HILL, W. F. (1963), *Learning: A Survey of Psychological Interpretations*, Methuen.

222   HINDE, R. A. (1967), 'The nature of aggression', *New Society*, vol. 9, pp. 302–4.

58   HIRSCH, J. (1964), 'Breeding analysis of natural units in behavior genetics', *Amer. Zoologist*, vol. 4, pp. 139–45.

219   HIRSCH, J., LINDLEY, R. H., and TOLMAN, E. C. (1955), 'An experimental test of an alleged innate sign stimulus', *J. comp. physiol. Psychol.*, vol. 48, pp. 278–80.

229, 245, 255   HOCHBERG, J. E. (1964), *Perception*, Prentice-Hall.

379   HOCKETT, C. F. (1960), 'The origin of speech', *Scient. Amer.*, vol. 203, pp. 89–96.

435   HOIJER, H. (1953), 'The relation of language to culture', in A. L. Kroeber (ed.), *Anthropology Today: An Encyclopaedic Inventory*, University of Chicago Press.

680 References

Page

322, 327, 344, 346   HOLDING, D. H. (1965), *Principles of Training*, Pergamon. [Legge*]

638   HOLLANDER, E. P., and HUNT, R. G. (eds.) (1963), *Current Perspectives in Social Psychology*, Oxford University Press.

480   HOLTZMANN, W. H., *et al.* (1961), *Inkblot Perception and Personality: Holtzmann Inkblot Technique*, University of Texas Press.

643   HOMANS, G. (1961), *The Human Group*, Harcourt, Brace.

136   HORN, G. (1965), 'Physiological and psychological aspects of selective perception', in D. S. Lehrman, R. A. Hinde and E. Shaw (eds.), *Advances in the Study of Behavior*, vol. 1, Academic Press.

485   HORST, P. (1965), *Factor Analysis of Data Matrices*, Holt, Rinehart & Winston.

177   HOSKINS, R. G. (1933), *The Tides of Life*, Norton.

295, 296, 625   HOVLAND, C. I. (1937), 'The generalization of conditioned responses', *J. gen. Psychol.*, vol. 17, pp. 125–48.

621   HOVLAND, C. I. (ed.) (1957), *The Order of Presentation in Persuasion*, Yale University Press.

624   HOVLAND, C. I., and JANIS, I. L. (eds.) (1959), *Personality and Persuasibility*, Yale University Press.

621   HOVLAND, C. I., JANIS, I. L., and KELLEY, H. H. (1953), *Communication and Persuasion*, Yale University Press. (Jahoda and Warren*]

618   HOVLAND, C. I., and WEISS, W. (1951), 'The influence of source credibility on communication effectiveness', *Publ. Opin. Quart.*, vol. 15, pp. 635–50.

272, 274   HOWES, D. H., and SOLOMON, R. L. (1950), 'A note on McGinnies's "Emotionality and perceptual defense"', *Psychol. Rev.*, vol. 57, pp. 229–34.

235   HOWES, D. H., and SOLOMON, R. L. (1951), 'Visual duration threshold as a function of word probability', *J. exp. Psychol.*, vol. 41, pp. 401–10.

550   HSU, F. L. K. (1949), 'Suppression versus repression: a limited psychological interpretation of four cultures', *Psychiatry*, vol. 12, pp. 223–42.

Page

254 HUBEL, D. H., and WIESEL, T. N. (1962),
'Receptive fields, binocular interaction and
functional architecture in the cat's visual
cortex', *J. Physiol.*, vol. 160, pp. 106–54.

496 HUDSON, L. (1966), *Contrary Imaginations*,
Methuen. [P. E. Vernon *]

58 HUGHES, K. R., and ZUBEK, J. P. (1956),
'Effect of glutamic acid on the learning ability
of "bright" and "dull" rats. I', *Canad. J.
Psychol.*, vol. 10, pp. 132–8.

58 HUGHES, K. R., and ZUBEK, J. P. (1957),
'Effect of glutamic acid on the learning ability
of "bright" and "dull" rats. II', *Canad. J.
Psychol.*, vol. 11, pp. 182–4.

428 HULL, C. L. (1920), 'Quantitative aspects of the
evolution of concepts', *Psychol. Monogr.*, no.
123.

440 HULL, C. L. (1934), 'The concept of the
habit-family hierarchy and maze learning',
Psychol. Rev., vol. 41, pp. 33–54, 134–52.

311 HULL, C. L. (1943), *Principles of Behavior*,
Appleton-Century-Crofts. [Bindra and
Stewart *]

420, 425, 434, 437 HUMPHREY, G. (1951), *Thinking*, Methuen.

519 HUMPHREYS, L. G. (1957), 'Characteristics of
type concepts with special reference to Sheldon's
typology', *Psychol. Bull.*, vol. 54, pp. 218–28.

497 HUNT, J. McV. (1961), *Intelligence and
Experience*, Ronald Press. [Wiseman *]

215, 220, 483 HUNT, J. McV. (1963), 'Motivation inherent in
information processing and action', in O. J.
Harvey (ed.), *Motivation and Social Interaction*,
Ronald Press.

291 HUNT, J. McV., *et al.* (1947), 'Studies of the
effects of infantile experience on adult behavior
in rats. I. Effects of infantile feeding frustration
on adult hoarding', *J. comp. physiol. Psychol.*,
vol. 40, pp. 291–304.

366 HUNTER, I. L. (1964), *Memory*, Penguin Books,
2nd edn.

420 HUNTER, W. S. (1928), 'The behavior of
racoons in a double alternation temporal maze',
J. genet. Psychol., vol. 35, pp. 374–88.

Page

607   HURLOCK, E. (1964), *Child Development*, McGraw-Hill, 4th edn.

63   HUSEN, T. (1959), *Psychological Twin Research*, Almquist & Wiksell.

331   HYMAN, R. (1953), 'Stimulus information as a determinant of reaction time', *J. exp. Psychol.*, vol. 45, pp. 188–96.

42   HYMAN, R. (1964), *The Nature of Psychological Inquiry*, Prentice-Hall.

279   HYMOVITCH, B. (1952), 'The effects of experimental variations on problem solving in rats', *J. comp. physiol. Psychol.*, vol. 45, pp. 313–20.

509   INHELDER, B., and PIAGET, J. (1958), *The Growth of Logical Thinking from Childhood to Adolescence*, Basic Books.

508, 509   INHELDER, B., and PIAGET, J. (1964), *The Early Growth of Logic in the Child*, Routledge & Kegan Paul.

626   INSKO, C. A. (1967), *Theories of Attitude Change*, Appleton-Century-Crofts.

623   INSKO, C. A., ARKOFF, A., and INSKO, V. M. (1965), 'Effects of high and low fear-arousing communications upon opinion change towards smoking', *J. exp. soc. Psychol.*, vol. 1, pp. 256–66.

416   IRWIN, O. C. (1960), 'Language and communication', in P. H. Mussen (ed.), *Handbook of Research Methods in Child Development*, Wiley.

257   ITTELSON, W. H. (1952), *The Ames Demonstrations in Perception*, Princeton University Press.

477   JACKSON, D. N. (1967), 'Acquiescence response styles: problems of identification and control', in I. A. Berg (ed.), *Response Set in Personality Assessment*, Aldine.

162   JACOBSON, C. F. (1935), 'Functions of the frontal association areas in primates', *Arch. Neurol. Psychiat.*, vol. 33, pp. 558–69.

435   JACOBSON, E. (1932), 'Electrophysiology of mental activities', *Amer. J. Psychol.*, vol. 44, pp. 677–94.

Page

544, 548, 556   JAHODA, M. (1958), *Current Concepts of Positive Mental Health*, Basic Books.

188   JAMES, W. (1884), 'What is emotion?', *Mind*. vol. 9, pp. 188–205. [Arnold]

188, 247, 269, 347   JAMES, W. (1890), *The Principles of Psychology*, Holt.

33   JAMES, W. (1902), *The Varieties of Religious Experience*, Longmans, Green.

548   JANIS, I. L. (1958), 'Emotional inoculation: Theory and research on effects of preparatory communications', *Psychoanal. soc. Sci.*, vol. 5, pp. 119–54.

623   JANIS, I. L., and FESHBACK, S. (1953), 'Effects of fear-arousing communications', *J. abnorm. soc. Psychol.*, vol. 48, pp. 78–92.

625   JANIS, I. L., and KING, B. (1954), 'The influence of role-playing on opinion change', *J. abnorm. soc. Psychol.*, vol. 49, pp. 211–18. [Jahoda and Warren]

626   JANIS, I. L., and MANN, L. (1965), 'Effectiveness of emotional role-playing in modifying smoking habits and attitudes', *J. exp. Pers. Res.*, vol. 1, pp. 84–90.

370   JENKINS, J. G., and DALLENBACH, K. M. (1924), 'Obliviscence during sleep and waking', *Amer. J. Psychol.*, vol. 35, pp. 605–12.

311   JENKINS, J. J. (1963), 'Mediated associations: paradigms and situations', in C. N. Cofer and B. S. Musgrave (eds.), *Verbal Behavior and Learning*, McGraw-Hill.

311   JENKINS, J. J. (1965), 'Mediation theory and grammatical behavior', in S. Rosenberg (ed.), *Directions in Psycholinguistics*, Macmillan, New York.

299   JENKINS, W. O., McFANN, H., and CLAYTON, F. L. (1950), 'A methodological study of extinction following aperiodic and continuous reinforcement', *J. comp. physiol. Psychol.*, vol. 43, pp. 155–67.

298   JENKINS, W. O., and RIGBY, M. K. (1950), 'Partial (periodic) versus continuous reinforcement in resistance to extinction', *J. comp. physiol. Psychol.*, vol. 43, pp. 30–40.

684 References

Page

293   JENNINGS, H. S. (1906), *Behavior of the Lower Organisms*, Columbia University Press.

390   JENSEN, A. R., and ROHWER, W. D., JR (1965), 'What is learned in serial learning?', *J. verb. Learn. verb. Behav.*, vol. 4, pp. 62–72.

408   JOHNSON, N. F. (1965), 'Linguistic models and functional units of language behaviour', in S. Rosenberg (ed.), *Directions in Psycholinguistics*, Macmillan, New York.

600, 607, 611 JOHNSON, R. C. (1962), 'A study of children's moral judgments', *Child Devel.*, vol. 33, pp. 327–54.

545, 549, 557, 560 JONES, E. (1948), 'The concept of a normal mind', in *Papers on Psychoanalysis*, Baillière, Tindall & Cox, 5th edn.

638   JONES, E. E. (1965), 'Conformity as a tactic of ingratiation', *Science*, vol. 149, pp. 144–50.

132   JOUVET, M. (1967), 'The states of sleep', *Scient. Amer.*, vol. 216, no. 2, pp. 62–72.

266   JOYNSON, R. B. (1958), 'An experimental synthesis of the associationist and Gestalt accounts of the perception of size', *Quart. J. exp. Psychol.*, vol. 10, pp. 65–76, 142–54.

512, 520   JUNG, C. G. (1928), 'Psychological types', reprinted in B. Semeonoff (ed.), *Personality Assessment*, Penguin Books, 1966. [Semeonoff]

200   KAELBLING, R., *et al.* (1960), 'Reliability of autonomic responses', *Psychol. Rep.*, vol. 6, pp. 143–63.

505   KAGAN, J. (1958), 'The concept of identification', *Psychol. Rev.*, vol. 65, pp. 296–305.

586   KAGAN, J., and PHILLIPS, W. (1964), 'Measurement of identification: a methodological note', *J. abnorm. soc. Psychol.*, vol. 69, pp. 442–4.

70   KALLMAN, F. J., and SANDER, G. (1949), 'Twin studies on senescence', *Amer. J. Psychiat.*, vol. 106, pp. 29–36.

582   KANFER, F. H. (1965), 'Vicarious human reinforcement: a glimpse into the Black Box', in L. Krasner and L. P. Ullman (eds.), *Research in Behavioral Modification*, Holt, Rinehart & Winston.

Page

582   KANFER, F. H., and MARSTON, A. R. (1963), 'Human reinforcement: vicarious and direct', *J. exp. Psychol.*, vol. 65, pp. 292–6.

420   KARN, H. W. (1938), 'The behavior of cats on the double alternation problem in the temporal maze', *J. comp. Psychol.*, vol. 26, pp. 201–8.

417   KATZ, J. J. (1966), *The Philosophy of Language*, Harper & Row.

397   KATZ, J. J., and FODOR, J. A. (1963), 'The structure of a semantic theory', *Language*, vol. 39, pp. 170–210.

397   KATZ, J. J., and POSTAL, P. M. (1964), *An Integrated Theory of Linguistic Descriptions*, M.I.T. Press.

238, 240   KAUFMAN, L., and ROCK, I. (1962), 'The moon illusion', *Scient. Amer.*, vol. 207, no. 1, pp. 120–32.

455   KELLY, E. L. (1967), *Assessment of Human Characteristics*, Wadsworth.

479   KELLY, G. A. (1955), *The Psychology of Personal Constructs*, Norton.

427   KELMAN, H. C. (1961), 'Processes of opinion change', *Publ. Opin. Quart.*, vol. 25, pp. 57–78.

159   KENNARD, M. A. (1938), 'Reorganization of motor function in the cerebral cortex of monkeys deprived of motor and premotor areas in infancy', *J. Neurophysiol.*, vol. 1, pp. 477–96.

159   KENNARD, M. A. (1942), 'Cortical representation of motor function: studies on series of monkeys of various ages from infancy to maturity', *Arch. neurol. Psychiat. (Chicago)*, vol. 48, pp. 227–40.

574   KENNEDY, W. A., and WILLCUTT, H. C. (1964), 'Praise and blame as incentives', *Psychol. Bull.*, vol. 62, pp. 323–32.

68   KESSEN, W. (1960), 'Research design in the study of developmental problems', in P. H. Mussen (ed.), *Handbook of Research Methods in Child Development*, Wiley.

195   KESSEN, W., and MANDLER, G. (1961), 'Anxiety, pain and the inhibition of distress', *Psychol. Rev.*, vol. 68, pp. 396–404.

625   KING, B., and JANIS, I. L. (1956), 'Comparison

686 References

of the effectiveness of improvised versus nonimprovised role-playing in producing opinion change', *Hum. Rel.*, vol. 9, pp. 177–86.

151 KING, F. A. (1958), 'Effects of septal and amygdaloid lesions on emotional behavior and conditioned avoidance responses in the rat', *J. nerv. ment. Dis.*, vol. 126, pp. 57–63.

276 KIPLING, R. (1937), *Something of Myself*, Macmillan.

481 KLEINMUNTZ, B. (1967), *Personality Measurement: An Introduction*, Dorsey Press.

144 KLEIST, K. (1934), *Handbuch der ärtzlichen Erfahrungen im Weltkriege*, vol. 4, pp. 343–1408, Barth.

133, 338 KLEITMAN, N. (1939), *Sleep and Wakefulness*, University of Chicago Press.

135, 201 KLEITMAN, N. (1952), 'Sleep', *Scient. Amer.*, vol. 187, pp. 34–9.

133, 201 KLEITMAN, N. (1963), *Sleep and Wakefulness*, University of Chicago Press, 2nd edn.

480 KLOPFER, B., and DAVIDSON, H. H. (1962), *The Rorschach Technique: An Introductory Manual*, Harcourt, Brace.

479 KLOPFER, B., and KELLEY, D. M. (1942), *The Rorschach Technique*, Harcourt, Brace.

144 KLÜVER, H., and BUCY, P. C. (1937), '"Psychic blindness" and other symptoms following bilateral temporal lobectomy in rhesus monkeys', *Amer. J. Physiol.*, vol. 119, pp. 352–3.

144 KLÜVER, H., and BUCY, P. C. (1938), 'An analysis of certain effects of bilateral temporal lobectomy in the rhesus monkey, with special reference to "psychic blindness"', *J. Psychol.*, vol. 5, pp. 33–54.

144 KLÜVER, H., and BUCY, P. C. (1939), 'Preliminary analysis of functions of the temporal lobes in monkeys', *Arch. neurol Psychiat.*, vol. 42, pp. 979–1000.

482 KNIGHT, R. (1950), *Intelligence and Intelligence Tests*, Methuen, 5th edn.

243, 246, 250, 263 KOFFKA, K. (1935), *Principles of Gestalt Psychology*, Routledge.

547, 601, 603, 614 KOHLBERG, L. (1963), 'Moral development and

Page

identification', in H. W. Stevenson (ed.), *Child Psychology*, Yearbook of National Society for the Study of Education, University of Chicago Press.

255   KOHLER, I. (1962), 'Experiments with goggles', *Scient. Amer.*, vol. 206, pp. 67–72.

310   KÖHLER, W. (1925), *The Mentality of Apes*, Harcourt, Brace.

255   KÖHLER, W., and WALLACH, H. (1944), 'Figural after-effects: an investigation of visual processes', *Proc. Amer. Phil. Soc.*, vol. 88, pp. 269–357.

432   KRECH, D., and CRUTCHFIELD, R. S. (1958), *Elements of Psychology*, Knopf.

58   KRECH, D., ROSENZWEIG, R., and BENNETT, E. L. (1956), 'Dimensions of discrimination and level of cholinesterase in the cerebral cortex of the rat', *J. comp. physiol. Psychol.*, vol. 49, pp. 261–8.

518   KRETSCHMER, E. (1925), *Physique and Character*, Harcourt, Brace.

157   KRYTER, K. D., and ADES, H. W. (1943), 'Studies on the function of the higher acoustic nervous centers in the cat', *Amer. J. Psychol.*, vol. 56, pp. 501–36.

433   KUBIE, L. S. (1958), *Neurotic Distortion of the Creative Process*, University of Kansas Press.

444   KUDER, G. F. (1953), *Kuder Preference Record, Form A – Personal*, Science Research Associates, New York.

476   KUO, Z. Y. (1939), 'Total pattern or local reflex', *Psychol. Rev.*, vol. 46, pp. 93–122.

82   KURTZ, K. H. (1965), *Foundations of Psychological Research*, Allyn & Bacon.

36   LACEY, J. I. (1956), 'The evaluation of
42   autonomic responses: toward a general solution', *Ann. New York Acad. Sci.*, vol. 67, pp. 123–64.

183   LACEY, J. I. (1959), 'Psychophysiological approaches to the evaluation of psychotherapeutic process and outcome', in
188   E. A. Rubinstein and M. B. Parloff (eds.), *Research in Psychotherapy*, American Psychological Association.

188, 200   LACEY, J. I., *et al.* (1963), 'The visceral level:

Page

situational determinants and behavioral
correlates of autonomic response patterns', in
P. H. Knapp (ed.), *Expression of the Emotions in
Man*, International Universities Press.

407   LADEFOGED, P., and BROADBENT, D. E.
(1960), 'Perception of sequence in auditory
events', *Quart. J. exp. Psychol.*, vol. 12, pp.
162–70.

180   LADER, M. H. (1967), 'Pneumatic
plethysmography', in P. H. Venables and
I. Martin (eds.), *A Manual of Psychophysiological
Methods*, North-Holland.

570   LAMBERT, W. E., LIBMAN, E., and POSER,
E. G. (1960), 'The effect of increased salience of
a membership group on pain tolerance', *J.
Personal.*, vol. 28, pp. 350–57.

184   LANDIS, C., and HUNT, W. A. (1939), *The
Startle Pattern*, Farrar.

165   LANDSELL, H. (1962), 'Laterality of verbal
intelligence in the brain', *Science*, vol. 135, pp.
922–3.

189, 198   LANGE, C. (1885), *Om Sindsbevaegelser. et
psyko. fysiolog. studie*, Krønar, Copenhagen.
English translation in K. Dunlap (ed.), *The
Emotions*, Hafner, 1967.

129   LASHLEY, K. (1926), 'Studies of cerebral
function in learning: VII. The relation between
cerebral mass, learning and retention', *J. comp.
Neurol.*, vol. 41, pp. 1–48.

129   LASHLEY, K. (1929), *Brain Mechanisms and
Intelligence: A Quantitative Study of Injuries to
the Brain*, University of Chicago Press.

129   LASHLEY, K. (1931), 'Mass action in cerebral
function', *Science*, vol. 73, pp. 245–54.
LASHLEY, K. (1935), 'The mechanism of vision:
XII. Nervous structures concerned in the
acquisition and retention of habits based on
reactions to light', *Comp. Psychol. Monogr.*,
vol. 11, no. 52, pp. 43–79.

129   LASHLEY, K. (1943), 'Studies of cerebral
function in learning: XII. Loss of the maze
habit after occipital lesions in blind rats',
J. comp. Neurol., vol. 79, pp. 431–62.

Page

389 LASHLEY, K. (1951), 'The problem of serial order in behavior', in L. A. Jeffress (ed.), *Cerebral Mechanisms in Behavior: The Hixon Symposium*, Wiley.

274 LAWRENCE, D. H., and COLES, G. R. (1954), 'Accuracy of recognition with alternatives before and after the stimulus', *J. exp. Psychol.*, vol. 47, pp. 208–14.

156 LAYMAN, J. D. (1936), 'The avian visual system: I. Cerebral functions of the domestic fowl in pattern vision', *Comp. Psychol. Monogr.*, vol. 12, no. 58.

273 LAZARUS, R. S., and MCCLEARY, R. A. (1951), 'Autonomic discrimination without awareness: a study of subception', *Psychol. Rev.*, vol. 58, pp. 113–22. [M. D. Vernon *]

578 LAZARUS, R. S., *et al.* (1962), 'A laboratory study of psychological stress produced by a motion picture', *Psychol. Monogr.*, vol. 76, no. 34, whole no. 553.

585 LAZOWICK, L. M. (1955), 'On the nature of identification', *J. abnorm. soc. Psychol.*, vol. 51, pp. 175–83.

633 LEAVITT, H. J. (1951), 'Some effects of certain communication patterns on group performance', *J. abnorm. soc. Psychol.*, vol. 46, pp. 38–50.

543 LEE, S. G. M. (1961), *Stress and Adaptation*, Leicester University Press.

236 LEEPER, R. (1935), 'A study of a neglected portion of the field of learning – the development of sensory organization', *J. genet. Psychol.*, vol. 46, pp. 41–75.

580 LEFKOWITZ, M. M., BLAKE, R. R., and MOUTON, J. S. (1955), 'Status factors in pedestrian violation of traffic signals', *J. abnorm. soc. Psychol.*, vol. 51, pp. 704–6.

194 LEHMANN, A. (1914), *Die Hauptgesetze des menschlichen Gefuehlslebens*, Reisland, Leipzig. [Arnold *]

433 LEHMAN, H. C. (1953), *Age and Achievement*, Princeton University Press.

75, 318, 416 LENNEBERG, E. H. (1967), *Biological Foundations of Language*, Wiley.

Page

254   LETTVIN, J. Y., *et al.* (1959), 'What the frog's eye tells the frog's brain', *Proc. I.R.E.*, vol. 47, pp. 1940–51.

192   LEVI, L. (1965), 'The urinary output of adrenalin and noradrenalin during pleasant and unpleasant emotional states: a preliminary report', *Psychosom. Med.*, vol. 27, pp. 80–85.

277   LEVINE, S. (1956), 'A further study of infantile handling and adult avoidance learning', *J. Personal.*, vol. 25, pp. 70–80.

278   LEVINE, S. (1960), 'Stimulation in infancy', *Scient. Amer.*, vol. 202, pp. 81–6.

57   LEVINE, S., and BROADHURST, P. L. (1963), 'Genetic and ontogenetic determinants of adult behavior in the rat', *J. comp. physiol. Psychol.*, vol. 56, pp. 423–8.

641   LEWIN, K. (1948), *Resolving Social Conflicts*, Harper.

191   LEWINSOHN, P. M. (1956), 'Some individual differences in physiological reactivity to stress', *J. comp. physiol. Psychol.*, vol. 49, pp. 271–7.

572   LEWIS, M. (1965), 'Social isolation: a parametric study of its effects on social reinforcement', *J. exp. Child. Psychol.*, vol. 2, pp. 205–18.

362   LIBERMAN, A. M. (1948), 'The effect of differential extinction on spontaneous recovery', *J. exp. Psychol.*, vol. 38, pp. 722–33.

299   LICKLIDER, J. C. R., and MILLER, G. A. (1951), 'The perception of speech', in S. S. Stevens (ed.), *Handbook of Experimental Psychology*, Wiley.

229   LILLY, J. C. (1956), 'Mental effects of reduction of ordinary levels of physical stimuli on intact, healthy persons', *Psychiat. Res. Rep.*, vol. 5, pp. 1–9.

123, 184, 189, 200   LINDSLEY, D. B. (1951), 'Emotion', in S. S. Stevens (ed.), *Handbook of Experimental Psychology*, Wiley.

136   LINDSLEY, D. B. (1960), 'Attention, consciousness, sleep and wakefulness', in J. Field, H. W. Magoun and V. E. Hall (eds.), *Handbook of Physiology*, sect. 1, vol. 3, American Physiological Society.

Page

232   LINDSLEY, D. B. (1961), 'Common factors in sensory deprivation, sensory distortion and sensory overload', in P. Solomon *et al.* (eds.), *Sensory Deprivation*, Harvard University Press.

133, 134   LINDSLEY, D. B., *et al.* (1950), 'Behavioral and EEG changes following chronic brain-stem lesions in the cat', *EEG clin. Neurophysiol.*, vol. 2, pp. 483–98. [Pribram, vol. 1]

59   LINDZEY, G. (1951), 'Emotionality and audiogenic seizure susceptibility in five inbred strains of mice', *J. comp. physiol. Psychol.*, vol. 44, pp. 389–93.

479   LINDZEY, G. (1961), *Projective Techniques and Crosscultural Research*, Appleton-Century-Crofts.

515   LINDZEY, G., and HALL, C. S. (1965), *Theories of Personality: Primary Sources and Research*, Wiley.

555   LINTON, R. (1945), *The Cultural Background of Personality*, Appleton-Century-Crofts.

555   LINTON, R. (1956), *Culture and Mental Disorders*, Charles C. Thomas.

640   LIPPITT, R., and WHITE, R. K. (1958), 'An experimental study of leadership and group life', in E. Maccoby, T. M. Newcomb and R. E. Hartley (eds.), *Readings in Social Psychology*, Holt.

182   LIPPOLD, O. C. J. (1967), 'Electromyography', in P. H. Venables and I. Martin (eds.), *A Manual of Psychophysiological Methods*, North-Holland.

143   LISK, R. D. (1966), 'Inhibitory centers in sexual behavior in the male rat', *Science*, vol. 152, pp. 669–70.

52   LOEVINGER, J. (1943), 'On the proportional contributions of differences in nature and in nurture to differences in intelligence', *Psychol. Bull.*, vol. 40, pp. 725–56.

606   LONDON, P., SCHULMAN, R. E., and BLACK, M. S. (1964), 'Religion, guilt and ethical standards', *J. soc. Psychol.*, vol. 63, pp. 145–59.

281, 288   LORENZ, K. (1937), 'The companion in the bird's world', *Auk.*, vol. 54, pp. 245–73.

Page

222   LORENZ, K. (1966), *On Aggression*, Methuen.

639, 640   LOTT, A. J., and LOTT, B. E. (1965), 'Group cohesiveness as interpersonal attraction', *Psychol. Bull.*, vol. 64, pp. 259–309.

636   LUCHINS, A. S., and LUCHINS, E. H. (1955), 'Previous experience with ambiguous and non-ambiguous perceptual stimuli under various social influences', *J. soc. Psychol.*, vol. 42, pp. 249–70.

581   LUMSDAINE, A. A. (ed.) (1961), 'Student response in programmed instruction: A symposium', *Nat. Acad. Sciences: Nat. Res. Council Publ.*, no. 943.

566   LURIA, A. R. (1961), *The Role of Speech in the Regulation of Normal and Abnormal Behaviour*, Pergamon.

606, 610   LURIA, Z., GOLDWASSER, M., and GOLDWASSER, A. (1963), 'Response to transgression in stories by Israeli children', *Child Devel.*, vol. 34, pp. 271–80.

392   LYONS, J. (1968), *Introduction to Theoretical Linguistics*, Cambridge University Press.

179, 180   LYWOOD, D. W. (1967), 'Blood pressure', in P. H. Venables and I. Martin (eds.), *A Manual of Psychophysiological Methods*, North-Holland.

316   MACCORQUODALE, K., and MEEHL, P. E. (1948), 'On a distinction between hypothetical constructs and intervening variables', *Psychol. Rev.*, vol. 55, pp. 95–107.

300   MACFARLANE, D. A. (1930), 'The role of kinesthesis in maze learning', *Calif. Univ. Publ. Psychol.*, vol. 4, pp. 277–305.

602, 609   MACKINNON, D. (1938), 'Violation of prohibitions', in H. A. Murray (ed.), *Explorations in Personality*, Oxford University Press.

337   MACKWORTH, N. H. (1950), Researches in the measurement of human performance, *MRC Special Report Series*, no. 268, H.M.S.O.

601, 611   MACRAE, D. (1954), 'A test of Piaget's theories of moral development', *J. abnorm. soc. Psychol.*, vol. 49, pp. 14–18.

119, 133   MAGOUN, H. W. (1958), *The Waking Brain*, Charles C. Thomas.

Page

170   MAGOUN, H. W., DARLING, L., and PROST, J. (1959), 'The evolution of man's brain', in M. A. B. Brazier (ed.), *The Central Nervous System and Behavior*, Josiah Macy, JR, Foundation, New York.

546, 550   MAHER, B. A. (1966), *Principles of Psychopathology*, McGraw-Hill.

197, 559   MAHL, G. F. (1952), 'The relationship between acute and chronic fear and the gastric acidity and blood sugar levels in Macaca rhesus monkeys', *Psychosom. Med.*, vol. 14, pp. 182–210.

197   MAHL, G. F. (1953), 'Physiological changes during chronic fear', *Ann. N.Y. Acad. Sci.*, vol. 56, pp. 240–52.

440   MAIER, N. R. F. (1929), 'Reasoning in white rats', *Comp. Psychol. Monogr.*, vol. 6, no. 29.

426, 431, 432   MAIER, N. R. F. (1945), 'Reasoning in humans: III. The mechanisms of equivalent stimuli and of reasoning', *J. exp. Psychol.*, vol. 35, pp. 349–60.

223   MAIER, N. R. F. (1949), *Frustration*, McGraw-Hill.

163   MALMO, R. B. (1942), 'Interference factors in delayed response in monkeys after removal of frontal lobes', *J. Neurophysiol.*, vol. 5, pp. 295–308. [Pribram, vol. 3]

200   MALMO, R. B. (1959), 'Activation: a neuropsychological dimension', *Psychol. Rev.*, vol. 66, pp. 367–86.

188   MALMO, R. B., STAGNER, C., and DAVIS, F. H. (1950), 'Specificity of bodily reactions under stress: a physiological study of somatic mechanisms in psychiatric patients', *Res. Publ. Ass. Res. nerv. ment. Dis.*, vol. 29, pp. 231–61.

440   MALTZMAN, I. (1955), 'Thinking: from a behavioristic point of view', *Psychol. Rev.*, vol. 62, pp. 275–86.

426   MALTZMAN, I. (1960), 'On the training of originality', *Psychol. Rev.*, vol. 67, pp. 229–42.

236   MALTZMAN, I. (1962), 'Motivation and the direction of thinking', *Psychol. Bull.*, vol. 59, pp. 457–67.

194   MANDLER, G. (1960), 'Emotion', in T. M.

Page

Newcomb (ed.), *New Directions in Psychology*, vol. 1, Holt, Rinehart & Winston.

193   MANDLER, G., and KAHN, M. (1960), 'Discrimination of changes in heart rate: two unsuccessful attempts', *J. exp. anal. Behav.*, vol. 3, pp. 21–5.

194   MANDLER, G., and KREMEN, I. (1958), 'Autonomic feedback: a correlational study', *J. Pers.*, vol. 26, pp. 388–99.

194   MANDLER, G., MANDLER, J. M., and UVILLER, E. T. (1958), 'Autonomic feedback: the perception of autonomic activity', *J. abnorm. soc. Psychol.*, vol. 56, pp. 367–73.

634, 637   MANN, R. D. (1959), 'A review of the relationship between personality and performance in small groups', *Psychol. Bull.*, vol. 56, pp. 241–70. [Gibb*]

195   MARAÑON, G. (1924), 'Contribution à l'étude de l'action émotive de l'adrenalin', *Rev. franç. d'éndocrinol.*, vol. 2, pp. 301–25.

405   MARKS, L., and MILLER, G. A. (1964), 'The role of semantic and syntactic constraints in the memorization of English sentences', *J. verb. Learn. verb. Behav.*, vol. 3, pp. 1–5.

495   MARSH, R. W. (1964), 'A statistical reanalysis of Getzels' and Jackson's data', *Brit. J. educ. Psychol.*, vol. 34, pp. 91–3.

310, 576   MARSHALL, H. H. (1965), 'The effect of punishment on children: a review of the literature and a suggested hypothesis', *J. genet. Psychol.*, vol. 106, pp. 23–33.

582   MARSTON, A. R., and KANFER, F. H. (1963), 'Group size and number of vicarious reinforcements in verbal learning', *J. exp. Psychol.*, vol. 65, pp. 593–6.

191   MARTIN, B. (1961), 'The assessment of anxiety by physiological behavioral measures', *Psychol. Bull.*, vol. 58, pp. 234–55.

406, 407   MARTIN, E., and ROBERTS, K. H. (1966), 'Grammatical factors in sentence retention', *J. verb. Learn. verb. Behav.*, vol. 5, pp. 211–18.

219   MARTIN, R. C., and MELVIN, K. B. (1964), 'Fear responses of Bobwhite Quail (*Colinus*

Page

           virginianus) to a model and a live red-tailed hawk (*Buteo jamaicensis*)', *Psychol. Forsch.*, vol. 26, pp. 223–36.

310   MASSERMAN, J. H. (1943), *Behavior and Neurosis*, Chicago University Press.

475   MATARAZZO, J. D. (1965), 'The interview', in B. B. Wolman (ed.), *Handbook of Clinical Psychology*, McGraw-Hill.

289, 410   MCCARTHY, D. (1954), 'Language development in children', in L. Carmichael (ed.), *Manual of Child Psychology*, Wiley, 2nd edn.

150   MCCLEARY, R. A. (1961), 'Response specificity in the behavioral effects of limbic system lesions in the cat', *J. comp. physiol. Psychol.*, vol. 54, pp. 605–13.

102, 108   MCCLEARY, R. A., and MOORE, R. Y. (1965), *Subcortical Mechanisms of Behavior*, Basic Books.

604   MCCORD, W., and MCCORD, J. (1960), 'A tentative theory of the structure of conscience', in D. Wellner (ed.), *Decisions, Values and Groups*, Pergamon.

608, 609   MCCORD, W., MCCORD, J., and ZOLA, I. (1957), *The Origins of Crime*, Columbia University Press.

358, 362, 366, 371, 372   MCGEOGH, J. A., and IRION, A. L. (1952), *Psychology of Human Learning*, Longmans, Green, 2nd edn.

59   MCGILL, T. E. (1962), 'Sexual behaviour in three inbred strains of mice', *Behaviour*, vol. 19, pp. 341–50.

270   MCGINNIES, E. (1949), 'Emotionality and perceptual defense', *Psychol. Rev.*, vol. 56, pp. 244–51. [M. D. Vernon]

202, 231   MCGRATH, J. J. (1963), 'Irrelevant stimulation and vigilance performance', in D. N. Buckner and J. J. McGrath (eds.), *Vigilance: A Symposium*, McGraw-Hill.

77   MCGRAW, M. B. (1940), 'Neural maturation as exemplified by the achievement of bladder control', *J. Pediat.*, vol. 16, pp. 580–90.

42   MCGUIGAN, F. J. (1960), *Experimental Psychology: A Methodological Approach*, Prentice-Hall.

Page

621   McGUIRE, W. J., and PAPAGEORGIS, D. (1961), 'The relative efficacy of various types of prior belief-defence in producing immunity against persuasion', *J. abnorm. soc. Psychol.*, vol. 62, pp. 327–37.

434   McKELLAR, P. (1957), *Imagination and Thinking: A Psychological Analysis*, Cohen & West.

444   McKINNON, D. W., and DUKES, W. F. (1962), 'Repression', in L. Postman (ed.), *Psychology in the Making*, Knopf.

366   McNEILL, D. (1966a), 'The creation of language by children', in J. Lyons and R. J. Wales (eds.), *Psycholinguistics Papers*, Edinburgh University Press.

312   McNEILL, D. (1966b), 'Developmental psycholinguistics', in F. Smith and G. A. Miller (eds.), *The Genesis of Language*, M. I. T. Press.

28, 29   MEDAWAR, P. B. (1963), 'Is the scientific paper a fraud?', *Listener*, vol. 70, pp. 377–8.

601   MEDINNUS, G. R. (1959), 'Immanent justice in children', *J. genet. Psychol.*, vol. 94, pp. 253–62.

603   MEDINNUS, G. R. (1966a), 'Age and sex differences in conscience development', *J. genet. Psychol.*, vol. 109, pp. 117–18.

605, 606   MEDINNUS, G. R. (1966b), 'Behavioral and cognitive measures of conscience development', *J. genet. Psychol.*, vol. 109, pp. 147–50.

34   MEEHL, P. E. (1956), *Clinical versus Statistical Prediction*, University of Minnesota Press.

404   MEHLER, J. (1963), 'Some effects of grammatical transformation on the recall of English sentences', *J. verb. Learn. verb. Behav.*, vol. 2, pp. 346–51.

404   MEHLER, J., and MILLER, G. A. (1964), 'Retroactive interference in the recall of simple sentences', *Brit. J. Psychol.*, vol. 55, pp. 295–301.

347, 354   MELTON, A. W. (1963), 'Implications of short-term memory for a general theory of memory', *J. verb. Learn. verb. Behav.*, vol. 2, pp. 1–21.

415   MENYUK, P. (1964), 'Syntactic rules used by children from pre-school through first grade', *Child Devel.*, vol. 35, pp. 533–46.

Page

477   MESSICK, S. J. (1967), 'The psychology of acquiescence: an interpretation of the research evidence', in I. A. Berg (ed.), *Response Set in Personality Assessment*, Aldine.

152   MEYER, D. R., and MEYER, P. M. (1963), 'Brain functions', *Ann. Rev. Psychol.*, vol. 14, pp. 155–74.

576   MEYER, W. J., and SEIDMAN, S. B. (1960), 'Age differences in the effectiveness of different reinforcement combinations on the acquisition and extinction of a simple concept learning problem', *Child Devel.*, vol. 31, pp. 419–29.

604, 606   MIDDLETON, R., and PUTNEY, S. (1962), 'Religion, normative standards and behavior', *Sociometry*, vol. 25, pp. 141–52.

218   MILES, R. C. (1958), 'Learning in kittens with manipulatory, exploratory and feed incentives', *J. comp. physiol. Psychol.*, vol. 51, pp. 39–42.

682   MILES, T. R. (1957), 'Contributions to intelligence testing and the theory of intelligence: I. On definining intelligence', *Brit. J. educ. Psychol.*, vol. 27, pp. 153–65. [Wiseman]

402, 404   MILLER, G. A. (1962), 'Some psychological studies of grammar', *Amer. Psychol.*, vol. 17, pp. 748–62.

385, 388   MILLER, G. A. (1965), 'Some preliminaries to psycholinguistics', *Amer. Psychol.*, vol. 20, pp. 15–20. [Oldfield and Marshall]

397   MILLER, G. A., GALANTER, E., and PRIBRAM, K. H. (1960), *Plans and the Structure of Behavior*, Holt, Rinehart & Winston.

400   MILLER, G. A., HEISE, G. A., and LICHTEN, W. (1951), 'The intelligibility of speech as a function of the context of the test materials', *J. exp. Psychol.*, vol. 41, pp. 329–35.

405   MILLER, G. A., and ISARD, S. (1963), 'Some perceptual consequences of linguistic rules', *J. verb. Learn. verb. Behav.*, vol. 2, pp. 217–20.

400   MILLER, G. A., and LICKLIDER, J. C. R. (1950), 'The intelligibility of interrupted speech', *J. Acoust. Soc. Amer.*, vol. 22, pp. 167–73.

402, 403   MILLER, G. A., and McKEAN, K. (1964), 'A chronometric study of some relations between

Page

sentences', *Quart. J. exp. Psychol.*, vol. 16, pp. 297–308.

410, 415   MILLER, G. A., and McNEILL, D. (1969), 'Psycholinguistics', in G. Lindzey and E. Aronson (eds.), *Handbook of Social Psychology*, vol. 3, Addison-Wesley, 2nd edn.

336   MILLER, J. G. (1960), 'Input overload and psychopathology', *Amer. J. Psychiat.*, vol. 116, pp. 695–704.

339, 343   MILLER, J. G. (1961), 'Sensory overloading', in B. E. Flaherty (ed.), *Psychophysiological Aspects of Space Flight*, Columbia University Press.

623   MILLER, N. (1965), 'Involvement and dogmatism as inhibitors of attitude change', *J. exp. soc. Psychol.*, vol. 1, pp. 121–32.

222   MILLER, N. E. (1941), 'The frustration-aggression hypothesis', *Psychol. Rev.*, vol. 48, pp. 337–42.

220   MILLER, N. E. (1948a), 'Studies of fear as an acquirable drive', *J. exp. Psychol.*, vol. 38, pp. 89–101. [Bindra and Stewart *]

223   MILLER, N. E. (1948b), 'Theory and experiment relating psychoanalytic displacement to stimulus–response generalization', *J. abnorm. soc. Psychol.*, vol. 43, pp. 155–78. [Lee and Herbert]

220   MILLER, N. E. (1951), 'Learnable drives and rewards', in S. S. Stevens (ed.), *Handbook of Experimental Psychology*, Wiley.

211   MILLER, N. E. (1957), 'Experiments on motivation', *Science*, vol. 126, pp. 1271–8.

139   MILLER, N. E. (1961), 'Learning and performance motivated by direct stimulation of the brain', in D. E. Sheer (ed.), *Electrical Stimulation of the Brain*, University of Texas Press.

139   MILLER, N. E., BAILEY, C. J., and STEVENSON, J. A. F. (1950), 'Decreased "hunger" but increased food intake resulting from hypothalamic lesions', *Science*, vol. 112, pp. 256–9.

146   MILNER, B. (1962), 'Les troubles de la
147   mémoire accompagnant des lésions

Page

hippocampiques bilatérales', in P. Passouant (ed.), *Physiologie de l'Hippocampe*, C.N.R.S., Paris. Translated into English in S. Glickman and P. M. Milner (eds.), *Cognitive Processes and the Brain*, Van Nostrand.

161   MILNER, B. (1963), 'Effects of different brain lesions on card sorting', *Arch. neurol.*, vol. 9, pp. 90–100.

161   MILNER, B. (1964), 'Some effects of frontal lobectomy in man', in J. M. Warren and K. Akert (eds.), *The Frontal Granular Cortex and Behavior*, McGraw-Hill.

274   MINARD, J. G. (1965), 'Response-bias interpretation of "perceptual defense": a selective review and an evaluation of recent research', *Psychol. Rev.*, vol. 72, pp. 74–88.

163   MISHKIN, M., and PRIBRAM, K. H. (1956), 'Analysis of the effects of frontal lesions in monkeys: II. Variations of delayed response', *J. comp. physiol. Psychol.*, vol. 49, pp. 36–40.

182   MONTAGU, J. D., and COLES, R. (1966), 'Mechanism and measurement of the galvanic skin response', *Psychol. Bull.*, vol. 65, pp. 261–79.

216   MONTGOMERY, K. C. (1952), 'A test of two explanations of spontaneous alternation', *J. comp. physiol. Psychol.*, vol. 45, pp. 287–93.

217   MONTGOMERY, K. C. (1954), 'The role of exploratory drive in learning', *J. comp. physiol. Psychol.*, vol. 47, pp. 60–64. [Bindra and Stewart]

235, 400   MORAY, N. (1969), *Listening and Attention*, Penguin Books.

107   MORGAN, C. T. (1965), *Physiological Psychology*, McGraw-Hill.

143   MORGANE, P. J. (1961), 'Alterations in feeding and drinking behavior of rats with lesions in *globi pallidi*', *Amer. J. Physiol.*, vol. 201, pp. 420–28.

142   MORGANE, P. J., and KOSMAN, A. J. (1957), 'Alterations in feline behaviour following bilateral amygdalectomy', *Nature*, vol. 180, pp. 598–600.

Page

142   MORGANE, P. J., and KOSMAN, A. J. (1959), 'A rhinencephalic feeding center in the cat', *Amer. J. Physiol.*, vol. 197, pp. 158–62.

133   MORUZZI, G., and MAGOUN, H. W. (1949), 'Brain stem reticular formation and activation of the EEG', *EEG and clin. Neurophysiol.*, vol. 1, pp. 455–73.

332   MOWBRAY, G. H. (1960), 'Choice reaction times for skilled responses', *Quart. J. exp. Psychol.*, vol. 12, pp. 193–202.

220   MOWRER, O. H. (1939), 'A stimulus–response analysis of anxiety and its role as a reinforcing agent', *Psychol. Rev.*, vol. 46, pp. 553–65.

585   MOWRER, O. H. (1950), *Learning Theory and Personality Dynamics*, Ronald Press.

305, 603, 614   MOWRER, O. H. (1960a), *Learning Theory and Behavior*, Wiley.

377, 383, 384, 386, 387, 614   MOWRER, O. H. (1960b), *Learning Theory and the Symbolic Processes*, Wiley.

354   MUNTZ, W. R. A. (1967), 'Mechanics of visual form recognition in animals', in W. Wathen-Dunn (ed.), *Models for the Perception of Speech and Visual Form*, M.I.T. Press.

269, 444   MURPHY, G. (1947), *Personality: A Biosocial Approach to Origins and Structure*, Harper.

480   MURRAY, H. A. (and collaborators) (1938), *Explorations in Personality*, Oxford University Press.

479   MURRAY, H. A. (1943), *Thematic Apperception Test Manual*, Harvard University Press.

201   MURRELL, K. F. H. (1967), 'Performance differences in continuous tasks', in A. F. Sanders (ed.), *Attention and Performance*, North-Holland.

480   MURSTEIN, B. I. (1963), *Theory and Research in Projective Techniques (emphasising the TAT)*, Wiley.

586   MUSSEN, P. H., and DISTLER, L. S. (1959), 'Masculinity, identification and father–son relationships', *J. abnorm. soc. Psychol.*, vol. 59, pp. 350–56.

586   MUSSEN, P. H., and DISTLER, L. S. (1960), 'Child-rearing antecedents of masculine

Page

identification in kindergarten boys', *Child Devel.*, vol. 31, pp. 89–100. [Lee and Herbert]

169   MYERS, R. E. (1961), 'Corpus callosum and visual gnosis', in J. F. Delafresnaye *et al.* (eds.), *Brain Mechanisms and Learning*, Blackwell.

156, 157   NEFF, W. D. (1960), 'Sensory discrimination', in J. Field, H. W. Magoun and V. E. Hall (eds.), *Handbook of Physiology*, sect. 1, vol. 3, American Physiological Society.

275, 355, 376, 388, 396, 398   NEISSER, U. (1967), *Cognitive Psychology*, Appleton-Century-Crofts.

480   NEWCOMB, T. M. (1966), 'On the definition of attitude', reprinted in M. Jahoda and N. Warren (eds.), *Attitudes*, Penguin Books.

441   NEWELL, A., SHAW, J. C., and SIMON, H. A. (1958), 'Elements of a theory of human problem solving', *Psychol. Rev.*, vol. 65, pp. 151–66.

194   NEWMAN, E. B., PERKINS, F. T., and WHEELER, R. H. (1930), 'Cannon's theory of emotion: a critique', *Psychol. Rev.*, vol. 37, pp. 305–26.

383   NOBLE, C. E. (1952), 'An analysis of meaning', *Psychol. Rev.*, vol. 59, pp. 421–30.

383   NOBLE, C. E. (1963), 'Meaningfulness and familiarity', in C. N. Cofer and B. S. Musgrave (eds.), *Verbal Learning and Behavior*, McGraw-Hill.

335   NOBLE, M., FITTS, P. M., and WARREN, C. E. (1955), 'The frequency response of skilled subjects in a pursuit tracking task', *J. exp. Psychol.*, vol. 49, pp. 249–56.

477   NORMAN, W. T. (1963), 'Relative importance of test item content', *J. consult. Psychol.*, vol. 27, pp. 166–74.

186   OBRIST, W. D. (1965), 'EEG approach to age changes in response speed', in A. T. Welford and J. E. Birren (eds.), *Behavior, Aging and the Nervous System*, Charles C. Thomas.

323   OLDFIELD, R. C. (1959), 'The analysis of human skill', in P. Halmos and A. Iliffe (eds.), *Readings in General Psychology*, Routledge & Kegan Paul.

139   OLDS, J. (1958), 'Self-stimulation of the brain', *Science*, vol. 127, pp. 315–23.

Page

306 OLDS, J. (1961), 'Differential effects of drives and drugs on self-stimulation at different brain sites', in D. E. Sheer (ed.), *Electrical Stimulation of the Brain*, University of Texas Press.

305 OLDS, J., and MILNER, P. (1954), 'Positive reinforcement produced by electrical stimulation of septal area and other regions of rat brain', *J. comp. physiol. Psychol.*, vol. 47, pp. 419–27. [Pribram, vol. 4]

126 OLDS, J., and OLDS, M. (1965), 'Drives, rewards and the brain', in T. M. Newcomb (ed.), *New Directions in Psychology*, Holt, Rinehart & Winston.

127, 153 ORBACH, J., and FANTZ, R. L. (1958), 'Differential effects of temporal neocortical resections on overtrained and non-overtrained visual habits in monkeys', *J. comp. physiol. Psychol.*, vol. 51, pp. 126–9.

255 ORBISON, W. D. (1939), 'Shape as a function of the vector field', *Amer. J. Psychol.*, vol. 52, pp. 31–45.

313, 358, 362, 363, 418, 435 436 OSGOOD, C. E. (1953), *Method and Theory in Experimental Psychology*, Oxford University Press.

383, 388, 437, 479 OSGOOD, C. E., SUCI, G. J., and TANNENBAUM, P. H. (1957), *The Measurement of Meaning*, University of Illinois Press. [Hogg*]

626 OSGOOD, C. E., and TANNENBAUM, P. H. (1955), 'The principle of congruity in the prediction of attitude change', *Psychol. Rev.*, vol. 62, pp. 42–55.

569 PAIVIO, A. (1965), 'Personality and audience influence', in B. A. Maher (ed.), *Progress in Experimental Personality Research*, vol. 2, Academic Press.

621 PAPAGEORGIS, D., and MCGUIRE, W. J. (1961), 'The generality of immunity to persuasion produced by pre-exposure to weakened counterarguments', *J. abnorm. soc. Psychol.*, vol. 62, pp. 475–81.

144 PAPEZ, J. W. (1937), 'A proposed mechanism of emotion', *Arch. neurol. Psychiat.*, vol. 38, pp. 725–43.

Page

326   PASK, G. (1961), *An Approach to Cybernetics*,
Hutchinson.

426   PATRICK, C. (1935), 'Creative thought in
poets', *Arch. Psychol.*, vol. 178.

426   PATRICK, C. (1937), 'Creative thought in
artists', *J. Psychol.*, vol. 4, pp. 35–73.

293, 295   PAVLOV, I. P. (1927), *Conditioned Reflexes*,
Oxford University Press.

528   PAWLIK, K., and CATTELL, R. B. (1964),
'Third-order factors in objective personality
tests', *Brit. J. Psychol.*, vol. 55, pp. 1–18.

586   PAYNE, R. W., and MUSSEN, P. H. (1956),
'Parent child relations and father
identification among adolescent boys', *J. abnorm.
soc. Psychol.*, vol. 52, pp. 358–62.

604   PECK, R. F., and HAVIGHURST, R. J. (1960),
The Psychology of Character Development,
Wiley.

167   PENFIELD, W. (1959), 'The interpretive cortex',
Science, vol. 129, pp. 1719–25.

168   PENFIELD, W., and BOLDREY, E. (1937),
'Somatic, motor and sensory representation in
the cerebral cortex of man as studied by
electrical stimulation', *Brain*, vol. 60, pp.
389–443.

168, 169   PENFIELD, W., and RASMUSSEN, T. (1950),
The Cerebral Cortex of Man, Macmillan.

168   PENFIELD, W., and ROBERTS, L. (1959), *Speech
and Brain Mechanisms*, Princeton University
Press.

206   PETERS, R. S. (1958), *The Concept of Motivation*,
Routledge & Kegan Paul.

351   PETERSON, L. R., and PETERSON, M. J. (1959),
'Short-term retention of individual verbal
items', *J. exp. Psychol.*, vol. 58, pp. 193–8.
[Postman and Keppel]

604   PETTEL, S. M., and MENDLESOHN, G. A.
(1966), 'Measurement of moral values: a review
and critique', *Psychol. Bull.*, vol. 66, pp. 22–35.

436, 506   PIAGET, J. (1926), *Language and Thought of the
Child*, Routledge.

600   PIAGET, J. (1929), *The Child's Conception of the
World*, Routledge.

Page

598   PIAGET, J. (1932), *The Moral Judgment of the Child*, Routledge.

497   PIAGET, J. (1950), *The Psychology of Intelligence*, Routledge.

505   PIAGET, J. (1951), *Play, Dreams and Imitation in Children*, Routledge.

503   PIAGET, J. (1952a), *The Origins of Intelligence in Children*, International Universities Press. [M. D. Vernon*]

506   PIAGET, J. (1952b), *The Child's Conception of Number*, Routledge.

503   PIAGET, J. (1954), *The Construction of Reality in the Child*, Basic Books. [Dodwell*; M. D. Vernon*]

436   PIAGET, J. (1962), *Comments on Vygotsky's Critical Remarks Concerning 'The Language and Thought of the Child' and 'Judgment and Reasoning in the Child'*, M.I.T. Press.

165   PIERCY, M. F. (1964), 'The effects of cerebral lesions on intellectual function: a review of current research trends', *Brit. J. Psychiat.*, vol. 110, pp. 310–52.

363   PILKINGTON, G. W., and McKELLAR, P. (1960), 'Inhibition as a concept in psychology', *Brit. J. Psychol.*, vol. 51, pp. 194–201.

180   PLUTCHIK, R. (1956), 'The psychophysiology of skin temperature: a critical review', *J. gen. Psychol.*, vol. 55, pp. 249–68.

254   POLYAK, S. L. (1941), *The Retina*, University of Chicago Press.

31   POPPER, K. R. (1957), 'Philosophy of science: a personal report', in C. A. Mace (ed.), *British Philosophy in the Mid-Century*, Allen & Unwin.

19   POPPER, K. R. (1963), *Conjectures and Refutations: The Growth of Scientific Knowledge*, Routledge & Kegan Paul.

309   POSTMAN, L. (1962), 'Rewards and punishments in human learning', in L. Postman (ed.), *Psychology in the Making*, Knopf.

235   POSTMAN, L., BRUNER, J. S., and McGINNIES, E. (1948), 'Personal values as selective factors in perception', *J. abnorm. soc. Psychol.*, vol. 43, pp. 142–54.

Page

236   POSTMAN, L., and LEYTHAM, G. (1951),
      'Perceptual selectivity and ambivalence of
      stimuli', *J. Personal.*, vol. 19, pp. 390–405.

235   POSTMAN, L., and ROSENZWEIG, M. R. (1956),
      'Practice and transfer in the visual and auditory
      recognition of verbal stimuli', *Amer. J. Psychol.*,
      vol. 69, pp. 209–26.

74   PRESSEY, S. L., and KUHLEN, R. G. (1957),
      Psychological Development Through the Life Span,
      Harper & Row.

163   PRIBRAM, K. H. (1950), 'Some physical and
      pharmacological factors affecting delayed
      response performance of baboons following
      frontal lobotomy', *J. Neurophysiol.*, vol. 13, pp.
      373–82.

128   PRIBRAM, K. H. (1954), 'Toward a science of
      neuropsychology', in R. A. Patton (ed.), *Current
      Trends in Psychology and the Behavioral Sciences*,
      University of Pittsburgh Press. [Pribram, vols. 1
      and 2 *]

111, 168   PRIBRAM, K. H. (1960a), 'A review of theory in
      physiological psychology', *Ann. Rev. Psychol.*,
      vol. 11, pp. 1–40. [Pribram, vol. 1 *]

111, 168   PRIBRAM, K. H. (1960b), 'Intrinsic systems of
      the forebrain', in J. Field, H. W. Magoun and
      V. E. Hall (eds.), *Handbook of Physiology*,
      sect. 1, vol. 3, American Physiological Society.

232, 256, 257   PRITCHARD, R. M. (1961), 'Stabilised images
      on the retina', *Scient. Amer.*, vol. 204, pp. 72–8.

610   RABIN, A., and GOLDMAN, H. (1966), 'The
      relationship of severity of guilt to intensity of
      identification, in Kibbutz and non-Kibbutz
      children', *J. soc. Psychol.*, vol. 69, pp. 159–63.

366   RAPAPORT, D. (1942), *Emotions and Memory*,
      Menninger Clinic, New York, monograph
      series, no. 2.

641   RAVEN, B. H., and RIETSEMA, J. (1957), 'The
      effects of varied clarity of group goal and group
      path upon the individual and his relation to his
      group', *Hum. Rel.*, vol. 10, pp. 29–45.

426   RAY, W. S. (1955), 'Complex tasks for use in
      human problem solving research', *Psychol. Bull.*,
      vol. 52, pp. 134–49.

Page

606   REBELSKY, F. G. (1963), 'An inquiry into the
        meaning of confession', *Merrill-Palmer Quart.*,
        vol. 9, pp. 287–94.

602   REBELSKY, F., ALLINSMITH, W., and
606   GRINDER, R. (1963), 'Resistance to temptation
        and sex differences in children's use of fantasy',
        Child Development, vol. 34, pp. 955–62.

432   REED, H. B. (1946), 'Factors influencing the
        learning and retention of concepts: 1. The
        influence of set', *J. exp. Psychol.*, vol. 36, pp.
        71–87.

363   REID, R. L. (1960), 'Inhibition – Pavlov, Hull,
        Eysenck', *Brit. J. Psychol.*, vol. 51, pp. 226–32.

442   REITMAN, W. R. (1965), *Cognition and Thought:
        An Information-Processing Approach*, Wiley.

316   RESCORLA, R. A., and SOLOMON, R. L. (1967),
        'Two-process learning theory: relationships
        between Pavlovian conditioning and
        instrumental learning', *Psychol. Rev.*, vol. 74,
        pp. 151–82.

300   RESTLE, F. (1957), 'Discrimination of cues in
        mazes: a resolution of the "Place-vs.-Response"
        question', *Psychol. Rev.*, vol. 64, pp. 217–28.

606   RETTIG, S., and PASAMANICK, B. (1959),
        'Moral codes of American and Korean college
        students', *J. soc. Psychol.*, vol. 50, pp. 65–73.

607   RETTIG, S., and PASAMANICK, B. (1964),
        'Differential judgment of ethical risk by cheaters
        and noncheaters', *J. abnorm. soc. Psychol.*, vol.
        69, pp. 109–13.

475   RICHARDSON, S. A., DOHRENWEND, B. S.,
        and KLEIN, D. (1965), *Interviewing: Its Forms
        and Functions*, Basic Books.

262, 263   RIESEN, A. H. (1947), 'The development of
        visual perception in man and chimpanzee',
        Science, vol. 106, no. 2744, pp. 107–8.

551   RIESMAN, D. (1950), *The Lonely Crowd*, Yale
        University Press.

365   RILEY, D. (1962), 'Memory for form', in
        L. Postman (ed.), *Psychology in the Making*,
        Knopf.

392   ROBINS, R. H. (1964), *General Linguistics: An
        Introductory Survey*, Longmans, Green.

Page

58   RODERICK, J. H. (1960), 'Selection for cholinesterase activity in the cerebral cortex of the rat', *Genetics*, vol. 45, pp. 1123–40.

479   ROGERS, C. R., and DYMOND, R. F. (1954), *Psychotherapy and Personality Change*, University of Chicago Press.

601, 626   ROKEACH, M. (1960), *The Open and Closed Mind*, Basic Books.

626   ROSENBERG, M. I., and HOVLAND, C. I. (eds.) (1960), *Attitude Organization and Change*, Yale University Press.

157   ROSENZWEIG, M. R. (1946), 'Discrimination of auditory intensities in the cat', *Amer. J. Psychol.*, vol. 59, pp. 127–36.

369   ROSENZWEIG, S. (1943), 'An experimental study of "repression" with special reference to need-persistive and ego-defensive reactions to frustrations', *J. exp. Psychol.*, vol. 32, pp. 64–74.

553   ROSENZWEIG, S. (1944), 'An outline of frustration theory', in J. McV. Hunt (ed.), *Personality and the Behavior Disorders*. vol. 1, Ronald Press.

135   ROUTTENBERG, A. (1966), 'Neural mechanisms of sleep: changing view of reticular formation function', *Psychol. Rev.*, vol. 73, pp. 481–99.

230   RUFF, G. E., LEVY, E. Z., and THALER, V. H. (1961), 'Factors influencing the reaction to reduced sensory input', in P. Solomon *et al.* (eds.), *Sensory Deprivation*, Harvard University Press.

180   RUSSELL, R. W., and STERN, R. M. (1967), 'Gastric motility: the electro-gastrogram', in P. H. Venables and I. Martin (eds.), *A Manual of Psychophysiological Methods*, North-Holland.

201, 205   RYAN, T. A. (1953), 'Muscular potentials as indicators of effort in visual tasks', in W. F. Floyd and A. T. Welford (eds.), *Fatigue*, H. K. Lewis.

279   SACKETT, G. P. (1965), 'Effects of rearing conditions upon the behaviour of rhesus monkeys', *Child Devel.*, vol. 36, pp. 855–68.

284   SACKETT, G. P., PORTER, M., and HOLMES, H.

Page

(1965), 'Choice behavior in rhesus monkeys: effect of stimulation during the first month of life', *Science*, vol. 147, pp. 304–6.

137 SAMUELS, I. (1959), 'Reticular mechanisms and behavior', *Psychol. Bull.*, vol. 56, pp. 1–25.

435 SAPIR, E. (1949), *Selected Writings*, University of California Press.

431 SAUGSTAD, P. (1957), 'An analysis of Maier's pendulum problem', *J. exp. Psychol.*, vol. 54, pp. 168–79.

382 SAUSSURE, F. DE (1915), *Cours de Linguistique Générale*, 5th edn. Translated by W. Baskin as *Course in General Linguistics*, Philosophical Library, 1959.

403, 407 SAVIN, H. B., and PERCHONOCK, E. (1965), 'Grammatical structure and the immediate recall of English sentences', *J. verb. Learn. verb. Behav.*, vol. 4, pp. 348–53.

191 SCHACHTER, J. (1957), 'Pain, fear and anger in hypertensives and normotensives', *Psychosom. Med.*, vol. 19, pp. 17–29.

642, 643 SCHACHTER, S., ELLERTSON, N., MCBRIDE, D., and GREGORY, D. (1951), 'An experimental study of cohesiveness and productivity', *Hum. Rel.*, vol. 4, pp. 229–38.

196 SCHACHTER, S., and SINGER, J. E. (1962), 'Cognitive, social and physiological determinants of emotional state', *Psychol. Rev.*, vol. 69, pp. 379–99.

220 SCHAFFER, H. R. (1966), 'The onset of fear of strangers and the incongruity hypothesis', *J. child Psychol. Psychiat.*, vol. 7, pp. 95–106.

215 SCHAFFER, H. R., and EMERSON, P. E. (1964), 'The development of social attachments in infancy', *Monogr. Soc. Res. child Devel.*, vol. 29, no. 3, pp. 1–77.

137 SCHARLOCK, D. P., TUCKER, T. J., and STROMINGER, N. L. (1963), 'Auditory discrimination by the cat after neonatal ablation of emporal cortex', *Science*, vol. 141, pp. 1197–8.

161 SCHERER, R. W., WINNE, J. F., and BAKER, R. W. (1955), 'Psychological changes over a

Page

three-year period following bilateral prefrontal lobotomy', *J. consult. Psychol.*, vol. 19, pp. 291–8.

136　SCHLAG, J. D., and CHAILLET, F. (1962), 'Thalamic mechanisms involved in cortical desynchronization and recruiting responses', *EEG clin. Neurophysiol.*, vol. 15, pp. 39–62.

195　SCHNEIRLA, T. C. (1959), 'An evolutionary and developmental theory of biphasic processes underlying approach and withdrawal', in M. R. Jones (ed.), *Nebraska Symposium on Motivation*, University of Nebraska Press.

219　SCHNEIRLA, T. C. (1965), 'Aspects of stimulation and organization in approach/withdrawal processes underlying vertebrate behavioral development', in D. S. Lehrman, R. A. Hinde and E. Shaw, (eds.), *Advances in the Study of Behavior*, vol. 1, Academic Press.

289　SCHNEIRLA, T. C., and ROSENBLATT, J. S. (1963), '"Critical periods" in the development of behavior', *Science*, vol. 139, pp. 1110–15.

204　SCHNORE, M. M. (1959), 'Individual patterns of physiological activity as a function of task differences and degree of arousal', *J. exp. Psychol.*, vol. 58, pp. 117–28.

149　SCHREINER, L. H., and KLING, A. (1953), 'Behavioral changes following rhinencephalic injury in cat', *J. Neurophysiol.*, vol. 16, pp. 643–59.

148, 149　SCHREINER, L. H., and KLING, A. (1954), 'Effects of castration on hypersexual behavior induced by rhinencephalic injury in cat', *Arch. neurol. Psychiat.*, vol. 72, pp. 180–86.

282　SCHUTZ, F. (1965), 'Sexuelle Prägung bei Anatiden', *Z. Tierpsychol.*, vol. 22, pp. 50–103.

283　SCOTT, J. P. (1958a), *Animal Behavior*, University of Chicago Press.

288　SCOTT, J. P. (1958b), 'Critical periods in the development of social behavior in puppies', *Psychosom. Med.*, vol. 20, pp. 42–54.

283, 289　SCOTT, J. P. (1962), 'Critical periods in behavioral development', *Science*, vol. 138, pp. 949–58.

Page

289   SCOTT, J. P. (1963), 'The process of primary socialization in canine and human infants', *Monogr. Soc. Res. child Devel.*, vol. 28, no. 1, pp. 1–47.

59, 75   SCOTT, J. P., and FULLER, J. L. (1965), *Genetics and the Social Behavior of the Dog*, University of Chicago Press.

555   SCOTT, W. A. (1958), 'Research definitions of mental health and mental illness', *Psychol. Bull.*, vol. 55, pp. 29–45.

58   SEARLE, L. V. (1949), 'The organization of hereditary maze-brightness and maze-dullness', *Genet. Psychol. Monogr.*, vol. 39, pp. 279–325.

522   SEARS, R. R. (1944), 'Experimental analyses of psychoanalytic phenomena', in J. McV. Hunt (ed.), *Personality and the Behavior Disorders*, vol. 1, Ronald Press.

585   SEARS, R. R. (1957), 'Identification as a form of behavioral development', in D. B. Harris (ed.), *The Concept of Development*, University of Minnesota Press.

594, 606, 610   SEARS, R. R., MACCOBY, E. E., and LEVIN, H. (1957), *Patterns of Child Rearing*, Row, Peterson.

592, 594, 597, 602, 605   SEARS, R. R., RAU, L., and ALPERT, R.
606, 609, 610, 911   (1966), *Identification and Child Rearing*, Tavistock Publications.

566   SECORD, P. F., and BACKMAN, C. W. (1964), *Social Psychology*, McGraw-Hill.

204   SHAW, W. A. (1956), 'Facilitating effects of induced tension upon the perception span for digits', *J. exp. Psychol.*, vol. 51, pp. 113–17.

209   SHEFFIELD, F. D., and ROBY, T. B. (1950), 'Reward value of a non-nutritive sweet taste', *J. comp. physiol. Psychol.*, vol. 43, pp. 471–81. [Bindra and Stewart]

518, 519   SHELDON, W. H. (with S. S. STEVENS) (1942), *The Varieties of Temperament: A Psychology of Constitutional Differences*, Harper. [Semeonoff *]

634   SHERIF, M., and SHERIF, C. W. (1956), *An Outline of Social Psychology*, Harper.

190   SHERRINGTON, C. (1906), *The Integrative Action of the Nervous System*, Yale University Press.

Page

62, 63   SHIELDS, J. (1962), *Monozygotic Twins*, Oxford University Press.

62   SHIELDS, J., and SLATER, E. (1961), 'Heredity and psychological abnormality', in H. J. Eysenck (ed.), *Handbook of Abnormal Psychology*, Basic Books.

218   SHILLITO, E. (1963), 'Exploratory behaviour in the short-tailed vole', *Behaviour*, vol. 21, pp. 145–54.

69   SHOCK, N. W. (1951), 'Growth curves', in S. S. Stevens (ed.), *Handbook of Experimental Psychology*, Wiley.

211   SIEGEL, P. S. (1947), 'The relationship between voluntary water intake, body weight loss, and number of hours of water privation in the rat', *J. comp. physiol. Psychol.*, vol. 40, pp. 231–8.

59   SIEGEL, P. B., PHILLIPS, R. E., and FOLSOM, E. F. (1965), 'Genetic variation in the crow of adult chickens', *Behaviour*, vol. 24, pp. 229–35.

455   SIEGEL, S. (1956), *Non-Parametric Statistics*, McGraw-Hill.

550   SIEGMAN, A. W. (1961), 'The relationship between future time perspective, time estimation and impulse control in a group of young offenders and a control group', *J. consult. Psychol.*, vol. 25, pp. 470–75.

236   SIIPOLA, E. (1935), 'A group study of some effects of preparatory sets', *Psychol. Monogr.*, vol. 46, no. 210, pp. 27–38.

557   SILBER, E., and TIPPETT, J. S. (1965), 'Self-esteem: clinical assessment and measurement validation', *Psychol. Rep. Monogr. Supp.*, vol. 4.

297, 385   SKINNER, B. F. (1938), *The Behavior of Organisms*, Appleton-Century-Crofts.

316   SKINNER, B. F. (1950), 'Are theories of learning necessary?', *Psychol. Rev.*, vol. 57, pp. 193–216.

300, 383, 388   SKINNER, B. F. (1957), *Verbal Behavior*, Appleton-Century-Crofts.

354, 359   SLAMECKA, N. J., and CERASO, J. (1960), 'Retroactive and proactive inhibition of verbal learning', *Psychol. Bull.*, vol. 57, pp. 449–75.

404   SLOBIN, D. I. (1966), 'Grammatical

Page

transformations and sentence comprehension in childhood and adulthood', *J. verb. Learn. verb. Behav.*, vol. 5, pp. 219–27.

214, 280, 291   SLUCKIN, W. (1964), *Imprinting and Early Learning*, Methuen.

220   SLUCKIN, W., and SALZEN, E. A. (1961), 'Imprinting and perceptual learning', *Quart. J. exp. Psychol.*, vol. 13, pp. 65–77.

127   SMITH, C. J. (1959), 'Mass action and early environment in the rat', *J. comp. physiol. Psychol.*, vol. 52, pp. 154–6.

335   SMITH, M. C. (1967), 'Theories of the psychological refractory period', *Psychol. Bull.*, vol. 67, pp. 202–13.

274   SMOCK, C. D., and KANFER, F. H. (1961), 'Response bias and perception', *J. exp. Psychol.*, vol. 62, pp. 158–63.

36   SNEDECOR, G. W. (1956), *Statistical Methods*, Iowa State College Press, 5th edn.

116   SNIDER, R. S. (1958), 'The cerebellum', *Scient. Amer.*, vol. 204, no. 8, pp. 84–90.

636   SNYDER, A. F., MISCHEL, W., and LOTT, B. E. (1960), 'Value, information and conformity behavior', *J. Pers.*, vol. 28, pp. 333–41.

184, 185   SOKOLOV, E. N. (1960), 'Neuronal models and the orienting reflex', in M. A. B. Brazier (ed.), *The Central Nervous System and Behavior*, Josiah Macy, Jr, Foundation, New York. [Pribram, vol. 2 *]

185   SOKOLOV, E. N. (1963), 'Higher nervous functions: the orienting reflex', *Ann. Rev. Physiol.*, vol. 25, pp. 545–80.

230   SOLOMON, P., *et al.* (eds.) (1961), *Sensory Deprivation*, Harvard University Press.

310   SOLOMON, R. L. (1964), 'Punishment', *Amer. Psychol.*, vol. 19, pp. 239–53.

230, 310   SOLOMON, R. L., KAMIN, L. J., and WYNNE, L. C. (1953), 'Traumatic avoidance learning: the outcome of several extinction procedures with dogs', *J. abnorm. soc. Psychol.*, vol. 48, pp. 291–302.

491, 492   SPEARMAN, C. (1927), *The Abilities of Man*, Macmillan.

Page

355   SPERLING, G. (1963), 'A model for visual memory tasks', *Hum. Factors*, vol. 5, pp. 19–31.

122, 169   SPERRY, R. W. (1961), 'Cerebral organization and behavior', *Science*, vol. 133, pp. 1749–57.

122, 169   SPERRY, R. W. (1964), 'The great cerebral commissure', *Scient. Amer.*, vol. 210, no. 1, pp. 42–52.

254   SPERRY, R. W., and MINER, N. (1955), 'Pattern perception following insertion of mica plates into visual cortex', *J. comp. physiol. Psychol.*, vol. 48, pp. 463–9.

574   SPIELBERGER, C. D. (1962), 'The role of awareness in verbal conditioning', *J. Pers.*, vol. 30, pp. 73–101.

574   SPIELBERGER, C. D. (1965), 'Theoretical and epistemological issues in verbal conditioning', in S. Rosenberg (ed.), *Directions in Psycholinguistics*, Collier-Macmillan.

286   SPITZ, R. A. (1945), 'Hospitalism: an inquiry into the genesis of psychiatric conditions in early childhood', *Psychoanal. Stud. Child.*, vol. 1, pp. 53–74.

286   SPITZ, R. A. (1946), 'Anaclitic depression', *Psychoanal. Stud. Child.*, vol. 2, pp. 313–42.

579   STARCH, D. (1911), 'Unconscious imitation in handwriting', *Psychol. Rev.*, vol. 18, pp. 223–8.

637   STEINER, I. D., and VANNOY, J. S. (1966), 'Personality correlates of two types of conformity behavior', *J. Pers. soc. Psychol.*, vol. 4, pp. 307–15.

195   STEINSCHNEIDER, A. (1967), 'Developmental psychophysiology', in Y. Brackbill (ed.), *Infancy and Early Childhood*, Free Press of Glencoe.

141, 142   STELLAR, E. (1954), 'The physiology of motivation', *Psychol. Rev.*, vol. 61, pp. 5–22.

141   STELLAR, E. (1960), 'Drive and motivation', in J. Field, H. W. Magoun and V. E. Hall (eds.), *Handbook of Physiology*, sect. 1, vol. 3, American Physiological Society.

204   STENNETT, R. G. (1957), 'The relationship of performance level to level of arousal', *J. exp. Psychol.*, vol. 54, pp. 54–61.

479   STEPHENSON, W. (1953), *The Study of Behavior:*

Page

Q-Technique and its Methodology, University of Chicago Press.

147   STEPIEN, L. S., CORDEAU, J. P., and RASMUSSEN, T. (1960), 'The effect of temporal lobe and hippocampal lesions on auditory and visual recent memory in monkeys', *Brain*, vol. 83, pp. 470–89.

467   STERN, W. (1912), *The Psychological Methods of Testing Intelligence*, translated by G. M. Whipple, Warwick & York, 1914.

184, 185   STERNBACH, R. A. (1960), 'Correlates of differences in time to recover from startle', *Psychosom. Med.*, vol. 22, pp. 204–10.

205   STERNBACH, R. A. (1966), *Principles of Psychophysiology*, Academic Press.

205   STERNBACH, R. A. (1968), *Pain: A Psychophysiological Analysis*, Academic Press.

451   STEVENS, S. S. (ed.) (1951), 'Mathematics, measurement and psychophysics', in S. S. Stevens (ed.), *Handbook of Experimental Psychology*, Wiley.

573   STEVENSON, H. W. (1961), 'Social reinforcement with children as a function of CA, sex of E and sex of S', *J. abnorm. soc. Psychol.*, vol. 29, pp. 136–47.

573   STEVENSON, H. W. (1965), 'Social reinforcement of children's behavior', in L. P. Lipsitt and C. C. Spikes (eds.), *Advances in Child Development and Behavior*, vol. 2, Academic Press.

573   STEVENSON, H. W., and ALLAN, S. A. (1967), 'Variables associated with adults' effectiveness as reinforcing agents', *J. Pers.*, vol. 35, pp. 246–64.

571   STEVENSON, H. W., and HILL, K. J. (1966), 'Use of rate as a measure of response in studies of social reinforcement', *Psychol. Bull.*, vol. 66, pp. 321–6.

573   STEVENSON, H. W., KEEN, R., and KNIGHTS, R. M. (1963), 'Parents and strangers as reinforcing agents for children's performance', *J. abnorm. soc. Psychol.*, vol. 67, pp. 183–6.

74   STONE, C. P., and BARKER, R. G. (1939), 'The attitudes and interests of pre-menarcheal and

Page

post-menarcheal girls', *J. genet. Psychol.*, vol. 54, pp. 27–71.

565   STOTLAND, E. (1965), 'Experimental social psychology and its neighbours', *J. soc. Psychol.*, vol. 67, pp. 315–23.

632   STRODTBECK, F. L., and MANN, R. D. (1956), 'Sex role differentiation in jury deliberation', *Sociometry*, vol. 19, pp. 3–11.

475   STRONG, E. K. (1955), *Vocational Interests Eighteen Years after College*, University of Minnesota Press.

254   SUTHERLAND, N. S. (1964), 'Visual discrimination in animals', *Brit. med. Bull.*, vol. 20, no. 1, pp. 54–9.

272   TAFFEL, C. (1955), 'Anxiety and the conditioning of verbal behavior', *J. abnorm. soc. Psychol.*, vol. 51, pp. 496–501.

71   TANNER, J. M. (1962), *Growth at Adolescence*, Blackwell, 2nd edn.

71   TANNER, J. M. (1963), 'The regulation of human growth', *Child Devel.*, vol. 34, pp. 817–47.

433   TAYLOR, C. W., and BARRON, F. (1963), *Scientific Creativity: Its Recognition and Development*, Wiley. [P. E. Vernon *]

139   TEITELBAUM, P. (1955), 'Sensory control of hypothalamic hyperphagia', *J. comp. physiol. Psychol.*, vol. 48, pp. 156–63.

139   TEITELBAUM, P., and STELLAR, E. (1954), 'Recovery from failure to eat produced by hypothalamic lesions', *Science*, vol. 120, pp. 894–5.

333, 334   TELFORD, C. W. (1931), 'Refractory phase of voluntary and associative responses', *J. exp. Psychol.*, vol. 14, pp. 1–35.

457   TERMAN, L. M., and MERRILL, M. A. (1937), *Measuring Intelligence*, Houghton Mifflin.

607   TERMAN, L. M., and ODIN, M. H. (1947), *The Gifted Child Grows Up*, Stanford University Press.

576   TERRELL, G., and KENNEDY, W. A. (1957), 'Discrimination learning and transposition as a function of the nature of the reward', *J. exp. Psychol.*, vol. 53, pp. 257–60.

Page

145 TERZIAN, H., and ORE, G. D. (1955),
'Syndrome of Klüver and Bucy: reproduced in
man by bilateral removal of the temporal lobes',
Neurology, vol. 5, pp. 373–80.

128 TEUBER, H.-L. (1955), 'Physiological
psychology', *Ann. Rev. Psychol.*, vol. 6, pp.
267–96.

161 TEUBER, H.-L. (1959), 'Some alterations in
behavior after cerebral lesions in man', in
A. D. Bass (ed.), *Evolution of Nervous Control
from Primitive Organisms to Man*, American
Association for the Advancement of Science.

156 TEUBER, H.-L. (1960), 'Perception', in J. Field,
H. W. Magoun and V. E. Hall (eds.), *Handbook
of Physiology*, sect. 1, vol. 3, American
Physiological Society.

161 TEUBER, H.-L. (1964), 'The riddle of frontal
lobe function in man', in J. M. Warren and
K. Akert (eds.), *The Frontal Granular Cortex and
Behavior*, McGraw-Hill.

161 TEUBER, H.-L., BATTERSBY, W. S., and
BENDER, M. B. (1949), 'Changes in visual
searching performance following cerebral
lesions', *Amer. J. Physiol.*, vol. 159, p. 592.

643 THIBAUT, J. W., and KELLEY, H. A. (1961),
The Social Psychology of Groups, Wiley.

59 THOMPSON, W. R. (1953), 'The inheritance of
behavior: behavioral differences in fifteen mouse
strains', *Canad. J. Psychol.*, vol. 7, pp. 145–55.

58 THOMPSON, W. R., and BINDRA, D. (1952),
'Motivational and emotional characteristics of
"bright" and "dull" rats', *Canad. J. Psychol.*,
vol. 6, pp. 116–22.

279 THOMPSON, W. R., and MELZACK, R. (1956),
'Early environment', *Scient. Amer.*, vol. 194,
pp. 38–42.

491 THOMSON, G. N. (1939), *The Factorial
Analysis of Human Abilities*, University of
London Press.

418, 427 THOMSON, R. (1957), *The Psychology of
Thinking*, Penguin Books.

421 THORNDIKE, E. L. (1898), 'Animal intelligence:
an experimental study of the associative processes

Page

in animals', *Psychol. Rev. Monogr. Suppl.*, vol. 2, no. 4. [Riopelle]

297, 421, 422   THORNDIKE, E. L. (1911), *Animal Intelligence*, Macmillan. [Bindra and Stewart *]

308, 355   THORNDIKE, E. L. (1932), *The Fundamentals of Learning*, Teachers College Bureau of Publications, New York.

459   THORNDIKE, R. L. (1949), *Personnel Selection*, Wiley.

472   THORNDIKE, R. L., and HAGEN, E. (1959), *Ten Thousand Careers*, Wiley.

219, 223, 580   THORPE, W. H. (1963), *Learning and Instinct in Animals*, Methuen, 2nd edn.

381, 423   THORPE, W. H. (1966), 'Ethology and consciousness', in J. C. Eccles (ed.), *Brain and Concious Experience*, Springer Verlag, Berlin.

247, 265, 266   THOULESS, R. H. (1932), 'Individual differences in phenomenal regression', *Brit. J. Psychol.*, vol. 22, pp. 216–41.

369   THUNE, L. E. (1950), 'The effect of different types of preliminary activities on subsequent learning of paired-associate material', *J. exp. Psychol.*, vol. 40, pp. 423–38.

489   THURSTONE, L. L. (1940), 'Current issues in factor analysis', *Psychol. Bull.*, vol. 37, pp. 189–236.

308   TILTON, J. W. (1939), 'The effect of "right" and "wrong" upon the learning of nonsense syllables in multiple-choice arrangement', *J. educ. Psychol.*, vol. 30, pp. 95–115.

219   TINBERGEN, N. (1948), 'Social releasers and the experimental method required for their study', *Wilson Bull.*, vol. 60, pp. 6–51.

213   TINBERGEN, N. (1953), *Social Behaviour in Animals*, Methuen.

310   TOLMAN, E. C. (1939), 'Prediction of vicarious trial and error by means of the schematic sowbug', *Psychol. Rev.*, vol. 46, pp. 318–36.

302   TOLMAN, E. C., and HUNZIK, C. H. (1930), 'Introduction and removal of reward, and maze performance in rats', *Univ. Calif. Publ. Psychol.*, vol. 4, pp. 257–75.

479   TOMKINS, S. S. (1949), 'The present status of

Page

the Thematic Apperception Test', *Amer. J. Orthopsychiat.*, vol. 19, pp. 358–62.

481   TOMKINS, S. S., and MESSICK, S. J. (eds.) (1963), *Computer Simulation of Personality: Frontier of Psychological Theory*, Wiley.

576   TRAVERS, R. M. W., *et al.* (1964), 'Learning as a consequence of the learners' task involvement under different conditions of feedback', *J. Educ. Psycholl*, vol. 55, pp. 167–73.

136, 235, 248   TREISMAN, A. M. (1964), 'Selective attention in man', *Brit. med. Bull.*, vol. 20, pp. 12–16.

401   TREISMAN, A. M. (1966), 'Human attention', in B. M. Foss (ed.), *New Horizons in Psychology*, Penguin Books.

169   TREVARTHEN, C. V. (1962), 'Double visual learning in split-brain monkeys', *Science*, vol. 136, pp. 258–9.

57   TRYON, R. C. (1940), 'Genetic differences in maze learning ability in rats', *39th Yearbook Nat. Soc. Stud. Educ.* (Part 1), Public School Publishing Co., Illinois.

595, 606, 607   UGURAL-SEMIN, R. (1952), 'Moral behavior and moral judgment of children', *J. abnorm. soc. Psychol.*, vol. 47, pp. 463–74.

367   UNDERWOOD, B. J. (1949), *Experimental Psychology: An Introduction*, Appleton-Century-Crofts.

361, 362, 374   UNDERWOOD, B. J. (1964), 'Forgetting', *Scient. Amer.*, vol. 210, pp. 91–9.

374   UNDERWOOD, B. J., and EKSTRAND, B. R. (1966), 'An analysis of some shortcomings in the interference theory of forgetting', *Psychol. Rev.*, vol. 73, pp. 540–49.

643   VAN ZELST, R. H. (1952), 'Validation of a sociometric regrouping procedure', *J. abnorm. soc. Psychol.*, vol. 47, pp. 299–301.

182   VENABLES, P. H., and MARTIN, I. (1967), 'Skin resistance and skin potential', in P. H. Venables and I. Martin (eds.), *A Manual of Psychophysiological Methods*, North-Holland.

181   VENABLES, P. H., and SAYER, E. (1963), 'On the measurement of the level of the skin potential'. *Brit. J. Psychol.*, vol. 54, pp. 251–60.

Page

266, 267, 268   VERNON, M. D. (1962), *The Psychology of Perception*, Penguin Books.

483   VERNON, P. E. (1955), 'The psychology of intelligence and g', *Bull. Brit. psychol. Soc.*, vol. 26, pp. 1–14.

471, 474   VERNON, P. E. (1960), *Intelligence and Attainment Tests*, University of London Press.

488, 489, 492, 530   VERNON, P. E. (1961), *The Structure of Human Abilities*, Methuen, 2nd edn. [Wiseman *]

496   VERNON, P. E. (1964), 'Creativity and intelligence', *Educ. Res.*, vol. 6, pp. 163–9.

427   VINACKE, W. E. (1952), *The Psychology of Thinking*, McGraw-Hill.

333   VINCE, M. A. (1948), 'Intermittency of control movements and the psychological refractory period', *Brit. J. Psychol.*, vol. 38, pp. 149–57.

518   VIOLA, G. (1909), *Le legge de correlazione morfologia dei tippi individuali*, Properini, Padua.

573   VITELES, M. S. (1962), *Industrial Psychology*, Cape, 2nd edn.

264   VON SENDEN, M. (1932), *Space and Sight: The Perception of Space and Shape in the Congenitally Blind before and after Operation*, translated by P. Heath, Methuen, 1960.

436   VYGOTSKY, L. S. (1934), *Thought and Language*, translated by E. Haufmann and G. Vakar, M.I.T. Press, 1962.

163   WADE, M. (1947), 'The effect of sedatives upon delayed responses in monkeys following removal of the prefrontal lobes', *J. Neurophysiol.*, vol. 10, pp. 57–61.

219, 259, 260, 263   WALK, R. D., and GIBSON, E. J. (1961), 'A comparative and analytical study of visual depth perception', *Psychol. Monogr.*, vol. 75, no. 519. [Dodwell *; M. D. Vernon *]

597   WALLACE, J., and SADALLA, E. (1966), 'Behavioral consequences of transgression. I', *J. exp. Res. Pers.*, vol. 1, pp. 187–94.

619   WALSTER, E., ARONSON, E., and ABRAHAMS, D. (1966), 'On increasing the persuasiveness of a low prestige communicator', *J. exp. soc. Psychol.*, vol. 2, pp. 325–42.

Page

581   WALTERS, R. H., and AMOROSO, D. M. (1967),
        'Cognitive and emotional determinants of the
        occurrence of imitative behavior', *Brit. J. soc.
        clin. Psychol.*, vol. 6, pp. 174–85.

581   WALTERS, R. H., BOWEN, N. V., and PARKE,
        R. D. (1964), 'Influence of the looking behaviour
        of a social model on the subsequent looking
        behaviour of observers', *Percept. mot. Skills*,
        vol. 18, pp. 469–83.

572   WALTERS, R. H., and KARAL, P. (1960),
        'Social deprivation and verbal behavior', *J.
        Pers.*, vol. 28, pp. 89–107.

572   WALTERS, R. H., and PARKE, R. D. (1964),
        'Emotional arousal, isolation and
        discrimination learning in children', *J. exp.
        child Psychol.*, vol. 1, pp. 163–73.

284   WALTERS, R. H., and PARKE, R. D. (1965),
        'The role of distance receptors in the
        development of social responsiveness', in
        L. P. Lipsitt and C. C. Spiker (eds.), *Advances in
        Child Development and Behavior*, vol. 2,
        Academic Press.

582   WALTERS, R. H., PARKE, R. D., and CANE,
        V. A. (1965), 'Timing of punishment and the
        observation of consequences to others as
        determinants of response inhibition', *J. exp.
        child Psychol.*, vol. 2, pp. 10–30.

572   WALTERS, R. H., and RAY, E. (1960),
        'Anxiety, isolation and reinforcer effectiveness',
        J. Pers., vol. 28, pp. 358–67.

159   WARD, A. A., JR, and KENNARD, M. A.
        (1942), 'Effect of cholinergic drugs on recovery
        of function following lesions of the central
        nervous system in monkeys', *Yale J. Biol. Med.*,
        vol. 15, pp. 189–229.

303   WARDEN, C. J., and JACKSON, T. A. (1935),
        'Imitative behavior in the rhesus monkey',
        Pedagog. Sem. & J. genet. Psychol., vol. 46, pp.
        103–25.

159   WATSON, C. W., and KENNARD, M. A. (1945),
        'The effect of anticonvulsant drugs on recovery
        of function following cerebral cortical lesions',
        J. Neurophysiol., vol. 8, pp. 221–31.

Page

635   WATSON, J. B. (1914), *Behavior: An Introduction to Comparative Psychology*, Holt.

348, 352, 371   WAUGH, N. C., and NORMAN, D. A. (1965), 'Primary memory', *Psychol. Rev.*, vol. 72, pp. 89–104.

471   WECHSLER, D. (1958), *The Measurement and Appraisal of Adult Intelligence*, Williams & Wilkins, 4th edn.

180   WEINMAN, J. (1967), 'Photoplethysmography', in P. H. Venables and I. Martin (eds.), *A Manual of Psychophysiological Methods*, North-Holland.

127, 150   WEISKRANTZ, L. (1956), 'Behavioral changes associated with ablation of the amygdaloid complex in monkeys', *J. comp. physiol. Psychol.*, vol. 49, pp. 381–91.

340   WELFORD, A. T. (1953), 'The psychologist's problem in measuring fatigue', in W. F. Floyd and A. T. Welford (eds.), *Symposium on Fatigue*, H. K. Lewis.

321, 342   WELFORD, A. T. (1958), *Ageing and Human Skill*, Oxford University Press. [Legge *]

332   WELFORD, A. T. (1960), 'The measurement of sensory-motor performance: survey and reappraisal of twelve years' progress', *Ergonomics*, vol. 3, pp. 189–230. [Legge *]

206, 207   WELFORD, A. T. (1962), 'Arousal, channel capacity and decision', *Nature*, vol. 194, pp. 365–6.

202   WELFORD, A. T. (1965), 'Stress and achievement', *Austral. J. Psychol.*, vol. 17, pp. 1–11.

344, 346   WELFORD, A. T. (1968), *Fundamentals of Skill*, Methuen.

342   WELFORD, A. T., and BIRREN, J. E. (1965), *Behavior, Aging and the Nervous System*, Charles C. Thomas.

189, 198   WENGER, M. A. (1950), 'Emotion as visceral action: an extension of Lange's theory', in M. L. Reymert (ed.), *Feelings and Emotions*, McGraw-Hill.

192, 195   WENGER, M. A., *et al.* (1960), 'Autonomic response patterns during intravenous infusion

Page

of epinephrine and norepinephrine', *Psychosom. Med.*, vol. 22, pp. 294–307.

198   WENGER, M. A., JONES, F. N., and JONES, M. H. (1956), *Physiological Psychology*, Holt.

81   WERNER, H. (1948), *Comparative Psychology of Mental Development*, Follett.

243   WERTHEIMER, M. (1923), 'Untersuchungen zur Lehre von der Gestalt. II.', *Psychol. Forsch.*, vol. 4, pp. 301–50. Translated by W. D. Ellis, *A Source Book of Gestalt Psychology*, Routledge, 1938.

218   WHITE, R. W. (1959), 'Motivation reconsidered: the concept of competence', *Psychol. Rev.*, vol. 66, pp. 297–333.

606   WHITEMAN, P. H., and KOSIER, K. (1964), 'Development of children's moralistic judgments', *Child Devel.*, vol. 35, pp. 843–50.

610   WHITING, J. W. (1959), 'Sorcery, sin and the superego', in M. R. Jones (ed.), *Nebraska Symposium on Motivation*, University of Nebraska Press.

290   WHITING, J. W. M., and CHILD, I. L. (1953), *Child Training and Personality: A Cross-Cultural Study*, Yale University Press.

624   WHITTAKER, J. O., and MEADE, R. D. (1967), 'Sex and age variables in persuasibility', *J. soc. Psychol.*, vol. 73, pp. 47–52.

435   WHORF, B. J. (1956) in J. B. Carroll (ed.), *Language, Thought and Reality: Selected Writings of Benjamin Lee Whorf*, M.I.T. Press.

326   WIENER, N. (1948), *Cybernetics*, Wiley.

182   WILDER, J. (1957), 'The law of initial value in neurology and psychiatry. Facts and problems', *J. nerv. ment. Dis.*, vol. 125, pp. 73–86.

205   WILKINSON, R. T. (1960), 'Effects of sleep deprivation on performance and muscle tension', in G. E. W. Wolstenholme and M. O'Connor (eds.), *The Nature of Sleep*, Little, Brown for CIBA Foundation.

203   WILKINSON, R. T. (1961), 'Interaction of lack of sleep with knowledge of results, repeated testing and individual differences', *J. exp. Psychol.*, vol. 62, pp. 263–71.

Page

203, 204 WILKINSON, R. T. (1963), 'Interaction of noise with knowledge of results and sleep deprivation', *J. exp. Psychol.*, vol. 66, pp. 332–7.

204 WILKINSON, R. T. (1965), 'Sleep deprivation', in O. G. Edholm and A. L. Bacharach (eds.), *The Physiology of Human Survival*, Academic Press.

289 WILLIAMS, E., and SCOTT, J. P. (1953), 'The development of social behaviour patterns in the mouse, in relation to natural periods', *Behaviour*, vol. 6, pp. 35–64.

383, 574 WILLIAMS, J. H. (1964), 'Conditioning of verbalization: a review', *Psychol. Bull.*, vol. 62, pp. 383–93.

131 WILLIAMS, R. L., AGNEW, H. W., and WEBB, W. B. (1964), 'Sleep patterns in young adults: an EEG study', *EEG clin. Neurophysiol.*, vol. 17, pp. 376–81.

475 WISEMAN, S. (1964), *Education and Environment*, Manchester University Press.

81 WITKIN, H. A., DYK, R. B., FATERSON, H. F., GOODENOUGH, D. R., and KARP, S. A. (1962), *Psychological Differentiation*, Wiley.

547, 548 WOLF, S., and WOLFF, H. G. (1942), 'Evidence on the genesis of peptic ulcer in man', *J. Amer. med. Ass.*, vol. 120, no. 9, pp. 670–75.

198 WOLF, S., and WOLFF, H. G. (1943), *Human Gastric function*, Oxford University Press.

148 WOOD, C. D. (1958), 'Behavioral changes following discrete lesions of temporal lobe structures', *Neurology*, vol. 8, pp. 215–20.

475 WOODWORTH, R. S. (1920), *Personal Data Sheet*, Stoelting.

341 WOODWORTH, R. S. (1938), *Experimental Psychology*, Holt.

249 WOODWORTH, R. S. (1948), *Contemporary Schools of Psychology*, Methuen, 2nd edn.

314, 330, 347 WOODWORTH, R. S., and SCHLOSBERG, H. (1954), *Experimental Psychology*, Holt.

162, 353 WOULDRIDGE, D. E. (1963), *The Machinery of the Brain*, McGraw-Hill.

576 WRIGHT, D. (1968), 'Social reinforcement and maze learning in children', *Child Devel.*, vol. 39, pp. 177–83.

Page

406, 407   WRIGHT, P. (1969), 'Two studies of the depth
              hypothesis', *Brit. J. Psychol.*, vol. 60, pp. 63–9.

364   WULF, F. (1922), 'Über die Veränderung von
              Vorstellungen (Gedachtnis und Gestalt)',
              Psychol. Forsch., vol. 1, pp. 333–73.
              Translated by W. D. Ellis, *A Source Book of
              Gestalt Psychology*, Routledge, 1938.

223   YATES, A. J. (1962), *Frustration and Conflict*,
              Wiley.

405   YNGVE, V. H. (1960), 'A model and an
              hypothesis for language structure', *Proc. Amer.
              phil. Soc.*, vol. 104, pp. 444–66.

254   YOUNG, J. Z. (1964), *A Model of the Brain*,
              Clarendon Press.

143   YOUNG, W. C., GOY, R. W., and PHOENIX,
              C. H. (1964), 'Hormones and sexual behaviour',
              Science, vol. 143, pp. 212–18. [Pribram, vol. 1]

568   ZAJONC, R. B. (1965), 'Social facilitation',
              Science, vol. 149, pp. 269–74.

568, 569   ZAJONC, R. B. (1966), *Social Psychology: An
              Experimental Approach*, Wadsworth.

129   ZANGWILL, O. L. (1960), 'Lashley's concept of
              cerebral mass action', in W. H. Thorpe and
              O. L. Zangwill (eds.), *Current Problems in
              Animal Behaviour*, Cambridge University Press.

368   ZEIGARNIK, B. (1927), 'Über das Behalten von
              erledigten und unerledigten Handlungen',
              Psychol. Forsch., vol. 9, pp. 1–85. Translated by
              W. D. Ellis, *A Source Book of Gestalt Psychology*,
              Routledge, 1938.

638   ZETTERBERG, H. (1957), 'Compliant actions',
              Acta Sociol., vol. 2, pp. 179–201.

77   ZIMMERMAN, R. R., and TORREY, C. C.
              (1965), 'Ontogeny of learning', in A. M.
              Schrier and H. F. Harlow (eds.), *Behavior of
              Non-Human Primates*, vol. 2, Academic Press.

230, 231   ZUBEK, J. P. (1964), 'Effects of prolonged
              sensory and perceptual deprivation', *Brit. med.
              Bull.*, vol. 20, no. 1, pp. 38–42.

Penguin Modern Psychology Readings

Acknowledgements

Acknowledgement is due to the following for permission to use figures and tables in this volume.

Figure 2, Humanities Press and Routledge & Kegan Paul; Figure 5, Addison-Wesley Publishing Co.; Figure 6, BBC Publications; Figure 12, Basic Books; Figure 13, University of Chicago Press; Figure 15, Blackwell Scientific Publications; Figure 16, McGraw-Hill Book Company; Figure 17, Basic Books; Figure 18, Basic Books; Figure 19, Blackwell Scientific Publications; Figure 20, Blackwell Scientific Publications; Figure 24, *EEG and Clinical Neurophysiology*; Figure 25, American Psychological Association; Figure 26, Basic Books; Figure 27, The Williams & Wilkins Co.; Figure 28, McGraw-Hill Book Company; Figure 29, *Brain*; Figure 30, Brain; Figure 31, The Macmillan Company; Figure 33, W. W. Norton & Co. Inc. ; Figure 34, North-Holland Publishing Company; Figure 35, North-Holland Publishing Company; Figure 36, North-Holland Publishing Company; Figure 37, Charles C. Thomas; Figure 42, Humanities Press and Routledge & Kegan Paul; Figure 43, Weidenfeld & Nicolson; Figure 44, *Scientific American*; Figure 46, *Scientific American*; Figure 48, Journal Press; Figure 49, American Psychological Association; Figure 51, *Quarterly Journal of Experimental Psychology* and W. E. Hick; Figure 52, *Quarterly Journal of Experimental Psychology* and G. H. Mowbray; Figure 54, Humanities Press and Routledge & Kegan Paul; Figure 56, John Wiley & Sons Inc.; Figure 58, Appleton-Century-Crofts; Figure 64, Journal Press and E. Heidbreder; Figure 65, Alfred A. Knopf Inc.; D. Krech and R. S. Crutchfield; Figure 74, Methuen & Co. Ltd; Figure 75 John Wiley & Sons Inc.

Table 2, Elsevier Publishing Company and D. B. Lindsley; Table 4, New York Academy of Sciences and Frances M. Davis; Table 8, John Wiley & Sons Inc.; Table 9, Methuen & Co. Ltd; Table 10, Methuen & Co. Ltd.; Table 12, *American Sociological Review*.

Index

Ability, concept of, 484
Absolute refractory period, 94, 95
Accommodation–assimilation, 500
Achievement tests, 471, 474–5
Adaptability, and autonomy, 554
Adjustment, and normality, 554
Adrenal glands, 177–178
Adrenalin, 175, 176, 184, 191–3, 195–7
Affectionless character, 287
Age and effects of brain damage, 126, 157, 159, 162, 163, 165, 496
Aggression, 221–3
  intraspecific, 221, 222
All-or-none principle, 94
Allport, G. W., 17, 32, 33, 82, 513–16, 522–3, 541
Altruistic behaviour, 590, 595
Amygdala, 107–9, 142, 148–50
  and avoidance behaviour, 149, 150
  and eating, 142, 148
  and fear, 148, 149
  location of, 107–9
Anaclitic depression, 286
Anxiety, 220, 596
  and normality, 547, 548, 549
Aptitude tests, 471–4
Arousal, 117, 118, 136, 137, 200–206, 338, 549
  and A R A S, 117, 118, 136, 137
  and audience effects, 569
  and efficiency, 200–206
  and inverted-U relation, 202, 203, 204, 205

and physiological measures, 200, 204, 205
Ascending reticular activating system (ARAS), 116–19, 130–37, 338
  and arousal, 117, 118, 136, 137
  and attention, 136, 137
  and discrimination, 136, 137
  and wakefulness, 132, 136
  structure of, 116–19
Assimilation
  see Accommodation–assimilation
Association areas, 109–12, 159–70
A-thinking v. R-thinking, 444–6
Attachment, 281, 284
  and moral development, 608–11
Attitude scales, 479–80
Audience effects, 567–70
Autokinetic effect, and norm formation, 634–5
Autonomic nervous system (ANS), 86, 87, 88, 171–205
  and arousal, 200–5
  and behaviour, 171–205
  and emotion, 188–99
  measurement of autonomic variables, 178–83
  structure of, 171–6
Autonomy, and normality, 556
Avoidance learning, 149–51, 298–9, 510
Axon, 91–4
  see also Nervous transmission

Bales, R. F., 631–2
Bandura, A., 223, 576–80, 602, 608

'Gritty, authentic and superbly written'
INDEPENDENT

Ian
Rankin
The Hanging Garden